NO ACCESS TO LAW

Alternatives to the American Judicial System

NO ACCESS TO LAW

Alternatives to the American Judicial System

Laura Nader
EDITOR
Department of Anthropology
University of California
Berkeley, California

ACADEMIC PRESS
A Subsidiary of Harcourt Brace Jovanovich, Publishers
New York   London   Toronto   Sydney   San Francisco

ACADEMIC PRESS, INC.
111 Fifth Avenue, New York, New York 10003

United Kingdom Edition published by
ACADEMIC PRESS, INC. (LONDON) LTD.
24/28 Oval Road, London NW1 7DX

Library of Congress Cataloging in Publication Data
Main entry under title:

No access to law.

Includes bibliographies.
1. Consumer protection––United States––Addresses,
essays, lectures. 2. Complaints (Retail trade)
I. Nader, Laura.
HC110.C63N6   381'.34'0973   80–526
ISBN 0–12–513560–2 (Cloth)
ISBN 0–12–513562–9 (Paper)

PRINTED IN THE UNITED STATES OF AMERICA

80 81 82 83   9 8 7 6 5 4 3 2 1

To citizens whose actions provided much of the material for this book, to undergraduate researchers who took up the challenge of this study, and to the discipline of anthropology as it expands its studies to benefit the public

CONTENTS

I
STRUCTURE AND IDEAS

1
ALTERNATIVES TO THE AMERICAN JUDICIAL SYSTEM — 3
Laura Nader

2
OLD SOLUTIONS FOR OLD PROBLEMS — 57
Laura Nader and Christopher Shugart

II

VOICING COMPLAINTS

3

4

III

MECHANISMS FOR REDRESS

5

10

EASY TERMS, HARD TIMES: 379
COMPLAINT HANDLING IN THE GHETTO
David I. Greenberg

11

GRASS ROOTS SOLUTIONS: 417
SAN FRANCISCO CONSUMER ACTION
Gregory Wilson and Elizabeth Brydolf

12

GRIEVING AND FEUDING: 461
THE ORGANIZATIONAL DILEMMA OF A LABOR UNION
Elaine Combs-Schilling

13

MEDIA IN THE MIDDLE: 485
A STUDY OF THE MASS MEDIA COMPLAINT MANAGERS
Michael C. Mattice

CONTRIBUTORS

Penny Addiss received a B.A. in Romance languages and Spanish literature from Radcliffe College in 1960. She pursued her graduate studies in anthropology at the University of California, Berkeley (1962–1970) and did fieldwork in an urban upper-class neighborhood in New Delhi, India.

Elizabeth Brydolf received her B.A. in anthropology from the University of California, Berkeley, in 1975. Her publications include a critical study, *Down Sesame Street,* and freelance articles on various aspects of urban culture and women's issues for both local and national publications.

Elaine Combs-Schilling earned a B.A. with honors in anthropology from Stanford University in 1972, and an M.A. in social anthropology from the University of California, Berkeley, where she is currently a Ph.D. candidate. Combs-Schilling spent 2 years (1976–1978) in Morocco conducting research for her doctoral dissertation, "Traders on the Move: a Moroccan Case Study of Organizational and Symbolic Adaptations to Change."

Marian Eaton received an A.B. in anthropology from the University of California, Berkeley, and an M.A. in anthropology from the University of Chicago. She is currently conducting research on the handling by U.S. Congressmen and their staff of constituents' government-related complaints.

Eric E. Freedman received a B.A. (1975) and M.A. (1976) in anthropology from the University of California, Berkeley. From 1976 to 1977 he was a Research Student in Archaeology at Peterhouse, Cambridge. Freedman spent two summers as a research assistant in anthropology at the Smithsonian Institution in Washington, D.C., and has participated in archaeological fieldwork in the El Morro Valley of New Mexico and at Sardis, Turkey. He is currently a J.D. student at the Yale Law School.

David I. Greenberg attended Williams College, Williamstown, Massachusetts (1972–1975) and is presently enrolled at the University of Chicago where he is a candidate for a combined law degree and masters degree in business administration.

Angela Karikas earned a B.A. magna cum laude with highest honors in social anthropology from Harvard University in 1974, where she was a member of Phi Beta Kappa. In 1977 she graduated from the U.C.L.A. School of Law. She is a member of the California State Bar and practices law in San Francisco.

Michael C. Mattice is a general practice and trial attorney in Fairfield, California. His undergraduate studies commenced at Cornell University but were interrupted by military service. After receiving an A.B. degree in Anthropology from the University of California, Berkeley, he acquired a Juris Doctorate at the University of California, Hastings College of the Law. He is a member of the State Bar of California, the California Trial Lawyers' Association, the Solano County Bar Association, and Phi Beta Kappa.

Laura Nader, professor of anthropology at the University of California at Berkeley, has studied law among the Zapotec of Mexico, the Shias in Lebanon, and in the United States. The author of *Talea and Juquila: A Comparison of Zapotec Social Organization* (1964), she has produced a film on Zapotec court procedure (1966) and with her students published *The Disputing Process—Law in Ten Societies* (1978).

Rena Rosenwasser attended Sarah Lawrence College (A.B., 1971). She is presently completing her M.A. at Mills College in a combined writing and English Literature program.

David Serber has a B.A. and Ph.D. in anthropology from the University of California at Berkeley and was a postdoctoral fellow at the Health Policy Program, School of Medicine, University of California, San Francisco. Serber's publications include articles on reform and regulation and on complaint management. He is currently an assistant professor at Carnegie-Mellon University, Pittsburgh.

Christopher Shugart received a B.A. in history (1971) from the University of Wisconsin, Madison, where he graduated Phi Beta Kappa. Shugart holds a J.D. (1978) from Hastings College of the Law, San Francisco, and is a member of the California Bar.

Tom H. Stanton, a Washington, D.C. attorney, received his B.A. from the University of California at Davis, M.A. from Yale University, and J.D. from the Harvard Law School. He is co-author of the book *Tax Politics* (Pantheon 1976). He has been director of the Public Citizen Tax Reform Research Group and the Housing Research group of the Center for Study of Responsive Law. He is now Deputy Director of the Office of Policy Planning of the Federal Trade Commission.

Gregory F. Wilson holds a B.A. (1973) from Harvard College and a J.D. (1977) from the Harvard Law School. He was admitted to the State Bar of California in 1977, and currently practices law in San Francisco.

PREFACE

The maintenance of order is a problem that human beings every-where must deal with. For over a century scientists have made an effort to understand the range of alternatives that human societies have devised to handle problems of order. They have discovered that there can be much law with no courts, and much order with little government, or the reverse. They have found that law functions as one form of social control, but that in most societies of the world where there are viable alter-natives, law is not necessarily the most important form of control. They have learned something about choice making: Whether people choose to mediate or adjudicate a case depends on the rank relationship between the parties and as well on the type of conflict; for example, whether they choose plea bargaining over court trial depends on who the advocates are and what components of a case they choose to act on. The context in which things happen gives meaning. As a way to delineate more specifi-cally the perspectives that underlie the work in this volume, I should briefly review where I started and why.

I initiated anthropological research in 1957 when I began to investi-gate patterns of social control and problem solving among the isolated mountain Zapotec villagers of Oaxaca, Mexico. I started with a study of Zapotec courts—their functions, purposes, and users—but I quickly realized that in order to have any kind of profound understanding of how the courts worked, I had to have an idea of the alternatives that people felt they had to the courts, and I had to understand the perspective of the complainants as well as that of the judge. As I began to look at the alterna-tives, I gradually came to realize that the relation between the various alternatives available to Zapotecs was an interdependent one; that is, if extended families were successful in solving their own family troubles, there would be fewer family cases in the courts; if the courts did not give satisfaction, alternative remedy agents might do so. In my publications on

Zapotec law (Nader, 1964, 1965, 1969, 1977), I describe it as a system that is problem solving in intent, educative, preventive, deterrent, and simple enough for citizens to understand and use. In addition, Zapotec law has a built-in set of priorities for determining the seriousness of an action in terms of its effect on the society and on sheer numbers of people. Traditionally, pollution of the water supply would be considered more serious than murder.

After completing my research among the Zapotec, I began to train graduate students to do fieldwork on law and functionally equivalent institutions in other cultures among people who for the most part lived in small, relatively stable, face-to-face communities or in face-to-face communities that were in transition to relationships between strangers (Nader & Todd 1978). The problems certain other cultures are facing have often encompassed within a decade the changes that have been with us in America at least since the onset of industrialization. Other cultures provide an invaluable historical reminder of processes that have been evolving worldwide since industrialization and irrespective of the particulars of a culture. While this cross-cultural work was going on, I became interested in United States law. In the late 1960s I began querying my colleagues at the law school of the University of California at Berkeley, asking them the kinds of questions I had asked the Zapotec: Who uses the legal system? We found one serious article on the subject. How much does it cost to run the American legal system? We found one article, after a search by the Yale Law School librarian. What happens after a law is passed? Few studies could be pointed to that followed the impact of new laws. Why is the law so complicated? Why are Americans so uneducated about their law? What alternatives to the law do citizens have? Do we have a competitive system of dispute settlement? What is it like here, anyway?

Responses to such questions were revealing a way of thinking that is professionally closed. Law professors (not unlike other professionals) wrote for each other and for other members of the practicing profession; yet the fact that they knew so little, and cared less, about the users and potential users of the system was a disappointment. I also gradually came to realize that anthropologists probably knew more about living law among the Booga Booga than the legal profession knew about that in the United States; most certainly anthropologists knew more about the pattern of legal remedy usage.

Sociologists working on law have reflected some of the biases of the legal profession itself. Empirical sociological studies of law got underway only sometime in the 1950s, and then at a snail's pace. Much of the work by political scientists and sociologists was jurisprudential or philosophical in orientation, and concerned either with high-level professionals such as Supreme Court justices or with lower-income people found in the nation's prisons. Clearly, exceptions could be found, but these were the dominant trends in the late 1960s.

The picture that began to form in my mind was that of a legal system that did not seem to have a place for "most people's legal problems," but I was not certain. I encouraged Berkeley anthropology students to study the small claims courts in the San Francisco Bay Area and to review the social science literature on the subject. Some small claims courts were used for handling people's individual problems; mostly, however, they were used as collection agencies. I would catch a glimpse of action line columns in newspapers now and then and would remark that the kinds of problems taken to action liners seemed to be of a kind that the Zapotecs would take to their courts. The question "What do Americans really do with their legal problems?" though formulated, remained in the back of my mind for lack of knowing exactly how to explore such a broad question.

In 1971 I began to look systematically at the information contained in consumer and other complaint letters sent to Ralph Nader. As I read these letters, I realized they would be extremely useful in getting a general picture of how Americans actually handle legal problems. Often the letters written to Nader are chronicles of problems: the life history of what happened from the inception of a problem through a maze of real or perceived remedy agents, and details of coping attempts on the part of the citizen. I began to get a sense of some of the alternatives that people use in problem solving when they feel they have no access to law, and some ideas about their perception of the legal system as contrasted with the perspective of the professional law person. These letters reflect a select group of people: People who would at least write a letter in their own behalf; people who would voice objection, who would advocate; people who were motivated by a sense of injustice. I might add also that these were people who said they did not usually write in a fit of anger but who, on the contrary, had experienced an injustice and were telling about it. Despite this selection in favor of people who actively voiced, I was impressed by an overwhelming feeling of powerlessness in many of the letters. The questions began to come one on top of the other. What were the mental health consequences of consumer problems? What were the more pervasive consequences for our democratic system of the felt powerlessness to cope? What did legal rights mean if there was no forum in which to exercise them?

The analyses of complaint letters opened a new world of research for us. With the exception of Gellhorn (1966) and a small number of other researchers, few had ever paid intellectual attention to the fact that Americans are probably the biggest complaint letter writers in the world, and few had looked into such coping behaviors as were mentioned in the letters. But we also had our frustrations in using the letters: Who were these complainants? How did they plan their strategies? How did they learn where to take a problem? How did it all finally end?

With minimal research funding, I began to work with undergraduates in the study of some of the old and new institutions that were developing as alternatives to a legal system that was unresponsive to legal problems. The undergraduates who participated in this project were not all students at Berkeley, nor where they all anthropology majors. There were students from Northwestern, Radcliffe, Harvard, Williams, and Sarah Lawrence, in addition to Berkeley. None were recruited; all were volunteers who came to my office. We began to pursue studies on the People's Law School as it operated in San Francisco; on hot lines; action lines; consumer offices; volunteer citizen bureaus; department store complaint-managing systems; government agency complaint handling; corporate ombudsmen; and patterns of problem solving as handled by politicians. A fascinating picture emerged. During the decade of the 1960s Americans seemed to have entered a period of wanting to do something about their complaints, and institutions developed in response. For example, the first newspaper action line column appeared around 1961; a decade later there were close to 200 such columns. We were in the middle of a rapidly changing situation.

What we began to uncover was only the tip of the iceberg. There has been much written about alienation, but there has not been enough attention given to the actual means by which people become alienated. Political lip service is paid to the silent majority without knowing whether the American is silent or whether he is silenced. We have not adequately studied where Americans speak and are heard.

This research had great interest for students. In addition, I was impressed with the way in which research on this topic affected students who did the research. The subject matter was alive and of the sort that provided a link between academia and action. Although they were not action agents, the students were studying incidents of action or voicing on subject matter they could well empathize with. Students studying patterns of complaint management—institutions seen as alternatives to the legal system—were studying the possibility of a truly competitive series of institutions used to solve and prevent people's problems, and not a locked-in system. Along with the students, I saw in this research opportunity a chance to contribute as a citizen as well as a scientist.

In 1973 a proposal was submitted to the Carnegie Corporation from the Center for the Study of Responsive Law in Washington, D.C., the organization headed by my brother, Ralph Nader. It proposed to establish a Consumer Complaint Research Center to learn in greater detail about the actual operation or nonoperation of existing grievance-handling mechanisms in government, business, volunteer, and individual complaint management in the United States and to determine American attitudes about these processes. The intent was to analyze the consequences of the present system of complaint handling and to understand better

what works and what does not, and for whom. Those of us who participated in the writing of this proposal hoped for various changes as a result
of the research: faster reform of small claims courts, realistic corporate
complaint systems, and the establishment of citizen complaint centers
around the country through volunteer and self-financing efforts. Basic
concepts were to be examined: the actual operation of the market mechanism with its consumer feedback for higher quality competition and improved product quality; the possibility of aggregating the grievances of
people into structural reform of the law to prevent recurring grievances;
and an examination of the meaning for our society of having evolved a
nation-state law as the sole source of law. The proposal was funded, and
work was carried out both in Washington, D.C. and at the University of
California, Berkeley.

This book is an examination of the various alternatives to the American legal system and, as such, reflects only part of the work supported
through the Complaint Research Center. A good deal of research was invested in life histories of consumer complaints about corporate products,
services, or policies, which, as I mention in the Acknowledgments, will
be published as a separate book by Arthur Best. The life-history cases
were selected by a number of criteria, such as the importance of the complaint as it related to health, income, population at-risk, future risk expansion, or the extent to which the complaint represented a grievance perceived by others in a neighborhood or group. The complaint case studies
were designed to elicit data about complaint response patterns unobtain-
able or unavailable for reasons of "protection of the complainant and
complainee" or of protection of trade secrets. The researchers were to
probe the extent to which the various government agencies respond and
under what stimuli they will use their authority to act justly. They were to
test complaint management strategies to ascertain what works and how,
when, and where. Some dozen of these cases were then selected for even
more intensive study in order to capture and highlight the issue of "what
is a big trouble and what is a little trouble." How a layman defines a large
versus a small problem may be quite different from the professional's
view, and, as in all our work, we wished to explore complaint management from the complainant's view. What we have found is a serious indictment of the types of relationships that have evolved along with our
evolving GNP. We have a mass phenomenon in which large segments of
the population, reflective of all socioeconomic groups, are exposed to
low-profile, undramatic, petty exploitation that is ruinous to the quality of
democratic life. Despite our high GNP, access to purveyors of justice is
more readily available in some underdeveloped parts of the world than it
is in this country (Nader & Todd 1978).

ACKNOWLEDGMENTS

I wish to express my gratitude to Carnegie Corporation of New York for its direct leave support of my work at Berkeley during one quarter in 1975, and for its support of student researchers. The support from Carnegie allowed what had started as a voluntary research operation to move into more rigorous pursuit of knowledge about complaining in America. In particular, I wish to thank Mr. Eli Evans, then of the Carnegie Corporation, for encouraging an application that tries to incorporate the academic research interests at Berkeley with the more practical and activist interest of the Carnegie Corporation-funded Complaint Research Center at the Center for the Study of Responsive Law in Washington. Our advisory panel was an interested group. Judge George Brunn, Municipal Court Judge in Berkeley, California, Gordon Sherman, former president of Midas Muffler Corporation, David Caplovitz, Professor of Sociology at CUNY Graduate Center, and Albert Hirschman, fellow at the Institute for Advanced Study at Princeton, all made substantive contributions to the overall work on complaints of which this book is but a part.

The undergraduate students who contributed to this book were stimulated to explore new terrain when graduate students, already tied to a career line, were more timid. The book is testimony: Undergraduates are capable of important contributions to scholarship, and were we to harness their energies, both undergraduate teaching and anthropological research could be substantially improved.

There are many people who do not appear as authors whose work has been important to this book. Arthur Best, presently deputy commissioner of New York City's Department of Consumer Affairs, completed a manuscript entitled *When Consumers Complain: Consumer Justice, Problems and Prospects* (Columbia University Press, in press), and published the results of a survey of consumer complaint behavior in urban America in the *Law and Society Review*. Political Scientist Christopher Wheeler,

Polly Tyson, now a practicing lawyer, Jan Agee, who has since contributed to a directory on more effective consumer complaint-handling for Californians, and many others helped in research and case worker positions. Belinda Johns, my research associate, herself a student of law, has for the past 2 years contributed at one time or another to all phases of the work. Grace Buzaljko has edited these chapters and young authors have learned to respect the importance of quality editing. Enid Satariano and Laura Watkins helped with the typing of the manuscript.

In particular, I would like to acknowledge the work of Christopher Shugart who assisted me with the introductory and policy chapters in this volume. Mr. Shugart volunteered many hours of his time, while a student of law, to research essential background materials. The introduction also benefited from independent research completed by Andrew Sharpless (1978) on the economic costs of complaining and by a graduate student in history at the University of Chicago, Peter Samson, on the historical beginnings of the consumer movement in the United States. Both the works of Samson and Sharpless have been funded through the Complaint Research Center.

In addition, I would like to acknowledge those who chose not to participate in a study that required that data be attributed. The Ford Motor Company, with whom we negotiated for months for permission to study their complaint-handling process because it was reputed to be the best among car manufacturers, chose not to allow us access, as did Whirlpool, a corporation also reputed to have success in complaint handling. At differing times some of the trade associations, in particular the MACAP organization, as well as The Better Business Bureau of Oakland, I. Magnin of San Francisco, and Macy's in San Francisco, and as well, The United States Post Office, also chose not to cooperate despite the contributions that we might have made to these organizations as a result of external evaluation. The general observation may be made that cooperation and research is not easily forthcoming from companies accustomed to operating within the protection of confidentiality.

There are many other people in the field of law who inspired and/or challenged my thinking in this work on complaint mechanisms. Chief Justice Warren Berger allowed me the privilege of attending and addressing the First Pound Conference on Popular Dissatisfaction with the Administration of Justice in St. Paul in 1977. Because the Chief Justice comes to the subject of little injustices from a perspective quite different from that of the anthropologist, our interaction at that conference served as an invitation to rethink the meaning of alternative justice forums in this country. The invitations from the California Bar Association to attend its Conference on Law in the Year 2000 and from the American Judicature Society to celebrate the bicentennial in Philadelphia on the subject of justice in America allowed me further opportunity to communicate my ideas to people in another and more predominantly practicing profession than my own (see Nader 1976, Nader & Singer 1976). Michael Lowy was always helpful in seeing to it that I did not become affected by operating for so long in the midst of legal professionals; he has helped me to keep the legal paradigm separate from the anthropological paradigm. However, Ralph Nader, more than all other lawyers, inspired me as an academic anthropologist to fulfill the promise of anthropology, to make a contribution to the problem of devising appropriate complaint mechanisms for an industrial society operating in a runaway world.

I thank my family for supporting my work, for questioning my ideas, for protecting my time, for giving me a very personal reason to wish to contribute to the world into which our children are growing.

I

STRUCTURE AND IDEAS

1

Laura Nader

ALTERNATIVES TO THE AMERICAN JUDICIAL SYSTEM

Introduction

The observation that Americans have no access to law for certain types of cases has appeared in numerous law review articles since the turn of the century and probably before.[1] The reasons for lack of access have usually been documented by these same authors—the type of case and lack of time, money, and knowledge. Most of these same scholars not only have called attention to the access problems and the reasons that have caused no access but also have provided a series of possible remedies. Many of the remedies developed into movements: the small claims courts movement, the regulatory movement (as in the work of the ICC and FTC), the legal services movement, the prepaid legal services effort, and the public interest law movement. Although many books and articles have been written defining the problem of access and although many solutions have been suggested, few researchers have asked how people with complaints but no access to law do handle their problems. Nor have scholars explored in any depth the consequences of citizen alternative action or inaction.

This book is about what Americans do with their legal problems when they perceive, objectively or subjectively, that for them there is no access to law and yet they wish to respond to injustice or what Lerner (1975) calls the justice motive. We have found that some people in trouble can be ingenious and persevering in their search for justice; in the face of obvious discouragement they have invented or searched out a number of

[1] See, e.g., Fox (1965); Harley (1915); Maguire (1923); Pound (1913); Vance (1917).

nonjudicial mechanisms. We have also found that the impact of their actions and the consequences of a lack of access to judicial remedy have had a serious effect on the machinery of government, on the mental health of Americans, and on the crime rate. The absence of prosecution has encouraged an escalation of criminal behavior among those who have consciously or unconsciously capitalized on the fact that the American criminal justice system is not organized to handle widespread petty thievery accomplished by a series of small, economic crimes committed against individual Americans.

It is not surprising, perhaps, that American inventiveness in the area of remedy generally has been ignored by researchers in law as well as by those in the social sciences. Heavy dependence on the case method in law schools, with its focus on individual problems usually at the appellate level, makes unlikely any systematic approach to recognizing mass problems or to earning a living by the handling of block cases. Scholars have ignored this area for many of the same reasons that the law has ignored them: As individual cases they are not important enough to warrant a position high on the list of research priorities. It is only when we address the question of consequence that we realize how serious the absence of attention has been.

The reason for an interest in little injustices is, on the other hand, perhaps more obvious to the anthropologist: People care about them. Little injustices are the greater part of everyday living in a consumption society, and, of course, people's attitudes toward the law are formed by their encounters with the law or by the absence of encounters when the need arises. If there is no access for those things that matter, then the law becomes irrelevant to its citizens, and, something else, alternatives to law become all they have. As we shall see later on, these alternatives appear in many forms; in this book we do not address violent response, nor do we include studies of apathetic response. We concentrate our attention on people who voice their complaints in a responsible manner, in settings where the expressed goal, at least, is to arrive at a solution.

Individual responses to no access add up, causing a drift in the legal system itself. For what happens outside the system is as likely to have repercussions on the legal system as is the reverse situation, in which legal actions reverberate beyond the law and affect other institutions. Judicial and nonjudicial mechanisms should be viewed as parts of one social-control system. It may be useful to remind ourselves that our legal system had its roots in a much smaller society, characterized by the opposite of anonymity: People knew each other or knew of each other. Public opinion was an important mechanism of social control. As Ehrlich (1936) notes: "It is only when the state has grown extremely powerful and has begun to tend towards an absolute form [that the idea arises] of making the state the authoritative, and in course of time the sole, source of law [14]."

Ours is a nation of strangers, a country where the greatest number of potential abuses occurs between people who are strangers to each other. Parties that buy and sell are often strangers to each other; production is centralized; and large organizations control information, condition the terms of purchase, and shape perceptions through advertising. These forces have culminated in increased dependency, which has brought with it a redistribution of power in our society; most product and service complaints are between people of greatly unequal power.

The direction of law seems to be evolving in similar ways worldwide, although with different consequences in places where the social and cultural structures are different (Nader 1978; Nader and Todd 1978). When nation–state law begins to predominate, as it does in industrial states, extrajudicial processes and social-control mechanisms are replaced. At the same time most actual and potential disputes are those between strangers; the true plaintiff becomes only secondarily important, and the courts decline in personnel relative to population growth and need. Court functions shift away from dispute settlement; access to courts decreases; the function of law as power equalizer diminishes, and law decreases in its role relative to issues that affect the quality of everyday life (see Colson 1976; Friedman 1973). Then we return full circle: Extrajudicial processes begin to develop in direct response to these trends, and with them the struggle between the legal system and the litigant for control or influence over the extrajudicial processes that are evolving as a result of the failure of law (Lowy 1978). Although many non-Western countries are at different points of the circle, this book is about the struggle occurring in a highly evolved industrial country over the problems of how to achieve a certain kind of justice in a mass society.

In this chapter I describe how we as researchers proceeded in our study and what we were able to learn as well as report on the broader implications of this work. I begin with a summary of our approach and findings in the study of individual complaint responses and the dynamics of complaint organizations. I then analyze the constraints on third-party handlers in the United States as they affect their abilities to perform to stated goals. The final portion of this chapter is an analysis of the meaning and consequence of extrajudicial complaint handling in the United States. I purposely have set apart any policy recommendations for the following chapter in the belief that understanding must precede recommendation.

This subject matter is fraught with emotional responses and irrational procedures. It is my hope that we can begin to address the issues raised by a frank consideration of complaint handling from the point of view of the parties specifically concerned as well as from that of the society at large. Our starting point is the complainant, the actual operation of the market mechanism with its consumer feedback for higher-quality competition, the use of prevention, the examination of the meaning for our society of having evolved a "state" law as the sole source of law.

Discovering the Content of Extrajudicial Complaint Handling

How does an anthropologist who was trained to study small communities in a holistic manner proceed in a study of complaint processing in a nation of over 200 million people? From the outset it was clear that our techniques would have to be eclectic, our approach unorthodox and the result of teamwork. We commenced our journey with a careful scrutiny of complaint letters. Along with newspaper clippings, these letters were invaluable as a means of scanning the mundane concerns of people around the country.

We began to delimit the study. We would, as Gellhorn did (1966), study nonjudicial mechanisms; by the 1970s there was a small cadre of social scientists and lawyers looking into strictly legal mechanisms. We would focus on people who voice their concerns, although we did make a feeble attempt at studying nonvoicers in a door-to-door study in a California community (Parnell 1973). We would choose for study a number of organizations that are not generally studied in this context, that represent both public and private attempts at dispute settlement, and that illustrate both honest and devious attempts by government, business, unions, and the voluntary sector to provide a forum for voicing dissatisfactions. Our starting point was always the complainant: What do these various public and private systems look like to him or her? Finally, where possible, our work was carried out over a period of time, sometimes as long as 7 or so years. The emphasis from the beginning was purposely panoramic in order to develop a broad framework for understanding the continuum or process of complaint handling that ranges from legal to extralegal.

The Individual Complaint Responses

As I said, we began with complaint letters, letters written to Ralph Nader. If from personal experience we had guessed that people experience varying degrees of frustration and disillusionment in grievance handling, such personal experience certainly was borne out in letters from consumers of food, automobiles, housing, insurance, appliances, finance, drugs, and medical, legal, and other professional services such as repair and utility services.[2] But the letters were also interesting from a purely intellectual perspective; there were patterns and styles of complaining. Styles were related to instrumental goals in letter writing: requests for aid and information, giving of aid and information, confessionals, the use of Ralph Nader as a pressure strategy. Our study of styles led to an analysis of strategies of complainants, such as "calling in the outsider." When an individual sees that her opponent (a company or government bureaucracy) is too big for her, she attempts to balance the power situation by sending letters to opponents, with carbon copies to one or more people. These multiple- and single-pressure letters seem to correlate with the requests made; that is, the more a situation is perceived as serious or harmful, the more likely there are to be multiple carbon or duplicated copies.

What we found is akin to what Gulliver (1969) has described for African societies—a way of balancing power by political means, by developing a support network. We also observed a power–impotence dimension in these letters ("I have been deeply hurt." "This didn't hurt me, but what if my child had eaten the wood splinters in the oatmeal?" "Nothing happened this time, but the whole family could have been burned when the TV shorted." "My husband, a veteran, is sick, and these frustrations cause him grief he can ill afford and doesn't deserve." "To whom it may concern, if anyone." "I hope this gets to you because no one else seems to care about my problems."). I do not believe it is simply the result of a view of complaints as symptomatic of social pathology that leads us to suggest that the costs of unresolved complaints must be enormous. Grievance often feeds alienation, anomie, frustration, anxiety, and kinship friction, and is an enormous waste of money, time, and resources for individuals and the economy in general.

The importance of these letters cannot be overstated for gaining a wide-angled view. It is most difficult to study complainants in a mass society like ours because they are geographically dispersed and often remain unknown by virtue of the confidentiality maintained by companies and nonjudicial dispute-settlement mechanisms. In addition, it has been true that even those most concerned with complaint handling are rarely interested in analyzing the nature of their clientele. In Chapter 3, Eric Freedman attempts to systematize what can be learned from the letters beyond the generally cumulative educational effect that reading several hundred letters has on one.

---

[2]Ralph Nader, of course, is not the only recipient of letters from troubled consumers:

The FTC, for example, gets complaint letters, some 60,000 a year as a matter of fact, in which often the major problem is simply that the consumer has no means of getting a fair resolution of the dispute at any price he can afford to pay [Statement of James DeLong, FTC Bureau of Consumer Protection, in U.S. Congress 1977:21].

The analysis of the complaint letters proved somewhat elusive in response to measurement techniques; there was too much variability, as Freedman notes. Beyond the sense of powerlessness and the loss of trust, the very advertising techniques and packaging devices that companies use to sell their products are the source of expectations of justice and also of widespread disillusionment and lack of faith. Customers believe that products and services should meet the standards set forth by the business community and their advertisers, although these buyers differ in their expectations concerning the likelihood of difficulties with their purchases.

One does begin to believe that there is indeed a justice motive (Lerner 1975) operating universally. The very fact that people of all socioeconomic brackets write these letters is an indication that they are motivated to write by a sense of injustice rather than by pure and simple economic need.[3] It is morality and economic justice that often count when people are either unaware of the legal aspects or think them irrelevant. The gravity of the complaints is always described in relation to individual circumstances—economic, physical, social, and mental. From the letters (which are usually written as a last resort and after a case has acquired a history) I discern that Americans have certain expectations with regard to their business transactions that are not being met.

It is also clear from analysis of these letters that thresholds of complaint differ widely. At the onset of this study, I had thought that the world was divided into people who voice and others who do not. An incident on an airplane convinced me otherwise. My seat partner was served breakfast, and immediately afterward his tray broke; he found himself sitting in coffee and orange juice. I was surprised at his calm response, at the almost timid way in which he asked for a napkin, and I asked him if he ever complained. His answer was revealing: "Yes, I complain, when something causes me to lose time. Time is all I've got. When the phone company overbills and I have to cross the city to get it straightened out, that makes me angry, and I complain. But right now I'm just sitting here goin' nowhere; my suit is dirty and needs cleaning anyway, and mistakes do happen." Freedman observes that people often relate just how an incident caused them to cross their tolerance threshold. They also pass judgment on just how much of their complaining is appropriate and how much is "just plain bitchin'."

There is also a practical utility to these letters that does not come out in the Freedman analysis but that Ralph Nader has pointed to re-

---

[3]In fact, complaint letters seem to be written more often by those with less economic need. Liefeld, Edgecombe, and Wolfe (1975) conducted a mail survey of over 17,000 Canadian consumers who had written complaint letters to consumer agencies in 1972. The average complainer turned out to be middle-aged, well-educated, affluent, and in the managerial–professional occupational strata.

peatedly in his contact with business and consumer people. An analysis of trends in complaints dealing with particular products or services can yield early alerts to potentially severe problems. Consumer complaints have served to alert appropriate regulatory agencies to the problems of faulty automotive engine mounts and defective intravenous fluid containers (both resulting in significant recalls) as well as to problems encountered by women in obtaining credit.[4] Consumer complaints from small businesspeople have often alerted the Justice Department antitrust division to widespread anticompetitive practices. Although academic researchers may think of these letters as being highly anecdotal or inconsequential and although the complainants themselves may sometimes feel that their letters perform mainly an expressive function, complaining by letter has been a powerful tool. It is interesting that companies sometimes value such letters to the degree that they would steal them from a competing company or, if written to themselves, would keep them in secret hiding places away from the scrutiny of the public.[5]

It was one of the arguments made by Albert Hirschman (1970) that companies might do well to listen to voicers; the advice they get is often valuable free consultation on how to improve their products. Yet the most frequent response by industry to complaint letters is denial or "runaround." When people do receive an honorable response from a company or service, they are also willing to give credence, glad to know that integrity is not dead and that their beliefs are not unfounded. The analyses and opinions of American business found in these letters are often sophisticated and to the point; they are also sometimes deferential of business leaders and always rich in commentary on the social scene. People in positions of responsibility might do well to read these letters themselves rather than to pass them off to public relations people.

Several issues were pursued through a selected few of the more successful complaint cases: evaluation of seriousness, the difference between

[4]Other examples: Consumer columnist Margaret Dana (1971) recounted for her readers how their complaint letters to her had revealed three major problems in 1971 and how efforts were being made to bring the problems to the attention of the appropriate government agencies and manufacturers. The problems were: "(1) cans that won't open and can openers that won't work; (2) slippery plastic heels that are dangerous; (3) fitted bed sheets that don't fit mattresses [p. 12]."

Adrian Stungo (1976) has described how the institution of the local ombudsman in England aided in recognizing a widespread pattern of complaints about town planning; over 40% of the complaints made in the first year of the ombudsman's existence concerned this subject.

[5]As testimony to the attempt of companies to keep complaints secret, we note in passing General Motors' avid interest in buying 19 boxes of microfilmed complaint letters sent to a Chevrolet customer relations department that accidently wound up in the hands of scrap dealers. It would be overgenerous to presume that GM quickly paid $20,000 out of a desire to better understand the nature of customer dissatisfaction (*San Francisco Chronicle* 1971:2).

specific complaining and more general or public citizen complaining, the cultivation of a sense of justice—or exercise of the justice motive—the making of public citizens, and the consequences of complaining.

The problem central to deciding the importance of a case is the contrast between the personal meaning of a case and the professional evaluation of the same case. Legal scholars have speculated for many years on the issue of what legal problems are important. A legal problem may be defined as of little importance if the amount of controversy is small, if one of the parties is too poor to wage a legal battle, or if the problem appears to be trivial, such as one that deals with interpersonal hostilities. A problem that is seen as a single issue rather than as part of a broad process will probably be seen as trivial by an attorney. From the personal view of a lower-income family, a tenant deposit not returned at a time the family is receiving a new baby into the house can cause a change of direction in family development and an escalation of problems that may leave the family undone in the end (Small Claims Study Group 1972). In our culture, such are the makings of novels. In other cultures, the ramifications are the makings of law cases. A published report of a similar situation appeared in a book on old age in America (Townsend 1971), when a car accident and serious injury to one member of a family led to a chain of events that destroyed the homestead of an elderly couple. A striking case that we investigated was that of the stove that turned itself on and off unexpectedly. By the time the owner sent Nader her 3-inch-thick packet of correspondence, she still could not claim to have attracted help or attention from the parties she had contacted: the seller, the producer, the utilities, and a dozen government offices. Finally her house burned down, and she felt vindicated. At the onset it was hardly a case that a lawyer would think worth his or her time. It is essential that the multifaceted nature of individual complaints be clearly understood by the complainants themselves as well as by government and legal planners.

The evidence is overwhelming that complaint experience in this country is not cumulative in impact. The lady who complained about diapers that disintegrated when used and asked that something be done to improve their quality lest a child swallow a piece of cotton and perhaps choke to death, got in response a new box of the same diapers from the producer. Research to date suggests that companies believe that people use general complaints as a strategy to "get a specific something" rather than accept a complaint for what it's worth—namely, a suggestion that the company change its policy. Similarly, rather than streamline or change the bureaucratic system that makes Social Security a nightmare in this country,[6] congressmen accept it as a duty to do something about a missing

[6]A study in 1975 found that congressmen in Washington were receiving 9300 com-

Social Security check, but they do not accept the challenge to "do something about this crazy system." One complainant succeeded in getting the New York Department of Consumer Affairs to slap a $50 fine on a company for its fraudulent disc-brake special—but that is all that happened.

Of the general complaint cases that we followed in detail, the consumer complaint process at the third-party stage generated basic action in only a small number of instances. In the extended case discussed by P. Addiss in Chapter 4, a southern couple with no tradition of voicing found themselves in a months-long battle with Chevrolet. Like the many other experiences we have encountered, the experience served as an education; they really did not know how business handled complaints before they embarked on their experience. It also served to damage their faith in fair treatment from business and was a blow to their self-esteem. They were tenacious in their pursuit of justice, but they really never saw beyond the specific case—they never saw themselves as members of a class of people with the same problems. We specifically searched for people who did take the next step and became public citizens concerned beyond their own specific problem to the general problems involved in defective products and deceptive advertising. The question still remains: Why do we as a people handle problems one by one rather than by block solutions? I found myself returning to this question in the research.

Business Complaint Handling

It was appropriate, after having given a good deal of attention to the complainants' point of view, that we look at business organizations in order to see "the other side" and to examine for ourselves the successes and failures in the complaint mechanisms that business had set up in response to the increasing numbers of consumer complaints they were receiving. Again we tried to get at this information using a variety of strategies. First, we looked for self-reputed and other defined successes. Whirlpool, for example, had informed the world of the availability of attention through hotlines and other means for consumers with complaints.[7] We wrote to Whirlpool for substantive information on their complaint mechanisms, and in return we received a number of public relations notices. We then wrote and asked if one of our students could spend some time studying "how they did it." Again there was little cooperation and response. We dropped the idea. With Ford Motor Company it was the

plaints a week about Social Security benefits, a volume that represented half of all public inquiries received by many congressional staffs (Fialka 1975).

[7]Whirlpool was the first U.S. company to receive customer complaints on a toll-free telephone line. Initiated in 1967, its system became the prototype for a number of other company hotlines (Prestbo 1971).

same, only the correspondence was more extended. Our Washington-based researcher negotiated for over 7 months for permission to study the complaint mechanisms of Ford, which had the reputation of being the best among automobile companies. In the final analysis the company said no, because car sales were down and there was a general agreement among American car manufacturers to stick together. It was a different story with businesses that had an open return policy of handling complaints; they not only had an open return policy but were willing to tell the world about it. The most successful businesses with open return at that time were department stores, the most famous being Marshall Field in Chicago, and small-product companies like Midas Muffler.

As part of our investigation of business attitudes toward consumer complaints, we explored the open return policy and the reasons why businesses may have aversion to open return. There is, in some commercial quarters, an overriding fear that ceding ground in the arena of consumer complaints will produce an avalanche of unsubstantiated complaints that would in turn reduce corporate profits. To date we know of no systematic study that substantiates this position and, in fact, have found some evidence to the contrary. A regional spokesperson at Sears Roebuck, a company that successfully has made use of an open return policy since the 1890s, told us that the number of product returns that are not made in good faith is insignificant—.5%, as he puts it. Judge George Brunn, who has had extensive experience in the Berkeley, California, small claims court, stated bluntly: "The charge that many claims are frivolous is just another bit of corporate mythology." One of our informants pointed out that the cost of the near-absolute return policy could be compared to the corporate advertising budget to demonstrate that the suggested return policy is reasonable and manageable. Nevertheless, there is considerable resistance to open return.

Midas Muffler, under the guidance of businessman Gordon Sherman, during the years 1950–1970, demonstrated that a corporation could readily adopt consumer complaint policy to replace a product that a consumer complained about and that it could do so without a statistically significant impact on corporate profits. Simply put, Midas promised to replace a defective muffler as long as the purchaser of the muffler owned the car. Determination of product failure was simple enough: A muffler is defective when it fails to muffle, that is, when one can hear the engine noise. There was no time limit on the guarantee, and Midas made money.

In our preliminary survey of a dozen retailers and a like number of manufacturers, we gleaned the following patterns. Retail stores uniformly stated that some version of an "automatic return policy" (sometimes called a customer satisfaction policy) is essential to everyday retail business. One store's published policy has been: "Your money is only on deposit until you are perfectly satisfied with your purchase." Leaving aside the difference between policy and action, it is probably fair to say that retailers, particularly those dealing with well-to-do customers, respect the impact of a rebuff in a face-to-face complaint. The retailers are caught between sloppy manufacturing and the customer. From the manufacturing viewpoint, policies are sometimes made to ensure performance on the part of the retailers. One manufacturer limited the merchandise returns from retailers to actual defects and misorders, the purpose being to reduce the incidence of retailers returning slow-moving merchandise.

In general, manufacturers of low-cost items, such as recording tape, do not hesitate to replace a complained-of item. Moderately priced goods, in particular clothing, can be replaced inexpensively within the limits of the "use time" of an article ("use time" referring to style changes). Large, high-cost items are reluctantly replaced because of high inventory costs, shipping expenses, and the belief that maintenance teams are less expensive to fund than product replacements would be.

Although the options were many, we finally settled on three studies that would tell us something about the dynamics of complaint-handling in areas in which there was a high degree of interaction between people and business. We studied a Better Business Bureau (BBB) in a northern California city; we described the complaint-handling organizations of six department stores in the Bay Area; and we studied self-governing mechanisms devised by several trade associations. The Better Business Bureau study began in 1971 and followed throughout the research period (to 1976) in the context of what was happening at the national level of the BBB. The trade association study commenced in 1973 and continued for 3 years, and the department store research was begun in 1972 and followed up in 1975 and 1978. In all these organizations there have been changes that naturally affect anything as fragile as a complaint mechanism; for example, since our study of the department stores, several of them have been bought by large firms whose home bases are outside California. From our experience, such shifts in ownership often mean a deterioration in complaint handling. In fact, some of the large department stores of San Francisco that did not originate in San Francisco, such as Macy's, simply refused to cooperate with us in spite of arguments that they might benefit from our study. As to the trade associations and the BBB, changes in their structures and policies may be directly correlated with the climate for business in the nation's capital.

A 1974 Roper Report asked consumers where they would turn should they fail to get satisfaction from the seller or manufacturer for a product problem. Over 50% responded that they would go to the Better Business Bureau (Conference Board 1973:6).[8] Marian Eaton's work (Chapter 6) on

---

[8]See also King and McEvoy (1976). The BBB ranked third out of 21 public and private

the BBB analyzes the performance of a branch of the Bureau, an organization that presents an image of itself as an outfit after shoddy, "fly-by-night" business practices. Her study essentially substantiates the findings in the report of Rep. Benjamin Rosenthal (1971), which documents problems stemming from a conflict of interest: Better Business Bureaus are financially dependent on local businesses but at the same time are expected to serve consumers.[9] Although the BBB is one of the best-known and most frequently contacted of all third parties that process consumer complaints, many complainants come away from the BBB dissatisfied.[10] Self-regulation has never been successful (except with parachute makers who have to test their own products). As an arm of the established business community, especially of larger businesses, its goal is to give consumers a favorable impression of the business community without causing much inconvenience for the businesses themselves.

From the first contact with the BBB, consumers must persist if they are to win; the first obstacle is presented when consumers are required to register their complaints on BBB forms rather than tell their story or write a letter to BBB personnel. Eaton sees the greatest value of the BBB system in the opening up of a channel of communication between the local merchant and the consumer that occurs when the BBB forwards the complaint to the business—most businesses pay attention to BBB complaints. The BBB, however, does not take the role of an active mediator. In keeping with its ideal of self-regulation by the business community, the BBB assumes that businesses will voluntarily resolve complaints in an equitable fashion once the lines of communication are opened.

Even if it tried to take a more active stance, the BBB would be limited by its lack of power to compel a settlement. The major sanction it will bring to bear on a recalcitrant company—in the absence of gross illegality—comes through the preparation of a "bad reliability report," which the BBB will give to any inquirer, and in this way does influence

---

organizations of potential help to consumers in terms of familiarity to consumers. Only the U.S. Postal Service and the Social Security Commission were better known.

[9]Dean Determan, Vice President of the Council of Better Business Bureaus, confirmed our observation that since the Rosenthal report in 1971, there has been no other published independent study of complaint handling at the BBB (personal communication, 26 January 1979). In 1970, the Council of Better Business Bureaus was formed to address public criticism, and in 1977 the Metropolitan New York BBB made news by naming as its President James Lack, a recognized consumer advocate. (Lack has since left this post to become a state senator.) Whatever changes may have taken place in the BBB system in the last few years, the Rosenthal report and Eaton's study in Chapter 6 represent the last independent word on the subject.

[10]Note also a random survey in 1971 of 51 complainants who had used the Washington, D.C., Better Business Bureau (Levy 1971). The poll revealed 26% satisfied and 67% dissatisfied. This result contrasted sharply with the local BBB's claim that it "routinely" settled 90% of all complaints against businesses that it received from residents of the area.

public opinion. For reasons she states in her study, Eaton does not believe that reliability reports are very effective in pressuring businesses to change their practices.

If a just resolution cannot be achieved, the BBB's interest is best served by pacifying the complainant. The BBB educates the consumer to accept the "reasonableness" of certain business practices. The consumer may be told, for instance, that agreements are binding only if they are in writing—a misstatement of the law. Moreover, the consumer is led to believe that the BBB has done all that can be done outside the courts. Eaton concludes that the regulation of business by the BBB holds potential value but should not be overestimated. It is more effective in dealing with small, local businesses than with large national or multinational ones—an observation that also applies to the complaint panels set up by the trade associations, as we shall see.

David Greenberg and Thomas Stanton (Chapter 5) analyzed data collected by fieldworker Ruth Darmstadter while she was studying the Consumer Action Panels (CAPs) sponsored by six trade associations for the processing of consumer disputes. The central purpose behind the CAP programs was to forestall government regulation by demonstrating that the industries, dealing in new houses, new cars, major appliances, furniture, carpeting, and moving and storage, could regulate themselves.[11] In other words, the CAPs (like the BBBs) exist primarily to serve the trade association members, not the consumers. Their aim is to increase consumer satisfaction, or rather to decrease overt dissatisfaction, at the smallest cost and without alienating the businesses that constitute their membership.

Because the trade association systems can act only when there is a broad consensus among members and the members naturally are reluctant to give up their autonomy, these dispute-processing mechanisms have little power. In the first phase of the process, the consumer action panel serves as an intermediary by transmitting a complaint from the consumer to the company (manufacturer or retailer). As in the BBBs, the larger companies prevail. The CAPs review complaints that cannot be resolved (by company and consumer), but they are empowered only to give nonbinding advisory opinions, and they generally make no follow-up to see if the businesses have complied.

The authors detail the various ways in which the complaint process is structured to encourage consumers to drop out. Some of these CAP complainants are the unsung persevering heroes of our time. For example, at each stage of the review process the initiative must come from the con-

---

[11]As Virginia Knauer, then the President's consumer advisor, warned: "We're encouraging voluntary action, but time is running out. If industry doesn't shape itself up soon, the government will step in and do it for them [*Wall Street Journal* 1971:1]."

sumer; consumers often are not told that they can continue to press their case if they remain dissatisfied with the company's response; and a CAP will not review a complaint until the company has refused several times to give the consumer satisfaction.

Of all the trade association programs, the Office of the Impartial Chairman (OIC) for the moving industry in New York City was most receptive to being studied. This program was set up jointly by the movers' trade associations and a local chapter of the Teamsters' Union. OIC's position gives it more power and independence than that of the other systems. It has the authority to resolve disputes between moving companies and their customers by the use of binding arbitration, and it helps prevent complaints by screening members' estimates of moving costs.

The Greenberg–Stanton study concludes that, with the exception of OIC, the trade association programs are of no real help to the consumer. One might think that if the CAPs do little good, at least they can do no harm. But the authors call attention to the pernicious influence of ineffective dispute-processing institutions, even if effective institutions also exist in the society. The experience of dealing with such institutions contributes to the frustration that causes so many American consumers to give up trying to resolve their grievances—to "lump it." For the most part, the trade association programs probably have this effect as well as that of "cooling out" the federal government; if it looks as if industry is attending to its customers' dissatisfactions, the government will not lean toward further regulation or preventive means to relieve the consumer.

Anela Karikas and Rena Rosenwasser's study (Chapter 7) of department store complaint handling is particularly interesting because it is an example of complaining directly to the seller—and two-party negotiation is the most common consumer response.[12] It is also interesting, and perhaps related to the impact of a rebuff in face-to-face situations, that customers probably have more success in settling complaints in their favor with department stores than with industry or the telephone company or government, for example.

Karikas and Rosenwasser studied the complaint-managing systems of six department stores in the San Francisco Bay Area. Although the six systems differ in organization, the researchers found that if a customer is persistent enough in pursuing her complaint, the upper levels of the store's management will usually resolve it in her favor—especially if she is a steady customer with a good credit record—and even if the complaint seems unreasonable. Department stores are in competition with each other, and their managements have concluded that the benefits of keeping

[12]Best and Andreasen discovered that only 3.7% of complaints were taken to third parties (1977:713). For a recent discussion of the process of negotiation and how it is affected by the context of legal norms, see Eisenberg (1976).

the steady customer satisfied are worth the costs to the store. As we shall see later, this policy is exactly the opposite of the telephone company's.

But the complainant's path may not be completely smooth, for in most of the stores the complaint process begins at the level of the salesperson. The authors examined various aspects of this encounter and the bargaining that goes on between the salesperson and the customers. A major problem is that the procedure for appealing a decision reached on the floor is not always made clear to the customer. The customer service department, if there is one, is often hidden away in an obscure office, although customer service in family firms such as Hinks' in Berkeley has been anything but obscure. It is not surprising that the (then) most successful complaint system was found in a leading luxury store. As the lady complaint manager at Gump's explained, "Honey, there ain't nothin' in this store you couldn't live without." At Gump's the salespeople immediately refer all complaints to a central office. Centralized complaint processing simplifies procedure and makes the outcome more predictable.

One theme found in all the department store complaint-handling systems, whether they were centralized or decentralized, is that individual complaints have little effect on the general policy of the store. Furthermore, manufacturers are rarely made aware of customer complaints; complaints about quality thus have little influence in inducing manufacturers to change their products.[13] Again, complaining does not have a cumulative impact and is usually ameliorative, at best.

Government Complaint Handling

Does government do any better than business?[14] We found early in our research that referral from agency to agency rather than resolution of complaints seems to characterize the overwhelming number of citizen experiences with both government offices and their elected officials (Darmstadter 1973; Tyson 1973). But others had been and were saying the same thing. As noted in Nader and Singer (1976), Justice William O. Douglas, concurring in the case of *Johnson v. Avery* (1969) 393 U.S. 483,

---

[13]Sears Roebuck, however, which has an open return policy, is an example of a company that has instituted a system for recognizing and dealing with patterns of complaints. Reports on every complaint are sent to headquarters in Chicago and compiled. Sears then tries to work with manufacturers to improve products that are continually failing to satisfy customers. The important point is that where there is an open return system, the store has an increased incentive to make sure it carries only products that will please. Making one-by-one complaint resolution easier can lead to a large cumulative impact and to preventive changes.

[14]The experience of complaining citizens is testimony to the ineffectiveness of government complaint processing. A survey conducted for *U.S. News & World Report* (1978) revealed that although 80% of consumers who return goods to retailers come away satisfied, only 37% of those who lodge complaints about government services gain satisfaction.

attempted to call attention to the plight of a citizen with a complaint against a government agency:

> The increasing complexities of our governmental apparatus both at the local and federal levels have made it difficult for a person to process a claim or even to make a complaint. Social Security is a virtual maze; the hierarchy that governs urban housing is often so intricate that it takes an expert to know what agency has jurisdiction over a particular complaint; the office to call or official to see for noise abatement, for a broken sewer line, or a downed tree is a mystery to many in our metropolitan areas [p. 491].

Furthermore, citizens lack access even to the information on which critical bureaucratic decisions concerning their welfare and livelihood are made. For example, the state agencies that make initial determinations of eligibility for disability payments under Social Security do not allow rejected applicants to see either the specific reasons why they were considered ineligible nor the reports of the applicants' medical examinations. Petitions for reconsideration must be based on the applicants' guess as to why the original application was denied (Hendry 1975; Stewart 1975). One of our team attempted to collect information on a Department of Labor decision and was informed that the California Public Information Act did not apply to intraoffice memos, the type of document that was at issue in this case.

A survey of federal agencies that was sponsored by the Administrative Conference of the United States in 1972 revealed the low priority placed on handling citizens' complaints (Rosenblum 1974). For example, of 64 agencies responding to a questionnaire, 51 reported having no office specifically responsible for handling citizen-initiated complaints, excluding formal adjudicative procedures (1974:10). Furthermore, the agencies without special complaint offices generally had no specific procedures for handling complaints; fewer than half the agencies publicized their complaint procedures or kept any statistics on their complaint mail; fewer than a fifth asserted that changes in agency practice had resulted from complaints. As Rosenblum notes:

> Without statistical records of the nature, categories, frequencies, distribution, and dispositions of complaints, agencies can hardly be expected to integrate complaint data into their regular operations or sustain standards of meritorious performance in their direct relationship with the public [1974:12].

More recent surveys (TARP 1975, 1978) elaborate on these findings.[15] And there have been other studies since the classic by Gellhorn (1966)

[15]In early 1978, TARP (1978) conducted a follow-up study of the complaint-handling

that echo Gellhorn's observations that national, state, and local government safeguards and complaint procedures look much better on paper than in practice (see Rosenblum 1974; TARP 1975). Chapters 8 and 9, by Serber and Karikas, respectively, explore how grievances are handled or not handled by government and why. Beyond that, our interest was in understanding the structural processes inherent in the failure of agencies to respond to grievances.

David Serber studied the Policy Services Bureau (PSB) of the California Department of Insurance in 1971–1972 and during 1975–1976 observed similar phenomena at the Insurance Commission of Pennsylvania. PSB, the only California state bureau where one can bring insurance complaints, has great formal power over insurance companies: It is able to suspend an insurer's certificate of authority in response to many kinds of unfair practices. Yet Serber found that this power has not made PSB an effective mechanism for the resolution of customers' complaints. From the start of a grievance to the final disposition of the case, PSB exhibits a syndrome of bureaucratic inertia and accommodation to the needs of the insurance industry. Few customers know of its existence, because the bureau has no public information policy designed to secure public attention. Because PSB is understaffed, underfinanced, and overworked, the bureau discourages many consumers from pressing their complaints by giving them lengthy forms to fill out, bombarding them with technical explanations, or simply failing to answer their complaint letters. Serber found that the "deselection" procedure in its operation favors the polite, articulate, middle-class male complainant and discriminates against women, racial minorities, and lower-class complainants.

Most of the work of PSB involves the use of an insurance officer as a mediator between the customer and the insurance company. The officer plays a useful role in straightening out bureaucratic mix-ups, but the mediation tends to be passive; in cases involving underpayment of claims, PSB rarely challenges an insurance company's final offer. Furthermore, PSB never presses insurance companies to make general reforms; it treats each case in isolation. PSB's bias toward the insurance

---

mechanisms of 22 federal agencies. TARP found a substantial improvement: "[A]lmost two-thirds of the Federal agencies were found to be performing most of the complaint-handling functions satisfactorily [1978:ES-3]." But there are still areas of weakness. Over one-third still do not systematically analyze complaint data so that underlying problems can be dealt with. Input to the policymaking levels is performed only on an ad hoc basis in almost half of the agencies. And, most important, very few agencies have follow-up procedures to determine if consumers understand the responses given by the agency and find them useful. We should note a significant weakness of the methodology of the TARP follow-up study (attributed by TARP to a lack of time and funds): In evaluating the effectiveness of the complaint-handling mechanisms, TARP made no attempt to contact the complaining consumers themselves to see if they were satisfied with the treatment they received.

industry is shown in its reluctance to launch investigations of large companies. Although PSB can request a public hearing, it rarely does so.

In his analysis Serber discusses the many ways in which PSB is reduced to impotence: lack of funds; bureaucratic methods that emphasize the routine processing of cases; hiring practices that result in homogeneity and conservatism in the personnel; an open channel of job mobility between the insurance industry and the state Department of Insurance that leads to overlapping loyalties; and informal relationships between the insurance officers and representatives of the insurance companies. Serber suggests further that the inferior position of the insurance officers within the department causes resentment that is expressed both directly toward the complainants and indirectly by a lack of interest and innovation that reinforces the passive, routine nature of the officers' work. Elsewhere Serber, in a comparison between California and Pennsylvania regulatory commissions, spells out the aspects of the workplace that serve as structural impediments to good complaint handling (Nader and Serber 1976; Serber 1976).

Since Serber began his research there has been some additional research published on the handling of consumer insurance complaints. Whitford and Kimball (1974) examined the Office of the Commissioner of Insurance in Wisconsin and came to essentially the same conclusion as did Serber. Whitford and Kimball, however, take a more standard approach to explaining the operation of complaint handling; for example, they note that the volume of complaints effectively prevents the office from generally being an effective settler of close legal and factual disputes. Serber is most interested in the subculture of such agencies that generate the processes and results that Whitford and Kimball speak about, and in his work he includes many of the same variables that Ross (1970), for example, uses in dealing with the social process of claims adjustment within insurance companies: the nature of white-collar occupations and the structure of bureaucracy as it affects the negotiation process occurring inside real organizations.

Whereas Serber's work deals with a regulatory agency, Angela Karikas' study of constituent complaint-handling in Philadelphia describes how myriads of daily grievances are dealt with by an elected official. In 1973 Karikas studied the way complaints were handled in the district office of the late U.S. Congressman William Barrett in southern Philadelphia. Although Gellhorn (1966) has much to say that is germaine to the role of elected officials' constitutent complaint handling and public administrative policy, Karikas, building on her earlier work (1974), reminds us with considerable descriptive detail of the kinds of problems that people bring to their congressmen, why they do so, and with what consequences. Congressman Barrett, who held his position for some 30 years (until he died in 1976), operated in the style of the political machine that in the past has prevailed in many cohesive ethnic communities in American cities. Machine politics was based on reciprocal favors within the local ward: Barrett's constituents delivered the vote in return for his personal aid. But there was an even more reciprocal exchange: The personal aid that Barrett received for his constituents was given in exchange for Barrett's lobbying for local industry through his Washington office.

Barrett made a ritual of attending to the problems of his predominantly black constituents who poured into his district office in the evenings. There was no need for special publicity; everyone knew about the Congressman. The problems covered the full gamut, with those related to employment, welfare, and Social Security being the most numerous. Consumer problems, in the strict sense, were handled only occasionally.

Karikas found Barrett remarkably adept at resolving his constituents' complaints. For the most part, Barrett handled the problems himself, without the aid of his staff and without bureaucratic procedures. He dealt with the constituent personally, and with his long experience he could analyze a problem immediately. He rarely referred a constituent elsewhere. The key to his effectiveness, when more was required than merely giving information or advice, was the wide network of influential contact that Barrett had built up over the years—people who would do a favor for Barrett in return for a past or future favor from him. The network gave Barrett great range of method and flexibility—even the power to "bend the law" when necessary. Another important ingredient in his proficiency was that he played the role of advocate rather than neutral mediator. Karikas compared Barrett's techniques with the more impersonal administrative methods in three other congressional offices and found that Barrett processed more complaints than any of the others.

Karikas concludes that Barrett's system failed in the last analysis because it was totally dependent on the unique position of one man and because Barrett handled cases on an isolated basis and did nothing to create lasting changes in the structure against which his constituents complained. In a sense, Barrett had a stake in the continuation of people's problems. Indeed, this was one of Gellhorn's conclusions in his book *When Americans Complain* (1966:75–76).

On the one hand, he had a successful record as measured by constituent satisfaction; on the other hand, by virtue of his success Barrett did not change the system that caused the repetition of the same problems he solved. This, of course, is the dilemma that runs throughout our data and our analysis: individual complaint handling versus organizational change or prevention. Both Karikas and Serber discuss these questions within the larger economic and political context. Their primary concern, unlike that of Whitford and Kimball, for example, is not to invent ways to improve the hearing of individual complaints within an organization but rather to see grievances as a means by which to reorganize structures larger than an insurance commission or a congressional office. More lasting than investigating specific grievances is understanding and preventing the causes of grievance.

Whatever we may think of the comparative success of business and governmental complaint-handling, nowhere in this book are the organizational constraints made clearer than in David Greenberg's study (Chapter 10) of three organizations that handle complaints in a black ghetto neighborhood in Washington, D.C.: (a) a furniture store that sells on credit and deals with customers' complaints about the terms of payment; (b) a private service organization, the Neighborhood Development Center (NDC), which helps local residents cope with a variety of problems, including problems that concern welfare benefits; and (c) the city government's local "service area committee" (SAC), in which leaders of community organizations and city agency personnel meet once a week to discuss complaints about municipal services. Greenberg, who did his field research in 1975, finds that none of the organizations resolves complaints in an effective manner, and in analyzing their weakness he focuses on three concepts: monopoly, informality, and control of information.

The aim of the store, which has a near monopoly on easy credit in the community, is not to resolve customers' complaints in a fair manner but to hold onto its customers and to prevent their going elsewhere to complain. The creation of a warm, personal relationship between the salesman and the customer, in which the salesman seemingly shows great concern for the customer's needs and feelings, pacifies him, blocks his awareness of his manipulation by the salesman, and dulls his interest in discovering and asserting his legal rights. Furthermore, as a last resort in its efforts to keep the customer from complaining to a third party, the store uses intimidation practices and threatens to reveal damaging information that it has gathered on a customer, for example, illegal activities in which the customer has engaged.[16]

The weakness of NDC is that, although it has good intentions and a friendly, supportive relationship with the community, it lacks formal power over the government agencies that distribute benefits to the residents. Indeed, it must rely on the influence it has gained through its informal contacts with the public agencies; and even here its greatest

---

[16]Compare the comment of a consumer investigator for the City of Boston. Referring to the black ghetto of Roxbury, where many neighborhood merchants hold the ghetto residents as a captive clientele, Eleanor Joy exclaimed: "Every time I see a merchant around here on a consumer problem, he tells me he's been in business for 40 years without a complaint. . . . But the only reason he hasn't gotten complaints is that people are afraid to speak up [Business Week 1972:43]."

success is merely to facilitate the processing of applications in certain cases—at the discretion of the public agency personnel. NDC's basic acceptance of the way the agencies operate helps reinforce the community's acquiescence in established practices.[17]

The SAC operates within severe constraints that are set by the way in which resources for municipal services are allocated at higher levels of city government and by its dependence on the city government for its continued existence. Greenberg explores the ways in which SAC attempts to preserve its legitimacy despite its inadequate resolution of complaints. The weekly meeting between city agency representatives and community leaders is characterized by a friendly atmosphere and takes on the appearance of a congenial gathering of well-intentioned people, all doing their best to solve the problems; in fact, the informality helps shift the focus away from the formal rights and duties of the parties and lowers the expectations held by the community. Community leaders tend to accept the rationalizations given by the city officials, who often place blame on the community, and frame their grievances in the form of requests when they should be making demands. In addition, the way in which SAC handles complaints tends to divide the community by causing its leaders to compete for the fixed amount of municipal services made available to them. Finally, Greenberg shows how SAC shores up its legitimacy by carrying out special projects that serve as symbols of its concern for the community while accomplishing little that is lasting.

Greenberg concludes that "complaint handling serves the needs of ghetto stores, the social agencies, and the city departments rather than those of low-income people." Complaints are defined away by the organizations' selective control of information, and a just resolution is impeded by making the complaint process too difficult and costly. Apathy in the low-income consumer is seen as a rational response. To improve his or her position, the consumer will require more than technical adjustments in complaint-handling institutions; what is needed is a shift in the balance of power, and this requires political change.

---

[17]Not all community groups that set out to help people in their dealings with welfare agencies are reduced to the powerlessness of NDC. Tripi's study (1974) of several groups of activist welfare clients in a large metropolitan area on the West Coast shows that clients who organize can exercise effective control in encounters with welfare officials. Unlike Greenberg's NDC, the welfare rights organizations (WROs) have chosen not to use informal relationships with the welfare agency personnel as a means of influence. The WROs' sources of power are their knowledge of clients' legal rights and their ability to harrass the agency with constant personal appearances and demands for meetings. The WROs have overcome some of the problems discussed by Greenberg in his sections on "informality" and "control of information," but one should note that less than 1% of the county caseload is represented by the WROs. Agency reaction would possibly be less accommodating if WRO clients were more numerous.

Volunteer Complaint Handling

The range of devices for complaint handling covers a wide spectrum, from public to private, from formal to informal. Yet regardless of the mechanism, successful functioning of dispute resolution by third-party handlers generally requires a relatively equal balance of power between the individuals or groups involved in disputes, or so San Francisco Consumer Action learned through experience.

San Francisco Consumer Action was founded in 1971 to remedy the need for individual complaint handling, a need that was not being met in either the public or private sector. Our research with SFCA was initiated by Gregory Wilson in 1973, followed up 3 years later by Elizabeth Brydolf, and revisited by Christopher Shugart and myself in 1978. Our intent was to follow a voluntary consumer organization through a long enough period of development so that we could plot the process and direction of organizational and ideological change. Throughout its early development the organization was characterized by strong and continuous leadership.

SFCA started as a complaint switchboard; each complaint was handled by an individual. As functions began to be differentiated, the shape of the organization changed. Individual complaint handling was replaced by staff-run grievance committees; a separate, SFCA-sponsored organization, San Francisco Consumer Advocates, was formed to handle political lobbying. There were further changes in complaint handling which involved the creation of consumer complaint committees; consumers, rather than staff, now handle their own complaints, with advice and counsel from staff members.

Both the educational function and the financial insecurity of the organization were helped by a series of publications such as *Break the Banks* (1973), a shopper's guide to banking services; by such books as *Deceptive Packaging* (Schulman and Geesman 1974), an evaluation of the California State Department of Consumer Affairs; and by a series of pamphlets that resulted from various task forces, such as the one on food. Furthermore, SFCA realized that the power imbalance had to be remedied by the use of strategies such as picketing or boycott—strategies that were reinforced by attention from the press.

Notice the direction of development: SFCA moved from individual complaint handling to group complaint handling, a policy designed to create a sense of unity among consumers. Such a policy direction has never characterized either government or business dealings with consumer complaints. SFCA's educational publications were informative and analytical. The SFCA staff members early realized the importance of political lobbying and encouraged the use of available government forums. Their creativity in learning to live by their wits because of the perennial shortage of funds resulted in ideas that were borrowed by nearby government agencies. To date SFCA has trained hundreds of Bay Area residents in how to exercise their rights in small claims courts and elsewhere; a smaller number have gained experience in citizenship and the participation it entails; and still others have learned the futility of any complaint-handling policy that concentrates sole attention on the handling of individual cases. The process of watchdogging must be continuous in a democratic society; it must also be private as well as public.

There are important lessons to be learned from the experiment at SFCA. One stems from a comment by one of its founders that anyone can start such an organization. For all those people leading, by their view, dull lives in this country and wondering how they can contribute, this is an important lesson. In evaluating SFCA, the results of Wilson's survey of complainants at SFCA are particularly instructive; they showed a strikingly high satisfaction rate. In particular, faith in SFCA was high; 88% of those polled said they trusted SFCA. In comparison to trust in government and business these days, such a finding is indeed out of the ordinary.[18]

Union Complaint Handling

Our decision to study how unions handle worker problems with the union stemmed not only from noticing that action liners often receive complaints from workers about their unions, but also from the hope that some unions might have developed good ideas in this field that would be transferrable. With such in mind we chose for study the union reputed to have the best-developed mechanisms for handling worker–union complaints, and one that indeed can be proud of having invested in the development of a formal mechanism for handling complaints. The Public Review Board of the United Auto Workers Union was established in 1957. Like judicial mechanisms, the UAW mechanisms are oriented toward specific grievances rather than toward the handling of underlying worker unrest.

The author of Chapter 12, Elaine Combs-Schilling, studied the UAW's formal mechanisms for handling complaints during two separate periods: in 1973, when the auto industry was in relatively good health, and again in 1975, when the industry was in crisis. When times are good, workers are more willing to complain about the union leadership; when times are bad, they keep their "family" problems to themselves. It was more complex than that, however. As Combs-Schilling describes the pro-

---

[18]A poll by Peter Hart (U.S. Congress 1975) found that 58% of the public believes that public officials in Washington are dominated by big corporations; 61% believes that there is a conspiracy among big businesses to set prices as high as possible. Pollster Pat Caddell (U.S. Congress 1975) discovered that 79% of the public feels that big business does not care whether they live or die; it only cares about selling its products.

cedures used for processing complaints, she notes that they resemble American legal procedures in their formality and complexity: They include the initiation of charges, the choosing of a trial committee, the trial, and further procedures for several levels of appeal. Her most important finding: The system was hardly ever used. Why wasn't it? The answers varied depending on whom she spoke to and when.

Committee members say that the system is not used because there are no complaints. The workers have another perspective: "The more paperwork involved, the less likely the men are to use the procedure"; or "It'd have to be something really big to go through all the trouble it is to file an appeal." Combs-Schilling summarizes her data on this point by pointing to the workers' lack of familiarity with the complexities of the complaint system; to possible discouragement by union officers and committee members, who make a virtue of not complaining; to a general sense of fatalism among the workers; and to a strong pressure to "lump it" if jobs are on the line. The pressures from union officials are strong. People who complain about the union, they say, are antiunion.

As noted earlier, the perspective of the line workers is quite different. Beyond reasons having to do with the formality and complexity of the system, there are structural reasons why union men "lump" their complaints. The worker runs a risk in complaining about union practices. Most of the line worker's grievances are against the district committee members, whose role it is to initially handle complaints the worker has against company management. Because the worker cannot afford to alienate the committee member, he is often forced to swallow his grievance. Feuding with company management creates an environment that protects the union hierarchy from thinking about grievances in their own house. Workers are intimidated, and their rights continue to be inadequately upheld by the very organization that was set up to improve the worker's position. Combs-Schilling suggests that a third party, independent of both union and management, would be an improvement over the present system. It is odd to think that handling worker complaints could threaten the image of union solidarity rather than provide outsiders with an image of a dynamic, caring union.

Media Complaint Handling

Chapter 13 investigates the role of the media (radio, television, and newspapers) in handling people's complaints.[19] Since the 1960s, activity in complaint handling has expanded dramatically along with other

---

[19]See, in addition, Hannigan (1977), who conducted a survey of 282 users of a Canadian newspaper ombudsman. One finding was that the action line was considered helpful in resolving the consumers' problems in 46.5% of the cases.

forums that have developed during the same period, such as city consumer departments, consumer fraud offices of attorneys generals' offices, company toll-free hotlines, advertising review boards, consumer voluntary complaint centers, and neighborhood legal services. By the early 1970s we had located over 350 action-line newspaper columns in the United States.[20]

Michael Mattice studied four media action lines in the San Francisco Bay Area, one in a newspaper, one associated with a television station, and two with radio stations. His basic research in 1972 was followed up during several succeeding years.

Action lines serve principally as information and referral services, but they are most effective in opening up new channels of communication with the complainee organizations.[21] Most action-line complaints are resolved by circumventing the cumbersome bureaucracies of the organizations to ensure that the complaint is heard by someone who has the power to take corrective action. This accomplishment is made possible by a carefully constructed but informal network of contacts close to the centers of power within the organizations, for instance, the secretaries. Thus action lines avoid routine processing, delay, and haphazard rejections. There is something here reminiscent of the wardheeling strategies of Barrett and other congressmen and of Greenberg's CDG ghetto group.

In their communications with a complainant, action lines help clarify the complaint by toning down the emotions and giving the complainants objective information that may help them reshape their expectations. Even though the action lines can exert no direct pressure on offending organizations, there is always the threat of bad publicity. It is true that bad publicity is used only as a last resort, but the possibility that it will be used surely helps guarantee an attentive ear and helps make the complainee organization more amenable. Action liners are go-betweens and structurally not so very different from the go-betweens described for some native Philippine groups (Barton 1919).

An important aspect of action lines is the way individual complaints are translated into calls for general reform. First, Mattice reports that action lines give more publicity to recurrent complaints. Second, he notes that one of the radio stations he studied monitored the complaints in order to spot community problems that deserved editorial comment.

---

[20]Since then, however, their growth seems to have tapered off. See Hannigan (1977:681n.).

[21]In this context, consider one conclusion of Hannigan (1977), who conducted a survey of the users of a Canadian newspaper ombudsman: "The complainant was most likely to find *Sound Off* helpful where the complainee's [initial] response was noncommunicative, and less likely where the complainee was hostile or evasive. This suggests that *Sound Off* can overcome problems of communication and mild opposition by the complainee, but not determined resistance [p. 695]."

A limitation of the action-line approach is that, regardless of how independent the action line is from the parent newspaper or broadcaster, the goal from the latter's perspective is to please the audience. Action lines are expensive to maintain and may be difficult for the broadcaster or newspaper to justify. Complaints may be rejected because they are repetitive and hence uninteresting to the audience or because they are difficult and require judgment. Finally, there is a reluctance to name uncooperative businesses for fear of upsetting advertisers.[22] On the other hand, Mattice notes that the goal of an action line is not simply to make a pretense of processing a dispute, because a solid victory for the consumer is what makes good news.

Despite their drawbacks—not the least of which is the money-making motivation of media organizations that tends to gloss over or dramatize certain aspects of complaints—action lines have good potential in their roles as go-betweens and as revivers of a very important social-control mechanism that has been decreasing in mass societies. Public opinion can be encouraged to develop and to diffuse through the media. Fraudulent business practices become part of our shared knowledge and influence our future business dealings. The media can also play an important role in creating a consumer-group consciousness. What spurred Barbara Zinsky to persevere in her complaint against Caloric stoves were the letters that she received from many other sufferers from defective Caloric stoves after her problem had been published in a local newspaper. Consciousness that others suffer from the same problem can become the training ground for public citizens.

Discovering How Well Complaint Organizations Work

An ideal complaint-handling system would, with speed and fairness, resolve grievances and would be part of an early alert to head off future similar complaints by providing public agencies with data with which to do their jobs better. An ideal system also would disclose aggregate patterns of abuse or injustice and would provide people with a competitive number of private and public avenues and forums within which to pursue just treatment. It would work for prevention and deterrence.

Our research has shown that in practice our society rarely adheres to any part of this ideal pattern, not because of the absence of norms and legally recognized rights and duties but because of poor application, nonaccessible forums, and a refusal to recognize that our law, rooted in a

---

[22]For examples of advertiser pressure on action lines, see, e.g., Bowler (1971); Waters (1975).

small-scale agricultural period where face-to-face relationships predominated, is no longer appropriate in an industrial society where most of the real and potential complaints are between strangers of unequal power. What we have found is a serious indictment of the types of relationships that have evolved along with our evolving GNP. We have a mass phenomenon in which large segments of the population, reflective of all socioeconomic groups, are exposed to low-profile, undramatic, petty, and illegal exploitation.

At the start of this essay I noted that whether the absence of access to law is a deficiency within our society depends on whether there are successful alternatives to law. We initiated the study of extrajudicial alternatives expecting to find that alternative mechanisms were meeting the goals of an ideal complaint-handling system. Instead, our conclusions have led us in the opposite direction. We are left with the need to spell out why the systems we studied fail in the long run and how extrajudicial systems might be made to work.

As an anthropologist I believe that an increase in complaints and disputes is a sign of disorganized communities, a situation that cannot be fixed by arbitration boards, improved small claims courts, CAP organizations, and so on. We have to get into deterrence and prevention by working back from the case studies down the chain to the source of the problem. An adversary legal system is predicated on the idea of a balance of power before the judge, but the imbalance is such that an individual cannot ever get to a forum and success does not necessarily follow even if he or she does have access. More driver-training courses alone will not solve the problem of traffic accidents; trying to fit the complainant to existing mechanisms is not enough. We have to redesign the complaint system to fit the present social reality. Let us first turn to the reasons for success and failure in the private and public mechanisms that we studied.

If we place our examples on a continuum from most successful to least successful in handling individual complaints, San Francisco Consumer Action and Congressman Barrett's district office would come as close to the most successful as any examples we could locate. These two organizations depended in great part on the charismatic qualities of the leadership. When the leaders left, either because they died (as in the case of Barrett) or because they decided to run for public office (as in the case of Kay Pachtner), the organizations suffered a decline. First rule: Complaint organizations that are dependent on individual personalities may be short-lived, or at least their success is short-lived.

There are other organizations of good potential that do not classify as successful complaint mechanisms because of a conflict of interest between the organization and the complaint-resolving task: The BBB, the CAP organizations, the California Insurance Commission Complaint Division, and the media mechanisms all suffer from constraints put upon them by the supporting power. Second rule: Complaint mechanisms operating under the constraints of conflict of interest cannot operate as third-party handlers of complaints.

The union complaint mechanisms were not used because of their complexity, a lack of knowledge on the part of the potential users, fear of retaliation, and a number of other factors. Third rule: If complaint mechanisms are complicated and not easy to use, they will not be used. Fourth rule: If the party settling the case is also the party being complained against, the chances for the complainant to achieve success are small.[23]

Voluntary organizations such as San Francisco Consumer Action, which do not have stable funding, are constantly trying new experiments to attract support and funding. Fifth rule: Voluntary organizations are excellent places for experimenting with dispute-settlement mechanisms, but lack of adequate funding leads to instability and discontinuity in service.

Perhaps the most general conclusion from the evidence accumulated over 8 years is that third-party intermediaries have been of little help to the consumer. A final rule that applies to all cases is: Without the force of law as back-up, third-party complaint handlers will be of limited use.

We will now look at the drawbacks of third-party complaint handlers in greater detail. To begin with, complaint intermediaries are hardly ever used. Best and Andreasen (1977) conducted a survey of 2419 households in 34 cities in 1975 in order to discover how consumers respond to unsatisfactory purchases of goods and services. A remarkable finding was that buyers did not complain at all concerning 57.7% of the problems they perceived that involved more than just the price of the purchase. In 30.7% of all the cases in which buyers did perceive problems, the only complaint they made was to the seller. In only 1.2% of the cases did the buyer take his or her gripe to a third party. One might think that the buyers found no need to resort to third parties because the sellers were so quick to give redress, but the data show otherwise. Overall, only 56.5% of the voiced complaints (disregarding the few that concerned only price) were settled to the full satisfaction of the purchaser—and we should note that a *partial* refund of money was classified as a fully satisfactory result unless the respondent indicated otherwise. This means that many consumers who complained without success to the seller did not go on to contact a third party.

Their reluctance to use complaint intermediaries is remarkable in view of the number of newspaper and magazine articles that aim to in-

---

[23]This rule applies to all the organizations mentioned earlier in the discussion of conflict of interest, including in addition the ghetto business studied by Greenberg. In retail selling, the majority of complaints deal with defective products and are not complaints against the store itself. In this respect, the retailer is indeed the middleperson.

struct the reader in the art of complaining. Why don't more consumers make use of this information? Probably the main reason is that third-party complaint handlers have a low success rate. Best and Andreasen (1977:726) found that when consumers do take their problems to third parties, they come away satisfied only about one-third of the time. Many consumers have learned that these mechanisms do not work for them.

This is not the whole story, however. The same study suggested that people are reluctant to consider themselves complainers. Only 9.1% of the households questioned believed that they complained more often than other households. Being a complainer evidently has negative connotations for many people. Best and Andreasen (1977) continue: "If voicing complaints is generally disfavored, it is likely that households would be even more reluctant to complain to third parties [721]."[24]

Another reason that consumers ignore third-party complaint handlers is that they cannot always figure out which one to consult. The consumer columns in newspapers and magazines often list a dozen or more complaint bureaus. New intermediaries with fresh images come onto the scene each year, and others fade into oblivion. Consumer agencies are found at every level of government—city, county, state, and federal. The private sector has many other species of consumers' helpers (business councils, professional associations, ombudsmen, "watchdogs," self-help groups, gripe centers, action lines, hot lines, and religious cults.[25] One might think that greater diversity would lead to better choice, but the consumer is more likely to be unable to distinguish the truly helpful intermediaries that are submerged in a crowd of worthless ones. The more a person has found any of the organizations in his environment to be unresponsive and the more his feelings of powerlessness have been reinforced by encounters with them, the more will he treat these lists of complaint handlers with skepticism. Studies have shown that when people feel powerless, they turn their attention away from the kind of information that could help them gain control over their lives.[26] It appears

[24]Friedmann (1974), in a study of complaint behavior is Canadian and British populations, also notes the respondents' possible "reluctance to appear as complainers or malcontents. This impression could be gained from reports by interviewers that some respondents claimed with pride: 'I never complain' [pp. 33–34]." Friedmann found that four-fifths of the respondents reported that they had never made a complaint about their dealings with government.

[25]Zaretsky and Leone (1974:xxx–xxxiv) observe that some religious cults develop to immunize complaint handlers from the laws that protect the professional interests of doctors and lawyers.

[26]Melvin Seeman (1967) has tested the notion that "the structural conditions of mass society (e.g., high mobility, rationalization of industrial processes, bureaucratization) encourage a sense of powerlessness which leads the individual to be insensitive to, and uninformed about, an environment over which he believes he has little influence [p. 106]."

In one study Seeman (1963) found that reformatory inmates with strong feelings of powerlessness learned less about matters that were immediately relevant to the control of

that there is a vicious circle at work: Lack of knowledge leads to power-lessness, which leads to apathy toward acquiring new information, which reinforces a lack of knowledge. The critical question is whether the circle can be cut by providing consumers with more information about their legal rights and procedures for complaining. The answer probably is that this information will not penetrate as long as consumers continue to ex-perience failure in their attempts to redress grievances.

Why are intermediaries generally ineffective in handling complaints for the consumer? Many complaint handlers have an official goal to help consumers resolve their complaints, but the pressures they face push them in other directions. Anthropologists doing fieldwork systematically differentiate what people say they do from what people actually do from what people think they ought to do. To find out what an organization is actually trying to do, we have to look at what the in-house rules are, how the complaint intermediaries actually behave, who selects and who makes up the top echelon, how they hire, and where they get their funds and other means of influence.

The source of funds is the best clue to the operating as contrasted to the official goals of third-party complaint handlers. Many are supported by business—for example, the Better Business Bureau and the trade as-sociation complaint mechanisms. The personnel of these organizations may be ardent consumer advocates at heart, but if they want to keep their jobs and if they want their organizations to continue receiving support, their primary purpose will be to strengthen the hand of business.

The history of business-supported complaint organizations supports the hypothesis that they are born in response to dwindling consumer confidence and that they exist in order to forestall government control and regulation. In 1972 H. Bruce Palmer, President of the Council of Better Business Bureaus, warned that consumer dissatisfaction was creat-ing an "almost frightening prospect for every businessman in the coun-try"; unless business could meet rising consumer expectations, the whole free enterprise system could be jeopardized (*Palo Alto Times* 1972:8).[27] The situation today reflects ever-increasing consumer dissatisfaction.

Turning to government complaint intermediaries, we see that the official goals are subverted in more complex ways. Funds may come ulti-

their future—information about parole—than did other inmates. The inmates showed no difference in their readiness to absorb other kinds of knowledge. Seeman extended the applicability of his findings in later studies of hospital patients' knowledge of health mat-ters, workers' political knowledge, and university students' knowledge about nuclear war-fare (see Seeman 1967). Consumer education advocates should take heed and temper their enthusiasm. See also, Nader (1977) for a comparison of powerlessness among members of U.S. society and the Zapotec of southern Mexico.

[27]See also the report on the Better Business Bureaus by Rep. Benjamin Rosenthal (1971:E13764).

mately from the taxpayer, but they are funneled through legislatures where business lobbies exert tremendous pressure. Persons appointed to fill key positions in the agencies often have close ties with the business community. In his study of the complaint bureau of the California Department of Insurance, Serber describes the open, informal channel that exists between people in the bureau and people in the insurance industry: Individuals frequently move from one job to the other, and their loyalties are colored by their past experience or their hopes of future employment in the industry. Herbert Denenberg, formerly the Pennsylvania Insurance Commissioner, has publicly noted many times that the industry often selects a state's candidate for insurance commissioner or has veto power over the person considered. One solution suggested by the late Justice William O. Douglas is to abolish and reconstitute every regulatory agency every 10 years. In this manner the inevitable ties with industry might become less pervasive and secure.

Industries spend millions of dollars each year to present their cases before government regulatory agencies. According to Senator Abraham Ribicoff, Chairman of the Senate Governmental Affairs Committee, in a period of time during which 11 of the major airlines spent $2.8 million to be represented before the Civil Aeronautics Board (money which, by the way, could be deducted as a business expense), major public interest spokespersons could muster only $40,000 (Christian Science Monitor 1977:16).

Action lines, too, are crippled by a conflict of interest. The goal of the newspapers and radio and television station action lines is to further the interest of their sponsors. Because they aim to please their audiences, action lines may reject a complaint because it is repetitive and hence uninteresting to the audience. An advertisement placed in the San Francisco Chronicle (1972:11) by "Action 7" of KGO-TV announced that it was "looking for unusual problems that can't seem to get resolved in usual ways." The real problem for action lines, however, is that the media depend on advertising, and so they tread softly for fear of antagonizing their benefactors—the business community. The media have good reason to be fearful. An auto association in Atlanta decided that it had had enough of WXIA-TV's proconsumer broadcasts and retaliated with a 1-year advertising boycott (Waters 1975).

It is true that complaint handlers often suffer from poor management, careless organization, inefficient operating procedures, and lack of concern, but these factors are only superficial causes of ineffectiveness. The fundamental cause is that the forces controlling many complaint intermediaries are not interested in creating effective mechanisms for consumer as well as producer.

The resources of complaint handlers are limited—often severely limited—and so they must find ways of weeding out many of the complaints they receive. Screening recurs throughout the entire process of handling the complaint. Intermediaries look at whether the subject of complaint is legitimate and important, and they try to determine whether the consumer in fact has been treated unfairly and whether the problem is serious and justifies the cost of processing. If intermediaries judge a complaint on legal grounds rather than on commonly accepted ideas of fair play, some complainants with just causes will not be heard. A consumer may feel she has a valid complaint about the short life of a product, even though there is no legal cause for action. Many intermediaries reject such complaints, even though legal duties define only the minimum standards of good conduct expected by society.

Of course complaint handlers must have some way of separating the valid complaints from the frivolous.[28] The point to be stressed here is that the selection process may be misused if the intermediary has too narrow a conception of a legitimate and important complaint. In addition to the complaint itself, intermediaries also use grounds for selection that depend upon personal characteristics of the complainant. In the state Insurance Department Complaint Bureau, Serber reports, the calm, articulate, white, male, middle-class complainant received Bureau attention over the excited or hysterical, black, or female complainant.

The way the complaint is processed may lead the consumer to drop out before his or her problem has been solved. By and large, it is up to the complainant to initiate at each step of the process. Some intermediaries transmit a complaint to the offending organization and take no further action unless the consumer contacts the intermediary again. The trade association CAP organizations presume that the consumer has been satisfied if they hear nothing to the contrary. In a 1975 report, MACAP claimed that 97% of its cases were satisfactorily resolved during the first phase of its procedure, but Greenberg and Stanton (in this volume) examined a sample and found that less than half were actually resolved in a way that the complainants considered satisfactory. The other complainants had dropped out.[29] Another of our researchers examined the success file of Virginia Knauer's White House Consumer Office and found that when the office received a return communication from the business or company being complained about the case was placed in the success file, whether

[28]An Auto Safety Research Center in Cleveland made the point in these terms: "The fact of the matter is that the person complaining will not always tell you all of the facts involved in his particular complaint. . . . After reviewing all the facts, the staff member may conclude that the consumer's complaint is unfounded, and that the consumer had not carefully read his warranty [Vacar and Banta 1971:E12799]."

[29]Cf. NICJ (n.d.:41–42) for MACAP's own follow-up study (conducted around 1972) according to which almost three-fourths of the respondents indicated satisfaction with the way their complaints had been settled in the initial "communications phase." In any event, it is not correct to assume that all consumers who do not recontact MACAP are satisfied.

the reply was positive or negative. A common procedure among inter-mediaries is to terminate a case after a certain sequence of steps, regard-less of the outcome. Sometimes full treatment consists, as with Virginia Knauer's office, of simply forwarding the complaint with a covering let-ter. Although there are exceptions to these observations, a *New York Times* report discovered that "some of the [action line] help centers are so understaffed that they rarely give personal attention to complaints, never mediate disputes and rarely follow up to see if a complainant has been satisfied [Cerra 1976]."

Is it true that these organizations do not have power? Serber tells us that the California Department of Insurance can have an insurance com-pany ordered to a public hearing and can suspend the insurer's "certifi-cate of authority." However, the Department rarely resorts to such mea-sures. Even when an insurance officer decides that an investigation of an insurance company is called for, his or her request is frequently denied after a company official pays a friendly visit to the higher-ups in the Insurance Department. There is little difference between saying that the department has power but does not use it and saying that the department simply does not have much power.

The business-sponsored complaint mechanisms, with few excep-tions, have no authority to order a business to resolve a complaint or to punish a company for not doing so. Their members have not given them the right to interfere in company affairs; the most they can do is to make recommendations, and this they do ever so gently. At any rate, such organizations do not have ties with all the businesses in their field. Most of the trade association mechanisms represent less than half the manufac-turing companies in a particular industry.[30]

Power comes in many guises. In a mass society, an individual's report of unfair treatment will not circulate widely, and so it will have little impact on the offender. English towns in the Middle Ages relied heavily on public opinion to deter abuses in the marketplace. Dishonest craftsmen and merchants were paraded through the streets, were placed in stocks for all to see, and their wares publicly burned (Hamilton 1931:1152). We do not resort to such measures today, but third-party complaint handlers may have the ability to give the offending business a bad name. They can amplify the sound of a consumer's complaint and make it reverberate through a huge city just as it would through a small village. The head of a county consumer fraud division in Texas made it a habit to bring the news media in on his activities. Businesspeople, of course, objected to such methods as trial by the media (Fallon 1972). Pennsylvania's former Insur-

---

[30]According to Dean Determan, Vice President of the Council of Better Business Bureaus, in areas covered by BBBs, on the average only 5–7% of business firms are members (personal communication, 26 January 1979).

ance Commissioner, Herbert Denenberg, conducted televised investigations because he believed that it was necessary to "create intense public pressure, or else changes don't take place [Time 1972]." "Action 4" in New York City (WNBC-TV) was having difficulties getting Macy's department store to settle customers' complaints, but Macy's cooperated after Action 4's Betty Furness discussed the problem on the air (Cerra 1976). SFCA also mobilizes public opinion through picketing and boycotts to pressure settlements in favor of consumers.[31]

Pressures on media action lines, however, usually prevent them from making effective use of public opinion. The experiences of one newspaper action line in Atlanta are typical. When advertisers began complaining, the action-line staff was told to discontinue publishing the names of companies. In addition, a local lawyer began worrying that the action line was treading too close to the practice of law. The problem wound up before the state bar association, and, in the end, the newspaper adopted the policy of no longer including commercial items in its action-line column (Bowler 1971). Action lines are often so subdued that all they give is bland advice, and many consumers' help centers have followed the counsel of lawyers who say that the best way to avoid the unauthorized practice of law is to avoid giving specific answers to individuals' specific questions (Schwartz 1969).

Better Business Bureaus shy away from publicizing consumer disputes. They prepare a bad "reliability report" on the misbehaving company that is passed on to prospective customers who think to telephone the BBB before making their purchases. But the telephone reports almost never describe actions that government agencies have taken against the companies, and the BBBs keep the reports toned down out of fear of being sued for slander.[32] Eaton believes that most of the time it is ordinary self-interest rather than the desire to avoid a bad reliability report that causes the offending company to comply. One can imagine a BBB that published monthly lists of unfair practices engaged in by local companies—along with their names—as recommended by U.S. Congressman Benjamin Rosenthal in 1971 (1971:E13765).

As with any form of power, adverse publicity is more effective when it is used rarely and judiciously. Even so, the effectiveness of public

[31]Some consumer organizations rely heavily on their contacts with the news media. When a dispute reached a stalemate, COMBAT, a consumer organization in Maine, found that the merchant complied readily when COMBAT mentioned that it might air the dispute at an upcoming press conference scheduled for other purposes (West and Reben 1971). COMBAT also built up useful relationships with reporters. Newspeople are hungry for news, and once COMBAT had developed a good reputation, there was no problem in getting publicity: "When we tell a reporter something, he thinks he is getting a scoop [West and Reben 1971:16]," said Howard Reben, COMBAT's general counsel.

[32]Moreover, a study by Munns (1978), based on tests carried out in 1976, concluded that many BBB reliability reports were misleading, inaccurate, and incomplete.

opinion has its limits. When an organization has a monopoly or a near monopoly over the products or services it offers, prospective customers have nowhere else to go. Greenberg's study of ghetto residents documents that residents may be well aware of the inadequacies in the products or services they receive, but they have no real choice because they rely so heavily on one business for easy credit or on one social agency for welfare benefits.

Government service providers, too, are in the short run relatively immune to the effects of bad public opinion; their revenue does not come directly from the individual consumer. Hence a shifting of consumer demand for their services has little impact.

Prestige is a diffuse kind of influence that is of use to some complaint intermediaries. It helps congressmen who try to work out the problems of their constituents; as I have noted, Congressman Barrett is a good example. On the other hand, a lack of prestige hurts many consumer organizations. Consumers often give less weight to statements made by local volunteer consumer groups than to the pronouncements of established organizations because the influence of prestige is so strong.

Complaint handlers may claim that their contacts within the complainee organizations give them a good deal of influence. Action lines rely heavily on such networks of contacts. Actually, however, informal networks are not in themselves a genuine source of power for intermediaries; rather, networks are effective because of another kind of power that the intermediary may possess: the ability to dispense favors in return for favors. Congressman Barrett's control over patronage positions and other benefits, his close ties with the local judiciary, and his ability to sponsor national legislation made him an effective complaint handler. When a supermarket executive lobbied for new legislation, Barrett told him, "It'll cost you jobs," which Barrett's constituents would fill. Barrett possessed an extraordinary way of dealing with his constituents' complaints about unemployment benefits: He could eliminate the basis of the complaints by finding them jobs—an example of how an intermediary can redefine a complaint to yield even greater benefits for the complainant.

There is yet another kind of power. Because it takes skill to complain, knowledge is power. Offers to settle are more common when the complainant is knowledgeable. One couple bought a new house through a Department of Housing and Urban Department (HUD) arrangement whereby HUD was to pay the interest on the mortgage. When sewage from their septic tank began seeping into the basement, they complained to HUD, who told them there was not much that could be done. Only when they learned that HUD in fact could force the builders to make repairs and confronted HUD with this knowledge, did HUD force the builders to make the repairs (Schorr 1975). Greenberg, in this volume, provides another illustration of this principle in his description of how a private service organization in Washington, D.C., was blocked in its efforts by the welfare agencies' control of information.[33]

Despite a general lack of power and position, however, third-party complaint handlers do manage to resolve some of the complaints that are brought to them. Why does an organization decide to settle a dispute in the consumer's favor if the intermediary has so little power? Organizations see that it is in their own interest to clear up some of the problems of their customers and clients. But if it is in the organizations' own interest to take care of at least the clear-cut injustices, why does the consumer need an intermediary? We can see that the consumer might benefit from third-party assistance when the grievance is more complicated and involves a disagreement with the organization's policy. But it is in that kind of case that the intermediary has the least to offer, because most intermediaries cannot or will not then put much pressure on the complainee organization. Are complaint intermediaries superfluous in that they are only of use when the consumer can do without them?[34]

Discovering the Meaning of Third-Party Complaint Handling

In our society, complaint intermediaries play a role that yields important benefits to the organizations against which the complaints are brought. Only the most blatant cases of unfair treatment are resolved, and only the most persistent of complainers—the potential troublemakers—are satisfied. From the complainee organization's perspective it is better to let third parties handle complaints. Intermediaries save the organizations the cost of processing complaints themselves, and such organizations can set up almost insuperable barriers for consumers who complain directly. Most important, however, the handling of complaints is given legitimacy by being placed in the hands of "neutral" third parties. A third party is in a good position to pacify the complainant. A kind of symbiosis exists between the organizations that provide goods and services in our society and third-party complaint handlers. The organizations are a source of problems for the intermediaries to process, and the intermediaries in turn help the organizations by diverting all but the real troublemakers while taking the edge off the anger felt by those whose

[33]Tripi (1974), on the other hand, found that several activist welfare groups in a West Coast city had become experts in the intricacies of the welfare codes and rules. They were able to challenge arbitrary decisions, and they could make it clear when the responsibility for inadequate service lay with the welfare agency and not with the client.

[34]Hill (1974) said the same of ombudsmen: "Often the ironic comment is made that ombudsmen exist where they are least needed, and it is true that standards of public administration are quite high in all of these jurisdictions [that have ombudsmen] [p. 1085]."

complaints have not been settled fairly. Most intermediaries are probably unaware of this functional fit.

It is only part of the story to say that complaint handlers cause many consumers to decide not to press their complaints even though they have not received full satisfaction. More important, complaint handlers tend to reduce the distress that complainants otherwise would feel when their grievances are not resolved. If, at the moment a grievance arose, consumers believed that there was no means of redress, the resulting feelings of outrage could have unpredictable results for the offending organization. And if, at the same moment, consumers believed that their only hope lay with the judicial system, they might be more likely to sue in small claims court than they are at present.

Complaint handlers ensure that consumers are not too suddenly and unambiguously confronted with their powerlessness. In Goffman's (1952) terms, the consumer must be "cooled out." His anger must be tempered; the wound to his self-esteem must be assuaged. His situation must be defined "in a way that makes it easy for him to accept the inevitable and quietly go home [451–452]." First, the consumer is placated by being shown that help indeed exists. He is not alone in his struggle against the organization. The next strategy is delay—one of the most important methods of cooling out. The anger from frustrated expectations diminishes with time. The "cooler's" strategy: Give the complainant hope in the beginning, then slowly take it away.[35] Another way to cool out the complainant is to let him vent his anger or to give him the opportunity to displace it ritualistically in the routine activities of making telephone calls and filling out forms.[36] Complaining to an intermediary may provide a substitute achievement for the consumer. As least he is doing something about his complaint; it has generally been observed that even when citizens' problems are not resolved, they feel better after going to an intermediary.

Complaint handlers sometimes actively help the complainant reformulate his complaint, a process referred to variously as "clarification," "objectification," or "interpretation." The process may cause the consumer to reevaluate his initial feeling that he had been treated unfairly. The complaint-handler can also help the consumer come to see his rights as they are defined by the complainee. Greenberg and Stanton (Chapter 5)

[35]Nader (1978:93–94) gives an illustration of the linguistic techniques used by a Bell Telephone supervisor to cool out the complainant; these techniques have been called the "hot–cold treatment."

[36]It is ironic in this context that the Whirlpool Corp., the first U.S. company with a toll-free complaint line, dubbed its service the "Cool Line." Though, in the case of Whirlpool, the name may not reflect the primary purpose, in general it is easier to set up toll-free telephone lines to let consumers rid themselves of their anger than it is to improve the product that caused the problem.

state it this way: "The trade association programs garb industry perspective in objective, independent third-party clothes." Eaton's study describes how the Better Business Bureau tries to explain to customers that agreements should be in writing to be binding. How many go away believing that it is unfair of them to make a complaint when there has been no written agreement? The consumer may end up feeling that it was peevish of him to demand redress for such a minor problem: He learns to see people who complain as deviants.

By slowly increasing the perceived costs of a complaint instead of presenting the consumer with a closed door initially, the intermediary gives the complainant the opportunity to rationalize away his powerlessness by letting him view his dropping out as a calculated decision of his own. At least he has the power to choose *when* to drop out. A final alternative of the complaint handler is to shift the blame for failure of product or service onto the complainant. Greenberg describes how the sanitation department representative to a community complaint forum blamed the trash in vacant lots on the lack of community participation when the real problem was that the community was not able to discover the department's procedures or times for trash removal.

We can see why third-party complaint handlers are of such value to the complainee organizations in our society. Cooling out is best performed by third parties, for otherwise the complainant would be too ready to suspect that he is being manipulated.[37] The consumer is made to believe that his problem does not result from personal or corporate inadequacy. Possible solutions retreat from view, and he comes to accept the difficulty as a fixed aspect of the world to which he must resign himself. In short, he learns not to care. As Clark (1960) has put it: "The general result of cooling-out processes is that society can continue to encourage maximum effort without major disturbance from unfulfilled promises and expectations [576]." In the present context, "maximum effort" means maximum activity as a complacent, malleable consumer.

Despite differences between cases heard by the same intermediary and differences in case loads processed by different organizations and despite the fact that our research was geared to discovering successful instances of third-party handlers in order that successes might be replicated, I would have to conclude that third-party complaint intermediaries do not fulfill the requirements for an ideal complaint system; they do not even come close.

One might argue that in this book we have skewed the picture by concentrating our attention on complaints and the complainants. Only by

[37]As an official of the Furniture Industry Consumer Action Panel (FICAP) stated: "[A] letter [from FICAP] to an unreasonable customer can often end a problem when the same letter from the manufacturer would make the consumer more angry and the problem more difficult [Greenberg and Stanton in this volume]."

moving into a discussion of the consequences of inadequate complaint mechanisms can we fully appreciate the magnitude of the problem that is merely alluded to in discussions of complaint handling in particular settings. The consequences of present complaint-management systems in the United States touch every aspect of American life. I will address briefly the question of "endemic powerlessness" as well as the economic and political consequences of the present system of complaint management.

A salient characteristic of industrialized nation–states is the ease with which the strong, wealthy, and aggressive members of society can influence, manipulate, and intimidate the poor, powerless, outcast, and even the "average" citizen. This characteristic is related in great part to a legal system in which dominant members of society are able to influence (and sometimes even to buy off) legislators, lawyers, the media, and other public policymakers in order to strengthen their own economic and political positions. I believe that one of the reasons anthropologists idealize isolated indigenous groups is because they themselves come from cultures where the feeling of powerlessness is widespread.

In his contribution to the complaint literature, Albert Hirschman (1970), an economist, is concerned with two kinds of responses to a perceived wrong: "voicing" complaints and "exiting" in apathy, futility, or disgust. Hirschman argues that individuals' decision to voice or to exit is related to what they see as the probability of influencing a decision, to the calculated advantage to be gained from the outcome, and to the availability of alternative products and services. The tendency to voice also depends on a population's general readiness to complain and on the availability of institutions and mechanisms for communicating complaints cheaply and effectively. Elsewhere (Nader 1977) I have suggested that the exercise of voice for handling everyday complaints can be treated as an index of the degree of what I call "endemic powerlessness"—the feeling of powerlessness that is independent of any realities of power distribution in a society. The Small Claims Study Group report, *Little Injustices* (1972), puts it this way:

> The person of modest income, barred from seeking redress for a real grievance by the cost of legal assistance, may feel a sense of powerlessness just as great as the unattended patient.... The luxury price of lawyers is however only part of the problem ... [p. 5].

> The point is that such grievances are the stuff of everyday life and the outcome of the attempt to redress them has much to do with whether people feel empowered, active agents controlling their own destinies, or exploited, victims of forces beyond their control [p. 9].

Powerlessness takes major economic toll when it permits predatory economic activity to proliferate (Caplowitz 1963). Good complaint management would solve economic grievances and discourage criminality. It is estimated, for instance, that price fixing and other anticompetitive practices cost the economy billions of dollars in inflated prices or devalued products and services. The point here is that if consumers are not heard, the influence of law, either deliberately or through neglect, will tend to protect and institutionalize economic crime rather than detect, redress, and prevent it. If an orange juice producer in Philadelphia has a competitor who adds 10% more water to his product, the competitor will make more money. The other producer who does not wish to do this is at a competitive disadvantage if the fraud is allowed.

What costs have arisen that would not have appeared if the product had functioned as expected? Costs directly associated with the act of complaining are the time and effort spent writing letters, making phone calls, and paying personal visits to the complainee. The most obvious economic toll, perhaps, is the fiscal and manpower inefficiency of chain referrals. Our society is at present extremely inefficient in its handling of product failure. The cost of dealing with an average important product or service failure is often as large or larger than the original purchase cost, and consumers absorb the greater part of such costs.

Even if we could develop a method for measuring costs in a rational manner, the intangible costs would probably never be measurable, though they would be felt. Three months without teeth has emotional and psychological costs for a patient that far exceed the $200 involved. The possibility that a disputed bill will be collected through garnishment and may lead to a worker's dismissal causes him or her anguish. The hazardous and dilapidated condition of a new mobile home causes mental and physical health problems.

The most significant determinant of intangible costs associated with a given product or service failure is the household income of the family involved. A specific dollar loss is serious for a poor family that has no savings, cannot qualify for a loan or for a replacement product or service, and has no relatives with spare funds. The breakdown of a washing machine can be a real crisis for an individual or a family without an automobile. Another factor is the predictability of the failure. Living with an intermittently unreliable product produces repeated psychological strain because one does not know what might go wrong next. The owner of a Volkswagen that stalled in the path of an oncoming cement truck never again felt safe driving it. Another intangible cost that permeates many of our cases is the effect of consumer problems on family and other personal relationships.

Most of all, the complaint process itself is full of emotion. Our intensive case investigations illustrate that complaints impose costs on the consumer who purchased the product, expecting to use it a certain period and then finding he or she will have to do without it. The time factor needed for formulating and carrying out strategies is particularly significant for the consumer who is trying to decide whether to exercise warranty rights, seek repair at an independent dealer, or drop the entire matter and take a loss. Most warranties do not provide compensation for any of the major costs of failure: lost service, contingent expenses, or time spent complaining.

Surprisingly enough, there may be intangible benefits. Rewards arise from joining an activist consumer group and from winning something from the seller. Some consumers continue to attend meetings of consumer groups long after their own problems have been resolved. Sometimes the consumer's experience in the complaint process has an exhilarating impact.[38] It is also an educational experience. However much we might romanticize the benefits, however, the number of consumers who participate in an activist consumer group is very small; such groups exist in only a few major American cities. The amount of actual wins, especially when we are dealing with amounts over $500, is negligible.

Consumers and businesses are unable to communicate to each other their true interest in complaint resolution. The businessperson is not sure that the consumer appreciates the expense he or she has absorbed in complaint resolution by gratis repairs, for example. The intangible expenses to the consumer are shrugged off by business. Disparity between the consumer's and the businessperson's valuation of the same complaint may be a partial explanation for business' failure to carry more of the costs of product or service failure.

The costs of not having systems of dispute settlement that work are massive in the political arena as well. Because "little injustices" are ignored by those who generate them, by the legal system, and by government agencies, and because they are so personally important to individuals, paying attention to them, as I have noted earlier, has become a prime currency of politics. At the federal level, it has been documented that dispute-settlement efforts cost members of Congress and their staffs at least one-third of their time (Gellhorn 1966; Green, Fallows & Zwick 1972).[39] Because many complaints fall into block areas (Social Security, Veterans Administration, and government bureaucracy generally), congressmen could handle these problems legislatively; but as I mentioned

---

[38]Compare John Weiss' comment (1974) on the possible benefits of complaining in small claims court: "The enshrinement of professionalism in American society makes the gap between expert and layman increasingly difficult to bridge. Yet arguing one's own case in small claims court can help to overcome a sense of dependence on experts. If a person can act to influence his own destiny in small claims court, why not in other spheres as well? [p. 52]."

[39]Note also an early 1970 newspaper article on the activities of Rep. Lester Wolff (Dem. N.Y.) that reported that troubleshooting for constituents took up one-third of the district staff's time (Connor 1972).

they prefer for the most part to handle problems in a personal way because it pays off politically. Even at the 10% success rate usually cited for congressional offices, people appreciate the attention they receive from politicians, and it pays off in votes. Because pressure for resolving personal problems will not be denied, complaints continue to find their way into the legislative political machinery in greater and greater numbers. Moreover, if we look at local governments such as Daley's machine in Chicago or Congressman Barrett's ward in Philadelphia, we find that political machines are built on the very stuff of grievance handling and dispute settlement. The figures may vary, but the use of legislators and congressmen in the complaint arena is striking because of the time they spend on individual problems rather than the structural changes they achieve in a country of over 200 million people.

As a nation we have been riding until recently on a wave of abundance and expansion. Wars have bailed us out of tight economic pinches and increasing dissatisfactions. Wives entering the work force have bailed us out of excessive inflation. Institutions have been invented to "cool out the mark." An individuated population whose main contact with other citizens is through television and radio programs planned and sponsored by business interests can hardly develop class consciousness, let alone consumer consciousness. A strong anticomplaint ethic is part of the ideology sold to consumers along with goods and services ("you're the first person to complain"; "it's not that simple"; "go with the flow"; "let it slide"). Complainants are immediately labeled deviants.

Theoretically, Americans have access to a great number of both old and recent institutions where disputes may be processed. The overall picture, however, leads one to conclude that in the United States, unlike many countries with fewer forums for justice, the justice motive is starving for lack of attention. This slow death is, I believe, related to the absence of power of the law, for there is a direct relationship between what is happening in extrajudicial complaint mechanisms and the potential for judicial recourse. One of the most important findings of our intensive case analysis was that even with perseverance, complaining pays only up to about $500, which is roughly the average upper limit in small claims courts around the country. Disputing without the force of law, as I argue in the final section of this chapter, is structurally doomed to fail.

Discussion

What have we said thus far? That there has been increased activity in the area of individual complaint handling among citizens, business, government, and, last but not least, scholars. That there is an obsession with handling specific individual complaints and with finding the right way to go about dealing with specific complaints. Access, simplicity, arbitration, inexpensiveness, speed are all words that enter our vocabulary when we think of what to do with specific mechanisms; yet these characteristics have not been prominent in the operation of third-party complaint mechanisms.

Finding block or wholesale solutions for classes of complaints that are either preventable or remedial seems to be antithetical to business and government although both groups claim an interest in efficiency. Secrecy, intimidation, and distancing mechanisms all protect self-interested groups. The experience that business has accumulated from product and service complaints is not utilized. Secrecy shrouded in the rationale of confidentiality characterizes the way business uses information it receives from complaint letters. Business benefits from setting up trade association centers, because such action serves to postpone public accounting in Washington. Congressmen benefit from constituent complaint handling; complaints become primary currency in elections. Trusting citizens are deceived daily and experience a loss of faith in their system. Voluntary groups that develop to fill the void created by business and government contribute to building community and citizen participation but may also accelerate citizens' realization that handling complaints one by one in a country of over 200 million people benefits many but not, in the long run, the entire body of taxpayers–consumers. The practical utility of complaints is underrepresented in our data: Business, by virtue of its defensive stance, does not learn from the users of its products how to improve these products; neither do professionals at large seek to learn how to improve services—they are interested only in service delivery. Complaints do not seem to be widely used as early alerts; indeed, they are hidden from view whenever possible. Those that render professional services do not seem to use their intelligence in admitting problems and setting about to right abuses; rather, along with business, they fall prey to public-relations tactics that cover what is with what might be. When trade associations are effective in handling inside messes, it is usually in relation to the performance of small business, not big business. More satisfaction is generally achieved if complaint handling is face-to-face in all arenas, but the overall picture is as Schrag (1972), a law professor at Columbia University, described it after his attempts to deal with everyday problems in New York City. Schrag suggests there is a breakdown in law and order: large landlord corruption; loan sharks; nonenforcement of health codes; nonpayment of property taxes; abuses relating to cars, medicine, food, and appliances; and the constant exposure of large segments of the population to low-profile, undramatic, petty exploitation. Endemic lawlessness was the conclusion of the Harvard Small Claims Study Group report, *Little Injustices* (1972). If there is popular dissatisfaction with the administration of justice in our country, there is good reason for it, grounded in daily encounters and having worsened since Pound's famous lecture to the American Bar Association in 1906, "The Causes of Popular Dissatisfaction with the Administration of Justice."

A few years ago I attended a ceremony in San Francisco to celebrate the opening of a complaint mobile as part of the community activities of the antifraud division of the district attorney's office. In plain view the public was invited to present their complaints; access was most certainly easy. An agitated woman hurried forward and sat down in front of the complaint-handler. She began her complaint: "I haven't received my Social Security check for 6 months." The complaint-handler put down her pencil. "I'm sorry, we don't handle Social Security problems." The woman walked away. There is a lack of fit: The sign on the truck did read "Complaint Mobile."

In that small incident is summarized the attitude associated with most complaint technologies; the attitude is more generally paralleled by the way we usually build technologies in the United States. The user perspective is ignored. Whether we build a car or an educational system, we adjust (or attempt to adjust) human behavior to the instrument after the fact. We build nuclear reactors, and only afterward do we examine the fit or lack of fit between the technology on the one hand and our form of government or the implications of human frailty for health and safety on the other. In designing new instruments for dispute processing, the social and cultural setting must be the source of the design. Our age is a time of increasing consumer goods and services and an even greater increase in governmental services. There is more opportunity for grievances to arise, not solely because there is more of everything but also because of increased complexity; goods are more intricate, and more things can break down that consumers cannot fix themselves. In addition, increasingly monopolistic production patterns and the monopolistic character of providers of service, together with anonymity in the relations between producer and consumer, have come to mean that there are fewer nonjudicial ways to prevent consumer problems.[40] Bureaucratization seals off personnel from influences of the outer environment, and responsibility is dispersed within organizations. Advertising increases expectations. Educational patterns do not train people to cope with living in a mass society.

It has been said that scholarly treatments of Western law have tended to view law as something independent of the society in which it is em-

---

[40]The result of these developments has found expression in consumer polls. A recent survey of consumer attitudes commissioned by the Sentry Insurance Co. (1977:22–23) found that 61% of consumers interviewed thought that the quality of goods and services in the marketplace had worsened in the past 10 years, and 78% said that products did not last as long as they did a decade ago. Complaints about shoddy products and sloppy service are on the increase, according to a nation-wide survey of 5873 respondents conducted for *U.S. News & World Report* (1978). It was found that 70% of respondents had returned products to retailers in the past year, as compared to the 59% revealed by a similar poll in 1976.

bedded (Abel 1974). Although the view of law as an interesting process in itself may generate interesting questions, it would be sheer folly to ignore the issue of social and cultural constraints in attempting to understand the role of law and extrajudicial mechanisms in dispute processing; complaint systems cannot be invented by computer. It may be interesting to study, as Sir Henry Maine did, the role of legal fictions (1861), but a closed-system perspective does not lead us to better understand the relation between the law and its clients.

We know the probable concomitants of disputing without the force of law when the parties are grossly unequal. Yet we recognize a fiction of equality before the law and proceed to ignore the sociological characteristics of the parties; pretending things are not the way we know they are can cause stress in the social system. Fictions were developed to fit a changing social order into traditional concepts. For example, the newly emerging corporation was treated as a "person." But this has led to the employment of sanctions that are inappropriate, given the fact that corporations are in fact not real persons (see Stone 1975).

Most pre-nation–state customary law focuses on the relations between groups and not on those between individuals. In modern nation–state, common-law countries such as the United States, the three main branches of the private sphere of the law reveal the law as focusing traditionally on the relations between individuals.[41] Modern social reality lies in neither of these models in terms of complaint handling. Today when a customer walks into a store, the contract is no longer arrived at through bargaining. It is interesting to speculate on how this feature of modern life has affected consumers' competence and confidence in complaining. In a society where goods are acquired by bargaining in a market—where there are no fixed prices—the buyer's first move is a complaint, namely, an objection to the high price set by the seller. In these circumstances, buyers are continually practicing the art of effective complaining. Today the customer is handed a warranty, or a new kind of contract—the one-sided contract of adhesion.[42]

[41]To express the traditional view in a highly simplified way: For resources to be freely exchanged between individuals in the market, the nature of each individual's ownership has to be clearly specified. Property law accomplishes this end. The function of tort law is to protect the autonomy of the individual by providing compensation for interferences with an individual's person or property. The law of contracts enables individuals to enter freely into binding agreements with one another to make the exchange of resources orderly and predictable. Of course, the law sometimes allows an "artificial person" (a corporation, for instance), to be substituted for a real person, but the essential point is that such an artificial person is treated in most respects as if it were an individual.

[42]Reference to the classic treatment of contracts of adhesion by Kessler (1943) lends a historical dimension to my discussion:

> With the decline of the free enterprise system due to the innate trend of competitive capitalism towards monopoly, the meaning of contract has changed radically. . . . Society, by proclaiming freedom of contract, guarantees that it will not interfere with the exercise of power by con-

The contract of adhesion allows the seller to decree to the buyer what his or her power will be, and the relationship reflects unequal power. In anticipation of a dispute all is conceded; the seller can do no wrong. Relations are no longer between groups, nor are they between individuals; rather they are between a social group on the one hand and an individual on the other. Such is the relation between a modern corporation and the individual consumer, and no amount of legal fiction can mask the fact that we are dealing with a business group vis-à-vis an individuated citizen. Regardless of access patterns, remedies for the individual will not yield a long-term result until the legal system has fully recognized the nature of the power differentials that exist in our society. Class action law must be reformed to take into account the collective nature of the complaint,[43] and the two-sided contract must be returned, permitting the law to operate from an equivalence in the power base of complainee and complainant. New instruments must consider the realities in social relations.

National law is a mechanism and a process that may be used to distribute or centralize power, or it may be used to legitimate and maintain present power groups. In the complaint arena in the United States, it appears that the law tends to maintain power groups and that extrajudicial processes are built in this same mode. In disputing, the cost advantage is on the side of the business group: Business legal expenses are tax-deductible; the consumers' legal expenses are not. Although fines can inflict painful wounds on real persons, they do not have a large effect on the corporation. Fines do not, for example, decrease the salaries of top executives (see generally Stone 1976).

The plethora of articles I have reviewed on what to do about the absence of remedies for the exercising of the rights we hold dear are technical in orientation and rich in ideas on ways to make individual justice work better. We will make use of this material in Chapter 2. The overall issue that needs to be addressed is one pursued by the late Herbert Packer (1968) when he stressed the limits of the law, and particularly the criminal sanction, and reminded us that we do not have the funds to do all and so must set our priorities. In the field of minor disputing, the

---

tract. . . . Standard contracts in particular could thus become effective instruments in the hands of powerful industrial and commercial overlords enabling them to impose a new feudal order of their own making upon a vast host of vassals [1943:640].

Since these words were written, American courts have become more willing to "interfere with the exercise of power by contract." But these changes have influenced the theory more than the behavior of the law; the courts move with caution when considering whether to void an unreasonable standardized contract.

[43]The law continues to be resistant to the idea of seeing class actions as anything more than aggregated individual lawsuits. Witness many courts' reluctance to adopt fluid recovery techniques. See generally McCall (1974).

priorities should be ordered along a continuum of prevention, aggregate justice, and individual justice.

The public health movement in the United States was organized in the first decade of this century. We need a counterpart movement in the law, a movement that would center on the individual's ensured access to legal institutions, on simplified law, on techniques for dispute avoidance, and, most important, on a scheme to prevent or get at the source of legal controversies. These mechanisms need to be fashioned by professionals at ease with prevention; lawyers will need help, in this case, because their profession is one that focuses on the disputing process rather than on prevention. There are whole societies that practice avoidance and prevention in the law, and their organizational profiles might be of use here (see Cox 1968; Li 1977).

To accomplish a new direction in priorities we need a major commitment to make a reality of the old maxim of equity courts: "Every right should have a remedy." One of the greatest challenges facing the legal profession is to create forums that can resolve disputes between distant, unequal parties with both fairness and credibility. The courts have so far refused to extend the constitutional right to counsel to civil litigants. It is only when there is a real possibility of using the force of law that the extrajudicial, third-party complaint handlers will work—from the complainant's perspective.

References

Abel, Richard L.
    1974   A comparative theory of dispute institutions in society. *Law and Society Review* **8**:217–347.
Barton, Roy F.
    1919   *Ifugao law*. University of California Publications in American Archaeology and Ethnology **15**(1):1–186.
Best, Arthur, and Alan R. Andreasen
    1977   Consumer response to unsatisfactory purchases: A survey of perceiving defects, voicing complaints, and obtaining redress. *Law and Society Review* **11**:701–742.
Bowler, Mike
    1971   Action line gets answers. *Columbia Journalism Review* **10** (2) (July–August): 29, 32.
Business Week
    1972   A new kind of consumer watchdog. **22** (July): pp. 42–43.
Caplowitz, David
    1963   *The poor pay more: Consumer practices of low-income families*. New York: Free Press.
Cerra, Frances
    1976   Free "action" services a help to consumers—well, some. *New York Times*, 29 March: pp. 31, 57.

Christian Science Monitor
    1977   15 August: pp. 16.
Clark, Burton J.
    1960   The "cooling-out" function in higher education. *American Journal of Sociology* **65**:569–576.
Colson, Elizabeth
    1976   From chief's court to local court: The evolution of local courts in southern Zambia. *Political Anthropology* **1**(3/4):15–19.
Conference Board
    1973   *The consumer affairs department: Organizations and functions.* New York: Conference Board.
Connor, Michael J.
    1972   Keeping in touch: Congressional offices in home states can be big political asset. *Wall Street Journal,* 2 October.
Cox, Bruce A.
    1968   *Law and conflict management among the Hopi.* Ph.D. dissertation, Dept. of Anthropology, University of California, Berkeley.
Dana, Margaret
    1971   Gripes: What's being done. *San Francisco Sunday Examiner & Chronicle,* 7 November (Section: Women Today): pp. 12.
Darmstadter, Ruth
    1973   *All you want to know about the office of consumer affairs.* Unpublished paper prepared for the Berkeley Complaint Management Project.
Ehrlich, E.
    1936   *Fundamental principles of the sociology of law.* Harvard Studies in Jurisprudence, Vol. 5. Cambridge: Harvard University Press.
Eisenberg, Melvin A.
    1976   Private ordering through negotiation: Dispute-settlement and rulemaking. *Harvard Law Review* **89**:637–681.
Fallon, Craig V.
    1972   In Houston, nowadays, cheating a consumer is a risky business. *Wall Street Journal,* 6 January: pp. 1, 10.
Fialka, John
    1975   Social Security scandal: Complaints swamp Congress. *Washington Star,* 12 September: p. A1.
Fox, Cyril A., Jr.
    1965   Providing legal services for the middle class in civil matters: The problems, the duty, and a solution (comment). *University of Pittsburgh Law Review* **26**:811–847.
Friedman, Lawrence M.
    1973   *Some historical aspects of law and social change in the United States* (Working papers from the Program in Law and Society, No. 2). University of California, Berkeley.
Friedmann, Karl A.
    1974   *Complaining: Comparative aspects of complaint behavior and attitudes toward complaining in Canada and Britain.* Sage Professional Papers in Administrative and Policy Studies, Vol. 2, No. 03–019. Beverly Hills: Sage Publications.

Gellhorn, Walter
  1966 *When Americans complain: Governmental grievance procedures.* Cambridge: Harvard University Press.
Goffman, Erving
  1952 On cooling the mark out: Some aspects of adaptation to failure. *Psychiatry* **15**:451–463.
Green, Mark J., James M. Fallows, and David R. Zwick
  1972 *Who runs Congress?* New York: Bantam.
Gulliver, P. H.
  1969 Dispute settlement without courts: The Ndendeuli of southern Tanzania. In *Law in culture and society,* edited by L. Nader. Chicago: Aldine Press.
Hamilton, Walton H.
  1931 The ancient maxim caveat emptor. *Yale Law Journal* **40**:1133–1187.
Hannigan, John A.
  1977 The newspaper ombudsman and consumer complaints: An empirical assessment. *Law and Society Review* **11**:679–699.
Harley, Herbert
  1915 The Small Claims Branch of the Municipal Court of Chicago. *The American Judicature Society Bulletin,* **8**:25–49. Chicago: Barnard and Miller Print.
Hendry, H.
  1975 *Selected observations of the operation of the Social Security Administration.* Unpublished.
Hill, Larry B.
  1974 Institutionalization, the ombudsman, and bureaucracy. *American Political Science Review* **68**:1075–1085.
Hirschman, Albert O.
  1970 *Exit, voice, and loyalty.* Cambridge: Harvard University Press.
Karikas, Angela
  1974 *Complaint management in Philadelphia.* Unpublished B.A. honors thesis, Harvard College.
Kessler, Friedrich
  1943 Contracts of adhesion—some thoughts about freedom of contract. *Columbia Law Review* **43**:629–642.
King, Donald W., and Kathleen A. McEvoy
  1976 *A national survey of the complaint handling procedures used by consumers.* Conducted for the Office of Consumer Affairs under subcontract from Technical Assistance Research Programs. Washington, D.C.: U.S. Department of Health, Education and Welfare.
Lerner, Melvin J.
  1975 The justice motive in social behavior: Introduction. *Journal of Social Issues* **31**(Summer):1–19.
Levy, David L.
  1971 The Better Business Bureau: Whom does it really protect? *Washington Post* (*Potomac Magazine*), 7 November: pp. 16–17, 38.
Li, Victor H.
  1977 *Law without lawyers: A comparative view of law in China and the United States.* Stanford: Stanford Alumni Association.

Liefeld, J. P., F. H. C. Edgecombe, and Linda Wolfe
  1975 Demographic characteristics of Canadian consumer complainers. *Journal of Consumer Affairs* **9**:73–80.
Lowy, Michael J.
  1978 *Efficiency and community empowerment: A short review of the cooptation of decentralizing the management of interpersonal disputes.* Paper prepared for the Law and Society Association meetings, Minneapolis, 18–20 May.
Maguire, John M.
  1923 Poverty and civil litigation. *Harvard Law Review* **36**:361–404.
Maine, Sir Henry
  1861 *Ancient law: Its connection with the early history of society and its relation to modern ideas.* Boston: Beacon Press (1963).
McCall, James R.
  1974 Due process and consumer protection: Concepts and realities in procedure and substance—class action issues. *Hastings Law Journal* **25**:1351–1410.
Munns, Joyce M.
  1978 Consumer complaints as pre-purchase information. An evaluation of Better Business Bureau reports to consumers. *Journal of Consumer Affairs* **12**:76–87.
Nader, Laura
  1977 Powerlessness in Zapotec and U.S. Societies. In *Anthropological Studies of Power*, edited by R. Fogelson and R. Adams. New York: Academic Press.
  1978 The direction of law and the development of extra-judicial processes in nation state societies. In *Cross-examinations: Essays in memory of Max Gluckman*, edited by P. H. Gulliver, Leiden: E. J. Brill.
Nader, Laura, and David Serber
  1976 Law and the distribution of power. In *The uses of controversy in sociology*, edited by Lewis A. Coser and Otto N. Larsen, New York: Free Press.
Nader, Laura, and Linda R. Singer
  1976 Law in the future: Dispute resolution . . . what are the choices? *California State Bar Journal* **51** (4 Supp.):281–286, 311–320.
Nader, Laura, and Harry F. Todd, Jr.
  1978 Introduction: The disputing process. In *the disputing process—law in ten societies*, edited by Laura Nader and H. F. Todd, Jr. New York: Columbia University Press.
NICJ (National Institute for Consumer Justice)
  1973 *Business-sponsored mechanisms for resolving consumer disputes* (Staff study prepared for the NICJ). Washington, D.C.
Packer, Herbert L.
  1968 *The limits of the criminal sanction.* Stanford: Stanford University Press.
Palo Alto Times
  1972 April 21: pp. 8.
Parnell, Philip C.
  1973 *Consumer behavior in problem management.* Unpublished manuscript.

Pound, Roscoe
   1906   The causes of popular dissatisfaction with the administration of justice. *Reports of the American Bar Association* **29**:295–417.
   1913   The administration of justice in the modern city. *Harvard Law Review* **26**:302–328.
Prestbo, John A.
   1971   "Seller beware": Consumer ire grows as some firms ignore complaints and queries. *Wall Street Journal,* 1 July: pp. 1, 13.
Rosenblum, Victor G.
   1974   Handling citizen initiated complaints: An introductory study of federal agency procedures and practices. *Administrative Law Review* **26**:1–47.
Rosenthal, Benjamin S.
   1971   Report on the Better Business Bureaus. *Congressional Record,* 17 December: E13764–E13778.
Ross, H. Lawrence
   1970   *Settled out of court: The social process of insurance claims adjustment.* Chicago: Aldine Press.
San Francisco Chronicle
   1971   GM pays to get letters back. 29 April: p. 2.
   1972   Open the door in the wall you're up against (Advertisement by KGO-TV). 28 August: p. 11.
San Francisco Consumer Action
   1973   *Break the banks! A shopper's guide to banking services.* San Francisco: SFCA.
Schorr, Burt
   1975   Federal handling of complaints is criticized. *Wall Street Journal,* 7 October: p. 46.
Schrag, Philip G.
   1972   *Counsel for the deceived: Case studies in consumer fraud.* New York: Random House.
Schulman, Michael, and John Geesman
   1974   *Deceptive packaging: A close look at the California State Department of Consumer Affairs.* San Francisco: SFCA.
Schwartz, Ted
   1969   Avoid practicing law in "action" columns. *Editor and Publisher,* **102**(46) 15 November: p. 56.
Seeman, Melvin
   1963   Alienation and social learning in a reformatory. *American Journal of Sociology* **69**:270–284.
   1967   Powerlessness and knowledge: A comparative study of alienation and learning. *Sociometry* **30**:105–123.
Sentry Insurance Co.
   1977   *Consumerism at the crossroads.* Commissioned in 1976 and conducted by Louis Harris and Associates, and Marketing Science Institute. Stevens Point, Wisconsin.
Serber, David
   1976   *The politics of insurance regulation: An ethnographic study of the process of insurance regulation in California and Pennsylvania.* Unpub-

lished Ph.D. dissertation, Department of Anthropology, University of California, Berkeley.

Small Claims Study Group (J. Weiss, Project Director)
1972 *Little injustices: Small claims courts and the American consumer.* 2 volumes. Cambridge Mass.: Quincy House, Harvard College.

Stewart, J.
1975 *A look at Social Security from the ground level.* Unpublished.

Stone, Christopher
1975 *Where the law ends: The social control of corporate behavior.* New York: Harper & Row.
1976 Stalking the wild corporation. *Working Papers for a New Society* **4**(1):17–21; 87–89; 92–93.

Stungo, Adrian
1976 The impact of the local ombudsman on planning offices in London. *Journal of Planning and Environmental Law* (London) (December):725–731.

TARP (Technical Assistance Research Programs, Inc.)
1975 *Feasibility study to improve handling of consumer complaints: Evaluation report, first portion.* Washington, D.C.: U.S. Department of Health, Education and Welfare.
1978 *Feasibility study to improve handling of consumer complaints. federal agency complaint-handling: Evaluation update.* Washington, D.C.: U.S. Department of Health, Education and Welfare.

Time
1972 They are all afraid of Herb the horrible. 10 July: pp. 80, 82.

Townsend, Claire (Project Director)
1971 *Old age—The last segregation.* Ralph Nader's Study Group Report on Nursing Homes. New York: Bantam Book with Grossman Publishers.

Tripi, Frank
1974 The inevitability of client alientation: A counter argument. *Sociological Quarterly* **15**:432–441.

Tyson, P. W.
1973 *Governmental consumer protection agencies: A comprehensive study of multi-leveled complaint management.* Unpublished paper prepared for the Berkeley Complaint Management Project.

U.S. Congress
1975 Joint Economic Committee. *Pollsters report on American consumers and businessmen 1.* Hearing, 94th Congress.
1977 Senate Committee on Commerce, Science, and Transportation, Subcommittee for Consumers. *Consumer Controversies Resolution Act.* Hearing. 95th Congress, 1st Session, 5 May.

U.S. News & World Report
1978 Why people gripe about business. 20 February: pp. 16–18.

Vacar, Thomas, and Michael Banta
1971 A guide for establishing public interest consumer auto complaint organizations. *Congressional Record,* 1 December: E12794–E12801.

Vance, William R.
1917 A proposed court of conciliation. *Minnesota Law Review* **1**:107–116.

Wall Street Journal
1971 Consumer ire grows as some firms ignore complaints and queries. 1 July: pp. 1, 13.
Waters, Harry F.
1975 Consumer Galahads. *Newsweek*, 15 September: pp. 69–70.
Weiss, John H.
1974 Justice without lawyers: Transforming small claims courts. *Working Papers for a New Society* **2**(Fall):45–53.
West, Michael G., and Howard T. Reben (Eds.)
1971 *Building a consumer organization—COMBAT, Incorporated.* Presented at the Northeast Regional Consumer Law Conference, Brandeis University, Waltham, Mass., 13 October.
Whitford, William C., and Spencer L. Kimball
1974 Why process consumer complaints? A case study of the Office of the Commissioner of Insurance of Wisconsin. *Wisconsin Law Review* 1974:639–720.
Zaretsky, Irving I., and Mark P. Leone
1974 Introduction: The common foundation of religious diversity. In *Religious movements in contemporary America*, edited by Zaretsky and Leone. Princeton: Princeton University Press.

2

Laura Nader
Christopher Shugart

OLD SOLUTIONS FOR OLD PROBLEMS

Introduction

This chapter focuses on an old social problem in mass and industrialized societies, an old and unresolved problem—the equitable settlement of minor disputes—which is not, as we have discovered, minor at all. In the words of the California Supreme Court, "Protection of unwary consumers from being duped by unscrupulous sellers is an exigency of the utmost priority in contemporary society."[1] Three recent surveys reveal in quantitative terms the seriousness of the problem we are considering (Best and Andreasen 1977; King and McEvoy 1976; Sentry Insurance 1977).[2] The studies in this book explore the problem in organizational terms.

The difficulties of dispute resolution have continued despite a burst since the late 1960s of new laws designed to protect consumers. The federal government entered the warranty field with the Magnuson–Moss Warranty Act of 1975 in an attempt to make warranties more easily understandable and assure a basic minimum coverage. Some states, such as California, for example, also passed new consumer warranty laws.

By the mid 1970s, almost every state had some kind of deceptive sales practices act aimed at abuses in the marketplace that might not fall under

[1]See *Vasquez v. Superior Court,* 4 Cal. 3d 800, 808 (1971), cited in *Fletcher v. Security Pacific National Bank,* 23 Cal. 3d 442, 445 (1979).

[2]A comparative examination of problems of access to the legal system and an exploration of promising approaches and new institutions were the goals of the 4-year "Florence Access-to-Justice Project." The results, based in part on reports from 23 countries, are found in Cappelletti and Garth (1978) and Cappelletti (1978–1979). Volume II of the latter work focuses particularly on small claims and consumer problems.

NO ACCESS TO LAW
Alternatives to the American Judicial System

the common-law definition of fraud. At first, the tendency was to allow only the state attorney general to sue under these acts, but increasingly, the consumer who is injured by deceptive practices is being given the right to sue and recover money damages (Sheldon and Zweibel 1978:103–104). In addition to these general laws, state and federal legislators have enacted measures covering special problems such as door-to-door sales, unsolicited goods, consumer credit transactions, and automobile repairs. Especially important is the fact that many of these new laws attempt to encourage the consumer to sue by providing for minimum recovery (for example, $100 or $200 even if actual damages are less), double or treble damages, punitive damages, or recovery of attorney fees. Despite these changes in the law, few people have sued under these statutes (Bernstine 1977:263). The reasons are apparent. The cost of legal services is too high, and even when attorney fees are provided for the winner, plaintiffs still face a gamble—they may lose and end up having to pay the legal costs themselves. Furthermore, few members of the public know about these new laws; few lawyers specialize in consumer cases; and judges are reluctant to award attorney fees that adequately compensate the attorney when the case involves only a small claim (Bernstine 1977:341; Berke and Stern 1974:104). The prognosis for major social change by these consumer fraud laws of the past decade thus far looks bleak.

The Consumer Controversies Resolution Act (CCRA) bill was first introduced into the Senate in 1974 and was passed twice. An amended version with a new name, the Dispute Resolution Act, and with a reduced emphasis on consumer disputes was passed by the House on December 12, 1979, the Senate on January 30, and signed by the President February 12, 1980 (#96–190). The original purpose of the CCRA was to set out broad national guidelines for handling consumer grievances and to provide financial assistance to the states for establishing or improving dispute mechanisms. The findings of Congress, enunciated in the last version of the CCRA bill (before it was amended) are worth quoting because they demonstrate that our assessment of the problem is hardly novel: "For the majority of American consumers, mechanisms for the resolution of controversies involving consumer goods and services are largely unavailable, inaccessible, ineffective, expensive, or unfair [Congressional Record 1978: S10143]."

At this point we might well ask whether it is really to society's advantage to spend more money and effort in trying to redress consumer grievances. One might argue that the cost to society of setting up machinery to handle small grievances will be large compared with the benefit of having minor grievances resolved. What is often overlooked in this view are the preventive and therapeutic benefits to be gained.

In the neoclassical model of economics, products and services are kept at high quality by forces of competition; consumers control quality by their decisions to accept or reject commodities. This model presupposes that "perfect competition" obtains in practice and that consumers have perfect knowledge of market commodities, including the probabilities of product failure and service shortcomings. But consumers today do not have this kind of knowledge, and therefore the consumer's "dollar vote" in the market is not an adequate means to stimulate business to maintain high quality.[3]

Instead consumers try the products of one firm and then move on to another. Advertising and continual changes in style on the one hand, and dissatisfaction on the other, accentuate switching behavior. "New and improved" products, often manufactured by the same companies under new brand names, encourage the consumer to try again in a "futile search for the 'ideal' product [Hirschman 1970:28]" or for one that meets reasonable expectations. The result may sometimes be an "ineffective flitting back and forth of groups of consumers from one deteriorating firm to another without any firm getting a signal that something has gone awry [p. 26]."

Today's market gives a competitive edge to companies that cut costs by engaging in deceptive practices, producing low-quality products and services, and failing to honor warranties (cf. Jones and Boyer 1972:361; Spence 1973:2). As noted in the report from the Council of State Governments, "The more honest operator is forced to the level of the less trustworthy in order to remain solvent [1970:12]."

The nonproductive consumer today bears a substantial part of the risk of product and service defects. Effective redress of consumer grievances, by shifting that risk to business, would give manufacturers a stronger incentive to invest in improving quality. Better-served consumers should be the goal of a societywide quality-control system. Well-intentioned businesspeople, too, would benefit if the competitive advantage to be gained from shoddy and dishonest practices were removed.

The Processes of Control

In discussing solutions to social problems as divergent as poverty, sickness, child abuse, and consumer complaints, American writers have regularly constructed two models of reform. One model has focused upon the individual; the other upon the wider structures of society. By and large, solutions to social problems have been based on the first model and have emphasized improving a person's lot through educating, improving

---

[3]Various economists have explored these ideas. See, e.g., Akerlof (1970); Darby and Karni (1973); Hirschman (1970:21–29); Leland (1977); Spence (1973).

public services, advocating rights, enlarging the pie, and promising that the rewards of such strategies will be harvested in the next generation. As for the present, amelioration is the best that can be expected. If we look at the history of reform in the United States, various combinations of such solutions have often been successful in at least "cooling out" demand.

The focus on the individual and on assistance to the individual, which is often associated with liberal reform movements, distracts attention from economic forces, power differential, and the inequality of distribution of remedies to rights in the United States. The extent to which social class and institutional structures affect the options of individuals is minimized. The assumption that change is to be achieved preeminently through individual reformation is so deeply embedded that there has developed a cultural blindness to the importance of the social and cultural structure that produces the problem in the first place.

In the consumer field the individual has also been the object of reform. Agencies such as the Federal Trade Commission have placed reliance on educating consumers, emphasizing the theme "Let the buyer beware." We are a people who psychologize everything, so it is not surprising that we tend to locate the cause of social problems within the individual and to look for solutions there also, with an assist from the government.

In this chapter we look at both individuals and social structures, because both must be dealt with if we are to change the situation. We address first the obstacles to improved complaint handling arising from ideology and social institutions. We then consider what happens in the complaint-handling chain, for this is the key to improving both the judicial and extrajudicial ways of handling individual complaints. And finally we look at both private and public bloc solutions from a number of perspectives. In our concluding remarks we focus on the question of motivation and success: How can consumers and sellers be brought to cooperate in solving minor disputes and by whose standards do we measure success in this area? The purpose of the chapter is to delineate the role of individualization, ideologies, and social structure in the complaint process to indicate why it is that mere tinkering or experimentation with pieces of the process, such as binding arbitration, only serve to postpone solutions.

Observations of how Americans complain indicate the pivotal importance of three features: power, confidentiality, and a focus on single cases rather than issues. The relation between power and control goes beyond having access to lawyers and courts; in fact, in any society, central power processes probably have less to do with the judicial system than most legal thinkers might wish to admit. Anthropologists have studied societies where there is no judicial system, no third-party decision makers, and yet there is order and control. They have been greatly interested in the informal processes that govern peoples in both preliterate and industrial societies, in part because these processes often seem little affected by change in the formal structure of government. Both ideologies of control and networks of social relations have major impact on disputing and dispute settlement whether governmental institutions are present or absent.

In working with the American complaint materials we have been struck by the following ideologies as being controlling concepts that interpret the working out of the play of power, the emphasis on confidentiality, and the handling of single cases. They curtail the ideal development and function of complaint processes and weaken the impact of new laws that are intended to make a difference in dispute processing.

Caveat Emptor ("Let the Buyer Beware")

In 1966, a law review article could state: "The consumer is faced by a set of legal concepts traditionally premised on the 'caveat emptor' doctrine. He is unprotected by state legislatures since no lobby exerts pressure for laws to protect him . . . [*University of Pennsylvania Law Review* 1966:397]." Taken broadly, caveat emptor in its heyday in the nineteenth century meant that the sale of goods was a purely private affair between the participating parties; the government was to look the other way, except to enforce contracts and take action against extreme forms of fraud. A major consequence was that if a product had a hidden defect (hidden from the consumer) and if the merchant made no guarantees and uttered no false statements, the buyer had very little chance of securing a remedy even if the product fell to pieces the next day (see Biddle 1884). As time went on, the law began to show more concern, and many manufacturers provided warranties, but these were often vague and riddled with exceptions, disclaimers, and limitations that frequently had the effect of removing protection for the consumer in just those circumstances in which he or she was most in need of it (see, e.g., Roberts 1978:1845; Rothschild 1976:341).

For those who assume that recent moves away from the doctrine of caveat emptor represent a strikingly new direction in Western law, a glance at history will show that caveat emptor was instead the abnormal principle. Most legal systems probably have recognized in at least some circumstances what lawyers call an "implied warranty"—a warranty of quality that the law itself establishes—the message being, "Let the seller beware." In mature Roman law, for example, implied warranties insured the buyer against latent defects for a broad range of goods. Buyers could cancel a sale and get their money back (with interest) for some defects, or they could have the price reduced to compensate (Morrow 1940:352–360). Hamilton (1931) has shown convincingly that the doctrine of caveat emptor was held in little regard in medieval England. Merchants and craftsmen were strictly regulated by the authorities of fairs and markets. In Western Europe during the Middle Ages, many direct controls were placed on the quality of products. Between the thirteenth and sixteenth centuries, when this development reached its peak, all the major trades and industries were subject to detailed regulations.[4] Rules in Barcelona in 1330, for instance, specified the exact number of rivets to be put in breastplates (Cipolla 1963:422–423).

Its Latin name suggests that the doctrine of caveat emptor has an ancient heritage; in fact, in England the term first appeared in law reports only in the beginning of the seventeenth century and had a growing success from then on (Hamilton 1931:1165). Morrow points out how odd it is that the law increasingly left the buyer to his or her own devices just as trade began to expand and protection for the buyer became a more and more pressing need (Morrow 1940:330).

In the early days of the United States, caveat emptor gained a secure place in the legal imagination. Because the buyer and seller were presumed to have equal bargaining power, the judicial system thought it best to avoid any interference with what it regarded as "freedom of contract." From the middle of the nineteenth century to the mid 1930s, the courts, acting under the influence of a strong pro-business climate, almost routinely struck down the state legislatures' attempts to pass consumer protection laws. For example, in 1930 the legislature of Connecticut passed an act fixing minimum standards for motor oils that the federal district judges pronounced null and void, reasoning that because buyers

---

[4]Caveat emptor involves access to effective means of redress as well as laws governing market transactions and product quality. The institutions that preindustrial state societies developed to settle disputes in marketplaces and fairs demand further study. Easy access and speedy resolution are recurring themes. Overseers of the market, located in or near the marketplace, were found, for example, in ancient Greece and Rome, medieval Europe, and Aztec Mexico. A composite picture shows that their functions included keeping order, receiving complaints, preventing falsification, controlling weights and measures, and enforcing product regulations. Forums for the settling of disputes between buyers and sellers appear generally to have been located in the marketplace itself or close at hand. Though we cannot easily ascertain the quality of justice dispensed by these forums, we know that in medieval Europe and in the great Aztec market of Tlatelolco, the goal was to render a verdict on the spot (see Huvelin 1897:72–74, 113–117, 386–419; Morrow 1940:351; Soustelle 1955:27–28.

The account given by Daniel Defoe, the famous novelist and pamphleteer, of his visit in 1723 to Sturbridge Fair, the most important in Great Britain at the time, is worth quoting, for it captures the essence of an institution found in one variation or another in diverse societies:

> I should have mention'd that here is a Court of Justice always open, and held every Day in a Shed built on purpose in the Fair; this is for keeping the Peace, and deciding Controversies in matters Deriving from the Business of the Fair: The Magistrates of the Town of Cambridge are Judges in this Court . . . : Here they determine Matters in a Summary way . . . ; and they have a final Authority without Appeal [quoted in Walford 1883:142].

can seek out exactly what they want in our competitive market, they should be allowed to take their own chances (Hamilton 1931:1133). The courts ignored the fact that buyers were having an increasingly difficult time judging the rapidly changing goods in the market and exerting effective economic and social pressure on business.

Although our legal system has moved away from the old idea of caveat emptor (e.g., recent legislation has put implied warranties on firmer ground), the doctrine is still with us. Much of the recent reform tries to eradicate the hardships of caveat emptor by placing the consumer and the business on an equal footing so that the buying-and-selling game can be played more fairly within the context of a single transaction. Caveat emptor remains but with the provisio that the consumer be given better information through labeling requirements, disclosure laws, and policing of advertising (see Creighton 1976:83). Pervading the Magnuson–Moss Warranty Act of 1975, for example, is the belief that if warranties are easily understandable, consumers can protect themselves by making careful choices (see Rothschild 1976:380; *Temple Law Quarterly* 1976a:461). Caveat emptor now means that the consumer must beware in choosing among warranties.[5] Yet, few consumers spend much time in careful comparison shopping for warranties (cf. Bryant and Gerner 1978:32), and few can accurately weigh increased warranty coverage against increased price for a number of brands and determine the best bargain.

The Insistence on Custom Treatment of Complaint Cases

There is a tradition in our law that favors the handling of legal complaints one by one. An institutional fit exists between such a tradition and the manner in which lawyers have evolved their businesses, and indeed the way that Christopher Columbus Langdell, the first dean of Harvard Law School, imagined the teaching of law would most profit its students. The case method of legal education, Langdell's innovation, is predisposed to the custom treatment of complaints. There is also a functional fit with the individualistic spirit of American culture. Just as the welfare and progress of society as a whole is expected to result from individuals'

---

[5]The Magnuson–Moss Act (15 USC Sec 2301 et seq.) does make it impossible for a warrantor to disclaim implied warranties, though they can be limited in duration. But caveat emptor lives on in ways such as the following: The Act does not impose any requirements at all on a supplier of consumer goods who decides not to provide a written warranty; important differences in coverage exist, depending on whether a warranty is labeled "full" or "limited" (even "full" does not necessarily indicate complete warranty coverage, including consequential damages; see Roberts 1978:1849); and the Act provides that an informal dispute settlement used by the warrantor must conform to government specifications only if the warrantor mentions the mechanism in the written warranty.

pursuit of economic self-interest in the market, so too should the public good emerge out of people's assertion of their individual rights in court and from individual handling of cases.

In Alfred Conard's terms (1971:420), legal thinking has been preoccupied with "microjustice"—a focus on particular plaintiffs and defendants—rather than with "macrojustice"—a perspective in which cases are viewed in the aggregate and the broad consequences of laws and legal institutions are analyzed. Eric Steele's description (1975b) of a state consumer fraud bureau that was set up to deal en bloc with the problem of consumer fraud and over a 10-year period came to conduct most of its business by righting the wrongs of individual customers illustrates how strong the ideology of custom treatment is. The Federal Trade Commission during the 1950s and 1960s concentrated on individualized complaint resolution to the neglect of corrective action and law revision—a "truly staggering waste of resources [Krattenmaker 1976:94–99]." Also at the national level, congressmen deal with their constituents' complaints individually for the most part. The newspaper success stories that describe new and better ways of handling complaints—for example, expanded automatic return policies, simplified small claims courts, or increased use of consumer arbitration—almost always stay within the realm of individual complaint handling. So deep is this ideology that we insist on its use even when the chances of achieving justice are hampered, as they may be in a search for a pattern of fraud that can emerge only when cases are viewed together.

In general, finding bloc or wholesale solutions for classes of complaints—solutions that are either preventive or remedial—seems to be antithetical to corporations, government, some private citizens, and the law. At a time when interest groups were complaining about congestion in the courts, the same groups were unfriendly to the idea of class-action suits or other aggregate solutions. Part of the control inherent in liberal ideology is solving cases one by one rather than making structural changes such as mandating simplicity in design where possible.

Equal before the Law

The ambiguity of the sentence "Everyone is equal before the law" is a source of both confusion and control. Intrinsic to our idea of the rule of law is the premise that the law should be applied impartially, with no exceptions made for parties with high status or special power. The adversary system has been developed to equalize litigants before the court. In another context, anthropologist B. Cohn (1959) has noted that to an Indian peasant the picture is not so simple. Indian peasants would argue that men are not born equal and that they have widely differing worth. Most Americans would probably agree, although we at the same time know people to be equal in the sense that each one has a life to lose, well-being to gain, etc.

We concentrate attention on rights in our culture, often to the exclusion of remedies. It is much easier to guarantee universal rights than it is to guarantee universal remedies that necessitate dealing with the distribution of power. One could argue that rights without remedies are not rights at all. Yet we presume that right implies remedy, and we legislate as if that were indeed the case. Concepts such as caveat emptor rest on the assumption of equality in buyer–seller relations both outside and inside the courts.

Law governing consumer transactions has increasingly moved away from pure contract—where the two parties are treated as abstract entities, A and B—to a conception that recognizes one party as a "consumer" who is occupying a role with inherently weaker bargaining power. The California Consumers Legal Remedies Act in fact implies that in construing the act, the court should resolve ambiguities in favor of the consumer (Cal. Civil Code Sec. 1760). There are provisions in new laws that award attorney fees only to the winning consumer, not to the winning business. These are examples of a kind of inequality of treatment before the law that is intended to compensate for real inequality of an economic sort.

Most aspects of the complaint process, however, in both the extrajudicial and judicial spheres, claim to treat the consumer and the business as basically equal, with the result that the business is given an advantage whenever time, resources, or know-how are required, as in filling out forms, gathering evidence, learning the law, securing expert factual information, going to hearings, and presenting a case. While the insistence on custom treatment of complaint cases continues, the result can be that access is virtually barred to the individual litigant. The consumer usually bears the burden of initiating each step of the complaint process and in court bears the burden of persuasion. In small claims courts, it falls upon the plaintiff to collect on the judgment—a trying experience sometimes; in arbitration, it is up to the plaintiff to go to court to enforce an award if the defendant does not pay. The practitioners of law must weigh the chances of the parties, as determined by their positions in the real world, to obtain satisfaction in a case.

Confidentiality

Organizations like to keep confidential the complaints they receive, a practice usually justified as protection of the consumer's privacy or as a way of preventing attack by competitors. On the other hand, an examination of complaint letters to corporations and the responses received makes it clear that the complainant is less interested in confidentiality than is the complainee. In fact, confidentiality is used by business to monopolize knowledge about complaints against it. An important strategy used by complaint-letter writers is to send carbon copies of their complaints to people they think might help them. At the present time, however, there is no way of knowing whether or not internal complaint-handling mechanisms are indeed dealing with problems except by locating and contacting the dispersed complainants.

Government agencies, too, are often stymied by businesses' unwillingness to disclose complaints. Donald Kennedy, Commissioner of the Federal Food and Drug Administration (FDA), in testimony before a House subcommittee, lamented that the FDA cannot compel cosmetic manufacturers to submit consumer complaints, a procedure that would enable the FDA to keep check on adverse reactions experienced by cosmetic users (U.S. Congress 1978:384–385).

Business- and government-sponsored complaint intermediaries usually have the same secretive policy toward the complaints they receive. Their files may reveal whether a company has a "bad" complaint record, but that is all. Consumer arbitration is often praised because of the privacy of its hearings and records. But the business firm concerned about its reputation is the party that has the most to gain from this arrangement. Again, confidentiality protects the organization; more public scrutiny would be in the public interest (see Friedman 1977:196, 212).

Some consumer laws exact a penalty from the defendant in addition to the consumer's actual damages. The consumer who sues using these laws is helping to enforce them as a "private attorney general." But many consumers may feel uncomfortable in this role, which allows them to come away with a windfall, when they have no idea whether the defender is a repeat offender and deserves this punishment. Here, the justice motive backfires. In one case in which a complainant used such a law against an auto repair shop, it was impossible to discover from the Better Business Bureau or the state auto repair bureau whether other complaints had been filed against the shop. The complainant felt reassured when the small claims court bailiff told him after the hearing that the defendant had been in court many times before for similar complaints.

Confidentiality of complaints also increases the difficulties of proof. In Better Business Bureau arbitration, neither the complainant nor the arbitrator is allowed access to other complaints that the BBB may have received against the same company, evidence that in some cases could be crucial in proving, say, that false promises were made to the consumer.

In most societies, and ours is no exception, a most powerful tool of law and order is public opinion. Although we are a mass society with sophisticated communications technologies, we have seldom used our communication system to reveal and publicize the records to be found in the variety of complaint organizations that exist. The victim has a different idea of what is private and what is public knowledge, as do some third-party complaint handlers, such as the head of the consumer fraud division in Harris County, Texas, who regularly invited the press to witness his confrontations with accused companies (Fallon 1972).

The control of information is an important form of power in our society. Confidentiality of complaints, in a market where it is impossible for the consumer to be adequately informed through word of mouth, prevents consumers from being able to learn from the experience of others. It prevents them from seeing themselves as part of a group when they have occasion to complain.

The Complainant as Deviant

One and a half centuries ago de Tocqueville (1835/1840) observed that as a people Americans are intolerant of deviant or eccentric behavior; the observation has been repeated many times over the years. A prime technique in handling complainers is to make them feel like deviants. Comments such as "You are the first person to complain" are intended to communicate to complainers that they are out of line or at least that their experience is abberrant. Consumers then learn to "go with the flow" or "let it ride," that is, not to cause any bumps. Another strategy for making complainers feel peripheral and uncomfortable is to suggest that they are complaining because they cannot pay their bills; the justice motive is denied.

One way to discover how complaints are stereotyped is to notice how complainers try to avoid being labeled deviant or malcontent; that is, there are acceptable reasons for complaining in our culture. Sickness is one—"Please don's smoke; I'm asthmatic." Another such reason is illustrated by a woman returning a sale item: "My husband didn't like it." (If the woman does not like it, she is a malcontent; if her husband does not like it, his dislike is legitimate because he supposedly pays the bills.)

In a sense, the idea of consumer complaints contradicts the idea of consumerhood. Being a consumer has been culturally defined to mean that one deals not with a world of people who can be influenced and swayed, but with a world of things to be chosen and things to be rejected. In the market model of society, consumers satisfy their desires from an array of commodities that have been produced and displayed by economic, political, or ideological entrepreneurs; the only role of the consumer is to choose among alternatives. In this model, it is not the dissatisfied consumer's role to try to alter any particular commodity. As people internalize the role-image of the consumer, they adopt the strategy of "exit" as a way of dealing with problems they face as consumers. But as Hirschman (1970) has pointed out, when consumers cannot exit, whether because of absence of real choice or because of monopoly patterns, they may begin to voice and take an active role in participating in the marketplace. The concept of consumer in this model merges with the idea of citizen.

The Guardian of Public Rights

Many people would probably say that in the American legal system it is the proper role of the attorney general or district attorney to act on the public's behalf and that private parties should concern themselves only with furthering their own interests. Such a view echoes the traditional legal doctrine of most Western nations that permits only the state (that is, the government at any level) to bring legal action to protect the welfare of the general public.[6]

This cleavage has not always existed in the law of nation–states. In England and the Continent before the twelfth century, private parties were the sole avengers of wrongs committed against them; the state did not prosecute what we would call crimes against the person (Diamond 1971:97; Langbein 1974:142–148, 217; Plucknett 1956:424–430). As the state developed, however, criminal prosecution came more and more under its control, the European Renaissance having been a crucial period for this shift (Langbein 1974). In considering the evolution of legal systems, other scholars (for example, Black 1973:147) have noted that there seems to be a movement toward a state monopoly of the exercise of social control.

For our purposes it is useful to take note of the offense known as public nuisance, offenses such as obstructing a public highway, keeping diseased or vicious animals, storing explosives, maintaining a bawdy house, polluting the air with dust or foul odors, practicing medicine without proper qualifications, and performing an opera that threatens to cause a riot (see Prosser 1966:999–1000). It is an accepted principle in the United States today that private individuals may not sue to restrain a public nuisance; such suits can be brought only by the state.[7]

A recent case illustrates the doctrine. Aileen Adams of Washington, D.C., felt advertisements that boasted that Excedrin was twice as effective as aspirin were false and misleading, and she sued Bristol-Myers Corporation to stop their unrelenting barrage of these ads, arguing, among other things, that they amounted to a public nuisance. The court did not have to

---

[6]Our sketch is a simplified one. There have been notable exceptions to the general rule. For instance, the English had the institution of the "common informer," a kind of private attorney general who received part of the fine in return for initiating legal action, which was of special importance in the eighteenth and nineteenth centuries (see Radzinowicz 1957:138–155).

[7]A provate party may be able to bring a tort action for a *private* nuisance, but that is an entirely different kind of offense, involving interference with a person's property interest in realty (see Prosser 1966:999).

decide whether the ads were in fact a public nuisance; it answered Ms. Adams by reminding her that she, as a private person, had no right to bring an action against a public nuisance.[8]

By contrast, in England by the thirteenth century, representative bodies of the public could initiate nuisance actions in some of the courts (see Hudson 1892; McRae 1948:35), but these forums went into decline in the fifteenth and sixteenth centuries in response to the growth of royal institutions (Holdsworth 1922:76–81, 135–143). Self-help, the oldest method of dealing with public nuisances, was a lawful extrajudicial remedy in England until the middle of the nineteenth century (see Turner 1964:1391). The California Supreme Court relied on this doctrine as late as 1851 in the case of *Gunter v. Geary* (1 Cal. 462, 466), which held that, since a common nuisance is an injury to the whole community, "[e]very person in the community is aggrieved, and consequently every person has the right to abate the nuisance." Over time, the state monopolized social control both by denying private parties the right to sue and by prohibiting individuals from taking the law into their own hands.

The division between public law and private law received a special justification within the nineteenth-century ideology of liberal democracy and the free market. The public welfare was to be maximized by the cumulative effect of individuals' self-interested activity in the market, private individuals being restricted to the pursuit of their private interests. The state was to play only a limited role in furthering the public interest.

The emergence in this century of new public or collective rights in modern legal systems throughout the world in the areas of civil rights, consumer protection, labor relations, and urban development is one of the most remarkable of recent legal developments (Cappelletti 1975, especially 807–808; 1976:645–648).[9] This growth springs partly from a realization that the market economy cannot by itself prevent economic oppression and misallocation of resources in the modern world. The outstanding

---

[8]For further details see *Holloway v. Bristol-Myers Co.*, 327 F Supp. 17 (1971), affd. 485 F. 2d 986 (1973).

[9]One way to characterize public rights is to say that they are directed more toward prevention than compensation and do not focus on injury to any particular person. If a person loses money by relying on deceptive advertisements, he or she may have the right to sue the advertiser to recover damages. This is an *individual right* to be compensated for injuries resulting from deceptive advertising. On the other hand, there now exists in this country at several legal levels the right to be free of deceptive advertising irrespective of whether any individual has yet been harmed. At the federal level, it is the FTC's job to take action based on this particular right. In some states—for example, California—*any* person is permitted to sue to enjoin (that is, to stop) deceptive ads. Since the individual who is suing must already know that the ads are false and misleading, he himself is not likely to be led astray and harmed. The individual plaintiff is best thought of as a "private attorney general," acting on behalf of the public who are likely to be misled.

problem for the individual today is how to cope with the huge bureaucratic organizations that have become the salient actors in our society. The laissez-faire market system was never meant to be able to control government organizations, which have become so important and widespread; and in the private sector, market pressures are effective only where products and services are simple and do not change rapidly, firms are numerous and well known, and information flows freely among consumers so that the mistakes of some can guide the purchases of others. These preconditions can no longer be taken for granted, if they ever could be. But who should be able to use the legal system to enforce these rights? For example, there has been a recent push to permit consumers to sue government agencies for not enforcing the laws or to force them to comply with the existing laws. But the traditional model lingers on, casting its shadow on many aspects of the legal system. The state still has a monopoly over many areas of public interest law; the awarding of adequate attorney fees to "private attorneys general" is disfavored or prohibited; class actions continue to be regarded as aggregated private rather than public actions; and, most important in the present context, the legal system underrates the importance of minor consumer claims because it views them as merely private affairs.

The Corporation as Person

There are two general models of a corporation. The first model never forgets that a corporation is not a real person but rather an entity that owes its entire existence—including its will—to the law. Hence, according to this view, a corporation has no natural rights (though the individuals that stand behind the corporate entity do have a right to freedom of association). The second model, on the other hand, sees the corporate personality as something like human personality and as deserving of similar treatment and respect. American history has shown a shift in emphasis from the first to the second model, a development that has enabled the concept of the corporation to be reconciled with a dominant ideology of individualism.

Most of the business enterprises incorporated in the early years of U.S. history were chartered for a clear community purpose—public utilities of a sort—such as water supply, transport, banking, insurance, fire-fighting.[10] It was accepted that the charter did more than give birth to an autonomous being; it determined the content and scope of the corporate organization through the mid nineteenth century. Some people believed that corporations should be so restricted because they would not have the sense of moral responsibility that individuals have; critics

---

[10]The following brief description is based largely on Hurst (1970).

charged that corporations were "soulless" (Hurst 1970:43). In 1839, the U.S. Supreme Court held that the corporation was not a "citizen" and therefore should not be accorded the constitutional rights guaranteed to "citizens."

After the middle of the nineteenth century, however, the corporation began to be treated more like a human being. In the late nineteenth century the courts used the Fourteenth Amendment guarantee of due process to protect corporations from economic regulation by states; the Supreme Court had accepted the idea that a corporation was a "person" for the purposes of the Fourteenth Amendment. The legislative restrictions on corporate organization and purposes began to have less practical importance, and before the 1930s general incorporation acts were prevalent, thus permitting businessmen free rein in creating the kind of corporate arrangements that suited their purposes.

These changes did not go unnoticed by social critics of the era. In 1937, Thurman Arnold wrote a book that contained a chapter entitled "The Personification of Corporation," in which he explained "how great organizations can be treated as individuals, and the curious ceremonies which attend this way of thinking [Arnold 1937:183]." Arnold's point was that our system of symbols had allowed the corporation to fit neatly into the creed of "rugged individualism": "The laissez faire religion, based on a conception of a society composed of competing individuals, was transferred automatically to industrial organizations with nationwide power and dictatorial forms of government [pp. 188–189]."

The underlying conception of a corporation as a person essentially like human persons has had consequences for sanctions employed by the legal system (Stone 1976:87). There is little evidence that present criminal sanctions have been able to control white-collar crime, for instance (Ogren 1973:960). Fines may work with human beings, but should we expect them to deter corporations? Fines may be passed on indirectly to shareholders or almost imperceptibly to consumers without having much deterrent effect. This is not to deny that fines and penalties, though inadequate now, could be useful if they were raised, but it might be more effective to calculate them as a percentage of corporate profits or income to guarantee a forceful impact.

Much of the deterrent effect of heavy fines on individual businesspeople comes from the social stigma of a criminal conviction (Elkins 1976:77). But individuals within a corporation may feel shielded from any stigma that attaches to the corporate entity; then, too, a corporation's conviction may not produce the same degree of moral revulsion among the populace. Pecuniary sanctions often fail to touch the persons responsible for making the decisions that led to the offense. One suggestion is that fines and prison sentences be directed against individuals within the corporate structure. In a huge, complex organization, however, it is difficult to determine which individuals are responsible for violating the law (Elkins 1976:83; Stone 1976:87). Also there are usually formal or informal ways for a corporation to indemnify key individuals who have been fined (Stone 1976:20, 87). Jail sentences hold more promise of deterring executives from leading their corporations down the path of criminal conduct.

In sum, ideologies can block reform just as cost constraints, technical barriers, and vested interests can. The patterns of ideology that we have sketched interrelate in various ways, forming a thick net that ensnares and entangles: Caveat emptor is based on a belief in existing equality; protection of confidentiality is connected with the personalization of the corporate entity and contributes to a reliance on the custom handling of complaints; handling individuals' cases one by one encourages the belief that public rights should be in government hands; and so on. Together, the ideologies induce a passivity that helps reinforce the self-image of the complainant as rule breaker and of the consumer as the person at a smorgasbord who consumes from a wide display but cannot change the menu and would not think of doing so.

When these ideologies are accepted without being examined and questioned, movement in new directions seems not only difficult but contrary to the essential nature of things. Piecemeal organizational reforms that do not challenge the present mind-set can have only limited effect; they are weakened from within by the assumptions on which they are based and eroded through meshing with other pieces of the system. Even substantial reforms that keep within the present framework, such as removing the cost barrier that prevents consumers' access to lawyers, may not be able to make much headway toward achieving social justice (Abel 1979b). To be sure, causation moves in both directions: Incremental changes in the complaint-making system do make themselves felt in ideology as shifts in thought and symbol work their way into the structures of the system.

The Complaint-Handling Chain for Individual Cases

Complaint-resolution mechanisms must be seen as interrelated parts of a process or chain. In the discussion that follows we will break the complaint process into three stages: (a) Stage 1: *internal mechanisms* (those that are set up within a company); (b) Stage 2: *nonbinding third-party mechanisms* (intermediaries and mechanisms that decide a case without formally compelling either party to accept the decision); (c) Stage 3: *mechanisms for adjudication* (those that make a binding decision, such as government courts or agencies or forums for voluntary arbitration). The point of breaking the process down into three stages is that they form a usual progression: Those complainants who have arrived at Stage 2 have usually gone through Stage 1, and those who make it to Stage 3 generally come by way of stages 1 and 2. The three stages represent an escalation of the dispute: The first stage corresponds to negotiation, the second (roughly) to mediation, and the third to adjudication. We can take it as a principle that is in little need of argument that it is better to resolve a dispute at a lower stage than at a higher one—provided, of course, that the outcome is a fair one. So let us being with Stage 1 and work our way through the process much as a complainant would do.

Internal Mechanisms

The ideal way to resolve consumer disputes would be between the consumer and the business. Apart from the fact that resolution through negotiation often brings less disharmony than do other methods, there are a number of other advantages: The consumer knows where to go; a complaint that results from a misunderstanding, unrealistic expectations, or the consumer's ignorance (say, in how to operate an appliance) can easily be straightened out; and no time has to be spent educating a third party about the nature of the business, product, service, or dispute. In short, negotiation between two parties is easier and costs less to society.

However, as we have learned from survey material (Best and Andreasen 1977; King and McEvoy 1976), sellers resolve only about half the complaints to the satisfaction of the consumer.[11] The springing up of so many third-party complaint handlers during the 1970s is testimony to that fact. This does not mean that all businesses handle complaints inadequately. Some do an excellent job, as can be seen in Chapter 7. Some retail businesses, such as Sears Roebuck, have open return policies by which they will refund the customer's money for any reason within a reasonable time after purchase.

Ross and Littlefield (1978) looked at the in-house complaint handling of a TV and appliance distributor in the Denver area and found that the company seemed to resolve complaints in a favorable way for its customers. They conclude with the policy implication that efforts should be

---

[11]Best and Andreasen (1977) found that only 56.5% of voiced nonprice complaints were resolved to the full satisfaction of the consumer. Since only 3.7% of voiced complaints are taken to third parties, the first figure gives a good estimate of the satisfaction rate for complaining to businesses. King and McEvoy (1976) found that about 92% of households who took action went to the seller or manufacturer as a first step. One-half of the households that complained reported that they made 3 or more contacts with the first source they went to; 22% made 5 or more contacts; 9% reported that 10 or more contacts were necessary. Only 78% of households received a response (not necessarily satisfactory) from the first source contacted; only 58% of the same group received a final response within a month after the initial contact.

concentrated on enhancing internal complaint mechanisms. Many businesses created such offices in the 1970s (see Fornell 1976:161), but a majority (53 versus 41%) of business consumer-affairs executives themselves agree that it is often very difficult for people to get their consumer problems corrected (Sentry Insurance 1977).

Direct controls over how business handles complaints would require constant policing; moreover, there are always ways to sabotage the purpose of regulations. Though better internal handling must be the ultimate goal of a complaint-resolution system, it is best, we think, to try to achieve this end by settlement incentives built into Stages 2 and 3 (see Johnson 1978:27–34 for a good discussion of settlement incentives).

A good complaint system (encompassing all levels) must be one that encourages good internal procedures by making it unprofitable or uncomfortable for businesses to let valid complaints reach Stage 2 or 3. We will discuss this aspect in the next section. The other part of the solution is to allow businesses the opportunity to rectify a problem but not allow them to wear the consumer down in interminable negotiations (see Eovaldi and Gestrin 1971:304). This book should make us sensitive to the great dangers of procedures that tend to "cool out" the complainant.

One approach is to fix a time limit to the business's efforts to resolve the complaint and to provide for Stage 3 handling immediately afterward. A similar kind of provision is found in some laws at present. In California a consumer who wishes to sue under the state deceptive trade practices act must first give the business 30 days to correct the problem or agree to do so within a reasonable time (Cal. Civil Code Sec. 1782). Thirty days is too long a time, especially considering the additional delays consumers face after they file their complaint, but the basic idea has merit.

Nonbinding Third Parties

We now turn to the second stage of the complaint process: the nonbinding intermediaries. Many complainants pass through this stage on their way to Stage 3 if they persist that long. A study of small-claims consumer cases in the Philadelphia municipal court found that the plaintiffs had contacted a wide range of public and private organizations before going to court. Almost half the consumers had sought help from more than one source. "The pattern appears to be one of considerable floundering around [NIC] 1972:474–475]." In Chapter 1 we referred to the cooling-out function of many intermediaries and of the system of which they are a part. Perhaps we do not need Stage 2; perhaps there should only be internal mechanisms and then final adjudication.

Today, for many Americans, the complaint intermediaries are the only hope. Whatever their weaknesses, intermediaries do help some consumers resolve their complaints, and a few of them help a fair number, even if they achieve only a compromise solution. The Boston Consumer Council, for example, arranges voluntary settlements in 75% of the cases it mediates (statement by Mark Green, U.S. Congress 1977:54). By looking at why intermediaries fail, we can come up with an idea of what would make a fairly effective organization under present constraints.

Common sense can tell us the superficial requirements of a good complaint-handling process: It must be accessible, easy to use, informal, speedy; it must keep the procedure rolling without waiting for the consumer to reinitiate each step; it should make a point of checking up to see whether the consumer is truly satisfied; it should be able to advocate for the consumer when it sees that the consumer's cause is just; and, most important, it must have some way to put pressure on recalcitrant businesses.

Underlying the weaknesses of complaint handlers are certain structural handicaps that were discussed in Chapter 1. The key question is independence from sellers; without it, third-party handlers are crippled. Independent groups are thus the best choice to operate complaint processes. Under certain conditions, such as open review, government mechanisms function well. But, in general, business-sponsored mechanisms just do not have the necessary ingredients for equitable complaint handling, as the National Institute for Consumer Justice has attested: "If a car dealer believes that a car in question works and that the consumer is simply being unreasonable, neither an internal procedure nor the Better Business Bureau is likely to make him change his mind [NICJ 1973:1]." The importance of securing funds for independent consumer groups that operate complaint intermediaries becomes a top priority.

At the present time there are few controls over extrajudicial complaint handlers in our society. The Federal Trade Commission's jurisdiction covers unfair or deceptive practices affecting commerce, but there has not been even minimal regulation of consumer complaint handlers (unless a warrantor specifically refers the consumer to one in a written warranty—a rare occurrence so far). For example, no one controls the practice of some intermediaries who consider a complaint settled if nothing more is heard from a consumer once a business says it will perform. For an intermediary to derive its "consumer satisfaction rate" in such a way is both unfair and deceptive.

Rules that compel certain disclosures are one way that some present abuses could be dealt with. Consumers should be given the information to enable them to choose a complaint-resolution forum that meets their own requirements (see Budnitz 1977). Third-party intermediating bodies might be required to inform the consumer of the sources of their funding.

An appropriate authority could require every complaint handler to keep a record of all those complaints it handles that have first been taken to the retailer or manufacturer (cf. Lurie 1972). The record should contain the names of the business complained against, the nature of the complaint, the product complained about (for certain categories of products), and the outcome of the case. The records would be compiled centrally by a government office. Businesses and complaint handlers could be required to keep a copy of the relevant comparative report on hand for examination by customers.

The complaint bank just described is one of the most important changes that could be made in the present system of consumer complaint handling. It is a simple idea, requiring little policing and involving few technical problems. It might be an excellent way to encourage businesses to resolve complaints right away with internal mechanisms (no report would be made in that case) and to prevent their using dubious third-party handlers as a cooling-out device. The proposal would also encourage businesses to do their best to settle complaints when outside intermediaries contact them. The complaint bank would give business, the public, and offical government authorities a way to look for general trends in grievances.

The proposal we have just made is not a new one.[12] One version of the Consumer Controversies Resolution Act (CCRA) that passed the Senate in 1976 specified that if a mechanism was to be responsive to national goals, it would have to provide for "the identification and correction of product design problems and patterns of service abuse by ... maintaining public records on all closed complaints [*Congressional Record* 1976:S13303]." This provision was deleted in later versions of the CCRA.

If this country had a workable system of consumer dispute adjudication as the final link in the chain, we might then question the need for intermediaries between Stages 1 and 3. *Mediation seems to work best for disputants who are relatively equal in power and who are involved in a broadly defined, multipurpose, continuing relationship, and both of whom have something to gain from a resolution of the dispute.* These conditions do not hold for most consumer disputes. The gravest danger of mediation is that it can make the dispute appear as a conflict between equals that should be worked out on amicable terms for both, inducing the feeling of the consumer that he should compromise, regardless of the justice of his claim (cf. Ison 1972:30).[13]

---

[12]Complaint banks have been put into practice in this country on a limited scale. "Consumer H-E-L-P," a telephone action line in Washington, D.C., developed a computerized system that produced monthly fraud reports that were sent to the U.S. Attorney's Office (Fax 1978:19). In Sweden, the official Central Consumer Complaints Board, which in 1 year in the mid 1970s received 19,000 telephone complaints, has no enforcement powers but blacklists firms that do not go along with its decisions by publishing their names in the government consumer journal and in several newspapers (Thorelli and Thorelli 1977:214–216).

[13]It is well to beware of certain misguided "anthropological" ideas currently in vogue in some quarters that assume that mediation is the ideal form of dispute handling for all minor

There may be special situations where mediation would be quite appropriate—for example, disputes between consumers and small merchants in tightly knit communities (see Danzig and Lowy 1975) or cases where a misunderstanding rather than an actual conflict exists. How then, should Stage 2 fit into our system? We have already suggested setting aside a short period of time before government adjudication can take place, during which the business and the consumer can try to work things out by themselves. Stage 2 can fit in this time period also. The business firm can pass the complaint along to an intermediary of its choice if it cannot bear to deal with an obstreperous consumer. A consumer can try out an intermediary of her choice as a last attempt before adjudication if she gets a negative or indifferent response—or no response at all—from the business firm or if she has a good personal relationship with a particular merchant that she does not want to jeopardize if she can help it.

What needs to be carefully examined is one trend of thought that favors mandatory intermediaries. A scheme suggested by the U.S. Chamber of Commerce, in a leaflet entitled "The Consumer Redress Program," implies that every complaint should pass through the first two stages to get to number 3. The Model Small Claims Court Act of the Chamber of Commerce adds yet another possible layer of intermediaries: An optional provision of the act (optional for the state legislatures, not for consumers) would allow the small claims courts to establish a mandatory mediation mechanism to precede all court hearings (Chamber of Commerce 1976: Sec. 5.1). There may be merit to the idea of mandatory informal session to be held right before the hearing in order to save court costs. But as we have stressed, making consumers wend their way through a bothersome maze before getting to adjudication is likely to tax their persistence and encourage them to settle for an unjust compromise. Mark Budnitz, Executive Director of the National Consumer Law Center, an organization that provdes assistance to lawyers with low-income consumers, has opposed mandatory mediation or arbitration for the same reason, especially for low-income consumers, who "just don't have the time or resources to keep pursuing their case until they finally get before a judge [U.S. Congress 1977:32–33]." (See also Budnitz 1977.)

---

grievances. In proposals for neighborhood justice centers, we see allusions made to the idealized village elder or tribal head who brings the parties together for a friendly chat and encourages them to see that some kind of compromise would be the best way to put an end to their feuding. We read that the "entire justice system" today should "stand at the greatest possible remove from Authority's thumb" and encourage "fellowship in mutual endeavor for the common good [Strick 1977:211, 217]." What anthropologists have shown is that different modes of dispute handling are appropriate for different kinds of disputes (see Nader and Yngvesson 1973:909–911). As Yngvesson and Hennessey (1975:264) have noted, the most relevant features are the type of case and the nature of the relationship between the disputants, not the size of the claim.

Despite such warnings on mandatory complaint mechanisms, provisions for them have been enacted in the important federal Magnuson–Moss Warranty Act of 1975, which provides that a consumer cannot first sue under the act if a dispute mechanism has been incorporated into a warrenty.[14] One commentator has noted that a warrantor might want to create such a mechanism so that "the availability of an early, expeditious dispute procedure may facilitate compromises between the disputants [Schroeder 1978:35]." In the area of consumer disputes, past experience should make us suspicious when we see the word "compromise." If Stage 2 mechanisms, chosen by the business, are made a prerequisite to the use of Stage 3 adjudication, there should be provisions that allow the consumer who goes on and wins in Stage 3 to be reimbursed by the business for all the expenses incurred and inconvenience suffered in going through Stage 2. This will discourage businesses from choosing mechanisms that are stacked against the consumer and from not complying with fair, Stage 2 decisions that are in the consumer's favor.

Adjudication

In Stage 3 we come to mechanisms whose decisions are binding on the parties, or at least on the business. The proposals that are heard most often concerning Stage 3 are (a) reform small claims courts; and (b) set up and greatly expand programs for voluntary consumer arbitration. We will look at voluntary arbitration first.

In voluntary arbitration the consumer and the business agree to submit their dispute to an arbitrator. As the system presently operates, the arbitrator is generally someone chosen by the parties from a list provided by the organization conducting the arbitration. The decision reached by the arbitrator is binding on the parties, and there is generally no appeal to a court unless some gross impropriety has been committed by the arbi-

---

[14]The Magnuson–Moss Warranty Act (15 USC Sec. 2301 et seq.) provides that if (and only if) a business refers to an informal dispute-settlement procedure in its written warranty (a rare occurrence so far), the dispute mechanism must meet certain minimum requirements, to be specified by the FTC. The regulations the FTC has drawn up (16 CFR Sec. 703) specify that the decisions of the mechanism shall not be legally binding on either party—a kind of advisory arbitration. The consumer's required trip through the mechanism may become but one more runaround on the way to the courthouse. The FTC requires the business to act in "good faith," but what this means is unclear, and the FTC is the sole authority to police this provision. The FTC has imposed a number of requirements that attempt to ensure the independence and integrity of the mechanism (though it may be business-sponsored), but there is no telling how well these safeguards will work. Congress conspicuously left the door wide open for a requirement that there be participation by government or consumer representatives in the mechanism's procedure (see 15 USC Sec. 2310 [a][2]; U.S. Congress 1974:26), but the FTC did not accept this invitation in devising its regulations.

trator. Even though the arbitration itself is extrajudicial, the law will stand behind and enforce the award. The first potential difficulty with arbitration appears at this point. The consumer may need to use the judicial system to enforce the award, and hence all the problems with that system that the consumer has been hoping to avoid crop up again.

A number of organizations have established programs for voluntary arbitration in recent years. A National Center for Dispute Settlement (NCDS) was set up by the American Arbitration Association in 1968. The NCDS formulated rules of consumer arbitration and set up several pilot projects, but the program has not shown much success (Best n.d.; Eovaldi and Gestrin 1971:310–311). Another experiment that foundered involved several Montgomery Ward stores in New York state in 1974–1975; not a case actually went into arbitration (Best n.d.).

The most significant program of voluntary arbitration, apart from those connected with some small claims courts, as in New York City, is that administered by local Better Business Bureaus under the National Council of Better Business Bureaus (CBBB). The formal program was launched in 1972 (Best n.d.). As of September 1977, 91 local BBBs offered arbitration to customers, with voluntary arbitrators chosen by the parties from a list provided by the BBB. Between 1972 and September 1977, 6900 hearings were conducted. In the year ending in September 1977, 4600 cases were arbitrated with amounts awarded averaging about $340 (Council of Better Business Bureaus 1977). When we consider the enormous number of unresolved consumer complaints in this country every year, 4600 cases is only a drop in the bucket.

Many companies are unwilling to participate in BBB arbitration, a fact attested by Dean Determan (1975:837), Vice President of the Council of Better Business Bureaus. On the other hand, General Motors Company precommitted itself to use BBB arbitration for several cities beginning in 1978. Also, the FTC has required several companies to precommit themselves to BBB arbitration in exchange for the FTC's refraining from legal action against them.

To our knowledge, no independent study has been carried out to examine the actual operation of BBB arbitration, and available BBB data on the percentage of decisions in the consumer's favor are ambiguous.[15] If the CBBB (1977) is reporting correctly, there have been few difficulties with collection in BBB arbitration: Losers refuse to comply in less than 1%

[15]BBB data show that about 40% of the decisions are in the consumer's favor; 40% go for the businessperson; and the rest are split decisions (Readers Digest 1976). But in trying to sell the concept of arbitration to businesspeople, the U.S. Chamber of Commerce, in its pamphlet "Consumer Complaint Mediation–Arbitration Programs" (1976), chose to give a brief description of one BBB program, the Seattle program, in which the cases were described as follows: 23% for consumers, 47% for businesspeople, and 30% compromise.

of the cases. But the problem may become more acute if arbitration becomes widespread.

Getman's (1979) evaluation of labor arbitration applies in some ways to voluntary consumer arbitration. The important determinant of its success or failure is the nature of the underlying relationship between the parties; *where arbitration seems to help the weaker party, it is because that party has already gained power—for example, through organizing.*

It would be best if private arbitration were competing with effective government adjudication mechanisms; in any event, the disclosure and reporting rules that we have suggested for nonbinding third-party intermediaries should apply as well to private arbitrators. One of the touted advantages of private arbitration is that programs can be developed to meet the special needs of particular industries and the customs of the trade. These programs should be developed, but a good system of *government adjudication* of consumer grievances is even more important.

The small claims courts are the other major area of interest to those who are looking for ways to improve the consumer dispute system. Emerging from relative obscurity, the small claims courts began to attract renewed attention in the early 1970s as many voices were heard charging that these courts had not lived up to their promise to provide informal and inexpensive forums for the speedy resolution of disputes involving small amounts of money. The goals of the present reformers have not changed much from the goals of those who initiated the small claims courts over half a century ago.[16]

Cases brought by consumers do not make up a large part of the caseload of small claims courts which are so frequently used by businesses as collection agencies. It is probably true to say that no more than one-quarter of the cases are brought by individuals against businesses (see statement by Mark Green in U.S. Congress 1977:53; Small Claims Study Group 1972:126). Data collected during a 5-month period in 1977–1978 in six judicial districts in California for an official report show that only 12% of cases filed were suits by individuals against businesses or government agencies (California Department of Consumer Affairs n.d.).

Even though consumers often win in small claims courts, very few take their complaints there (see Best and Andreasen 1977:713–714).[17] If

---

[16]For a good review of the literature on small claims courts, see Yngvesson and Hennessey (1975). See also Chamber of Commerce (1976), Frierson (1977), Kosmin (1976), Lowy (1978), National Institute for Consumer Justice (1972, 1973), Ruhnka and Weller (1977), Small Claims Study Group (1972), Weiss (1974), and Weller and Ruhnka (1978).

[17]A 1977 study of 15 jurisdictions by the National Center for State Courts (NCSC) found that small claims courts were meeting the goals of speedy and inexpensive justice better than previous studies had suggested (Ruhnka and Weller 1977:11; see also Weller and Ruhnka 1978). But "justice" for the NCSC seems to pertain only to what happens once a case enters the court system and not to whether a case is able to enter it in the first place. The appro-

they were to begin doing so, the capacity of the system would have to be greatly expanded. The Best and Andreasen survey (1977) gives us a very rough idea of the volume of consumer problems that an effective system should be processing. In every 100 urban households each year, there are about 28 perceived problems (that concern more than just price) that lead to complaints and to *full* dissatisfaction with the results of complaining. In the urban California counties of Alameda, Contra Costa, Los Angeles, Orange, Sacramento, San Francisco, San Mateo, and Santa Clara in 1976–1977, there were about 4.5 small claims court dispositions for every 100 households.[18] Noting that only a small proportion of cases are brought by consumer plaintiffs at present, we can say as a gross estimate that the present small claims caseload would have to be expanded many times over to take all the cases in which consumers have voiced complaints about products or services but remain fully dissatisfied with the results of their action. Remember that we have used California as our example, a state considered to be in the vanguard of small claims court reform. And we have not yet begun to think of the 136 nonprice problems per 100 households that are never voiced. If complaint mechanisms were more popular, surely many of the present noncomplainers would begin to complain.

We are not suggesting that it is necessary for all unresolved complaints to reach the stage of adjudication; nevertheless, at the start a certain critical mass of complaints must be handled by adjudication in order to pull the complaint system out of its present morass. As more complaints are adjudicated, more also will be settled by in-house mechanisms and intermediaries.

Small claims courts as we know them may not be able to meet this new challenge; the changes required to make them more popular while keeping their present form would probably increase the government's cost. One approach to solving this problem would be to combine the compulsory nature of small claims courts (compulsory for the defendant) with the informal, uncourtlike nature of an arbitration proceeding. The

---

priate question to ask is why consumers do not make more use of small claims courts. In addition to the various costs and inconveniences involved, there are certain psychological barriers. Most important, perhaps, is that everything about the court model reminds one that this is a forum usually reserved for experts. Patricia Kennedy (1978:72–73) describes the case of a physician who was reluctant to sue an airline in small claims court on a claim of $400: "My speciality is medicine, not law." This example brings to mind Veblen's concept of "trained incapacity" (see Merton 1968:251–252).

[18]Sources: Judicial Council of California. *Annual Report of the Administrative Office of the California Courts*. Table 32. 1 January 1978: pp. 213–216 (small claims dispositions); U.S. Bureau of the Census. *1970 Census of the Population* 1, Part 6, Sec. 1, Table 36, pp. 330–334 (number of households). Our estimate of dispositions per household errs on the large side because the counties under consideration have on the whole grown in population since 1970.

procedure that emerges is usually called compulsory or mandatory arbitration. (There is an added Constitutional requirement that compulsory, as opposed to voluntary, arbitration must provide some sort of appeals procedure to a regular court.) The distinguishing feature of true arbitration—selection of the arbitrator by the disputants—is missing in most examples of compulsory arbitration. The latter may be thought of as "adjudication with a judge."

A number of proposals have been made to set up special mechanisms for the compulsory arbitration of consumer disputes. In 1967, an appliance warranty bill in the Senate, which never became law, set out a procedure for settling warranty disputes. The customer would first be sent an "arbitration demand form" by the manufacturer, who would then be required to provide arbitration adhering to government specifications. The expenses of arbitration would be borne by the manufacturer as long as the consumer's claim was made in good faith, and a way provided for the consumer to enforce the arbitration award in court if necessary, with court costs and attorney fees to be paid by the manufacturer.[19] In the field of consumer dispute resolution, good ideas have been around for a long time.

Some proposals have provided a rough sketch of how a mechanism for compulsory arbitration or informal adjudication should work. We will look briefly at three of these ideas.

In 1972, the adventurous Special Committee on Consumer Affairs of the New York Bar Association proposed a model of a "neighborhood consumer court" for claims under $3000 (City of New York 1972). The Committee felt it essential to impress upon the public the idea that a forum was available that encouraged consumer suits and enabled adjudicators (called "referees") to develop the needed expertise. The referees would not have to be lawyers, but they would decide cases by applying the regular rules of law. Every community would have a consumer court; procedures would be informal; and appeals to a regular court would be severely limited so that the purpose of the new forum would not be defeated.

A statewide system of neighborhood centers for the resolution of consumer disputes under $1000 was proposed in a law review note in 1976 (*Temple Law Quarterly* 1976b:420–427). The centers could be located in schools or libraries, and hearings could even be held in a consumer's home, for example, when the complaint concerned home improvements. If the case could not be resolved through mediation, it would go before an attorney arbitrator. Arbitrators would be free to make decisions based on general standards of fairness; legal counsel would be barred; and deterrents would be placed in the way of appeal. Especially

---

[19]For details on Senate Bill 2728, Sec. 4, see *Congressional Record*, 6 December 1967: pp. 35285–35286.

noteworthy is the method suggested by which the successful consumer could collect on the judgment. He would be paid immediately from a fund, and the center would collect from the defendant.

The final proposal we mention is one made by James Frierson (1977), an attorney and professor of business administration. Entitling his article "Let's Abolish Small Claims Courts," Frierson proposed state-operated small-disputes agencies in storefront offices, perhaps in shopping centers. Most of the components are familiar to us by now: informality, simplicity, and finality. The main difference is that Frierson's agency would handle all kinds of claims for money damages under a specified dollar ceiling (at least $1000), not just consumer actions.

Ideas and laws like these represent a step in the right direction. As well as physically removing the dispute process from the courtroom, such ideas signal a healthy trend away from the adversary model of adjudication that dominates our court system.[20] Even though most small claims court judges play a more active role than they would in an ordinary courtroom, small claims courts still operate within an adversary framework (Yngvesson and Hennessey 1975:263); the usually inexperienced consumer litigant has to prepare a convincing case to be presented in just a few minutes. Few small claims litigants bring an attorney to the hearing (though only eight states actually prohibit attorneys), but a sizable number do seek the advice of an attorney before the trial (Weller and Ruhnka 1978:35–36). It is understandable that there has been a call for assistance by trained personnel to nonbusiness litigants in small claims courts after the example of the successful "community advocate" program in the Harlem Small Claims Court in New York City. But providing assistance to disputants increases costs for the dispute handler. If the adjudicator took a more active, investigatory role, some of these costs could be avoided without sacrificing the quality of justice. As Ison (1972:28) has argued, the closest analogy for the small claims adjudicator should be that of detective or inspector of weights and measures rather than that of regular judge (see also Mentschikoff 1961:846–848).

We need to move far away from adversary and court models if we

---

[20]In the adversary model of adjudication (admittedly not to be found in our courts in its purest form), the litigants raise the issues and develop and present the evidence; the judge (together with the jury if there is one) plays the relatively passive role of maintaining order, weighing the evidence, and interpreting and applying the relevant law.

There have been criticisms of the adversary ideal even as applied to our regular courts (see, e.g., Judge Marvin Frankel, 1976). When small claims are involved, the adversary process is bound to be either too biased or much too costly to justify the advantages it purportedly brings. To reduce bias, both parties have to be equally matched in their skill and capacity to investigate, to produce evidence and witnesses, and to make a persuasive argument (Morgan 1956:34). The consumer would therefore need a lawyer or other advisor to equalize his or her chances against the business litigant, who can pour more resources into the case and often has skill gained from experience.

want a mass justice system for small consumer claims. Let the adjudicator be mobile and go to the defendant if that is most convenient. The idea of a single trial or hearing could well be dispensed with; the adjudicator could consult with court-affiliated experts on the telephone. In fact, when the consumer first files a complaint, the adjudicator might be able to decide straightforward cases by a quick call to the retailer (Ison 1972:28). We should remember Judge Shirley Hufstedler's advice to beware of thinking in terms of "a little-bitty court" when we should be working with an entirely different methodology (in Winters and Schoenbaum 1976:217).[21]

Stage 3 presents a dilemma: On the one hand, mechanisms that render a very precise kind of justice are considered too costly to society, given the small amounts of money involved in most consumer cases; on the other hand, some will say that extremely simplified procedures impose too heavy costs in wrongly decided cases.

Lawyers as a whole tend to be preoccupied with the search for individual, case-by-case justice. They have a fixation on the risk of error, and it is this worry about the unjust decision that causes the impasse.[22] When we look through a wide-angle lens, however, we see that there are enormous "error costs" right now from valid complaints that are never satisfied and never come before a forum for adjudication. A good case could be made that even a rudimentary system would be to society's benefit if it reduced error costs by an amount greater than the added costs of running the new system (cf. Posner 1973:399–400). Professor Maurice Rosenberg quipped when looking at how legal reformers approach the problem of congestion in the courts, "When the Titanic is sinking, there is no use in bailing water with thimbles [1971:800]."

Although it may well be that the best solution would involve simplified mechanisms that preserve a thorough case-by-case consideration, there may be even more inexpensive approaches. Rosenberg (1971) suggested that in certain kinds of cases it might be best to provide for "compensation without litigation [813]." He proposed the creation of a Department of Economic Justice that would give on-the-spot relief for minor consumer grievances (say, up to $200) without proof that the business was at fault. The department could then sue the business if it wished. The idea of no-fault justice is not without precedent. Some stores already have a "satisfaction guaranteed or your money back" policy. And as Jones

[21]Richard Abel (1979a) points out a related obstacle to informal methods of dispute resolution: The ideology of our society holds informality and delegalization to be incompatible with the legitimate exercise of power; thus informal mechanisms are often consigned to a weak and marginal role. We should distinguish, however, among different kinds of informality.

[22]Johnson (1978) gives an excellent discussion of the risk of error, the capacity of organizational disputants to absorb and redistribute error costs, and the possible desirability of a skewed distribution of the burden of error. See also Posner's (1973) exploration of the interaction between direct costs and error costs for many aspects of the legal system.

and Boyer (1972) have commented, "In essence, we already have a manufacturer–retailer 'no-fault' system for those claims which the consumer cannot afford to take to court [366]"; in other words, business wins regardless of fault.

Many legal reformers are loath to contemplate a system that is intentionally designed so that a greater proportion of wrongly decided cases falls on one class of litigants. Such a system offends our ideas of procedural fairness. Yet the legal system tends to make a fetish of the individual due process when a macrojustice perspective would recommend another approach as being more equitable.

At present, the major burden of unjustly concluded cases is placed on consumers. Let us suppose the tables were turned, and a simple, inexpensive system were devised to roughly screen complaints so that consumers would be stuck with almost no error costs and business would have to bear the major burden of incorrectly decided cases. This idea does not seem so unfair when we compare it with the present situation. There are important differences between what happens when an individual consumer is made to suffer an unfair loss and what happens to a business, especially a large business. The consumer suffers a monetary loss, or a loss of the use of a product, that may cause anxiety and disrupt his or her life; the large business can better absorb the loss and may be able to pass it on in diluted form to dispersed stockholders or customers. One could argue that a simple screening or no-fault model would be more equitable than the present haphazard system, biased against consumer complainants or the small business that is frequently caught in the middle.[23]

There are other, less extreme, alternatives: A study by Earl Johnson (1978) reveals the wealth of ideas that designers of complaint-handling mechanisms can draw on. Our point is that the problem should be attacked in a new way: Instead of starting with the ideal of "perfect, never-fail, hand-crafted justice in each and every case [Rosenberg 1971:799]" and then reluctantly moving away a little from that ideal for reasons of

---

[23]The criticism might be made that we have ignored the problem of "moral hazard," a term used in economics and insurance literature to refer to the idea that shifting the risk of loss away from a party can lead that party to alter his or her behavior intentionally so that the risk is increased. In the present context, the worry is that a system of rough justice, by increasing the likelihood that an invalid claim will receive compensation, will cause more people to come forward with invalid claims. Though this would undoubtedly occur to some degree, it is not clear that the resulting increase in error costs would nullify the benefits to be gained. The most telling response to such a criticism, however, is that here, as opposed to usual systems of insurance, moral hazard cuts both ways. When the likelihood of a consumer's *not* receiving compensation for a *valid* claim is high, as in present circumstances, businesses alter their behavior by investing less in correction of product and service failures. This moral hazard diminishes as a greater proportion of valid complaints is redressed. Thus it is not easy to tell what would be the net effect of the moral hazard involving dishonest complainants in a system of rough justice for consumer claims.

efficiency toward a rougher system of justice, let us begin with the idea that every valid consumer complaint should be redressed, even if that means a margin of unjustified complaints that are also decided in favor of consumers. We can then move back toward a more careful (and costly) case-by-case scrutiny until the margin of wrongly decided cases decreases to an acceptable size.

Cost considerations and technical barriers are often put forward as arguments for maintaining the hit-or-miss system that now exists for settling consumer grievances. What must be stressed is that the present set of institutions reflects our society's decision to place the burden of many valid grievances on consumers themselves.

Aggregate Complaint Handling

There are fundamental inadequacies in a complaint system that makes use primarily of individual complaint handling. Individual complaint handling is directed toward individual redress—generally repair, replacement, or refund—toward compensation and not prevention. Purchasers may be able to get their money back on a malfunctioning stereo, but this outcome, by itself, does nothing to change the quality of the product. As a result, other purchasers will meet the same abuse. Of course, when taken together, the individual complaints of many purchasers can have a preventive influence by cutting profits to such an extent that the manufacturer would have an incentive to change its product. That the cumulative impact of separate complaints could serve as a societal system of quality control is an important argument in favor of reforming the one-by-one system, whether this be by expanding automatic return policies, radically simplified small claims courts, or independent consumer arbitration.

Unfortunately, the cumulative impact of individual complaints will not always act as a powerful enough preventative because the system will not be used as much as it should be if it is to have a therapeutic effect on the economy. Products are so complicated that the consumer may not even know that a product or a defect in a product has caused a problem. Asbestos has been shown to be carcinogenic, but how many people suspected that their hairdryers might be blowing asbestos into their faces? One woman who suffered burns when her car overturned and caught fire had no trouble realizing that she had a problem, but she did not regard it as a grievance against the car manufacturer until she read an article explaining that the manufacturer knew the gas tank cap was defective and could burst during an accident.

Complainants do not always know their legal rights, either. Anyone would be annoyed when a bill collector calls late at night, but few of us know that a new federal law may give the debtor a right to sue under these circumstances. Many Californians would be surprised to learn that they do not have to pay for auto repair work if they were not given an initial written estimate, even if there were oral agreements with the mechanic. It is doubtful whether better consumer education can keep up with the constant surge of new products and services and the continually changing body of consumer law; rather, action needs to be brought on behalf of consumers who do not complain.

Sometimes the nature of an offense makes proof extremely difficult when only one case is under consideration; fraud is a classic example (Steele 1975a:1233). In its strict legal sense, fraud requires an intent to deceive, and although fraudulent intent is hard to prove directly, a pattern of complaints can be strong circumstantial evidence. Automobile repair fraud, for instance, is a serious trouble to many communities (Ogren 1973:985), but individual lawsuits do little to correct the problem. Rarely can the car owner tell for sure whether the repair shop's diagnosis was dishonest or whether the mechanic neglected to make the repair he said he made. But when complaints are looked at together, a suspicious pattern of fraud may emerge. At that point, a consumer fraud bureau can use specially rigged cars as decoys to get evidence that clinches the case.

A group response is also required when each individual injury is very small. A utility rate above the legal maximum may result in an overcharge of only a few pennies or dollars per person. A "gallon" container of milk may actually contain 5% less than a gallon. In such cases, who would make the effort required to obtain individual redress, and what court would grant an expensive hearing on such a miniscule claim? An old maxim is that the law does not bother with trifles. In fact, in any case in which a large number of people have been harmed in a similar way, even if the aggrieved parties are able and willing to take individual action, it will cost less per person if the claims are aggregated. This advantage is highlighted when the complexity of the case or difficulties of proof make it very costly to handle, as in antitrust cases against businesses that engage in price fixing.

When people complain in groups, they can be more persistent, and when individuals focus on the public benefit to be gained by their efforts, the process of working to bring about change can be its own reward, a phenomenon Albert Hirschman (1975:4; see also 1974:8–11) has described as a "mutation of cost into benefit" (cf. Bachrach 1975). Furthermore, organized complaining increases the possibility of counteracting the powerful lobbying groups that have an interest in maintaining the status quo. For example, a good deal of criticism has been directed against the corps of professional middlemen in the home-buying business—title companies, searchers, insurers, real estate lawyers, and others—that have been estimated by Senator Proxmire to cost the country $14 billion a year

(Wright 1974). To bring about needed legislative changes will take organized complaining.

Perhaps Marc Galanter (1974) offers the best example of the advantages of bloc organizing of consumer interests in the confrontations that occur in legal forums. Galanter elaborates on ways in which parties that use the legal system with great frequency—"repeat players"—have an edge over "one shotters." Because organizations are better equipped to become repeat players, consumers, by organizing, can deal with corporations on a more equal footing. "Delegalization" of disputes may occur when opposing parties are both repeat players in the legal system; equal parties in a continuing relationship tend to find ways to adjust their differences out of court (Galanter 1974:111, 145). We need to remember the interplay between judicial and extrajudicial processes: Organizing the consumer interest can work changes within the judicial system, and these changes in turn can have further consequences for the extrajudicial sphere of dispute-processing (cf. Morrison 1977).

In the sections that follow, we look at how aggregate or collective interests can be pursued in courts and administrative forums. Since government may seem the logical public representative, we look first at its role as enforcer of laws and as regulator of industry and the marketplace. The consumer agency proposal rejected by Congress in 1978 is discussed as one way that government's role could have been strengthened and brought more into accord with the consumer interest. We examine the class-action suit as a device with good potential, and we conclude the discussion by suggesting ways that access for nongovernmental public representatives could be increased and preventive sanctions that could be applied in and out of the judicial realm.

We wish to make it clear that we are using the term "aggregate" to mean action brought on behalf of a group of individuals or the public as a whole, regardless of whether such action is brought by the government or by private parties and whether against the government or private companies.

Who Brings Aggregate Cases?

Remedies that go beyond individual solutions involve us in the question of who should represent the consumer interest in the legal system—the government, private parties, or both. The mental association of public legal action with the state suggests that it should be the government's role to vindicate collective rights. Mauro Cappelletti (1975) argues differently: "Most Western experts seem to have reached a consensus ... that the public administration acting alone cannot adequately deal with the 'public interest' aspects of the growing economic, social, and environmental problems of modern societies [843]." He concluded that governmental efforts must be supplemented by the initiative of private individuals, groups, and organizations—private attorneys general, so to speak.

The special advantages of government action derive from the government's visibility, resources, and authority. Individual complaints to government agencies are of great use in detecting problem areas and in establishing persuasive evidence (see Steele 1975a:1234). In addition, agency resources can be used to ferret out abuses. The disadvantages of government agencies have been more frequently documented than the advantages. Agencies are often subject to the maladies of large bureaucracies generally—inertia, inflexibility, and lack of imagination. Some states still operate under antiquated preconsumer-era provisions and often do not use the remedies available to them.[24] Most agencies are underfunded and understaffed as compared to the activities they are supposed to police (see Bernstine 1977:339; Cappelletti 1975:799).[25]

Government prosecutors also are criticized. Their priorities and strategies change sluggishly; most district attorneys still concentrate on traditional, nonbusiness offenses and give little attention to the growing rate of white-collar crime (Bequai 1977:6ff.). Looking at all levels of enforcement, Bequai, a former federal prosecutor, concludes, "The present system is too cumbersome, politicized, and antiquated to be of any real value [1977:10]." Nor does the situation look better in terms of compensation. Although at least 39 states now permit restitution (recovery of losses) for aggrieved consumers (Bernstine 1977:254), this remedy is seldom used by attorneys general. It is still too early to tell what use will be made of federal laws that have recently made it possible for the government to sue for compensation to consumers in such areas as consumer product safety, deceptive trade practices, and antitrust.

And yet we cannot do without the efforts of government agencies in overseeing the marketplace. One way to ensure that the public interest is

[24]In general, see Bernstine (1977) and Gold and Cohan (1977). State fraud bureaus are reluctant to bring criminal actions, and courts have gingerly avoided imposing effective penalties for white-collar crime (Ogren 1973:961; Rothschild and Carroll 1977:928). Civil penalties are more popular because civil offenses are easier to prove and do not carry the stigma of a criminal conviction. But they are often too small to do much good, and state bureaus have not used them frequently or aggressively enough (Bernstine 1977:253). As of 1976, only 27 states could impose civil penalties for initial violations of their consumer protection acts (Gold and Cohan 1977:936). Moreover, government agencies rely heavily on assurances of voluntary compliance, consent decrees, and injunctions, none of which subjects the wrongdoer to a penalty for the offense.

[25]The Attorney General of California noted in an amicus (friend of the court) brief filed in support of a consumer class-action suit brought by private parties: "The actual number of cases which can and do get filed by law enforcement agencies to vindicate the rights of aggrieved consumers is infinitesimal in comparison to the number of legitimate consumer complaints received [quoted in *Hogya v. Superior Court*, 75 Cal. App. 3d 122, 137n.12 (1977)]."

adequately represented in regulatory proceedings would be to create an official consumer advocate who would counterbalance the powerful voice of business. The idea of a consumer representative at the federal level has had a long history of rejected proposals and shattered hopes, beginning with the unsuccessful attempt of a delegation of consumers in 1938 to convince President Roosevelt to establish a Consumer Department that would, among other things, represent the consumer before regulatory bodies and in the administration of laws (Leighton 1973:289–290).

A new concept of a consumer office, conceived by Rep. Benjamin Rosenthal of New York and Ralph Nader, was taken up by Congress in 1970.[26] The new version would have established an independent federal agency rather than a cabinet-level department. Congress considered various bills based on this idea over the next 7 years; the House of Representatives rejected the last version in February 1978.

In basic terms, the bill would have created a consumer advocacy agency to assert the consumers' position in federal regulatory proceedings, challenge the decisions of regulatory bodies in court, and act as a clearinghouse for consumer information and complaints. The head of the Federal Trade Commission, Michael Pertschuk, was among those in government who understood the value of such an agency: "It'll be a pain for the FTC, but we need it. We have recognized the facts of life in Washington, that only one side has the trade association and lawyers [quoted in Jenkins 1977:52]."

The proposed agency would have had no regulatory powers, and a net savings of federal funds would have resulted in the first year from the consolidation of consumer offices and activities, at present scattered throughout the federal government, that was to accompany the creation of the agency.

The bill was defeated through a ferocious campaign of publicity and lobbying by business interests, including the U.S. Chamber of Commerce, National Association of Manufacturers, and Business Roundtable. The strength of the opposition touched off by the consumer agency proposal showed the formidable forces that must be overcome in this country if substantial reforms are to be instituted. After the bill was defeated in the House, Esther Peterson, the President's consumer affairs adviser, said, "I am frightened for my country after seeing this demonstration of corporate power [quoted in Shabecoff 1978:1]."

To sum up our arguments: Although there are major remedies that the government plaintiff or agency at the federal, state, and local levels can use, the enforcement and redress efforts of the government are not sufficient. The FTC, the state attorneys general and consumer affairs depart-

---

[26]Sources of the following discussion of the consumer advocacy agency include Cerra (1977), Green (1978), Jenkins (1977), Leighton (1973), and Shabecoff (1978).

ments, and the district attorneys at the local level all might operate more effectively if private parties were given greater means to represent the public interest in the courts.

How can private parties vindicate the public interest, and what are the obstacles?

Devices for Aggregate Complaining: Class Actions and Suing on the Public Behalf

A class action is a device by which a lawsuit can be brought on behalf of a large group of people by a representative of that group. In our legal system, the absent members are fictionally considered to be before the court. On the one hand, they receive any benefits that accrue from the lawsuit; on the other hand, they are considered bound by the judgment. Whether they win or lose, they cannot sue the defendant again on that issue. This last characteristic of class actions has important consequences, as we shall see.

The increased use of class actions in recent times has resulted from the changed conditions of our society in which one action taken by a large organization can easily affect many people. A good example of how class actions can be used is found in an important California case, *Daar v. Yellow Cab Company* (1967). Daar sued on behalf of himself and other taxicab riders in Los Angeles who, he claimed, had been overcharged over a 4-year period by Yellow Cab through the use of rigged taximeters that charged a rate in excess of the maximum allowed by the Public Utilities Commission.[27] Daar's individual claims were only just over $7. One can see how impractical it would be to handle a dispute such as this on an individual basis. Virtually no one would take the trouble even to go to a small claims court for such a small grievance.[28] Hence, if private parties are to get legal redress at all, some device such as the class action must be available. In fact, class actions derived their justification originally from the maxim of equity courts in England that every right should have a remedy.

The range of situations in which class-action procedure is of the utmost need is almost unlimited, as a sampling of cases will show: 300,000 consumers buy meat that has been falsely upgraded by the packer; several million car owners with defective engine mounts are subject to a charge for correction of the defect; 100,000 people purchase a brand of camera that fails to perform as it reasonably should; a travel company misrepresents the quality of service and accommodation

[27]For further details see *Daar v. Yellow Cab Company* 67 Cal. 2d 695 (1967).

[28]The cost barrier is much higher in regular courts. Fraud in the travel industry, for example, has become a problem of increasing concern, and yet it appears that few travel complaints under $1000 are taken to regular courts (Dickerson 1977:850).

supplied on a package tour to a Caribbean resort; all 600 passengers on a pleasure cruise fall seriously ill while on board. Class actions can help provide what is especially lacking in modern times: the ability to form a community of action (see Dole 1968; Starrs 1969).

Unfortunately, class-action suits face severe barriers at the present time. Supreme Court decisions have seriously eroded the feasibility of consumer class actions in federal courts. In the 1973 Zahn case[29] the Court laid down the general rule that each member of the class that is suing must have a claim of over $10,000 if a case is to get into federal court; the members cannot aggregate their claims. It is obvious that this rule by itself would bar virtually all consumer cases from federal court, but it should be noted that some federal laws, such as antitrust laws and the Truth in Lending Act, specifically open doors to plaintiffs who have smaller claims.

The Eisen case in 1974 effectively closed whatever doors remained open in federal courts for large class suits with small individual claims. The Supreme Court held that class representatives at their own expense must provide *individual* notice of the suit to all the class members who could be located through reasonable effort; publication in a newspaper would not be sufficient.[30] Notification by mail to large classes, of course, poses an insuperable cost barrier for many cases.

The Eisen decision represents a fixation on the custom handling of complaints. It rests on a blind creed of individual initiative and freedom in the private sphere in times when new solutions are called for. The Court, or the legislators of the federal rule that the Court was interpreting, believed that if every member of a class is bound by the judgment, due process requires that each be given notice so that he can opt out and sue on his own if he wishes. Due process here gives individuals an empty freedom.

A point to be noted is that when attorneys general bring an action for restitution for aggrieved consumers—in effect a class action initiated by the government (Monaghan 1973:1383)—onerous notice requirements do not apply; then there is no attempt to bind all injured consumers by the court's judgment. Here it is recognized that the primary purpose of the action is deterrence and the prevention of unjust enrichment—an attempt to protect the rights of citizens generally—and there is no need for the fiction that all the aggrieved consumers are before the court, because the action is being brought by one who is seen as a fitting representative of

[29]See 414 U.S. 291 (1973).

[30]See 417 U.S. 156. Eisen brought an antitrust suit on behalf of several million investors who had been injured by their stockbrokers' conspiratorial activities. The average individual claim was about $3.90. Notification by mail to the 2,000,000 class members who could be identified through reasonable effort would have cost $225,000. Eisen himself stood to recover about $70.

the public—the attorney general. Seen in this light, the invocation of due process in the Eisen case resembles something from Kafka: the lawsuit can proceed only when those who have a real stake in the outcome do not bring it.

State legislatures and courts do not have to follow the federal lead in this area. California, for instance, allows for dispensing with individual notification where it would be unreasonably expensive, and the courts have interpreted this liberally, looking at the benefits to be gained by the lawsuit in determining what is "unreasonably expensive."

Every state allows some form of class action. Some are more liberal than others, but on the whole they do not permit satisfactory relief for consumers (Rothschild and Carroll 1977:933). One major problem is the so-called "commonality requirement": The members of the class have to have something more in common than simply that they have all been harmed by the same defendant, and just what these common factors need to be depends on the law of the state. In many states, the usefulness of class actions is curtailed by the limited circumstances in which they can be used.[31]

Other barriers to class actions come from the problems of calculating and distributing the money damages that will come out of a successful action. Many courts, for example, reject antitrust class actions with large consumer classes because they are said to be unmanageable (see Mandig 1976:944–947). The problem arises from slavish adherence to the fiction that individual members are before the court and hence that the amount of money to be paid by the defendant should be the sum of the individual claims. What should the court do when many class members are unidentified and the amount of their individual claims is unknown? The most reasonable solution is to assess damages on the basis of the injury to the class as a whole by examining the defendant's own records. Once that is done, class members can come forward and claim their share (McCall 1974:1401). This method, know as "fluid recovery," has met with hostility from many courts that are especially concerned with what should be done with the unclaimed portion of the money. One solution is to require the defendant company to reduce its prices until it has returned to the mass of future customers the amount for which it is liable. Such a solution was adopted in an out-of-court settlement in the case of *Daar v. Yellow*

---

[31]Many states will not permit class actions where, as in most consumer cases, the class members have been harmed through separate seller–buyer transactions, even where a common scheme can be shown (Bernstine 1977:271; Sheldon and Zweibel 1978:108). Other states that do allow class actions under these circumstances may have strict standards for determining whether the separate transactions have enough in common: Must all members have bought the same kind of product or is it sufficient that a uniform sales routine was used to deceive customers? See Bernstine 1977:264; Lovett 1971:284; Sevell 1973:330; Sheldon and Zweibel 1978:108.

Cab; the cab company agreed to reduce its fares by a specified amount each year until all its illegal gain had been returned.

Judges who cannot escape from the idea that compensation to individuals is the only proper concern of private law are reluctant to adopt such solutions, for the money recovered may not go to the same individuals who were injured. From a prevention point of view, however, it matters little what happens to the money recovered, whether a few pennies or even a few dollars go to Jones, who actually suffered the loss, or to his consumer neighbor Smith, who suffered no loss. A report of The Consumer Protection Section of the New York Trial Lawyers Association expresses the opinion that the primary purpose of class actions should be to deter wrongdoing and prevent unjust enrichment (Burman 1978:47).

Judges' attitudes affect class actions in other ways. American judges are accustomed to the role they usually play in our adversarial mode of litigation—that of a passive referee who helps the truth emerge by making sure that the opponents stick to the rules of the game. Class actions require the judge to play a much more active role of supervision in order to protect the interests of the absent members (Homburger 1974:349). At a minimum, the judge must ensure that the party bringing the action adequately represents the class. All in all, American judges may feel uncomfortable in a role that leans toward court prosecution of a case.

By looking at an action only from within the legal system, lawmakers and courts are blocked from seeing that giving consumers an effective class-action remedy is merely giving them equal opportunity of response. In a society in which control of resources by large organizations is the rule, a single action outside the legal system can often harm a multitude of individuals. We need a consumer class-action act at the federal level (see, e.g., Hinds 1976).

It would be a great stride forward for the law to abandon the view that class actions are aggregated individual actions[32] and to recognize that many class actions could be better thought of as public interest actions brought by a plaintiff acting as a private attorney general, even if the "public" in question is only a limited segment of the general public (for example, all the taxicab riders in Los Angeles or all the purchasers of a particular brand of camera) (Homburger 1974:408–409). This point leads us to the next topic: standing to sue.

The legal concept of "standing" deals with the question of who the proper party is to bring a particular issue before a court. If Schwartz is hit by a negligent driver, the court ordinarily will not permit Anderson,

---

[32]The legal system did not hold such a view in the earliest cases of group litigation in seventeeth-century England, which involved the collective grievances of manor or parish communities (see Yeazell 1977).

Schwartz' neighbor, to sue the driver on behalf of Schwartz. Only Schwartz has standing to sue the person who caused him harm.

Again, our legal system tends to give private parties standing to sue only to vindicate their own private rights—only when they have a personal stake in the action. The government alone has standing to bring criminal or public nuisance charges; generally speaking, private persons lack standing to act as advocates for the public at large rather than for themselves or any particular persons.

In 1972, a U.S. district court ruled that a citizens' group associated with Ralph Nader had no standing as a public representative to intervene in the Justice Department's antitrust suit against ITT after the Justice Department was pressured into settling the case. Nader's attempts to establish the idea that courts should not rely only on government agencies to protect the public interest in the area of economic regulation were rejected.[33]

In *Holloway* v. *Bristol-Meyers Corp.* (1973),[34] which we discussed earlier, a U.S. court of appeals ruled that private parties could not sue to enforce the Federal Trade Commission Act, which broadly covers unfair and deceptive commercial practices; the FTC was left as the sole enforcer. The plaintiffs in that case argued that only by giving private litigants the right to sue under the FTC Act could meaningful consumer protection be guaranteed because a lack of resources prevents the FTC from providing effective enforcement itself. The court decided, however, that a private right of action would run contrary to the intent of Congress in enacting the Act and would create an incoherent, inflexible, and inexpert system of enforcement. In 1977, the House of Representatives, in its turn, rejected provisions of a bill that would have allowed private parties to sue when FTC trade regulation rules or cease and desist orders were violated.[35]

Oddly enough, the U.S. Supreme Court has held to a very narrow conception of "standing" even in cases where citizens challenge laws as being unconstitutional. Generally, the plaintiff must show actual or threatened injury to a concrete personal interest. Raoul Berger (1969) has shown that the Court's restriction of standing is a development that arose around the turn of the century. In fact, when the Constitution was adopted, "strangers" could challenge illegal government action in the courts without showing a special personal interest (Homburger 1974:390). This makes sense: The public should have the right to clear the air of the pollution of unconstitutional laws even before they threaten concrete personal harm.

---

[33]For details, see *U.S.* v. *ITT*, 349 F. Supp. 22 (D. Conn. 1972), affd., 410 U.S. 919.
[34]See 485 F. 2d 986.
[35]See H.R. 3816, 95th Congress.

There are exceptions to this direction, especially where the available remedy is an injunction (a court order requiring the defendant to stop engaging in a particular activity). Nineteen states specifically allow private consumers to seek injunctions against deceptive trade practices (Sheldon and Zweibel 1978:102); the federal Clean Air Act of 1970 allows any citizen to sue any polluter without needing to show that personal harm is threatened; and under the federal Consumer Product Safety Act of 1972, consumers, acting in effect as private attorneys general, can sue for injunctive relief when companies have violated product safety rules.

Some recent laws that are primarily aimed at individual compensation also try to encourage enforcement by private parties by allowing money recovery above actual damages—for example, the federal Truth in Lending Act (1968) and Fair Debt Collection Practices Act (1977). But this approach remains basically within the sphere of private rights and in addition suffers from the obstacles that all small claims face in our courts (see Flink 1978).

The "standing" requirement has been carried out thus far on a piecemeal basis by legislative statutes. There is a pressing need to develop more general solutions. Cappelletti (1975:849–852) has suggested that one concept worth examining is the true "relator action" that is found in England and other countries of the common-law (English-speaking) world, especially in Australia. By this device, used a great deal in public nuisance and related cases, an individual who has no personal stake can bring certain kinds of public actions in the name of the attorney general. The French have a system of private prosecution by which a criminal proceeding (with its greater potential for deterrence) can be initiated even against the will of the public prosecutor by a private plaintiff suing in a civil action (Cappelletti 1975:838n.).

We need new concepts of standing in public interest cases that, instead of focusing on the injury to the plaintiff who brings the case, scrutinize the plaintiff's qualifications to represent in a responsible way the segment of the public whose interests are at stake; we need functional rather than formal criteria (Homburger 1974:400, 408). As Homburger (1974:407) has noted, neither the public attorney general nor the "private attorney general" are really parties to the litigation; both are merely spokespersons for the various sides of a public issue.

In 1973, a high court in Italy granted standing to a private environmental association, Italia Nostra, to sue the government as an organization representative of the public interest (Cappelletti 1976:679–680). This enlightened approach should be compared with a 1972 decision of the U.S. Supreme Court, in *Sierra Club v. Morton* (405 U.S. 727), in which a similar organization in similar circumstances was denied standing to sue as a representative of the public. The Italia Nostra idea represents a growing trend in much of Western Europe (see Cappelletti 1975:863–868;

1976:678–680; see also Fisch 1979). The French, for example, in 1973 enacted the "loi Royer," a law that grants standing to certified consumer associations to sue in civil cases where there is prejudice to the "collective interest of consumers" (Cappelletti 1975:863).

Outcome of Aggregate Actions: Preventive Sanctions

Finally, we turn to the outcome of public or aggregate actions in the courts and administrative agencies (regardless of who brings the action): the preventive sanctions that are applied. The legal system should have at its disposal an array of special sanctions to be used when large-scale organizations are the lawbreakers, sanctions that mobilize the forces of public opinion. One such form of sanction is publicity. Publicizing a corporation's misconduct can detract from its reputation and serve to warn consumers. As we have noted, English towns in the Middle Ages relied heavily on publicity to deter abuses in the marketplace (Hamilton 1931:1152). In 1481 a French law provided the following punishment:

> Anyone who sells butter containing stones or other things [to increase the weight] will be put into our pillary, then the said butter will be placed on his head and left until entirely melted by the sun. Dogs may come and lick him, and people offend him with whatever defamatory ephithets they please without offense to God or the King [quoted in Breeden & Lovett 1973:307n.].

Today we consider such sanctions to be cruel and inhumane, as applied to persons, that is. But corporations are not real persons, and we should not have the same qualms over publicizing their misdeeds. Of course, corporations cannot be put in stocks, and butter cannot be placed on their heads. But in place of putting the product on the offender, why not put the offense on the product, that is, make the products or advertisements carry notices stating that the manufacturer has recently violated consumer laws? Imagine a small box at the bottom of magazine ads, like the present cigarette warnings, that would contain a message such as the following: "Notice: The FTC has recently found that XYZ Co. has violated a trade regulation rule concerning . . . . For more information, call (800) 123–4567."[36]

Formal publicity sanctions have been rare in the United States (Fisse 1971:115). Government agencies use news releases, but these are often ignored. The Food, Drug, and Cosmetic Act of 1938 provides that reports are to be published summarizing all judgments and court orders, but these reports appear in a special bulletin of the agency, *FDA Papers* (Fisse 1971:116)—a practice hardly calculated to achieve widespread publicity.

---

[36]See Flynn (1967:1332) for a related suggestion in the area of antitrust violations.

Under the FTC Improvement Act of 1975, courts were expressly given the power to order public notification in the case of a company's violation of the FTC Act. It remains to be seen how extensively this remedy will be used.

Capital punishment for seriously offending corporations is another sanction that may be effective. Statutes that require the licensing of certain businesses and provide for revocation of licenses in the case of misconduct already exist. The idea should be extended to cover more kinds of businesses.

Finally, if we get away from the view of the corporation as a "person" with human qualities, we see that there is nothing inhumane about probing beneath the skin of the corporation in order to control its behavior. Some corporations may very well deserve rehabilitative neural surgery. Christopher Stone (1975; 1976:87, 93) has been a leading exponent of the view that the law must reach into the inner world of the corporation to prevent and help deter misconduct.

If the law created positive legal duties to be attached to certain corporate roles (e.g., chief test engineer), then individual responsibility would be easy to determine and individual sanctions would have greater deterrent value (Stone 1976:88). If individual product defects continually pose a safety hazard, perhaps courts should be able to rehabilitate the corporation by assigning a "probation officer" to the company's quality control staff (see Stone 1976:89). Given that some level of the corporate structure usually is aware of legal violations even though the news may not be transmitted to a person who will take corrective action, perhaps the law should require internal information systems to ensure that all crucial developments are conveyed to top officers (see Stone 1976:89). These suggestions and others like them will be thought about more seriously once our culture has depersonalized the concept of the corporation (which involves, in addition, repersonalizing the people who actually govern the corporations) and once we realize the importance of the problem.

It has sometimes been noted that our legal system does not fit the needs of an individualized society because it is rooted in an agricultural era. Although such an observation undoubtedly explains much about the lack of fit between legal needs and legal remedies in the consumer product and services area, what is more striking is the recent history of the obstacles to consumer justice. The concept of caveat emptor; the idea that individuals should not have standing to sue the government in public matters; the concept of a corporation with the characteristics of human personality—all these arose or attained preeminence in the nineteenth or twentieth century. The idea that courts should serve mainly to handle business transactions rather than settle ordinary disputes is also of recent origin. What appears in recent times is the extraction from court schedules of "minor grievances" and the absence of use of public opinion to support law and order, and instead an increasing reliance on professional law enforcement. It is as if increased professionalization of the bar in recent decades has had as its purpose the creation of a legal system to serve the sole needs of the corporation.

What are we to conclude?

Concluding Remarks

Here and in Chapter 1 we have described the reasons for failure of particular complaint mechanisms and the consequences of failure. In this chapter we have also considered how we might develop a better fit between the judicial and extrajudicial mechanisms, and between complaint-handling devices and salient features of our society, fitting the law to the need for law. Essentially, we have underscored that changing technologies usually render a consumer's knowledge inadequate, that unduly complicated products discourage simple repair, that unequal power between consumer and producer makes mediation and arbitration problematic, and that controlling use is made of such ideologies as the personalizing of social failure or of concepts such as confidentiality at great cost to consumers and to our nation.

We have also reviewed the obstacles to solving this now century-old problem by means of the law. None of the solutions we have discussed are new: negotiation, mediation, arbitration, adjudication, aggregate techniques—these have all been written about for decades. What is new perhaps is that all these solutions are now begging to be dealt with at once rather than serially. It would be interesting to plot the swings in legal reform from delegalization as panacea to legalization as panacea. We might find that liberal reform never works because the reform plan always postpones the payoff to the future. The swing from adjudication to mediation or arbitration distracts our attention from worrying about the problem because the results of reform are at least 20 years away; the small claims courts movement was not truly evaluated until at least 5 decades after the first small claims courts were constituted; binding arbitration programs of the BBB have been in operation close to a decade now with little outside evaluation of what has been touted as success. We would not wish to be part of any set of recommendations where improvements in complaint handling could not be measured within a year against the ideal system we described earlier.

Recommendations we have alluded to are largely but not wholly within the realm of the law. We noted first that "solutions" or "techniques" that have been described as if they could fly solo and make a difference are an illusion, or worse, public relations gimmicks. A better BBB mechanism, a better hotline is not what we aim for. We envision a system of complaint handling that starts with consumer needs. Negotiation, mediation, and adjudication become a process along which the consumer travels—with increasing clout. If there is increased litigation, it will be as a result of increasingly equal clout; experience teaches us that this increased legalization will soon be followed by the delegalization characteristics of repeat players.

We have pointed out that the costs rather than the benefits are always emphasized when discussing policies for better dispute management. There are important benefits from redressing consumer grievances that we alluded to earlier: Improvement in the quality of products and services and a decrease in criminal behavior were two. Policymakers might be willing to allocate more resources toward the creation of effective grievance-resolution systems if they were to bear in mind that there is much more at stake than just the individual losses of the complainants.

We have purposely not spoken here in greater detail because focusing attention on a few key principles would almost guarantee change. For example, simply to require that cases dealt with by mediators or third-party handlers, such as the BBB, be part of the public record could dramatically affect the operation of all in-house complaint handling. Public banking (via the media) of complaints to government agencies such as the post office or social security or to state and federal legislators' offices could also have immediate effect in forging public opinion. Requiring public notice of fraud or other criminal violation on the product itself and in advertising related to it would also be a simple and yet crucial change toward greater public knowledge of criminal behavior. In New York the media since the late 1960s has been publicizing health inspectors' reports on major New York restaurants. All these strategies are preludes toward a shifting of the law itself toward a recognition of the devastatingly unequal balance of power of producer, seller, and consumer before the law, in fact and not solely in the books. De facto there is no law governing claims between the amounts of $1 and $75, which rarely get to small claims court, and between the top amount of small claims court and what is worth taking to a lawyer. These two areas between $1 and $75 and between $500 (on the average) and $5000 are indeed the areas where crime pays very well. When a more equal balance is established between consumers and their adversaries, either by means of a complaint chain as described earlier or by broadening the concepts of public standing to sue or of class-action suits, then mediation and arbitration may indeed become useful solutions because such measures are successful between parties of relatively equal position.

But our critics will remind us that it is one thing to make suggestions, another to institute them. These ideas have not been enacted because they are difficult to think up; rather, there is resistance to their being adopted. Such resistance, we argue, is deeply embedded in ideologies such as individual handling of cases, confidentiality, private versus public rights, short-term profit, "progress," and the fact that law is a business for legal professionals. Solutions that would downplay the role of lawyers or yield an unprofitable venture for them will not likely be supported by the organized bar. Auto manufacturers have little to gain by manufacturing cars that produce less pollution. In the same vein, the legal profession has little to gain by promoting solutions that help prevent legal problems from arising—unless doing so involves the creation of new kinds of legal problems; the social benefit would reduce rather than add to their sales volume.

In our legal profession, justice is a commodity, and it has its price; for small claims the price is too high. Just as mass transit systems clash with the needs of the auto industry, a mass justice system for small claims clashes with business goals of the legal profession (as presently defined) and hence with the predispositions of our legal system. The legal profession, as a profit-making business, does not offer its services at a price that would encourage the bringing of small claims. Courts wait passively and respond only to the cases brought to them by the legal profession; lawyers are the gatekeepers to the legal system in our society.

But one might make the reverse argument by the example of class actions: Consumer class actions do have a potential for big profits for lawyers. So, we would expect to press hard for ways to facilitate class actions. We cannot use the "law as a business model" alone to explain the resistance to effective class actions. It would be better to say the law is a business whose outlook is shaped by its major clients, business corporations. Yet, if the law of a society is to preserve its legitimacy it must be available in fact to all strata of that society. Remedies must accompany rights. And the solution cannot be a two-tier system, with minor disputes relegated to extrajudicial mechanisms, while the judicial is reserved for those who can afford it.

Despite the fact that we have posed consumer rights and remedies as a legal problem, and one with legal solutions, we know that consumer complaint problems are but symptoms of larger societal problems and that the problem as well as the solution may be played out in other than the legal arena. For example, a dramatic increase or decrease in energy supply, a gradual worldwide decrease in natural resources could bring great change in consumer problems and how they are handled. The self-reliance movement, the rise of consumer cooperatives, the movement towards decreasing dependence, which is part and parcel of the move toward regionalism within the country, may also be important in the very definition of the consumer complaint problem. If we see the consumer complaint problem as though it were a problem of developing adequate mechanisms for the individual handling of complaints, we will not find effective ways of dealing with it. Consumer complaints are symptoms of fundamental and systemic problems in our society, one of the most important being the absence of democratic control over society's resources (see Edwards 1976). Consumers are not a class-bound group; the problems of consumers are those that affect all Americans, albeit differently. The consumer complaint arena is as good as any to work out the differences between theory and practice in our society. It strikes at questions of production, management-labor, distribution, equity, and law in a democratic society. Solving the consumer complaint problem will allow people to stop focusing their discontent on this level and allow them to move on to grapple with the more fundamental questions. Solutions may come through imaginative recombinations of old solutions, or they may come from new problems that stem from changing availability of natural resources. We should not be deceived by the rhetoric of the day: Delegalization does not offer hope per se, and neither does legalization. The struggle is over the monopolization or distribution of power. The challenge is straightforward and fundamental to basic structure: Can we have a society where it pays to be law-abiding?

References

Abel, Richard L.
    1979a Delegalization: A critical review of its ideology, manifestations, and social consequences. In *Alternativen Rechtsformen und Alternativen zum Recht, Jahrbuch für Rechtssoziologie und Rechtstheorie* (6), edited by E. Blankenburg, Opladen, West Germany: Verlag.
    1979b Socializing the legal profession: Can redistributing lawyers' services achieve social justice? *Law and Policy Quarterly* 1(1):5–51.

Akerlof, George A.
    1970 The market for "lemons": Quality uncertainity and the market mechanism. *Quarterly Journal of Economics* **84**:488–500.

Arnold, Thurman W.
    1937 *The folklore of capitalism*. New Haven: Yale University Press.

Bachrach, Peter
    1975 Interest, participation, and democratic theory. In *Participation in politics*, Nomos XVI, edited by J. Roland Pennock and John W. Chapman. New York: Lieber-Atherton.

Bequai, August
    1977 White collar crime: The losing war. *Case and Comment* **82**(5):3–10.

Berger, Raoul
    1969 Standing to sue in public actions: Is it a Constitutional requirement? *Yale Law Journal* **78**:816–840.

Berke, Stephen P., and David M. Stern
    174 Recent developments in truth in lending class actions and proposed alternatives. *Stanford Law Review* **27**:101–123.

Bernstine, Nancy T.
   1977   Prosecutorial discretion in consumer protection divisions of selected
          state attorney general offices. *Howard Law Journal* **20**:247–345.
Best, Arthur
in press *When consumers complain: Consumer justice problems and prospects.*
          New York: Columbia University Press.
Best, Arthur, and Alan R. Andreasen
   1977   Consumer response to unsatisfactory purchases: A survey of perceiving
          defects, voicing complaints, and obtaining redress. *Law and Society Re-
          view* **11**:701–742.
Biddle, Arthur
   1884   *A treatise on the law of warranties in the sale of chattels.* Philadelphia:
          Kay & Brother.
Black, Donald J.
   1973   The mobilization of law. *Journal of Legal Studies* **2**:125–149.
Breeden, Patrick D., and William A. Lovett
   1973   Louisiana's new unfair trade practice and consumer protection law.
          Louisiana Bar Journal **20**:307–322.
Bryant, W. Keith, and Jennifer L. Gerner
   1978   The price of a warranty: The case for refrigerators. *Journal of Consumer
          Affairs* **12**(1):30–47.
Budnitz, Mark
   1977   Consumer   dispute   resolution   forums.   *Trial   Lawyers   Quarterly*
          13(12):45–49.
Burman, Sheldon V.
   1978   Class action update. *Trial Lawyers Quarterly* **12**(2):43–47.
California Department of Consumer Affairs and Project Advisory Committee
   1979   A report to the legislature on the court assistance experiment. Part of
          Small Claims experimental project. August.
Cappelletti, Mauro
   1975   Governmental and private advocates for the public interest in civil litiga-
          tion: A comparative study. *Michigan Law Review* **73**:793–884.
   1976   Vindicating the public interest through the courts: A comparativist's
          contribution. *Buffalo Law Review* **25**:643–690.
Cappelletti, Mauro (Ed.)
1978–1979 *Access to justice.* 4 vols. Leyden/Boston: Sijthoff.
Cappelletti, Mauro, and Bryant Garth
   1978   Access to justice: The newest wave in the worldwide movement to make
          rights effective. *Buffalo Law Review* **27**:181–292.
Cerra, Frances
   1977   8-Year skirmish continues on agency for consumers. *New York Times,*
          26 September: p. 24.
Cipolla, C. M.
   1963   The Italian and Iberian peninsulas. In *The Cambridge economic history
          of Europe III: Economic organization and politics in the Middle Ages,*
          edited by M. M. Postan. Cambridge, England: Cambridge University
          Press.

Cohn, B. S.
1959 Some notes on law and change in North China. *Economic Development and Cultural Change* **8**:79–93.
Conard, Alfred F.
1971 Macrojustice: A systematic approach to conflict resolution. *Georgia Law Review* **5**:415–428.
Congressional Record
1976 S. 2069, Sec. 8(b)(6), 4 August: S13303.
1978 S. 957, 29 June: S10143.
Council of Better Business Bureaus
1977 Status report: BBB consumer arbitration program. 28 November.
Council of State Governments
1970 *Consumer protection in the states.* Lexington, Kentucky.
Creighton, Lucy Black
1976 *Pretenders to the throne: The consumer movement in the United State.* Lexington, Mass.: Heath.
Danzig, Richard, and Michael J. Lowy
1975 Everyday disputes and mediation in the United States: A reply to Professor Felstiner. *Law and Society Review* **9**:675–694.
Darby, Michael R., and Karni, Edi
1973 Free competition and the optimal amount of fraud. *Journal of Law and Economics* **16**:67–88.
Determan, Dean W.
1975 The arbitration of small claims. *Forum* **10**:831–842.
Diamond, Arthur S.
1971 *Primitive law, past and present.* London: Methuen.
Dickerson, Thomas A.
1977 Travel consumer fraud: Rip-offs and remedies. *Syracuse Law Review* **28**:847–873.
Dole, Richard F., Jr.
1968 Consumer class actions under the Uniform Deceptive Trade Practices Act. *Duke Law Journal* **1968**:1101–1135.
Edwards, Richard C.
1976 An appeal to tired activists: A radical looks at the consumer movement. In *Consumerism: A new force in society*, edited by Mary Gardiner Jones and David M. Gardner. Lexington, Mass.: Heath.
Elkins, James R.
1976 Corporations and the criminal law: An uneasy alliance. *Kentucky Law Journal* **65**:73–129.
Eovaldi, Thomas L., and Joan E. Gestrin
1971 Justice for consumers: The mechanisms of redress. *Northwestern University Law Review* **66**:281–325.
Fallon, Craig V.
1972 In Houston nowadays, cheating a customer is a risky business. *Wall Street Journal*, 6 January: pp. 1, 10.

Fax, Leslie
    1978   Consumer protection against unfair trade. *New Directions in Legal Services* **3**:18–23.
Fisch, William B.
    1979   European analogues to the class action: Group action in France and Germany. *American Journal of Comparative Law* **27**:51–79.
Fisse, Brent
    1971   The use of publicity as a criminal sanction against business corporations. *Melbourne University Law Review* **8**:107–150.
Flink, Marc D.
    1978   Private enforcement under the Fair Debt Collection Practices Act. *Case Western Reserve Law Review* **28**:710–738.
Flynn, John J.
    1967   Criminal sanctions under state and federal antitrust laws. *Texas Law Review* **45**:1301–1346.
Fornell, Claes
    1976   *Consumer input for marketing decisions: A study of corporate departments for consumer affairs.* New York: Praeger.
Frankel, Marvin E.
    1976   From private fights toward public justice. *New York University Law Review* **51**:516–537.
Friedman, Aryeh
    1977   The effectiveness of arbitration for the resolution of consumer disputes. *New York University Review of Law and Social Change* **6**:175–215.
Frierson, James G.
    1977   Let's abolish small claims courts. *Judges' Journal* **16**(4):18–21, 50–52.
Galanter, Marc
    1974   Why the "haves" come out ahead: Speculations on the limits of legal change. *Law and Society Review* **9**:95–160.
Getman, Julius
    1979   Labor arbitration and dispute resolution. *Yale Law Journal* **88**:916–949.
Gold, Paula W., and Robert D. Cohan
    1977   State protection of the consumer: Integration of civil and criminal remedies. *New England Law Review* **12**:933–954.
Green, Mark
    1978   Why the consumer bill went down. *Nation*, 25 February: pp. 198–201.
Hamilton, Walton H.
    1931   The ancient maxim caveat emptor. *Yale Law Journal* **40**:1133–1187.
Hinds, James A., Jr.
    1976   To right mass wrongs: A federal consumer class action act. *Harvard Journal on Legislation* **13**:776–844.
Hirschman, Albert O.
    1970   *Exit, voice, and loyalty.* Cambridge: Harvard University Press.
    1974   "Exit, voice, and loyalty": Further reflections and a survey of recent contributions. *Social Science Information* **13**(1):7–26.

1975 Exit and voice—Some further distinctions. Paper presented at the Annual Meeting of the American Economic Association, Dallas, December.

Holdsworth, W. S.
1922 *A history of English law* 1. Boston: Little, Brown.

Homburger, Adolf
1974 Private suits in the public interest in the United States of America. *Buffalo Law Review* **23**:343–410.

Hudson, William
1892 Leet jurisdiction in the City of Norwich during the XIIIth and XIVth centuries. In *Selden society* 5. London: Bernard Quaritch.

Hurst, James Willard
1970 *The legitimacy of the business corporation in the law of the United States, 1780–1970.* Charlottesville: University Press of Virginia.

Huvelin, P.
1897 *Essai historique sur le droit des marchés et des foires.* Paris: Rousseau.

Ison, Terence G.
1972 Small claims. *Modern Law Review* (London) **35**:18–37.

Jenkins, John A.
1977 Jimmy Carter's proposed consumer agency. *Student Lawyer* **6**(2):23–24, 50–52.

Johnson, Earl, Jr., with Elizabeth Schwartz
1978 *A Preliminary analysis of alternative strategies for processing civil disputes.* National Inst. of Law Enforcement and Criminal Justice, LEAA, U.S. Dept. of Justice.

Jones, Mary G., and Barry B. Boyer
1972 Improving the quality of justice in the marketplace: The need for better consumer remedies. *George Washington Law Review* **40**:357–415.

Kazanjian, John H.
1973 Consumer protection by the state attorneys general: A time for renewal. *Notre Dame Lawyer* **49**:410–427.

Kennedy, Patricia
1978 *Flying dilemmas: Consumer problems and complaint mechanisms for airline passengers.* Washington, D.C.: Center for the Study of Responsive Law.

King, Donald W., and Kathleen A. McEvoy
1976 *A national survey of the complaint-handling procedures used by consumers.* Conducted for the Office of Consumer Affairs under subcontract from Technical Assistance Research Programs. Washington, D.C.: U.S. Department of Health, Education, and Welfare.

Kosmin, Leslie G.
1976 The small claims court dilemma. *Houston Law Review* **13**:934–982.

Krattenmaker, Thomas G.
1976 The Federal Trade Commission and consumer protection. *California Management Review* **18**(4):89–104.

Langbein, John H.
1974 *Prosecuting crime in the Renaissance: England, Germany, France.* Cambridge: Harvard University Press.

Leighton, Richard J.
1973 Consumer protection agency proposals: The origin of the species. *Administrative Law Review* **25**:269–312.

Leland, Hayne E.
1977 *Quacks, lemons, and licensing: A theory of minimum quality standards* (Research Program in Finance, Working Paper No. 60). Berkeley: Institute of Business and Economic Research, University of California at Berkeley.

Lovett, William A.
1971 Private actions for deceptive trade practices. *Administrative Law Review* **23**:271–290.

Lowy, Michael J.
1978 *Community legal education and the use of Small Claims Court.* Unpublished manuscript.

Lurie, Howard R.
1972 Consumer complaints: A proposed federal trade regulation rule. *University of Michigan Journal of Law Reform* **5**:426–435.

Mandig, D. Michael
1976 Restitution: A solution to *Illinois Brick Co.* v. *Illinois* and to the manageability problems of antitrust and other problems of consumer class actions. *Arizona Law Review* **18**:940–986.

McCall, James R.
1974 Due process and consumer protection: Concepts and realities in procedure and substance—class action issues. *Hastings Law Journal* **25**:1351–1410.

McRae, William A., Jr.
1948 The development of nuisance in the early common law. *University of Florida Law Review* **1**:27–43.

Mentschikoff, Soia
1961 Commercial arbitration. *Columbia Law Review* **61**:846–869.

Merton, Robert K.
1968 *Social theory and social structure,* enlarged ed. New York: Free Press.

Monaghan, Henry P.
1973 Constitutional adjudication: The who and the when. *Yale Law Journal* **82**:1363–1397.

Morgan, Edmund M.
1956 *Some problems of proof under the Anglo-American system of litigation.* New York: Columbia University Press.

Morrison, Alan B.
1977 An overview of consumer protection and public interest groups: The need for a multiple approach. *New England Law Review* **12**:849–858.

Morrow, Clarence J.
1940 Warranty of quality: A comparative survey. *Tulane Law Review* **14**:327–360, 529–572.

Nader, Laura, and Barbara Yngvesson
1973 On studying the ethnography of law and its consequences. In *Handbook of social and cultural anthropology,* edited by J. Honigmann. Chicago: Rand McNally.

NICJ (National Institute for Consumer Justice)
  1972 Staff report on the small claims courts, by David S. Gould. Washington, D.C.
  1973 *Redress of consumer grievances.*
Ogren, Robert W.
  1973 The ineffectiveness of the criminal sanction in fraud and corruption cases: Losing the battle against white-collar crime. *American Criminal Law Review* **11**:959–988.
Plucknett, Theodore F. T.
  1956 *A concise history of the common law,* 5th ed. Boston: Little, Brown.
Posner, Richard A.
  1973 An economic approach to legal procedure and judicial administration. *Journal of Legal Studies* **2**:399–458.
Prosser, William L.
  1966 Private action for public nuisance. *Virginia Law Review* **52**:997–1027.
Radzinowicz, Leon
  1957 *A history of English criminal law and its administration from 1750 2: The clash between private initiative and public interest in the enforcement of the law.* New York: Macmillan.
Readers Digest
  1976 You can get your money back. **108**(649) May: 106–109.
Roberts, Barry S.
  1978 The Magnuson–Moss Federal Warranty Act. *Business Lawyer* **33**:1845–1858.
Rosenberg, Maurice
  1971 Devising procedures that are civil to promote justice that is civilized. *Michigan Law Review* **69**:797–820.
Ross, H. Lawrence, and Neil O. Littlefield
  1978 Complaint as a problem solving mechanism. *Law and Society Review* **12**:199–216.
Rothschild, Donald P.
  1976 The Magnuson–Moss Warranty Act: Does it balance warranty and consumer interests? *George Washington Law Review* **44**:335–380.
Rothschild, Donald P., and David W. Carroll
  1977 *Consumer protection: Text and materials,* 2nd ed. Cincinnati: Anderson.
Ruhnka, John C., and Steven Weller
  1977 15 Small claims courts examined. *Judges' Journal* **16**(4):11.
Schroeder, Milton R.
  1978 Private actions under the Magnuson–Moss Warranty Act. *California Law Review* **66**:1–36.
Sentry Insurance Co.
  1977 *Consumerism at the crossroads.* Commissioned in 1976 and conducted by Louis Harris and Associates, and Marketing Science Institute. Sentry Insurance Co. at Stevens Point, Wisconsin.
Sevell, Robert D.
  1973 Private and public remedies for fraudulent business practices in California: The importance of a strong public role. *Loyola of Los Angeles Law Review* **6**:312–349.

Shabecoff, Philip
    1978   House rejects consumer agency. *New York Times,* 9 February: pp.
            A1,B10.
Sheldon, Jonathon A., and George J. Zweibel
    1978   *Survey of consumer fraud law.* Washington, D.C.: National Institute of
            Law Enforcement and Criminal Justice, Law Enforcement Assistance
            Administration, U.S. Dept. of Justice.
Small Claims Study Group
    1972   *Little injustices: Small claims courts and the American consumer.*
Soustelle, Jacques
    1955   *The daily life of the Aztecs on the eve of the Spanish conquest.* Trans-
            lated by Patrick O'Brian. London: Weidenfeld and Nicolson.
Special Committee on Consumer Affairs of the Association of the Bar of the City of
            New York
    1972   Toward the informal resolution of consumer disputes. *Record of the
            Association of the Bar of the City of New York* **27**:419–434.
Spence, Michael D.
    1973   *Consumer misperceptions, product failure, and producer liability.*
            (Memo No. 158.) Stanford: Center for Research in Economic Growth,
            Stanford University.
Starrs, James E.
    1969   The consumer class action II: Considerations of procedure. *Boston Uni-
            versity Law Review* **49**:407–513.
Steele, Eric H.
    1975a   The dilemma of consumer fraud: Prosecute or mediate. *American Bar
            Association Journal* **61**:1230–1234.
    1975b   Fraud, dispute, and the consumer. *University of Pennsylvania Law Re-
            view* **123**:1107–1186.
Stone, Christopher
    1975   *Where the law ends: The social control of corporate behavior.* New York:
            Harper & Row.
    1976   Stalking the wild corporation. *Working Papers for a New Society*
            4(1):17–21, 87–89, 92–93.
Strick, Anne
    1977   *Injustice for all.* New York: G. P. Putnam's Sons.
Temple Law Quarterly
    1976a   The Federal Trade Commission rule for informal dispute settlement
            mechanisms. **49**:459–475.
    1976b   Nontraditional Remedies for the Settlement of Consumer Disputes.
            49:385–427.
Thorelli, Hans B., and Sarah V. Thorelli
    1977   *Consumer information systems and consumer policy.* Cambridge, Mass.:
            Ballinger.
Tocqueville, Alexis de
    1835/1840 *Democracy in America.* Translated by Henry Reeve. London: Saun-
            ders and Otley.
Turner, J. W. Cecil
    1964   *Russell on crime 2,* 12th ed. London: Stevens.

United States Chamber of Commerce
   1976   Model consumer justice act: A proposed model small claims court act for state legislatures. Washington, D.C.: Chamber of Commerce.
U.S. Congress
   1974   House of Representatives. *Consumer Product Warranty and Federal Trade Commission Improvement Act.* Conference Report. 93rd Congress, 2nd Session, Report 93-1606.
   1977   Senate, Committee on Commerce, Science and Transportation, Subcommittee for Consumers. *Consumer Controversies Resolution Act.* Hearing. 95th Congress, 1st Session.
   1978   House of Representatives, Committee on Interstate and Foreign Commerce, Subcommittee on Oversight and Investigation. *Cancer-Causing Chemicals 1.* Hearings. 95th Congress, 2nd Session.
University of Pennsylvania Law Review
   1966   Translating sympathy for deceived consumers into effective programs for protection. **114**:395–450.
Walford, Cornelius
   1883   *Fairs, past and present: A chapter in the history of commerce.* London: Elliot Stock.
Weiss, John H.
   1974   Justice without lawyers: Transforming small claims courts. *Working Papers for a New Society* **2**(3):45–53.
Weller, Steven, and John C. Ruhnka
   1978   Small claims courts: Operations and prospects. *State Court Journal* **2**(1):6–7, 34–41.
Winters, Glenn R., and Edward J. Schoenbaum (Eds.)
   1976   *American courts and justice.* American Judicature Society to Promote the Effective Administration of Justice.
Wright, Cabot
   1974   House buyers bilked by greedy middlemen. *National Star,* 8 June: p. 2.
Yeazell, Stephen C.
   1977   Group litigation and social context: Toward a history of the class action. *Columbia Law Review* **77**:866–896.
Yngvesson, Barbara, and Patricia Hennessey
   1975   Small claims, complex disputes: A review of the small claims literature. *Law and Society Review* **9**:219–274.

II

VOICING COMPLAINTS

3

Eric Freedman

"DEAR MR. NADER":
A Study of Consumer Complaint Letters

Introduction

Few studies have been undertaken of American public letter writing, and of the research done, nearly all has involved political rather than economic mail. Jeanette Sayre briefly summarized a study of radio fan mail in a 1939 issue of the *Public Opinion Quarterly* in an attempt to ascertain what use, if any, might be made of messages sent to "America's Town Meeting of the Air" for the 1937–1938 season. A question of central interest to her was whether letter writers are deviates or simply normal members of the public who write letters, such that their letters would be representative of the problems faced by all. Sayre found that mail differed from one "Town Meeting" program to another in factors of age, sex, social status, and geographic origin of the writer, but she was unable to answer the question of how fan-mail writers compared with the total audience for any given broadcast.

In 1941, Rowena Wyant and Herta Herzog conducted an extensive analysis of about 30,000 letters sent to the Senate during debate on conscription (specifically the Burke–Wadsworth Selective Service Bill) (Wyant 1941; Wyant and Herzog 1941). Wyant and Herzog were interested in such variables as geographical region, class, age, and sex of the writers. The authors found that people were more likely to write to a senator with whom they agreed and to a senator representing their own state rather than another (unless their own senator disagreed with their position) (Wyant 1941:365–368). Well-known senators received more out-of-state mail than did their lesser-known colleagues (p. 368). People tended to write when they believed their side was losing (about 90% of

NO ACCESS TO LAW
Alternatives to the American Judicial System

the letters analyzed expressed disapproval of the Burke–Wadsworth Bill, although a Gallup Poll conducted during the same period reported that most citizens favored conscription) (pp. 359, 364). Wyant and Herzog noted a variance in the letter-writing strength of different states, and related this variance to differences in the age composition of the population and the degree of industrialization and urbanization of the states.[1]

Leila Sussmann, in her book *Dear FDR: A Study of Political Letter-Writing* (1963), reviews the history of American political letter writing (beginning with the "deluge" of mail urging General Washington to accept a draft for the presidency), and indicates that four major factors have contributed to the growth of such mail: first and foremost, the increased educational attainments of Americans; second, the growth of mass communications media; third, the greater role of the federal government in the day-to-day lives of individuals; and finally, the encouragement of letter writing by prominent political figures (Sussmann 1963:13–18). From extensive analysis of the mail received by Franklin D. Roosevelt[2] during his 1932 and 1940 presidential campaigns,[3] and during selected years of his terms in office, Sussmann determines that letter writers are not representative of Americans as a whole (i.e., their differences from the general public extend beyond mere possession of a greater propensity for self-expression).[4] She agrees with Wyant and Herzog that letter writers can differ considerably from one another, too, and that the characteristics of

[1]Wyant and Herzog found rates of letter writing on the conscription issue highest in big cities and small towns, next highest in medium-sized cities, and lowest in rural areas, and they noted that states having large proportions of people over 40 tended to produce larger volumes of mail, although the correlation between age and quantity of mail was less marked than that between urbanization and quantity of mail (Wyant 1941:362–64).

[2]According to Robert K. Merton, author of the introduction to the Sussman study, Roosevelt gave "letter-writing on the large scale a new functional character, converting it into a circuit of communication between the holder of political power on the one hand and both organized groups and unorganized masses on the other. It was he, more than any other person, who turned mass mail into the functional equivalent of an episodic plebiscite [1963:xv]." With Roosevelt's assumption of the presidency, letters began to reach the White House in record numbers; some 450,000 arrived during only his first week in office (Sussmann 1963:9).

[3]Sussmann groups Roosevelt's mail from his first and third presidential campaigns into six broad categories: issue mail, political fan mail, campaign-strategy mail (a small block of letters concerned primarily with campaign strategy and tactics and offering assorted advice on propaganda techniques), congratulatory mail (given a separate label from the fan mail), personal service mail (asking favors of the candidate—half the letters in this category contained pleas for financial aid), and self-expressive mail (in which the writers discussed their personal lives more than political matters). Although the contents of most letters fell into more than one of these types, a single type ordinarily predominated (Sussmann 1963:88–125).

[4]Sussmann cites Gallup, National Opinion Research Center, and Roper surveys which show that individuals ranking high on scales of economic, educational, and occupational status far exceed people standing low on these scales in their rate of political letter writing

any given group of writers will vary with the topic under consideration (Sussmann 1963:146–148).[5] According to her own and previous examinations, concludes Sussmann, the following comprise the most important patterns of political letter-writing behavior:

> ... the preference for writing letters of support, which can be overcome only if the writers are convinced of participating in a large, collective effort; the tendency to write when one's political goals are endangered rather than when they seem assured; and the importance of the mass media as carriers of the events, information, and sometimes the direct appeals which stimulate letterwriting [p. 166].

This chapter summarizes a study of 300 consumer complaint letters sent to Ralph Nader. These letters, written between 19 November 1969 and 20 December 1971, form part of a collection of approximately 5000 such missives, all dating from the late 1960s and early 1970s and filed in the office of Professor Laura Nader. Our analysis of these materials came out of a desire better to understand individuals who write about specifically consumer, rather than political, affairs. We were interested in what consumer complainants wrote about, how they reacted to problems, how they communicated their dissatisfaction, and what kind of remedies they sought. Seeking a varied and representative data base for our examination, we sampled, at random, 100 letters each in the categories of food, medical, and appliance problems.[6]

(Sussmann 1963:135). Roosevelt's mail differed from this average pattern for political letter writers in that it contained an unusually large component of low-income writers.

Sussmann notes a rise, between the early 1930s and the early 1950s, in the number of women political letter writers; the ratio of men to women in Roosevelt's 1932 campaign mail was nearly four to one, whereas by the 1950s, after Roosevelt's death, females comprised half of political letter writers, according to a National Opinion Research Center poll [pp. 143–144].

[5]Thus, while inhabitants of heavily urbanized areas are generally more disposed than rural populations to write political letters, letters of rural origin can occasionally outnumber those from urban centers. In general, Roosevelt received relatively more campaign mail from urban than rural places; the rate of letter writing increased fairly steadily with the size of the community (Sussmann 1963:145).

[6]This study owes much to the seminal work of Marion Eaton and Margaret Rader, who in 1971 and 1972, and 1977, respectively, examined and wrote about portions of the letters on file in Professor Nader's office. Among the letters available for study were many dealing with subjects other than complaints about products and services; we focused on product complaint letters however as the most directly linked to an understanding of the remedy system. Although the majority of the letters are from the early 1970s, a follow-up study showed that today's letters are virtually indistinguishable from the earlier ones in content and form; except that writers seem to realize they are not alone in their complaint, and increasingly express concern for others as well. Examples from 1979 are found at the end of this chapter (I–M).

The Letters and Their Writers

Each of the 300 sample letters we examined would more appropriately be termed a packet, because a "letter" actually represents all material forwarded by a single writer rather than simply an individual piece of correspondence. Many packets contain more than the minimum of one postcard or letter. Complainants may have written to Nader repeatedly during the span of time covered by the universe of 5000 letters, in which case their correspondence was filed together; and, even if a complainant wrote only once during this time, he may have sent, with or without a cover letter, copies of previous correspondence between himself and a particular company. Quite a few letters, in addition, contain documentation of one kind or another—labels, receipts, guarantees, and, on occasion, at least part of the product itself.[7]

The correspondence falls into two general types: letters sent originally to Nader and letters sent in the original to another addressee (either to an individual—such as a company official, a politician, a government consumer representative, a medical doctor, or a media personality—or to an organization, such as a business firm or a newspaper) with a carbon or photocopy to Nader. Letters written specifically to Nader (or to politicians or government consumer representatives and sent in copy to Nader) normally belong to at least one of several subtypes: simple complaint (either a statement of the problem only or a statement of the problem with a request for aid or remedy); request for information; suggestion that Nader investigate a given product or situation; offer of information or aid (as when individuals write specifically to grant Nader permission to use their knowledge or experience in an investigation or for any other purpose he may wish); declaration of the writer's determination to achieve satisfaction; proselytism; and request to publicize some fact or condition. Letters written originally to companies and sent in duplicate to Nader normally display a more limited range of variability, falling into one or more of three subtypes: simple complaint (either a statement of the problem only

---

[7]Analysis of the letters was carried out largely by means of a code developed specifically for this study. Each four-page coding form contained sufficient space for extensive quoting from letters, because we wished our presentation to draw amply upon the writers' own words. Our original intention was to undertake a more systematic quantitative analysis. We found, however, that the letters do not lend themselves well to highly systematic examination. The sheer variability of the material—in content, format, and packet makeup—means that data on almost any except the most straightforward variables will be very incomplete, with large portions of the sample furnishing no or only partial information. We were, furthermore, unable to establish objective measures for many items (such as willingness to fight, degree of futility and sources of futility–frustration-–gloom, degree of problem specificity, length of time from problem onset to writing, number of previous attempts to solve the problem, basis and intensity of appeal, and whether or not a reply was requested by the writer).

TABLE 3.1
Marital Status of Sample Complaint Writers

	Married	Single	Widowed	Unknown	Inapplicable[a]
Medical	34%	4%	7%	51%	4%
Appliance	69%	7%	7%	17%	—
Food	49%	7%	1%	42%	1%

[a] These letters usually originated from groups rather than individuals.

or a statement of the problem with a request for remedy–restitution), demand, and reply to a company letter or demand for payment.

The letter writers, although varied, are not representative of the nation's population. In each complaint category, women write more letters than do men. It may be that the female writers, most of whom are housewives, generally have more free time for such correspondence than do men; or that in our society, women on the whole possess a greater propensity than do men for letter writing; or that women tend to have closer contact with the goods and services considered in this study. Not surprisingly, food complaints display the greatest disproportion between men and women; 37% of food complainants are men and 57% women (with 1% couples and 5% unknown). Of the medical writers, 38% are men and 52% women (with 3% group and 7% unknown), and of appliance complainants, 42% are men and 56% women (with 2% couples). The majority of all writers in each category are between 30 and 65 years of age, it would seem;[8] one would expect such to be the case, as demand for consumer goods and services is stronger in this age group than in any other. The elderly contribute a modest proportion of letters (especially, as one might expect, in the area of medical problems), whereas the population under 20 writes almost not at all.[9]

The marital and employment status of approximately half the letter writers can be ascertained from the contents of their correspondence.[10] Of the medical writers, 34% are married, as are 69% of the appliance writers and 49% of the food writers (see Table 3.1). Of the medical writers, 22% are

[8] Only a small proportion of writers in each category mentioned their exact ages. When a figure was not given, we made as precise an estimate as possible of the writer's age (if we could make any estimate at all) on the basis of letter content or handwriting.

[9] Forty-nine percent of the medical letters come from writers aged 50 or over, and 13% from people 65 or over. Sixteen medical writers give their exact ages, ranging from 33 to 83, with a mean of 63. Twenty-four percent of the appliance letters come from writers 50 or over; 5 give their exact ages, ranging from 61 to 85, with a mean of 72. Forty percent of the food letters come from writers aged 50 or over; 4 give their exact ages, ranging from 57 to 82, with a mean of 70.

[10] Determination of marital status, when made, came from letter content rather than from the writer's title, except in the case of women who signed themselves as "Miss."

TABLE 3.2
Employment Status of Sample Complaint Writers

	Employed	Unemployed	Retired	Housewives	Unknown	Inapplicable[a]
Medical	22%	3%	22%	1%	49%	2%
Appliance	23%	—	11%	19%	47%	—
Food	8%	—	11%	26%[b]	51%	1%

[a] These letters usually originated from groups.
[b] Another 3% are classified as farm wives.

employed, and an equal percentage are retired; 23% of the appliance writers are employed, and 19% are housewives. Of the food writers, 26% are housewives—the highest proportion, as one might expect, of any category (Table 3.2).

More than three times as many medical (10%) as appliance and food letters (each with 3%) are written by insiders, those having personal access to inside information on the product or subject about which they are complaining. Many of these medical writers have relatives in nursing homes or state hospitals for the mentally ill, and are complaining about the treatment given patients and the conditions existing in these institutions. Linked to the higher proportion of letters from insiders in the medical category is the comparatively high proportion of anonymous letters in that group. Seven percent of medical letters carry no signature, whereas 5% of food letters carry none; all appliance letters, on the other hand, have been signed (appliance letters contain far fewer sensitive complaints and revelations—such as might jeopardize the livelihood or even safety of the writer—than do food and medical). Also, a greater number of medical writers than appliance and food writers have written on more than one occasion; six have written twice, and one individual has written four times.[11]

A higher proportion of appliance (74%) than medical (44%) and food (35%) letters is typewritten; that the food category contains the fewest typewritten letters may be due at least in part to the fact that women (largely housewives, many of whom might not have access to a typewriter) have written here in highest disproportion to men. Also, a higher proportion of appliance letters has been dictated (8%) and written on business letterhead stationery (12%).[12]

Of all the letters taken together, by far the largest number (112 out of 300) come from the Northeast (Table 3.3). The second greatest number (69)

[11]Six medical writers have written on the same topic, and two have written about the same incident. Four appliance writers have written more than once (two writing twice, one three times, and one four times); all four individuals have concerned themselves with the same subject and same incident on each writing. No food writer has written more than a single letter.

[12]Only 2% of medical letters have been dictated, whereas no food letters have been. Nine

TABLE 3.3
Geographical Origin of Complaint Letters

	Northeast	Midwest	South	West
Medical	32	30	21	23
Appliance	30	34	21	15
Food	50	15	18	17
Totals	112	69	60	55

is from the Midwest, whereas the South and West contribute almost equally (60 and 55, respectively). The Northeast provides most of the food and medical letters (see Table 3.3), with the other three areas accounting for approximately equal numbers in each of these two subject categories. Most appliance letters come from the Midwest, although the Northeast furnishes virtually as many. Northeastern writers complain most about food (50) and second, in nearly equal numbers, about medical and appliance problems. The Midwest complains most about appliances; the South complains nearly equally about all three subjects; and Westerners write most concerning medical difficulties.

Cities account for a high proportion of all three categories of complaint letters (see Table 3.4). This fact is apparent even when places of origin are designated as rural (having less than 10,000 people), town (having between 10,000 and 50,000 people), or urban (having more than 50,000 people) solely on the basis of population size. The United States, however, has many communities with populations of less than 10,000 or between 10,000 and 50,000 that are only suburbs of cities or are otherwise located within a relatively short distance (say, 30 miles) of urban centers. These places would have comparatively easy access to the offerings (both in terms of marketing and of complaint resolution) of such nearby cities and therefore deserve to be considered as urbanized. When one takes into account not only population size but also distance from a city (i.e., when one includes among urban letters not only those from centers having populations of 50,000 or more, but also those from rural communities or towns located within 30 miles of a city), an even greater proportion of the letters in each subject category is found to be of urban origin. The number of urban centers then increases to about an equal level in each category (85% in medical and food and 81% in appliances).[13] Concomitantly, of course, the proportion of places considered rural or town falls (rural regions make up 10% of appliance, 8% of medical, and 6% of food complaints; towns account for 7% of appliance, 6% of medical, and 4% of food complaints).

---

percent of medical and only 3% of food letters appear on business letterhead stationery; this higher proportion, like that of typewritten letters, probably derives from the fact that more men have written about appliance than about food or medical problems.

[13]The overrepresentation of urban residents among those who write to Nader is made

TABLE 3.4
Size of Community in Which Sample Complaint Letters Originated

	Rural areas (less than 10,000 population)	Towns (10,000–50,000 population)	Cities (over 50,000)	Community size unknown
Medical	18%	19%	61%	2%
Appliance	20%	27%	50%	3%
Food	24%	24%	43%	9%

Across subject categories, only the proportion of urban letters (when the assignation has been made by population alone) varies significantly. The highest proportion of urban letters (61%) is found in the medical category. This relatively high proportion may be due to the fact that city dwellers are often exposed to more crowded and less caring medical facilities than are residents of small communities. The fewest urban letters (determined by population alone) occur among food complaints. This fact is rather hard to explain but may have its origin in the comparatively greater selection and availability of different foodstuffs and relatively greater variety of food stores that cities offer their residents. Two letters from rural areas illustrate problems resulting, or deriving much of their significance from, the small size of the communities in which they occur (see Sample Letters A and B.). (These and other sample letters mentioned later are reprinted in full, except for names and addresses of the writers, at the end of this chapter.)

Specifics of Complaints

Medical Letters

The medical letters in our sample contain complaints about medical professionals, hospitals, medical costs, drugs and drug manufacturers, Medicare, and government restrictions or bans on controversial treatments and preparations. The most common subject of complaint is the medical profession, and especially doctors. The writers of these letters, which number 29, describe doctors as incompetent, unethical, unconcerned about the welfare of patients, and too highly profit-oriented. Vari-

---

clear by figures of the 1970 U.S. census, which finds that only about 60% of the U.S. population (118,447,000 out of the nation's total population of 203,212,000) live in "urbanized areas" (areas consisting of a central city, or twin cities, with a total of 50,000 or more inhabitants, together with contiguous, closely settled territory) (U.S. Bureau of the Census 1977:2, 18).

December 17, 1970

Mr. Ralph Nader
Washington, D.C.

Dear Mr. Nader,

Philipsburg is a small cattle town, population 1035, 25 miles from Anaconda, Montana.

In 1953, we dedicated a 10 bed hospital—built with participating Halburton funds and a county bond issue. We needed it desperately as our winter roads sometimes make it impossible to get residents to nearby hospitals. At the time it was built, there was a good deal of mining going on and it was necessary for protection of our miners to provide medical care. Now, we have 2 sawmills in operation and various loggers cutting in our woods. Young people usually leave and go to greener employment fields, so most of our town is made up of middle agers and senior citizens.

Our problem, now, is that the existence of our hospital is threatened now by stringent rules laid down by Medicare. We have trouble finding RN's to staff each shift but we have responsible LPN's that have been working one shift due to the RN shortage.

Conditions here vary from urban institutions. Our Doc. is one of the last of his species—a G.P. that works 7 days per week—on 24 hr. call and one who cares about the welfare of his patients. His office and home are within a block of the hospital and he keeps constantly in touch so that all nursing is closely supervised.

Who can we see to state our plight? If we lose our Medicare coverage, our hospital could not exist without this revenue.

(continued)

Sample Letter A—Continued

Our elderly and all other citizens are panic stricken, facing
the possibility of having to leave town for medical attention
or perhaps, even losing our doctor. Surely, rules should be
tailored to fit the needs of each community. We would not want
to accept inferior conditions in our medical care but we are
limited to our supply of RN's. We have long ago, learned to
"make do"—with what we have. Many of our elderly would not have
transportation out of town and they would get upset to have to
leave home. Their mental attitude, often, is 65% of their
illness—we have a county nurse that makes home visits because
Medicare patients could not qualify for home nursing under
their rules.

Could you tell us where to turn in order to save our little
hospital? Many other small hospitals in our state are in the
same boat.

Would appreciate any guidelines you could give us.

Sincerely,

Sample Letter B

July 8, 1971

Dear Sir:

I would like to know what help that I can receive from your
office regarding a business deal with the Our Own Hardware
owned by Mr. Phil Anderson Staples Minn.

(continued)

Sample Letter B—Continued

On March 18, 1969 my wife and I entered the store to buy a new freezer the one they had was too small so Mr. Anderson asked about a good used one he said it was 3 years old and he would give us a five year written guarantee on it. He opened the door and we did not see the name on the door it looked alright and then I asked what make it was and he said it was a Gamble machine and I said alright they brought it out and installed it in our basement.

As my wife had just been released from the hospital I was busy assisting her the evening they delivered the freezer and did not check until the next morning when the name on the machine was Crosley Shelvadore which went out of business approximately in 1954. They want $6.00 for taking the machine out and 18% per month interest charges total now $14.50 and threaten to sue. We have had to rent a public locker $18.00 per year and have suffered a lot of mental anguish on acc't we think this is a plain fraud and intent to cheat.

I am a retired Northern Pacific employee with a good record and a fine letter from our supt. and my check is as good as my word.

We have always paid our bills and never intend to hurt or defraud anyone, and want this settled.

---

ous complainants relate experiences involving misdiagnoses or mistreatment either of themselves or of others (see Sample Letter C). They express agreement with Nader's contention that medical care would be much improved were doctors required to undergo continuing education and regular evaluation from outside the profession.

Many individuals express the sentiment that doctors are driven not so much by a humanitarian spirit as by an enormous desire to increase profits, even at the expense of adequate medical treatment. An elderly Midland, Michigan, woman writes that her doctor too long allowed her glaucoma to go unchecked, with the result that she is now completely blind in one eye and nearly so in the other. She concludes, "There are no more dedicated doctors any more. Can't blame them much tho [sic] everyone is grabbing trying to get all the money as everyone else is." A New Jersey attorney who has retired to Florida suggests that Nader conduct an investigation of the latter state's doctors, asserting that "a life to them is worth as much as a mouse being used for laboratory study." A

Sample Letter C

June 8, 1971

Dear Mr. Nader,

I was so glad to read you are investigating the medical profession. It would be impossible for me to describe what I've
undergone for 8 years due to a wrong medical diagnosis, and a
sloppy operation, performed by an unqualified surgeon. I've
lost piles of money considering what I've spent in medical fees
and not being able to work, but besides that, I'm a fairly young
woman, a college graduate with 11 years office experience, who
can't find a job now, because I haven't worked for so long and
because of this awful medical background. I'll never be able to
drive a car or do a few other things because my sight was parti-
cally impaired because of this mess, and the fellow I went
around with for 3 years married another girl, for which I don't
blame him, because I can't have children either. So this terrible operation, which I didn't need in the first place—I was a
normal woman, has cost me a normal life, and exposed me to the
largest group of racketeers in existence today—the doctors
and their all-powerful AMA.

Philadelphia woman writes that she and her friends have found that their
doctors no longer conduct as thorough an examination for cancer as they
once did. How, she asks, can physicians reconcile such neglect with the
American Cancer Society's declaration of the importance of discovering
cancer in its early stages? An M.D. from Chepachet, Rhode Island, disturbed by the medical profession's increasing abandonment of general
practice and house calls for lucrative specializations, suggests that an
increase in the number of women admitted to medical schools would
help to reverse this trend.

The American Medical Association, and doctors in the context of
their AMA membership, receive a good deal of criticism. Writers perceive
the AMA as self-interested and intransigent, both in reacting to medical
proposals coming from outside its ranks and to legitimate attacks upon its
members. A South Bend, Indiana, woman, both of whose parents died of

cancer and who herself has twice required surgery for the disease, decries the Ohio Medical Board's ban on a cancer treatment device, "although claims were made that it reduces cancerous tumors." "As you know," she comments to Nader, "the AMA has always refused to accept anything that has not been invented by its own." A Miami, Florida, history professor describes how he "was swindled by an unethical or inept (or both) doctor" who treated him for coronary problems:

> The Dade County Medical Association has failed to give me any satisfaction in writing. . . . Last June a secret committee of the local medical association phoned me to say that Dr. G was "respected by the community." Ha! and bah! . . . When will able, honest doctors stop protecting crooks and mediocrities, stop acting like a senatorial club? We teachers, the poorest profession, may soon get so mad at doctors (and maybe at shysters) to work for socialized medicine or tough reform legislation short of it.

A 63-year-old Capistrano Beach, California, woman, having received an outrageously high bill from her dermatologist, describes the delays and frustrations she has encountered in registering her complaint with the Orange County Medical Association (OCMA) and her inability to locate any other organization to handle her grievance:

> It evolves that the only place where one may present information regarding what one may consider an overcharge in the medical area, is to a membership in which all doctors in the County of Orange pay dues. What kind of unbiased public service is this? I wonder how many people before me have complained and how their cases were handled. An individual has no other recourse than to either pay the bill, or have a nervous breakdown trying to prove the organized OCMA wrong.

Two letters report that physicians have used their special relationship with and access to patients to monopolize allied paramedical and other health services. A physical therapist with a private practice in South Gate, California, informs Nader that doctors, by establishing unlicensed therapists in their offices, are driving licensed, independent operators out of business. He explains that M.D.'s, now able to manipulate the profession of physical therapy, are greatly increasing their own revenues, and he asks for a public exposé of the situation. A Monroe, Wisconsin, man, unhappy about doctor-owned pharmacies, cites two examples of such from his own community. He observes, furthermore, that an article in The Progressive shows that such ownership, with its opportunities for profiteering, exists nationwide. "The AMA," he concludes, "has never been very sensitive to ethical issues where its income is concerned."

Several writers are concerned about the current state of education for health professionals. Disturbed by the national shortage of doctors and the financial problems of medical schools, an Arlington, Virginia, man suggests that Nader conduct an investigation of "the American Medical Association's possibly not permitting construction of additional medical schools or not allowing expansion of existing facilities." He anticipates that the doctor shortage will "become more serious in the near future and will certainly result in needless deaths." A registered nurse who once served as president of the Georgia State Nurses' Association blasts the Association's efforts to move schools of nursing out of hospitals and into colleges and universities. The demise of hospital nursing schools, she argues, has brought with it skyrocketing training costs and a decline in the amount of practical experience given students.

Two letters sent by physicians defend doctors from what the writers see as threats from Nader and members of the public. An M.D. in Agana, Guam, attacks Nader's proposal, designed to upgrade and standardize the quality of medical care, that physicians be required to participate in continuing medical education and to undergo periodic examination by the federal government. A Bethlehem, Pennsylvania, doctor notes that the rise in the number of malpractice cases is proving very costly to the consumer, as higher costs for medical liability premiums are passed on to patients in fees for treatment and increased "protective" measures such as laboratory analysis, X ray, and consultation. Calling the situation a "crisis," the writer advises Nader to "take a long look down the malpractice judgment road. Plaintiff attorneys are the only winners in the 'malpractice cases.' The consumer is the big loser in the long run."

Eighteen medical letters—nearly 20% of the total—contain complaints about hospitals. A number of individuals provide accounts of neglect and abuse suffered while in general hospitals. An Eau Claire, Wisconsin, man believes that his asthma may be due to administration of an improper anesthetic during surgery. A Charlotte, North Carolina, woman, whose sister contracted a staphylococcal infection while hospitalized for hip surgery, has subsequently heard that one-quarter of all operations cause such infections and asks, "Will you PLEASE do everything possible to correct this situation. . . . Why aren't they more careful in hospitals to sterilize the operating rooms and instruments?" Several letters contain even more serious complaints. A New York City widow, writing to her late husband's doctor, forwards a copy of the letter to Nader with directions to use the "information in any way you see fit in the investigation that you are doing on hospital abuses." To the doctor she writes:

> I have been trying to get you repeatedly, but to no avail. I am considering filing a suit against Columbus Hospital for malpractice and/or criminal negligence, but before taking such a step, I want to know if you would also be implicated. . . . I have waited until now to take this step because I wanted to be certain that I was being rational and not emotional.

She goes on to describe how her husband, hospitalized for a heart attack, had been moved during the middle of a heat wave without doctor's orders from intensive care to a room lacking air conditioning. He subsequently suffered a second coronary but was unable to summon aid from within the hospital because the call light above his door did not function properly. The writer concludes:

> Doctor, it is my contention that: (1) if my husband had not been moved out of Intensive Care Unit 3; and (2) if he had not had to wait for such a long time to get help and not been required to call me at home, he would still be here today.... I consider that the hospital was extremely negligent and absolutely irresponsible. If the hospital cannot take care of the patients entrusted to its care, it should cease to operate.

After her release from a famed Los Angeles hospital, where she had spent 2 weeks recovering from a routine hysterectomy, a 49-year-old public relations worker responded to a hospital query concerning her stay. She chose to reply to the hospital by letter (a copy of which she forwarded to Nader), rather than on the form provided because, she declares, "I sincerely and genuinely hope it will serve in some way to help to sustain both physically and emotionally those patients who are now following me." The "ability to relate professionally and humanly," she explains, was "sadly, even tragically missing" among most of the hospital's salaried staff:

> I find myself in an intolerable position, that of being forced to pay outrageously high medical coverage for neglect, indifference and costly carelessness while hospitalized.... It is common practice for LVN's and Aides to force patients to cower under physical abuse.... It is well perceived that your staff attempts to keep patients sufficiently sedated to meet first and foremost the needs and desires of staff rather than patients.... I feel... grossly insulted and cheated by your continuance of a **high standard of inefficiency and inadequacy.**

Errors in hospital billing and techniques of bill collection are another source of complaint. Despite repeated attempts, an 82-year-old resident of Washington, D.C., who suffers from diabetes and a heart condition, has been unsuccessful in persuading a local hospital to remove undeserved private-room charges from his bill. The hospital now threatens to turn the matter over to its attorney. "This I will welcome," states the writer, adding that it "will give me great pleasure to air some of the complaints I have re. the most unsatisfactory service I received." An 81-year-old St. Petersburg, Florida, woman, who was told upon her release from the hospital that she owed nothing on her bill, learned 1 month later that a misunderstanding with Medicare makes her liable for nearly $600 of her hospitalization charges. She has now received "several threatening letters and two phone calls" from the hospital's billing office.

Several writers express grave concern about the treatment received by patients in nursing homes and state mental institutions. A resident of Lehigh Valley, Pennsylvania, has written two anonymous letters beseeching Nader to investigate state schools and hospitals for the mentally ill and retarded. "At these hospitals you will see man's inhumanity to man at its worst. . . . Please, please, please do something for these helplessly sick people who can't tell it like it is." A former nurse's aide living in Grand Rapids, Michigan, describes conditions in a nursing home where she worked and a state hospital where a relative was confined. The latter place she describes as a "Hell Hole I'd like to tell you about—any time. . . . These places are cesspools that starve people to death." A letter (Sample Letter D) from Southport, North Carolina, describes particularly well the kinds of experiences and emotions communicated by a number of these writers.

Twenty percent of the medical letter writers complain about the high costs of medical treatment and supplies. Most of these writers ask Nader to conduct a thorough inquiry into the pricing policies of doctors, hospitals, pharmaceutical houses, and drugstores. Predictably, many of these letters come from retired individuals. One such writer in Minneapolis, suggests that Nader "look into the awful bills people receive after being in a hospital for three weeks." A Southfield, Michigan, woman who has just read a Detroit News item concerning a heart attack victim asks, "How does a hospital charge $1634.80 for a patient dying in 8½ hours after being admitted? I am fuming! How does a hospital charge $569.80 for drugs alone?" A 74-year-old retired nurse from New York City asks that Nader look into the "milking of Medicare patients" by private hospitals and doctors. And a resident of Arkansas, which does not help needy victims of kidney disease to meet the high costs of artifical kidney machines, declares, "You can see that people in Arkansas cannot afford to live should they have kidney failure."

Drug prices, too, arouse the ire of complainants. An Albany, Oregon, couple writes to inform Nader of the sudden, seemingly arbitrary doubling in price of a painkiller upon which they are dependent. A San Franciscan, perturbed by the price differences between name-brand and generic aspirins, claims that "since 1930 the Bayer company has stolen over $100,000,000 from the American people thru [sic] its criminal price for aspirin." Writers are bothered not only by the fact that drugs are costly but also that the same drugs sell for different prices, depending on where they are purchased. An elderly Mattituck, New York, man congratulates Nader for his investigation of doctors and adds, "It is my hope that you are also going after all druggists and drug manufacturers. I have bought medicine of like kind and each druggist had a different price." A 79-year-old Silver

December 20, 1970

Dear Mr. Nader:

I am a widow, since my husband died in July of this year, he spent 30 years in the Marines and Air Force. You have been look-ing into the nursing home situation, but have you thought of the state retarded centers?

I want to tell you what happened to my son a little over three years ago. He is retarded and my husband and I sent him to the O'Benny Center for the retarded which is part of Cherry Hospital in Goldsboro, N.C. He spent eleven days there, in the little hospital there. I had a feeling something was wrong on the eleventh day and went to see him. They brought him out to us with two swollen black eyes, bruises of a man's fist covering his body, with cigarette burns on the bottoms of his feet. I took him to the hospital at Seymour Johnson at Goldsboro, N.C. where the doctor on duty looked at his black eyes and simply said he has two black eyes, and did not examine him at all. We took him home and he lay on the bed unconscious. I then took him back to Seymour Hospital where another doctor put him in the hospital for two days and he said he had done all he could so I took Michael back home and since that time he has had fits two and three times a day. When my husband died I could do nothing but send Mike to another retarded center since I could not take care of him alone and I have no money to help with him since they have cut off my social security for no reason that I can find unless the state of North Carolina had something to do with it and I mean the Congressman from this district because I had made so much noise about the whole thing. Please investigate and make a loud noise about it and I will thank you with all my heart. I have nothing to do now so I would like to join your raiders as the news papers call them. The things I could tell you about O'Benny would make your hair stand straight up be-cause I have done some snooping on my own. I have a letter from a doctor to prove what I have told you if you want it. I would love to go before Congress and tell them what I know so retarded children would get better treatment. Thank you.

Spring, Maryland, woman who writes to Nader at "Wherever You Are, Washington, D.C.," expresses especially poignantly the burden that high drug and other medical costs place upon senior citizens (Sample Letter E).

Not only the pricing but the marketing, availability, efficacy, and possible side effects of various drugs are of concern to writers. A Palm Springs, California, retiree questions the potency of the Squibb Theragran-M vitamins which she has been taking for 2 years; her husband's doctor has informed her that the tablets are "no good, just fake junk," but she considers that "Squibb is a big-name company and should be reliable." A Lake Park, Florida, woman, who has found Walgreen's

---

Sample Letter E

November 15, 1970

Ralph Nader

Bless your heart for being a crusader and trying to help the underdog a break. My husband and I are 79 and 80 yrs old. We have our aches and pains and don't run to the Dr. every time because they sock it to you so we suffer and the drug stores have no mercy at this writing. We in need of all kinds of medication. I have an old age care and supposed to get a cheaper price, they should live so long they up the price then tell you they'll give you 10% off. The fakes—Where will it all end and one day you go to the grocery store bread 39¢ 2 days later 42 and 43¢. There are so many injustices they mete out to the old folks. I worked so hard all my life raised a family of 4. I shouldn't have to fret that after I've saved for my old age I should have to dish it all out to the blood suckers—get after the Drs and drugs—etc. etc. Bless you. I am just a 79 yr old but my brain is still O.K. My body Eh?

Respectfully,

vitamin C tablets ineffective in stopping her gum bleeding, wonders if the company might be defrauding the public, whereas a Brooklyn writer worries about the severe heart palpitations she has suffered as a result of taking Mellaril No. 25 under doctor's prescription.

A number of writers assail the production and merchandising practices of certain drug manufacturers and retailers. From Parma, Ohio, comes a complaint about the "cheating going on in large chain drug stores," the writer saying that he has on several occasions received fewer pills than called for in his prescription. A New London, Connecticut, man delivers a detailed and well-documented attack on Parke-Davis' tactics in producing and marketing the antibiotic Chloromycetin (the generic Chloramphenicol). A knowledgeable San Diego, California, consumer questions Abbott Laboratories in almost accusatory terms about the contents of that company's Surbex T (high-potency Vitamin B) tablets. And an Inglewood, California, man sees carelessness on the part of large pharmaceutical houses and the government as responsible for the easy and widespread availability of amphetamines.

About 10% of all medical letters contain complaints about various forms of government financial assistance to the needy. Medicare is by far the commonest subject of such dissatisfaction. Various writers detail the huge amounts of time and energy they have expended in attempting to settle claims, often reaping only enormous frustration. Others describe the horror of learning after expensive hospital care that their coverage has expired or has been changed without notice, or is not so extensive as informational bulletins have led them to believe. A Freeport, New York, woman writes about the difficulties she has experienced in attempting to obtain Medicare payments for her 84-year-old mother, who is stricken with cancer:

> I have been trying to collect the claims for her, and have had such difficulty that I am about to give up. If we cannot get these claims paid she will have to go on welfare as we are running out of money. However this personal problem is not my major reason for writing you. I believe from my experience that probably one third of the justified claims submitted to Medicare are never paid. I can assure you that my aged and ill mother could never go through the aggravation and continuous correspondence [herself].

A Rockford, Illinois, woman, whose 85-year-old father-in-law is in an approved nursing home for treatment of a broken hip, finds that Medicare will not cover his expenses because it excludes "pinned" hips from those conditions deemed to require skilled attention in extended-care facilities. But, protests the writer, "I do not understand how it could take anything but skilled care to get a man up and down 3 times a day without putting weight on that leg or without possible further injury." A Chicago retiree condemns what she feels are the arbitrary and inconsistent payment policies characterizing Blue Cross's administration of Medicare:

> From what I have seen there is no consistency or regulation in what they are doing, except a keen desire to cut the bills, whether it is logical or not. . . . Insofar as I am concerned, and the figures will bear me out, this out-patient program is one of the biggest frauds ever perpetrated on a gullible public. . . . Any program initiated by Congress should emphasize preventive medicine and try to keep people out of the hospital by paying for out-patient care and keeping them well. . . . There is no question that we need radical changes in the delivery of health care for everybody.

Two writers concern themselves chiefly with the effectiveness and promise of current efforts in the battle against cancer. One, a retired Navy captain living in Wheaton, Maryland, and himself a cancer victim, sends Nader a carbon copy of a letter written to Senator Edward Kennedy (who was then in charge of handling recommendations made by a national panel of cancer experts) in which he suggests that any increase in federal funding for research might prove a wiser investment if it were to be redirected toward other, perhaps more fruitful, areas of medical investigation, such as the causes of and cures for heart disease. A Hollywood, Florida, woman, on the other hand, wishes to see the fight against cancer made all the more vigorous: "The safety factors in cars can wait, the foods on the shelves can wait," she declares, while we concentrate on finding cures for cancer. "Talk about it! Write about it! Ask about it! For God's sake help!!! . . . Are these clinics and researchers getting the monies allotted? New equipment? Are our cancer research centers manned with capable, dedicated men or fatalists?"

A number of other writers adopt a somewhat different perspective on government involvement in the search for cancer cures. They see the Food and Drug Administration, along with major pharmaceutical houses and the American Medical Association, as depriving citizens of their health freedoms by either refusing to sanction or actually banning purported anticancer agents such as Laetrile, the Rand Vaccine, and Krebiozen. Many letters on this subject come from representatives of organizations sponsoring drives for legalization of controversial therapies. The director of one group in Philadelphia writes "regarding the withholding of cures for cancer by an illegal conspiracy. The matter in question concerns cancer cures which appear to be sound and ought to be properly tested, but which it seems are being intentionally withheld by drug companies, the FDA and/or the AMA." And a Wyckoff, New Jersey, woman asserts that:

> It is inconceivable that in this free land of ours, an American cancer victim who is declared "hopeless" has to cross the border to Mexico in order to

obtain a harmless preparation which he feels may be beneficial. Even if Laetrile were completely useless, as the FDA so adamantly declares, this person has as much right to freedom of choice as does the cigarette smoker or those that take the birth control pills (both of which have known adverse effects).

Restrictions on drugs other than anticancer agents are also a source of complaint. A Los Angeles resident wonders why Gerovital, a drug claimed to revitalize the aged and heal the crippled, is available in Europe but not in this country: What gods keep it off the market or what sacred cows think it's too cheap for profit?" A San Francisco man whose severe bursitis has been completely relieved by experimental administration of Dimethyl Sulfoxide (DMSO) believes that the lobbying of major drug cartels has prevented the government from releasing the preparation to the public. And a Schillington, Pennsylvania, woman upset by an FDA ban on Sulfaguanidine, which she has taken for 6 years with favorable results, appeals to Nader for aid.

A final group of medical letters comes from writers who bemoan generally the quality of health care, diet, and life faced by most Americans. A number of these letters have been sent by groups devoted to achieving healthful living through special diets, cures, and forms of exercise. A Doylestown, Pennsylvania, woman writes, "I think it a statement of the priorities of our society when one realizes that the average citizen knows more about the repair of his car than the repair of his body." And a sergeant in the Air Force is appalled that "we are the richest country in the world and only the tenth or twelfth healthiest. Doesn't made sense . . . our medical system is the laughing stock of the world."

Appliance Letters

Appliance letters contain complaints about defective and poor-quality products, warranties and equipment life span, design failures, service representatives and repairs, replacement parts, and fraud.

Nearly half of all the appliance letters in our sample involve complaints about defective merchandise. Most of the writers sense that occasional "lemons" are to be expected among mass-produced items (a Chandler, Arizona, woman asks, "If there can be serious mistakes in space-flight mechanics, why not in a small Amana purchased by a housewife in the desert?"), but that awareness does not much ease their disappointment at finding themselves the owners of such equipment. Often merchandise has shown itself to be faulty on its arrival or only shortly thereafter. A Port Clinton, Ohio, housewife, describing her deluxe refrigerator, states, "The doors never closed tight from the very beginning, and the bottom rack which holds the vegetable bin drawer has been broken from the day of purchase. Cussin and Fearn store has sent serviceman after serviceman, but it was never fixed right." And a La Mesa, California, woman writes:

> At the present time—and since the day it was put into my home—this refrigerator has sounded like the proverbial "threshing machine." It is . . . the loudest refrigerator I have ever heard—anyone who is in my home when the refrigerator begins a cycle immediately asks "What's that?". . . I feel it is one of the so-called "lemons" that occur in the best of companies and are really no one's fault.

Initial problems with defective appliances frequently provide only a hint of what lies in store for the consumer. Original failings often continue or worsen despite repeated service calls and are often joined by new difficulties. A Brightwaters, Long Island, man sounds a common theme when recounting his experiences with his General Electric appliances:

> Upon delivery, the refrigerator was not working, the range came through with a bent and crooked drawer handle, and the first time I used the large oven, in March, it shorted out. This was followed by a call in June for sudden and yet unexplained excessive draining of water from the refrigerator and non-function of the P7 cleaning device, which I used for the first time. In July the glass in the door cracked clear through while the oven was in operation for three hours. In November, the door, which had been making a binding noise right along, although none of the service men seemed to notice, refused to close in the middle of a roasting operation.

Complainants commonly find that they are the prisoners of their defective appliances. Unable in most cases to exchange their purchase for an entirely new item, they must content themselves with replacement parts and whatever service their dealer is able and willing to provide them. From Chicago, the owner of a defective furnace writes that his "dealer finally refused to make any more service calls because, he advised, he did not know how to correct the problem." Faced with continuing problems and financial loss, some writers portray themselves as almost ready to abandon hope. A woman from Irving, Texas, for example, writes:

> We gave a lot of money for this refrigerator and it isn't worth it and will be ruined besides giving very poor service, before it's paid for. We cannot afford this loss. We thought we were buying a good product. The repair man has been very diligent in his job and I suppose he has done his best, but I hesitate to call him again. He has been out four or five times on the box and I am thoroughly disgusted. The refrigerator is a mess from being torn down and I have the mess in the house to put up with as well as the inconvenience.

Problems not solved before expiration of an appliance's warranty may continue thereafter to plague consumers who cannot afford to replace the defective merchandise at their own expense. And each new investment in the equipment obliges the owners to make any further repairs that become necessary. A Barrington, Illinois, woman writes: "Yesterday my husband and I were told that our three-year-old diswasher was probably not going to be worth repairing. Indeed the estimate came back that it would cost us $100 to repair the machine. We feel we will have to go ahead and invest this money because we don't think we can dispose of a three-year-old dishwasher." If fortunate, the owner of a defective appliance, even at his or her own expense, finally may put the appliance into satisfactory working order. One such consumer, from Dayton, Ohio, says that his Frigidaire had failed three times within the first year of ownership; on each occasion no cause for trouble could be found. "Then six months after the parts warranty expired, the motor went out and has to be replaced. Needless to say I must now pay for the parts and labor. Since having this replaced my box runs like a different refrigerator. This was probably the trouble all along."

Approximately 10% of the appliance complaints involve merchandise that writers consider not aberrantly defective but simply of a poor quality assignable to the normal materials and production methods of the manufacturer. A Dillon, Montana, woman declares, "I have had it right up to the teeth with overpriced, poor quality merchanidse...." An attorney from Warren, Ohio, in a letter to the manufacturer of his central heater, writes, "Surely you cannot claim to make a quality product when a motor that has been in actual use for something less than seven months cannot satisfactorily perform its function."

Inseparable from product quality is the issue of life span, a matter of explicit concern in 10% of the letters in the appliance category. Writers expect that major appliances, because they represent a considerable investment, will serve them not only well but long—at least a decade and perhaps two. Many individuals, or their parents, have previously owned equipment that has lasted for such periods of time with little if any need for service. When complainants find that their newer appliances require major repairs only 6 or 7 years after their purchase, and often just after expiration of the warranty, they blame their difficulties on a general decline in standards of manufacture or even on built-in obsolescence.

Warranty complaints, found in 20% of the appliance letters, also frequently encompass concerns about product life span. Warranties normally extend only 1, 2, or 5 years, depending upon the particular parts involved. Some people find, to their horror, that repairs become necessary just as this coverage expires, and they wonder whether warranty periods are not actually statements of life expectancy. One such complainant, a Miami Beach lawyer whose dishwasher carries only a 12-month guarantee, says that he has had to pay over $50 for repairs to the machine, which "was just barely a year and a half old," when "even [Westinghouse's] own mechanic stated that he could not understand how [the part involved] could go bad." Writers whose appliances have caused them considerable trouble and expense during the warranty period commonly fear that they will suffer more of the same, only at even greater cost, after coverage expires.

Several owners of products that were accompanied by assurances of "satisfaction guaranteed" have learned that their own expectations for satisfaction differ from those of the manufacturer. A Parma, Ohio, man appeals to Amana for reconsideration of a claim he has made for food spoilage resulting from malfunction of his refrigerator–freezer: "You denied my claim saying I should have been able to spot the damage as this appliance is used often. . . . Yes it is used often—when I am home, but it so happens that I was at my brother's in Toronto, Canada. . . . Upon further scrutinizing, the guarantee I have does not say anything like you did about having to be a freezer only." A Baltimore, Maryland, woman writes that although her freezer is new, fully guaranteed, and backed by an optional 2-year service policy, she has "been refused even a service call."

Writers often find that their warranties leave them responsible for repair labor charges—charges that may be so considerable that they make the warranty coverage seem almost nonexistent. A retired doctor living in Miami writes to his heater service company, "Your various attempts to justify $280.39 for installing a new compressor for one that you say shorted out while on warranty makes the York warranty a joke. . . ." A retired accountant living in Hughes Springs, Texas, complains that his daughter has had to pay $39.05 for 20 minutes of labor to replace the transmission on her guaranteed General Electric washer. "Since the transmission in washers is simple, consumers are paying an inflated price on parts as well as labor. Just a selling gimmick is the guarantee."

The warranties accompanying small appliances especially frustrate consumers, who find that the labor costs involved in repairing them even once may approach or exceed the original purchase price. Two consumers in Peoria, Illinois, and Kensington, California, have learned only with the breakdown of their minor appliances that they are repairable solely at the factory (for which repairs, even when made under warranty, a labor and postal charge must be paid) or not at all.

Some writers are bothered by what they consider unfair restrictions contained in the warranty of a particular appliance. A businessman who has recently bought a house in Shaker Heights, Ohio, discovers that Westinghouse will not permit transfer of the warranty on the home's central heater–air conditioner from the original purchaser to him, despite the former owner's express agreement to the transfer. The system now requires balancing, which would normally be performed without charge under warranty. Furious at being denied this service, the writer has hired an attorney in an attempt to hold the company to its "legal and moral obligations." A Louisville, Kentucky, homeowner objects to the fact that the guarantee on his Sears water heater applies only if replacement parts are purchased at Sears: "Needless to say I told [Sears] to keep their heater, I wanted no more of this junk. They could well afford to give me a 100-year guarantee if I would buy from them each time. To install a tank costs $40.00 or $50.00, of which they probably get 10%."

Design defects, some of them involving product safety, are of concern in nearly 10% of the appliance letters. A 73-year-old Corona del Mar, California, man, whose new vacuum cleaner has clogged repeatedly, writes to the Hoover Company, "It seems apparent to me that the trouble lies in bad design—the heavily corrugated plastic tube which impedes the flow of lint. A smooth tube would never do this. Yet you continue to put out one new model after another with this same defect. One would think that a company as old as yours would learn, but no." The Fullerton, California, owner of a Hotpoint refrigerator sarcastically observes that "one of the first things the family noticed about this appliance was the skill that had gone into its design. The door shelves and juice brackets in the freezer have such sharp corners that cleaning the appliance is a hazard." One writer from Eatontown, New Jersey, is bothered by a dryer whose motor gathers sufficient lint to pose a fire hazard, and two writers (one in Burbank, California, and the other in Bayside, New York) are plagued by stoves with inexplicable gas leaks and knobs that can be turned to "on" positions by the mere brush of a passerby. A Euless, Texas, physicist, whose family has narrowly escaped being asphyxiated by a faulty central-heating unit, demonstrates extreme patience and accommodation in advising the manufacturer of the experience and in defining the source of the problem (Sample Letter F).

By far the greatest proportion of appliance letters—a full 70%—contain complaints about service. Problems can arise even before delivery, when strikes, poor communication, and ineptitude cause long manufacturing and shipping delays. A Palatine, Illinois, woman who ordered a stove in September was assured on several occasions that the range was on its way, before being informed in mid November that the company's Chicago warehouse had no record of her purchase order; reordered, the appliance finally arrived, after further broken promises, on 23 December. Problems can develop, too, during delivery and installation. A La Mesa, California, housewife reports that improper connection of her new refrigerator by a commercial freight company caused her troubles that remained unsolved for months.

Most service complaints, however, involve repairs made after delivery and installation. Letter after letter recounts tales of difficulty and delays in obtaining service, of repeated service calls that bring little or no remedy, and of unconcerned, unskilled, and dishonest company representatives, dealers, and repair personnel. Once problems appear, consumers can have grave difficulties in reaching a responsible individual. A

September 7, 1970

... ite—Rodgers Valve Company
& Fedder Corporation
2969 Lake Shore Drive
Muskegon, Michigan 49443

Dear Sir:

One of your heater controls is installed in a Fedders central heating and air conditioning unit in my home at... , Euless, Texas. It is original equipment and is only two years old. (Model #3601, Type 404, 24 V., 60 CY., 4 Amps., Max Pr. $\frac{1}{2}$ PSI, Filter Cap 2 CFH Air) Other markings include ""AGA'', ""1167B'', ""E—1'' and ""Reg $3\frac{1}{2}$''

It has always been my impression that these controls with their pilot—heated thermocouple and electromagnetic latching safety valve were designed to provide ""fail—safe'' operation in the event of pilot flame—out, by preventing unburned gas from being supplied to the burners and... accumulation in the phlegm chamber (and home!)

Last night, I awoke with a headache. I went through the hallway past the heating unit, on my way to the kitchen in search of some aspirin. As I passed the heating unit, I heard the sound of escaping gas issuing from the unit's louvered door. Upon checking I found the gas going full blast! The pilot was extinguished! I turned off the gas at the main valve.

My wife then woke up, apparently by my clamoring. Together we checked on the children and opened doors and windows to air out the house.

I realize how lucky we were that I was alert enough, after breathing that damned gas and after just waking up, to discover

(continued)

the valve failure. Otherwise, none of us might have awakened at all! Or, had the gas accumulated long enough for an explosive mixture to exist, the whole house might have been blown to smithereens with us in it, when the light was turned on!

The purpose of this letter is not just to "bitch," as I'm already over being mad as Hell about the incident. I have diagnosed the problem with your valve and will impart it to you for the benefit of other users of your product. I feel qualified to do this as I am a physicist working in a well-known hospital with various respiratory gas devices and have several designs, innovations and improvements to my credit. I have found in the past that some manufacturers (or at least their engineering departments) do not seem to appreciate honest criticism of their products. I don't know how you will take this one, but here's the critique, and now it's on your conscience.

The little red reset knob is a piece of junk! Your otherwise fine (and expensive) valve failed because of the quality of plastic in the stupid knob! It split and slipped on its shaft when the pilot was first lit. When the pilot went out, friction between the knob and the shaft prevented it from allowing the fail-safe valve to close.

Suggested Remedy: Spend another 50¢, pass it on to the consumer for his own welfare, and have the knobs made out of cast iron, aluminum, brass or even pot metal, so it won't split the first time some strong fisted jerk tries to light the pilot.

A good part of my position is also spent evaluating various mechanical and electrical devices that will be used in the treatment of patients in the hospital. I can sympathize with anyone trying to design something foolproof and think of all the "what if's."

Respectfully,

Delaware, Ohio, woman is one of many writers who tell of getting nothing but delaying tactics when trying to arrange for necessary repairs: " . . . the man from whom we purchased the ice box was on two-week vacation—nothing possible there. The president of the company was 'out for lunch'—until 5 P.M. the next day, when he was honorable about returning my call." Repeated assurances that a service representative will call may have absolutely no meaning, as a Mission, Texas, housewife, among others, has found: " . . . the last word I had from the repair man (who, incidentally, is as difficult to get to come and do anything as anyone could possibly imagine) was that he would come back and check his work. . . . To date, I have not seen him. The door still leaks, the gasket was not installed properly . . . and countless telephone conferences with the dealer result in nothing but promises, promises—no action."

Writers are enormously bothered by having to deal with—and especially to contribute to the salary of—disinterested, rude, and seemingly unskilled repair personnel. Some writers tell of service personnel who pronounce on appliance problems without even touching the machine. A West Orange, New Jersey, couple notes that "[the repairman] came to the house two days after the call was placed, looked at the refrigerator (and we mean looked; we guess he didn't wish to get his hands dirty) and told us . . . there was nothing he could do but have a Ford field representative come to the house." A Miami building contractor states that the men sent to pick up his defective air conditioner were "very uncouth and had very little good behavior," and a Cleburne, Texas, resident whose complaints have been ignored by her appliance dealer writes: "I'm a 69-year-old widow living on my social security. I don't believe they would treat a man like I have been treated."

Several writers claim that service personnel have intentionally given them false information. More common, however, are complaints that dealers and repairers are themselves either misinformed about or wholly ignorant of their merchandise. A Fullerton, California, woman reports: "Each time we call the service representative we are asked what brand of appliance needs service, but the person who is sent to our home doesn't seem to know anything about Hotpoint refrigerators." She adds that each of her repair calls elicits two or three visits by service representatives who confess unfamiliarity with the appliance, contradict one another, and perform work that fails to solve the problem of the refrigerator's inability to cool. A Los Angeles man, describing the results of several attempts to repair his appliance, writes, "Our refrigerator looks and acts more like it has been vandalized than serviced." And a Uniontown, Pennsylvania, housewife complains that a repairer has "ruined" her stove: "The front panel pushes in. He ruined the oven door; one side in, one side out. Same way with the storage door. One side piece is out. The red signal light, he busted that up. Chrome strip along the side was loose; I wanted that fixed, he put a big piece of paper under it."

High repair charges are a common source of complaint. Writers are appalled at some of the labor costs that confront them. Service companies franchised by the manufacturer charge from $7 to $9 (plus tax) simply to send a repairman to the consumer's house; thereafter, installation of each part varies in cost according to a predetermined "job price." Some writers convert house call and job price amounts into an hourly wage, and find that they represent charges of $20, $30, or even $60 per hour. Writers consider such labor charges unjustified, especially if they suspect that the repairer has exaggerated the amount of time spent on the job. An Armonk, New York, orthodontist claims in a letter to General Electric that he has been charged for 35 minutes of labor when, according to his wife, the repairer worked for no more than 20 minutes. Furthermore, the writer complains:

> Your man arrived with his tool kit still in his truck and borrowed our vacuum cleaner to clean the coils. He also managed somehow to adjust the fan, miraculously, without the use of tools. After enjoying a cup of coffee, he spent a few minutes writing out our bill while discussing the fact that doctors overcharge their patients. Our bill was over $25.

The high price of replacement parts and labor is another major source of irritation. Some writers consider that the exclusive control of parts sales by authorized distributors creates a monopolistic situation and allows price fixing. A 72-year-old Akron, Ohio, widow, who has had to pay $4.05 for a water hose available only through General Electric outlets asks, "Just how far can this go?" One writer notes a 335% increase, over the course of 2 years, in the cost of humidifier filter pads. "Such a percentage rise," he claims, "cannot be due to normal rise in cost of production of such an item—I can only conclude that it is another example of the greed that has led to the inflation we find in our country today." And a New Orleans woman writes, "Three years ago, Sears replaced a tiny $.25 part in my dryer. Cost: $9.86. Last week the same part . . . was replaced. Cost: $15.06. For one living on Social Security, that is quite an item. Would feed me for almost two weeks."

Some writers have found that the replacement part they require is available only as a portion of a larger assembly; thus, they are forced to purchase more than they need or want, and they consider such sales tactics outrageously unfair. Various other writers are bothered not so much by the cost of parts as by the long delays involved in obtaining them. A Fitchburg, Massachusetts, man writes that he has been without the use of his refrigerator for a full month while awaiting the arrival of a replacement thermostat. From Stoughton, Wisconsin, a woman writes that she has failed, despite numerous complaints, to receive the nylon refrigerator rollers she ordered and paid for more than a year earlier.

Several writers, finally, claim to have been either misled or actually defrauded when making their purchases. In one case an elderly couple has been sold an ancient freezer as a much newer one (Sample Letter B), and in three instances complainants have received floor models that were sold as, and at the cost of, brand-new merchandise. Another individual, a resident of New York City, has just found that her refrigerator ceases operation entirely during power cutbacks such as Consolidated Edison institutes as part of normal procedure during the summertime.

Food Letters

Food letters contain complaints about nutritionally deficient and highly processed foods, additives, product labels, the presence of foreign objects in packaged or canned goods, fraud, food prices, and grocery stores.

The most common subjects of complaint among the sample letters about food are the poor quality and dangers of the average American diet. Writers despair of vitamin-depleted packaged and frozen foods; of the pesticides and other poisons present in fruits and vegetables; of mercury contamination in fish and eggs; of foods high in cholesterol; of products containing insects and rat excreta (and of the fact that the Department of Agriculture permits, by virtue of its "filth tolerances," even the most minute quantities of such material to be lawfully accepted as fit for human consumption); and soft water. Writers believe that the food industry cannot be trusted to produce safe, wholesome consumables and doubt that the Food and Drug Administration is truly dedicated to ensuring the safety of foods sold to citizens. Many consider dietary deficiencies responsible for illnesses—such as cardiovascular disease and cancer—widespread among Americans. Some provide testimonials to the nutritional benefits of natural foods and specific diets.

Several writers condemn the quality of specific brands of processed foods. A Rockville, Connecticut, couple, in a letter to the Campbell Soup Company, complains that "your chicken soup has been, for years and years, mostly water." Other complainants decry the quality of general categories of foodstuffs, such as most of the flour and bread available in the United States. A Teaneck, New Jersey, housewife asserts that mills across the country have since 1960 been producing flour of a lower grade. And a Redwood City, California, man, disgusted with the insubstantial, fluffy white bread he has purchased, writes, "I know we have to pay, someday, to clean our air. What I didn't know was that we were already paying to EAT it!"

Nearly 20% of all food letters contain complaints about additives. Writers are bothered by artificial flavorings in ice cream; hydrogenated fats, monoglycerides, diglycerides, and sweeteners in peanut butters; preservatives in canned sandwich spreads and "Space Food Sticks"; dyes in maraschino cherries; and stabilizers in nondairy creamers. Complainants recall days when they could purchase basic foodstuffs free of such chemicals; a New Bern, North Carolina, housewife remembers that "there was a time when one could buy a good wholesome peanut butter that was made *only* from peanuts and salt." Other writers ask why many products require preservatives; "after all," writes a resident of West Palm Beach, Florida, "we have the best in refrigeration in all our houses and stores. We use preservatives in cereals that contain more wrappings and boxes than the actual weight of the air-blown cereals themselves."

Writers are concerned about the harmful effects of additives. A Chicago woman who works for an insurance company is disturbed by the large number of cancer deaths recorded in the firm's files. She wonders whether cancer-causing chemicals in food might not bear some responsibility for this loss of life. Several writers describe their own severe reactions to specific additives. A San Diego, California, woman writes to Nader, "I am informed that you investigated the health hazards of monosodium glutamate. . . . I am a living example of what is does to adult humans." She says that the MSG in canned broth has twice given her sharp, piercing head pains and has left her suffering from memory lapses. Another woman, from White Hall, Maryland, tells of the dramatic improvements in her life that have followed the dismissal from her diet of foods containing large numbers of additives:

> I have risen above it. Cutting out all junk including ice cream—I am thinking clearly and am even joining women's clubs—through a diet of less starches—no sugar except what is in natural foods. I feel like a million—and this is every day. Our farm looks good again—my husband's business does not upset me—we live with it. I am president of one club—never before in my life has this happened. None of this could be without a complete switch in eating habits. . . . I am 57—and just beginning to live—tomorrow I'll probably drop dead from overwork—but it is worth it.

Twenty percent of all letters in the food category contain specific complaints about the quality of the meat sold to the American public. Many who write on this subject have just read newspaper or magazine articles exposing unhealthy practices in the meat industry, and have been appalled by what they have learned. One such individual, from Ballston Spa, New York, comments: "Have been nauseated to even look at meat, it is so shocking! You cannot believe what you read! . . . Thirty states permit *every bit* of offal to be included in meat products. Have you ever wondered why meat doesn't taste like meat anymore?" Two complainants are concerned that leukosis in chickens may be affecting consumers, but most writers worry more about the condition of beef being offered for sale. They are especially bothered by use of the known cancer-causing hormone diethylstilbesterol (DES) to stimulate abnormally fast weight gain in beef cattle. Half of all the sample letters regarding meat have been sent in response to the FDA's doubling of DES allowances for cattle in late 1970. Complainants are shocked that regulations have been eased rather than tightened and recommend that DES be banned altogether. They are outraged that the meat industry is, in the words of a Pittsburgh housewife, "given such frightening freedom to slowly kill its customers."

Writers complain also about the injection of water into beef and ham. An Ossining, New York, man recalls that "several years ago, after cooking a steak or roast, you had grease left in the pan. Now you have water. On Sunday we had a 4-lb. pot roast and although no water was added [by us], we wound up with enough water to make two small bowls of soup." Other writers describe other forms of what they see as cheating by meat packers. A Schenectady, New York, man claims that hams, though still advertised as smoked, are in fact now little more than salted. And two writers (one in Union City, New Jersey, and the other in Salem, Oregon) tell of having purchased canned hams which, though labeled as having had excess fat removed, contained great quantities of the substance.

Nearly one-seventh of the food writers register dissatisfaction with the labeling of products they have purchased. Some are bothered by the partial or total failure of companies to list the contents of food products. Others complain about labels that describe ingredients in general rather than precise terms. The wife of a man stationed at Norton Air Force Base in California fears that the oil described on many food packages only as "vegetable" is in fact coconut oil and states, "I would prefer to see the exact name of the oil listed, instead of a general term, for those who have a problem with cholesterol." A Wall, New Jersey, housewife directs a similar complaint to the makers of Best Food mayonnaise, stating, "I am convinced of my right to know exactly what my family is ingesting." Two writers complain that they cannot understand many food labels because they are not familiar with the names of most chemical additives, and two others say that they cannot even read certain labels because of the small size and poor quality of the print. Several complainants have noticed discrepancies in the lists of dietetic beverage ingredients, finding that labels for the same brand contradict each other as to the product's cyclamate content.

Among those who express greatest dissatisfaction with food labels are diabetics. They complain that incomplete and imprecise listings of ingredients lead them unknowingly to purchase foods containing sugar. An Olive, California, man notes that foods marked as "dietetic" are especially troublesome, as their labels often give little indication of their sugar content: "... this leads a lot of diabetics to think the food is alright for them. My wife is one of these people; she buys these foods and eats them, then her tests are all out of kilter." Other diabetics complain about having difficulty not only in recognizing but simply in locating suitable foods.

The (then) recently imposed ban against cyclamates resulted in the addition of sugar to many products formerly containing the artificial sweetner and thus forced diabetics to abandon some of their favorite purchases. One anonymous diabetic from South Bend, Indiana, after proclaiming that "the diabetics in this country represent some of the most powerful and smartest people in the world," asks Nader to work toward a repeal of the ban against cyclamates.

Nearly 17% of all food letters recount the writers' unexpected discovery of alien objects in packaged or canned goods. Most of the foreign matter mentioned—such as a hair in a package of scrapple, a fly in a can of clam chowder, a cockroach in a box of frozen stringbeans, and insects in cereals and cake mixes—has disgusted the writers but has not seriously threatened their health. Other finds—among them a screw in a box of brown sugar, broken glass in a can of tuna, and a stone in a bag of peanuts—have not inflicted harm but have had the capacity to do so. In several instances, however, the inclusions have actually injured or sickened complainants. An Albuquerque, New Mexico, man states that a woodlike contaminant in a recently purchased candy bar has caused him "immeasurable mental and physical anguish." And a Ventnor, New Jersey, housewife describes the following unpleasant experience, which occurred while she and her husband were driving to Florida for a holiday and stopped one night at a motel in Myrtle Beach, South Carolina:

> We were sitting outside in the evening and were drinking king-sized Cokes from the machine there. As I tipped the bottle up, when I had almost finished it, I felt something go in my mouth which was not liquid. I went into the room to where the light was and was amazed to see a small piece of plastic in my hand. I held the bottle to the light and immediately ran to the bathroom and lost my dinner. There was a large plastic thing about 8 or 10 inches long that had been all curled up in order to get it into the bottle.

Fifteen percent of all individuals writing about food recount how they have been cheated in purchases of processed edibles. A Chester, Pennsylvania, woman claims that the king crab meat she bought had been adulterated with fish. Letters describe packages of frozen breaded shrimp that contain largely batter, "beans-and-franks" TV dinners lacking frankfurters, beer whose alcoholic content falls below that allowable by law, and large cans of fruit that provide a sea of syrup but only four apricot halves. A Teaneck, New Jersey, housewife relates that she has opened a can of beets labeled "contents 16 oz. (1 lb.)" that not only has yielded more than twice as much water and salt (by weight) as beets but its total contents has weighed only 15 ounces.

About 10% of all food letters contain reports of false advertising, deceptive packaging, or other fraudulent sales tactics. A Winchester,

Massachusetts, woman says she cannot tell any difference between Ocean Spray's deluxe and ordinary cranberry jelly (the former selling for 39¢ a can, and the latter for 23–27¢). Three writers complain about package photographs that misrepresent the products contained within. One of these individuals (living in Jeannette, Pennsylvania), referring to a can of stew, claims that "any resemblance between the photograph and the actual product is strictly coincidental." Another, who has received 5 won ton rolls in a package picturing 10, says that "since there is no mention anywhere on the box about the number of won ton rolls in the package, I relied on the picture. I was cheated by the company . . . ." Two complainants write with inside information on deceptive labeling and packaging; one, from Angola, New York, reveals that many eggs sold as "fresh Grade A" have in fact sat in cold storage for periods of up to a year; the other, from Huntington, Massachusetts, reports that a well-known cookie and biscuit company, without decreasing package size or price at all, has cut back on content weight. Two other writers denounce what they consider fraudulent practices in food coupon offers.

Several writers complain about high food prices. One, from Shreveport, Louisiana, has seen the price of whole cloves at her local supermarket almost double (from 25¢ to 49¢) in the span of several weeks. "I am on Social Security and disabled," she reports, "and this kind of price hurts. Can anyone help?" A Summit, New Jersey, woman asserts that supermarkets charge unfair prices for diet foods and foods packaged in single-serving portions—items for which there is great demand from the overweight, the poor, and the elderly living on fixed incomes. A third writer, living in Woodbury, New York, has been outraged at seeing prices raised on products already sitting on her supermarket shelf. Addressing the president of the market chain, she states:

> Every time I walk into one of your stores it costs me more than the week before. This has been going on for over a year now and it is time that someone makes an effort to stop it. It seems to me that you people are cashing in wherever and whenever you can and the devil with the economy and especially the devil with your customers, one of whom you have just lost for good. You would be the first to scream and cry about free enterprise if the President finally found that he had to impose wage and price guidelines.

Several other letter writers assail elements of grocery-store policy, along with various practices of food delivery and sales personnel. A Knoxville, Tennessee, man is appalled that markets allow frozen vegetables to become defrosted while in the top layer of their freezers and then transfer the affected items to the bottom of the chests. A housewife from Pelham Manor, New York, who purchased moldy and discolored pork chops at her local market, relates that she had been unfairly denied a refund; she went back to the market with the meat wrappers, she states, "but the manager told me he could not refund my money since I did not bring back the pork chops. I was to save the moldy things until Monday and return them for a refund. My word was not good enough although I have traded in that store for seven years . . . ." Two writers concern themselves especially with the unhealthy or deceptive practices existing at some supermarket meat counters. One, a former employee at a counter in Coventry, Rhode Island, offers an anonymous exposé of conditions and procedures at that establishment; the second writer is the source of Sample Letter G.

These writers, finally, complain about the quality of pet foods. One, living in Glendale Springs, North Carolina, reports that she opened six cans of a chicken-flavor cat food, only to find that each one contained a high proportion of liquid to solids. A Houston housewife asks that Nader investigate the quality of pet foods, as "the old saying 'That's not fit for a dog' has got to mean the food the companies are putting out for pets now." And a Portland, Oregon, family writes that its cat recently died of urinary blockage and kidney damage resulting from a diet consisting entirely of dry cat food. The food in question is advertised as a complete diet for cats, the writer points out, whereas in fact cats require fresh meats to dissolve the crystals that dry food creates in their urine. "Someone," the writer concludes, "is being negligent in providing information to cat owners in the use of dry cat food."

Discussion

Consumer complaint letters, as they nearly always involve expressions of dissatisfaction, provide considerable insight into certain expectations of their writers. Most writers indicate that they have entered into business transactions with high hopes for product and service performance. They portray these expectations as originating from a number of sources in their sociocultural environment—sources such as the experiences of friends, relatives, and the writers themselves; the companies concerned, through their reputation, advertising, and packaging; the price paid for a specific product, on the commonly expressed assumption that higher price and quality go hand-in-hand; and the kind of transaction involved (writers often rue having paid cash for items, in the belief that a company's and dealer's sense of responsibility disappears once full payment has been received). Complainants believe that appliances, food, and medical care should meet reasonable standards of quality. They ask that service be performed honestly and reliably, and that charges be commensurate with the kind and amount of work done. They believe that consumers should be fully informed, at the time of purchase, of all aspects of the

October 22, 1970

Dear Mr. Nader:

I am infuriated and disgusted with the chain grocery stores in this town.

I don't ask that they sell me pheasant under glass for 49¢ per pound, but I _do_ ask and expect to receive honest meat at an honest price.

Last Saturday I purchased two small packages of stew beef at 95¢ per pound. That's a pretty stiff price, because when I started to prepare it, I discovered there were two or three small pieces on top of big hunks of meat _full_ of tendons and heavy connective tissue.

It was all prettily dressed up with cellophane that sported a little, blue stick-on sign that said "tender cuts."

I spent over an hour removing the tissue and tendons. I left the fat on because stew beef has to have fat on it.

The beef also had lots of blood clots and it was _old_ and tough. Also, it was cow beef. How do I know? Well, I lived 25 years with a meat man who started as a truck driver, then meat cutter, then a "box man" and _finally_ boss of the whole meat section in a warehouse _so_ big he rides around in an electric car. I lived, breathed and slept _meat_ for years and years.

But even _I_ cannot see through a cellophane package. At least, not more than the top layer.

Well, I had a pile of tissue and tendons that weighs 4 or 5 ounces—or more and I'm marching _right_ back to Shop-Rite, Slater Road, New Britain and I'm going to tell a few people off. I'm not a red head for nothing! I may just belt someone—ha!

(continued)

Oh, Mr. Nader, they cheat like the devil himself—all of them. How many times I have bought boiled ham in a cellophane wrapping, only to find when I lifted up the top two slices, the rest was bits and pieces heavily laced with fat.

We are prisoners of cellophane wraps! They refuse to open the wrapping and let you see what you are buying.

It's especially bad in this town because it is a mill town and has an awful lot of uneducated, and at least, <u>previously</u> deprived people. They simply think things <u>have</u> to be like this. They don't know <u>what</u> to do, so, they accept it!

I am <u>not</u> a modern day suffragette... , I'm just a hard working woman who supports a not too-well husband and myself. I don't make very much, but I try to spend wisely.

I wrote to the Dept. of Agriculture once and the Secretary of the Dept. of Agriculture is a "ding-a'ling" and you may <u>quote</u> me. Some dame there, who <u>gets</u> a salary ten times what she is worth, sent me the silliest letter I ever read! Next time we send people to the moon, <u>they</u> should go—hand in hand.

I allow myself $15 a week for all my groceries, including soaps and paper goods and I set a good table, but, I just <u>have</u> to get my money's worth and I have to use good common sense. Also, you have to do things that are a little extra trouble.

Why, I even make my pet's cat food—it's a snap and costs much less than the stuff you buy. He's a Blue Persian that looked so bad when he was little that he was going to be destroyed. I begged for him and you should see him now—he is gorgeous.

Stores should have big signs that tell the customers their guaranteed rights as customers.

Including the fact that a customer has the right to have cellophane wrapped meat opened if requested and weighed on demand.

This and other customer rights should be in plain sight, with big letters and in the languages other than English, popular in the particular area.

(continued)

Sample Letter G—Continued

Grocery stores offend or out and out cheat in every department. The big bosses are rich and complacent. They have fancy
lawyers and sneaky tricks, but when they put their sticky fin-
gers in _my_ pocket, they better be prepared to lose the arm too.

I think the work you do is simply wonderful....

Most sincerely,

---

product and transaction, both positive and negative. Too often, they
think, buyers are ill-equipped to deal with businesses as equals or to
sensibly and knowledgeably select among competing products (when,
after all, one of the consumer's single greatest powers is his or her ability
to exercise options). A commonly expressed belief is that some public or
private body should be looking out for the safety and well-being of consumers. A number of writers suggest that companies themselves should
bear this responsibility, or at least share in it, whereas others feel that
government agencies charged with this task must bear the heaviest burden. Writers nearly universally observe, however, that neither business
nor government has performed, or perhaps can perform, an adequate job
of consumer protection.

Writers differ considerably in their expectations concerning the
likelihood of problems with the goods and services they have purchased.
Some are astonished to meet with difficulties. Others have a sense that
occasional irregularities and imperfections are to be expected and tol-
erated. Still others claim, when confronted with an unsatisfactory purchase, that they have only had their worst fears realized.

All complainants are motivated to write by a sense of injustice. In
letter after letter appear such comments as "I feel it is a little unjust," "It's
not fair," and "This is an outrage to us." Writers differ, however, in the
relative importance that they assign to simple economics, as opposed to
moral principle, when naming the impetus for their complaint. To a degree, of course, this difference stems from variations in the size of the
investment the writers have made. Quite often those who claim moral
rather than economic injustice as the chief basis for their complaint have
not incurred a heavy financial loss. Many of those who have spent several

hundred dollars for an appliance, on the other hand, are not about to dismiss the importance of their monetary sacrifice.

The problems related by the writers differ, of course, in their basic seriousness. Some are matters of life and death; others appear, at least on the surface, fairly innocuous. But vexing problems occur in each category of complaint. Many medical writers convey reports of months or even years of poor health resulting from malpractice. Appliance writers commonly report that the purchase of defective merchandise has led to a repetition and buildup of problems stretching through the entire warranty period and beyond. And although most complaints about food involve only a single, minor source of dissatisfaction, a number of food complaints contain descriptions of illnesses stemming from the presence of foreign objects or additives in purchases.

The life situation of the complainant and the specific time at which problems occur affect the seriousness of the difficulties. The elderly on fixed incomes suffer disproportionately from high medical and food costs, and senior citizens often express the belief that unscrupuluous appliance dealers and repair personnel have seen them as especially easy prey for fraud and poor service. The necessity of taking clothes to a laundromat while awaiting repair of a washer or dryer most inconveniences those with large families. People whose appliances fail during strikes or on holiday weekends encounter abnormally long delays in repairs—often at times when elaborate preparations are underway for holiday meals and entertaining. Breakdowns in heaters and air conditioners are most likely to occur during seasons of their greatest use and need. Ten days without heat during a severe Michigan winter or a summer without air conditioning in Texas forms understandable grounds for anger and frustration.

Complainants demonstrate that their problems have exacted a myriad of costs—economic, physical, social, and mental. Most writers in each category of complaint have suffered some financial loss; in certain cases this loss has been very considerable. Writers in every category suffer emotional distress, whether caused by the initial appearance of a problem or by the sense of frustration and futility that often accompanies repeated, unsuccessful attempts to achieve remedy. Those who have had difficulty with major appliances frequently betray the greatest anger and misery; they, more often than medical or food writers, find themselves confronting repeated, long-lived problems. Appliances play an indispensable role in the lives of most Americans. A single failure of a refrigerator can mean the loss of $100 or more in perishable food and requires changes in shopping habits until repairs have been made. Consumers, having arranged for service at the convenience of the dealer, frequently must take time off from work to be present for the service call. Two writers (residents of Burbank, California, and Bayside, New York) tell of the worry of living with leaky gas ranges. Many describe the anguish of facing repeated breakdowns, intervals without the use of an appliance, and hollow assurances that just-completed repairs have finally solved the problem. A Binghamton, New York, housewife shows especially vividly the toll that appliance problems can take (Sample Letter H).

Writers vary considerably in their thresholds of complaint. Some fire

---

Sample Letter H

August 9, 1971

Ralph Nader
Washington, D.C.

Dear Ralph Nader:

    Two years ago I bought a Tappan Gallery stove at "Olums," a reliable furniture store in Binghamton, New York. At first I thought I had to get used to the new stove, for ever since I have the stove, nothing comes out good for me. The side panels of the stove are not baked enamel. When I was washing the stove with "Easy Off" according to directions, the paint came right off. Olums had replaced one panel, and now the other panel's paint is coming off. I took off the door to soak it so it would be easier to clean, and water seeped in between the glass and now I have a streaked glass door. I had my other stove for twenty-five years and it never spattered inside the oven as this stove does. It is so hard to clean, I never had to scrub so hard on the old stove.

    Every cake I baked, it only half rose in the oven, then when I took it out, the rest of it flopped! I hate it, I hate it, I hate it! Not one of my roasts comes out good, my pigs in the blankets get burned on top and bottom and the inside is raw. The same happens to all the pies.

(continued)

Sample Letter H—Continued

I have been embarrassed too many times, and apologized too many times, that I'm a nervous wreck from this stove.

Three hundred and fifty nine dollars is a lot of money for us to pay for a stove, as my husband only earns between five and six thousand a year. With 2 children and me to support.

I've had the man from Olums three times to adjust it, he finally said that he couldn't do any more. So I got the man from the gas company, and he had three different settings, and he said that there was nothing wrong with the stove.

Olums said had I complained before the years guarantee, they might have done something about it. Well I didn't complain before because I thought that I had to get used to the stove. HELP! Now my husband is constantly hollering at me that I wanted a new stove, that I wanted to go modern. This is modern?

I hope something can be done about this situation.

Sincerely yours,

off letters to Nader (and officials of government and industry) as soon as they perceive problems, whereas others wait days, weeks, months, and even years before complaining, at least to anyone beyond their local dealer or service representative. Those who wait to complain often mention some development which they may call "the straw that broke the camel's back" or "the last turn of the screw," at which they are moved to write to Nader. A few mention that the compounding of like but unrelated experiences has provided the instigation for their complaint. A Middletown, Connecticut, man who discovered bones in a can of chicken and dumplings states, "I would put this down as an isolated incident if I had not, in the past, found other foreign matter in canned food...."

Attitudes toward complaining, which vary considerably among writers, play an important part in determining the point at which consumers make the decision to register a grievance. Many people display a reluctance to complain. Such individuals apologize for writing at all, or for bothering the addressee, or for sending long letters; mention that they have put off writing for some time; complain anonymously (or ask that their name not be used publicly); or minimize the importance of their problem. A number of writers evince the attitude that frequent complaining, or complaining for its own sake, is to be avoided. Others view complaining more positively. Some describe themselves as regular complainers, and one Houston resident calls himself a "one man army," though "fighting a losing battle." These writers wish that a greater portion of the public would voice complaints (a Tulsa, Oklahoma, woman laments, "So many people are so passive and unconcerned about problems"). Several people acknowledge that it is the rise of the consumer movement, and of a new consumer consciousness spawned particularly by the arrival of Nader on the public scene, that has given them higher expectations and has made them more ready to complain.

Nearly all the sample letters written specifically to Nader express solidarity with the consumer movement. They speak of problems that their writers know will interest the consumer advocate, in terms with which they can be certain he will sympathize. A few individuals caution Nader that his efforts are misplaced. One, a resident of Palm Springs, California, writes: "I wouldn't say you are a total failure but not much success. The hot dogs and hamburgers are still excessively fat. The maraschino cherries are not only too red but too highly flavored. I could keep on reminding you of the things you have tried to do but no *luck*. . . . Do some real good." Many complainants, on the other hand (nearly half of those in the medical and food groups and 20% of those in appliance), express gratitude to Nader for his efforts on behalf of the public, and a goodly number add praise (often lavish) or exhortations. Only a limited number of writers cite a specific publication or particular media coverage as having familiarized them with the activities of Nader, and only a few evidence any very sophisticated knowledge of the work of the Center for Study of Responsive Law. But many state that they have written to Nader because they consider him to have power, stamina, and an efficacy that they lack as individuals. They have faith in Nader's will and capacity to improve the quality of life, and trust in his vision of the future. A resident of White Hall, Maryland, for example, postscripts her letter with "you are normal, just 20 years ahead of your time."

It is clear that the writers of all letters registering a complaint, whether originally to Nader or to another addressee, wish to inspire some form of action. They are usually seeking a solution to a more or less general problem. There is evidence that this intention lies behind even those letters that have commonly been considered pure voicing (Hirschman 1970), that is, attempts not to achieve redress but merely to communicate dissatisfaction. Within our sample are carbon copies of a number of letters addressed to manufacturers and purporting to be no more than expressions of dissatisfaction; the writers of these letters, however, have made it clear in accompanying notes to Nader that they are actually seeking some form of redress. Most letters sent in the original to companies contain direct requests, and often demands, for compensation. Few writers propose punitive settlements; most, instead, ask only that their problems be solved and that they be reimbursed in the exact amount of their monetary losses. Letters to Nader frequently embody solicitations of aid, but these are less often requests that Nader explicitly involve himself in solving the problem than that he give whatever support and advice he can.[14] Those writing to Nader quite often declare that they wish at least to contribute to solving the problems bothering them, but are uncertain how they may most effectively do so. These individuals wish to avoid complete reliance on Nader for assistance and seek to confront problems by more than employing their option to exit from further dealings with a company or individual (Hirschman 1970). Only 3 medical writers, 21 appliance writers, and 14 food writers in the sample mention their intent to exercise that option.

Writers utilize a variety of devices to lend authority and precision to their letters. Some send actual objects or products, packaging, or bills and receipts as documentation. Others enclose newspaper and magazine clippings that either have provided some impetus for the complaint or show that the problem is not confined to the writer alone. Complaints about food are supported in certain cases by the results of careful weighing and measuring of products. And a limited number of writers in each subject category have carried out personal research in order to better understand the meaning and context of their individual difficulties.

Thirteen of the medical packets, 21 of the food packets, and 71 of the appliance packets contain 1 or more carbon copies of letters addressed elsewhere than to Nader—usually to manufacturers. The original letters involved in nearly every case have contained a listing of the recipients of all carbon copies, ranging from Nader alone to upward of 10 individuals (usually government officials involved in consumer protection activities, but also including representatives of the media, attorneys, local dealers and service agencies, and, in more than one instance, President Nixon); these listings have the dual purpose of informing presumably interested parties and of putting pressure on original addressees. Some individuals (1 in medical, 6 in food, and 18 in appliances) have tried to pressure companies by threatening to publicize (even if only among friends and neighbors) their negative experiences and to warn others away from the companies' products. Interestingly, only a comparatively small number of writers (1 in food, 5 in medical, and 14 in appliances) threaten to take, or announce that they have taken, legal action.

---

[14]Consumer groups associated with Mr. Nader examine letters in aggregate, to follow trends in consumer dissatisfaction and to identify troublesome products and situations.

Many individuals write to Nader only after having engaged in correspondence with representatives of business or government. Frequently they comment upon the nature of this exchange or send photocopies of at least part of the correspondence. These comments, along with any letters enclosed, demonstrate important deficiencies in government and business complaint handling. On occasion, writers report, the addressees do not even bother to answer. At other times, they respond but avoid answering the questions raised or otherwise dealing with the specific complaint. For example, companies may simply send out a form letter along with a certain amount of printed product information or related material, such as, in the case of food companies, recipes. Even when businesses do respond with a personal letter, the results may be, in the eyes of the consumer, grossly inadequate. Manufacturers frequently wish to avoid any responsibility for the problems of the complainant and may suggest that the writer seek remedy from his or her nearest dealer when a basic aspect of the consumer's complaint is that he or she has already failed, despite repeated efforts, to gain satisfaction from that same establishment.

When manufacturers do assume responsibility, it is often to deny the request of the complainant. This denial normally is made as impersonally and vaguely as possible, company letters would indicate. Business representatives may write using the first person plural and credit the denial to some unnamed higher authority. A branch service manager for the Westinghouse Appliance Sales and Service Company, for example, turns down a Lomita, California, resident's plea with a simple "we would not be allowed to reimburse you for the parts as you have requested." Or business people may respond with a denial formulated in paternalistic terms purportedly to protect the majority good. A Florissant, Missouri, man forwards such a response from the administrative assistant to the general service manager of the Maytag Company, received in reply to the consumer's complaint that he had had to buy a complete assembly, at considerable expense, simply to replace a worn plastic gear in a washing machine. The Maytag representative explains the rationale for this sales procedure with the following:

> There are rare cases where a gear only may resolve the timer problem. . . . As a general rule, however, and since we serve millions of customers through our parts distribution system, it is in the best interest of most people to have a new or completely reconditioned timer. . . . Years ago we found that providing small replacement gears and other items penalized customers more than it benefitted them . . . .

Responses such as the foregoing do not endear companies to complainants. In response to the quoted letter of the Maytag representative, the Missouri recipient writes, "Your correspondence has helped me to make up my mind about one type of dryer that I will not buy, and that is Maytag. I couldn't take the chance on too many plastic gears that might fail. I probably would have to buy a whole new dryer." A Los Angeles man relates that he has been so infuriated by the delaying tactics and falsehoods that have met his appliance complaint that he has fought a court battle (and has obtained a judgment) against his local dealer, and has proceeded also, in different fashion, against the manufacturer. To the latter, the Fedders Corporation, he writes: " . . . the sum and substance of your response to my service complaint was a runaround and a brush-off. . . . The anger generated by your miserable conduct caused me to become an owner of stock in your corporation so that I might be more fully informed about the way you do business . . . ." The writer then goes on to relate that he tried to air his complaints to the president of the Fedders Corporation during the annual stockholders' meeting, but was informed that the time and place were not appropriate for such discussion:

> I have always understood that good company management considers cus-
> tomer service and purchaser satisfaction a matter of importance equal to
> that of sales and profits. Since your management does not consider these
> matters of sufficient importance to be considered by ownership at stock-
> holders' meetings, it appears quite obvious that you do not agree with this
> principle, and place such matters below such subjects as sales, profits,
> acquisitions, executives' stock options, salary raises, and retirement bene-
> fits. . . . One of these days, enough customers will get so fed up with poor
> products or bad service that they will expend the necessary time, effort, and
> expense to get rid of them. . . . I already have.

Many of the letters in this study, particularly those in the food and appliance categories, convey something of the complainants' attitudes toward a particular company or toward business in general. A number of individuals, despite their own difficulties with a product, retain faith in the manufacturer's goodwill. A Brooklyn, New York, woman, whose vacuum cleaner had not been returned to her after more than 6 months at her local Sears repair shop, and who has called concerning the machine "time and time again and [only] been given the 'runaround,'" still can state, "I know Sears prides themselves on taking care of their customers." And a Fairfield Highlands, Alabama, resident, in a letter to the Sunbeam Corporation, shows that she maintains respect for that company's products despite more than 5 years of problems with one of its electric percolators: ". . . this I could hardly believe would happen to any Sunbeam product. . . . I feel that this is simply an inferior product, not up to your usual high standards. . . ."

Some of those writing to a manufacturer express concern for the company's well-being, effectiveness, and reputation, and wish to alert the addressee to weaknesses in its products or organization. An Eatontown,

New Jersey, couple, in a missive to the Hoover Company, advises, "This letter is to make you aware of a service problem which could very well be damaging to your company's reputation in the New Jersey area.... It is unfortunate that a company of your reputation does not give better service." An Orinda, California, resident writes the president of the Amana Company, "I am sorry to bother you with this letter but I think it is important for you to know that your parts service is so much below expectancy and need that you are alienating customers such as myself from later purchases of equipment manufactured by you." Several such writers make specific recommendations as to how a company can improve its products or operations.

Many individuals have faith in the willingness of manufacturers to handle complaints decently, honorably, and fairly, and express their sentiments in such phrases as "we feel confident that having your reputation, you will promptly and properly fulfill the above request," "I know you will use your best judgment," or "I know you will do the right thing." In a couple of instances, people who have written to Nader initially, with copies of their complaints addressed to manufacturers, write him later to tell him that their problems have been solved and offer praise for the companies responsible. A Dillon, Montana, woman, reports: "My gripes seem to have all been taken care of.... Truly there is some integrity left in the business world." This writer, although assured and forceful in her original complaints to the Kelvinator company, now seems rather contrite; she closes her note with "believe me, I have not made a life's work of finding fault."

Far outnumbering those expressing positive sentiments about business, however, are those who communicate criticisms, suspicion, and antagonism. A good many complainants write to industry despite concern that their voices will not be heard, or at least will not elicit much sympathy; they fear that their letter will be read only by a computer, that their question will remain unanswered, or that they are "just yakking and getting no place." Some have had their respect for a particular company shattered by the source of their complaint ("I am writing this to you to tell you how disappointed I am in Frigidaire ..."). The writers criticize business on a variety of grounds: They suggest that companies generally lack a sense of decency ("I just could not refrain from expressing an opinion on [Nader's] wonderful courage in launching out against companies who have no conscience"), are motivated by a desire to increase profits even by unscrupulous means ("I still feel that Lightolier has cheated me and is a dishonest company. Perhaps you feel that if you stall long enough I will lose interest, and you can increase your profits with my money. I am very tempted to talk to an attorney over the principle rather than the dollars; you have displayed a complete and utter lack of ethics and consumer interest"), practice deception ("mixing old and new hamburger to sell as fresh hamburger is pure fraud"; "it may be true that the average American is dumb enough to continue buying such shoddy workmanship and materials and that you are able to exploit such stupidity . . . but let me assure you that growing numbers of Americans are fed up with nearly worthless goods and are turning more and more to foreign goods in which one still sees a little pride in workmanship"), are not concerned about the welfare of the general public or even of their own customers ("there are too many [food companies] pushing ideas that haven't been tested properly or long enough"; "I was never contacted by your company, which leads me to believe that Kelvinator is not *really* interested in their customers"), and are granted too much protection and are subject to too little control ("it is appalling that the food industry is given such frightening freedom to slowly kill its customers").

Complainants differ in their views concerning not only business in general, but specifically big business. There are those who attribute greater good to and have higher expectations for larger companies. A West Orange, New Jersey, couple states, "It utterly amazes us that a company as big as Ford . . . does not care about or take steps to insure that the consuming public gets what it pays for." Many writers, however, have special contempt for big business. They refer to the "evils of big business," the "cheating going on in large chain drugstores," and the reprehensible manufacturing and sales practices of major drug companies. Various complainants describe the growth of monopolies among appliance service and parts companies and dairy cooperatives. These individuals realize that increase in size is an important trend in business, and they see it as a disturbing, even frightening, one.

Writing to the presidents of large industries, a few complainants demonstrate considerable deference and respect; they apologize for disturbing the addressee and may even add such pleasantries as "I hope this reaches you in good health and high spirits." Other people, however, address corporate executives on an informal basis. In a letter to William N. Austin, President of Gaffers & Sattler, Magic Chef, Inc., a woman describes the numerous problems she has had with her range over 6 years of ownership and then asks, "Tell me, Mr. Austin, would you buy a Gaffers and Sattler range for your wife or mother right now?"

Consumer complaint letters are rich in commentary on political and social conditions in the United States. Writers expound on a variety of topics that either form the substance of or bear some relation to their complaints. Medical writers decry the ineffectiveness, arbitrariness, and lack of communication characterizing government administration of health care, and particularly Medicare. Many food writers complain about the lack of protection afforded consumers by the Food and Drug Administration and the Department of Agriculture: "What is wrong with the Department of Health when they make no objection to the sale of [maraschino] cherries?" and "... it's a well-known fact that government agencies frequently work at cross purposes, even going so far as to seriously challenge one or more department's programs or intents." Another complainant reports:

> The U.S. Department of Agriculture in a letter dated April 15, 1969, stated "The Department of Agriculture has no control over the grade or quality of flour that is sold in food markets." If such is the case apparently it has no control over anything including weights and measures. If so, why do we have this Department at taxpayer's expense? Better it be disbanded.

A retired accountant living in Hughes Springs, Texas, attacks the quality and effectiveness of government consumer advocates:

> The consumer protection analyst that's on the President's staff is only interested in that job salary, travel allowances, and other fringe benefits that go with her office. Why does the President appoint politicians to such jobs? I once heard Betty Furness say on TV she had never purchased any groceries in a store. How would persons like these know how to protect the public? ...

Nearly all comments of a social nature revolve around economics and the American economic system. Complainants refer to "our highly competitive, buck-grabbing economy," and consider that "all too many of our people are willing to sell their very souls for a fast dollar." And a 61-year-old Dillon, Montana, resident contrasts the buying habits of the young with those of her own generation:

> There seems to be a whole generation of young people growing up who must have everything new that appears on the market. They don't keep things long enough to wear out but they must buy everything in sight. Some of us older people ... can remember working hard to have enough cash to buy something necessary and to cherish and take care of it because we knew what it cost us. The market is definitely appealing to the young customers and cash seems to be a dirty word any more. Surely this bubble must burst one day and there will be a rude awakening. ...

Inherent in most writers' conceptions of society is the idea of progress. Especially disappointing to these individuals, and figuring largely in a high proportion of complaints, thus, is the failure of business, professionals, and government to improve conditions. Writers feel that the nation is "getting nowhere faster and faster in our solution of the drug horror." They report a decline in the state of the goods and services about which they are writing, asserting that the new drugs are more expensive but not more effective than the "old and cheap" ones, that today's General Electric appliances possess neither the quality nor workmanship of the old ones, and that the quality of canned corn, peanut butter, ice cream, and pet foods has fallen. Some writers are haunted by a fear that conditions may have to worsen before they receive the attention needed to bring about their improvement (see also Nader and Beckerman 1978:10–17).

Concluding Remarks

The form and content of the approximately 2000 complaint letters sent weekly to Ralph Nader vary enormously, just as do the experiences and motives of the letter writers. Yet at some level and in some degree, virtually all these missives express a common theme—a loss of trust. Writers declare that they have lost faith in companies, their products, and their local representatives, as well as in professionals and government. They complain of fraud and dishonesty in business—of deceptive advertising and warranties; of false claims and assurances from companies, dealers, and service personnel; of evasive and dishonorable responses to complaints; and of dealer and repair company employees who do not divulge the truth for fear of jeopardizing their employment. They bemoan incompetent and dishonest professionals, especially doctors and lawyers. They lament disreputable behavior in government: corrupt officials; influential lobbying by powerful vested interests; suppression of basic rights by various government agencies; dereliction of duty by officials, departments, and administrations; and poorly conceived and ill-managed health and welfare programs.

Many writers, disappointed by organizations they had presumed to be concerned and responsible, question whether anyone has regard for their troubles: "I feel something should be done about this but no one seems interested"; "Who gives a damn? Does Con Edison care, or Delmonico, or Gimbels?" For the 300 letter writers sampled in this study, a consumer advocate often represents the only interested and knowledgeable recipient for their complaints, fears, and worries. They communicate their trust and appreciation in such words as the following: "I hope you let me know the truth"; "I am happy that someone cares somewhere who has the power to do something about it . . . I am happy you are aware of what is around us!"; and "I've been wanting to thank you for all you have done for us poor unsuspecting ones." These are people who have learned from experience the need for protection; they well recognize that our educational, political, and economic systems have done little to provide consumers with the knowledge and resources they need for self-reliant handling of their complaints.

May 8, 1979

Dear Sirs:

Enclosed is a copy of a letter that was sent to the Caloric Company to express our dissatisfaction with their product and service.

We feel that it is an absolute disgrace that we, the consumer, are defenseless in dealing with an organization such as this.

Yours truly,

April 11, 1979

Dear Mr. Nader:

Enclosed is a copy of a few random answers to a question of food avoidance. When so many people seem to want to avoid certain additives—chemicals, sugar, preservatives—<u>why</u> must we be forced to use foods containing these additives. That is, as an American housewife, I do use many fresh foods in season, but also buy occasional canned foods or packaged foods for variety and I realize now that I cannot take the time to read all the ingredients listed, nor do I understand the chemicals involved. Is anything being done to eliminate this constant use of hazardous additives in our food?

Very truly yours,

March 19, 1979

Dear Sir:

The enclosed carbon is being sent to you for information and such action or disposition as you may deem appropriate.

It refers to a complaint registered with the Penney Company against my washing machine, Penncrest label, which has required excessive repairs due to improper design and faulty manufacture and/or quality control. It is now about 25% through a normal expected life, but required extensive attention within the first two years of use, the cost of which was only partly borne by the Penney Company under Warranty. The operation of the washer is still not completely satisfactory, in spite of all the repairs.

Specifically, the filling and discharge pump was repaired four times in the first 15 months of light household use, and the casing of the washer began to rust _from the inside_ after about two years of similar use. The rusting area is continuing to spread, and the pump continues to leak.

I suggest that this information be made a part of your complaint file against the subject company. Additional details can be willingly furnished if required, promptly at your request. My basic intent is to protect other consumers from acquiring in good faith Penncrest products which may be faulty and for which the Company refuses to acknowledge responsibility, thereby placing the entire burden upon the consumer who has no knowledge of the fault at time of purchase, and no recourse after the expiration of the ridiculously short Warranty period.

Cordially,

Sample Letter L

January 14, 1980

Ralph Nader:

I write you for advice and assistance to solve my problem and help make the public aware of such activities as I am about to relate.

What has happened to us could easily happen to any average family that makes a purchase through their local auto dealership authorized by a corporation that provides a warranty as a purchase incentive.

In August, 1978, we considered this warranty a major portion of our decision to purchase a recreation vehicle involving a commitment of such expense. A "dream" vehicle; impressive to look at, cosmetically ideal—just like the brochure. Oh yes, it's warranted—nothing to worry about, any problems will be taken care of—it's a good warranty that implies specific defects will be made right.

What they don't tell you is how many trips to the garage will be necessary, how many trips to referrals to service depots, how many phone calls, taxi expenses due to lack of courtesy cars and the time loss inconveniences you are expected to tolerate. These are all required to get the company to perform this warranty work.

Our problems started at 2601 miles (see attachment) when it was discovered that drive shaft, wheel bearing, etc. work needed to be done. This meant going to the garage where it was purchased, only to be referred by them to a garage that "does their RV work for them". They don't tell you it will take from a week to nearly a month to get it repaired... or what will happen if the work is not done properly. You are at their mercy to trust the facility and labor performed. The public would, in general (myself in particular), believe in the dealer. However, you can see by the attached police report that the facility was

(continued)

totally irresponsible in the security of my vehicle. They left
the key in the ignition, vehicle unlocked and it became a prime
target for theft. A TV, CB radio, cookware and custom tailored
clothing with an appraised value of over $900.00 were stolen.
To date restitution has not been made. This facility submitted
warranty repair orders for specific labor. But there is no cost
identified. I do not know how much they were reimbursed for
warranty work done. Good or bad, someone had to pay for it.

I was not given a choice of where our vehicle would be
serviced—it had to be a special garage authorized to cover services under warranty. We bought from a local dealer trusting
his judgment in this department—after all, that's supposed to
be part of their way to establish and keep business. An authorized dealer is expected to be more reliable than "Honest Joe
Blow" from some used car lot. (Certified Customer Care?)

We are not rich businessmen, only a hard-working family and we
have to be responsible for our bills. We question the validity
of them when it is necessary. Doesn't the Chrysler Corporation
question theirs? The bank didn't care if we could use the vehicle or not, just as long as they got their $2228.94 interest
this year from us.

From the attachments (warranty repair orders) there is proof
of mechanical problems—severe ones—requiring repeated servicing of these items under warranty. Forty-four days worth.
Quite a record for a "dream vehicle", less than 100 miles on the
road for every day in the garage. If all this work was done
properly we would not have suffered expensive towing charges
(see attachment), and the mental anguish of being stranded for
three days in a town where there is no authorized dealer as well
as phone calls (long distance) to get direction from my dealer
and transportation for my family home. My dealer gave me a
number and name in Detroit, I called in desperation only to be
told to "stick it in my ear". For a call to the local Chrysler
Corporation representative in Dallas, I was told "Sorry,
buddy, it's your problem. Chrysler is not responsible!"

This vehicle was released from the garage indicating repairs
were completed and my vehicle safe for the road. I had no reason
to believe it would develope the same rear-end problem while

(continued)

parked undisturbed in my yard for four months. It is only 3.5 miles from the garage to my home.

My vehicle has been extremely well cared for. From the police report (attached) you can see that installation had been made of items to make this motor home the "home away from home" it was designed to be. This required personal time and much expense to make trips more enjoyable. Instead, our RV has made ill feeling between our local dealer and us; money for the insurance company; $2228.94 interest for the bank; I believe a warranty service "rip-off" for Chrysler Corporation; embarrassment to us to say "I don't know" when people ask us "Don't they stand behind their product?"; not to mention the expenses for towing (attached invoice); assistance in getting my family transported home on the holiday weekend and still having a disabled vehicle many miles from home and not knowing if it will be damaged if they tow it back (if the dealer authorizes it's return) or if I will be forced to pay storage fees at the lot where it is now parked—disabled; or be forced to pay expenses for the same work Chrysler Corporation thinks was done before— and paid for.

Needless to say, the thought of our "dream vehicle" puts fear in our hearts. We will be hesitant to use it—if we ever get it on the road under it's own power.

Our problems have been related to our local Better Business Bureau; a local TV studio is very interested and we have been asked of the possibility of the use of our experiences in a human-interest type story for a popular publication.

I believe that something must be done to provide the consumer with an avenue of protection and self defense that will enable one to protect himself against this sort of thing happening.

When a new vehicle (under warranty) is in the garage more than once for the same work (attachments—work repair orders), the Corporation that pays for this labor should be in communication to find out WHY? Is there a public relations representative or someone whose job it is to account for and follow-up on warranty services that I might contact in my efforts to protect myself and get restitution for my own expenses? I also want to

(continued)

Sample Letter L—Continued

publicize through as varied media methods as are available, what has happened to us and perhaps can prevent the same thing from happening to others.

I have attached copies of various personal records to verify my statements and will be glad to correspond with anyone that can help me or share a similar problem.

Any assistance you can render me will be deeply appreciated. I await your reply.

Regards,

attachments: Police Record
Repair Order—028—
Repair Order—046—
Repair Order—062—
Towing Invoice
Trouble Stop Invoice
Correspondence to Better Business Bureau

Sample Letter M

October 30, 1979

Dear Mr. Nader:

Why does everyone ignore the rip–offs the retired people are getting who live in mobile home parks, by the owners, cartels, and monopolies?

Why aren't there laws, federal, state and county governing M/H Park owners? Why are all the rules, requirements, penalties, and restrictions made by the park owners? Where has self–government gone??

Why aren't park owners required to keep the parks, drainage, sewerage, and roads in repair without a huge raise in rent? Why aren't there restrictions on dumping weed, brush and trash by the park that is a fire hazard?

Park owners get a profit; salesmen get a commission; we get cheap sinks, cheap faucets, knobs that you can't grip, windows that won't open, doors that won't close, gouged linoleum. Under warranty??? Yes, when you pay for it.

I have been flooded five times while living in this park. No NOT FROM HARD RAINS! From lack of drainage. My heater/air conditioner was ruined. $170.65 repairs from a man who claimed to have put in a new motor AND DIDN'T; he put in a 110 transformer instead of a 220 and didn't wire correctly. It burned out in a month.

I've had rotting fish and rotting vegetation. When I came here the salesmen told me the sewer pump directly in back of my place was just electrical equipment. I had sewer gas for months in my

(continued)

Sample Letter M—Continued

home——the park did absolutely nothing. I filed a complaint with the Sanitation Dept. and finally got a plywood cover over it.

Promises: contract read the streets would be cleaned. New contract omits street cleaning. Heated pool—lovely for arthritis——no longer heated. How long will it be before we have to mow our own lawns, pay water/sewer bills, & garbage collection? As soon as the park fills up with residents and it was no longer necessary to have attractive advertisements to lure people here.

These cartels don't even consider us human beings, just so much income to them. We move into parks for security reasons, companionship with those of our age and we can afford the rent if REASONABLE.

Is there no one interested in retired citizens, taxpayers and voters? The cry is to save the BOAT PEOPLE. Good. How about retired people? Will no one look into it?

Very truly,

References

Hirschman, Albert O.
  1970 *Exit, voice, and loyalty.* Cambridge, Mass.: Harvard University Press.
Nader, Laura, and S. Beckerman
  1978 Energy as it relates to the quality and style of life. *Annual Review of Energy* **3**:1–28.
Sayre, Jeanette
  1939 Progress in radio fan-mail analysis. *Public Opinion Quarterly* **3**(2):272–278.
Sussmann, Leila
  1963 *Dear FDR: A study of political letter-writing.* New Jersey: Bedminster Press.
U.S. Bureau of the Census
  1977 *Statistical abstract of the United States,* 98th ed. Washington, D.C.: U.S. Government Printing Office.
Wyant, Rowena
  1941 Voting via the Senate mailbag I. *Public Opinion Quarterly* **5**(3):359–382.
Wyant, Rowena, and H. Herzog
  1941 Voting via the Senate mailbag II. *Public Opinion Quarterly* **5**(4):590–624.

4

Penny Addiss

THE LIFE HISTORY COMPLAINT CASE OF MARTHA AND GEORGE ROSE:[1] "Honoring the Warranty"

Introduction

One of the approaches to understanding the consumer complaint process is to follow in depth the course of specific consumer grievances from the complainant's point of view. The life history approach to studying complaint management (Langness 1965) was selected for the concrete, specific, in-depth, and contextual data about the complaint process that it provides, allowing us to analyze and contrast different decisions, styles, and strategies that consumers have chosen in complaining.

Although every consumer complaint case is, in some respects, unique, by using the life history approach to gather intensive data on the complaint process, we were able to see significant patterns and issues common to voicing complaints in America in the 1970s. "Honoring the Warranty" is an example of the case method approach to the ethnography of conflict resolution and dispute settlement that has a long history in anthropology (Nader, Koch, and Cox 1966; Collier 1975).

In this chapter we describe and analyze how and why Martha and George Rose, who considered themselves an average, middle-class suburban family, chose to do something about a complaint. Their efforts to remedy a grievance illustrate the costs and benefits of engaging in the consumer complaint process in our society.

Like other complainants who make the decision to complain, something in the Roses' interaction with the complainee triggered their anger and made them determined to pursue their grievance with third-party

[1]Martha and George Rose are pseudonyms.

NO ACCESS TO LAW
Alternatives to the American Judicial System

remedy agents. The complainants' sense of outrage and injustice is often validated and encouraged by friends, colleagues, and even supervisors who empathize with and may urge them to complain. In the process of complaining, consumers like the Roses, who have not "voiced" a complaint before, go through a series of expectations regarding the outcome of their dispute. It is not unusual for complainants to believe at first that their claim is self-evident and that once they state their case, their problem will be resolved without further delay. Most first-time complainants do not keep copies of their initial round of complaint letters, for example. Nor is it unusual for consumers who have invested heavily in their complaint, like the Roses, to believe they will get action from the top that will serve not only to resolve their grievances but also to modify the company's complaint-handling policy with other customers. Complainants who do not resolve their first complaint and yet go on to complain about a second, though unrelated, grievance invariably believe, nonetheless, that they made a mark in the first instance—that by pursuing that first grievance they made a difference and that the party they complained against will be more responsive to other consumers' complaints in the future.

In "Honoring the Warranty" we see General Motors applying the "no job." This is a common tactic that large-scale organizations use to forestall consumer "voicing" (Nader 1978: see pp. 93–94). No negotiation is offered the complainants, who are often confused and defused by the varying explanations (the "Rashomon approach") given by the different respondents who deny their claim. Martha and George Rose, like most consumers, never knew who in the Chevrolet complaint-handling system had authority over their case. Their strategies in complaining, then, were sometimes misguided, for they had no map with which to navigate their way effectively through the bureaucratic and impersonal maze of multiple Chevrolet Customer Service personnel. Moreover, once the local Chevrolet office had made a decision on the grievance, there was no disinterested person or board within the company to whom the Roses could appeal to review the validity of their case.

Before we began our study, we wondered how consumer complainants chose which third-party remedy agents to complain to. Was it critical whether the remedy agents were private or public? From the life histories of consumer complaints, we found that complainants selected their remedy agents on the basis of the size, power, and location of the party complained against. The Roses, for example, believed that only nationally based third parties had sufficient "clout" to intercede on their behalf with General Motors; they, therefore, ignored their local remedy agents. They also, like many other consumers who see themselves as the "little guy," rejected the alternative of retaining an attorney to file suit because, as they stated, they did not believe they could win in court against big business, an indictment which strikes at the roots of the American system of justice.

The objective of our study of the consumer complaint process as exemplified in "Honoring the Warranty," was to explore and delineate the incentives and constraints, the perceptions, strategies, and choices that lead consumers to pursue a grievance and "voice" a complaint to third-party remedy agents. Hirschman (1970), in his provocative analysis of the "voice" and "exit" options in the marketplace, finds that "voicing" is considerably more costly in time, effort, aggravation, and perhaps even money, than "exiting" or "lumping it." He therefore suggests that "voicing" will be the exception rather than the rule. How is it, we ask, that Martha and George Rose, and others like them, are willing to assume the costs of "voicing?" What benefits do they derive from "voicing" that offset such costs? Under what circumstances will the costs of "voicing" turn into benefits? The rationale in each case may be different. With the Rose family, for instance, the financial burden of replacing the engine of their car, the injury to their self-esteem, and their moral indignation at their treatment by Chevrolet provoked and sustained their determination over a period of 20 months to "voice" initially to Chevrolet and then, when faced with Chevrolet's intransigence, to third-party remedy agents. Complainants, we found, without exception, experience "voicing" as a recuperative mechanism against feelings of powerlessness or ennui.

A Case Analysis

On the morning of 23 January 1974, Martha Rose was driving the family 1970 Chevrolet station wagon to work as usual when the engine began missing. By the time she reached the office, a 6-mile drive from the Rose home in suburban Jackson, Mississippi, white smoke was pouring out of the tail pipe. Martha immediately asked a mechanic who worked for the firm and who had arrived the same time as she that morning to take a look at the car. He later testified that the temperature light on the dashboard "was not burning" and the radiator under the hood "was not boiling over" at the time. But the excessive white smoke coming out of the exhaust suggested to him that the trouble "could be a cracked head or a blowed head gasket."

In the office that morning, amid her secretarial chores, Martha tried to contact her husband. George Rose was the district product service manager for General Electric products in the Mississippi area, a job of which he was proud. He handled consumer complaints on GE products and dispatched 11 service trucks to make home and commercial repairs on large appliances. Martha Rose was anxious to ask her husband what she should do about the car. But George Rose was out of his office that morning. Unable to reach him by lunchtime, Martha decided to go ahead and take the car over to the independent garage where George always had his GE trucks serviced. The owner was a well-known and trusted mechanic, and the independent shop was closer to her workplace than the Chevrolet dealer in downtown Jackson.

In the independent repair shop, the car was torn down to diagnose the problem. "Pressure was pumped up on the cooling system and water came out of one cylinder. The cylinder head was removed and the block was found with a hairline crack." For the second time that day, the radiator was checked and was found to be in "satisfactory condition" with no evidence of overheating.

A cracked cylinder block meant that the car would need a new engine. This would be a major and extensive repair and, the Roses anticipated, a large expense. But they had driven their 4-year-old car less than 50,000 miles (49,169 to be exact), and so it was still under the 5-year or 50,000-mile warranty, in effect until either the stated time or mileage had been reached.

Martha Rose looked up the terms of the warranty:

> Chevrolet (Chevrolet Motor Division, General Motors Corporation) warrants to the original retail purchaser that it will repair or replace, at its option, any parts of each new 1970 Chevrolet passenger car vehicle and chassis, including all equipment and accessories thereon (except tires) manufactured or supplied by Chevrolet which are returned to an authorized Chevrolet dealer at his place of business and which examination discloses to Chevrolet's reasonable satisfaction to be defective in material or workmanship under normal use and service. Such repairs and replacements shall be performed by such dealer without charge.

The Roses concluded that the new engine block their car required would be covered under the warranty and that Chevrolet would bear the cost of both parts and labor.

The next day George Rose called the independent garage owner to tell him to leave the car as it was, with the engine disassembled. He then spoke to the service manager at the local Chevrolet dealer and explained to him what had happened. Rose arranged with the service manager to have the car towed into the dealership later in the week.

A Chevrolet dealer is allowed only to repair and replace individual parts on cars under warranty without notifying Chevrolet. Replaced assemblies and extensive paint jobs require the authorization of a Chevrolet representative. As the Rose car needed a new engine assembly, the local dealer could not install the block without explicit permission from the Chevrolet area service manager, a field representative who deals with warranty problems and consumer complaints that the 20–25 dealers in his assigned area cannot handle. So the Roses had to wait until the local field rep next visited their Jackson dealership, while on his thrice-monthly round of northern Mississippi dealers, before warranty work on the car could begin.

The Rose car had been sitting at the dealership for nearly a week when the Chevrolet area service manager arrived. The Rose family was there to present their case. They watched as the field rep and the dealer's special "heating" mechanic looked under the hood. The area service manager was critical of the fact that the car had been torn down at the independent repair shop. It is more difficult to locate the cause of a problem when an engine has been disassembled earlier by someone else. But it took the field rep and the mechanic only a few minutes to size up the trouble and reach a conclusion.

The thermostat had stuck shut, they maintained, so that no coolant reached the cylinder walls as Martha Rose drove to work on 23 January. The intense heat that accumulated in the engine caused the head gasket to blow and a cylinder wall to crack. Water then got into the fuel line, which caused white smoke to pour out of the exhaust. All this damage, the mechanic explained, could have occurred that morning if the car had been driven as little as one-fourth of a mile after it began missing.

The Rose family, on buying their car, had received a 5-year/50,000-mile warranty on the engine. But the thermostat was guaranteed for only 12 months/12,000 miles, as it was for all Chevrolet models. As it was a faulty thermostat that had caused the engine to overheat and as Martha Rose had continued driving the car after the engine trouble began, Chevrolet denied responsibility under the warranty. The Roses, reported the field rep, would have to bear the cost of replacing the cylinder block and parts themselves.

Martha and George Rose were stunned by the news. They could not accept the field rep's decision. The car was not excessively hot, they contested. Two mechanics had checked out the radiator the day of the engine trouble, and each of them had asserted there was no evidence of overheating. The Roses argued instead that the block was inherently defective. "That was why it cracked. The engine looked like new. If we hadn't taken such good care of the car," they said, "the cylinder wall would have given way long before now."

In our interview, the Roses referred to themselves as "an average American family." Both Martha and George had grown up in the South. They were high school graduates, and they had worked hard to get where they were. George was a loyal "company man" with 15 years' service with GE. Martha was a secretary with a local business firm. They were responsible and good credit risks. They lived in a well-known and dignified suburb. They had two children, a boy and a girl. George was a Jaycee, and Martha belonged to the garden club. They displayed an upwardly mobile life-style. They spent what they earned each month. There was a second mortgage on their house. They voted in the last national and municipal elections. Martha and George considered themselves "moderate to conservative." They attended PTA meetings. They were regular churchgoers. And they cared about what others thought of them.

Perhaps only in one significant way did they differ from other American suburban families in the income range of $15,000. That was that the Rose family had only one car between them, the 1970 Chevrolet station wagon, which they had just finished paying off.

The Roses had never pursued a complaint before. But the Chevrolet area service manager's report provoked their anger and determination. They believed his decision was hasty, arbitrary, and inaccurate. The car was still under warranty and needed a new engine. It was only "fair justice" that Chevrolet should "honor the warranty" and replace the block assembly.

George Rose reacted immediately. He asked to use the dealer's phone and placed a call to the Chevrolet zone office in New Orleans. The Chevrolet owner relations manager in New Orleans listened to the Roses' complaint, spoke briefly with the field rep at the dealer's, and then told George Rose that he could not help him. "The field rep's word was final."

Rose did not accept that. He persisted. Who in Detroit could he call? The New Orleans office gave him the number of Customer Service at the central office. George then phoned Detroit. He finally reached two complaint-handling specialists who gave him inconclusive and equivocal replies.

Rose called back to New Orleans. This time he asked to speak to the fleet manager who handled complaints on Chevrolet trucks. Although only 1 out of the 11 GE service trucks George managed was a Chevrolet, he hoped this fact might give him some leverage with the Chevrolet office. The fleet manager responded that he "would look into the matter" and that, Rose reported to us, "was the end of it."

George then tried one notch higher in the Chevrolet organizational hierarchy. He called New Orleans for the third time that day and spoke with the assistant zone service manager, who was the field rep's boss and the number two man in the office. The assistant manager said, Rose recalled, that he would talk it over with the field representative. He suggested that the owner had some "obligations" on a car driven nearly 50,000 miles, and he promised that he would be back in touch.

So the Roses left the Chevrolet dealership that afternoon upset and dissatisfied, but hopeful that some accommodation would be forthcoming from Chevrolet. For George Rose, a complaint manager for GE, believed in "concession as a goodwill gesture toward a dissatisfied customer—even when the customer is in the wrong." He therefore interpreted his conversation with the assistant zone service manager in the light of this policy and anticipated that Chevrolet would make him an accommodating offer. He was prepared, he later admitted to us, to pay for the labor (approximately one-third of the repair bill) if Chevrolet would take care of the parts.

The very next day, however, George was bitterly disappointed. The field representative who had inspected the car returned the call on behalf of his boss and reiterated his stand that Chevrolet had "no obligation" under the circumstances. He offered the Roses no concessions whatever. The Chevrolet zone office thus closed off any possibilities for negotiation. George Rose recognized in the field rep's tone of voice the finality of his decision. He realized there was no point in contacting New Orleans again. So he tried another tack. He dropped by an attorney's office to consult him about the costs of suing Chevrolet. George told Martha that evening what the lawyer's fees would be: $125 to write letters to Chevrolet, one-third of the damages won if their case went to court, and one-half the amount awarded if the case were tried before a jury. Martha's response was adamant. The attorney was "too expensive," and they "wouldn't have a chance in court against a big corporation like General Motors."

Martha preferred to proceed another way—to offer Chevrolet a carrot rather than a stick. Instead of pursuing the complaint through an attorney and threatening a lawsuit, Martha Rose decided to write F. James McDonald, general manager of Chevrolet, a "firm but nice" complaint letter. She was convinced that she was in the right and that McDonald would "right the wrong" and "uphold the warranty" when he knew the problem. So on 6 February, the day after the New Orleans office confirmed its stand that Chevrolet had "no obligations" under the warranty, Martha Rose wrote her first complaint letter.

Martha did not bother to make a carbon copy of her typewritten letter. She was certain that once McDonald received the letter, he would review their case and reverse the zone office's decision. In fact, Martha Rose expected to receive in reply from McDonald both an apology for the trouble Chevrolet had caused them and reimbursement for the costs of replacing their engine.

She was so certain of a settlement that, at the same time she wrote McDonald in Detroit, she told the service manager at the local dealership to repair the car. The Roses had been without their car for 15 days by then. Martha had to get back and forth from work, the kids needed to be taken here and there after school, there were errands to run, marketing to do, and so forth. It was no longer feasible for George to chauffeur the family in the GE truck he used, which was his for business purposes only. So the Roses had decided to have the dealer install a new engine, pay the bill themselves, and assume that Detroit would reimburse them for repairs.

They perceived that they had no alternative. Martha's brother was a used-car dealer in Memphis, and she understood from him the loss they would face in trading in the station wagon. The car had cost them nearly $5000, which they had finished paying off just a few months ago. Its wholesale value was now $1100. And, as it was, without an engine, the car was worth only $600. A new car, even on a trade-in, would cost them considerably more than repairing the old. It would strain the family finances even further, and Martha was already working to help make ends meet and their comfortable life-style possible. Living as they did from paycheck to paycheck, how far could they stretch themselves?

There was no way, the Roses realized, they could afford to trade in their station wagon. Although it meant they would have to borrow again from the bank to meet the $680 repair bill, that seemed to be their only viable course of action. So they had their car repaired at their own expense and pinned their hopes for compensation on F. James McDonald.

However, George Rose anticipated that it might not be easy to convince McDonald of the validity of their claim. George, we remember, had already spoken with five different Chevrolet complaint managers from New Orleans and Detroit, each of whom had either equivocated or refused to "honor the warranty." So when he went in to pick up the car at the dealer's, Rose collected the old parts that had been replaced. He saved these parts in a box in the garage at home to hold as evidence in furthering their case against Chevrolet. What the Roses did not realize, apparently, was that if the dealer had thought there was any chance that Chevrolet would reverse their position and replace the engine under the warranty, the dealership itself would have kept the replaced parts to turn in to the Chevrolet office, if so requested, for inspection and review.

A week after the car was repaired, the Roses received two letters from Chevrolet in response to their complaint. The Rose letter to McDonald had been passed along to Chevrolet Customer Service to be handled routinely. A central office staff member, probably a young trainee in the Chevrolet Owner Relations Management Program, contacted the appropriate zone office in New Orleans, informed its staff of the complaint received in Detroit, and then replied to the complainants, the Roses:

> Naturally we are concerned when an owner expresses any degree of dissatisfaction with our product. For this reason we are apprising the management of our New Orleans office of your comments since they have the authority and responsibility for Chevrolet in your area.
>
> (Reply from Detroit, 15 February)

The New Orleans owner relations manager also responded in writing to the Roses. His blunt letter pulled no punches but also offered no explanations:

*We have investigated this engine failure thoroughly with both our Area
Service Manager, Mr. J. D. Hall, and Mr. Tom Desper, Service Manager at
Herrin-Gear Chevrolet. The result of the investigation again clearly indicates that Chevrolet has no outstanding obligations, and we see no reason to
alter our decision.*

(Reply from New Orleans, 15 February)

So the Roses found themselves full circle. Their grievance had gone
through the usual channels, with no results.

The Chevrolet complaint process, like those of other motor companies and large national corporations, basically *withholds* any meaningful appeal process from the complainant. The consumer who is dissatisfied with an area office's decision regarding a grievance may write to the
central office, but the central office only sends the complaint back to the
area office for handling. There is *no independent and impartial person or
judiciary board within the organization* who might reassess the customer's complaint and field rep's evaluation of its validity.

In the Chevrolet system at present, the assistant zone service manager
is the number two man in the zone office. He is the immediate supervisor
of the local field representatives and may review a field rep's decision as a
matter of course. But it is in the *vested interest* of the supervisor to confirm, rather than to reverse, the judgment of his representative in a disputed case. This is so both because, holding a managerial position, he
may not have the technical expertise with which to challenge the field
rep's firsthand diagnosis of the problem and also because, being an organization man, he values company loyalty and staff morale over the
outcome of a particular complaint case. He is constrained, therefore, from
reversing a field rep's decision by the priority he gives to maintaining
trust and good relations with his representatives in the field.

The two letters the Roses received in reply from Chevrolet were the
"last straw." At this point, the Roses began discussing their grievance
with others in earnest. Martha, for example, complained to her boss, to the
staff at work, and to the neighbors. We recall that she had consulted two
mechanics—one a mechanic in her company and the other an owner of an
independent repair shop—on the day of the engine trouble, 23 January.
She now asked each of them to write out statements attesting to the
condition of the car at the time they inspected it.

George Rose, meanwhile, talked about their problem with the people
in his office, with his boss, with his colleagues in the GE offices in
Shreveport and Little Rock, and with the GE attorney in the zone office in
Memphis. The company lawyer urged him to complain but specified that
GE employees were not permitted to use their company affiliation in any
way. George's supervisor later clipped and sent to the Roses an interview

with F. James McDonald in which the Chevrolet general manager lauded Chevrolet's service and warranty program. The irony of McDonald's praise for Chevrolet's customer service compared with their own personal experience did not escape the Roses.

The friends, neighbors, mechanics, and colleagues whom Martha and George consulted commiserated with them. They related anecdotes of their own "bad luck" with cars. But they were unable to offer the Roses any specific recommendations on how to resolve their problem beyond urging them to complain.

Then, shortly after the new engine was installed, the station wagon began leaking antifreeze. The Roses took the car back to the Jackson dealership for repairs. After trying twice to plug the leak without success, the dealer replaced the water pump "with no questions and at no charge" under the warranty. The dealer did not know it, but he had added "fuel to the fire" as far as the Roses were concerned. On the one hand, Chevrolet had refused liability under the warranty for replacing the cracked cylinder block. Yet now, on the other hand, the dealer, under the same warranty, assumed responsibility for replacing the faulty water pump. If the warranty covered the water pump in February, why did it not cover the engine in January? What made the two cases different?

It is possible that if the dealer had not replaced the water pump under the warranty at that particular juncture, the Roses might have dropped their complaint against Chevrolet out of frustration and discouragement. The letters they had received from Detroit and New Orleans certainly made the successful resolution of their case appear hopeless. But the dealer's action in "honoring the warranty" with regard to the water pump reinforced their argument—that the warranty was still valid—and rekindled their anger at Chevrolet's denial of responsibility for replacing the engine.

Martha Rose was particularly indignant at their treatment by Chevrolet. She and George talked it over, and Martha decided to insist on "voicing" their grievance. She now had what she thought were two persuasive arguments with which to bolster her case against General Motors. She had the written statements of the two independent mechanics asserting that the car had not overheated. And she had the recent example of the dealer replacing the water pump under the warranty. Urged on by friends and colleagues, Martha resolved to pursue the complaint further.

So on 23 February, Martha Rose wrote a second complaint letter to Detroit. She enclosed copies of the two mechanics' statements, and she quoted extensively from the Chevrolet warranty, adding that it seemed to her that replacing the defective water pump indicated:

> ... that the warranty is in effect good and that it covers parts mentioned under the five year/50,000 mile clause. My question is why did it not cover

the defective block, when in the warranty clause both parts are listed in the same sentence and I quote: "Vehicle's power train components are: cylinder block, head, all internal engine parts, water pump and intake manifold."

(Rose complaint letter, 23 February)

What is notable about this letter is the tone of righteous indignation that pervades it. Moreover, in each of her subsequent complaint letters, whether addressed to Chevrolet or to third-party remedy agents, Martha continued to express her moral outrage. For she did not stop with her second letter to Detroit. Martha Rose also "voiced" to third-party remedy agents, appealing to them to use their "clout" and intercede on her behalf with General Motors.

She complained, for example:

I am extremely dissatisfied with the cold and unconcerned way that my problem was handled.

(second complaint letter to Detroit)

It takes all both my husband and I make to live, raise two children and pay taxes. I can't really afford a lawsuit with a large company like General Motors, but a person has to stand up against any odds when he knows he has been used.

(complaint letter to Ralph Nader)

Four years ago, I too was one of those new customers, who, after years of buying Ford, was swayed to General Motors after reading the service and warranty claims made at that time. Little did I know then that if I had a legitimate complaint it would be totally disregarded and shuffled off from one complaint desk to another and then completely ignored as "not the responsibility of General Motors."

(third complaint letter to Detroit)

Never before have I taken steps of this magnitude in proclaiming my rights as a consumer. I am not a crack pot who has nothing better to do than write letters. Nor am I one who lies or tries to defraud. I am, however, a hardworking mother of two children who believes in equal rights and fair justice. The only fair justice being that the responsibility be placed on General Motors.

(complaint letter to Sen. Eastland)

Martha knew of Ralph Nader whom, she believed, had had similar problems with General Motors and had "won." She also had heard of Virginia Knauer's Office of Consumer Affairs in Washington, D.C., which, she assumed, had the authority as a federal agency to order a full review of her case with Chevrolet. She hoped, too, that the powerful senior senator from Mississippi, James Eastland, would lend the weight of his office to support a constituent's claim against General Motors. So once she had obtained the addresses of Ralph Nader, Virginia Knauer, and Senator Eastland, Martha sent them each letters, requesting their help in her case, along with copies of the warranty, the repair order, the mechanics' statements, and all information pertinent to the complaint.

Consumer advocate Ralph Nader, however, does not intervene on the part of individual complainants. Nor does the Federal Office of Consumer Affairs have the "clout" Martha so wishfully ascribed to it of being able to demand a reassessment of a disputed consumer grievance. Virginia Knauer merely forwarded to Chevrolet—with an accompanying letter— the Roses' complaint, claiming that her office has no jurisdiction, unless a law has been violated, except to "bring consumer complaints to the industry involved and ask for equitable handling." Senator Eastland referred Martha's complaint letter to Chevrolet's special congressional liaison office. But he, too, received in acknowledgment only a reiteration of Chevrolet's official position on the case. Chevrolet once more replied to the Roses with letters from Detroit and New Orleans refusing to review the complaint or alter their stance.

Martha tried again. This time she sent an angry registered letter to F. James McDonald enclosing the interview article, received from George's boss, in which McDonald extolled Chevrolet's service and warranty policy. Martha anticipated that McDonald himself would read this letter and would be "stunned" into taking three actions: calling Customer Service to account in this case, reviewing and reversing the original decision, and revamping the Chevrolet complaint-handling process. For all her trouble, however, Martha Rose received just one more public relations letter from Chevrolet Customer Service in Detroit to put into her complaint file.

In the 4-month period, then, that elapsed between the time the engine trouble occurred and the time of our interview, the Roses, we observe, passed through five successive *stages of expectation* regarding the outcome of their grievance.

In the first stage, extending from the morning when the engine began missing to the afternoon a week later, when the Chevrolet field representative inspected the car, the Roses expected *no problem*. They believed that the warranty would be honored and the repair bill covered. All they had to do, they thought, was to bring in the car to the dealership and wait for the field rep to authorize the warranty work. They were dumbfounded when the field representative denied Chevrolet's liability.

In the second stage, which lasted only two days—from George's conversation with the assistant zone service manager in New Orleans to the field rep's call back on the following day—the Roses expected *an accommodation*. They believed that the number two man in the zone office would make a deal with them, allowing both sides to the complaint to save face and feel vindicated. George, we remember, was prepared to pay for the labor if Chevrolet would take care of the parts on the new engine. When the field representative called back the next day on behalf of his boss, however, the Roses realized that no concessions would be forthcoming.

In the third stage, when Martha Rose wrote her second letter to Detroit and appealed to third-party remedy agents for help, the Roses expected *a review and reimbursement* of their claim. Martha's letters were written in the hope that, on reviewing their case, Detroit would find the field rep's decision "hasty" and that Chevrolet would then reimburse them the full amount of the repairs—with an apology.

In the fourth stage, initiated by Martha's registered letter to McDonald, the Roses expected *action from the top*. They thought McDonald would personally sign for and read the complaint letter, which would propel him to "take action" immediately. Martha Rose had no doubt whatever that once he heard about it, McDonald would "do something" about the case and "revamp the Chevrolet complaint program" in the process.

In the fifth stage, from the time Martha received Detroit's last public relations letter to the time of our interview, the Roses felt they had reached *a dead end*. They had received no positive feedback from Chevrolet or from remedy agents that either encouraged them to pursue their grievance or brought them any closer to resolving the problem. They were disillusioned and defeated in the face of Chevrolet's intransigence.

Chevrolet had given the Roses what has been called the "no job," mediated through a consumer complaint-handling program that seemed to the Roses designed primarily for public relations purposes. To each phone call they placed or complaint letter they wrote to Chevrolet, George and Martha received a courteous, processed reply by a different Chevrolet Customer Service correspondent. Clearly there was no one person responsible and accountable for the Rose file—no one person with whom the Roses could maintain contact to find out exactly why Chevrolet had denied their claim. At no time did Chevrolet's response reassess, reconsider, or modify in any way the company's original position: no engine replacement under the warranty. Despite George and Martha's efforts and expectations, Chevrolet refused to negotiate with the Roses over their complaint.

Under what conditions will a manufacturer honor its warranty on a product? According to an attorney specializing in auto warranty problems at the Federal Trade Commission, there are four circumstances under which auto manufacturers revoke their obligations under the warranty. They are: when repairs are made that are not explicitly covered in the warranty, when repairs are necessitated by improper maintenance, when repairs are performed in an independent repair shop (by nonauthorized mechanics), and when repairs are attributable to owner negligence or abuse.

There are interesting facets to Chevrolet's "no job" in refusing to honor the warranty in the case of the Roses' claim. First of all, the local dealership and Chevrolet personnel who were involved in the case each offered a different explanation for the problem and Chevrolet's denial of responsibility. When I interviewed the mechanic who had examined the car, the service manager at the dealership, the Chevrolet area service manager in New Orleans, and his boss—the number two man at the zone office—it was like watching the movie *Rashomon*, in which each person presents a different interpretation of an event.

The dealer's special "heating" mechanic, for example, who inspected the car with the field rep, declared that the problem was due to a freakish accident. The thermostat had stuck shut, causing the engine to overheat and the cylinder block to crack; there was nothing the owner could have done to have anticipated this. The service manager at the dealership, however, stated that the trouble occurred because of improper maintenance of the cooling system. The thermostat should have been replaced every 24,000 miles. This the Roses had not done. The field rep argued that the car had been torn down at an independent garage and was worked on by nonauthorized mechanics. The assistant zone service manager placed the blame squarely on owner negligence and abuse. He insisted that Martha Rose had continued to drive the car after the temperature gauge on the dashboard indicated that the engine was overheated, notwithstanding Martha's testimony to the contrary.

The Roses could have presented a stronger case to Chevrolet in two ways. They could have substantiated their claim by taking the replaced thermostat and engine to be checked at a diagnostic center in order to determine whether or not the thermostat had indeed stuck shut and whether or not there was in fact a hairline crack on the cylinder wall, necessitating the expensive repairs the dealer made on the car. Then, too, Martha and George could have submitted their maintenance records on the station wagon over the past 4 years and argued that if the engine had overheated, the trouble was caused by faulty parts or service—to a bad head gasket blowing or to improperly torqued head bolts—and that the dealer's service department had never suggested replacing the thermostat.

As it was, the Roses' denial that the thermostat had stuck shut and that the engine had overheated was weak, and their contention that the cylinder block was inherently defective was misguided. But if they had demonstrated that their car had been maintained regularly and exclusively by Chevrolet dealers and that, for example, the head gasket was faulty and had blown, causing, in turn, the engine to overheat as Martha Rose drove to work that morning in January, then they might have made and put forward a case for their claim as viable and as cogent as Chevrolet's case against them.

In any event, despite the phone calls and letter-writing strategies that George and Martha Rose pursued, it seems clear that their case was doomed to fail, regardless of the extent to which their complaint was justified. For the Roses were appealing to the wrong people in the Chevrolet organization to resolve their grievance.

The key person in the Chevrolet complaint process, who makes policy decisions as to whether or not the warranty applies in any particular case, is the area service manager—the field rep. (His equivalent in the GE complaint process would be the GE district product service manager, the position which George Rose held in Jackson, Mississippi.) The field representative is the crucial person for consumers to convince that their complaint is valid, their claim has merit, and their case is worth considering. The Roses, however, did not voluntarily contact the area service manager either before or after the decision was made on their car. Their appeals to other Chevrolet personnel were largely futile.

The owner relations manager, whom George Rose phoned to protest the field representative's decision, is an equal to, and the office counterpart of, the area service manager. He therefore does not have the authority to countermand the area service manager's on-site decision in the field. His job is to listen to complaints, assuage complainants, open and close "Owner Relations Reports," and handle the administrative details of the complaint process in the zone office.

George Rose's call requesting the local Chevrolet fleet manager to intercede in the case was an interesting gambit. One wonders if the fleet manager would have intervened on his behalf if the GE district office in Jackson had owned or leased more than 1 Chevrolet truck out of a fleet of 11.

George's phone call to the assistant zone service manager, the number two man in the zone office, was the single contact the Roses made with Chevrolet that might have influenced their case. The assistant zone service manager reviews complaint cases and can ask the area service manager to reassess his decision regarding a disputed claim. The field representative did so in the Rose case without, however, taking another look at the car or at the replaced parts that Martha and George had saved. His supervisor, the assistant zone service manager, did not challenge or override his decision.

Finally, the letters that the Roses wrote to Detroit expecting that the Chevrolet central office would "do something" were essentially useless. Despite George's position with GE, the Roses did not understand the decentralized structure of the Chevrolet complaint-handling system, in which authority to settle grievances lies with the zone offices.

The Roses continued to contact other remedy agents, some of whom were suggested to them in the course of our interview. For nearly 2 years, in fact, whenever they heard of an appropriate remedy agent to whom they might appeal, the Roses "voiced" a complaint. They complained to as many third parties as they believed might possibly be helpful in resolving their complaint.

There were, however, avenues of redress that Martha and George did not pursue. They chose not to proceed with hiring an attorney to file suit against General Motors on account of the expense. Like numerous consumer complainants in our study, the Roses threatened but then hesitated to go to court against a large corporation because they believed they could not win—that litigation between "the average guy" and "big business" is decided on the basis of power rather than of justice. They dared not risk incurring legal fees.

Another recourse the Roses considered but rejected was to take out a full-page newspaper ad explaining their grievance and expressing their dissatisfaction with Chevrolet. They thought that bad publicity might both shame and stimulate General Motors to respond to their claim and negotiate with them over it. But once more the Roses stopped short of following through on this action because of the expense involved.

Other third parties of which George and Martha Rose were aware, but to whom they did not complain, were local remedy agents, such as the Better Business Bureau of Jackson, Mississippi. Here, again, the Roses provided us with an example of an approach to complaint "voicing" shared by many other consumers in our study. Complainants, we found, often select remedy agents on the basis of such rational considerations as the *size, power,* and *location* of the party complained against. We would classify this as the *selective approach* to consumer complaining. The Roses chose to appeal to nationally known remedy agents (Ralph Nader, Virginia Knauer's Office of Consumer Affairs, and Senator Eastland's office) operating out of the nation's capital, Washington, D.C. These were the third parties they initially believed had the "clout" to make Chevrolet review and modify the original decision on the case.

Concluding Remarks

We might well ask why the Roses, whom we have described as an average, middle-class American family who had never proceeded with a formal complaint before, chose to "voice," given the apparent futility of their complaining. For neither by their own efforts nor through the intercession of third parties were the Roses able to win either financial restitution or psychological satisfaction from Chevrolet before, disheartened at last, they gave up trying.

In his book, *Exit, Voice, and Loyalty,* A. O. Hirschman (1970) discussed "voice" and "exit" as viable options in the marketplace. He describes at least three circumstances that apply in the Rose case in which "voice will be preferred to exit." First, dissatisfied consumers will "voice," he states, when the "exit" option is unavailable. The Roses were stuck with their 4-year-old station wagon, we saw, for replacing the car would have cost them far more than repairing it.

Second, Hirschman notes, the decision to "voice" will be taken if there is a "reasoned expectation" that the performance of the organization is remediable "provided the attention of management is sufficiently focused on the task." The Roses, we observed, contacted the management of the local zone office, Customer Service in Detroit, and even F. James McDonald, the general manager of the company, believing that their complaint would be resolved "from within" once Chevrolet was made aware of the problem.

Third, Hirschman points out that customers will "voice" when their estimate of their ability to influence the party complained against convinces them that "voicing" will be effective. The Roses assumed that they could turn Chevrolet around, appealing initially to the "justice" of their claim and relying later on the "clout" of selected remedy agents intervening on their behalf.

The question that engages us at this point is how we account for the Roses' determination and persistence in "voicing" their complaint to the limit of the means they perceived at their disposal. Why, in the face of Chevrolet's "no job," did Martha and George deem bearing the costs in time, effort, and energy of repeated "voicing" preferable to "lumping it" or "exiting"? What motivated and sustained their exhaustive quest over 20 months to persuade Chevrolet to "honor the warranty"?

For one thing, the Roses were faced with a bill for $680 in unanticipated repairs on a car they had just paid off after nearly 4 years of monthly installments. Replacing the engine was a shock and a strain to their finances. They did not have a sufficient cash flow or bank balance to meet the new expense. We recall that they had to borrow money from the bank, taking out yet another loan, in order to pay the repair bill. This unexpected expense meant cutting back on the family budget—buying fewer clothes, eating less meat, cancelling a planned vacation trip, driving the station wagon a year longer. It was obviously to their own financial benefit for the Roses to persevere in trying to persuade Chevrolet to "honor the warranty."

For another, Martha and George experienced Chevrolet's "cold and unconcerned way" of handling their problem as a blow to their self-esteem. Martha Rose in particular felt herself under attack, and with good reason. Chevrolet impugned her integrity, first, by contradicting her story that the dashboard temperature light was not burning and, second, by citing her "negligence and abuse" (in driving the car after the engine overheated) as the cause of the $680 damage. When Martha protested to Chevrolet and challenged the company's version of what had happened, she became the target of the second of two approaches not uncommonly used in the auto industry to frustrate a woman "voicing" a complaint, as our study of the consumer complaint process revealed.

We discovered that as long as a woman who complained was appreciative, courteous, and "nice," she was often flattered and cajoled by the party complained against with the "Sir Walter Raleigh" approach. But as soon as a woman demanded satisfaction and insisted that something be done about her grievance, she was likely to be treated with the "crazy lady" approach. She would then be blamed for the problem, which would be made out to be her fault, and she would be ignored or put down, as Martha Rose was by the Chevrolet zone office, as a liar, a chronic complainer, and an unreliable witness.

In addition, then, to the unexpected burden of carrying another loan, the Roses, at Martha's instigation, persevered in "voicing" their grievance in an attempt to heal and to restore their self-esteem. We would go so far as to suggest, in fact, based on the example of George and Martha Rose, that a consumer's persistence in "voicing" a grievance may depend as much upon that complainant's need to redeem injured self-esteem as upon the strength of his or her claim. Complaining, then, may be a recuperative mechanism.

Finally, there is no question that the Roses were morally shaken by Chevrolet's refusal to "honor the warranty." George Rose was a "company man" who, with a rural background and a high school education, had worked his way up, over 15 years, to his present position as a district product service manager for GE. He handled consumer complaints, including warranty problems, for GE with loyalty to his company and pride in big business. Chevrolet's "no job" in the face of what the Roses perceived to be their just complaint raised for them a troublesome question about the ethics of large corporations in their dealings with consumers. George reiterated several times in the course of our interview that GE meets its obligations, negotiates with dissatisfied customers, and reassesses disputed cases when contacted by third-party remedy agents.

The Roses' determination and perseverence in complaining was, in part, an effort to vindicate their confidence in the ethics of big business. They "voiced" their complaint because they believed they were in the right and that to "lump it" would be to condone an injustice. We have noted that an indignant and moralistic tone pervaded the Roses' quest for a resolution of their grievance. It was important to them to stand up to, and dissociate themselves from, collusion with Chevrolet's denial of its obligations under the warranty. For such denial potentially threatened the values, life-style, and identity upon which the Roses had built their life.

References

Collier, Jane
    1975   Legal processes. In *Annual review of anthropology*, edited by Bernard J.
           Siegel. Palo Alto: Annual Reviews, Inc.
Hirschman, Albert O.
    1970   *Exit, voice, and loyalty*. Cambridge: Harvard University Press.

Langness, L. L.

    1965   *The life history in anthropological science* (Studies in anthropological method). New York: Holt, Rinehart & Winston.

Nader, Laura

    1978   The directions of law and the development of extra-judicial processes in nation–state societies. In *Cross-examinations: Essays in memory of Max Gluckman,* edited by P. Gulliver. Leiden: E. J. Brill.

Nader, Laura, Klaus Koch, and Bruce Cox

    1966   The ethnography of law: A bibliographic survey. *Current Anthropology* **7**(3):267–294.

MECHANISMS FOR REDRESS

5

David I. Greenberg
Thomas H. Stanton

BUSINESS GROUPS, CONSUMER PROBLEMS:
The Contradiction of Trade Association Complaint Handling[1]

Introduction

Barbara Zinsky's new $250 Caloric oven quickly became a nemesis. Within a month of its purchase from Harvey Hall's, the gas oven began unexpectedly turning itself on and off, failing to warm even simple frozen foods and dropping its metal racks in the middle of cooking roasts.

Service attempts proved fruitless; Barbara's husband, Bob, became so angry at the total lack of effective response from the store, the complaint handlers, and the government, that he wanted to "lump it"—throw the

[1]The research on the six trade association programs was conducted between January 1974 and March 1976. Several people participated in the data collection: Project Director Christopher Wheeler, and Ruth Darmstadter, David Greenberg, Tom Stanton, and Pilar Markley.

The data are drawn from observations at panel meetings and in trade association offices; from interviews with panelists, trade association staff members, and ranking officials, regional administrators of the Automobile Consumer Action Panels (AUTOCAPs) and the National Association of Home Builders (NAHB), Home Owners Warranty program (HOW), and consumer complainants to all the programs; from review of documents both in the trade association programs and in the files of the Federal Office of Consumer Affairs; follow-up of random samples of actual complaints from the files of the Connecticut AUTOCAP, the NAHB Office of Consumer Affairs, and the Office of Impartial Chairman (OIC) of the moving and storage industry of New York City; a similar follow-up of complaints to the Carpet and Rug Industry Consumer Action Panel (CRICAP), which were selected from the files of the Prince William County (Virginia) Office of Consumer Affairs; and a follow-up of complaints to the Major Appliance Consumer Action Panel (MACAP), which were forwarded to MACAP from complaints received by various Ralph Nader offices in Washington, D.C. (This survey is explained in more detail in n. 78).

Much of the data were drawn from a series of working papers written by Ruth Darmstadter over a 2-year period (Darmstadter 1975a, b, c; 1976a, b, c). These papers and all the data—the

stove out and absorb the loss. Barbara was afraid to use the oven, fearing that the racks would fall and that she or one of her children might be scalded by hot drippings; the family began to impose on neighbors for cooking facilities and finally purchased a counter-top oven.

But Barbara did not give up. She wrote letters to the vice president, president, and chairman of the board of Hall's; to the manufacturer, Caloric Corporation; to a newspaper action line in Philadelphia; to the Better Business Bureau; and to Virginia Knauer, among many others. She made phone calls: dozens to the store, either to be told that the manager was out to lunch or to be visited by ill-prepared and inebriated service personnel; to the local office of consumer affairs; to the Legal Aid office, only to find that the cost of an attorney might well quadruple the oven's original cost. But, in contrast to many consumers in similar circumstances, Mrs. Zinsky found several sources of support that convinced her to pursue a solution to her problem for over a year: a power and light company serviceman, who told her that the oven's expandable hose was prone to gas leaks and was, in his opinion, a hazard; the Philadelphia action line, which reported that stores were selling out their stocks of Calorics because they were causing so many problems; and her letter to the editor of the *Wilmington Journal*, which prompted 27 similarly dissatisfied customers to call Mrs. Zinsky in order to voice their own grievances.

In the end, however, Barbara wished she had rid the family of the oven at the first sign of trouble. For one night the Zinskys returned from church to find their entire home ablaze. The fire marshall informed them that the fire had started in a corner of the kitchen near the oven. The likely cause? Gas. The house was completely ruined, and yet as Mrs. Zinsky cleaned up she could not help thinking that even this dark cloud had a silver lining: The troublesome stove was finally and utterly gone.

Of all the responses the Zinsky family received from remedy agents, perhaps one best illustrates the breakdown of the complaint process in this country. As the problems with the Caloric oven unfolded, the Zinskys contacted the Major Appliance Consumer Action Panel (MACAP),[2] one of

---

sheer volume of which makes it impossible to catalogue here—are on file with the Center for Study of Responsive Law in Washington, D.C.

The division of responsibility for this study was as follows: Ruth Darmstadter did the major research and authored working papers on all six of the trade association programs between January 1974 and March 1976. David Greenberg and Thomas Stanton supplemented Ms. Darmstadter's research during February, March, and April 1976. Thomas Stanton helped provide the overall context and approach to the study, aided in the initial organization of the final paper, and reviewed early drafts. David Greenberg was responsible for general organization, conceptual scheme, and writing of the final version.

[2] All material from the Zinsky case is drawn from Janice Lowen Agee's (1975) life history, *Barbara Zinsky*, on file with the Consumer Complaint Project. Actually the Zinsky case was handled by one of MACAP's three sponsoring trade associations, the Gas Appliance

the six dispute-resolution mechanisms sponsored by trade associations, which constitute the subject of this chapter.[3]

The only action MACAP took was redundant. As all the trade association mechanisms make a tremendous effort to give their members every opportunity to solve their own consumer problems (for the panels have no power to compel a business to respond), the appliance industry panel directed Barbara to Harvey Hall's and Caloric Corporation; that she had already contacted them many times and had received no tangible result was irrelevant. Given the limited resources and consensus-seeking procedures of these Consumer Action Panels, this was a fairly typical directive.

In MACAP's files at least, Barbara Zinsky is a satisfied consumer. Because she did not recontact the panel after being given the useless referral, Barbara, MACAP assumes, must have been satisfied. Thus, the Zinsky file at MACAP's Arlington, Virginia, headquarters reads: "Closed to the Consumer's Satisfaction."[4]

In the real world of consumer dispute settlement—as Barbara Zinsky experienced it—MACAP's simple assumption shifts yet another burden onto the shoulders of those seeking complaint resolution: "Lumping it" can become a more certain and less costly approach than enduring the intangible frustration and real costs of unanswered complaint initiatives.

MACAP is not alone in imposing heavy burdens on the consumer complainant. The structure and functioning of all the trade association consumer action panels in this study create similar roadblocks to complaint resolution. The underlying forces that produce such a process are neither arbitrary nor purposely insidious. Instead, they are a logical and fairly predictable outgrowth of: (a) business's perception of and approach to consumerism and complaints; and (b) the institutional weaknesses of trade associations.

Barbara Zinsky's single complaint experience colored her entire perception of business: She now views it with distrust. Since the mid 1960s, the opinions of the general population have undergone a similar shift. The American business community (to the extent that it can be considered an entity) has closely observed this rise of dissatisfaction—and that of its progeny, "consumerism."

In a relative sense, the confidence placed in business by consumers

---

Manufacturers Association (GAMA), headquartered in Arlington, Virginia. As the first step in the MACAP procedure, the trade association itself makes this initial contact with a complainant, in what is called the prepanel phase. These procedures are explained on pp. 199–200.

[3]Ruth Darmstadter completed several studies of trade association complaint handling as part of the initial research for this paper (see References). The authors wish to acknowledge her contribution to our analysis of such dispute-processing mechanisms.

[4]Three months after the referral, GAMA closed the case because it had not heard from Mrs. Zinsky. Later, after the house had burned down and the Zinskys had disposed of the stove, Barbara did write GAMA to state, sarcastically, that since the stove was gone she *was* finally satisfied.

fell by more than 50% between 1968 and 1975 (Wirthlin 1975:1).[5] In absolute terms, 56% feel that "business doesn't give [them] a fair shake [Wirthlin 1975:4]." And 65% hold that business profits to the detriment of the general public (Wirthlin 1975). This disillusionment translates into support for corrective action: 63% of a nationwide sample of 3240 in 1973 agreed that government regulation is a good way to make business more responsive to the average consumer; 70% felt that breaking up large corporations would, prima facie, be a good thing (Wirthlin 1975:12).

In its corner, business perceives these changes in attitude and fears the proffered alternatives. For example, 76% of middle- to high-level management executives polled in 1974 noticed a much greater degree of consumer disillusionment than had existed a decade earlier (Greyser and Diamond 1974).[6] There was mild disagreement among the executives as to the cause, but there was a general consensus that a likely result of this dissatisfaction would be more government legislation (see also Barksdale and French 1975; Greyser 1973; and Seelye 1975). A survey of business review commentaries revealed that business and marketing executives expected this legislation to increase the costs of marketing, raising overall costs (Barksdale and French 1975:63).[7] These surveys indicated that such legislation would represent an overreaction on the part of government agencies to consumerist pressures (Greyser and Diamond 1974:54);[8] that the result would be to increase retailers' costs, squeeze profits, and raise prices (Rosenberg 1975:43); that the legislation would be pointless and reflective of political opportunism (Rosenberg 1975:42); and that it would represent the onslaught of welfare statism and be a knee-jerk reaction that would "impinge heavily on customary business practices . . . , change the rules of the game and narrow the parameters of independent business decision-making, . . . adding billions to the cost of production [Seelye 1975:8–10]."[9]

This continuum of response reveals a common thread: Consumerism

[5]Business leaders ranked sixteenth out of 16 occupations rated in terms of public confidence. Religious leaders ranked highest, retaining 73% of their 1966 base.

[6]Greyser and Diamond (1974) surveyed 3418 middle- to high-level executive subscribers to the *Harvard Business Review*: 96% felt consumers were more critical of business generally than they had been 10 years earlier (p. 43); 86% felt that consumerism was "here to stay" (p. 39).

[7]Eighty-five percent of 597 chief marketing executives polled in a spring 1974 mailing agreed that consumerist demands had increased production costs and raised prices (Barksdale and French 1975:63).

[8]Nearly 60% of the 3418 respondents in the Greyser and Diamond survey agreed with the statement "government agencies have overreacted to consumerist pressure."

[9]Seelye (1975) cites six movements that are now shaping the course of history in the United States: the youth movement, the consumer protection movement, the ecology movement, the civil rights movement, the women's liberation movement, and the egalitarian movement. "Although their objectives are different . . . they all converge at one point: pressure on government to pass legislation to attain their goals [p. 8]."

threatens business with increased regulation, rising costs, and consequent increased consumer dissatisfaction. There has been, since 1970, one response that appears to be a practical way to help satisfy business' concerns: the trade association-sponsored Consumer Action Panel (CAP).

Trade associations are the logical actors to assist business in avoiding legislation with minimal expense. Trade associations can establish industrywide complaint-handling programs much more cheaply than can each of their member firms separately. Second, although individual business complaint-handling programs may be unacceptable to legislators contemplating industrywide standards, the trade association panels appear, on the other hand, to provide this necessary breadth. Third, trade associations can point to clear self-regulatory precedents, for example, voluntary product standards and safety requirements (Hunt 1975:34–55).[10] Finally, the trade associations' strategic position renders them capable of designing programs most likely to make legislation *seem* unnecessary. With professional staffs, industrywide data, and legislative monitoring experience, the trade associations can implement programs less costly to industry than government standards and yet just strong enough to preempt them (Hunt 1975:45).[11] Clearly, then, trade associations can help to solve *business's* consumer problems—the costs of consumer complaint handling and the fear of restrictive legislation.

However, one question remains: Can trade associations establish programs to solve *consumers'* consumer problems—complaints about unsatisfactory goods and services? Past experience and the traditional institutional role of the trade associations within industries—their lack of power, their orientation toward providing services to their members, and their need to work through consensus—raise doubts.

The six programs in this study tend to confirm past findings about trade associations (Finkelstein 1973:25; Rosenberg 1975:37; and Wilson 1975:149–152). They have succeeded in preventing threatening legislation, in providing public relations benefits, and in protecting the handling of complaints from outside scrutiny. In short, the trade associations' dispute-settlement mechanisms serve their members well; unfortunately, with one exception, they do not substantively improve consumer complaint handling.

[10]Hunt (1975:46–47) cites the safety standards of the Association of Home Appliance Manufacturers, which specify minimum levels of characteristics or performance for a home appliance and a certain performance continuum to allow manufacturers to compare their products with those of their competitors and to provide consumers with standardized data to help them compare brands.

[11]"It [self-regulation] has only to elevate the performance of the industry to the point where it does not represent a relatively attractive target to the resource-constrained regulatory agency. A similar argument applies to attracting the attention of the legislature [Hunt 1975:45]."

The Trade Association Complaint-Handling Mechanisms

Trade association-sponsored consumer action panels (CAPs) were encouraged by the Nixon–Ford administrations, Congress, the Federal Trade Commission, and the Federal Office of Consumer Affairs. This study focuses on six trade association programs:

1. The Major Appliance Consumer Action Panel (MACAP), established jointly in 1970 by the Association of Home Appliance Manufacturers (AHAM), the Gas Appliance Manufacturers Association (GAMA), and the National Retail Merchants Association (NRMA).

2. The Automobile Consumer Action Programs (AUTOCAPs), created in July 1973 by the National Association of Automobile Dealers (NADA) and the Automotive Trade Association Managers (ATAM).

3. The Furniture Industry Consumer Action Panel (FICAP), begun in August 1973 by the Southern Furniture Manufacturers Association (SFMA).

4. The Carpet and Rug Industry Consumer Action Panel (CRICAP), established in October 1973 by the Carpet and Rug Institute (CRI).

5. The Office of the Impartial Chairman of the Moving and Storage Industry of New York City (OIC), a product of the 1956 collective bargaining agreement between six movers' trade associations and the Teamsters Union Local 814.

6. The Home Owners Warranty program (HOW), adopted in September 1973 by the National Association of Home Builders (NAHB).

Conceptually, the programs fall into two categories: (a) the Consumer Action Panels (CAPs), which concentrate almost entirely on handling specific consumer complaints and mediating between trade association members and their customers; and (b) the prevention programs, combined with complaint handling, of HOW and OIC. The HOW program provides buyers of new homes with insurance against major home defects; the OIC protects businesses by scrutinizing commercial movers' job estimates before a move takes place, and it attempts to rid the market of unlicensed "gypsy" movers.

The CAPs

Conceived in answer to the express threat of federal legislation embodied in a 1969 study critical of major appliance warranties[12] and mid-

[12]The President's Task Force on Appliance Warranties and Service (report dated 8 January 1969) made two recommendations relating to consumer complaint handling: "Manufacturers of major appliances should . . . not attempt to pass on to the consumer or to

wifed by Virginia Knauer,[13] MACAP was born in 1970. The MACAP model was reproduced in AUTOCAP, FICAP, and CRICAP between July and October 1973 (Knauer 1975a:24–25).

Funded, staffed, and housed by their respective trade associations, the CAPs serve two functions: (a) as a communications intermediary forwarding consumer complaints to business, even in cases where such contact has already taken place; and (b) as a panel of consumer and industry experts reviewing stalemated complaints several times yearly, empowered only to render nonbinding advisory opinions.

The procedures of the national CAPs (FICAP, CRICAP, MACAP) can be considered together; the AUTOCAPs consist of several local panels. Basically, three stages comprise the complaint-handling process of the national CAPs:

Stage 1: Referral. The CAP forwards complaints to the manufacturer or retailer unless the consumer provides positive evidence of his or her prior contact with them.[14]

Stage 2: Communication. (a) The CAP acknowledges complaints and sends copies of the correspondence to the manufacturer–retailer requesting that he advise the CAP when the complaint has been resolved; (b) the CAP requests the consumer to supply any missing data; (c) if the manufacturer does not respond within a specified period, the CAP follows up by a letter or phone call; (d) if the manufacturer–retailer notifies the panel that the complaint has been resolved, the panel assumes consumer satisfaction unless the consumer advises differently; (e) if the manufacturer–retailer refuses to act or the consumer voices continued and specific dis-

---

the retailer a part or all of the financial burden of replacing defective parts or of correcting defects in design or manufacture. . . . If retailers or servicing agencies are responsible for any obligations stated in the guarantee, insure that such parties are provided with sufficient incentive and resources to encourage them to fulfill those obligations promptly and conscientiously and if they fail to do so take remedial action [pp. 3–4]." The threat of legislation was embodied in the final recommendation: "At the end of one year if it appears that substantial progress is not being made toward the solutions of these problems, the mentioned officials [Secretaries of Commerce and Labor, the Chairman of the Federal Trade Commission and the Special Assistant to the President for Consumer Affairs] should consider the nature and scope of legislation necessary to achieve the desired results [p. 5]."

[13]Mrs. Knauer was appointed by President Nixon to head the newly created Office of Consumer Affairs, now in the Department of Health, Education, and Welfare; her title was Special Assistant to the President for Consumer Affairs. She calls herself an "ardent advocate" of business self-regulation and refers to the trade association panels as "an innovation of this decade [Knauer 1975a:23–24]."

[14]"The first contact regarding a customer's dissatisfaction must be made with the retailer from whom the product was purchased. Then if necessary and appropriate, the retailer communicates with the manufacturer. If by this time no satisfactory resolution has been reached, the complaint may then be brought to the attention of FICAP [FICAP 1974c:8]." CRICAP and MACAP have similar operating rules (CRICAP 1973:5; MACAP 1975:10).

satisfaction, the CAP informs the manufacturer–retailer that the case will proceed to the panel unless resolved by a specified date (CRICAP 1973:5; FICAP 1974c:8; and MACAP 1975:16).

Stage 3: Panel Consideration. (a) Assigned trade association staff members prepare a summary of the cases, suggesting alternative solutions,[15] and place it on the calendar for the next panel session, which is sometimes months later;[16] (b) The case is reviewed by the panelists[17] and, if no further information is needed, the panel suggests an action that the manufacturer may choose to accept or reject. In general, the panel undertakes no follow-up to monitor the outcome of the case.[18]

MACAP must function in a slightly different manner, because it is sponsored by three trade associations whose headquarters are in three different cities (AHAM in Chicago, NRMA in New York City, and GAMA in Arlington, Virginia). Complaints received by MACAP at its Chicago AHAM offices are forwarded to either New York or Arlington if they involve members of NRMA or GAMA, respectively. All three trade associations then forward the complaints to the head offices of their member companies.[19] But as a complaint may involve, for example, a local Sears store, it must be forwarded from the national to the local level of Sears. It may be several weeks, then, before the complaint finds its way to the specific retail store where the problem began.

In contrast to the national CAPs, the AUTOCAPs function through several local panels administered by local offices of the Automotive Trade Association. Although the creators of the program originally envisioned expert panels composed of new car dealer members and manufacturer and consumer representatives, often only a single AUTOCAP administrator handles complaints.[20] The AUTOCAP procedure is generally similar to

[15]This was the procedure observed by Consumer Complaint Project researchers Christopher Wheeler and Ruth Darmstadter at MACAP meetings of 18–20 July 1974 and 9–10 May 1975.

[16]At the June 1975 FICAP meeting, for example, two of the five complaints discussed had originally been filed over 7 months previously (Ruth Darmstadter observation).

[17]Panelists in general are "distinguished" representatives from industry, academia, and consumer affairs. The panels meet infrequently, and panelists are reimbursed only for their expenses.

[18]"The only way MACAP can be certain a consumer is satisfied is through written or telephone confirmation of this fact." If consumers do not so communicate, confirmation is assumed. Assumption of confirmation was made in at least 26% of 1974 cases (MACAP 1975:10, 16).

[19]A change in this procedure was being considered, according to a 16 December 1975 letter from Joyce Viso, MACAP staff member, to Ruth Darmstadter. If so, the MACAP office in Chicago would no longer forward NRMA or GAMA complaints to the respective trade association headquarters but would instead acknowledge them directly.

[20]As of May 1975, of the 32 AUTOCAP programs, 15 were of the single-mediator variety (Alan Marlette, NADA AUTOCAP Administrator, interview with Darmstadter, 16 May 1975).

the national CAPs'. Complaints against new car dealers[21] are filed, and the local administrator attempts to conciliate in cases where a mere referral proves unsuccessful (Marlette, Administrator, AUTOCAP, interview with Darmstadter, 16 May 1975). The consumer must often inform the AUTO-CAP of this breakdown in negotiations. If conciliation, too, fails, the case is taken up by the panel (if one exists), and a nonbinding opinion rendered. Once again, the AUTOCAP does not follow up to determine whether or not the dealer involved heeds the AUTOCAP opinion.

In general, the procedures of all the CAPs reflect an orientation toward providing services to trade association members. The member is provided with many opportunities to resolve consumer problems in any way it sees fit. Meanwhile CAP communicates with the consumer and assembles documentary evidence about the case—which is made available to the member in some instances. If the manufacturer or dealer absolutely refuses to respond, the panel—in its apparently quasi-judicial role—evaluates the evidence and makes a decision that the member need not comply with. Throughout the entire procedure, the consumer must continually take the initiative to show why the panel should handle the case to begin with (instead of simply referring it to the retailer or the manufacturer); why the panel should continue communicating with the business (instead of assuming consumer satisfaction); and why the panel should review the case (instead of assuming that the business has already responded adequately). Yet even with continual vigilance, the consumer cannot receive anything more than the dealer or manufacturer wishes to give.

HOW and OIC

The National Association of Home Builders' HOW and the Movers' and Teamsters' Office of Impartial Chairman in New York City provide services of a more far-reaching nature than those of the CAPs. Each provides a form of precomplaint protection to both members and consumers, as well as postproblem complaint handling.

Based on the British warranty insurance program of the National House-Builders Registration Council[22] and prompted by the specter of

[21]Because manufacturers have declined to participate in the panels, the AUTOCAPs cannot successfully handle complaints that are manufacturer-related.

[22]The British National House-Builders Registration Council (NHBRC) is considered both the best and the most comprehensive home warranty program in operation. Founded in 1936, the NHBRC is an independent, nonpolitical, nonprofit body composed of all the interests concerned with housing: It has representatives of builders, developers, bankers, trade unions, and professional associations related to private housing. The core of the program is its National Register of over 17,000 approved house builders, or about 99% of the industry. The ultimate strength of the program lies in a 1966 agreement between the Council and the Builders Societies Association (similar to the U.S. Savings & Loan League) which

federal, state, and municipal legislation—as well as an increasingly broad interpretation by the courts of builders' civil liabilities—the Home Owners Warranty was adopted by the NAHB in September 1973 (HORC 1974b [May]).[23] The program—which systematizes (and limits) builder responsibility for major structural defects, provides the buyer of a new home with up to 10 years of protection against those defects, and establishes a conciliation and arbitration program for settling disputes—is administered through the Home Owners Registration Corporation (HORC), a wholly owned subsidiary of the NAHB.

The responsibilities for HOW are distributed among HORC, locally established (through NAHB affiliate home builders associations) warranty councils, the builders, and the program's private insurer. HORC markets the program and licenses the local warranty councils. These councils, in turn, adopt quality standards, screen applicant builders for past performance and financial stability in light of the standards, monitor local inspection procedures, and create specific conciliation and arbitration guidelines for handling complaints (HORC 1974c).[24]

The HOW builder[25] guarantees to cover faulty workmanship and defective materials as well as major construction defects during the first year after purchase.[26] During the first 2 years, the builder also provides a warranty for plumbing, heating, electrical and cooling systems, and repair of major construction defects (HORC 1974c:5–7).

American Bankers Insurance Company of Florida underwrites the builder's performance during the first 2 years if for any reason he or she cannot or will not meet his or her warranteed responsibilities. Additionally the insurance coverage extends to major construction defects during the third through tenth years (HORC 1974c).

---

established the ruling that all member associations issue mortgages only for those houses carrying the NHBRC warranty. That agreement, in effect, forced builders to become part of the program. (For descriptions of the NHBRC, see HUD 1974a).

[23]The first councils were licensed 22 May 1974 (HORC 1974d). The first builder was enrolled on 29 May (HORC 1974b [July]:3), and the first home received the warranty on 6 August 1974 (HORC 1974b [August–September]:1).

[24]Local councils may vary in jurisdiction. They may serve a city, county, a part of a state, or an entire state, but their function is the same in any case (HORC 1974c:5).

[25]A builder may choose whether or not to enroll particular houses. If a house is enrolled, the policy, which is transferable to a subsequent homeowner within the original time limits, is then mandatory for the buyer. The buyer can probably purchase a similar house without HOW coverage from the same builder if he or she chooses.

[26]The HOW program defines major construction defects in the following way: "Actual damage to the load-bearing portion of the home which affects its load-bearing function and which vitally affects or is imminently likely to produce a vital effect on the use of the Home for residential purposes [HORC 1974c:16]." One commentator has pointed out that defects in plastering, wall tiling, flooring, and drains and wet rot in window frames, doors, and other millwork are excluded from the coverage of the 10-year major construction defect umbrella (Kempner 1976:359).

The program is financed by a one-time fee of .2% of the closing price of the house (e.g., $100 for a $50,000 home). One-half of the fee pays for the insurance protection, whereas the other half is divided between the national corporation (HORC) and the local warranty council.[27] Builder-members also pay annual registration and reregistration fees established and collected by the local warranty councils. These membership fees vary from council to council but normally approximate $200.

Complaints arising under the HOW program proceed as follows: The buyer submits his or her grievance in writing to the builder. Consumers unsatisfied with builder response may request conciliation administered through the local warranty council. Council-selected conciliators investigate complaints and meet with the buyer and builder in an attempt to resolve disputes satisfactorily. If the conciliation process fails or breaks down, either party may request binding arbitration through a HOW arbitration program designed by the American Arbitration Association (AAA) and directed by former AAA President Lester Woolf (HORC 1974c).

It is too early to judge the dispute-settlement process provided by HOW; indeed, the program is still gestating.[28] On the one hand, the program seems to offer an impartial dispute-resolution mechanism, binding on the builder as well as the consumer. On the other hand, the problems NAHB has faced in marketing HOW—the shifting fortunes of the building industry, the inability of the trade associations to impose costly decisions on its members, and the precarious political calculus that the trade association faces in dealing with many different state and local associations and their members—dovetail with our major findings about the more developed trade association mechanisms for dispute handling.

From its position between the Teamsters Local 814 and the six movers' trade associations, New York City's Office of the Impartial Chairman emerges as the most powerful and effective of the dispute-resolution mechanisms in this study. The OIC sets its own complaint-handling procedure, largely controls its own budget and staffing, is vested with the authority to render binding, court-enforceable arbitration decisions between customers and moving companies, and serves as a catalyst to state (and as an ally to potential federal) regulatory efforts. Chairman James O. Harley's strong and visible posture is no accident; it is

---

[27]None of the fee goes to the builder, but the program presumes that the fee is reflected in an incremental increase of the price of the HOW home.

[28]As of this writing (1976) the HOW program is running into difficulties complying with Federal Trade Commission provisions promulgated under the Magnuson–Moss Warranty Act. Specifically, provisions of HOW regarding industry-selected conciliators and binding arbitration foreclosing consumer access to judicial remedies have been unacceptable to the FTC. HOW officials successfully won a postponement for compliance until January 1, 1977 and vigorously lobbied Congress for a complete exemption from the Magnuson–Moss/FTC requirements.

only from such a stance that the OIC can serve the interests of the OIC's approximately 260 members and their union employees. In a market characterized by easy entry and exit and fairly lax state enforcement of transportation licensing codes, the OIC provides positive economic benefits to its member firms through self-regulation of the New York City moving market.

Specifically, the OIC: (a) screens the commercial moving estimates of its members to ensure compliance with state-imposed rates (tariffs);[29] (b) distributes educational materials to the public, including a much-requested list of "approved movers" (all of whom are members of the sponsoring movers' trade associations); (c) informally mediates disputes between consumers and members, conducts formal arbitration at either disputant's request, and provides information on other avenues of redress for those with complaints against nonmember movers; (d) employs field inspectors to provide on-the-spot mediation at new housing projects and apartment buildings (where the sheer volume of moves tends to attract unlicensed movers and generally causes more problems); (e) reports the existence and illegal activities of nonlicensed movers to the State Department of Transportation; and (f) to the same end of eliminating unlicensed movers, proposes legislative changes to bring Interstate Commerce Commission regulation to the New York City commercial "exempt" zone (Harley, interview with D. Greenberg, 8 March 1976).[30]

Ultimately, the OIC's strength derives from the same incentives and purposes as do the weaknesses of the other five trade association programs. All exist to serve their members; different circumstances demand different approaches and have different impacts upon consumers.

The Institutional Dilemma of the Trade Association Mechanisms

The Director of NAHB's Office of Consumer Affairs commented, "One really shouldn't expect a trade association to be able to resolve consumer complaints [Les Blattner, interview with Greenberg and Stanton, 1 April 1976]." The NAHB official understands his institutional position well. Questions relating to the panels' breadth of representation, continuity of service, degree of independence, and membership consen-

---

[29]These tariffs were imposed in 1955 legislation that required all New York State movers to be licensed (Harley, interview with David Greenberg, 8 March 1976).

[30]Several other exempt zones exist in metropolitan areas that encompass parts of more than one state, for example, St. Louis, Missouri–East St. Louis, Illinois (Harley, interview with David Greenberg, 8 March 1976).

sus all affect a complaint-handling mechanism that is the offspring of a trade association.

Breadth of Representation

Of the six trade association programs, only MACAP—representing 95% of the major appliance market—gives consumers nearly industry-wide complaint handling, according to Guenther Baumgart, AHAM President (interview with Darmstadter, 18 July 1974). By contrast, the OIC membership accounts for only about one-third of the New York City movers.[31] NAHB affiliates build approximately half the nation's homes (Sumichrast and Frankel 1970:213–216); however, the HOW program, in the first 2 years of its existence, enrolled only 2800 builders out of a total of 110,000 and, in its second year, covered only 40,000 homes (out of nearly 900,000 housing starts) (HORC 1975:3–4). Even optimistic estimates by HOW President Richard Canavan place the ultimate HOW market at only 25–30% of the total new-home market (interview with David Greenberg and Thomas Stanton, 15 March 1976). FICAP is sponsored by only one of the three major furniture trade associations (the National Association of Furniture Manufacturers and the National Home Furnishings Association declined to participate), representing 35–37% of aggregate furniture sales (FICAP 1973). Because 59% of the FICAP complaints relate to fabric (FICAP 1974c), the inability of the furniture industry panel to involve the textile industry has weakened its breadth.[32] And 2 years after AUTOCAP's founding, the program claimed 17 existing local panels; however, only 10 of that small number have even met.

Certain aspects of trade association structure suggest that the programs lack not only present breadth but future growth potential as well; HOW provides a good example. Although the HOW program is nominally open to NAHB members and nonmembers alike (NAHB 1973b), local associations in the past have informally excluded nonmembers (Joseph Rodele, HOW Administrator, Delaware, interview with Darmstadter, 22 October 1975).[33] Although the original report to the NAHB envisaged a

---

[31]Approximately 260 movers belong to the six trade associations that comprise the OIC's sponsorship; there are, in addition, approximately 340 other licensed movers in the metropolitan area. Estimates of unlicensed (and therefore illegal) movers range from 150 to 200. (Harley, interview with David Greenberg, 8 March 1976).

[32]An informant on the staff of FICAP panelist Nell Weekley, Director of the New Orleans Office of Consumer Affairs, told the Consumer Complaint Project that he seldom sends a complaint to FICAP. Moreover, he states, "If it has to do with fabric, it's a dead end [10 June 1975]."

[33]However, it appears that local councils have a more difficult time turning away NAHB builders who might not meet HOW guidelines. See n. 39.

mechanism for builders in nonwarranty council areas to join HOW, no such procedure has been established (Kempner 1976:360). Kempner (1976) finds it "unclear" why the original report's conclusions have not been implemented; on the contrary, however, the reasons for both the NAHB exclusionary practices and the seeming omission of the nonwarranty council membership provision run true to the political problems of the trade association. Including non-NAHB members in HOW would be a contradiction of the very purpose of the local home builders' associations: to provide services and higher public status to their members. By systematically allowing builders from nonwarranty council areas to participate in HOW, the NAHB would be providing a potential competitive advantage to certain nonmember builders in areas where the consensus of local home builders' associations runs against participating in the warranty program. This tactic would surely anger the local NAHB affiliates, something the national is unlikely to risk for the benefit of a small number of builders.

Finally, HOW experience in Memphis suggests that the trade association is not always in an advantageous position to market its own program. Even though HOW participation was nearly 50% in 1975, Memphis realtors were reluctant to stress the program to potential buyers, fearing that they might begin to request it in situations where the realtor did not have HOW-builder houses among his stock (J. B. Bell, HOW Administrator, Memphis, Tenn., interview with Greenberg, 15 March 1976).[34]

There are many reasons, then, why a trade association may not be able to offer a broad-based program. Several noncooperating trade associations may be part of a given industry; nonmembers may make up a large part of an industry; problems and complaints may go beyond the specific jurisdiction of the trade association into that of another industry (e.g., FICAP and the textile industry); and, most importantly, trade association incentives may lead to limited membership.

Continuity of Service

The trade association complaint mechanisms often cannot provide a guarantee of uninterrupted service. Because trade associations' financial status reflects the current economic conditions in their industries, their dispute-resolution programs are also subject to change. CRICAP provides an example. Eighteen months after its inception, the panel was abandoned by the sponsoring Carpet and Rug Institute.[35] A letter from a prominent industry executive to Virginia Knauer explains:

[34]Mr. Bell also explained that only a few large builders actually sell their own homes.
[35]The total consumer affairs budget for CRI—including the approximately $32,000 annually for CRICAP—was $100,000 (CRICAP 1973:4–5).

The Carpet Industry is going through a very difficult period, which in turn is reflected in the Institute's [CRI] financial position. These pressures necessitate the tightest cost controls. Faced with a reduced membership and rising costs, the discontinuance of CRICAP apparently was just one of the economy moves CRI was forced to take [Bandy 1975].

Expansion of the HOW and AUTOCAP programs faced similar economic problems. A severe downturn in the housing industry was cited by all top NAHB and HOW officials as the single greatest marketing difficulty: Many builders, they contended, were too close to insolvency to bear the initial and continuing costs of HOW membership (Richard Canavan, President, HOW Program, interview with Greenberg and Stanton, 15 March 1976; Stan Baitz, Executive Vice President, Communications, NAHB, and Les Blattner, Consumer Affairs Director, NAHB, interviews with Greenberg and Stanton, 1 April 1976). Regional market economies also plague HOW. A slow year in Memphis, for example, may force up to 35% of HOW builders to drop out of the program; the local HOW administrator pinpoints a large inventory of apartments as the major factor in this decline (J. B. Bell, interview with Greenberg, 15 March 1976).

Regional difficulties threaten to decimate the AUTOCAPs as well. Largely dependent on the varying resource capabilities of local Automotive Trade Associations, the "panels" are designed in disparate ways.[36] Some, for example, are actually panels; others consist of only an administrator–mediator. Surveying the variation in August 1975, Virginia Knauer did not like what she saw:

> I feel very strongly that the present lack of conformity among complaint programs . . . is not only confusing to the consumers and industry alike but runs the danger of debasing the AUTOCAP reputation and name [Knauer 1975c].

Degree of Independence

The panels and programs are variously characterized by their parent associations as "completely independent" (FICAP 1974a,b,c) and "free of industry control or influence" (MACAP 1972) and as composed of

---

[36]"We have heard that some of the AUTOCAPs are less successful than others, that some have fallen by the wayside, that others never got off the ground [internal Office of Consumer Affairs memo dated 20 March 1974 from staff member Louise Duffy to Virginia Knauer regarding meeting with James Garfield, President of Automotive Trade Association Managers]." The memo went on to point out that Alan Marlette, NADA AUTOCAP Administrator, faced a similar resource strain: "He [Marlette] has had the almost impossible task of single-handedly selling the program to NADA members, keeping the AUTOCAPs already set up 'on track,' publicizing the program, and providing our office with feedback."

"independent professionals" (CRICAP 1973), but their structure and actions belie these descriptions. The CAPs cannot make decisions backed by any force: Peer pressure and moral suasion must suffice. Thus, FICAP renders "advisory opinions" (FICAP 1974c:8); MACAP makes "final recommendations" (MACAP 1972:6); CRICAP members pledge to give "full consideration" to panel "suggestions" (CRICAP 1974:4); and the AUTO-CAPs provide "non-binding arbitration and mediation" (NADA and ATAM 1973:24). The NAHB's Consumer Affairs Director provides the capstone: "You don't pay dues to an organization to have them tell you what to do. The trade association cannot enforce decisions, cannot impose mandatory standards ... it never has and never will [Blattner, interview with Greenberg and Stanton, 1 April 1976]."

The CAP mechanisms do not control their own procedures. Any amendments to MACAP rules must be approved by the three sponsoring associations (MACAP 1972:Art. VII). Changes in FICAP policy require ratification by the Southern Furniture Manufacturers' Consumer Affairs Committee, which is appointed by the trade association's president and executive committee (FICAP 1974a:Art. VII). The CRICAP charter empowers only the Board of Directors of the Carpet and Rug Institute to amend panel policies; moreover, only through panel unanimity can CRICAP even suggest procedural amendments; these, in turn, are referred to an oversight committee with similar lack of decision-making authority (CRICAP 1974:Arts. VII–VIII).

Neither do the dispute-resolution mechanisms control their own budgeting, staffing, and priorities; these, too, are largely dictated by the trade associations. The most conspicuous example is seen in CRICAP's termination. MACAP, however, provides two more subtle instances: As in all the CAPs, the day-to-day MACAP work is done by trade association staff members who have other responsibilities aside from complaint handling. One sponsoring trade organization, AHAM, is empowered to resolve any time conflicts caused by these dual staff roles (MACAP 1970b). And AHAM and the other two sponsors review MACAP meeting minutes before they are approved (MACAP 1970a).

The two programs composed of national federations of state and local groups—the AUTOCAPs and HOW—lack power over the locals. Virginia Knauer's pleadings notwithstanding, the National Director of the AUTO-CAPs states that he should not and cannot force the locals to do anything (Marlette, interview with Darmstadter, 19 April 1974); thus the regional disparities that Knauer labels "confusing" and "debasing" (Knauer 1975a) will inevitably continue. The national NADA office cannot ensure that programs using the AUTOCAP name actually function, cannot insist on information or statistical audits from its local affiliates, and cannot even require that statistics supplied be accurate. As of May 1975, 7 of the

17 existing panels had never met;[37] two had failed to provide NADA with statistics,[38] and the NADA summaries of another contained large discrepancies from information the AUTOCAPs gave to Consumer Complaint Project inquiries[39] (Marlette, interview with Darmstadter, 16 May 1975).

Apparently, local AUTOCAPs have wide discretion and may even directly contradict the program's philosophy and basic structure. The Administrator of the Central Florida AUTOCAP (and Executive Vice President of the Central Florida Dealers' Association) states that not only has his association chosen not to set up a dealer–consumer panel—using a single mediator instead—but that the entire panel concept is wrong. "If a complaint can't be settled by bringing the dealer and consumer together," he says, "a panel won't do any good [William Liddon, interview with Darmstadter, 16 May 1975]."

The administration of HOW reveals similar power relationships. Neither the national nor the local trade associations can compel builders to participate in HOW. Thus, only consumers who live in developed HOW markets can receive warranty insurance benefits. Furthermore, the local associations are expected to meet HOW quality standards covering only the most basic defects (Kempner 1976:377); beyond these they are empowered to establish (or not establish) their own. Moreover, the criteria by which builders are initially evaluated and possibly disqualified or expelled from the HOW program vary widely among different associations.[40] Nationwide, then, consumers enrolling in the HOW program cannot rely upon uniformity of financial soundness and technical competence from builders or fair treatment of their claims. Locally, the situation is equally variable. The local builders' associations—of which the HOW warranty councils are a part—have no power. They need members and

[37]These were Central Florida, Idaho, Kentucky (exclusive of Louisville), Louisville, Delaware, Indianapolis, and Toledo.

[38]Denver and Utah.

[39]Oregon.

[40]Indeed, the very name of the guidelines—"Suggested Local Council Procedures for the Review of Applicant Builders"—intimates this result (HORC 1974a:5–9). Interviews with local council administrators confirm this: The Milwaukee council "concentrates on getting them [builders] in . . . ; we'll kick 'em out later if we have to [Stephen Wohl, HOW Administrator, Milwaukee, interview with Darmstadter, 25 November 1975]." The Lancaster, Pa., council stretched its standards to allow participation by one NAHB member who "had to upgrade his standards," caused three complaints, and then withdrew (Earl Cramer, HOW Director, Lancaster, interview with Pilar Markley, 18 March 1976). The Delaware council states that it makes a very "broad interpretation" of national guidelines and has included in HOW some houses built several months before the program began—an action allowable under the HOW "grandfathering" provision (Joseph Rodele, HOW Administrator, Delaware, interview with Darmstadter, 22 October 1975).

offer services in pursuit thereof. This tension between service to members and protection to consumers—as well as the way trade associations inevitably resolve such conflicts—is perfectly distilled in the rhetorical question of one local HOW administrator: "How can you tell an NAHB member that he doesn't meet HOW standards? [Stephen Frye, HOW, Kansas City, Mo., interview with Markley, 11 March 1976]."

Membership Consensus

By their very nature, trade associations can act for the industry as a whole only in situations of fairly broad membership consensus (see Finkelstein 1973; Wilson 1975). In their dispute-resolution mechanisms, the trade associations seek consensus through raising membership expectations—sometimes falsely—and minimizing costs (in both money and foregone autonomy).

As originally conceived by the trade associations, the AUTOCAPs were to be a cooperative effort between dealers and manufacturers (NADA and ATAM 1973:24).[41] The presidents of NADA and ATAM called for the creation of a national CAP involving manufacturers (Knauer 1973a:2, 6). NADA's then Consumer Affairs Director, Bertrand Feiber, cited a "rising tide of consumer discontent" in four automotive areas—all, he said, manufacturer-related.[42] Clearly no member of either association would have opposed a mechanism helping to shift complaint resolution from dealers to manufacturers. Yet, as described by Mrs. Knauer, the AUTO-CAPS were not actually such a proposal; indeed, her references to manufacturer assurances of participation bordered on the disingenuous.[43]

---

[41]"The second phase of the program, which should come after the accumulation of data required to show the need for a national panel composed of representatives from the domestic car and import car and truck manufacturers, will be a national AUTOCAP to whom local and state panels can forward complaints that cannot be resolved without the aid of manufacturers [NADA and ATAM 1973:24]."

[42]The four he listed were: lack of quality control on factory assembly lines, the national recall program, warranties whose ambiguous and confusing language led too frequently to misunderstanding, and insufficient parts supply for new models (Feiber 1973:4–5). NADA's and ATAM's own publication, The Automobile Dealer and the Consumer, shows that the implications of Feiber's statement—that the major problems were manufacturer-related—were misleading. That booklet lists NADA's findings about "the most common causes of consumer dissatisfaction"; of these only three were manufacturer-caused. The four dealer-related problems listed (Feiber 1973:3) were: unsatisfactory dealer repairs, inaccurate estimates, consumer out-of-pocket transportation expenses while waiting for repairs, and discourteous and unhelpful dealership personnel.

[43]While Virginia Knauer stated at the White House press conference that "we have received assurances of support from Toyota, American Motors, Ford, Fiat, Chrysler, General Motors, and the American Imported Automobile Dealers Association [Knauer 1973a:5]," correspondence from Ford and AMC shows the support to have been nominal: AMC indi-

Although NADA and ATAM could initially sell AUTOCAPs to their members by this tactic, it ultimately helped to undermine the program when manufacturer participation failed to materialize. Evidently, the dealer–panel concept did not confer adequate perceived benefits on trade association members.

The marketing of the HOW program also reveals this consensus-seeking through the discretion granted to locals and the attempt to minimize costs. One former HOW official, who asked to remain anonymous, explained:

> They [NAHB officials] really thought of the trade association first and the consumer second and made acceptance standards too flexible in order to get more members in. Many hard-headed business decisions were not made because of not wanting to antagonize builders [interview, 25 November 1975].

The need for trade association consensus also weakens the complaint-handling programs because of their low priority (at least once the threat of legislation has passed). The NAHB's President stated quite openly that the did not want his industry split over HOW at a time when it needed to present a united front in its lobbying efforts for changes in government housing policies and mortgage interest rates (J. S. Norman, interview with Darmstadter, 27 October 1975). Similarly, HOW's President Canavan revealed that the "too democratic" procedures of the NAHB hurt the strength of the 1976 HOW policy statement on consumer affairs.[44]

Ultimately, it is the ability of the dispute-settlement mechanism to serve its members that determines the scope of its power and its priority. Even the most effective mechanism in this study—the Office of Impartial Chairman—is limited by precisely this membership consensus on how it should serve. Chairman James O. Harley failed in his attempt to define as a breach of contract the noncompliance of a mover with one of Harley's arbitration decisions (Harley, interview with Greenberg, 18 March 1976). Harley's attempt was an eminently logical step, since the OIC's power to regulate is fully established by the collective labor agreement and since his arbitration decisions carry the force of law. But as Chairman Har-

---

cated that if an AUTOCAP needed its "expertise" or "clarification," it would be "responsive" (Brown 1973). Ford was more explicit, stating that "the dealer appeal boards should retain clear identification as a dealer program . . . I believe the auto manufacturers should keep a low profile as regards these panels [Williams 1973]." A copy of this letter is in Mrs. Knauer's files.

[44]Evidently grassroots opposition by some locals to the HOW program caused the HOW President's prepared statement to be weakened (Canavan, interview with Greenberg and Stanton, 15 March 1976).

ley points out, it is not in the interests of either the movers or the union to have a strike result from a small consumer–mover dispute. (A strike might be caused in such a situation if noncompliance were defined as a breach of contract.)[45] For if the OIC has three constituencies—the movers' trade associations, the Teamsters, and the consumers—the consumer clearly has the least priority. The priorities of the other five programs examined here seem to follow suit.

Services

> Trade associations by their very nature must provide their members with services if they are to endure.... In a sense it would be counter-productive to evict a member because of morals or ethics [Les Blattner, Consumer Affairs Director, NAHB, in an interview with Greenberg and Stanton, 1 April 1976].

> You should note that the Panel has given an advisory opinion in favor of the manufacturer 19 times and the consumer 8 times in the 27 cases they have reviewed [FICAP 1974b].

The actual functioning of these trade association dispute-resolution mechanisms contradicts neither the attitude of the NAHB official in the first quotation nor the practice of FICAP: The panels exist primarily to serve their members. Costs or benefits to consumers are almost incidental. Even though many of the programs' sponsors and staff may support consumer protection quite strongly, more than intent to lead is necessary. However, the programs can and do provide important services for their members. Their original purpose of avoiding or weakening legislation, the consequent need to balance public relations against members' desire for privacy, and the way in which complaints are processed, with business foremost in mind, illustrate the means by which the programs solve their members' problems.

Defusing Legislation

Even before they handle a single complaint, the CAPs provide possibly their most important benefit to trade association members—helping to preempt or delay unwanted government intervention. It is in the context of exactly such an external political threat that Harvard political scientist James Q. Wilson found the real strength of the trade association (Wilson 1975:149). Thus, MACAP was created in the wake of a critical President's

---

[45]"The union wouldn't want to be putting men out in the street for a broken piece of furniture," Harley stated (interview with Greenberg, 8 March 1976).

Task Force report on Appliance Warranties and Service (1969), which scored the major appliance industry for its 1968 complaint record and recommended action under the express threat of legislation. AUTOCAPs were necessary, Virginia Knauer repeatedly told the industry trade associations, because automobiles represented the number one consumer complaint.[46] Responding to Knauer's comments, James Hinkley, President of NADA, revealed, somewhat paradoxically, the underlying purpose of the new CAPs: "The programs are in no way intended to be a substitute for legislation because we hope they will be so successful that legislation won't be necessary [Hinkley 1973:6]." And the stated rationale for the initiation of the Office of Impartial Chairman for New York City's moving industry explicitly contained similar intentions. As the first Chairman, Seymour Halperin, stated in the late 1950s: "Only through constant self-supervision of our own trade practices can we prevent government agencies from imposing exceedingly strict legislation [Nightengale 1973:3]."

Because they involve the broad issues of home warranties and the extent of builder responsibility, the NAHB's incentives for establishing HOW best illustrate the observation that these trade association programs can be conceived in fear. The final report to the NAHB leadership on the HOW proposal outlined the movement toward detailed government housing regulation at the national, state, and local levels (Gulledge 1973). Citing measures that would force builders to post bonds of 10% of home construction costs (Gulledge 1973:6),[47] to undergo rigorous licensing requirements (Gulledge 1973:8–10),[48] and to face an extended span of liability (Gulledge 1973:10–11)[49] and a broader definition of builder responsibility for defects,[50] Eugene Gulledge, former NAHB President, concluded

[46]Knauer began the AUTOCAPs press conference by stating that her office received 6500–7000 automobile complaints per year, approximately 20% of the total complaints (Knauer 1973a:1).

[47]This bill, introduced by Rep. Eugene F. Schlickman in the Illinois Assembly on 18 April 1972, would have required that builders deposit a bond or cash equal to 10% of the construction cost for each home when they applied for a permit. One year after the permit was issued, the builder would have received his funds back, without interest, providing there was no judicial action awaiting decision on a home buyer claim of "defective, substandard or other inadequate materials or workmanship."

[48]Gulledge stated that about half the states have licensing requirements for builders and more are moving toward passing such laws (Gulledge 1973:8–9). County licensing has also been proposed, he added (p. 10).

[49]"For builders the most unnerving governmental actions afoot are those defining the span of time for which a home builder can be held accountable for defects in construction [Gulledge 1973:10]." Because of the increasingly unlimited liability findings by courts, the Pennsylvania Builders Association persuaded the legislature to enact a 12-year statute of limitations; Oregon builders' efforts assisted in passage of a 9-year statute; and the California Builders Council took credit for the 10-year statute in California (Gulledge 1973:10–11).

[50]See, generally, Bixby 1972. He concludes: "At this writing, at least 21 states recognize the existence of implied warranties in the sale of a new house by a builder. . . . This author

that the momentum toward regulation was increasing in all strata of government, including the courts' interpretations of builders' civil liabilities.

HOW, on the other hand, and in other states, limited the length of the builders' liability,[51] narrowed their range of responsibility, provided flexible standards of financial soundness and building quality, and cost the builders less than many of the proposed laws.[52] Trade publications trumpeted these advantages.[53] NAHB officials admitted that HOW was a direct response to the possibility of federal legislation,[54] and many builders themselves saw HOW as a way to maintain optimum independence.[55]

Since its adoption, HOW has at least slowed the momentum of federal housing warranty proposals. Chief staff counsels of the relevant Senate and House Committees rated housing warranty issues as of very low priority, nor did the Department of Housing and Urban Development contemplate any action.[56] And Senator Charles Percy of Illinois—formerly active in warranty legislation—stated that HOW would "make legislation unnecessary and prove that private industry can perform better than government in the area of consumer protection [NAHB 1975:26]."

Clearly, then, the trade associations render a useful service to mem-

---

believes that courts will expand the protections afforded home buyers until they are protected to the same extent as the purchasers of goods [cited in Gulledge 1973:12–13]."

[51]Under a HOW warranty, the builder is not liable for faulty materials after 1 year, and for major construction defects and plumbing, heating, electrical, and cooling system defects after 2 years (HORC 1974c:16). The builder is not responsible for defects outside these definitions. For specifics see footnote 25.

[52]The Schlickman bill, for example, would have cost the builder on the average of several hundred dollars for each home, in the opinion of Illinois building officials (Gulledge 1973:7). HOW, on the other hand, costs on the average $83.

[53]The late 1973 and early 1974 issues of the *NAHB Journal–Scope* stressed that the warranty premiums would be indirectly paid by the home buyer (1973a:51), that the program would boost local home builder association memberships (1973a:51), that many items were excluded from coverage (1974:31), and that the local warranty councils were to have "maximum flexibility" in implementing the program (1974:31).

[54]For example, Charles P. McMahon, NAHB Vice President, said, "We don't see any need for federal regulation if we can do it ourselves. It's time to face up to responsibilities. Let's avoid legislation if at all possible—any restrictive laws—if we can satisfactorily prove that we can police ourselves [Szabo 1974:392]."

[55]Charles Adams, a St. Louis builder interviewed by Pilar Markley, cited the expense, encroachment, and tendency to self-perpetuation of a federal agency (29 March 1976). He was joined unanimously by several Kansas City builders (interviews, 12 March 1976), Richard D. Claffey of Lancaster, Pa., and Courtney Waldon and Dean McFarland of Indianapolis, Ind. (interviews, 30 March 1976). Almost every builder with whom Markley and other CCP interviewers spoke favored HOW over governmental action.

[56]Carl A. S. Coan, Staff Director of the Subcommittee on Housing and Urban Affairs of the Senate Committee on Banking, Housing, and Urban Affairs, interviewed by Greenberg, 16 March 1976; Benjamin B. McKeever, Counsel to the Subcommittee on Housing and Community Development of the House Committee on Banking, Currency, and Housing, interviewed by Greenberg 15 March 1976.

bers by instituting a largely voluntary, internally designed and operated program in place of unwanted government intervention. It is much less clear that builders' warranties provide similar benefits to consumers; indeed, well-designed national, state, and municipal housing legislation could ensure wider protection for home buyers.

Perhaps the clearest illustration of the trade associations' basic approach to government regulation—and certainly the one with the greatest relevance for the future—lies in their response to the 1975 Magnuson–Moss Warranty Act (Public Law 93-367).[57] This legislation seeks to encourage the establishment of informal, third-party dispute-settlement mechanisms.[58] Under the Act, the Federal Trade Commission is empowered to set up minimum requirements for incorporation of these grievance mechanisms into the warranties of either single companies or groups of companies. These minimum provisions must be met if the warrantors— either manufacturers or home builders—desire consumers to use the complaint mechanisms before pursuing rights guaranteed to them under Section 110 of the Act (relating to the commencement of civil actions and class action suits and recovery of attorneys' fees).[59]

Considering the trade associations' attempts to weaken the rules, "minimum requirements" is an excellent description of what they sought to accomplish. Their key concern, unsurprisingly, centered around the proposed mechanisms' costs, their degree of independence from sponsors, and their openness. In essence, the trade associations proposed a restructuring of the rules to conform to their own weak dispute-resolving programs.

For example, AHAM opposed all time limits for decision making (FTC 1975:R-1-4-1, 504), sought to delete the important explanation to consumers that they must proceed through the mechanism only before pursuing in court their *newly* guaranteed rights,[60] and proposed that the

[57]Public Law 93-637 (15 U.S.C. 2309, 2310). The Magnuson–Moss Warranty–Federal Trade Commission Improvement Act seeks to encourage the incorporation of informal, third-party dispute-resolution mechanisms into the warranties of single companies or groups of companies by requiring consumers to proceed first to the mechanism before pursuing newly created rights under the Act.

[58]"Congress hereby declares it to be its policy to encourage warrantors to establish procedures whereby consumer disputes are fairly and expeditiously settled through informal dispute settlement mechanisms [15 U.S.C. 2310, Section 110a1]."

[59]"If a warrantor incorporates a complying dispute settlement mechanism into the terms of the written warranty, and the warrantor requires that the consumer resort to the mechanism before pursuing any rights or remedies under Section 110, then the consumer may not commence a civil action under Section 110(d) (except for the limited purpose of establishing the representative capacity of a class of plaintiffs), without first seeking redress through the mechanism [15 U.S.C. 2310, Section 110a3]."

[60]"Detailed legal–technical consequences will only confuse consumers [AHAM comments to FTC, R-1-4-1, 504]."

mechanism be allowed to consult with the sponsor *only* (FTC 1975:512). SFMA opposed allowing consumers direct access to the mechanism (FTC 1975:TR 609); NRMA argued for weaker and more discretionary funding provisions and stated that regulations seeking to protect mechanism independence were clearly unjustified (FTC 1975:R-1-4-1, 49); GAMA said that the entire set of requirements was too costly and complex (FTC 1975:79).

Comments like the foregoing backed the FTC into a corner. The implicit—and often explicit—threat of all the trade associations was that strong regulations would "discourage" the creation of independent mechanisms.[61] They were, in part, successful in watering down the regulations: Warrantors do not have to disclose clearly and conspicuously the fact that consumers have direct access to the mechanisms;[62] it is only the sponsor's "good faith" that impels him to abide by mechanism rulings; and warrantors have flexibility in the way they choose to explain the limitations on consumers' legal rights.

Although the FTC did not wish to frustrate Congressional intent to encourage the creation of informal dispute-handling mechanisms, the agency did the consumer no favor by encouraging weak mechanisms. Indeed, it appears likely that the trade associations will attempt to come as close to "minimum" as possible.

Publicity—The Right Kind

If the trade associations' self-regulatory programs are to continue to forestall governmental regulation, they must attain a reputable public image. In their public relations efforts, the mechanisms face essentially two separate groups: potential government regulators, their peer professional community, and the press on the one hand; and the public on the other. The two represent different costs and benefits to the trade association and are approached in different ways.

Business, government, and media-related public relations are pursued with relish by the trade associations. High association officials and panelists write laudatory articles on the dispute-handling mechanisms for professional journals;[63] CAP panelists travel throughout the country

---

[61]The FTC stated: "One common theme among those opposed to the record-keeping requirements as proposed was that the cost would deter warrantors from establishing informal dispute settlement procedures [FTC 1975:60211, n. 236]." Regarding consumer comments that mechanism decisions should be binding on the warrantor, it said: "The Commission is not persuaded that making this impact on the warrantor even greater would benefit consumers more than it would discourage warrantors from adopting mechanisms [p. 60211, n. 236]."

[62]"In response to such comments, the Commission has eliminated the provision requiring warrantors to clearly and conspicuously disclose that direct access to the mechanism is always available at the consumer's option [FTC 1975:60199]."

[63]See, for example, Guenther Baumgart, AHAM President, writing in *California Man-*

speaking to business groups;[64] and all vigorously participate in major consumers' conferences, public policy forums,[65] and Congressional hearings.[66] The programs also regularly release press packets and statements.[67]

Virginia Knauer does an even better job in publicizing these trade association initiatives. Calling the CAPs a "breakthrough," Knauer has conducted major press conferences replete with statements about the mechanisms' broad promise,[68] has written about them in glowing terms to state and local consumer protection specialists,[69] has called conferences

---

agement Review, Spring 1974. Baumgart states rather surprisingly, "They [the panels] are attracting commendation from some of the most caustic critics of business [p. 55]." Baumgart alleges that "not only does the Panel offer . . . personal concern, but when the complaint reaches the company involved, it goes to the top executive and he, himself, reviews that specific problem and follows through to solution [p. 56]." Several of the correspondents in our own survey (see n. 75) told us that their hopes were raised falsely by the tone and wording of such statements in their MACAP correspondence. For example, Mrs. Norman Boysen's complaint was acknowledged by a form letter from General Electric's Consumer Relations Representative, who stated that the next correspondence would come from a district supervisor, hardly akin to Baumgart's claim.

[64]In 1974, for example, MACAP panelists collectively made more than 70 public appearances at conferences and workshops in 18 states (MACAP 1975:11). MACAP, at the request of business groups, has also held its meetings in different cities around the country. San Diego Gas and Electric Company invited MACAP to hold a meeting in San Diego in December 1973 (Federal Office of Consumer Affairs 1973).

[65]MACAP presented a special program in Hartford, Conn., in May 1974 at a Consumer Forum held in conjunction with the state's Consumer Information Week (MACAP 1975:11). Officials from CRICAP, AUTOCAP, MACAP, and FICAP attended the September 1974 Washington forum entitled "Consumer Complaints—Public Policy Alternatives" sponsored by George Washington University's School of Business and Public Administration and by the Federal Office of Consumer Affairs. Panelists from MACAP and CRICAP wrote articles for the published proceedings (Knauer 1975a) as did Robert Longnecker, an administrator for AUTOCAP.

[66]The hearings on the Magnuson–Moss Warranty–Federal Trade Commission Improvement Act provide an example. FICAP was represented by its Executive Director, Margaret Ward, on 17 September 1975. MACAP testimony was presented by then Chairwoman Virginia Habeeb, panelist John Rose, and AHAM President Guenther Baumgart on 15 September 1975. CRICAP submitted testimony the same day. John Hart, then First Vice President, testified for NAHB on September 17. Testimony is in the Federal Office of Consumer Affairs files.

[67] CRICAP, for example, sent out as a press release 1657 copies of Longnecker's "Complaint-Handling by the Consumer Action Panels" (see footnote 65). And MACAP claimed to have released a special detailed report on its activities and procedures to 10,000 consumer representatives, government officials, editors, and educators (MACAP 1975:11).

[68]"Based on the experience of . . . the Major Appliance Consumer Action Panel, we believe that approximately 75 percent of the consumers' complaints can be resolved satisfactorily to all concerned [Knauer 1973a:6]."

[69]Evidently, from their replies to Mrs. Knauer, some of the state and local officials do not agree with her. For example, regarding the AUTOCAPs: "Encouragement of industry self-regulation without comprehensive legislation and strong government enforcement powers is little more than window dressing and does not meet consumer needs [Matson 1973]"; "I

to discuss the panels' functioning,[70] and has presented her opinions on the trade association mechanisms to Congress.[71] In essence, Mrs. Knauer's role combines with the efforts of the trade associations and panels themselves to attempt to sell the programs politically.

Yet there is another facet to public relations, one involving the public's actual knowledge of the programs and one threatening increased costs through greater complaint workloads. The mechanisms have faced this side of public relations with more care. Citing "the strictures of time and money," MACAP panelists revealed their hesitancy about increasing the program's public exposure (Federal Office of Consumer Affairs 1973). Similarly, NADA turned down a Public Broadcasting System (PBS) request to film a special on the AUTOCAPs, fearing that the association would be swamped with complaints (Marlette, interview with Darmstadter, 16 May 1975). Besides threatening heavier workloads, increased publicity can also conflict with more important trade association goals. Nationwide advertising of the HOW program might well hold the key to greater consumer enrollments. On the other hand, such publicity would anger those state and local NAHB affiliate areas that have chosen not to participate. This internal political problem has combined with HOW budgetary constraints to minimize advertising, according to an anonymous informant in the Tulsa NAHM office on 16 March 1976.

Perhaps the most compelling illustration of the political tension involved in program relationships with the outside world comes through the trade associations' response to Consumer Complaint Project (CCP) requests to analyze the mechanisms' functioning. Project researchers were granted full access to panelists and to mechanism and trade publications, newspaper articles, charters, minutes, and annual reports—things in which the programs put their best foot forward but which prove little about actual functioning and results. However, CCP requests to follow up actual cases in order to assess the complaint-handling process were almost universally rejected. Negotiations with three of the trade associations stretched to 10, 13, and 14 months, during which time several concessions were made by the CCP,[72] and Virginia Knauer voiced her support

---

will reserve my opinion to a later date since the self-policing organizations sometimes leave much to be desired [Linber 1973]"; "It seems to me that this is a rather loaded panel [Merrill 1973]." All replies in Federal Office of Consumer Affairs files.

[70]On 8 April 1975, for example, Mrs. Knauer sponsored a CRICAP briefing to discuss an audit of CRICAP files and procedures by Dr. Maurice McDonald of Georgia State University.

[71]"Candor compels me to admit that we have used this movement by the major appliance industry [MACAP] as an example to stimulate the development of similar mechanisms by other industries.... These experiments are providing us with working models that illustrate the feasibility of certain procedures for further changes and improvements [Knauer 1974a:9–11]."

[72]Negotiations with MACAP over file access began about 1 June 1974 and ended 3 April 1975. Those with CRICAP extended from 2 May 1974 to 20 June 1975, and with FICAP from 1 May 1974 to 1 July 1975 (Wheeler 1976, and review of industry correspondence on file

for such an analysis.[73] Nevertheless, MACAP, CRICAP, FICAP, and several AUTOCAPs refused to open their files, even when granted complete anonymity for all businesses and consumers. The Connecticut AUTOCAP was the sole CAP to provide access. By contrast, Better Business Bureaus, media action lines, state and local consumer protection offices, small claims courts, and consumer groups all granted the CCP access to case files. Evidently, though, these groups did not face the potential wrath of their membership. Mrs. Knauer had gently foreshadowed this problem in her congressional testimony: "Corporate members are uneasy about the possibility that others may view their complaint files [Knauer 1974a:7]." Richard Hopper, Executive Secretary of CRICAP, put it more bluntly. He wrote: "To do so would put the program in great jeopardy [Hopper 1974]."

Complaint Handling

The dispute resolvers' complaint handling reflects the trade association imperative of service to members. Indeed, the mechanisms are sold to members as exactly that—a service. Thus, the FICAP invitation to furniture manufacturers prominently displays the 70% resolution rate in favor of manufacturers (FICAP 1974b). This solicitation to join continues: "As a member of FICAP your consumer problems can be resolved without publicity or the intervention of government or other consumer agencies [FICAP 1974b]."

Marketing trade association panels, with comments like the foregoing, in effect promise complaint handling from the industry's point of view. This perspective was crystallized in an April 1975 letter to FICAP members from SFMA Consumer Affairs Chairman Buck Shuford:

> I think we all prefer to have the FICAP panel, **who are reasonable people and understand our industry,** to handle our complaints rather than a government agency or newspaper action line [emphasis added].

Given this point of view, panel deliberations tend to ignore or label as stupid consumers with actual product expertise. Robert Wharton, an engineer, deeply resented his treatment by MACAP:

> I believe I had a valid complaint and did offer some constructive criticism. ... I am completely frustrated particularly in the fact that they all missed

---

with the CCP). Originally, the CCP did not want to guarantee anonymity to businesses. On about 1 January 1975, however, the CCP conceded this point and offered anonymity to all parties. Though this had seemed to be the point of contention, the guarantee ultimately did not succeed in opening CAP files.

[73]"The proposals for follow-up of selected cases and protection of complainants' rights of privacy seem necessary and fair to me [Knauer 1974c; copy on file with CCP]."

my point and insinuated that I am the one who is so stupid that I cannot comprehend [Wharton 1975].

And Mrs. R. M. Norton, a long-time housewife, was angered when MACAP rejected her complaint, implying that she could not understand the complicated process of doing her family's laundry. MACAP stated that her clothes dryer had been set at too high a temperature, when in fact the heat could not be further lowered on that particular model (Norton 1975).

Thus, CAP panelists tend to manifest a "victim-blaming" ideology toward consumers. At the FICAP meeting in June 1975, several complaints —filed 7 months previously—were finally coming to panel consideration. One panelist decided that because consumers were using their broken furniture while their complaints were being processed, any eventual settlement should be prorated; none of his colleagues voiced disagreement (Darmstadter 1976c). And MACAP panelist Professor Jason Annis remarked at the 9–10 March 1975 sessions that he failed to understand why a consumer had loaded a newly bought freezer with food. According to Annis, everyone knows that such appliances should be operated empty for several hours (Darmstadter 1975b).[74]

Opinions like these emerge from both the background of the panelists and the working environment of the CAPs. Many of the panelists have had years of contact with industry. MACAP's William White was ineligible for panel membership in April 1974 because he was employed by Commonwealth Edison of Chicago. After a 33-year stint with the company, he retired. In May 1974 he became a MACAP panelist (White 1974). Mrs. Virginia Habeeb, MACAP Chairwoman, has been employed by a Virginia electrical power company and an appliance manufacturer. She was also the recipient of AHAM outstanding communication awards in 1965, 1967, 1968, and 1969 (Habeeb, interview with Darmstadter, 19 July 1974). Panelist Mary Neil Alexander worked for Corning Glass and two natural gas companies for 18 of her 20 years prior to joining MACAP (interview with Darmstadter, same date). Such backgrounds undercut the MACAP claim of "total independence from industry." Indeed, Dr. Virginia Cutler, first MACAP Chairperson, related that "the industry people didn't want consumer advocates who were just out waving flags [interview with

---

[74]Not only was Professor Annis unrealistic in his expectations, but he was actually incorrect about the need for empty operation. We asked MACAP staff member Joyce Viso to explain Annis' comment. She originally supported his view, but later, after some research, she changed her mind: "I retract my statement that refrigerators and freezers ought to be given time to 'cool down' before storing warm food upon installation of the appliance. It is not absolutely necessary and not following the practice would normally only mean that the appliance would run longer at the outset to cool the interior of the appliance plus the food load [Viso 1975]."

Darmstadter, same date]." Moreover, Cutler remembers, she and the panel were to be "on trial" for an unspecified period.

The working environment of the panels seems to make them vulnerable to a form of "capture," a term commonly used to describe the relationship between regulatory agencies and their target industries. Robert Holding, MACAP Staff Director, states that the panel is akin to "a family that very much wants to be liked [interview with Darmstadter, 19 July 1974]." Dr. Cutler revealed in her interview that her attitude toward the industry changed when she saw how sincere the leaders were, what delightful families they had, and how they helped with schools and parks in their home neighborhoods.

Panelist attitudes like these may prove little in and of themselves, but they touch upon a deeper trade association fear of vigorous *consumer* representation. Virginia Knauer pointed out in a May 1974 press release that although consumer presence on the AUTOCAPs was the key to the programs' success, "a number of associations seem reluctant to open their doors [Knauer 1974b]." And when a member of HOW's Program Advisory Board suggested public representation on the HOW Board of Directors, he was told that, at that time, the program's leaders were having enough trouble selling HOW to builders (Benny L. Kass, interview with Stanton, 6 April 1976).

Moreover, in the context of mechanisms essentially funded, staffed, housed, and directed by the parent trade associations, panel bias is quite a logical, but nevertheless powerful, final blow to fair and responsive complaint resolution. Whereas the CAPs advertise themselves as expert bodies rendering quasi-judicial evaluations, their procedures and findings reveal deference toward industry.

First, the panels' refusal to review cases until a stalemate is reached holds down caseloads and provides maximum discretion to industry:

> It should be carefully noted that no effort is made to interfere with a manufacturer's opportunity to resolve his own complaint. If a consumer tries to by-pass this step, then MACAP will send the complaint back to the manufacturer. *Only if the manufacturer cannot obtain a resolution does the panel involve itself with the complaint* [CRICAP pamphlet 1973; emphasis added].

Not only does this practice increase the length of time consumers must wait, but it also heightens the possibility that they will give up in frustration. The panels' caseloads can severely limit the amount of time they devote to each case. Our observation of MACAP's meeting of 9–10 March 1975 illustrates. In the last 2 hours of the session, the panel decided 55 cases—barely 2 minutes per case (Darmstadter 1975b). Thus, the "individual attention to each complaint" that MACAP advertises (MACAP 1975:10) is hurried at best. Moreover, before the panel session, the trade association staff had analyzed each case and had recommended a specific decision to the panel. This recommendation was often adopted by the panel in its rush to dispose of its caseload. Thus, considerable power over a decision rests with staff personnel, who are actually paid by the business party to the dispute!

Second, CAP procedures assume consumer satisfaction unless the panels receive positive evidence to the contrary. MACAP, for example, claims that 97% of its communication phase (prepanel) cases are satisfactorily resolved (MACAP 1975:10). Our sampling of MACAP cases,[75] how-

[75]Since MACAP would not give the CCP access to its files, we conducted our own follow-up. In the fall of 1974 we started pulling from letters received at the various Ralph Nader offices those concerning on-going and past problems with MACAP-related products. The number of cases selected totaled 126. We could not reach some of the correspondents; many had already had their problems resolved; others had no wish to pursue them further or chose to drop out shortly after our initial contact. But after 9 months we had followed 66 cases through MACAP's prepanel and panel stages. (Included among this number were not only people who had followed our suggestion, after we explained the nature of our study, to contact MACAP for help, but also several who had already begun or completed the MACAP procedure before writing us.) The Federal Office of Consumer Affairs also cooperated by letting us search its files for MACAP-appropriate problems.

We then submitted the names of "our" complainants to MACAP, asking for permission to look at its complete files on these specific cases, so that we would not be dependent solely on the consumer's recollections of what had happened. If a complainant claimed he or she had never received, say, a closing letter from MACAP, of course, it would have been to the group's advantage if it could have shown that such a letter had in fact been sent. MACAP refused to release any files to us without the approval of the companies involved (all the consumers had already granted such approval) in spite of the fact that we already knew, from the complainants, all the firm names. Only Corning, Montgomery Ward, and Whirlpool (with 1, 1, and 3 cases, respectively) agreed to let us see the files of cases in which they were involved. The remaining 59 cases (we were unable to identify the manufacturer in 1 case and 1 non-MACAP member was not contacted), representing complaints against General Electric–Hotpoint (15), Westinghouse (7), Caloric (6), Norge (6), Kelvinator (5), Frigidaire (4), Tappan (4), O'Keefe & Merritt (2), Sears (2), and Admiral, Amana, Cory, Gaffers & Sattler, Hamilton, Jenn-Air, Magic Chef, and Roper, with 1 each, were withheld. However, MACAP did provide us with a status report on all the cases as of mid August 1975.

Our sample, although not as empirically random as we would have liked, turned out to be representative of the cases generally handled by MACAP.

Type of problem	Reported to MACAP	Reported to CCP
Service	35.9%	30%
Performance	32.5%	44%
Parts failures	10.4%	5%
Nonresponsiveness of manufacturer–dealer	3.6%	3%
Food loss	5.3%	5%
Warranties	3.5%	3%
Purchasing dissatisfaction	2.8%	2%
Safety	2.0%	8%
Other	4.0%	0%
	100.0%	100%

(continued)

ever, shows that only 14 of the 39 closed cases were considered satisfactory by the consumer. Five of this sample's consumers demonstrate the holes in MACAP logic; they were so discouraged by the manufacturer's or dealer's response (after the customary MACAP referral) that they deemed it useless to pursue the matter. Thus, MACAP's assumption of resolution might indeed create a perverse twist: Businesses may actually have the incentive to respond harshly, knowing that some consumers will give up in frustration at that point.

Third, the CAPs do not systematically inform consumers that, if they are dissatisfied with manufacturer response, they can continue to pursue their case with the panel. Many consumers therefore accept manufacturer offers or explanations because they think they have no other option. Mary Kolodny, an MACAP "satisfactory resolution," wrote to CCP on her return postcard: "I finally paid $57.50 for the part [on her Caloric range] plus labor. Wasn't really satisfied that this was fair but I really didn't have any choice at this point."

Fourth, many dissatisfied consumers, because of highly arbitrary panel definitions, find their way into the "satisfactorily resolved" column. Mrs. Laura Metcalf did not state a specific reason for her continued dissatisfaction; therefore she was classified as satisfied. Mrs. Arthur Martin's dispute with General Electric over labor costs ended after 6 months when MACAP reiterated the very same company offer that had prompted Mrs. Martin to contact the panel in the first place; yet she, too, in MACAP's files, was satisfied. Finally, even consumer politeness is misconstrued as satisfaction. For example, Susan Moratto wrote: "All claims were justified regardless of denial from Caloric Corporation. Corrections should be made where applicable to protect the unsuspecting consumer. Thank you for your service." (Copies of all correspondence are on file with CCP.) Mrs. Moratto, MACAP has decided, is satisfied. These industry-serving definitions, of course, stop cases dead in their tracks.

Fifth, it appears that panels give further deference to industry by tailoring decisions to accommodate traditional business responses. Most freezer manufacturers honor food loss claims of up to $150 during the warranty period. Thus, in considering a case with $400 in legitimate losses, MACAP recommended the standard $150 settlement. And in

---

Footnote 75—*Continued*

Type of appliance	MACAP	CCP
Refrigeration equipment	40.0%	36%
Cooking equipment	29.2%	38%
Laundry equipment	16.0%	18%
Clean-up equipment (dishwashers, disposal units)	10.0%	6%
Other	4.8%	2%
	100.0%	100%

another food loss case, MACAP authorized only part of a claim because "this manufacturer never covers labor [Darmstadter 1975b]."

Sixth, in not monitoring business promises of resolution, the panels avoid challenging membership credibility and alienating membership good will, as evidenced in our Connecticut AUTOCAP sampling.[76] In 11 of the Connecticut panel's 28 "satisfactorily resolved" cases, consumers stated that either the dealers had misinformed AUTOCAP or AUTOCAP had misinterpreted their responses. In fact, the cases had not been resolved at all; consumers had given up pursuing them instead, usually after repeated trips to the dealer.

Seventh, panel case dispositions result in consumers being treated arbitrarily. For example, an outside audit commissioned by CRICAP (McDonald 1974) found that: in 31 "invalid" cases, "the actual bases or factors upon which determination was made are not stated in files or records"; 24 of 62 "inquiries" should have been treated as complaints; on the average, CRICAP took 3½ months to make a finding of nonjurisdiction; the mechanism failed to inquire about what partial effort industry might have been willing to make in cases where it refused complaints; and, overall, CRICAP procedure revealed the "absence of a set of cohesive guidelines for handling cases and keeping records [McDonald 1974]." Not surprisingly, each one of these deviations from the governing rules benefited CRICAP's members.

Eighth, the trade association mechanisms take great pains to maintain the privacy of their member firms, further lessening any need for the firms to adopt panel findings. FICAP promises privacy, both in its charter and in its invitation to prospective members (FICAP 1974a and 1974b). CRICAP procedures ensure that "all case determinations shall be kept in confidence and may not be revealed by company name or product name [CRICAP 1974:5]"; consumer name is conspicuously absent from this commitment. MACAP holds itself to "constant confidentiality [MACAP 1975:5]." This concern for privacy in effect eliminates the one power the mechanism might have: the power to publicize. Talk of competitive pressure to the contrary,[77] this type of power is incongruent with the institutional stance of the trade association. It exists to eliminate competitive advantages among members and only to create consensus advantages for its membership as a whole.

This practice is weighted heavily against the consumer. Although

[76]We examined a random sample of 10% (28) of the 280 cases closed by AUTOCAP between July and December 1974.

[77]In Virginia Knauer's Congressional testimony (Knauer 1974a:7), she states, "Members of an industry are highly sensitive about a record which shows they may be generating more complaints than their competitors [p. 81]." The one exception is that MACAP will provide copies of the consumers' own correspondence with MACAP. Everything else is labeled "proprietary and confidential under MACAP's operating policy [Schroeder 1975]."

MACAP provides each AHAM company with file summaries of cases against it (Darmstadter 1975b), the panel will not release such information to the consumer. Thus, individuals who wish to take further action following a MACAP or company rejection are not even allowed to have copies of the material in their own files.[78] If a company refuses to accept a MACAP decision, MACAP does not inform the consumer of its own arguments in the customer's behalf. Instead, the closing letter from MACAP merely states that the company "did not agree with the Panel's judgment and has advised us that no further action will be taken on your complaint [MACAP 1970b:10]."

The basis of all these procedures is the need for the mechanisms to serve trade association members; they literally seem to have no power to do otherwise. FICAP's Buck Shuford puts it well in a letter to members:

> I'm sure that you have found FICAP does not interfere with your normal business practices or encourage more complaints. In fact some members find FICAP to be a help; a letter [from FICAP] to an unreasonable customer can often end a problem when the same letter from the manufacturer would make the consumer more angry and the problem more difficult [Shuford 1975].

Conclusion

In summary, the trade association CAP complaint-handling process is inadequate for several reasons. The process is slow, often consuming months, especially when the panels needlessly send consumers back to dealers or manufacturers. The panels are often partial, despite participation of nominal "consumer" representatives on some CAPs. This defect is more pronounced when the CAP depends on paid trade association staff members for support and even analysis of cases. The process places an immense burden on the complainant to pursue his or her case through numerous procedural obstacles, under pain of having the case lose its momentum and thereby be terminated by a panel eager to designate the file "closed to consumer satisfaction."

The rules and procedures of the process—critical in determining the outcome of a case—are weighted against the consumer and in favor of the trade association member. The business party to the dispute is provided with case materials, but access to them is denied to the consumer complainant. Arbitrary definitions are applied to designate a complaint as "invalid" or even a mere "inquiry," which are sufficient grounds to close a case in favor of the business defendant. Trade associations may boast to members that CAP procedures have been selected to minimize obstruc-

---

[78]Some exceptions are made to this rule (MACAP 1970b).

tions to the normal business operations of the defendants. The aggrieved consumer, however, may discover that the secrecy thrown up by the panels camouflages a long, arbitrary, and confusing process.

Many consumers are enticed into the trade association complaint-handling process and are thereby discouraged from pursuing potentially more effective remedies, for example, small claims courts. When the trade association process has dragged out enough months without providing actual redress, the consumer may be induced to give up his or her case altogether. The trade association panel may have lavished enough correspondence and attention on the case that the consumer accepts a negative decision without quite understanding the biased nature of the process; in carnival parlance, the "mark" is "cooled out."

Unfortunately, we can only conclude that the trade association CAP programs are of little value in the consumer complaint process. They have no power to enforce a decision against a recalcitrant business. Even at their best, they do not possess the statutory authority of state and local consumer protection offices; the media pressure of newspaper and radio action lines; the will or resources of mediating organizations to badger businesses; the economic threat of pressure groups that picket, leaflet, and boycott; or the fair, adversarial process of many small claims courts.

One might argue, as have some commentators,[79] that since the trade association panels resolve some complaints and do so without any direct economic costs to consumers, we are all, as a society, made better off by their existence. But such an argument would be valid only in a vacuum, for the complaint process is a highly complex one, imposing on consumers material and psychological costs, and literally tempting them to give up at various points along the way to resolution.

These comments apply to the CAP programs we have studied. While the HOW program and OIC do not involve the procedural unfairness of the CAPs, they too reflect the basic weakness of the trade association vis à vis its industry. Quite simply, both programs involve a reverse selection process: Those businesses—builders or movers—most likely to engender consumer complaints will simply remain outside the program.

Of course, in the end, one must be sympathetic to the institutional position of the trade association programs. Actually, as the NAHB official took pains to point out, the panels do about as much as can be expected from organizations without either the independent power or the incentive to respond to consumers' needs. But from the point of view of the con-

---

[79]"From a welfare viewpoint, MACAP seems noncontroversially desirable. It offered the consumer another channel for seeking a favorable ruling on a complaint. The total cost was extremely low (less than $100,000 per year) and insignificant on a per appliance basis. Hence, some consumers (i.e., those who received favorable rulings) were made better off while, given the extremely low cost, none were made significantly worse off [Hunt 1975:52]."

sumer seeking fair complaint resolution and from the point of view of a society seeking an array of accessible, understandable, dispute-resolving mechanisms, that is not enough.

Similarly, the finality and conclusiveness that we would seek in a dispute-resolution program is nowhere to be found in these trade association panels. Panel decisions need not be adhered to by member companies. And the panels do not undertake adequate follow-up procedures to determine whether or not member promises to resolve complaints are actually carried out. By contrast, a nondecision effectively denies the consumer redress through the mechanism.

Finally, a tremendous amount of potentially useful information is kept from the public by the panels' secrecy. Rather than campaigning to prevent legislation and regulation, trade associations could use the aggregate information collected from their panels to improve the regulatory process and spot problems requiring closer scrutiny by business or government.

One cannot propose reform of the panels without recognizing the institutional forces that constrain their complaint-handling efforts. Trade associations, since their inception, have sought to serve members, not coerce them. Here, in the complaint-handling process, we can see how this imperative obstructs adequate resolution of consumer complaints. Neither poor design nor inept administration—although evident—lie at the base of the panels' poor record with consumers. Instead, fundamental industry motivations manifest themselves in industry control of panel structure, funding, staffing, and decision-making power.

The real benefits of the trade association panel process—even setting aside the important benefit of preventing or weakening unwanted legislation—accrue to member businesses. Consider three points:

1. The panels handle complaints only after the manufacturer or dealer has refused to do so. Many consumers drop out of the complaint process during this referral and rereferral period. Therefore, if they so desire, businesses can turn complainants away, knowing that if the consumers eventually go to the trade association panel, business can still respond in an uncoerced fashion. It is possible that only the strongest, angriest, or most persevering of consumers will return to the panel.

2. The panels assemble complaints into tidy informational packages— collecting missing data, obtaining expert opinions if necessary, and even providing this information to the business involved, while at the same time denying it—by their pledge of privacy—to the aggrieved consumer and to government agencies in a position to use such information for the benefit of a large class of consumers. The trade association programs, in assembling case information, not only impose additional burdens on consumers—for example, requiring more case information—but

also may be said to help business discover which complaints will not fade away. In other words, the CAPs, by drawing out the complaint process, may even reduce industry's "complaint response dollar."

3. Most seriously, the trade associations garb their programs in objective, independent, third-party rhetoric. They sell the panels to their membership as a "help" with angry consumers while proclaiming to the outside world their freedom from industry influence.

References

Agee, Janice Lowen
1975 "Barbara Zinsky, a Consumer Complaint Project life history." Working paper on file. Washington, D.C.: Center for the Study of Responsive Law.
Babcock, James F. (President, Automotive Trade Association Managers)
1973 Statement at White House Press Conference for AUTOCAP. 20 July: p. 2.
Bandy, B. J. (Vice Chairman of the Board, Coronet Industries)
1975 Letter to Virginia Knauer. 30 September.
Barksdale, Hiram C., and Warren A. French
1975 Response to consumerism: How change is perceived by both sides. *Michigan State University Business Topics* (Spring) **23**(2):55–67.
Baumgart, Guenther (President, American Home Appliance Manufacturers)
1974 Industrywide cooperation for consumer affairs. *California Management Review* **16**(3):53–60.
Bixby, Michael
1972 Implied warranty of habitability: New rights for home buyers. *Clearinghouse Review* (December) **6**(8):468–476.
Brown, George (General Services Manager, American Motors Corporation)
1973 Letter to Frank McLaughlin, Director, Industrial Relations Division, Federal Office of Consumer Affairs. 19 July.
CRICAP (Carpet and Rug Industry, Inc.)
1973 *CRI Consumer Affairs Program* (pamphlet). 16 May.
1974 *Carpet and Rug Industry Consumer Action Panel charter.* 27 August.
Darmstadter, Ruth
1975a *Automotive Consumer Action Panels: A detour on the route to effective complaint handling in the automobile industry* (Consumer Complaint Project working paper). June.
1975b *Giving the consumer the business: A study of complaint handling in the major appliance industry* (Consumer Complaint Project working paper). September.
1975c *Better foundations needed: A study of the National Association of Home Builders Home Owners Warranty Program* (Consumer Complaint Project working paper). December.
1976a *The man on the shining white moving van: A report on the Office of the Impartial Chairman of the moving and storage industry of New York City* (Consumer Complaint Project working paper). January.
1976b *Carpet and Rug Industry Consumer Action Panel* (Consumer Complaint Project working paper). February.

1976c *Furniture Industry Consumer Action Panel* (Consumer Complaint Project working paper). February.

Duffy, Louise (Staff Member, Federal Office of Consumer Affairs)
1974 Memo to Virginia Knauer. 20 March.

Federal Office of Consumer Affairs (see also Knauer, Virginia)
1973 Internal memorandum. 12 December.

Feiber, Bertrand (Consumer Affairs Director, National Automobile Dealers Association)
1973 Statement at White House Press Conference for AUTOCAP. 20 July: pp. 4–5.

FICAP (Furniture Industry Consumer Action Panel)
1974a FICAP charter.
1974b *FICAP invitation* (pamphlet for prospective members).
1974c *FICAP: The first year* (pamphlet).

Finkelstein, Larry
1973 Some tough questions about trade associations. *Business and Society Review* (Summer) **1**(6):22–30.

Frye, Joseph J. (President, Southern Furniture Manufacturers Association)
1973 Statement at White House Press Conference for FICAP. 17 August: p. 3.

FTC (Federal Trade Commission)
1975 Regulations on Magnuson–Moss Federal Trade Commission Improvement Act. *Federal Register* (31 December): Title 16, Commercial Practices, Chap. 1, Subchap. 2, Part 703.

Greyser, Stephen A.
1973 Marketing and responsiveness to consumerism. *Journal of Contemporary Business* (Autumn) **2**(4):81–93.

Greyser, Stephen A., and Steven L. Diamond
1974 Business is adapting to consumerism. *Harvard Business Review* (September–October) **52**(5):39–50.

Gulledge, Eugene A.
1973 *An insured home warranty.* Washington, D.C.: National Association of Home Builders.

Hopper, Richard (Executive Secretary, CRICAP)
1974 Letter to Consumer Complaint Project. 24 May.

HORC (Home Owners Registration Corporation)
1974a *Criteria for registration of builders.*
1974b *Here's HOW* (monthly).
1974c *Know HOW.*
1974d News release. 22 May.
1974e *Understanding HOW.*
1975 *Consumer information booklet.*

HUD (Housing and Urban Development, U.S. Department of)
1974a *Housing in the seventies.* Washington, D.C.: U.S. Department of Housing and Urban Development.
1974b An insured builder's warranty plan for home buyers . . . British experience and an American proposal. *HUD International Foreign Information News Item.* Washington, D.C.: Office of International Affairs, Department of Housing and Urban Development.

Hunt, Michael S.
    1975   Trade associations and self-regulation: Major home appliances. In *Regulating the product*, edited by Richard E. Carejo and Marc J. Roberts. Cambridge, Mass.: Lippincott.

Kempner, Jonathan L.
    1976   The home owners warranty program: An initial analysis. *Stanford Law Review* **28**(7):157–380.

Knauer, Virginia (Special Assistant to the President for Consumer Affairs)
    1973a Press statement at White House Press Conference for FICAP. 20 July: pp. 1–15.
    1973b Press statement at White House Press Conference for FICAP. 17 August: pp. 1–20.
    1974a Statement before Subcommittee for Consumers of the Senate Commerce Committee and the Subcommittee on the Representation of Citizens' Interests of the Senate Judiciary Committee. 27 March.
    1974b Press release. 5 May.
    1974c Letter to Presidents of GAMA, AHAM, and NRMA. 3 July.
    1975a *Consumer redress—Some encouraging signs*. From Consumer Complaints—Public Policy Alternatives forum, December. Washington, D.C.: Acropolis.
    1975b CRICAP briefing. 8 April.
    1975c Letter to Bertrand Fieber (Chairman, NADA Consumer Relations Committee). 7 August.

Linber, Betty B. (Consumer Affairs Director, Montgomery County, Pa.)
    1973   Letter to Virginia Knauer. 10 September.

Longnecker, Robert
    1975   Complaint-handling by the Consumer Action Panels. In *Consumer redress—Some encouraging signs*, edited by Virginia Knauer. From Consumer Complaints—Public Policy Alternatives Forum, December. Washington, D.C.: Acropolis.

McDonald, Maurice E.
    1974   *CRICAP resolved consumer complaint audit and study*. Carpet and Rug Industry. 20 December.

MACAP (Major Appliance Consumer Action Panel)
    1970a MACAP prospectus.
    1970b Minutes to MACAP meeting. 1–2 May.
    1972   *MACAP, policies and procedures*.
    1975   *MACAP, fifth anniversary report*.

Matson, Robert W. (City Consumer Affairs Director, St. Paul, Minn.)
    1973   Letter to Virginia Knauer. 25 September.

Merrill, Wanda (Administrator, Consumer Services Division, Oregon Dept. of Commerce)
    1973   Letter to Virginia Knauer. 25 September.

NADA (National Automobile Dealers Association) and ATAM (Automotive Trade Association Managers)
    1973   *The automobile dealer and the consumer* (booklet).

NAHB (National Association of Home Builders)
    1973a *NAHB Journal–Scope*. 3 December: p. 51.

1973b Presidential memorandum to local and state presidents and executive officers. 15 October.

1974 *NAHB Journal–Scope.* 4 March.

1975 *NAHB Journal–Scope.* 3 July.

Nightengale, Margaret

1973 *The Office of Impartial Chairman: An example of industry-level complaint management* (Unpublished working paper). University of California, Berkeley. 16 July.

Norton, Mrs. R. M. (MACAP complainant)

1975 Letters to MACAP. 9 and 18 May.

President's Task Force on Appliance Warranties and Service

1969 *Final report to Secretaries of Commerce and Labor, the Chairman of the Federal Trade Commission, and the Special Assistant to the President for Consumer Affairs.* 8 January.

Rosenberg, Larry J.

1975 Retailers' responses to consumerism. *Business Horizons* (October) **18**(5):40–50.

Schroeder, Nancy (MACAP staff member)

1975 Letter to Barbara Snellbaker (complainant). 30 April.

Seeyle, Alfred L.

1975 Societal change and business–government relationships. *Michigan State University Business Topics* (Autumn) **23**(4):5–11.

Shuford, Buck (Chairman, Consumer Affairs Committee, Southern Furniture Manufacturers Association [SFMA])

1975 Letter to FICAP members. 12 April.

Sumichrast, Michael, and Sara A. Frankel

1970 *Profile of the builder and his industry.* Washington, D.C.: National Association of Home Builders.

Szabo, Joan C.

1974 Home warranties planned to forestall federal action. *National Journal Reports* (16 March) **6**(11):392–396.

Viso, Joyce (MACAP staff member)

1975 Letter to Ruth Darmstadter. 16 December.

Wharton, Robert (MACAP complainant)

1975 Letter to Ruth Darmstadter. 24 February.

Wheeler, Christopher (Project Director, Consumer Complaint Project)

1976 Interview with David Greenberg. 15 April.

White, William (MACAP panelist)

1974 Interview with Ruth Darmstadter. 19 July.

Williams, E. P. (Service Programs Manager, Customer Service Division, Ford Motor Company)

1973 Letter to Dr. William McClean, Motor Vechicle Manufacturers Association. 2 May.

Wilson, James Q.

1975 *Political organizations.* New York City: Basic Books.

Wirthlin, Richard B.

1975 Public perceptions of the American business system: 1966–75. *Journal of Contemporary Business* (Summer) **4**(3):1–15.

6

Marian Eaton

THE BETTER BUSINESS BUREAU: "The Voice of the People in the Marketplace"

Prologue

The Better Business Bureau system is composed of 143 local organizations, which concentrate on retail advertising and business practices in their respective market areas, and the Council of Better Business Bureaus, Inc., which provides support services to these organizations, handles government relations, and regulates national advertising. The field research upon which this chapter is based was conducted in 1971 (the "ethnographic present" of the description) in what was then a medium-sized, somewhat underfunded local office. The early 1970s was a period of rejuvenation and growth for the Bureau system. Only 2 years after my visits to the office, its staff of 7 had grown to 14; its contacts with the public had nearly doubled; and its aggressive campaign to recruit new members included arbitration services among its selling points. At the date of this writing, CBBB projects that were in the proposed stage in 1971 are in full operation. I have updated my observations where possible but have been unable to conduct a thorough restudy. I believe that despite the surface changes, the essential philosophy and intent of the BBB, which are the underlying issues of this essay, remain the same. But because of the lapse of time, the office I studied is identified merely as "City Bureau," and the names of local publications, firms, and businesspeople have been changed.

Introduction

This study was undertaken in an effort to understand the processes of information flow, dispute settlement, and social control in a complex

NO ACCESS TO LAW
Alternatives to the American Judicial System

market society through the intensive examination of one institution. The implicit aim of the project was to explore the extent to which the Better Business Bureau system, which has been called by advertisers "the voice of the people in the marketplace," actually does function in the interests of the American consumer and why. My investigation revealed that BBB activities related to areas of consumer needs are: disseminating information ("interpreting the marketplace"), providing channels for handling disputes between buyers and sellers, and promoting self-regulation of advertising and selling practices within the business community. This chapter will describe and evaluate the Bureau's work in these areas.

In the small, relatively "simple" societies that anthropologists habitually study, the acquisition of information is fairly straightforward: People learn in childhood most of the skills they will need as adults. In the local marketplace the range of goods to be exchanged is relatively small, and the criteria for their evaluation are widely known and easy to apply. There are traditional modes of judging products, and their prices are haggled over by the two parties to the transaction until both are satisfied with the bargain. Beyond having a body of common knowledge and evaluative criteria, the two parties are bound together by multiple bonds of relationship: kinship, ritual obligations, common residence, or ongoing exchange agreements, all of which introduce a moral dimension into the transaction. Everyone either knows everyone else's reputation or can learn of it through personal networks, gossip, and rumor (see Bailey 1971 for a discussion of the role of such communications in peasant village life). Thus, social control by means of public opinion can be effective: Sellers with bad reputations lose a significant number of customers if they do not mend their ways. Fear of public outrage and the necessity of continuing relations between parties to a dispute encourage redress of grievances (see Colson 1953 and Gluckman 1955 on multiplex relations and cross-cutting ties; Aubert 1969 and Nader 1969 on the relation between style of dispute settlement and the kinds of relationships desired between disputants).

Complexity and a wider range of communication bring new factors into the picture. As the number of goods and services expands and the technology of their production and operation increases in sophistication, the buyer has less evaluative competence. The prices of most goods and services are fixed in advance by the seller. Consumers can take or leave the offer; but their only control lies in their ability to shop around and compare prices and qualities before they buy. As more links intervene in the market network, the relationships between buyers and sellers become single-purposed and impersonal. Buyers have fewer personal holds on the producers and sellers, and must depend on the legal system to protect their rights. Furthermore, there is a huge discrepancy in size and resources between the individuals who have a grievance about a product and the production–distribution complex to which they must look for redress.

In the complex society, then, social relationships tend to be simplex rather than multiplex, interactions fleeting and impersonal rather than ongoing and familiar, and a multiplicity of groups bring a multiplicity of more or less conflicting values to the same transaction (see Bauer and Greyser 1971 for a discussion of the opposing values of consumerists and businesspeople regarding what is appropriate in advertising, for example). Parties to disputes include new combinations such as the state versus the individual, the individual versus the "corporate individual," and class actions (the people versus the industry).

In the United States today we depend upon specialists to provide services and often even to give us the criteria by which we are to judge their work.[1] Many of our transactions take place infrequently, which means that we may be totally inexperienced in evaluating what we pay for when we buy a large appliance, an insurance policy, or a vacation trip.

Likewise we may find ourselves incapable of obtaining redress for grievances when we think we have been misled or cheated. The eclectic and passive approach to problem solving upon which people in our society must often depend is illustrated by a thank-you letter quoted in a BBB newsletter:

> May I congratulate you and your office on handling the refund gripe I had with [a New York-based firm]. I was so provoked with these people for not refunding my money as they advertised, that I decided to try reporting them to every agency I knew. The Post Office had me come by three times, twice to send letters with certified receipt attached, etc., then a followup and finally a letter from the postal inspector stating that they had no authority to effect an adjustment. Action Line replied they had too many such complaints—it had no public appeal for their paper. A letter to our U.S. Senator was sent to the Federal Trade Commission. The FTC replied they were not authorized to intervene in individual complaints. I never got an answer from Virginia Knauer, the President's counsel for consumer affairs. Whatever you did must have been great because they sent me a refund by return mail. Again, may I say I am grateful [BBB/Westcoast (pseud.), April 1971, p. 2].

This study was initiated with the very general question: How does an individual in a mass society manage to operate in his complicated environment? My particular interest was in the marketplace interactions between the consumer and the organizations that provide him with the goods and services he requires, and so I chose to investigate the services provided to consumers by a Better Business Bureau office, one agency

---

[1]See Moore and Tumin (1949) for a rather general discussion of "ignorance as preservative of privileged position: the specialists and the consumer."

among several upon which citizens rely for aid in dealing with the business community. The BBB is the best-known "remedy agent" among consumers because it has been in existence longer than any other agency of its kind and has advertised its services with enthusiasm for many years.

Most people's knowledge of the Better Business Bureau is limited to the fact that it is an organization customarily contacted by telephone when a person has a question about the existence or dependability of a firm or a complaint against one that has failed to give satisfaction. Few go beyond these facts to ask whose voice is on the other end of the line, where she gets her information, or what actually happens to complaints sent to the BBB. And yet millions of people use the Bureau every year. A 1977 Harris poll showed that the Bureau was "the overwhelming choice for help when consumers refer complaints to third parties [CBBB 1977b:1]." Most people with complaints went directly to the companies involved, but 10% contacted a Better Business Bureau, in contrast to 3% who contacted government agencies and 1% who went to consumer groups. *Good Housekeeping Magazine* reported in October 1970 that in a survey of 1000 readers the BBB and congressmen ranked together as the parties most frequently contacted by readers about consumer problems. The Bureau's estimated annual caseload is even more impressive. In 1976, about 6.9 million people called Better Business Bureaus, including 803,500 who received help with complaints (CBBB 1977a:5). In the same year, the federal Office of Consumer Affairs received about 24,150 complaints.[2]

My original focus of research was the local-level information-dissemination and conflict-management activities of a particular office. However, as I learned more about the BBB, I realized that larger issues were involved. Beyond the basic descriptive questions, a social scientist (or a citizen who wants to evaluate the Bureau's service to consumers) needs to explore a more refined set of questions: What functions does the Bureau serve for the various groups with which it is involved? How do the interests of the business community affect the operation of the Bureaus they sponsor? How is the consumer affected by the way the Bureau works? What are the effects of self-regulation of business on the interaction of various interest groups in our society?

A Note on Methodology

The Bureau I chose to study is located on a quiet side street of a California city. This office, which I shall call the City office, serves a

---

[2]Personal communication with staff member of U.S. Office of Consumer Affairs, Consumer Complaints Division; telephone interview on 14 July 1977 concerning OCA monthly statistics for 1974–1976.

population of 1.7 million who patronize about 25,000 local business establishments.[3] The Bureau employees field calls and walk-in complaints from consumers and businessmen on weekdays from 10 A.M. to 3 P.M. It was during these open hours that I made nine visits of a few hours each to the Bureau in the spring of 1971 to observe its operations.

My data are based upon several interviews with the staff about their work and the problems they encountered in it. In addition, I sampled the day-to-day work of the office by going through the files of a few businesses and by spending about 4½ hours listening to the switchboard operator handle calls as they came into the office. I also sampled the Bureau's clipping file of stories and messages released to the public and listened to the recording of a public presentation on deceptive selling practices that was sponsored by the local Bureau president and a trade association.

In order to get a better idea of the Bureau's other aspects, I studied publications of the local and national BBB. The official literature included books intended for the Bureaus themselves, such as the 1947 *Manual of Operation;* publications, including newsletters, intended for the business community; and pamphlets and guides for the public. I checked the information I gathered against the findings of a study of the nationwide Bureau system, organized by the office of Congressman Benjamin Rosenthal of New York (*Congressional Record* 1971) and against the testimony of H. Bruce Palmer, President of the Council of Better Business Bureaus, before the House Subcommittee on Advertising and Small Business (U.S. Congress 1971). Finally, I supplemented my knowledge of consumers and their problems by surveying hundreds of letters from consumers to Ralph Nader, by interviewing other consumer advocates, and by consulting newspaper articles.

History and Philosophy of the BBB Movement

The history of the BBB falls into three major phases. First, there was an initial period during which businesspeople promoted self-regulation through a specialized agency in a spirit of moral fervor mixed with fear of government regulation. Second, there was a long period of growth, consolidation, and routinization during which most of the offices were established. And recently there has been a period of reorganization and revitalization of the organization to adopt higher standards of conduct in the interests of freedom from governmental interference.

---

[3]These figures are based on data provided by the local Chamber of Commerce for the two-county region that the Bureau serves. The best estimate for the number of businesses in the two-county area is a U.S. Bureau of the Census report, "County Business Patterns 1973" (California CBP-73-6), based on Social Security records for 1972. The publication is updated annually.

Most accounts of the history and purposes of the BBB movement are produced by the Bureau itself or by similar and closely allied groups. Official statements created by spokespeople of a group for the general public are only one version of the history and goals of an organization that the investigator observes; they are selective in what they reveal and biased in directions favorable to the image the spokespeople wish to present. Because such statements select and interpret the facts, they provide an excellent source of information on the world view of those who propound them. The Bureau's history—or myth of origin, as an anthropologist would be inclined to call it—appeared in a book written to commemorate the fiftieth anniversary of the Bureau's creation:

> Samuel C. Dobbs was a young man with a good job who liked his work. As a sales manager of the Coca-Cola Company—later to become its president—he watched the firm's rapid growth and felt the satisfaction of knowing that his efforts played an important role in the rising sales curve. Larger problems of advertising had rarely if ever occupied his thoughts—until that day in the courtroom in the summer of 1907.
>
> The Federal Pure Food and Drug Act was passed in 1906 and with more missionary zeal than care the Government had lodged charges against a number of firms. Dobbs' company found itself in a court on charges which the trial showed to be unfounded. During the proceedings Dobbs sat in Court and listened to the U.S. Attorney charge his firm with false advertising.
>
> "That was annoying enough," Dobbs recalled later. "But what shocked me was the way our attorney responded to the charge!"
>
> The company's attorney rose, shrugged his shoulders, and said with a wave of his hand, "Why *all* advertising is exaggerated. Nobody really believes it."
>
> The attorney didn't know it, but he started the Better Business Bureau movement with that remark.
>
> Dobbs could not forget what he had heard. After a few months he began to scan advertisements more carefully—and found plenty to criticize, along with plenty to praise. He saw easily enough how a careless indictment of all advertising could arise from areas of abuse [Smith 1961:7].

This account contains themes that run throughout the business community's explanations of its self-regulatory efforts. To begin with, the businessman–reformer is portrayed as an earnest, energetic man with a highly developed sense of responsibility, fully dedicated to the "free-enterprise system," proud of his active role in business, and willing to take the initiative to remedy any abuses he discovers. Second, the government is portrayed as overzealous, careless, or incompetent. In this tale it is attacking an "innocent" firm under the provisions of a regulatory law. Other explanations of the necessity of self-control allege that the government regulators are ineffective in preventing unfair forms of competition. Third, the majority of businesspeople are moral; a minority are crooks who damage not only the consumer but also the honest businessperson whose customers they attract and disillusion by their fraudulent practices. Finally, the hero of the tale discovers that there is public skepticism, and he realizes the implications of this attitude; the consumer may not believe *any* advertisements or, worse yet, may "carelessly" *indict* advertising in general. Besides rendering advertising campaigns ineffective, this public indictment might lead to the demand for restrictive legislation and government controls.

Because existing laws were not in themselves sufficient to bring order to advertising, Dobbs and others began forming vigilance committees of businesspeople to police themselves.[4] By 1946 these independent clubs had organized themselves into two national groups—the National Better Business Bureau and the Association of Better Business Bureaus. In 1970 the NBBB and ABBB merged to create the Council of Better Business Bureaus (CBBB).

Since the beginning of the BBB movement, government has lent a responsive ear to Bureau suggestions. The Council, which maintains its national offices in Washington, D.C., often represents advertising interests to legislators and provides information to such agencies as the Department of Commerce, the Federal Trade Commission, and the Office of Consumer Affairs. According to the Rosenthal group's report, the Bureau's dual reputation, as a friend to businessperson and consumer alike, has enabled it to ensure the success or defeat of many state consumer protection bills (*Congressional Record* 1971:E13767).

The third phase of BBB history began when the consumer movement came into full swing in the late 1960s, and consumer advocates began publishing exposés on the questionable practices of "reputable" national corporations. A report in *Business Week* (1972:46–54) describes the two types of reactions by the business community and Madison Avenue to the changing climate of public opinion. The first and immediate reaction was an outraged denial that business was as unprincipled as the modern-day Jeremiahs were making it out to be. The second reaction took a more serious view of the criticisms being leveled against the business community. Corporation executives such as James Fish of General Mills and Victor Elting, Jr., of Quaker Oats Company admitted that self-regulation of advertising at the national level had been largely ineffective (*Advertising Age* 1970b:18; Elting 1970:49).

Motivated primarily by fear of government control, many busi-

---

[4]The Association of National Advertisers (ANA) was founded in 1910, and the American Association of Advertising Agencies (AAAA) in 1917. The situation was serious enough that "the advertising community itself urged the establishment of the Federal Trade Commission in 1914 [Advertising Advisory Committee 1964:iii]." The National Association of Broadcasting, another major self-regulatory organization, was organized in 1922.

nesspeople advocated an expanded self-regulatory role for the BBB. In early 1970 the BBB organizations hired a management consulting firm to "explore ways to increase the effectiveness of the BBB movement [*Advertising Age* 1970a:118]." The consulting firm's recommendation was to merge the National Better Business Bureau and the Association of Better Business Bureaus, a suggestion that was implemented by August of the same year. Representatives of local Bureau members were required to ratify the proposal. The merger was explained as follows in the City BBB newsletter:

> Local Better Business Bureaus around the country may be members of the new Council, although their local autonomy will still be maintained. Most important is the provision whereby national business firms will maintain membership and control of the policies of the new organization.
>
> A 36-man Board of Directors has been elected with an additional 12 to be named by the new Board to represent government, educators, and consumer groups. . . . Its objectives are the following:
>
> 1. Develop programs in support of the self-regulation principle for the purpose of advancing ethical business standards.
>
> 2. Provide research, information and education services for both businessmen and consumers in recognition of the reciprocal rights, benefits and responsibilities essential to economic well-being.
>
> 3. Develop measures, programs and services for the protection of consumers against unscrupulous, fraudulent, deceptive and unethical business practices.
>
> 4. Participate actively in public affairs affecting business and consumer interests, and cooperate with legislative bodies and administrative agencies in providing vital information and expert counsel concerning such matters, and
>
> 5. Advocate public and business policies in the best interest of consumer protection and vitality of a free and competitive economy [July 1970:1].

In December 1970, H. Bruce Palmer, newly elected President of the new Council of Better Business Bureaus, called for an increase in the annual BBB budget from $9.5 million to $25 million in order to fund new services at the local level. One of the top-priority programs suggested was a central computerized data bank in which information about national and local firms would be stored. Also in 1970, Victor Elting proposed the formation of an independent council composed of advertising men and a wide variety of public representatives to review and regulate advertising. He said, "T.V. advertising needs help . . . and . . . what it doesn't need is government over-regulation [Elting 1970:49–50]." He treated his colleagues to an apocalyptic vision of what was in store for them if they did not join his crusade:

> Our effort is not a radical one, but more in the direction of conserving our system in heading off the alternatives that would destroy our freedom to

think and create, destroy the way advertising and marketing skills have been developed to bring us to our problems of plenty, destroy the force of competition and incentive, destroy the pluralism of many interacting forces in our society, and turn over to government the power to unilaterally determine everything that goes over the air to reach the minds of our children. . . . There are ticking sounds that we hear in all the pressure groups, congressional hearings, and other forums that are meeting to decide our fate. Let's defuse them by having the strength and courage to determine our fate for ourselves [pp. 49–50].

These exhortations met with some success. The Bureau's financial backing increased and then declined again, necessitating cutbacks in some new programs. In the recession year of 1975, the local Bureaus' income from memberships and CBBB grants was about $12.3 million, and the CBBB operated on about $2.3 million, most of it contributed by national advertisers (CBBB 1975:4, 13). An expanded program of national advertising regulation was instituted, but several of Elting's suggestions for fostering the "respectability and credibility" of self-regulation were not followed. Elting had envisioned a board independent of the advertising industry, composed largely of nonbusinesspeople, and employing sanctions—including resort to the legal system—against offending companies. What emerged was a two-stage process that featured minority participation and limited access by the public sector, and voluntary compliance sanctioned by "public exposure" in the reviewers' periodic activity reports.

The first stage is handled by the BBB's own National Advertising Division (NAD), expanded to enable it more effectively to review cases of questionable advertising initiated by its own monitoring staff, local Bureaus, consumers, and competing advertisers.[5] The NAD renders about 14 decisions each month, which are described in a monthly news release. For each case, the report details the staff's objections to an advertisement, the advertiser's substantiation of its claims, the staff's evaluation of this evidence, and the advertiser's final action. Reported outcomes are classified as: (a) claim substantiated; (b) advertising modified or discontinued; and, rarely, (c) referred for adjudication to the National Advertising Review Board (see following discussion). The list of "discontinued" cases is always prefaced by the explanation that withdrawing an advertisement is not an admission of any impropriety on the advertiser's part. In many of these cases, the company withdrew its ad for "marketing reasons unrelated to the inquiry," and the NAD closed its file without

[5]Of the 197 cases reviewed in 1976, these four sources contributed 51%, 10%, 11%, and 25% of the caseload, respectively. Competitors have been responsible for an increasing number of complaints over the past few years because of the current popularity of brand-name comparisons in national advertising. Calculations are based on raw figures provided in CBBB 1977a:3.

rendering a formal judgment. In others, the company went on record as disputing the NAD's evaluation but submitted to its suggestions "in a spirit of cooperation." Clearly, the NAD's primary goal is to get and keep questionable advertising out of the media rather than to punish the companies that disseminated it or to issue judgments on advertising practices.

Of the 1175 cases closed by NAD by 30 June 1977, 459 (39%) were concluded with the finding that the advertiser's claims had been substantiated, 412 (35%) ended with modification or withdrawal of the advertisement, 13 (1%) were referred to the NARB, and 291 (25%) were closed for a variety of "administrative" reasons (NAD 1977:1). The program's director, Robert F. Gertenbach, outlined some of these reasons in an interview (telephone interview with Eaton, 1 March 1977).

First, Gertenbach said, in the early days of the program, many product-related complaints were erroneously logged as false-advertising complaints (an example was a consumer who had bought a lemon accusing a car manufacturer of fraudulent advertising). When screening procedures improved, many of these complaints were dropped by the NAD. Second, with the rationale that it was a self-regulatory body, the NAD abandoned cases in which a government regulator (mainly the Federal Trade Commission) became involved. Finally, when the staff reached an impasse with a company, it might close the case and "give it to the cops."

When cases are dropped, they have to be accounted for in reports of processed caseload. By issuing detailed monthly descriptions of cases it resolves or appeals to a higher self-regulatory body, but burying in its quarterly statistical summary its encounters with belligerent advertisers and practices that eventuated in government action, the NAD stresses the successes of self-regulation and minimizes its limitations.

The second stage of the review process is the National Advertising Review Board (NARB), created in 1971 to accept cases on appeal from the NAD and from businesspeople (including competitors). It is funded by the CBBB, and 80% of its 50 members are representatives of advertisers or advertising agencies. By mid 1977, it had issued 31 decisions and 2 advisory reports, 1 on "product advertising and consumer safety" and 1 on "advertising and women." The CBBB offers a compendium of NAD and NARB decisions as a sourcebook for advertisers (CBBB 1977b:5; NAD 1977:1).

There seems to be a difference of opinion within the ranks of the advertising self-regulatory movement over whether self-regulation should be an alternative or a complement to more aggressive government action. On the one hand, some spokespeople readily admit that self-regulation has its limits and that the sanctioning procedures of the NARB, for instance, "recognize that the final regulatory jurisdiction rests with Government [U.S. Congress 1971:13]." The current NARB chairman, Kenneth A. Cox, commented on FCC intervention to regulate children's advertising on television after years of public dissatisfaction and industry inaction:

> Self-regulation broke down. There are very clear limits to what industry self-regulation can do. For one thing, you can't go too far or you may get in trouble with the antitrust laws. And you can't be too strict because the National Association of Broadcasters code is voluntary. Not even all the NAB members subscribe to it [Love 1977:D11].

On the other hand, it is clear that businesspeople such as Elting hope to head off increases in government regulation with well-publicized self-regulatory programs. Self-regulators often speak against new consumer protection laws, citing their own activities as evidence that there is no need for unsolicited interference by outsiders. They stress the advantages inherent in their voluntary standards, which may even go beyond the letter of the law, and maintain that all would be well if existing laws were adequately enforced.

The City BBB and Its Work

Although the national BBB organization has become a conspicuous advocate of the self-regulatory movement in business and advertising, the BBB has always staked its reputation on the work of the local offices. For instance, in his testimony before the House Subcommittee, H. Bruce Palmer, President of the CBBB, stated that "the primary role of the Better Business Bureaus is demonstrated at the local level. It is here that the Better Business Bureaus have shown the most unique competence to deal with a variety of self-regulatory activities—and we have done so for many decades with incredibly limited financial resources [U.S. Congress 1971:7]."

Description of the Office

THE STAFF

The City BBB, founded in 1919, is one of the oldest in the country. It is controlled by a board of directors, elected from among the businesspeople who are members of the Bureau. They meet four times a year and are responsible for appointing an executive committee, consisting of the president, chairperson, two vice-chairpersons, the secretary, the treasurer, two additional Board members, and the Bureau's legal counsel. The executive committee meets more frequently to act on matters of policy and to pass on membership and budgets. The list of committee members is a roster of some of the most successful businesspeople in the area and includes the local general agent of Northwestern Mutual Life Insurance Company; the business manager of the principal television station in the city; the vice-president of a computer service company; a division manager of Standard Oil of California; and a general merchandise manager of a department store chain.

According to the bylaws of the City bureau, its "objectives and purposes" are as follows:

> ... to further and promote honesty, truthfulness, and reliability in merchandising, and advertising of all kinds, discourage fraudulent and deceptive methods in business and thereby to increase public confidence in advertising, salesmanship, and business generally.
>
> By instruction and education, to increase the investing knowledge of the public and to teach prospective purchasers of securities to discriminate between legitimate investments, on the one hand, and illegitimate and fraudulent investments on the other.
>
> To investigate, give publicity to, and aid when necessary in procuring proper legal action against vendors offering securities or commodities of doubtful value, by fraudulent or deceptive methods [BBB 1967:1].

The Bureau staff is divided into managers and caseworkers. The group of Bureau managers includes the president, who is also president of the executive committee and has worked for the BBB for the past 25 years; the vice-president, an honorific title for the office manager, who previously worked for the Bureau in another city; and a "membership" man, whose duties are to keep track of the 1400-odd business members of the City Bureau. There are also three consultants or caseworkers who handle complaints initiated by consumers and a receptionist.

Most of the Bureau employees had business experience above the sales level before coming to work for the BBB. This suggests that they have a certain familiarity with and sympathy for the problems and attitudes of businesspeople. The consultants' familiarity with the business point of view is reinforced over the years of working at the Bureau as they cooperate with businesspeople, repeat the BBB position on consumer problems to innumerable callers, and come to know more about the marketplace than do the individual consumers whose disputes and mistakes they handle.

The staff members are all white, middle-class, native English-speakers. Although I could not discern overtly discriminatory handling of the cases of nonwhite complainants, I was aware of fear and resentment of minorities among one or two of the consultants. Racial attitudes in themselves do not seem to cause discriminatory handling of blacks and Mexican-Americans, but the situation is complicated by the preference of the harried office worker for polite and cooperative clients. The consultants are employees of the BBB, and their authority to effect settlements is limited; they are not legally obligated to do anything for anybody, and they cannot "make" anyone do anything. They resent angry, abusive, demanding clients for their ignorance of this state of affairs and for their personal hostility to the consultants, whom they see as representatives of the white business establishment. The demands of a particularly obnoxious caller, however, can be evaded. I heard of one instance in which a consultant who was temporarily operating the switchboard encountered an angry caller and told him, "Don't ask me that; I'm just the telephone operator here."

THE OPERATION

By observing the organization of the office, I found that the staff gives preferential treatment to the business member over the consumer. Whereas the public contacts the Bureau through a number in the telephone directory, the member businesses reach the Bureau through a series of unlisted extension numbers that are given priority when they flash on the switchboard. According to the staff, the members should receive some special consideration because the work of the Bureau is supported by their dues.

When a consumer phones the Bureau, his or her call is answered by Mrs. A, the switchboard operator. She attempts to answer the question herself but can refer the call to one of the consultants if a more involved problem arises. When a member or potential member calls, Mrs. A answers as quickly as possible and asks with whom he or she wishes to speak. She then refers the call to a consultant or to an officer, who spends as much time as is needed to handle the call satisfactorily. Over a 4½ hour period, I counted 7 calls by members, all referred to a consultant, and about 90 citizen calls, of which 70 were handled rapidly by the operator of the moment and 20 referred to a consultant. Although the BBB claims it does not recommend specific suppliers of goods and services to inquirers, I overheard one consultant make such a recommendation in a conversation with a member. I doubt that this happens frequently, but it would never happen if the caller were merely an anonymous citizen.

A partition in the office separates the reception area from the offices of the consultants and managers. In general, businesspeople have more access to the back regions of the suite than do consumers, whose problems are usually discussed in the reception area. A consultant or the receptionist is likely to invite a businessperson to go into the back region soon after his or her arrival at the office. However, walk-ins of any sort make up only a small fraction of all Bureau encounters; during the 4½ hours that I actually tallied contacts with the Bureau, I counted only five walk-ins.

There is a conflict within the consultant role itself that should also be mentioned. On the one hand, the BBB limits what its caseworkers can tell a consumer who calls in. On the other, because the BBB calls itself "P.R. for business," there is an implicit directive to be as helpful as possible to consumers. The consultant-as-individual is also inclined in this direction. The result of this conflict is that consultants must exercise some discretion in their jobs. They listen to some people blow off steam (which in terms of measurable office accomplishment is nonproductive); they volunteer some hints "as a courtesy"; they expend considerable energy on relatively insignificant cases; and at times even overstep explicitly stated rules against giving certain kinds of information. The daily workload of the Bureau includes about 400 telephone calls and 200–300 letters a day. In the City Bureau, each consultant specializes in certain types of complaints (Table 6.1). These area assignments are generally observed by the

TABLE 6.1
Types of Complaints Handled by BBB Consultants

Ms. B	Mr. C	Ms. D
Dry cleaning	Insurance (all types)	Business opportunities
Apparel	Advertising media	Collection services
Books	Advertising promotions	Loan, finance, discount
Magazines	Education (all types)	Banks
Camera and photo supplies	Employment agencies	Savings and loans
Photography	Employment (all types)	Real estate
Music, including record clubs	Personal services	Securities and investment
Miscellaneous merchandise;	Professional services	Miscellaneous financial
mail order	Funeral services	Moving and storage
Drugs and cosmetics	Home furnishings	Travel and transportation
(plus relief at switchboard	Furniture and bedding	Hotels and motels
and monthly report to	Floor coverings	Miscellaneous commercial
CBBB)	Gardening	Appliances
	Heating	Freezer food plans
	Home building (new)	Automotive repairs and
	Home improvement and	services
	remodeling	Automotive accessories
	Home maintenance	Tires
	Building supplies	New cars
	Upholstery	Mobile homes and trailers
	Solicitations	Used cars
	Pest control	Food and groceries
		Jewelry
		Sporting goods
		Games and toys
		TV and radio
		(also responsible for office
		supplies, addressograph,
		newsletter; tries to keep
		supply room in order)

receptionist when she refers a caller to a consultant for more detailed handling of a problem.

This concentration allows the consultants to gain familiarity and continuity in certain areas so that they can note trends in the performance of individual firms. In addition to a good deal of informal exchange of information among the consultants, there is also a weekly staff meeting to discuss problems and suggestions for improvements, such as the revision of Bureau reports on certain firms.

As a centralized complaint handler for the business community, the BBB is in a position to collect massive amounts of information on problems that firms have with their clients and to document patterns in complaints against both individual companies and trade groups as wholes. It tallies the number of inquiries, complaints, and customer-relations contacts for many business classifications, and from such data one can learn which classifications are responsible for the largest number of problems. For instance, Table 6.2 shows the total number of contacts for all categories, and the proportions of each kind of contact for new and used cars and for mail-order products recorded in the City BBB's 1970 activity report.

Such data suggest that consumers inform themselves less about mailorder houses than about car dealers before doing business and that the mail-order category is responsible for a much higher proportion of complaints than car dealers are. Information of this kind might be used by the City BBB in planning its consumer education activities, but it has done so only sporadically. For example, in 1973, when waterbeds became simultaneously popular consumer items and the subject of many complaints to the Bureau, a City BBB employee, in consultation with local marketers, developed a shopping guide on them (1973 reinterview). For the most part, however, the Bureau's use of statistics is limited to demonstrating to City businesspeople the magnitude of its services to the public and the general categories of most concern to consumers. In June 1970 its

TABLE 6.2
City BBB Consumer Services in Four Categories, 1970

Kind of product	Number of contacts	Proportions of complaints/ inquiries/customer relations[a]
All categories	39,543	1:6.8:3.7
New cars/New-car dealers	635	1:7:3.2
Used cars/Used-car dealers	211	1:3:2.5
Used cars/New-car dealers	812	1:7.4:4
Mail order (not including books and magazines)	673	1:2:2

[a] The national average for all categories is one complaint to eight inquiries.

newsletter carried a summary of the 10 top consumer concerns for the 1969–1970 fiscal year and compared them to those of the previous year (Table 6.3).

The CBBB undertakes a more detailed analysis based on standardized reports submitted by a sample of local Bureaus on roughly a quarter of the national caseload.[6] It keeps track of the numbers of inquiries and complaints in 86 business categories, the nature of these complaints, and the Bureau's settlement rates for complaints it handles in each category.[7] The CBBB supplies its results to the Bureaus to help them in their local self-promotion efforts and issues a press release on each report that is picked up by many consumer affairs columns across the country. The national organization uses its statistics to flag emerging problems for attention by trade-practices conferences and to document trends in problems already identified so it can encourage "sounder legislation by guiding efforts toward a more balanced consideration of issues in order to avoid unnecessarily restrictive regulation of business [CBBB 1977b:4]." The data are supplied to regulatory agencies, members and committees of Congress, which prepares issue briefs on proposed legislation (Tuttle 1977).

The top five concerns for 1969–1970 represent large investments for the consumer and involve questions of warranties and complicated services for both consumer and retailer. Service industries and retail stores present different types of problems for consumers. The Bureau found that misleading advertising and unfair selling practices are the most common complaints against retailers. In the case of service industries, many dissatisfied customers suspect they have been taken advantage of because they lack the entrepreneur's technical knowledge.

Functions of the Better Business Bureau

The categories listed in the foregoing tables represent major problem areas between business and consumers, but they are not the only categories the Bureau uses to record its own activities. The Bureau performs three kinds of services for the public and the business community:

[6]The local Bureaus' lack of interest in detailed record keeping is demonstrated by the methodology of the CBBB data collection program. The sample is composed of 11 local Bureaus that submit detailed information on their complaints and inquiries and 12 others that submit an abbreviated set of statistics on theirs. Nonetheless, the analyst still finds it necessary to allow for the possible inaccuracy of the information provided by some of the offices whose reports come in only sporadically.

[7]To determine whether or not a case is "settled," Bureau staffers apply their own standards of sound business practice rather than one based on the satisfaction of the complainant. However, cases that the staff regards as "controversial" are registered as unsettled in their statistics. CBBB's Director of Development said that he hoped soon to institute as part of the complaint-handling procedure a final call to the consumer to get his or her view of the outcome (Tuttle 1977).

TABLE 6.3
Major Consumer Problems Recorded by the City BBB

Category	Rank in 1969–1970	Rank in 1968–1969
Home improvement and remodeling	1	1
Automotive repair	2	5
Appliance sales and service	3	3
New and used automobile sales	4	6
Television sales and service	5	7
Magazine subscription sales	6	9
Business opportunities (franchises)	7	—
Insurance	8	4
Real estate	9	10
Transportation and travel services	10	—

services to individual businesspeople and consumers, regulation of advertising, and consumer education.

SERVICES TO INDIVIDUAL BUSINESSPEOPLE AND CONSUMERS

In the annual BBB activity report, business and consumer services are divided into inquiries, complaints, and customer relations. (Arbitration is a recent outgrowth of the complaint-handling function of the Bureau and is not listed in the report.) The simplest way to describe these activities is to follow the Bureau's development of an information file on a company that has opened for business in the Bureau's domain.[8]

The BBB begins to keep a file on a firm when the company itself requests one or when the BBB receives an inquiry or complaint about the company from the public. In either case, the BBB sends the managers of the business a questionnaire.[9] Most firms are willing to cooperate with the Bureau, at least to the extent of filling out the questionnaire. When a business fails to do so, subsequent callers are told that the firm did not

[8]It should be noted at the outset that files are kept on *companies*, for this is the primary orientation of the Bureau's work. It is less interested in evaluating its own performance or the kinds of complaints that come to it, and thus few statistics are compiled that could provide such information. This leads to the general observation that the files a group keeps are an excellent clue to what it sees as its most important activities. Action-line files (see Chapter 13) are classified according to product or problem categories rather than firm names.

[9]This form requests information on the firm's name, address, phone; time and place of incorporation; number of owners and of employees; names of affiliates, subsidiaries, and other trade styles; names, titles, and past business connections of its officers or principals; names of governmental agencies with which it is licensed or registered; description of the business, including nature of the clientele (public, franchised distributor, retailer, etc.) and nature of the firm's outlets; name and address of its advertising agency and types of advertising media used; names of people in the company to be contacted regarding inquiries, complaints from customers, and questions about advertising; and banking and business references.

cooperate. The uncooperative firm is at a definite disadvantage when callers request and receive information about competing firms that *did* answer the questionnaire. A consultant told me that a number of big insurance companies had been humbled into answering the Bureau's questionnaire after their original refusal resulted in the reporting of the "no information" response to the public for a few weeks.

Before a company returns the questionnaire, the BBB switchboard operator may give a favorable report to a caller about the company if the principals of the firm are known to be reputable. Negative information acquired about a company on which the BBB has no file is less readily divulged to callers for fear of libel suits. After a well-known weight-reduction specialist opened a mail-order service for Sauna Belts and Trim Jeans products, the BBB received several complaints about these items. The Bureau reported the complaints in their newsletter, but the threat of a possible libel suit prevented them from publishing the names of the firm's principals even in this privately circulated publication. On the other hand, the names of small operators whose fraudulent practices have come to the attention of the Bureau are frequently reported in the membership letter, though hardly ever in press releases to the public or in reports to individual callers.

After the questionnaire is returned, the staff prepares a file on the firm and adds an abstract of the information to the card file used by the telephone operator to answer callers' inquiries. These reports are updated as necessary to reflect the Bureau's knowledge of the firm's performance in the community. If the businessperson heading the firm is known to be reputable and cooperative with the BBB, the new company may be asked if it would like to join the local Bureau. An application for membership is reviewed by one of the consultants, and his or her recommendations are automatically put into effect by the board of directors, which must officially pass on all applications.[10] Members of the BBB are expected to sign and observe an advertising code, to substantiate their advertising claims if the Bureau so requests, and to avoid using their BBB membership in advertising claims, because this could be construed by consumers as a BBB endorsement.

Membership signifies a higher degree of cooperation with the BBB because members are expected to strictly observe all BBB standards as well as to support the Bureau's work with an annual membership fee. Nonmembership does not carry the stigma that noncooperation does.

---

[10]The membership application form asks no more information of the applicant than does the business questionnaire summarized above. The application form leaves space for staff recommendations and the appropriate authorization signatures as well as for service information such as to whom the Bureau "Monthly Report to Management" should be sent and to whom any advertising and selling standards for the relevant trade or industry should be sent if they have been developed.

After all, there are only about 1400 local firms that have invested the $75 or more in an annual membership subscription, and so it is obvious that there are many reputable businesspeople who are not members.

According to the 1970 activity report, the City BBB recorded 39,543 instances of business and consumer services,[11] of which inquiries accounted for 23,379, or about 59% of the total. Inquiries are defined as all requests for information made prior to doing business. Inquiries are made by individual consumers, businesspeople, organizations such as the Chamber of Commerce, and even banks checking on the performance of entrepreneurs who want to borrow money or to sell sales contracts. State licensing agencies also request information to add to their files of a firm's activities. Most calls seem to be made by consumers, however. In my small sample of telephone and walk-in contacts, very close to half were wholly or mainly concerned with preinvestment inquiries.

Of what use is the BBB to ordinary inquirers? If they are trying to predict the outcome of a business transaction—that is, if they ask about a specific firm—their chances of getting some kind of useful information are good. The BBB office is a clearinghouse for data gathered from its own research and from diverse external information sources, such as licenses, police reports, and court decisions, that are recorded in scattered places throughout the society. The customer will be told how long the particular company has existed, whether it has been the subject of complaints to the BBB, and how these have been handled by the management. He or she will also be told whether a firm is a BBB member. Membership is supposed to indicate the company's willingness to observe Bureau standards.

However, there are also limitations to the information released. First, the standardized statements reported to callers are very general. These are among the gradations:

> We have handled a few complaints about this company and have found that it is prompt to adjust those where it had a responsibility to do so. Accordingly, we have no reason to question the operation of this firm.

> This company has been the subject of some problems of customer dissatisfaction, some of which were controversial, but our records show that the company has adjusted those where it felt a responsibility to do so.

> This company has been the subject of a few problems and questions but since it has not responded to our follow-up communications concerning them, we have no way of knowing whether or not it ignores customer problems. Accordingly, we suggest that you satisfy yourself about the integrity of the company if you are interested in doing business with it.

[11]Because customer relations includes sending complaint forms, the total reflects a small amount of double-tallying of single cases. The figures are approximate also because some consultants were more conscientious than others about tabulating telephone calls when they acted as operators.

Were consumers to see these statements in series, they would realize that there is a progression having subtleties of difference; they mean more in series than they do if read one at a time. To get the maximum information from reliability reports, the consumer should inquire about several similar firms at the same time, but in fact only a small fraction of callers do this. In addition, the BBB may know somewhat more about a firm than it is willing to report; it cannot report bad business practices unless it has received written complaints about them. A "no information" report can mean that the company has something to hide or merely that its owner resents being interrogated by a self-appointed regulatory agency. The Bureau cannot directly state its interpretation of the situation.

If the consultant reports that a certain individual is licensed to conduct his or her business, the consumer cannot tell whether the license is still in effect or is in the process of being revoked. However, in the latter case the Bureau is likely to have received reports of malpractice, and such information is reportable to inquirers. In short, despite its limitations, the BBB is a valuable source of information. The Bureau's ability to establish the reliability of business concerns or expose frauds is not duplicated by any other organization in the community. A favorite BBB motto is, "If you don't know the merchandise, know the merchant; if you don't know the merchant, know the merchandise." The inquiry service of the BBB allows consumers to gain more information about the merchant.

Another phase of the BBB's service to individuals, termed "customer relations," accounted for 12,371 cases, or about 32% of the BBB caseload in 1970. A BBB office handbook providing instructions on categorizing office activities lists as examples of BBB consumer services: (a) contacts in which forms are provided or complainants are advised to submit a written report by other means (hence the "customer relations" tally includes the calls that later result in the processed complaints); (b) situations in which complainants have failed to contact the company involved first; (c) complaints unprocessed because they are regarded as unreasonable; and (d) "all other instances in which the Bureau provides assistance or advice to businessmen and consumers on matters related to customer relations activities."

When I listened to the switchboard operator, I found that most customer relations work consists of explaining to customers why the complaint is unjustified or unremediable, a process of consumer education the BBB calls "interpreting business to the consumer." The Bureau hopes that its explanation will lead the complainant to understand and accept the businessperson's logic behind the practice to which he, the consumer, has objected. For instance, consumers are told that agreements should be in writing if they are to be binding; exchange and return policies are not mandatory but merely courtesies; and a house call by a repairer results in service charges whether or not repair work is done because the overhead costs and the time expended on unnecessary trips must be paid for.

The BBB is self-consciously a public relations service, and as such it tries not to turn anyone away in ignorance, even if it cannot avoid sending some away angry or frustrated. The consultants live up to this "spirit of the BBB" by going beyond the minimum performance they are required to give, even though there are certain limitations to what they can do. For instance, one woman complained that after paying $2 to see a clairvoyant she was told that she would develop cancer and that for $9 extra the clairvoyant would pray for her. The BBB receptionist who handled the woman's call responded, "Oh, dear! We don't handle fortunetellers—they're too controversial. I suggest that you talk to the D.A. to see if she needs a license to operate, and if you are worried about your health you should check with a doctor." Although the Bureau does not give legal opinions, it will provide interested callers with the phone numbers of the County Lawyers Referral Service and the district attorney's office.

A good number of complaints are redirected to the proper remedy agents within the businesses themselves. When a complaint is made against a company considered by the BBB to be reputable, for instance, the consultant will immediately ask, "Did you talk to the manager of the store?" One national company, Chrysler Corporation, has requested that any complaint made to the Bureau about its operations be referred immediately to the corporation's "hot line" number so that the problem can receive special handling.

A complaint to the BBB must pass several tests before it is considered serious enough to warrant sending an official complaint form, called a "Customer Experience Record," to the company. When a consultant thinks that a caller is exaggerating or concealing self-damaging information, he or she may suggest that the caller send a complaint letter to the firm with the notation that a copy of the letter is going to the BBB. If the consumer is "off base" by Bureau standards, the business outlook on the matter may be quoted to him. If the complaint is regarded as valid, however, the customer is told that the complaint must be written in order to provide a record of his or her side of the story. This procedure is followed to discourage false complaints and to allow the consumer time to cool off and write "just the facts."

The philosophy behind the complaint procedure is that business wants to know when its performance has not been satisfactory to a customer and that it will want to remedy the situation in the interest of its reputation. A policy statement in the April 1970 edition of the local BBB newsletter indicates the Bureau's view of the purpose of the complaint procedure:

PR FOR BUSINESS. The investigation and mediation of consumer complaints brought to the [City] BBB are designed to first get at the facts. Should these facts disclose misunderstanding on the part of the consumer, careful discussion, without the emotional heat generated between buyer and seller ensues with the complainant. BBB consultants keep constantly in their considerations the objective of preserving good will for the business firm involved.... [p. 2].

Sometimes forms are sent out to a complainant with the verbal warning that although the complainant has a right to be upset, the chances for a settlement to his or her liking are slight. For instance, an acquaintance of mine reported to me that when the bobbin wheel on her sewing machine broke, she took the machine to a repair shop to get a replacement part. The attendant asked if she wanted just the replacement or a complete overhaul of the machine. "Only a new piece, no extra work, please," she said. A few days later the repairman himself called and again asked if she wanted only a replacement. Again she said that all she desired was the installation of the new wheel. When she went to retrieve the machine, she found it completely overhauled and accompanied by a bill for $25. She was told that she could not have the machine back until she paid the full amount, so she handed over the money and went home fuming. When she talked to a Bureau consultant later, she learned that although she had a legitimate gripe, she was unlikely to get an adjustment because she had never written down the terms of the repair agreement: There is no way to hold a repair service to a verbal agreement. (One may question this assertion. For example, a small claims court may have disposed of the case in another way.) However, the consultant said that a BBB form would be processed in hopes that the store would consider the problem worthy of remedy. The consultant also suggested to the owner of the sewing machine that in the future she write down all her instructions to repairpeople.

The complaint form is not automatically sent to callers whose complaints have been judged acceptable by the consultant. Rather, the customer is told to send a stamped, self-addressed envelope to the Bureau with a request for the form, which will be sent to him or her by return mail.[12] This policy was instituted recently as an economy measure. Because of the preliminary screening conducted during the first stage of the complaint process, the number of complaints actually processed is small: 3433 cases, or only about 9% of the total business and consumer contacts in 1970, were processed complaints. The effects of the screening process in the City office may also be reflected in the smaller proportion of complaints in its annual workload compared to the national average for BBB offices of 15–20% (see *Congressional Record* 1971:E13773; U.S. Congress 1971:19).

The Bureau retains one copy of the complaint form and sends three copies to the firm in question. After the company writes its explanations

---

[12]One of the early results of increased funding at City BBB was the abolition of the requirement that complainants send a stamped envelope for a complaint form.

and intentions on the copies it receives, it returns two forms to the Bureau. The BBB sends one of these to the complainant. It keeps the other in its file of completed complaints on the firm, and throws out its own pending copy.

The Bureau consultants claim that a complaint form is usually taken seriously by the offending company for several reasons. Sometimes the caller's failure to register a complaint with the company may have been the result of red tape or of ignorance; then the BBB merely expedites this process. In any case, a complaint that is referred to the company from the Bureau has been through the BBB screening process and is evidence that the customer was angry enough to have persisted in attempts to find redress for the grievance. The story, written in the consumer's own hand, may shed light on sales activities unknown to management or may reveal mistaken assumptions by the consumer that the manager failed to clear up.

Complaints submitted to companies by the BBB need not be settled by them; the Bureau has no power to directly force a settlement of a complaint. One day in the Bureau office I observed the owner of an electronics store waiting to speak to a consultant. The store owner was visibly distressed by a complaint ("the first in all these years") referred to him by the BBB. A customer had asked the proprietor to install an electric doorbell in his house to replace an old, battery-operated model. A technician for the store examined the wiring of the house and told the homeowner that it was faulty; although he was willing to sell the electric doorbell, he could not guarantee that the current in the house would be adequate to make the bell ring. The customer insisted that the bell be installed (at the price of the bell plus a labor charge). Several months later he phoned the store to report that he had torn the bell out because it did not work and he wanted all his money back. Because secondhand doorbells are not in great demand and because the work had already been done, the store refused to take the bell back and refund the customer's money. The complaint was processed by the Bureau, even though the consultant knew that the customer had no real case. It happened, however, that the owner of the store was about to go on vacation and did not want to leave the problem unsettled, so he left a check for the price of the bell at the Bureau. The consultant counseled the store owner that he was under no obligation to make the refund and that the Bureau had no desire to force businesspeople to do what was not their responsibility to do. But the store owner insisted, and the consultant reluctantly went along with the plan.

A company's refusal to consider a matter forwarded to it on a complaint form marks the end of the Bureau's participation in the consumer's case; it will not resubmit a complaint that has been returned by the firm's management, although it may pursue a case in which it does not receive an answer from the company to the initial complaint form.

In the event that an individual complainant does not get a seemingly justifiable grievance settled, the Bureau has indirect methods of pressuring a business to conform to acceptable standards in the future. An unsettled complaint contributes to the development of a bad reliability report about the firm. The BBB may report a company to the legal authorities if a law has been violated or if a licensee has been guilty of malpractice. Finally, the Bureau may report a firm's behavior to the advertising media and to relevant financial institutions. As the vice-president of the Bureau explained to me, if money and publicity are unavailable, the firm cannot survive for long. However, such action is taken only as a last resort, and it may be months before the company feels its effects.

According to a 1972 CBBB report entitled "Arbitration for Business and Customers: A National Program for Arbitrating Customer Complaints," slightly less than half (44%) of the consumers who complain to the BBB come away dissatisfied. The traditional BBB method of handling complaints obviously has not quelled what the report characterizes as "an increased awareness and confrontation by consumers of business practices in the marketplace." An example of the BBB's adaptation to deal with one kind of problem that frequently ends in an impasse between the businessperson and consumer is the Dry Cleaning Panel. The City BBB panel is one of several that have been organized in cooperation with local cleaning industries across the nation. In dry cleaning, as in many service industries, it is sometimes hard to evaluate the results of a company's work and to place the blame for an unsatisfactory result.

In March 1970 the cleaning industry and the City Bureau organized the arbitration panel in an attempt to eliminate dissatisfaction among customers. The program was initiated at the request of the California Drycleaners' Association, and more than 100 cleaners and laundries joined the Bureau to support it. The panel, which meets once a month with Mrs. B., the BBB's textile consultant, as moderator, deals only with complaints involving cleaners who have agreed to accept its decisions. The complaining consumer must also sign an agreement to accept this arbitration.

When complaints involving one of the cooperating firms reach the Bureau, they are referred to the panel. One of the Bureau consultants is responsible for recruiting volunteer panel members each month. The local Dry Cleaning Panel usually consists of two dry cleaning specialists, neither of whom is involved in the disputed cases, two retailers to help in assessing the original value of the garment, and two consumers. Arbitrators are sworn in by a justice of the peace or a notary and have the power to subpoena witnesses and evidence. Awards granted by recognized arbitrators are legally binding in California and in about half the other states in the Union.

Arbitration panels have advantages for consumers and businesspeople alike. They are easy and accessible complaint channels for the consumer. As the CBBB points out in its 1972 report on arbitration:

> The availability of volunteer arbitrators representing all segments of the community should lend greater credibility to the program for those who may feel alienated from more traditional institutions. Moreover, the clear and simple rules . . . are easily understood, encouraging participation of all consumers [CBBB 1972:3–8].

The panels provide the cleaning establishments with a group of judges that is weighted in favor of the technical and business orientations of the cleaner himself. The chances are relatively small that the panel will make what to the cleaner is a totally outrageous, unreasonable, and financially unsound assessment of the situation; yet it is an "impartial jury," and the cleaner's willingness to submit to its judgment is good public relations. The CBBB concludes its list of advantages for the businessperson by observing:

> In this age of "consumerism" some customers will simply not be satisfied regardless of the quality of product or services. Arbitration provides a "safety valve" for this kind of customer, forcing him to bring his claims under the scrutiny of an impartial member of his own community. Often frivolous accusations and unfounded disparagements can be silenced by the mere prospect of arbitration [CBBB 1972:3–6].

Both businessmen and consumers benefit from the program's low cost, its flexibility in the scheduling of hearings, and the efficiency of its procedures (awards are announced within 10 days of the hearing). In the panel's first year of existence, the complainant was found at fault in 23.4% of the 47 cases it heard; the cleaners in 38.3%; and the manufacturers in 31.9%. The National Institute of Drycleaning made restorations in the remaining 6.4%, and 17.1%, or $596.15, of the total requested damages against cleaners was awarded.[13]

The CBBB's plans for arbitration are still relatively new, and there is great promise in them if they are not unduly influenced by business interests. However, it is easy to see how panels like those of the City BBB may become biased. First, consumers are outnumbered by representatives

---

[13]By 1973 arbitration had been extended to all business categories; agreement to submit unreconciled complaints to arbitration had become a precondition for membership in the City BBB; and the service had become a selling point in the Bureau's recruitment drive. By 1975 the service was offered by 97 offices in the United States. A City Bureau official (1973 interview) observed that most cases scheduled for arbitration were never heard because once arbitration became a real possibility, one party to the dispute usually accepted a settlement proposed by the other.

of business interests. Second, the panel meetings are held at the Bureau in closed sessions; neither party to the dispute is actually in the office at the time of the hearing. And finally, the BBB screens cases as admissible or inadmissible before referring them to the panel. In the more general plans for arbitration drawn up by the CBBB, there is a provision for the two parties to be represented by legal counsel if they so desire. However, this provision may give an unfair advantage to businesspeople whose customers cannot afford to hire a lawyer—a problem that has developed in some small claims courts (Greenhouse 1972).

Paulson (1972) reports that although many Bureau members are in favor of the panel program, other businesspeople do not agree that it has advantages: "One businessman . . . said of the arbitration plan: 'They'll get a bunch of social workers who are presently out of a job.' [Another] said his store had inaugurated its own system for handling customer complaints, adding: 'We feel a personal contact is more advantageous for our company [p. 8].' " The cooperation of the business community is, of course, vital to the success of an arbitration program, but as Robert Cramton of the Administrative Conference of the United States has pointed out, the companies that cause the most complaints are not likely to be those who support arbitration (noted Paulson 1972).

As yet the BBB has only a dry cleaning arbitration panel, but it also tries to minimize consumer relations problems through the organization of trade practice conferences. The purpose of these meetings is to establish standards for the conduct of business and advertising in various industries in which BBB data show that there are a significant number of consumer problems. The standards adopted at the trade conference may remain the guidelines for self-regulation or may be used as the basis for legislation. The BBB position on most consumer protection laws, however, is that they are unnecessary: The problem is to enforce the laws already on the books rather than to create new ones.

REGULATION OF ADVERTISING

As emphasized in all the Bureau's accounts of its history and principles, private regulation of advertising was the original focus of the BBB movement. It still plays an important part in the Bureau's efforts to help build "merited public confidence in our competitive enterprise system." The Bureau staff has the primary responsibility for spotting faulty advertising, but competitors or customers can alert the agency to unfulfilled or unfulfillable claims by complaining or making inquiries about offers they see in the media.

An important point to remember here is that local Bureaus handle mainly local advertising: Most typically, they are concerned with the methods employed by local retailers to inform the public about their wares and the terms of sale. The task of creating a market is secondary in most local advertising. Whereas national advertisers are interested in creating a demand for their product, retailers focus directly on prices, guarantees, and relative quality. Naturally, there is some overlap between the two kinds of advertising. The Bureau must sometimes deal with national advertising appearing in local media. For instance, the January 1971 City Bureau newsletter reported the following case from its files, an unusual case for the local Bureau to have initiated because the offender was a large corporation and the questionable claims had emanated from a national advertising campaign.

> *Goodrich ad questioned.* The retail advertising supervisor of B. F. Goodrich Tire Company, Akron, Ohio, has admitted to the [City] BBB its offering of "the Long Miler" 4-ply nylon cord blackwall 7.00–13 automobile tire at $10.95 was in error. The Bureau questioned an advertisement which appeared in the October 12 issue of the *San Francisco Examiner* after a consumer complained of his inability to purchase the 7.00–13 in 4-ply construction. The company advised the tires in question were available in "most" sizes but not the 7.00–13. Clarification had been mistakenly omitted from the ad in question. The firm's representative did state, however, that "steps have been taken to insure that our future advertisements will include the proper information regarding tire construction." Prompt attention to advertising inaccuracies such as displayed by B. F. Goodrich assures a more acceptable and reliable sales market [p. 2].

It is probably relevant that the inaccuracy in the advertisement was brought to the attention of the Bureau by a dissatisfied customer. The newsletter item itself leaves one in doubt as to whether Goodrich is being lauded for its cooperative attitude toward the BBB or is being mildly punished by having the story reported to the business community.

There are several ways in which the BBB can check ads that are objectionable or questionable. If the BBB name has been used in the advertisement, a telephone call or letter to the advertiser and to the medium that carried the message points out that this is never an acceptable advertising practice for BBB members. For other objectionable practices, an "Advertising Double Check" form may be used; on this form the consultant details the Bureau's questions or objections about a specific advertisement and asks the advertiser to substantiate his or her claims.[14] The

---

[14]The form explains itself to the advertiser as an attempt to help him or her "maintain customer confidence in your advertising. The Bureau recommends that you double-check the accuracy of the advertisement as indicated [in the form], recognizing that the burden of proof lies with advertisers to substantiate their claims." The Bureau indicates the date, media, and location-time of the item in which a claim is challenged, and lists nine possible causes of the questioning: (a) availability of the advertised item; (b) characteristics of bait; (c) comparative price claim; (d) description; (e) illustration or layout; (f) use of word "guarantee"; (g) nondisclosure of material fact; (h) underselling or superlative claim; and (i)

Bureau expects the company to make a formal reply to the challenge and to correct the misleading advertising. Another method of advertising review by the BBB is to send a "shopper" to see if the goods advertised are actually available in the store. Because the City office is short-staffed, however, its consultants seldom act as investigative shoppers.

According to one consultant, most local entrepreneurs are aware of and observe the self-regulatory guidelines. It is the habitual misrepresenter and the new firms yet to be schooled in the proprieties of advertising that create most of the Bureau's advertising problems. The national Bureau (ABBB 1947:32) found that the most common unethical advertising practices were: (a) misdescription of seconds, irregulars, or imperfects; (b) unsupported superlative statements; (c) misstatements of material content; (d) incorrect description; (e) misleading trade names; (f) misleading use of trademark names; (g) bait advertising (items not on sale); (h) misstatements of sizes and colors; and (i) abuse of comparative prices.

In discussing misleading ads, the BBB's Advertising Advisory Committee to the Secretary of Commerce (1964) claimed that the "vast majority of cases . . . never reach the serious stage. BBB reports that 95% to 97% of all advertising which receives 'unfavorable' reports is corrected voluntarily by the advertiser, either on his own or after consultation with Bureau officials [p. 53]." Three kinds of cases are considered serious: (a) fraudulent advertising designed to victimize those who respond to it and clearly in violation of existing rules; (b) repeated misrepresentations by an advertiser who has previously had his errors called to his attention, in which cases the BBB assumes that he usually intends to deceive the public and that he will try to excuse his practices in the hope that the Bureau will not take drastic action; and (c) advertising by transient vendors who intend to sell their merchandise by any means and then to leave town.

When a firm balks at suggestions for improvements, the Bureau can apply pressure in several ways; the course of action taken seems to depend on the kind of culprit being dealt with. Transient vendors have often had previous run-ins with the law, and the police are alerted when the Bureau learns that one is in town. The City newsletter to its members almost always discusses some recent cases the office has handled. This kind of exposure reaches a limited audience and, moreover, deals largely with frauds that might injure the businesspeople who read the newsletter (e.g., solicitations of charitable contributions).

---

other. There follows a space for the consultant to elaborate on the basis on which the ad is questioned. The advertiser is expected to indicate his decision: that he will not repeat the ad, that he has revised the ad, that he will revise it by a given date, or that he is unwilling to revise it for reasons he has indicated. Again, a space is left at the bottom for Bureau comments.

The BBB may also interest the media in exposing questionable business practices. However, if the Bureau used this method too often, it would defeat its aim of presenting to the public the image of an ethical business community. The Bureau releases shopping tips at Christmastime and warnings on fraudulent magazine sales techniques when certain magazine subscription gangs are known to be in town, but much of its other work—even cases discussed in the newsletter—is not reported to the general press. For instance, in May 1971 the City Bureau newsletter carried the following story:

> *Mattress Firm Folds.* Complaints concerning nondelivery of mattresses for which deposits and full payments had been made began filtering into the [City] BBB in early March. An investigator who called at Factory to You Mattress Company discovered the premises padlocked and abandoned. Information developed by the Bureau disclosed the operation to be owned by Morris Sleight and Gladys Sleight, Morris Sleight said to be a retired disabled veteran. On April 1, a local newspaper reported Sleight was arrested in Manchester, Connecticut, on charges by California police for allegedly passing $3500 in bad checks and "losing" a $5000 rental truck. A detective also reported he had been contacted by an insurance company which said the Sleights had filed a $9000 claim for fur and jewelry stolen from their car in Tennessee in March. During a preliminary hearing in California on April 19, Sleight's attorney said his client had offered evidence in a Philadelphia extortion case in the 1960's which sent two Mafiosi to prison as part of his attempt to show Sleight had no intent to defraud in the local complaints.

The entire case was barely mentioned in the general press. When I asked the president of the Bureau if the BBB publicized the cases it took a part in solving, he used the incident just described as an illustration of why it did not. He said he had mentioned this case in an address to a group of consumers and immediately had to field a series of complaints from the floor about legitimate mattress stores that had made late deliveries. Discussing frauds creates a climate of suspicion that makes selling difficult for the legitimate firms in the area; it would not be long before the small store owners would cease to support the Bureau if it regularly publicized frauds.

Finally, if a law is broken, the Bureau may call for legal help after failing with lesser measures. One case involved an office equipment company that was using misleading comparative prices in its advertising. In its January 1971 newsletter, the City BBB cited the section of the State Business and Professions Code that the store owner had violated and also reported some of the details of the violations. It continued, "Mr. Invidio was asked to substantiate his claims under the section cited, but has failed to do so. Since advertising has continued and Mr. Invidio has failed to respond to a second attempt by the Bureau to obtain proof of his claims, the [City] BBB has asked the District Attorney's office to review the matter for action and to enforce applicable provisions of the law." In April (1971) the following story appeared in the newsletter:

> *Office Equipment Firm Recants.* Wayward Office Equipment Company, its president George Invidio, his legal counsel and advertising manager, met with a Bureau representative in the office of John Pate, Assistant District Attorney, at the Bureau's request. At the meeting, the Bureau representative detailed objections which had been made regarding the firm's advertising of comparative prices since the opening of the outlet in October 1970. After outlining provisions of Section 17501 of the California Business and Professions Code regulating the use of former prices in advertising together with details of the FTC Guides Against Deceptive Advertising, Mr. Invidio and his attorney agreed prior advertising had, indeed, been in violation of the regulations cited. The Bureau is pleased to announce that since that meeting the firm has discontinued the use of all comparative prices in its ads, demonstrating the sincerity of the firm and its principals [p. 1].

Referral to legal authorities is not favored by the BBB for most problems. In addition to making the business community look bad to the public, referral to the legal system is not a guaranteed remedy; Bureau consultants complained to me that the authorities give priority to solving violent crimes and that court proceedings may drag on for years. Especially in the case of license revocations, it may take years to accumulate the data needed to justify the agency's action.

The BBB prefers to pressure businesspeople into compliance with BBB standards by threatening to cut off their access to advertising media, banks, and customers, sanctions that are discussed in the following case history of the Bureau's efforts to regulate a firm I will call the Ripoff Carpet Company.

During one of my first visits to the City Bureau, the vice-president handed me a thick folder full of complaints that the staff had accumulated on the Ripoff Company and its manager, Mr. Schred. In June 1963 Ripoff published an advertisement in the local newspaper that Mr. W, President of the City BBB, found suspect. The carpeting was advertised at a very low price with a 5- or 10-year guarantee, a promise that very few manufacturers make, particularly for inexpensive carpeting.

Mr. W sent a "Double Check" form to Mr. Schred, challenging the use of the word "guarantee" and the tactic of underselling or superlative claims. He asked the regular price of the carpet that was advertised as being on sale and the conditions of the incredible wearability guarantee. According to guidelines laid down by the Federal Trade Commission, any advertised guarantee should clearly and conspicuously disclose three things: (a) the nature and extent of the guarantee; (b) the manner in which the guarantor will perform; and (c) the identity of the guarantor. Most media adopt these rules in publishing an advertiser's copy. Mr. Schred quickly replied:

> The information that you requested is available, and I am sure is above scrutiny, which my records would reveal. However, as a matter of principle, I will not forward you this information as I do not intend to be selected by your organization in conjunction with the big business that you represent in order to attempt to have me raise my carpet prices.

From 1965 to 1969 the Bureau received 104 complaints about the carpet company. Callers complained about late deliveries, improper installation, and faulty merchandise. The complainants recorded their stories on the Customer Experience Record form in styles that ranged from eloquent to almost unintelligible. The most detailed account came from a man who had been out of town on a business trip when his wife bought a carpet for the master bedroom: He even drew a map of the room, indicating the three unsightly seam lines that the carpet layer had made.

The local BBB continued to process complaints on the firm, but Ripoff's responses to the forms dwindled and then ceased. Then, in December 1969, Mr. Schred returned a complaint form to the Bureau with a letter that asked the staff not to send him any more forms "as they would no longer be answered under any circumstances."

During this period the Bureau several times changed its reports to callers inquiring about the company. In November 1965 the rubber-stamped message that was read to inquirers was still at a noncommital level:

> We have handled a few matters of minor customer dissatisfaction. The company has been prompt to adjust those where it had a responsibility to do so. Accordingly we have no reason to question its operation.

But in 1967 Mr. W prepared a new report on Ripoff:

> Numerous complaints have been filed during 1967 principally alleging failure to deliver carpeting when promised and wearability. Some complaints have been adjusted. Others are disputed by the firm on the basis of verbal agreements which were unprovable. We have had occasion to criticize the firm's advertising and request for change has met with no response from the home office. All guarantees should be examined prior to purchase for the restrictions, if any, involved. All agreements regarding delivery, installation, cost and wearability should be in writing to avoid dispute.

After Mr. Schred refused to receive any more complaints from the Bureau, its rating dropped to a clearly unfavorable level: "This company has been the subject of a considerable number of problems and questions. However, it has not responded to our follow-up communications. . . ." Shortly afterward, in February 1970, Mr. W instructed the staff to report to callers:

> The Bureau regrets it is unable to accept further complaints on this company since it has indicated its unwillingness to reply to complaints submitted through us. (Switchboard operator: If the consumer has a complaint, refer them to the State Contractor's License Board.)

Reliability reports represent the BBB's first and probably mildest sanction against an uncooperative firm: warning any potential Ripoff customers who inquire at the Bureau that they may encounter problems with the store. Unfavorable reports can have far-reaching effects, especially when they are given to financial institutions. An installment loan officer of a local bank received Ripoff's current reliability report in 1970 and undoubtedly refused to approve loans to the company or to people desiring money to spend on Ripoff carpets. The battle with Ripoff was fought on other fronts as well. In August 1970 the Bureau received a note from a representative of a local carpet association:

> In behalf of the almost fifty firm members of the Resilient Flooring and Carpet Association as well as the other one-hundred signatory firms in this four county area I pose a strong objection to the newspaper advertising of Ripoff Carpets. The most misleading factor is the inclusion of "free installation"; hardly possible when the area average is in the order of $1.75 per yard plus pad. As I mentioned on the telephone the girl at 123–4567 indicated it was a tackless installation and the pad ran from 99¢ to $1.99.
>
> The prices (and broad color range) are obviously suspect [sic] of switcheroo techniques. I have enclosed a copy of the last ad in the Metropolitan Herald (Sun 8/16/70) and two other typical local ads in the same paper to show price comparison at this gut level pricing. Hopefully the Contractor's License Board, the NLRB, and your office can resolve this customer trap.

Finally, in February 1971, another BBB office attempted to compile a case against Ripoff stores for exposure in the media, hoping that in addition to warning the public, the media would refuse to carry any more of Ripoff's misleading advertising copy. When I asked a Bureau consultant in May 1971 about the outcome of these efforts, he said that the newspapers were still carrying the ads. He shrugged in exasperation and suggested that the papers hated to lose Ripoff's lucrative business. As for the Contractor's License Board, it might take months or years for them to collect the materials necessary to revoke the firm's license.

In the summer of 1972 I encountered evidence of Ripoff's activities in a new context. I was interviewing a member of a local consumer action group dedicated to an aggressive pursuit of the consumer's rights in disputes arising in the marketplace. He told me that his organization had recently discovered the effectiveness of taking consumer cases to small claims court, especially when the group had done enough research on the offending company to be able to inform the sheriff where the company's attachable assets were located. I asked him if he relied on the area's BBBs for help. Not much, he said. As a matter of fact, "There was this lady who bought a carpet. . . ." The BBB told him it could not tell him the name of the company's owner, but it did suggest that he contact a Mr. Schred. However, Mr. Schred, it seemed, was perpetually on a vacation and unreachable. My informant told me that his next step would be to locate a secretary in the office who would admit that she was in charge while Mr. Schred was absent. Then he would serve her with a subpoena to make sure that a company representative appeared in small claims court on the required date.

The major lesson to be drawn from the case just described is that the Bureau's procedures are really intended for those firms who are already concerned with maintaining customer good will. The Bureau is, first and foremost, a public relations organization; it has little power to force quick reformations in the business world and cannot even be sure that local media will assist in its enforcement efforts. Without the cooperation of the firms involved, the Bureau can be of little assistance to an individual complainant.

In contrast to the outcome of the Ripoff case is that of an appliance store that used a clearly illegal promotion technique. It distributed notices that various individuals had won free stereos but did not mention that the winners had to buy several hundred dollars' worth of records in order to collect their prizes. There is a law specifically forbidding this kind of promotion. A consultant claimed that the store was driven out of business by the combined efforts of the D.A.'s office and the BBB's reliability report. The effectiveness of a reliability report lies in the number of people who phone and ask to hear it. In this case, many people must have checked with the Bureau.

Furthermore, the size of the company will have much to do with the impact of Bureau pressure. I think it is clear that small operators suffer more at the hands of a disapproving BBB than do larger firms such as Ripoff.

A final aspect of the Bureau's work in the advertising area, according to Ms. B, a consultant, is the encouragement of self-regulation by business through education of businesspeople and through organizing and participating in occasional trade-practice conferences to establish standards of advertising in various industries (see also ABBB 1947).

CONSUMER EDUCATION: MEDIA AND MESSAGES

The third major activity of the Better Business Bureaus, besides services to individuals and advertising regulation, is consumer education on the existence and uses of the BBB and on products, services, business practices, and frauds. As we have seen, this process occurs on an individual-by-individual basis through reliability reports, customer relations calls, and even the complaint procedure. But the Bureau also educates the public on a much larger scale through broadcast and printed media, BBB publications, and meetings of Bureau representatives and groups of consumers.

The Bureau's desire to expand its work in consumer education is explained by the fact that the consuming public has become increasingly dissatisfied with business. The same Harris poll that found that the nation's BBBs are better known than any other consumer protection agency in the nation (Clark 1973:62–66) also indicated that three-quarters of the respondents supported greater government regulation of business. Recognizing this trend, the CBBB announced in 1970 that a stepped-up education program was one of the highest priorities for the Bureau. The importance of consumer education was expounded in the August 1970 BBB newsletter:

> BBBs know that the average consumer is not confronted in a major way by fraud and deception. In fact, his unsatisfactory transactions may be both minor and very infrequent. It is also obvious that the average consumer should realize that, as the decision maker, he should know about fraud so he can avoid its traps. The consumer-education series of the BBB is designed to make a person a more sophisticated buyer, to learn about different types of merchandise, to check prices and quality of the product, to deal with those businesses who have proven over the years to be reliable [p. 1].

An example of the national Council's efforts to reach a larger audience with Bureau information and services is its sponsorship and coordination of Consumer Information Week, instituted in 1972 and refined in 1973. This program enlists the support or cooperation of national businesses and trade associations, as well as local Bureaus and their members, to publicize BBB services. The CBBB sees several benefits from an annual Consumer Information Week. First, it gives the Bureau an opportunity to reach the public with concentrated short courses in marketplace skills through newspaper supplements and an increased number of broadcast messages. Second, it increases the visibility of the Bureau and provides it with an opportunity to stress its role as a source of helpful buying information. Third, increased public visibility may make membership in the BBB more attractive to businesspeople. And fourth, it may serve to improve the BBB's relations with consumer protection agencies and consumer groups.

On a year-round basis, the BBB carries on consumer education activities at both the national and local levels. The most far-reaching form of BBB education is public service messages broadcast by radio stations and, to a lesser extent, by television. The national organization has also produced many short publications for widespread distribution. These are sold to local Bureaus at bulk rates, to be supplied free on request to consumers. The CBBB also publishes the *Consumer's Buying Guide*, some 200 pages in length, which is a digest of useful information on various products and services and advice on family budgeting and shopping.

Consumer education on the local level of the BBB appears to be less systematic. Although the City Bureau has a good reputation within the BBB, it is understaffed and cannot maintain an extensive consumer education program. It publishes a consumer advice column in small local newspapers but has only a cooperative agreement concerning advertising standards with the largest of the local papers. BBB members also sometimes appear on talk shows and speak before civic and senior citizens' groups and in classrooms.

In general, BBB consumer education is directed toward three goals. The first is to give general instructions on wise shopping habits. The basic warnings that appear over and over in BBB publications are variations on the themes of "You get what you pay for," and "As long as there's a market or a willing victim, the fraud will flourish." Other announcements give hints on shopping for particular products, such as steam irons. The second goal is to warn consumers about fly-by-night schemes by which many people are victimized. The Bureau frequently warns consumers that the transient salesperson will not be around later to back up his or her merchandise, so the customer may be wiser to pay higher prices at an established firm or for a well-known brand-name product. The third goal of consumer education is to explain legitimate business practices that frequently are misunderstood by consumers and create hostility toward local firms. For instance, the Bureau tells consumers that all promises and agreements should be put into writing if they are to be binding, that a binding agreement commits both sides of a transaction to its terms, and that records of all transactions should be retained by the consumer.

BBB messages vary little from medium to medium. Perhaps the most succinct statement of the Bureau's approach to consumer information is the list of eight rules that was published during Consumer Education Week in 1973 under the general admonition "Get the Facts!": (a) Read the label; (b) understand the guarantee; (c) shop price and quality; (d) know the cost of credit; (e) read use and care instructions; (f) check the seller's reliability (by calling the local BBB); (g) read the contract before signing; and (h) ask who services it.

The Bureau is also working to educate the public to use its reliability reports before buying rather than depend upon its complaint-handling facilities after purchases have proved unsatisfactory.

In its consumer education program, the Bureau operates under the same constraints as in its efforts to expose fraudulent businesspeople in the local marketplace (see page 26). One radio announcement issued by the Council in 1973 gave shopping tips to used-car buyers. Although the spot did not state outright that certain abuses are rife in the used-car business, it did advise consumers not to allow themselves to be pressured by salespeople on the lots and suggested that they visit at least three dealers before making a decision. Used-car dealers objected so strenuously to their local Bureaus that the CBBB withdrew the spot from the media (1973 reinterview).

Discussion and Conclusions

The BBB and the Selective Representation of Reality

The Bureau's mission is to promote a favorable atmosphere for business by providing services to the public: regulating business practices that harm consumers, mediating disputes, and preparing consumers to participate competently in the marketplace. But the manner in which these services are provided is affected by the concerns and outlook of the Bureau's other constituency—the sponsoring business community. Members of the BBB staff and board of directors either have professional backgrounds in business or are currently owners or managers of business enterprises. Local merchants pay the Bureau's bills and must be continually reassured of the wisdom of their investment. They must be convinced that the Bureau's activities are creating a favorable impression of business, giving consumers "confidence in our competitive enterprise system," conveying to the public the business view of the proper operation of the marketplace, and entertaining or encouraging only "legitimate" complaints from consumers. To be effective as a public relations instrument of business, the staff must also convince the public that as the authorized representative of the business community, the Bureau is promoting self-regulation so effectively that unsolicited intervention by government is unwarranted.

The BBB's two objectives—creating a good impression of business and providing services to the public—are often complementary. Thus, the Bureau brings customer grievances to the attention of business managers so that through fair handling of complaints the customer's favorable impression of business is maintained. To convince the public that government interference is unwarranted, some degree of control is exerted over business practices, and to that degree the public interest is served. However, in striving to maintain that favorable image, the Bureau necessarily imposes limits on the quality of assistance that it gives to consumers. How the Bureau's services are affected by its primary goal of impression management—the selective representation of reality—will now be discussed.

First of all, the Bureau must deal with the problem of the small businessperson's suspicion of big business (see, for example, Schred's self-justification on page 263). Throughout this chapter I have characterized the BBB as an organ of an interest group—the "business community"—as though this were a single body of entrepreneurs operating under a common set of values. Actually, although the BBB says that it "represents" business, only a small number of firms contribute materially to its support. This is true for all Bureaus across the nation; in New York there are 6300 members out of a possible 350,000; San Francisco reports 1200 out of 40,000; and Houston reports 2600 out of 37,000 (Clark 1973). Second, the BBB outlook is probably slightly different from that of many local businesspeople because it orients its behavior toward consumers and legislators and specializes in impression management for the entire business community. The Bureau is sensitive to the wider implications of the behavior of individual firms. Some businesspeople resent this professional conscience. A common complaint by businesses against the BBB is that it is really a means by which big businesses impose their standards upon small businesses, thereby giving an unfair edge to big concerns and driving little firms out of the marketplace.

The BBB, of course, challenges this contention. John O'Brien, Executive Vice President of CBBB, in congressional testimony, cited the fact that of the $9.5 million supporting the BBB in 1971, $8.2 million was supplied by companies other than the nation's thousand largest firms as listed in Fortune (U.S. Congress 1971:33). However, these statistics do not prove that small businesses actually control the policymaking of the local Bureaus, for there is a tendency for larger businesses with prestigious names to be heavily represented on the boards of directors of the BBB. The recent CBBB decision to try to increase the funding of the organization primarily from the contributions of national advertisers suggests that there will be a further drift toward big business in the balance of power in the BBB.

When deciding upon the phrasing of reliability reports or the release of a consumer alert to the media, the Bureau must weigh the dangers of alienating its members. The Bureau's staff members make frequent allusions to the threat of libel suits if it is too aggressive or critical in its reliability and press reports. These considerations, as well as those discussed later, cause the staff to limit the information it actually provides to the public.

Reliability reports provide predictability for the consumer or entrepreneur contemplating a transaction with a firm, but they serve another function for businesspeople. The BBB increases public confidence in the business community first simply by "being there" to research and report wrongdoers to the inquiring consumer and second by releasing a preponderance of favorable reports that corroborate the assertion that most businesspeople in the community are reliable. The bad reports, particularly those disseminated widely through the media as consumer alerts, tend to describe small, usually transient or remote (in the case of mail-order frauds), fly-by-nighters who make blatant misrepresentations about their merchandise or neglect to deliver goods for which they have received money—not the typical local businessperson at all.

The task of preserving the image of the responsible business community does not coincide with informing the public explicitly and frequently of all the illegal operations large and small, subtle and not so subtle, that exist at any given moment. Although the Bureau is willing to give some generally accepted guidelines for evaluating products and services, it does not leap at the chance to inform the consumer of ills that are widespread in the legitimate business world. For instance, BBB pamphlets provide information on how to shop for appliances and appliance repair services, but their major suggestion to the consumer for dealing with the high cost of repairs and the short life expectancy of appliances is to budget some money each month for repairs and replacements.

Another example of this policy of selective presentation of information is provided by the findings of the Rosenthal study (Congressional Record 1971:E13768–E13771). The task force found that Federal Trade Commission actions against BBB members were not mentioned in BBB reliability reports, that such members had not been ousted from the BBB, and that, in fact, few members had ever been ousted from the Bureaus that were studied. As the task force observed, "reliability" or "reputability" are primarily a reflection of the BBB's scorekeeping on the number of complaints sent to a company in relation to the number adjusted in some reasonable fashion; in short, "reliability" means cooperation with the BBB's complaint-screening procedure (E13771). A firm's membership in the BBB is included in reliability reports, and BBB membership status is meant to imply a very conscientious adherence to BBB guidelines.

The BBB says that it will not recommend firms to its clients but rather will give them "the facts" and let them judge for themselves. The facts that it chooses to reveal are those that it deems relevant criteria of evaluation. During my own fieldwork at the BBB, I found grounds on which to question the value of the reliability reports to consumers. As far as I could gather from the data, warnings to consumers are frequently couched in such subtle terms that only an educated or sophisticated person could understand their implications. Note, for instance, the shift in meaning between "It is prompt to adjust those complaints where it has a responsibility to do so," and "The company has adjusted those where it felt a responsibility to do so."

Through its consumer education activities, the BBB tells consumers what are legitimate or illegitimate practices, and reasonable or unreasonable expectations, and provides them with some basic guides to wise buying. They are advised to learn the reputability of the firms they are considering before they do business with them and to call on the Bureau for this "certification." Again, it must be emphasized that this instruction gives the consumer the business viewpoint on these matters. Providing the information is intended to make consumers confident and trusting in their transactions with the "right" people and to help them fit smoothly into the role of ideal "competent customers"—buyers who accept the legitimacy of the well-known brand name and are willing to pay extra for it to avoid the uncertainty of cheaper but unknown products, who conveniently keep records of their transactions, who understand and accept the responsibilities incurred in making a binding agreement by signing their names to a contract, who read and follow the instructions provided with their purchases. Such information is indeed useful to the public, especially to the poor, the semiliterate, the aged, and the sick. However, the BBB's educational activities provide less than all the information consumers should have. At least until recently, systematic pretransaction training in shopping skills and product knowledge has been a peripheral activity of the Bureau. The actual impact of the BBB's revitalized education program has yet to be gauged, but it may come to be much more important and useful to the public than it has been in the past.

COMPLAINT HANDLING AND ITS IMPLICATIONS

An important part of any program of impression management for business is to show that businesspeople are responsive to any customer dissatisfactions that they cause and to ensure that as many consumer–business disputes as possible are handled within the business community itself. The Bureau's complaint-handling activities are conceived and, in actuality, serve as a back-up system for the complaint-handling systems of the individual businesses. The Bureau's statistics on complaints processed indicate that a fairly large number of consumers are given an extra chance to get through to business managers with their grievances because the Bureau is there to help them. There are two phases of complaint management: putting the relevant parties in communication with each other and bringing some pressure to bear on the disputants to reach a fair settlement.

As we have seen, the Bureau is particularly well suited to perform the function of channeling the consumer's complaint back into the company. It deals primarily with the management personnel of the area's companies, and management is probably more image-conscious than are lower-level personnel. Because the Bureau evaluates complaints according to business criteria before referring them to the company and because the managers know that the referral process is intended to serve the long-term interests of businesspeople by enabling them to retain good will through the fair disposition of consumer complaints, most cases sent to companies by the Bureau receive serious consideration.

Despite these advantages for the consumer in the communication aspect of the complaint-handling procedure, there are also some disadvantages. As complaints come into the BBB office, the staff screens out those that it deems unjustifiable according to business criteria. The requirements that the complaint be written and that consumers send for the forms by mail also limit access to the complaint-handling service. This screening process is based not on considerations of what is just but rather on the pragmatic criterion of whether the complainant is determined enough to persist in registering his or her complaint in writing. The requirement of a written document makes filing a complaint particularly difficult for people with little education or for those who are not native English speakers.

In an office where there is continuous contact with disgruntled citizens, the staff's preference for polite behavior may also result in the screening out of certain complainants. What an angry person of an ethnic background different from that of the office worker may regard as blowing off steam, may be interpreted as threatening behavior by the BBB employee. As a result, the complainant may never be allowed to register his or her complaint. These statements are not meant to imply that the BBB is a hotbed of intentional discrimination, but rather simply to point out that the staff and procedures of the office make few provisions to prevent differential rates of success for consumers of other social and educational backgrounds.

The second phase of the Bureau's complaint-handling procedure—bringing pressure to bear to encourage equitable settlements—is very limited because it is organized on the assumption that most businesspeople will voluntarily make fair decisions. Once a BBB consultant has made the decision to refer a complaint to a store, his role as third party to the dispute is one more as liaison than as adjudicator or even mediator. If a businessperson decides not to adjust a complaint, the consultant will pursue the matter no further. As the local BBB vice president stressed to me during my first visit to the office, the Bureau has guidelines and preferred behavior patterns, not enforceable ideals; the rules have no teeth. If the consultants do not agree with a firm's disposition of complaints, they may eventually revise the company's reliability report. However, the data suggest that most entrepreneurs who handle complaints do so because they are already genuinely concerned with their customer relations, not because they are coerced by the prospect of receiving a bad report from the BBB.

The CBBB's attempts to improve services to consumers indicate its awareness of the Bureaus' shortcomings as complaint handlers. First, through its expanded national education program it tries to replace the Bureaus' traditional image as agencies specializing in fielding complaints with one that stresses their value as sources of reliability reports and consumer information. This measure in effect admits the BBB's shortcomings in complaint management and tries to redirect the attention of consumers to Bureau activities that are more successful and hence more valuable to the public. Second, the CBBB has encouraged the development of arbitration panels to handle controversial cases that previously might have been left unresolved. This program is certainly an improvement over abandoning dissatisfied clients to their own devices. However, it should be remembered that complaints are still subject to BBB screening before they are arbitrated and that one aim of arbitration is to silence what the CBBB calls "frivolous accusations and unfounded disparagements." Also, the program has no power to force arbitration on companies that do not wish to cooperate, and only about half the states in the Union recognize arbitration in place of court decisions.

A third CBBB effort, to increase budgets and staffs at the local level, could also lead to improvements in complaint handling if the increases were used creatively, since some of the present obstacles to complaining are caused by shortages in funds and staff time. If there were larger staffs, the BBB would not have to depend on the complaint-processing statistics on a firm in order to formulate its reliability reports; rather, it could conduct its own investigations prior to revising these reports.

An important criticism that can be leveled against the BBB is that it takes the heat off companies under attack by listening to complaints and going through the motions of attempting to remedy the grievances. If the basis of the complaint is not admissible evidence, according to the business view, the case is dismissed with no chance for appeal. This mode of action certainly does not benefit the consumer, but it does serve a useful purpose for the businessperson: The BBB first sets itself up as a legitimate interpreter of what is fair and reasonable in the marketplace and then, in this capacity, vindicates the businessperson. It is important to remember that there are other interpreters of the consumer's rights and obligations and that their conclusions may differ from the Bureaus:

> A couple of people who had first sent their complaints to the BBB said they found suing far more effective. "Before taking this case to court," one man said, "I contacted the [City] Better Business Bureau. I found, however, that this group seems to function not for the benefit of the public, but rather to protect businesses from complaints of the public. On discussing my case with the BBB I was advised not to sue. Perhaps reform of the BBB would be in order." Despite the BBB's advice, he won a $175 judgment for faulty repairs to his car's air conditioner. Another [City] consumer said: "In my case, the Better Business Bureau was totally unhelpful, and although I searched, I couldn't find any other agency or institution set up to protect the consumer [Consumer Reports 1971:627].

The implications of this state of affairs are great when we take into account the magnitude of consumer discontent and the exclusiveness (until recently) of the Bureau's claim to the title of complaint handler and interpreter of the marketplace to the public. For example, as long as consumers accept the Bureau's advice that shopping around for the best appliance and budgeting regularly for repairs and replacements (to be made at intervals deemed acceptable by appliance manufacturers and designers rather than by consumers) is the sensible way to purchase appliances, then products of greater durability and better design are unlikely to be developed.

Given the tremendous power that the business community has had by virtue of its near monopoly on interpreting the marketplace to most of the consuming public, it is not surprising that BBB spokespeople are opposed to consumer advocates and the protective legislation they demand (see, e.g., the anticonsumerist comments of New York City BBB President Wirsig in *Newsweek* 1970:60).

SELF-REGULATION BY BUSINESS AS A SOCIAL CONTROL

The Bureau's regulatory activities include developing standards of conduct for advertising and retail selling, educating businesspeople to follow these guidelines, and enforcing the rules by monitoring the behavior of businesspeople. Self-regulation by business is self-interested; it is intended to prevent competitive practices destructive to the business community itself and to manage a performance by the business community that will discourage further regulation of the marketplace in the public interest by nonbusinesspeople.

Self-regulation is more attractive to business than is its alternative, external social control, because it allows businesspeople to enjoy the comforts of being judged by their peers by their own standards. Because self-regulation is an "affair among gentlemen," the business community can justify keeping its problems, evaluative criteria, and methods of control concealed from the public audience, which possibly has dissimilar goals and values. Confidentiality works to the advantage of the business community by allowing it to conceal the exact nature and magnitude of the policing problem it faces and hence to foster the impression of an orderly and ethical marketplace. A third advantage for businesspeople is that self-regulation allows them to choose their own sanctions. In accordance with their view that self-regulation is an affair among gentlemen, they put great store in the effectiveness of public scorn as a sanction.

Self-regulation by business does not necessarily operate against the interests of consumers. It can be argued that insiders are the best judges of what are reasonable advertising promises and therefore know better than anyone else what must be guarded against. Interactions between colleagues (or at least sympathizers) tend to be more candid and cooperative than those between adversaries, and therefore it is possible that more can be accomplished through internal than through external regulation.

Once businesspeople establish rules for themselves, each person will probably keep a sharp eye out to make sure that no one takes unfair advantage of his or her law-abiding colleagues; thus, the self-regulatory system will be reinforced by the monitoring of the performance of the group by those subject to its rules. BBB spokespeople assert that in order to keep public confidence, self-regulating businesspeople often maintain a standard of performance higher than the legally required minimum. If self-regulation is indeed successful in achieving these high standards of performance, the public is saved not only the expense of maintaining a body of external regulatory personnel but also the delays caused by filing a lawsuit in the congested court system.

But the BBB's potential for acting as a regulator in the consumer's interest is not fully realized. There are two interrelated characteristics of the Bureau primarily responsible for its shortcomings. First, the model of the marketplace in accordance with which the BBB operates is unrealistic. According to this model, the marketplace is composed of responsible businesspeople taking individual initiative to answer the complaints of the consumers upon whose patronage their livelihood depends and cooperating to pressure recalcitrant merchants into living up to the business community's standards. That the model is inaccurate is demonstrated by the ineffectiveness of the Bureau's enforcement procedures. The unfavorable reliability report has little impact on most local firms (to say nothing of national advertisers) unless the BBB's evaluations are made known to a wide audience rather than to the relatively small number of people who consult it about any one firm. The BBB seems even more reluctant to broadcast its evaluations than to turn matters over to the legal system. Furthermore, advertising media are apparently less cooperative than they might be when the BBB seeks their assistance in dealing with unscrupulous businesses.

Limitations on what the BBB can do are also imposed by antitrust laws: If the Bureau is too aggressive in its attempts to force conformity to its standards, it can be accused of restraining trade and stifling competition. As long as the BBB and a firm agree on the proper way to conduct business, everything is fine, but when a disagreement arises, the BBB by itself is nearly powerless to enforce its views. The BBB depends ultimately on the legal system to supply the sanctions to enforce the rules against the most unscrupulous businesspeople. It is extremely difficult for the BBB to enforce rules not already backed up by laws, for if a Bureau cannot force a "disreputable businessperson" in its area to observe a BBB recommendation, it will have a difficult time convincing the reputable competitors to observe it unilaterally.

The BBB ideology contends that the marketplace is responsive to, and indeed is molded by, the desires of an informed public. This assumption may be true on some levels, but the picture is more complicated than that.

National corporations play a significant part in the local marketplace; they are more powerful than the consumers, who have dispersed power and lack organization, information, and communication. The consumers' complaints have more weight with the locally competitive retailer than with the faraway corporation making the product that the retailer sells. On the one hand, consumers are told that it is their responsibility to inform themselves and to exercise their power of choice to bring the market into line with their needs and desires, but on the other hand, they are confronted with a range of products from different manufacturers having no differences among them that appear to be significant.

The Bureau has been relatively successful at opening channels of communication between willing parties—the local merchant and his or her customer—but can it operate as efficiently to foster communication between the consumer and the national companies? My data are insufficient to answer this question, but the recent proliferation of hot lines and toll-free phone numbers to national corporations' complaint departments suggests that this role of the BBB has been less than satisfactory. There was some question in the 1971 congressional hearings as to whether individual consumers could complain directly to CBBB's National Advertising Review Board without first being screened through the CBBB (U.S. Congress 1971:7). If consumers are not given direct access to these national panels, both as complainants and as observers, the regulation of national advertising will remain entirely up to the CBBB, its member businesses, and, in the last resort, to the advertiser-dominated NARB.

In its role as self-regulator, the Bureau defines certain problems as appropriate areas of concern and limits its jurisdiction in other matters. Hence the BBB deals with "truth" and to some degree with "taste" in advertising, but not with relevance. It concentrates on how things are said in copy rather than on what is being advertised in it,[15] and, at least until recently, it has concentrated its efforts on local retail advertising rather than on national advertising.

Self-direction might be acceptable if business and other groups in the public were in agreement upon what are the most serious problems of the marketplace, the acceptable forms of advertising, the reasonable businessman, the most effective and just sanctions, and the rational expectations of consumers, but in fact they are not.

The BBB is fairly useful in protecting consumers who consult it about retail abuses and outright frauds (by its definition), but it defines itself out of the picture when it comes to problems such as noncompetitive pricing,

---

[15]As Kenneth A. Cox, Chairman of the NARB, has said, "A lot of complaints about advertising are really complaints about the product. And of course we don't control what's lawful to manufacture. For us to say something that is legal to distribute cannot be advertised would raise some very serious legal questions [Love 1977:D11]."

planned obsolescence, and the fairness of contract terms or billing procedures. Because the Bureau is a representative of the business community,
it cannot act as the "voice of the people in the marketplace." In fact, we
have seen that some of the complaints that consumers make against companies are not even admissible to a local Bureau.

Although my fieldwork at the City Better Business Bureau during the
spring of 1971 and my subsequent library research revealed much about
the workings and probable impact of the BBB system upon the nation's
consumers, there were some questions I did not explore. I learned much
about the day-to-day routine of the consultants but very little about the
work of the president, the membership representative, and the power
structure that makes the BBB's policy decisions. I focused on the
consumer-relations aspect of Bureau work rather than investigating directly the relationship between the Bureau and the businesses that sponsor it. A content analysis of the membership's newsletter and observation
of the directors' meetings would give a better idea of the motives and
deliberations of the businesspeople who make up the policies of the
Bureau at the local level. We need also to discover the status of the BBB in
the business community: What impels some businesspeople to join the
Bureau whereas many others do not?

In my interviews with staff members, they made explicit references to
the Bureau's decision not to publicize known frauds in the general press
for fear of alienating the businesspeople whose membership fees are the
sole support of the Bureau's work. It is important to know how great an
effect this concern for funding has on the decisions of the BBB management in their policy deliberations and on the staff's allocation of time,
effort, and money for promotional activities. And, of course, this concern
has serious implications for the manner in which the Bureau looks after
the interests of the consumer when these interests conflict with those of
BBB sponsors.

Further study might also reveal who uses the BBB and for what purpose. It would be interesting to learn if there are social class differences in
the use made of the Bureau. Who uses it as a preventive or predictive
agency? Who uses it as a complaint department after a purchase is made?
Are these the same people? Does the number of phone calls to the office
reflect a high or low rate of repeaters? In order to answer these questions,
the research must be carried beyond the BBB office walls in the form of
interviews or surveys of both businesspeople and consumers.

Today, the public, which has always harbored an incipient mistrust
of business, is provided with new sources of information, alternative values, and powerful spokespeople who demand changes in the laws and
their enforcement. On the local scene, the BBB's "territory" is being in-
vaded by public and private consumer protection groups with functions
parallel to those of the Bureau. The new groups pursue their tasks with

greater vigor and from a nonbusiness orientation. As a result, they can afford to take an adversary rather than a cooperative stance when dealing with firms for their consumer clients.

How will changes in the BBB's social environment affect its operation? As a body concerned with the quality of life in the business world, the self-regulators may be prompted to make innovations. A fine example is the development of the arbitration panel program to handle marketplace disputes in a society that fails to deal with "little cases." The sound and fury of the consumer movement have prompted enlightened businesspeople to press for new self-regulatory programs in areas that have been subject to severe criticism (for example, the practices of national advertisers). The scope of BBB activities has expanded to influence more directly the advertising practices of national companies and perhaps also to impose innovations upon the more conservative, locally oriented constituent Bureaus. But the sensitivity of business to its environment can have other results as well. The response can take the form of improvements, but it can also result merely in a new public relations theme. (For example, when the government issued a report on the damaging effects of abrasives in toothpaste, the toothpaste manufacturers quickly composed advertisement to the effect that X-brand toothpaste had fewer abrasives than other tooth whiteners did.) The BBB opposes consumer legislation on the ground that newly instituted "improvements" in self-policing program should be given a chance to work. In the words of ABBB's *Consumer Buying Guide*:

> The confidence man posing as a bona fide businessman seems to find loopholes in almost any law. The honest merchant abides by all the laws, but any new law means more red tape to contend with, another restriction on his merchandising, another brake on business and, therefore, on the economy. The weight of such laws seems too often to fall on the men who abide by the law in the first place [1969:200–201].

At present, public attention is focused on business, and so self-regulators are responsive to criticism. But consumerism may be a fad, and public interest may dissipate. Attention may drift to other issues. However, the BBB is entrenched both as a lobbying organization and as a frequently consulted consumer aid at the local level. In fact, BBB consultants told me that the Bureau's reputation is so well established that many people assume it is a governmental agency of some kind. Time is on the side of the Bureau, which can make dramatic surface changes without substantially changing the underlying assumptions upon which it operates. Its arbitration program is an innovation that responds to consumer needs in the marketplace, but it is promoted to businesses as a way to maintain privacy in their handling of disputes, to admit technical considerations that would be costly or inadmissible in the courts, and to avoid the courtroom (and any chance to establish new legal precedents in consumer law). In the Dry Cleaning Panel, business had a two-to-one majority in deliberations. And the Bureau does not have the sanctioning power to enforce any rule that is not backed up by law.

As Robert Choate, Chairman of the Council on Children, Media, and Advertising, pointed out so well in his testimony before the Hearings on Advertising and Small Business:

> Behind any system of self-regulation, Federal agencies must stand guard. They ... must remain a court of last appeal for any private self-regulation guidelines. Their vigor in employing their ultimate power to embarrass and coerce those who offend may be the key element in sustaining and strengthening the resolve of the private sector to make self-regulation work [U.S. Congress 1971:150].

As an editorial in *Broadcasting Magazine* stated:

> All systems of self-regulation develop as alternatives to systems of external regulation. The growing influence of the consumer movement is forcing the total advertising community to make that choice. If advertising does not opt for the voluntary way, it will fall under harsher and harsher regulation by government [1971:22].

If public attention and loud criticism are dissipated, the business world may return to its comfortable old ways unless the consumer movement is successful in getting its demands crystallized into laws with adequate provision for systematic enforcement. In short, consumers should not depend too heavily on a business interest group to look after their interests for them. Self-regulation by business is useful to all groups in society, as far as it goes. Its potentialities should be developed and encouraged but not overestimated.

References

*Documents by the Better Business Bureau and
Advertising Groups*

ABBB (Association of Better Business Bureaus)
  1947   *Manual of operation.* New York: ABBB.
  1969   *Consumer's buying guide.* New York: Rutledge Books and Benjamin Company (updated; now published by CBBB).
Advertising Advisory Committee to the Secretary of Commerce
  1964   *Self-regulation in advertising.* Washington, D.C.: U.S. Government Printing Office.

Better Business Bureau of City (pseud.)

    1970–1971 *BBB/Westcoast* (pseud.) (Newsletter to members). April, May, June, July, August, October, November, December 1970; January, February, April, May 1971.

    1967 By-laws of Better Business Bureau of City (Last amendment in 1967).

Burnett, Verne

    1950 *Self-regulation of advertising: A guidebook of major facilities* (Report prepared for the American Association of Advertising Agencies and the Association of National Advertisers). New York: Verne Burnett Associates.

CBBB (Council of Better Business Bureaus)

    1970 Newsletter. August.

    1975 Annual Report.

    1977a *News & Views* **2**(4).

    1977b *News & Views* **3**(2).

NAD (National Advertising Division of CBBB)

    1977 Eleven challenges to national advertising resolved by NAD in June (News release). 15 July.

Smith, Ralph Lee

    1961 *Self-regulation in action: Story of the Better Business Bureau, 1912–1962.* New York: ABBB.

Other Sources

Advertising Age

    1970a NBBB, ABBBI may merge. 25 May: p. 118.

    1970b "Credible, visible" self-regulation. 17 August: p. 18.

    1970c BBB to seek $25,000,000 fund to boost level of policing. 7 December: p. 2.

Aubert, Vilhelm

    1969 Law as a way of resolving conflicts: The case of a small industrialized society. In *Law in culture and society,* edited by Laura Nader. Chicago: Aldine.

Bailey, Frederick George (Ed.)

    1971 *Gifts and poison: The politics of reputation.* New York: Schocken.

Bauer, Raymond A., and Stephen A. Greyser

    1971 The dialogue that never happens. In *Consumerism: Search for the consumer interest,* edited by David A. Aaker and George S. Day. Glencoe, Ill.: Free Press.

Broadcasting

    1971 Out of sync (Editorial). 29 March: p. 122.

Business Week

    1972 Madison Avenue's response to its critics. 10 June: pp. 46–54.

Clark, Champ

    1973 Better Business Bureaus are getting better. *Money Magazine* **2**(4) (April):62–66.

Colson, Elizabeth

    1953 Social control and vengeance in Plateau Tonga society. *Africa* **23**:199–211.

Congressional Record
1971 Extension of remarks: Benjamin Rosenthal, 17 December: pp. E13764, E13767, E13768–E13771, E13773.
Consumer Reports
1971 Buyer vs. seller in small claims court. October: 624–631.
Elting, Victor, Jr.
1970 Ad federation chairman suggests independent council to curb abuses. *Advertising Age*, 12 October: 49–50.
Gluckman, Max
1955 *The judicial process among the Barotse of Northern Rhodesia.* Manchester (England): Manchester University Press.
Good Housekeeping Magazine
1970 GH consumer panel: How women feel about the products they buy. October: 179–181.
Greenhouse, Linda
1972 Small Claims Courts failing consumers. New York Times, 16 August: p. 1.
Love, Thomas
1977 Can TV ads be policed by ad men? *Washington Star.* 12 July: pp. A1 and D11.
Moore, Wilbert E., and Melvin M. Tumin
1949 Some social functions of ignorance. *American Sociological Review* **14**:787–795.
Nader, Laura
1969 Styles of court procedure: To make the balance. In *Law in Culture and Society,* edited by Laura Nader. Chicago: Aldine.
Newsweek
1970 Consumerism: Better business? 2 March: p. 60.
NYCBBB
1972 Final draft of Report by the Office of Consumer Arbitration, Division of Legal and Governmental Affairs, New York, New York. Not published.
Paulson, Morton C.
1972 Arbitration for consumer complaints. *National Observer,* 15 July: p. 8.
Tuttle, Robert L.
1977 Personal communication from Director of Information Systems and Development, CBBB Division of Bureau Affairs. Washington, 14 July.
U.S. Congress Select Committee on Small Business.
1971 Hearings before the Subcommittee on Activities of Regulatory Agencies Relating to Small Business. House of Representatives, 92nd Congress, First Session. 7, 11, 14, 18 and 25 June. Also referred to as Hearings on Advertising and Small Business.
U.S. Department of Commerce
1964 Self-regulation in advertising: A report on the operations of private enterprise in an important area of public responsibility. Submitted by the Advertising Advisory Committee to the Secretary of Commerce.

7

Angela Karikas and
Rena Rosenwasser

DEPARTMENT STORE
COMPLAINT MANAGEMENT

Introduction

Every day thousands of department stores across the nation receive hundreds of thousands of complaints regarding their merchandise and personnel. It is part of their daily routine to absorb such complaints in an effort to keep consumers satisfied. Although the subjects of many of the complaints are similar to those heard by governmental agencies, media hotlines, and legislative offices, there is one important difference: Department store complainants personally face their adversary in the arena of the sales floor or the store office.

In our complex society the opportunity for this kind of face-to-face confrontation appears to be extremely limited. Water and power companies include on their billing statements a telephone number that customers may call when they have questions or complaints. And consumers cheated by fly-by-night operators may resort to writing a letter to a newspaper action line or to calling the Better Business Bureau. For the most part, registering a complaint is an impersonal procedure. Letters are addressed to agencies, newspapers, television stations, and the like, and usually not to individuals.

The complainant who meets his or her adversaries in person undoubtedly carries a big advantage. For instance, consider the successful tactics of a "professional complainer," who was told that his confirmed hotel reservation could not be honored. He told the hotel clerk quietly but firmly, "I will give you three minutes to find me a room. After three minutes, I am going to undress in the lobby, put on my pajamas, and go to sleep on one of the sofas." The clerk handed him a key to a room (Nevy, *San Francisco Chronicle*, 16 December 1974).

Just as the hotel clerk could not easily escape the presence of the angered would-be guest, the salesperson or manager of a department store is forced to deal with the customer's problem at that moment. The immediacy of the situation works to the customer's advantage. He cannot be put off by being placed on hold or by having his letter filed at the bottom of the unanswered mail. The hotel clerk was undoubtedly pressured into resolving the man's problem favorably because he wished to avoid a scene. A ruckus in the hotel lobby is bad for business. The dissatisfied customer in a department store has a similar potential for creating a disturbance on the floor and scaring off other customers. In addition, the hotel clerk was more likely to be genuinely concerned about the problem of the man before him than he would for a disembodied voice on a telephone or a gilded letterhead. In the same way, a salesperson is more likely to be moved to help the customer if he or she has a face and a personality to deal with in addition to an account number.

Finally, there is another advantage for the consumer in the face-to-face confrontation. Both parties can examine the source of the complaint at the same time. The hotel clerk could not deny the fact that the man had a confirmed reservation in his hand, just as a salesperson is forced to accept the fact that an appliance does not work or that a zipper has been sewn incorrectly. A personal confrontation may not determine which party was at fault, but it will help to establish the fact that there is a complaint to be settled.

A Note on Methodology

The advantages that a face-to-face resolution of complaints seems to hold for the consumer led us to study the complaint-managing systems in department stores. Initially we wanted to determine if the uniquely personal nature of the complaint process made department stores successful in resolving their customers' complaints. In the fall of 1972 we interviewed salesclerks, department heads, buyers, and assistant buyers as well as the top managers of six major department stores in the San Francisco Bay Area. Although we called upon a number of other Bay Area department stores, not all of them were willing to be studied. As a result, the department stores that were studied varied both in volume of sales and in nature of merchandise carried.

Gump's is an exclusive gift store in which the average sale is higher than that of any of the other stores we studied. Joseph Magnin, I. Magnin, and City of Paris, all in San Francisco, have annual sales between $65 and $100 million dollars. Hink's and Penney's in Berkeley sell less expensive items and have much smaller annual sales. In 1973 the main store and the appliance concession at Hink's had $6.7 million dollars in sales. Its percentage of returned merchandise was .5%, far less than I. Magnin's rate of 15% for the same year.

The stores also represented a cross section of different types of ownership. City of Paris, I. Magnin, and Joseph Magnin were owned by conglomerates that own other department store chains. The owner of Gump's was an eastern publishing company, J. C. Penney's in Berkeley a branch of a single national chain of stores, and Hink's a locally owned store.

It is also important to point out that our investigation of department store complaints does not encompass all types of complaints made by customers. We studied store procedures for handling problems with merchandise only. Billing complaints are usually not registered in person, and in some stores these are referred to an administrative office in another building.

Complaint Management in Six Stores

Gump's: A Centralized System

Gump's of San Francisco claims to be "a legend in a legendary city." In a small brochure published for customers, browsers, and tourists, the store's management states, "This unique establishment has a world reputation as a mecca for lovers of fine art and merchandise of good taste." Agents from Gump's comb the world searching for unusual art pieces and gift items. The price tags on the merchandise do not always bear out the store's slogan: "Good taste costs no more." As one employee explained, "We are a prestige store with totally luxury items. There isn't a thing in this store that you couldn't live without."

On the first floor customers wander through the modern and Oriental gift departments where there are $50 marble bread boards from Italy and a selection of 10 different types of ice buckets. The street floor also houses the jewel room and a small salon that specializes in designer fashions for women. Unlike other department stores, Gump's displays its most valuable merchandise as a museum collection. The third floor is famous for its Jade Room, stocked with figurines displayed in locked glass cases. Around the corner from the Jade Room is a small art gallery with sketches by such artists as Picasso, Chagall, and Matisse.

According to Gump's managers, their unique department store–museum requires a special procedure for handling complaints. Gump's is the only store we studied that maintains a central office to process all complaints. Customers with billing, shipping, or exchange problems are immediately sent to the customer service department.

The customer service office is well marked and easy to find. A street-floor wall directory lists the department on the second floor, and a large sign near the elevator points the customer in the right direction. There is a reception area furnished with a couch and chairs in front of the counter where returns and complaints are received, thus giving every impression that the store intends the return procedure to be simple and convenient for the customer.

The customer service department has a regular staff of four employees. Ms. Willis, the office manager, has worked at complaint management at Gump's since 1957. She views herself as a professional complaint taker who is more interested in public relations than in sales. She said, "There aren't many people who like this job. I've had it the longest of anyone at this store, and I love the challenge."

Simple returns and exchanges are made at the customer service counter. The management prefers to have items returned within 90 days of their purchase, but Ms. Willis admitted that Gump's has a flexible policy. Customers with involved or unusual problems are asked to be seated in a comfortable chair while they explain their case to a department employee. Most of the problems that are not resolved by a return or exchange concern package deliveries. According to Ms. Willis, the most difficult complaints are cases in which the wrong gift was delivered or a price tag was not removed on a gift. The store is obviously at fault in these cases, and the only recourse for the customer service department is to send a letter of apology to the customer. Ms. Willis explained, "There is nothing that infuriates a customer more than an employee who makes excuses. We lay it right on the line. We've done it and I'm sorry." The store also calls customers to apologize for delivery delays.

The management of Gump's is proud of the consistent procedure they have developed for handling complaints. Ms. Willis noted, "Other stores are more erratic. Sometimes business is good, and they take returns on any complaint. And sometimes there is a slump, and their return policy tightens up. As far as Gump's is concerned, this department has the last say on returns. We have no really set rule; we deal with each case individually. Our business is to do right by the customer." However, when pressed to explain how she resolves a problem where the customer may be at fault, she had a different answer. "It boils down to this: If it's a good account, we don't want to jeopardize it. If there's a problem that's a bit unusual and we're going to have to stretch a point or two, we will check the customer's account. If it's good, we'll make the return."

Gump's believes that its centralized return system is the best method for serving its customers. As Ms. Willis explained, "We are a gift store, and our customers expect more from us than they do from Macy's or even I. Magnin's." According to the customer service department, most of the people who make returns at Gump's bring back more than one item at a time, and their work is made easier by the centralized office. The bride who has more than one gift to exchange makes a single trip to the second floor office rather than visiting several different departments.

Gump's has overcome the most obvious objections to a centralized complaint office. First, the store has made the customer service office accessible to the public. Returning an item to customer service is just as convenient, if not easier, than making the return to the sales department. The customer does not have to compete with shoppers for the salesperson's attention, and the office provides a comfortable and quiet atmosphere in which to register a complaint. An important criticism of the centralized return system is that salespeople are more qualified than office employees to judge customer complaints because they are familiar with the merchandise. However, in a store like Gump's, which specializes in unusual gifts from "Malaga and Mindinao, Bergen and Bora Bora"—to quote again from the public relations brochure—salespeople are often not experts on the merchandise they sell. And if the rule of thumb is never to jeopardize a good account, then extensive knowledge of the merchandise is not necessary.

The customer who registers a complaint at Gump's can expect predictable results. The employees of the customer service department handle only customer problems, and their goal is to maintain good public relations. During the busiest part of the Christmas season, a woman from out of town ordered six gifts for a total of $30. She called the customer service department and insisted that Ms. Willis personally take the gifts to the airport. They had already been sent, and there was nothing Ms. Willis could do. She said. "I was never consciously rude, but this woman had the audicity to scream and curse at me over the phone." Ms. Willis then spelled her name in a calm voice and told the woman that she (the customer) could report her to the store manager. She was attempting to show that even under the most trying circumstances her "business is to do right by the customer."

Ms. Willis explained that an important part of her job is letting the customer know that she cares about their problem. "The look on your face is important. You must show sympathy and above all let them know that there is no excuse for what has been done."

At Gump's customers are assured that their complaints will be heard by one of three regular employees. They have the alternative of appealing any decision to the manager of the department; and the procedure is the same for every type of problem. A predictable outcome is an important feature of the centralized system.

I. Magnin, the City of Paris, and Joseph Magnin:
Decentralized Systems

In the heart of San Francisco's shopping district are located three department stores specializing in women's clothing. I. Magnin, Joseph

Magnin, and the City of Paris share a prime location and many of the same customers and merchandise. In addition, the three stores also have developed similar systems for managing complaints. The correct procedure for a customer registering a merchandise complaint is to speak to a salesperson on the floor where the item was purchased. The stores refer to this system as an "on-the-floor" policy.

All three stores list a customer service department on their street-floor wall directories, but it is apparent that customers with merchandise problems are not encouraged to visit those offices. In each store, the department is located on the top floor along with houseware goods or sale items. It is necessary to ask directions to the office after stepping off the elevator. Perhaps it is no accident that I. Magnin's small customer service sign is partially hidden by a large plant. If a customer with a return or an exchange does find his way to the office, he is immediately directed down to the appropriate sales floor. The executives of the three stores firmly believe that the "on-the-floor" return policy is the easiest way to manage complaints.

Although each store maintains a decentralized complaint system, the customer's experience at I. Magnin, Joseph Magnin, and the City of Paris varies considerably. In each store the complainant may appeal the salesperson's decision to a higher authority, but the path up the executive hierarchy is not the same. Because the complaint policy is partly determined by the position of the person who handles the complaint, the resolution of a problem can differ significantly from store to store.

I. Magnin was a locally owned, exclusive women's store until it was bought in 1964 by a national conglomerate, Federated Stores. Although the procedure for a customer registering a complaint has remained the same, the store personnel have changed. Many of the loyal group of elderly salespeople have gone and have been replaced by much younger women. The third floor with its special designer collection is the only exception. According to one assistant buyer, "Probably the only girls still living in the glory of the old I. M. are the girls on the third floor. I still get the feeling myself that if you're not wearing a mink coat and a diamond ring, they won't wait on you."

On the other hand, most of the buyers at I. Magnin worked for the store before the change in ownership occurred. An assistant buyer complained that very few employees in the store are now promoted from salesperson to assistant buyer. "Then you worked your way up to department manager in a branch store and came back to I. Magnin as a buyer." Today, buyer's positions are filled mainly by employees from other Federated stores. Thus, at I. Magnin there is an important difference between the sales personnel and the executives. The limited chance for advancement obviously affects the younger employees' attitudes toward the store.

The complaint process at I. Magnin begins with the salesperson or the assistant buyer on the floor. A simple return, which is made within a month of the purchase date, is handled by the salesperson. If the item was charged, she writes down the customer's name, charge account number, address, and telephone number, as well as her own number and the department, on a refund slip. One copy is filed in the credit office, and another copy is given to the customer. Few cash refund slips are made because most customers at I. Magnin have charge accounts. The salesperson must have two other employees on the floor sign the slip before she sends it up to the sales audit office, where the purchase is verified. I. Magnin uses a pneumatic tube system to facilitate the process. According to the manager of the fifth-floor dress department, all returns are also entered in the "house book" on each floor.

Most other customer problems, including defective garments, are first registered with an assistant buyer. If an assistant buyer is not available to hear a customer's complaint, the customer fills out a short questionnaire on her problem. The assistant buyer then telephones her later at home. One assistant buyer said in a revealing jest, "Sometimes when a customer is being a nuisance, I'll make her fill out a slip, even though she doesn't have to." The slips are usually thrown out when the problem is resolved.

Complaints that concern store personnel or other complaints that cannot be resolved by the assistant buyers are sent to the department buyer or floor manager. According to one employee, "Buyers try not to get involved in complaints." However, it is only the buyer who can decide whether to send a garment back to the manufacturer. Defective garments returned by customers within 1 month of purchase are usually sent back to the manufacturer, from whom I. Magnin receives credit toward a future purchase. The return policies in the garment industry vary, and only the buyers know how far a company will back its merchandise. However, buyers have some latitude about passing a customer's mistake on to the manufacturer. When it is obvious that the customer has not followed proper washing instructions, a buyer may blame the fabric instead and send it back to the company. According to one employee, buyers set the example for the way complaints are handled on their floor. A buyer who values her good name among manufacturers will allow only flawed garments to be returned to the company.

If the buyer cannot resolve the problem herself and if she does not want to return the garment to the manufacturer, she may send the customer to the customer service department. The customer is often unaware that he or she can take a problem to someone above the floor buyer. An assistant buyer admitted, "Customers don't always leave here knowing they can appeal their complaint. Sometimes they have to ask to find out that customer service exists." But some customers, characterized as chronic complainers, usually make it to the customer service department no matter whom they deal with first.

The assistant store manager at I. Magnin estimated that the customer service department receives two complaints a month from the floor. He emphasized that the head buyers or managers are expected to handle their own merchandise problems. His estimation of the number of complainants who find their way to the upstairs office proved to be inaccurate. According to an employee at customer service, the office receives from two to six clothing complaints from the floor each day. The service department often decides on a case when a floor manager believes that a garment is too old to be returned. An employee described a recent case in which a customer wanted to return a sweater that had stretched when washed. The buyer who received the complaint on the floor did not believe that the woman had washed the sweater correctly. The head of customer service felt that the woman's complaint was justified and credited her account.

A buyer will sometimes forget what she stocks and then refuse to accept a customer's return. Customer service then checks the records to show the buyer that an item was actually purchased in her department. An office worker smiled and said, "Certain buyers have very poor memories and are always sending us customers." Some buyers in the cosmetics department, where small, relatively inexpensive items are sold, often refuse to accept a return.

Most of the verbal complaints that the customer service office receives concern package delivery. File cards contain the name, account number, address, phone number, and nature of the complaint and are filed alphabetically according to complainants' names. Complaint records and letters are kept on file for 6 months. Among 21 complaints chosen randomly, 14 concerned packages that were never delivered. Customer service resolved these problems by crediting the customer's account or delivering new merchandise. Five complaints were billing and credit problems. One letter described the rude conduct of a buyer who would not accept a return. The last complaint was from a customer who had purchased a half-empty bottle of lotion.

Four employees handle complaints in the customer service department. Mrs. Kilpack, the department manager, makes the final decision on difficult problems after an employee has researched the case. The customer service staff is dedicated to maintaining good public relations. An employee of the office explained, "I'm always courteous. I usually talk in a low voice, and if the customer is yelling, he has to stop to hear me." According to the assistant general manager of the store, I. Magnin's customer service department "handles complaints to the customer's satisfaction 99.9% of the time." A worker in the office explained that a dissatisfied customer may appeal a decision made by Mrs. Kilpack to Mr. Schultz, the store manager. However, she added, "He doesn't enjoy dealing with irate customers, and if possible, he will give the customer whatever she wants." All complaints about store policy are registered with Mr. Schultz. When a woman came in to complain that the music from a fasion show was so loud she could not shop, she was directed to see Mr. Schultz. His office is the very last stop in the complaint procedure.

The satisfaction a customer receives may vary at each point along the complaint path. The resolution of a problem may differ from floor to floor. The only official store policy regarding complaints is to avoid sending anyone to the customer service office. Mr. Trapp, the assistant store manager, explained, "At our weekly Tuesday meetings, I preach to my employees to satisfy the customer's complaints themselves." Thus, the buyers and assistant buyers are encouraged to devise their own methods for resolving customer problems.

At I. Magnin, the employees respond to merchandise complaints in three ways: They credit the customer's account, arrange a compromise, or send a customer up to the customer service office. Many of the assistant buyers automatically credit a customer's account without judging the merits of the complaint. More than one employee expressed the attitude of the assistant buyer who said;

> You may feel that the customer is obviously wrong, but it's not worth the aggravation to right her. And why should you? You get her upset, and you get yourself upset. If she goes above you, someone in customer service will give her credit anyway. So just give her credit yourself. Even the most absurd returns get credited.

This prophecy rang true in several cases.

A woman returned to the fifth-floor dress department with a white dress that she had worn for 1 year, dry cleaned, and then hung in her closet for another year. The dress had yellowed, and she demanded her money back. When the woman screamed at the sales personnel, the buyer quietly credited her account.

In another instance, a young woman wanted to return a pants suit that she had bought on sale. The buyer explained to her that all sales items are considered final sales. The customer countered that the sales slip did not print that information. The buyer accepted the garment, but she warned the woman that in the future all sales items would be nonreturnable. According to an assistant buyer, I. Magnin supposedly requires all returned merchandise to have the original sales tags. However, she admitted, "We take back anything, with or without sales tags."

Some buyers who feel that the customer does not have a legitimate complaint will try to bargain or make an adjustment. If the buyer reaches a compromise agreement with the customer, she minimizes the amount of credit the store will have to give. An assistant buyer described the process in the following way:

> You ask the customer what she feels is a fair adjustment on the problem. And you usually accept her answer, because if it goes up to customer service, they will give her whole credit. It is easier for us on the floor to give a $15 or $20 adjustment on a belt than to take a $160 credit on the whole garment. You run into some customers who are totally unfair about what their just desserts are. But if the customer is going to get credit in customer service, anyway, you might as well look like a good guy down on the floor.

At times, buyers will make adjustments on alteration fees as well as on the price of a garment. A woman returned a dress that she had purchased a year earlier but had never worn. When she took the dress out of her closet she discovered that the zipper was ripped. Because the dress was a sale item and had not been purchased recently, the assistant buyer had three alternatives. She could offer to split the $20 cost of putting in a new zipper, she could assume the entire cost of replacing the zipper, or she could credit the woman's account for the price of the dress. The assistant buyer later explained that the final decision would depend upon the customer's feelings. In this case, she was angry and insistent, and so I. Magnin assumed the cost of the alteration.

As a last resort, every buyer is authorized to send the most difficult problems to customer service. On the floor, the buyer's belief that customer service will "give the customer what she wants, anyway" affects the way she decides to handle the problem. The buyer either gives in immediately because she knows the customer will eventually receive credit, or she bargains because she feels that she has nothing to lose. On the other hand, Mrs. Kilpack's decisions in customer service are not influenced by what the executives above her will do. With only a few exceptions, the complaint process ends at her office door.

The criteria that Mrs. Kilpack uses to settle a complaint are illustrated in the following case:

> A woman entered the customer service office and demanded that her account be credited for two pairs of pants. She said the waists had stretched out of shape and that the salespeople in the sportswear department refused to accept the returns. One of the employees in the office asked the woman to fill out a request for adjustment form. She gave the woman a copy of the slip and told her that she would look into the matter. The employee then telephoned the buyer in the sportswear department. She discovered that the woman had bought the pants 7 months earlier. The buyer said that she didn't believe the waists were stretched out of shape. She added that the woman had probably lost weight and wanted to get rid of the pants because they didn't fit her anymore. The employee recorded the information for Mrs.

Kilpack and made her own recommendation. The next day the customer service office credited the woman's account for the two pairs of pants because she was a steady I. Magnin customer.

The deciding factor in a difficult case is the customer's own credit record. I. Magnin, like Gump's, will never jeopardize a good account. As a result, customers with charge accounts have an advantage over people who always pays cash, because they can prove that they are steady customers. Charge accounts are the most complete and permanent records of transactions in the store. They facilitate the return procedure because they verify where and when an item was purchased. Thus, customers with charge accounts bring additional bargaining power to their encounters with the store.

The policy on alterations and repairs varies according to the department and the price of the garment. An assistant buyer admitted that the quality of the clothing in the store has dropped and that I. Magnin no longer guarantees all its merchandise. She explained:

Stores cannot maintain profits now by buying the finest merchandise. There aren't that many customers that are willing to buy fine merchandise. As you drop your standards and go into mass merchandising, the quality is going to go down. There is no way you can service the life of a garment like you used to. In earlier days when a customer bought a $600 Norell dress and the seam split, the store was willing to put the seam in. And if the zipper needed replacing, the store would pay $35 for a new one to be put in. But there is no way that the store can keep up the life of that garment now. We'll be glad to do it the first time, but it's going to happen again. The clothes they are buying at I. Magnin they could have bought at Macy's and the Emporium. Other stores are not going to back their garments.

Thus, I. Magnin's policy on alterations and repairs is in a period of transition. The garments they are selling now do not last as long as the merchandise they once sold; so the store is attempting to "take a harder line on repair work" while still guaranteeing its merchandise. The assistant buyer said, "we're more lenient on $5 garments than another store would be, as far as repairing goes. There's this fine line that comes in. Some things you are willing to do and other things you won't."

The cost of the garment is an important factor when a buyer decides to make a repair or alteration at the store's expense. The customer who buys an expensive item expects the store to stand behind it. However, less expensive articles do not always have that guarantee.

An I. Magnin customer who bought a $20 skirt discovered that the buttonholes were poorly made and had begun to unravel. She returned to the store and insisted that I. Magnin make the necessary repairs. The store *accepted responsibility for the repair, but when the woman picked up her skirt, she noticed that very little had been done to improve the buttonholes. It was evident that the alterations department didn't want to take the time or effort to repair a $20 skirt.*

In another case, a buyer made every attempt to satisfy a customer who had purchased an expensive dress:

A woman claimed that a dress she bought fit perfectly but that the belt was too small. She wanted the belt altered immediately because she was going to wear the dress to a party that night. The dress was a size 6, and the woman was a size 10. The buyer checked with the alterations department to make sure the belt could be fixed, and then sent it to the seamstress. The belt was altered and returned in 20 minutes. The buyer later explained that it was obvious that the woman had bought a dress that was too small for her. The dress fabric would stretch, but the belt had to be lengthened. The alteration was made by I. Magnin, in spite of the fact that the dress was the wrong size.

An assistant buyer in the women's dress department noted that customers often attempt to return articles they have ruined. She said she explains to customers why certain fabrics cannot be washed in hot water and urges them to read the washing instructions on their garments. If a customer persists, she will credit her account. A woman returned a dress that she claimed had shrunk in the washing machine. The instructions stated "machine washable," and the fifth-floor buyer immediately credited her account.

When a dry-cleaning establishment ruins a garment, the buyer fills out a form that indicates the price of the article. She urges the customer to take the claim to the cleaners. If the dry-cleaning proprietor refused to pay for the mistake and insists that the fabric is faulty, the store may send the garment to Los Angeles for a laboratory analysis to determine how the garment was ruined. However, this procedure is costly, and I. Magnin rarely uses the test. A buyer on the fifth floor said that only two garments had been sent for a lab analysis from her department in the last 4 years.

Finally, two important factors in how a complaint is resolved are the appearance and attitudes of the customer and salesperson. An assistant buyer admitted that in a few cases in which the customer seemed "shaky" about her complaint and appeared unwilling to register her problem upstairs, she refused to make a return. However, she added that these instances were rare. Sometimes an employee's knowledge of store tradition conflicts with the customer's assumptions, and the store's point of view prevails:

A man recently complained to an employee that he had noticed a one-third off sale sign in the same window where a mannequin was dressed in a very glamorous fur coat. He wanted to buy the fur coat at the sale price, but a salesgirl had explained that the coat was not included in the marked-down merchandise. He accused the store of false advertising, but the customer service employee had no sympathy for his position. She knew that the department store displays only new merchandise in showcase windows and that new lines are never on sale.

Another I. M. worker explained, "In a way you become indoctrinated; the longer you've been working for the store, the better you adhere to their version."

There are other important differences between old and new employees that affect the final resolution of customer problems. According to the customer service staff, employees who have been with the store for a long time are more trusting of the merchandise complaints of customers with whom they have established a long-term professional relationship. They feel personally responsible for serving them well. In the fifth-floor better dress department, the older customers often request the help of particular employees. An elderly woman who always asks for the same salesperson explained, "She always knows just what I want, and I respect her opinion." But although the older employees are especially lenient with their good customers, some tend to be suspicious of those who do not conform to their ideas of a well-dressed I. Magnin customer. By contrast, in the Young Miss department on the seventh floor, the clientele is young and the merchandise less expensive. Loyalty between salesperson and customer does not seem to exist, and the buyer on the floor has a reputation for taking a hard line on returns.

The flow of complaints from I. Magnin's customers to garment manufacturers is not a steady one. The buyers on each floor keep their own records on returns and decide what to report to the manufacturers. An assistant buyer in the sportswear department estimated that at least 75% of the ruined or defective garments that are returned have not been cared for properly by the customers and that only 25% are the fault of the manufacturers. Most floors do not keep complete return records, and so it is not easy to spot defective lines from a particular manufacturer. One assistant buyer admitted that she and the other buyers on her floor had never analyzed customer complaints to determine whose merchandise was causing problems. She added that if a salesperson noticed that a particular line did not fit the customers well, she notified the assistant buyer. The assistant buyer then checked the floor roster on returns and reported her finding to the buyer. In the better dress department, there has been only one case in recent years in which the store stopped purchasing from a dress manufacturer who had produced defective garments. An assistant buyer said, "It's becoming harder and harder to get quality garments. But at the same time, we haven't had that many problems with any specific line. We may run into one dress problem on one line one season and another problem on another line the next season." The reporting of problems to the manufacturers varies from floor to floor, because "different buyers have different standards."

City of Paris has a recent history similar to that of its downtown neighbor, I. Magnin. When Liberty House, which is owned by the conglomerate Amfac, bought City of Paris in 1972, several changes occurred. The store, which was established in the late 1800s, underwent extensive remodeling on the inside. New merchandise began to be sold in order to appeal to a younger clientele, and the new owners hired outside personnel to fill the middle and top management positions, while retaining most of the salespeople. However, like I. Magnin, the store maintained the same complaint procedure.

City of Paris is the only store in the study that lists the manager's office on the first-floor wall directory. The fourth-floor credit counter and the sixth-floor Amfac offices are also listed. However, only a persistent customer can find the manager's office, which is tucked away from public view, on the second-floor circle. The store obviously does not encourage visits to the Amfac offices; the sixth floor cannot be reached by the main elevator, which is intended for use by the customers. The store's management believes that all complaints can and should be handled on the floor.

At City of Paris, the salesperson handles simple returns or exchanges that are made within 1 month of the purchase date. When an item is returned, the salesperson credits the customer's account or makes out a gift certificate or cash credit slip. Credit slips must be cashed at the cashier's desk on the fourth floor. All other complaints, including defective garment problems, are sent to one of the two managers on each floor. At least one of the floor managers is available at all times to hear customer complaints. Like I. Magnin, City of Paris instructs its floor managers to satisfy the customers themselves. The floor managers rarely send a customer to the credit department, which is the final step in the complaint process.

The head of the credit department has worked for the City of Paris since 1947. She assumed her present position in 1972, when the store changed owners. Mrs. Tarekko explained that she and the other two women who work in the department handle the special problems that resulted when Liberty House bought the City of Paris. Customers telephone the credit department to complain about credit mix-ups and about Liberty House charge plates that were never received. These credit complaints are recorded and filed, and they constitute the only record of complaints kept by the store. All billing problems on the new Liberty House accounts at City of Paris are referred to a central office in Dublin, California, nearly 50 miles away.[1]

---

[1]This office also serves several suburban Liberty House stores as well. Since this article was written, Liberty House has closed the former City of Paris store in downtown San Francisco.

Complaints about personnel are received at the personnel department office on the second floor. An employee from the office usually speaks to the floor manager about the salesperson against whom the complaint is lodged. They evaluate the complaint and decide whether to reprimand the employee. A written complaint by a customer about an employee is kept on permanent file. The management must send three written warnings to a salesperson before she or he can be fired. According to one floor manager, all the sales personnel at City of Paris are unionized, and the union protects their jobs.

The manager of the credit department said that the only official policy on complaints about merchandise is to treat the customer courteously and accept returns whenever possible. She added that the new management "tries to do right by the customer." Salespeople are especially encouraged to sell customers another item when they return merchandise. One floor manager said, "Any saleslady that cares about her job and is interested in a customer will take a return with a smile and at the same time try to sell the customer something else."

The floor managers have the same attitude toward resolving complaints as the buyers and assistant buyers at I. Magnin. A manager explained, "I usually grant the customer what he wants, because if the person is going to push the complaint higher up, he will always get credit." Another floor manager said, "We are supposed to make decisions in favor of the customer. When a floor manager lets a problem get to the office upstairs, it reflects on her ability."

A sample of complaints described by City of Paris employees shows that an irate customer eventually gets what he or she wants:

> Over a year after Liberty House bought the store, the floor manager in the dress department accepted several dresses from an angry customer who had purchased the garments when the store was under the old ownership. Although the garments had obviously been altered and could not be sold or returned to the manufacturer, the manager credited the customer's account.

Unlike I. Magnin, the City of Paris will automatically assume the cost of garments that are ruined by the cleaners:

> One manager accepted a pair of pants that had been incorrectly steamed and stretched out of shape by the cleaners. In another case, a woman returned a pair of pants which she claimed had stretched after dry cleaning. The floor manager noted that the pants were made of an acrylic fabric and they never should have been dry-cleaned. She told the customer that the label on the pants advised hand or machine washing. But the customer countered that she thought dry cleaning was always better. Although the label gave washing instructions, it did not specifically warn against dry cleaning. As a result, the floor manager credited the woman's account for the price of the pants.

The credit office also has an unofficial policy of giving the customer whatever he or she wants in nonmerchandise problems:

> The City of Paris once advertised in the local newspapers that it would give away framed pictures to customers who shopped at the store during certain hours on a specific day. There was a mailing delay, and the pictures did not arrive at the store on time. A very irate woman accused City of Paris of false advertising and threatened to report the incident to the Better Business Bureau. Mrs. Tarekko of the credit department calmly explained that there had been a mailing delay, and she would send the pictures to the woman when they arrived.
>
> In another case, a salesperson needed authorization from the credit department to allow a woman to use her employer's credit card. The woman was furious and stalked up to the credit department. She told Mrs. Tarekko, "I work for the old woman and she wants me to buy some furniture polish. I have always used her card to buy things for her." Mrs. Tarekko replied that the store needed written authorization from her employer. The customer insisted that "the old woman" could not write. Mrs. Tarekko finally gave the woman permission to buy the polish, and later phoned her employer to obtain authorization for future purchases.

Floor managers will sometimes "feel a customer out" before automatically accepting a return. One manager explained, "Some customers really believe they are right, and you can't dissuade them. But often someone comes in with a fishy complaint. They aren't quite sure of it themselves, and I try to feel them out." She described a case in which a woman returned a polyester garment that had instructions not to iron on high heat. The woman had obviously used high heat, and the fabric had melted. The customer appeared very nervous, and the floor manager said she was sure the woman would not take the complaint above her if she refused to credit her account. The customer accepted the manager's decision.

Although some employees attempt to test the customer's determination to return an item, others try to make an adjustment. According to one floor manager, most people would rather accept an adjustment in price than return a defective garment and have their account credited. "Often customers want to bargain with us. It doesn't bother a woman to wear a dress with a small hole in it if it cost $10 less. We want to make adjustments for higher priced items, but it doesn't pay to make them on inexpensive items."

If a salesperson notices that a certain dress line is causing problems, she reports the problem to the floor manager. The floor manager then discusses the line with the buyer, who decides whether to continue buying from that manufacturer. There is no systematic way of determining if a manufacturer has defective merchandise because City of Paris does not keep complete return records.

However, City of Paris rarely returns individual garments to the manufacturer because of the cost involved in shipping the items to the East Coast, where most of the manufacturers are located. When returns are made, credit for the merchandise is usually deducted from a future purchase from that manufacturer. One floor manager said, "It may cost $8 to send a dress back to the manufacturer. We save money by making an adjustment or doing the alteration ourselves." The manager continued, "Business is so bad now in the retail trade that you hate to lose customers. The cost of returns to the store is so small, and the payoff is very great in terms of satisfied customers who will always come back."

Some customers constantly abuse the lenient return policy, and they are treated differently from other complainants by the sales personnel. One of the floor managers at City of Paris described a "society woman" who was constantly purchasing expensive dresses and returning them. She believed that the woman bought the dresses to wear at specific social functions and returned them after the event was over. After the woman had been shopping at City of Paris for several months, the floor manager questioned her sharply about the returns. The woman was never seen in the store again. The same floor manager described the reception that chronic complainers received on her floor:

> After a while the girls on the floor will recognize a woman who is constantly complaining and returning dresses for no reason. They run the other way and try to avoid helping them. If you don't wait on a person, then she will be reluctant to come back. She is probably trying her tricks at another store, but at least she won't be bothering you.

City of Paris has processed a larger number of complaints since Liberty House became the new owner. The dress department once received no more than three complaints a week, but that number has tripled because many of the older customers are unhappy to find that the store is no longer stocking the same quality of merchandise. A remark about the unsettled situation at the City of Paris by an employee reveals an attitude that is prevalent at most of the stores in this study. She said, "Eventually people's expectations will fall into line with what the store actually carries." The complaint procedure at I. Magnin, City of Paris, and several other stores is not geared toward changing policies to accommodate the customers.

Joseph Magnin, like Liberty House, is owned by Amfac Corporation. It has a youthful image. The merchandise it sells attracts a young clientele, and unlike I. Magnin, Gump's, or the City of Paris, very few of its employees have worked for the store for more than 5 years. According to one employee in the downtown San Francisco store, "Life moves quickly at Joseph Magnin." It is not unusual for a salesperson to be promoted to an executive position after working in the store for only 3 months.

The executives who created this young, fast-paced image for the store also established a confusing and inconsistent procedure for handling complaints. The following case illustrates some of the problems involved in returning an item to Joseph Magnin:

> *A woman purchased two pairs of woolen knit slacks at the store for $88. She wore them two times and then sent them to the cleaners. When they came back, she discovered that they had stretched out of shape. With Joseph Magnin bag in hand, she returned to the second-floor sportswear department where she had purchased the pants. There were several salesgirls on the floor who didn't appear to be busy, but no one offered to help her. Finally, she told a salesgirl about her problem, and she was directed to the manager of the slacks department. The woman waited several more minutes before the manager looked at the pants. She told the customer that she did not remember stocking the merchandise in her department. The woman insisted that she had purchased the pants on that floor, but she did not have the sales receipt to prove it. The manager finally agreed to check with the department buyers. She wrote out a temporary receipt for the woman and told her she would telephone her later. After waiting for the phone call for several days, the woman called the store and found that no check had been made. Later, she found the sales tag for the slacks and returned to the sportswear department. The woman's account was finally credited for the price of the pants, but she vowed she would never shop at the store again.*

At Joseph Magnin, the procedure for registering a complaint is less standardized than at other stores. Sales personnel are instructed not to handle customer complaints, but they often do. Floor policy varies from department to department. The executives on each floor are officially responsible for resolving customer problems. Thus, a variety of employees, including department heads, floor managers, and assistant floor managers tackle complaints on the floor. An exasperated executive may sometimes direct a case to the customer service office. However, the customer is often unaware of the store's appeal procedure or the existence of the office. Although the customer service department is listed separately in the street-floor directory, it is actually part of the billing and payroll office. Two employees, questioned at random, said that Joseph Magnin does not have a customer service department. Only one–three customers a week find their way from the floor to the customer service office to register a complaint.

The office is currently staffed by one employee, Ms. Knoll, whose responsibilities include package delivery problems and some credit complaints. She refers most billing problems to Joseph Magnin's central office on Harrison Street in San Francisco. Customers' complaints about personnel must be registered in writing at the office. These forms are sent to the personnel manager, who then speaks to the employee involved. Both the customer's complaint and the employee's version of his or her dealings with the customer are submitted in writing to the store president, Cyril Magnin, for a final decision.

Merchandise complaints that reach Ms. Knoll's desk from the floor are recorded in triplicate on a customer service inquiry form. The original form is sent to the Joseph Magnin office on Harrison Street, and the other two copies are filed in the customer service department. Ms. Knoll researches these complaints and then turns the matter over to the store manager, who makes the final decision. She keeps unresolved problems in a folder on her desk. All resolved complaints are kept on file for 2 years before they are thrown out.

Ms. Knoll has handled customer complaints at Joseph Magnin since 1960. The position of assistant in the department is presently vacant. In 5 years 15 different women were hired for the job, but none of them wanted to stay. Ms. Knoll explains that it is a difficult job she enjoys. "You have to always assure the customer you really care." Most of the complaints she receives concern billing mix-ups. Customers call her office when payments or returns are not credited to their accounts or when items ordered are never delivered. She also replaces lost due bills and gift certificates.

Employees on the floor frequently call Ms. Knoll to ask her advice on how to handle a customer. A salesperson or department head sends a complaint to the office when the customer's request is unjustified or cannot be understood:

> A woman received a $20 due bill for an item she had returned, instead of a $20 credit on her account. [Due bills—the store's acknowledgement of a debt—are usually given to customers who do not have a charge account or a sales receipt for the returned merchandise.[2]] The woman did not understand what a due bill was, and she stormed into the store, convinced that Joseph Magnin was trying to cheat her. A floor executive sent her up to customer service. The woman spoke in broken English, and it took Ms. Knoll several minutes to establish the facts of the case. When she finally discovered what had happened, she explained that the store would gladly credit her account.

Ms. Knoll's desire to satisfy the customer is shown in the following two cases:

> A man bought a suit in the men's department of Joseph Magnin and requested that the tailor lengthen the sleeves. However, when he picked up the suit a few days later, he discovered that the sleeves had been shortened instead. The store did not have another suit in his size, and the department manager sent him to customer service department. Ms. Knoll spent two hours phoning all the other Joseph Magnin stores before she finally located the same suit in the right size.

[2]Due bills are usually good only in exchange for merchandise unless they specifically state otherwise.

*Another customer wrote a letter while on vacation in Ireland to complain
about a defective handbag. She had purchased the purse at Joseph Magnin
before she left San Francisco. Within a few days the leather began to crack.
She wrote that she expected the store to credit her account in the amount of
the handbag. Ms. Knoll wrote the woman that she would gladly credit her
account if she would send the purse back to the store.*

The customer service department at Joseph Magnin considers the
same factors as other stores do in settling a difficult complaint. Ms. Knoll
explained how she would handle the following hypothetical complaint: A
woman buys an expensive evening dress and wears it only twice in 2
years. She sends it to the cleaners, and the fabric comes apart. The customer service department must decide if the cleaner, the store, or the
manufacturer is responsible. She said, "That's a tricky one. First you have
to track down the customer's account. If it's a good account, you may
decide in her favor. If the customer doesn't have an account, you call the
buyers in. They will make the decision if they have received other complaints on the garment. If they don't decide, the decision is left to the store
manager." Once again, the crucial factor in settling a complaint is the
customer's own credit record. A store employee is hesitant to jeopardize a
good account.

The floor personnel at Joseph Magnin are less than eager to handle
complaints. The reluctance of the salespeople to wait on customers who
are making returns is illustrated by the case of the ruined slacks (discussed earlier) and the following comment made by two saleswomen.
When asked how they handle a customer complaint, the girls replied,
"We try to run in the other direction." Unlike the other stores in the study,
Joseph Magnin pays its sales employees on a commission basis, which is
added to a base salary. When an item is returned to the store, the price of
the article and the number of the saleswoman who made the original sale
are recorded. An employee explained that the saleswomen do not like
returns because "it goes against their salaries," and the floor managers do
not like returns because "they go against the department record." One
employee described the floor manager of the sportswear department as
"impossible about returns, but I think he is going to be set right by the
management." Ms. Knoll of the customer service department admitted,
"There are people on the floor who think the store is too lenient on returns
because they are working on commission. It's only natural that they feel
this way."

At Joseph Magnin the executive's desire to serve the customer and
accept all returns is tempered by his or her concern over thievery. A
department head explained, "The official store policy regarding complaints is 'The customer is always right,' but you have to watch out for the
person who is trying to cheat the store." Tracers are put on returned items

that do not have price tags or sales receipts, as well as on merchandise that is returned for no explicit reason. Such checks involve a call to the buyer or the credit department to determine if the merchandise was actually purchased from Joseph Magnin. All Joseph Magnin garments have store labels and clipped price tags to indicate that the merchandise was purchased in the store. According to one executive, the theft rate at the store is very high. She said, "Often someone will steal a garment and then try to return it for cash. We have to watch out for this."

A recent case illustrates the executive's point:

> The head of the dress department was about to give a customer credit for a return when a salesperson drew her aside. She informed her that the woman had taken the garment into a dressing room, but had not returned it to the clerk. The executive then told the woman that she had to put a check on the garment before the store would accept it. The woman left the store and was trailed to a parking garage, where she went into a restroom and changed her clothes. She then went to another department store, where she again tried to get credit for a supposed return. A security guard apprehended her.

The executive's belief that "such things are always happening" obviously affects the way she approaches merchandise returns.

At Joseph Magnin the customer's complaint is handled by sales personnel, floor executives, and the customer service department, and then may go to the buyer. Unlike buyers at the other stores in the study, buyers at Joseph Magnin do not work on the floor. They buy merchandise for several J. M. stores and depend upon other employees to detect and report a faulty line of clothing. If several garments in the same line have been returned, the buyer may stop purchasing from the particular manufacturer. However, the store never takes a systematic inventory of returns; and a department head admitted, "The store carries so much stock that it can't possibly make sure everything is of good quality. So much of what we sell is defective—the stitching is off, the buttons loose, and the colors fade in washing." She concluded by saying, "Customers have to complain to make us buy better merchandise." However, customers' complaints may be channeled through several employees at Joseph Magnin, including the store manager, and still not reach the buyer's desk.

J. C. Penney's and Hink's: National Chain Store versus Local Family Business

Penney's and Hink's are located on the main street in downtown Berkeley. Penney's is part of a national retail and mail-order chain whereas Hink's maintains only a single store in Berkeley. Mr. L. W. Hink, who is actively involved in his store's operation, decided several years ago not to expand. He was opposed to building more Hink's department stores because he realized that he could not personally supervise all of them, and he feared that expansion would affect the quality of his service and goods.

Today Hink's sells more expensive and higher quality merchandise than does Penney's. Both stores attempt to maintain the image of a "family-owned" store. (A large portrait of J. C. Penney, the founder of the Penney chain, is displayed on the first floor near the elevator.) However, unlike the employees at other stores, the personnel at Hink's have a special loyalty to the management and to Mr. Hink. Their attitude toward the store is obvious in the way they manage complaints.

Penney's slogan is, "Customer satisfaction is our goal." The management promises to refund the cost of any defective merchandise. However, that policy was modified several years ago when Penney's began to market major appliances under the Penney brand name. The Berkeley store no longer sells large appliances, but Penney's still does not give unconditional guarantees on all its merchandise. The store manager explained, "We want to be fair, but we don't want to give the store away."

Penney's maintains an "on the floor" return policy. Sales personnel handle simple returns and exchanges. When the responsibility for faulty merchandise is not clear, the salesperson refers the complaint to the selling supervisor, a position that was created in 1970. The supervisor reviews the problems in all the departments on his or her floor and helps with sales during busy periods. Most of the department managers and selling supervisors have worked at Penney's for at least 5 years. When a customer makes a return without a sales receipt, the supervisor asks her to fill out a refund slip with her name and address. The supervisor then matches the signature with the customer's personal identification. The store usually sends the customer a refund check in the mail. This procedure gives the store more time to check the legitimacy of a complaint. However, if the customer requests a cash refund, the supervisor is authorized to give it to her.

Customers who shop at J. C. Penney's are different from those who patronize I. Magnin, Joseph Magnin, or the City of Paris. They usually do not have charge accounts. Most of Penney's customers pay cash for the merchandise they buy. As a result, Pennys' system for resolving complaints differs from the other stores.

The deciding factor in resolving a problem at I. Magnin, Joseph Magnin, and City of Paris is the customer's credit account. If the customer is a steady patron, the complaint will be resolved in his favor. However, Penney's has a centralized credit office in Oakland and the Berkeley store cannot easily check a customer's account. Furthermore, as most customers do not have accounts, Penney's must use other criteria in resolving customer problems.

An important factor in how a complaint is resolved at Penney's is the customer's demeanor. Mr. Olander, the store manager explained, "It is important to listen to what the customer has to say. If it sounds like he is sincere, the salesperson will probably go along with him." He then described the following case:

> A man returned a jacket which he had worn in a rain storm and ruined. He claimed that the jacket was supposed to be water repellant and should have withstood the downpour. Mr. Olander explained that only rubberized items are water proof, and a water repellant garment is not guaranteed to withstand a heavy rain. The customer insisted that the jacket was defective, and Mr. Olander finally refunded his money.

Although the store manager knew that the man was wrong, he gave him a refund because the customer believed his claim was legitimate. The head of the shoe department maintained the same policy. He said, "When a person seems sincere, I will make almost any adjustment."

In difficult cases, the store usually makes a compromise adjustment:

> A woman returned a pair of shoes which her young son had worn out in two months. She complained that they were poorly made, and should have lasted longer. The head of the shoe department explained that the shoes normally lasted six months. He suggested that her son had been unusually active and that the shoes were not made to hold up under extreme wear and tear. The head of the department finally offered a compromise adjustment which was accepted by the customer. The store paid half the price of a new pair of shoes for the boy.

The manager of the store explained that compromise adjustments cost the store very little and that they help to preserve good customer relations.

The floor personnel also have the option of refusing a customer who seems insincere. An employee in the shoe department said, "Sometimes I get the same woman in here every month, insisting that the store should replace her children's worn shoes. One time when that happened, I told the woman to try a competitor's shoes and see if they would wear as well. The woman came back to us after two months, and she's been a loyal customer ever since." Customers who are not satisfied with the floor personnel's decisions may make a final appeal to Mr. Olander, whose office is in the basement.

Like the other stores in the study, Penney's does not keep a record of complaints. If a salesperson or department head notices that one-quarter of the garments from a single line have been returned, the store will ship all the garments back to the manufacturer. A central office in New York does all the buying for Penney's stores, and only the buyers there decide whether or not to continue dealing with the manufacturer. Thus, a complaint by a customer at the Berkeley store may never reach the buyer. Penney's does maintain a laboratory in New York where most of the store's standard merchandise, such as linens, are tested before distribution. Items under $5 are not returned individually to the manufacturer. They are collected throughout the year and are shipped back to the manufacturer at one time. The high cost of shipping returned items to manufacturers in the East prompts the store to make its own repairs on more expensive defective merchandise. Thus, important feedback from the customer to the manufacturer is eliminated.

A few years ago Penney's instituted a compaign to educate the consumer and decrease the number of complaints. The management has attempted to give the public more information about the merchandise it buys to prevent its misuse and damage. They recently published a J. C. Penney's "Home Laundry Reference Chart," which explains the washing or cleaning instructions attached to the woven, sewn-in tabs in garments. The chart also contains general laundering information. In the shoe department, salespeople are instructed to explain the type of wear a pair of shoes can withstand before making a sale. An employee in the department commented, "This warning helps eliminate complaints later on." J. C. Penney's was the only store in the study actively concerned with preventing merchandise problems.

A customer who returned a dress to Hink's department store recently wrote to the head of the adjustment department, "After fifty some years as a Hink's charge customer, I had to ask instructions as to how to return an item—my first offense. I was certainly treated well." Many of the store's customers have patronized Hink's for over 20 years, and their satisfaction with the service points toward one of Hink's most important assets. Like many of the customers, most of the employees have stayed with Hink's for several years. An assistant buyer explained that Mr. Hink runs the store personally and "he values and rewards loyalty in his employees."

In 1914 L. W. Hink was 20 years old and the President of Hink's department store.[3] The store was located in the White Cotton Hotel, across the street from its present site. A long-time employee of Hink's praised "old L. W.'s" ingenuity. "He was only twenty, but he had great foresight. He encouraged the hotel to expand across the block, and the store and the town expanded with it." Mr. Hink watched Shattuck Avenue in Berkeley change from a country orchard to a thriving business district in a university town. In 1927 the store expanded to three times its original size. Hink made the last addition in 1959, when he opened a new major appliance store three blocks away. He soon discovered that he could not manage two

---

[3]In October 1977 L. W. Hink died, and the store was bought by the C. H. Dunlap family of Modesto, California, owners of three other department stores. The Hink's name was retained by the Berkeley store.

stores satisfactorily, and so he decided to operate the appliance division as a concession.

According to one employee, Hink's has managed customer problems in the same way for almost 50 years. Merchandise complaints are handled in the department where the item was purchased. If a sales manager, buyer, or assistant buyer is not available, then the salesperson with the most seniority in the department handles the complaint. Like the other department stores in the study, Hink's does not give its employees special training in tackling customer problems. The management believes sales-persons promoted to managerial positions should be familiar with the merchandise and qualified to handle complaints.

Mrs. Scheikosky, the personnel manager and head of the adjustment department, receives problems that are not resolved on the floor. She explained that the managers and buyers can usually determine whether the customer has a valid complaint. When they refuse to accept a return, the customer is sent up to personnel. According to Mrs. Scheikosky, complaining at the department level is the only proper and considerate method of registering a complaint. She did not approve of customers applying pressure on the top management. Mrs. Scheikosky described a recent case in which a customer tried to return a worn and soiled sweater. She calmed the angry woman and explained that the store could neither return the article to the manufacturer nor resell it. However, she finally credited the customer's account as a "gesture of goodwill." Whenever a salesperson doubts that the merchandise was purchased at Hink's, he or she immediately sends the customer to the adjustments window. Customers who return items without a sales receipt must see Mrs. Scheikosky before they exchange the merchandise. Although Mrs. Scheikosky sees only the irate customer with the most difficult problems, she stresses that very few complaints are invalid. She keeps a record of the customer's problems when the store assumes a loss on the merchandise. She added that during some months, Hink's never receives an unjustified complaint.

Mr. Jelton, the assistant store manager, who describes himself as Mr. Hink's right-hand man, also handles complaints. When a customer refuses to pay his bill, the credit department sends him to see Mr. Jelton. He also receives all the complaint letters that are sent to the store. L. W. Hink comes into the store every morning at 10:30 and reviews the complaint letters that are addressed to him. He either follows up the complaint personally or leaves the problem for Mr. Jelton to handle.

At Hink's the procedure for handling merchandise complaints is less convenient for the customer than in most other stores. If the customer is dissatisfied with a salesperson's decision, he takes his complaint to the adjustments window. If the problem is resolved there, the customer must return or exchange the merchandise in the original department. On rare occasions, when Mrs. Scheikosky refuses to give a customer what he or she wants, the customer may make a third visit, this time to Mr. Jelton's office. Mr. Jelton admitted, "By the time a customer comes to my office, he's good and mad. Possibly he's gone through four people already." The hierarchy of complaint management at Hink's is similar to the procedure established by other department stores. However, at Hink's customers must carry their complaints up the hierarchy. Undoubtedly, the trips to the adjustment window or to Mr. Jelton's office and back to the department are an additional source of irritation to the complainant.

The dedication of Hink's employees in serving the customer seems to compensate for the "red tape" of the complaint procedure. Mr. Jelton, who began working at Hink's as a shipping clerk 49 years ago, said that the special pride he takes in doing his job well is not common among the employees of other department stores. "There just aren't too many people like us around." An assistant buyer said that her own 35-year record with the store was not unusual at Hink's. She explained, "Hink's is a unique store. It is one of a kind and prides itself on service."

Most departments in the store hold personnel meetings on Saturday mornings. At these meetings the younger workers learn about store policy from the older employees. Although complaint management is not usually discussed, customer treatment is always an important topic. One buyer said, "We like for all our employees to comply with Hink's high standards."

The following case illustrates one buyer's concern for giving the customer a fair deal:

> A woman placed a special order in the lingerie department, but the salesgirl on the floor failed to record the order. The woman waited several months for the store to call her when the article came in. One day while she was shopping at Hink's she noticed that the garment she had ordered was on display. She insulted the first salesgirl she encountered and demanded to know why she had never been notified. A buyer was called in to handle the problem. After several minutes of discussion and search, the buyer finally determined that the original salesgirl had neglected to fill out an order form. She explained the situation to the customer and apologized for the store's error, in spite of the customer's manner, and later explained that she felt she "had a wrong to right" for the customer and the store.

Mr. Jelton, the assistant store manager, expressed a similar belief. He said, "I want customers to understand that I'm a guy who really wants to help them." If a customer has a complaint against a store employee, Mr. Jelton brings the worker and the customer together in his office. He asks the customer if the employee should be fired. According to Mr. Jelton, "Most people back down. They just want to be heard, and we let them speak their piece."

Mr. Hink consideres the loyalty and dedication of his employees as a very important asset, and he believes in showing his appreciation to them.

Several years ago Mr. Jelton introduced the idea of a service pin for Hink's employees. A pin is given to every salesperson, buyer, and manager who works for Hink's for 5 years. Every 5 years thereafter, Mr. Hink gives his employees a diamond to place on the pin. According to Mr. Jelton, "It is nothing for an employee to have at least five diamonds and 30 years of experience at Hink's department store."

Unlike other stores, Hink's budgets an annual amount as a special customer relations fund. The money from this fund pays the cost of returned merchandise that is damaged and cannot be sent back to the manufacturer. In 1971 the amount spent on customer adjustments was $694. The average yearly figure is approximately $450. The money invested in maintaining good customer relations is only a small percentage of the $50,000–60,000 lost in theft at Hink's every year.

It is unofficial store policy to "take a loss" on invalid complaints. Mrs. Scheikosky, the head of adjustments, said, "It is profitable in the long run to satisfy all customer complaints. When customers are satisfied, business prospers." Like the employees of many other stores, those at Hink's realize that the top-level management almost always resolves a complaint in the customer's favor. A buyer in the lingerie department explained that she usually accepts the customer's story:

> The store is very lenient in granting credits and making exchanges. But we never totally ignore the nature of the complaint. I usually take a person's word, except in cases where it is apparent that the fabric has been through the dryer several times.

The buyer sized up her handling of a merchandise complaint in the following way. First, she examines the material and decides if the garment has been abused. When a customer returns a garment that is actually defective, a special form requesting authorization is sent to the manufacturer. Hink's then arranges for the cost of the merchandise to be deducted from the next remittance to the manufacturer. The buyer reported, "Hink's tried a new nylon gown, and we got so many returns because it was an inferior product that we dropped the line." Second, she assesses the customer's attitude. If the customer is reasonable, she is more responsive to her problem. The third step is a last resort that is used by most stores in resolving a complaint. The buyer checks the customer's credit account to determine if she is a good customer. Because most of the employees at Hink's have worked in the store for several years, they also know many of the steady cash-paying customers.

The employee's desire to satisfy almost any demand of a regular customer is illustrated by the following case:

> In December 1971, one of Hink's oldest customers wrote a letter of complaint to the management. For years his wife had purchased $2.50 pudding

molds from Hink's near Christmas time. In 1971 the price of the pudding mold jumped to $4, while a competitor was selling a very similar mold for $2.69. Mr. Hink wrote a personal reply to the customer, explaining, "If our housewares buyer could have located the $2.69 mold, she positively would have selected it instead of the one for $4.00." He also enclosed a slip crediting the customer's account for $2.42 plus 14¢ sales tax, the difference for the two molds. Mr. Hink added, "We do appreciate your taking time to bring these facts to our attention. It is only by the reactions of our patrons that we know whether we are in all departments maintaining our standards of quality, value, and service."

When an employee believes that a complainant has abused the merchandise, he or she will sometimes offer the customer a "compromise settlement" rather than take a total loss on the item:

A woman recently returned a teakettle with a broken handle and a bent spout to the buyer in the housewares department. The buyer firmly believed that the kettle had been damaged by careless treatment, but the customer insisted that she had never dropped the kettle. The buyer finally offered to charge the woman the minimal cost for repairs and parts.

However, Mr. Jelton's attitude toward customers whom he describes as chronic complainers is less accommodating. One customer wrote several detailed letters to Mr. Jelton, complaining about the personnel, the lighting in the store, and the quality of the merchandise she had purchased. He finally suggested that she close her account with Hink's. After the account was closed, Hink's sent the woman a letter stating:

We wish to apologize for any hardships or inconvenience caused you during your shopping at Hink's. Our aim is to please our customers both by our goods as well as our services. We are sincerely sorry that we have not accomplished this aim to your complete satisfaction.

In the housewares and small electrical appliance department, the same basic procedure for handling complaints is followed. Hink's guarantees all these appliances for 1 month. If an appliance fails to work properly and is returned to the store within 1 month, Hink's will give the customer a new appliance. The manufacturer then credits the faulty merchandise to Hink's account. If the appliance is returned after 1 month from the purchase date, Hink's services the item free. Older merchandise in need of repair is sent to the service department, where the customer is expected to pay a minimal service charge. The head buyer in the department explained that she urges customers who bring in faulty housewares to write to the manufacturer themselves. She added that most cookware companies replace defective wares 90% of the time.

Hink's handles complaints from its major appliance concession in a method different from that of the main store. Most problems are recorded and dealt with by the owner of the concession. Mr. Jelton hears an appliance complaint only when a dissatisfied customer takes their problem to the main store. Hink's has the right to make a final decision on any adjustment. In an incident that occurred a few years ago, Mr. Jelton overruled the decision made by the concession owner on a customer complaint:

> A man had bought a television set from the appliance store with a special repair insurance that Hink's offers its customers. Hink's extends the manufacturer's guarantee if the customer makes an additional monthly payment on his charge account. A year later the man divorced his wife and canceled their charge account at Hink's. The policy was automatically canceled. He later returned to the appliance division and wanted his TV repaired. The manager of the concession refused to do the repairs because, according to his books, the man's policy had been canceled. The problem finally reached Mr. Jelton, who decided that Hink's would take care of the repairs if the customer began paying the insurance premiums again. Mr. Jelton believed that the employees in the service department were responsible for the problem because they had failed to notify the customer that the insurance had been canceled.

According to Mr. Jelton, the major appliance service department at Hink's receives the largest number of complaints: "People don't realize the complexity of a machine, and they are forever placing the fault on the repairman." Hink's attempts to prevent servicemen from taking advantage of customers by paying them a monthly salary. Thus, there is no advantage for them to charge exorbitant rates.

A few years ago the TV repair devision received an unusually large number of complaints, because the concession's office refused to make adjustments. The business for that part of the concession decreased considerably. As a result, Hink's decided to eliminate the TV repair service.

In 1965 Mr. Hink added a new procedure to the complaint management process. He decided to ask customers who had returned merchandise to the store if their complaint had been handled satisfactorily. The adjustments department began sending form letters to customers whose accounts had been credited with more than $10. In January, July, and August 1972, 31% of the 909 customers who received a letter sent back a reply. Eighty-one percent of the 37 replies concerning the housewares department and 96% of the 195 replies concerning sportswear were favorable. Customers who wrote that they were dissatisfied with their treatment at Hink's complained about the "unnecessary red tape."

Although Mr. Hink initiated the letter program "to create good will," the replies he receives are also useful as a check on the quality of service and merchandise in the store. However, the letters represent only a portion of the people who register a complaint at Hink's. These customers were successful because their accounts were finally credited. Hink's cannot contact the customers who were refused a return or did not have a charge account because the store does not keep complete records of all complaints.

Conclusion

Although complaint procedures and the personnel who administer them may differ from one department store to another, the rationale behind the resolution of individual complaints is the same and produces the same results. Steady customers who are persistent do not often leave the store without satisfaction.

The management of I. Magnin, Joseph Magnin, City of Paris, Gump's, Penney's, and Hink's have a very lenient attitude toward merchandise returns. The executives of all these stores do not act like members of an impartial judiciary when they attempt to resolve complaints. Their goal is to satisfy customers and increase sales rather than to determine the merits of each customer's claim, and the most important criterion in resolving a customer's complaint is their own credit record. At Gump's the manager of the customer service department bluntly stated, "If [a customer's account] is good, we'll make the return." That policy was followed at I. Magnin, when a woman returned a dress that she had shrunk while washing, and at the City of Paris, when a floor manager accepted several dresses that had been altered and kept for over a year. In both cases the customer making the return was a regular patron who paid her bills promptly. Thus, a charge account can be an important source of bargaining power for the customer at stores like I. Magnin, City of Paris, and Gump's. The cash-paying customers who buy less-expensive items are at a definite disadvantage because they cannot prove they are regular patrons. The store has no record of their purchases, and salespeople are less likely to cultivate and remember them.

Although management usually resolves a complaint in the customer's favor, we found exceptions at all the stores we studied. The lenient policies of the top executives are not always executed by salespeople. If customers are not persistent in pursuing their complaints, they may never reach an employee who has the store's long-range interests in mind.

A comparison of the five decentralized systems studied shows that several factors may contribute to the successful resolution of a customer's complaint on the departmental level. The type of complaint, the quality and price of the merchandise, the management's relation to sales personnel, the employee's attitude toward his or her job, and the customer's own attitude are all important variables.

The five stores (excluding Gump's) with policies for settling complaints "on the floor" handle complaints about specific merchandise in a variety of ways. If a customer is dissatisfied with a recent purchase, the salesperson is authorized to exchange the item or refund the purchase price. The procedure is standardized. In all five stores a return is made by filling out a credit form and sending a copy to the store's accounting office. Another alternative employed at each of the stores is the making of adjustments in the selling price where either of the first two alternatives proves to be unsatisfactory.

The stores also have their own alteration departments, where an item can be repaired or altered to satisfy the customer. If the price and quality of the merchandise are high, the store is more likely to take the return or assume the cost of the repair. As the store managers at Hink's and Penney's made clear, however, expensive appliances that need servicing are usually exceptions to this rule. It is not surprising that the personnel of the cosmetics department at I. Magnin refused to accept returns and sent customers up to customer service more often than did the saleswomen who sold designer fashions on the third floor. And as one assistant buyer explained, the store no longer stands behind all its merchandise because the standard of quality has dropped. I. Magnin assumed the cost of lengthening the belt of an expensive dress for an overweight customer, but gave little attention to repairing a poorly made $20 skirt.

Two concerns of employees also seemed to affect the way complaints were handled at the stores we studied. First, store personnel were wary of shoplifters and disliked becoming innocently involved in fraudulent return schemes. The suspicion and delays that one customer encountered in returning two pairs of slacks to Joseph Magnin without a sales slip is partly indicative of this fear on the part of employees. From 1971 to 1973 the store averaged a 3% yearly inventory shortage. Employees began practicing delaying tactics in order to trace the merchandise before accepting a return. These additional safeguards have further complicated the complaint process. Second, although many employees might doubt the validity of a complaint, they realize that management usually resolves complaints in the customer's favor. This knowledge inspires an early resolution of problems on the sales floor. As one J. M. employee put it, "You might as well look like a good guy down on the floor."

The relationship between sales personnel and management is also an important factor affecting the resolution of a customer's complaint. The contrast between the employees at Hink's and those at Joseph Magnin is a case in point. Most of Hink's employees have worked there for a number of years. Mr. Hink has fostered a strong sense of loyalty in his employees by showing his appreciation through rewards. As a result, the salespeople feel personally responsible for resolving customer complaints. The lingerie buyer who believed she had a "wrong to right" for both the store and the customer because a salesperson had neglected to fill out a special order form is not atypical at Hink's. Comments regarding the courteousness and helpfulness of salesclerks were volunteered by many of Hink's customers.

On the other hand, Joseph Magnin does not place a high premium on years of service; the turnover among sales personnel is very high. Unlike the other stores in the study, Joseph Magnin pays its salespeople on a commission basis that is added to a base salary. As a result, they avoid customers who are returning merchandise because "it goes against their salaries." It is not surprising that the woman who returned two pairs of slacks to the Joseph Magnin sportswear desk was met by uncooperative clerks.

At I. Magnin it is obvious that the older personnel treat customers' complaints differently than do the new salesclerks. Like the Hink's employees, the older I. Magnin employees have worked toward cultivating customers who always ask for their help when shopping. While the long-term employees are more trusting of customers, the newer salespeople tend to take a harder line against complaints. The difference in the attitudes of older and newer employees seems to be explained by the recent changes in I. Magnin personnel practices. Because few salespeople or assistant buyers are promoted to buyership positions, the lack of career potential keeps many of the new employees from considering their jobs at I. Magnin as permanent. As a result, there is less chance for salespeople to develop their own following among the store's patrons.

In some cases the resolution of a problem depends ultimately upon the customer. At J. C. Penney's the store manager accepted the return of a water-repellent jacket because the customer seemed sincere. At I. Magnin an assistant buyer admitted she would give in to a customer who was angry and insistent. But the customer's most important source of bargaining power, as we have said, is a good credit record at the store.

Thus, the management of all six department stores were interested in resolving their customers' individual merchandise complaints. However, although the stores attempted to satisfy individuals, they failed to serve the mass of individuals who make up their consuming public. The stores' procedures for managing complaints were geared toward isolated actions. None of the stores was prepared to use what could be learned from a single complaint to improve its merchandise or its policies for all customers. Four of the department stores had complaint procedures that did not process policy complaints. With the possible exception of Gump's, with its centralized complaint system, and Hink's, with its follow-up inquiries, the stores discourage their customers from registering complaints with the management. The store managers' offices and the customer service departments are tucked away on the top floors and out of public view. The established procedure is for the customer to deal with the salesperson or assistant buyer on the floor. If a customer finds the customer service department first, he or she is directed down to the appropriate floor.

The salesperson is not in a position to affect policy decisions within the store. There is no form to fill out by which a customer's opinions on prices, store procedures, or the quality of merchandise can be relayed to policymakers. According to store employees, many customers are even unaware that they can take their complaints to a higher authority. An assistant buyer at I. Magnin said, "Sometimes they have to ask to find out that customer service exists." Managers and employees revealed on a few occasions that they did not expect customer complaints to shape store policy. This view was clearly expressed by the City of Paris worker who said, "Eventually people's expectations will fall into line with what the store actually carries."

Another important area where the stores fail to serve the customer is in their dealings with the manufacturer. Customer complaints rarely reach the manufacturer's ear. First, none of the stores keeps complete records of all complaints. Defective lines of merchandise are spotted only by impressions of current returns on the floor, rather than by systematic checks through complaint files. At Joseph Magnin, the buyers do not even work in their own departments. They depend on salespeople to alert them to defective merchandise.

Although most stores have agreements with manufacturers to return faulty merchandise, they often fail to do so. Much of the merchandise in Penney's stores is shipped from the East Coast. One manager admitted that by repairing garments in his own alterations department, the store saves the cost of shipping the article across the country to the manufacturer. Thus, manufacturers never receive important feedback about their products.

Finally, the terms of some of the agreements with manufacturers prevent the stores from applying pressure on the producer to make better products. When most departments at I. Magnin, City of Paris, and Hink's return items to the manufacturer, the cost of the merchandise is deducted from a future purchase made by the store. Thus, the return agreement ensures that the store will continue to buy from a manufacturer who is producing faulty merchandise.

A centralized office for the management of all complaints is a practical and desirable alternative to the current practice of "divide and conquer." Customers are more likely to learn the store's policies and procedures for handling complaints if they take all their problems to the same office rather than to different departments. Knowledge of the store's complaint process is valuable because if customers understand the complaint hierarchy, they are more likely to appeal to a higher authority when they do not receive satisfaction.

A centralized office also makes it easier for the store to keep accurate records of every complaint. Most salespeople fail to record all the problems they receive because their primary job is to sell merchandise. Complete records of customer complaints could serve management as reliable indicators of the quality of service and goods it offers.

A centralized complaint-management system will not automatically turn the grievance procedure at department stores into effective complaint channels for the public. Complaints about store policy and merchandise quality still may be ignored. But a system similar to the one employed by Gump's will give consumers the opportunity to express a stronger, collective opinion that is not filtered through sales personnel, assistant buyers, and buyers before it reaches management.

8

David Serber

RESOLUTION OR RHETORIC: Managing Complaints in the California Department of Insurance

Introduction

In small, face-to-face communities where relations are close and in-tense, all disputes take on a public character and are resolved in the context of an overriding concern for the stability of the entire community. In industrial societies, on the other hand, disputes are characteristically managed in the context of private bureaucratic and large-scale economic institutions[1] that may be far removed and sometimes directly opposed to the maintenance of good order in the community at large. This chapter will describe and analyze the complaint-management process of the Pol-icy Services Bureau [PSB], a unit in the California Department of Insur-ance. The resolution of disputes through intermediary agencies such as the Policy Services Bureau is extremely susceptible to the influence of powerful economic interests. Moreover, the decisions are affected by internal considerations within the agencies. In the PSB, for instance, budgetary constraints, public-relations needs, the class background of the

[1]How large is a "large scale economic institution"? The insurance industry and indi-vidual insurance companies transacting business in California are the institutions involved in disputes with one individual consumer. The assets of insurance companies operating in California were $226,262,231,000 in 1969. This figure was larger than the 1969 Gross Na-tional Product of any nation in the world except the United States. Just the premiums collected in 1969 by these companies in California ($6, 079, 416,000) were greater than the G.N.P. of any nation in Africa with the exception of South Africa. The total premiums collected in 1969 by these companies from consumers nationwide ($61,816,513,000) was larger than the combined G.N.P. of all African nations, and over half that of the combined G.N.P. of all Latin American countries (State of California 1969:53–72; *Official Associated Press Almanac* 1973:568).

personnel, and the politics of bureaucracy greatly affect the way complaints are managed. What is *not* at stake in the Policy Services Bureau's process of dispute resolution is the maintenance of the social order of a community or the mental health of its members. What *is* at stake are not only the interests of individual consumers, but also the interests of insurance companies and a government bureaucracy. The examination of the Policy Services Bureau presented in this chapter will show how these various interests affect the process of complaint management and so will begin to answer the question of "Who benefits?" from this process.

History of the Policy Services Bureau

The state legislature of California established the position of Insurance Commissioner in 1866,[2] vesting him with the full authority and duty to regulate the insurance industry by enforcing the insurance laws of California in the interests of the investing and consumer public of the state. Historically his two primary functions have been:

1. to so administer . . . the insurance laws as to achieve the highest possible degree of protection for the public in general and all policy holders and beneficiaries in particular.
2. to adequately supervise the maintenance of the financial stability of the insurance companies licensed in California [State of California 1940: 36–37].

Today this enforcement power potentially includes liquidation of unstable companies, conservatorship, the levying of fines, and suspension of a company's certificate of authority to transact business in California.

The stated function of public protection indicates an early public awareness of and legislative concern for the consumer. However, in the late nineteenth century, there were so few insured Californians that it was unnecessary to establish a separate bureau for handling consumer complaints about insurance companies. But by 1927 the need was growing, and the Commissioner of Insurance established the Bureau of Policy Complaints (today the Policy Services Bureau) to be solely responsible for the processing of consumer complaints (State of California 1940:35). The new bureau was established and justified under Section 704 of the California Insurance Code:

The Commission may suspend the certificate of authority of an insurer for not exceeding one year whenever he finds, after proper hearing following notice, that such insurer engages in any of the following practices:

[2]Stats. 1867–1868, c. 300, p. 336.

  a. Conducting its business fraudulently;
  b. Not carrying out its contracts in good faith;
  c. Habitually and as a matter of ordinary practice and custom compelling claimants under policies to accept less than the amount due under the terms.

For its first 13 years, the growth of the Bureau of Complaints was slow despite a 46% increase in the number of processed complaints (State of California 1940:34–42). But there was a massive increase in the funding of this bureau between the years 1940 and 1960. (In 1960 the Office of Insurance Commissioner was renamed the Department of Insurance, and the Bureau of Complaints was retitled the Policy Services Bureau.[3]) I was not able to discover why the Bureau underwent such expansion during this period: Perhaps the sharp rise in California's population and the greater number of insurance policies in force during that period were important factors, but a similar population increase in the 1960s generated no such expansion. In fact, since 1960, expansion of the PSB has fallen greatly behind the population and the rapid growth of the insurance industry. Informants in the PSB attribute the diminished expansion rate to the limited funds available from the state and the relatively low priority the PSB receives within the Department of Insurance as a whole. This is unfortunate, as the PSB is the only departmental bureau that is in communication with the consumer; it is the public's only access to the Department of Insurance. In fact, other than the courts, the PSB provides the only formal mode for the expression of complaints by the consumer against insurance companies.[4] No insurance company maintains a specialized department or staff to process consumer complaints.

---

[3]Insurance Code 12906, added by Stats. 1941, c. 1180, p. 2935; see also Gov. C. 15480, 15481, added by Stats. 1945, c. 118,3, p. 504.

[4]Unlike most national industries, there is little federal regulation of the insurance industry; rather, each state regulates independently of every other state. The U.S. Supreme Court in 1944, in the United States v. Southeastern Underwriters, held that insurance companies conducting their activities across state lines are subject to federal anti-monopoly legislation within the regulatory power of Congress under the commerce clause. Soon thereafter Congress passed the McCarran-Ferguson Act, permitting "the continued regulation and taxation of insurance by the several states. . . . No act of Congress shall be construed to invalidate, impair, or supersede any law enacted by any state for the purpose of regulating the business of insurance. . . . Provided, that after Jan. 1, 1948, . . . the Sherman Act . . ., the Clayton Act . . . and the Federal Trade Commission Act . . . shall be applicable to the business of insurance to the extent that such business is not regulated by the state." This returned the taxation and regulatory powers to the individual states, where they remain today. United States v. Southeastern Underwriters Association (Ga. 1944) 64 S.Ct. 1162, 322 U.S. 533, 88 L.Ed 1440, rehearing denied 65, S.Ct. 26, 323 U.S. 811 L.Ed 646; McCarran-Ferguson Act 2, ch. 20, 59 Stat. 34 (1945), as amended, 15 U.S.C. 1012(b) (1964). For legislative history, see Congressional debate, 91 Cong. Rec. 499–509, 1112–22, 1470–73, 1548–59 (1945). As introduced, the bill was based upon a draft by the Legislative Committee of the National Association of Insurance Commissioners. See 91 Cong. Rec. 504 (1945).

The Policy Services Bureau has undergone only minimal structural changes since 1927, and procedural and policy changes have been almost nonexistent. Very possibly, the entire Department operates as it did in 1927. Furthermore, not a single employee of the PSB is much acquainted with the history of the Bureau; apparently few events have affected the discharge of its services to the public. It is, on the whole, a static organization. For PSB employees, time is marked by changes in commissioners. There is a slogan in the Department that expresses this resignation to the repetitive nature of the events in the Policy Services Bureau: "The Commissioner, like the Governor, changes with a loud fanfare, but things will always manage to continue to remain the same."

The Policy Services Bureau in Rhetoric

The Formal Organization

In 1940 the Insurance Commission outlined the functions of the PSB that have guided its formal policy ever since. These duties were: "To investigate and adjust all claims or controversies arising out of or appertaining to the interpretation or enforcement of the provisions of contracts of insurance; and to conduct all necessary correspondence and maintain all files appertaining thereto [State of California 1940:36–37]." Today there are three PSB offices in the state that perform these functions—in San Diego, Los Angeles, and San Francisco at the time this work was carried out (1971–1972). Statewide, the PSB employs 32 of the Insurance Department's total of 271 employees; the San Francisco office, in which this research was conducted, has 13 employees. The employees perform specific duties and are given formal hierarchical titles that correspond to their functions. The Civil Service Board sets the qualifications and requirements for these positions and draws up the qualifying oral and written examinations. There are five categories of employment: "Supervising Insurance Officer," "Insurance Officers III and IV," "Senior Stenographer," and "Range B Typist." The Supervising Insurance Officer plans, organizes, and supervises the work of the rest of the staff while also handling the more complex cases. Insurance Officers III and IV perform the routine policy services work: gathering documentation, interviewing complainants, reviewing evidence, and evaluating claims. Insurance Officers IV are responsible for reviewing the work of Insurance Officers III. The Senior Stenographer is the secretary for the Supervising Insurance Officer. She also supervises the clerical staff, prepares reports, keeps records, and answers public telephone inquiries. Range B Typists do the necessary clerical and receptionist work.

All these workers are under the direct authority of the Supervising

Legal Counsel, who is in turn responsible to the Assistant Deputy Commissioner, who heads the Legal and Compliance Division in which the PSB is one of four bureaus (see Figure 8.1). As can be seen, the hierarchical character of the Department bureaucracy is quite marked. Clearly, the Policy Services Bureau is by no means an autonomous entity in the Department of Insurance. It is, in fact, totally under the supervision of the Insurance commissioner and the Chief and Assistant Chief of the Legal Division. These officials set policy for the PSB and maintain ultimate control over most of the decisions made by the Insurance Officers, specifically their decisions to send investigators into companies or to commence formal action. Thus, the primary organizational objective of the Supervising Insurance Officer and his staff—to ensure that the PSB recover a "reasonable" amount of money for the complainants—is severely constrained by policy decisions from "higher-ups." As will be seen, this strict hierarchy effectively ties the hands of PSB employees and contributes to a general lack of enthusiasm and imagination in prosecuting consumer complaints.

Formal Procedures for Processing Complaints

As stated earlier, the processing of complaints is the primary function of the Policy Services Bureau. The description of the procedure will be simplified by describing only the *formal* process here. We are concerned with the official criteria for making decisions concerning the acceptance and processing of a complainant's case. We will not consider the highly technical aspects of insurance law, which are the ideal bases for many of the decisions, though it should be kept in mind that all the decisions made by an Insurance Officer are supposed to be based on a technical evaluation of the legal aspects of each case.

An individual may appear in person at the Department to file a complaint. If he does, a secretary takes down the general vital information of the case. If she determines that the problem is within the sphere of the PSB, she calls an Insurance Officer out to the front desk. If the inquiry is a simple one, he answers it on the spot. Often, an issue cannot be accepted by the Policy Services Bureau, as there are many technical grounds for disallowing a complaint—for instance, if it is a claim against a company that is not licensed in California, or a claim that dates beyond the statute of limitations, or a claim that involves an unusually high monetary value.[5] If the case is of a more complex nature, the Insurance Officer invites the complainant into his office to explain his case in more detail. Here the Officer familiarizes himself with the specifics of the case, asking the complainant to fill out a simple form and, if necessary, to supply additional

[5]From interview with the Supervising Insurance Officer.

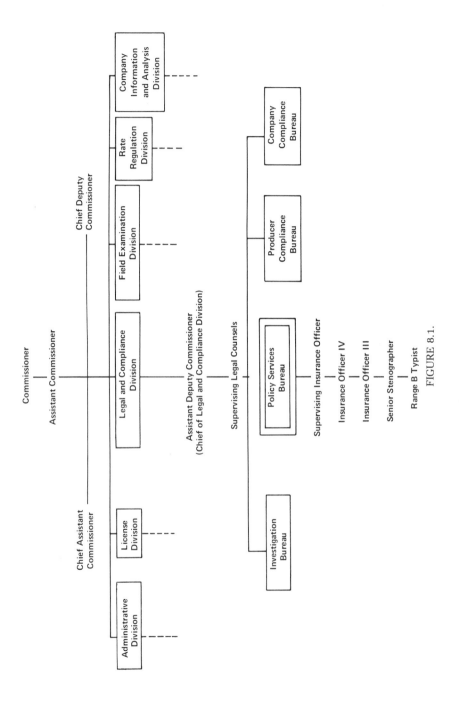

FIGURE 8.1.

materials such as receipts, copies of the policy, and any correspondence between the complainant and the company. Essentially the same procedure is followed when the Bureau receives a complaint by mail from either a consumer or his attorney.

When the Bureau accepts a case, a file is started containing copies of all correspondence and any comments that the Insurance Officer may make. The case is usually classified as to type of complaint and is then recorded on a reference index card.[6] Once the type of case has been determined, the secretary prepares a letter informing the complainant that the case has been opened and that the results will be relayed within 60 days. She prepares another letter for the company. In the case of a claim, she sends a form letter to the company, informing it of the complaint and requesting its explanation. She includes a copy of the complainant's letter and copies of the other correspondence in the Bureau's file on the case.

After the initial contacts have been made, there are three possible courses of action. In the first type of action, the company responds promptly, saying that the claim payment is in the process of being adjusted or that payment has been delayed because of a bureaucratic mix-up. In either case, the consumer is notified; the claim is settled; and the file is closed. This is the most direct and desirable outcome. In the second type of action, the company submits evidence that the claim is unjustified. The Insurance Officer then requests more specific evidence from both parties. If he and his superiors finally adjudge the claim to be unjustified, the Department notifies the claimant by letter and explains the judgment. The case is then closed, although dramatic new evidence may warrant its reopening.

In the third type of action, a controversy arises because the company does not honor a claim that an agent of the PSB has deemed valid. In this case, the Insurance Officer again contacts both the claimant and the company, specifically asking the company to defend its position of noncompliance. Under this mild pressure, the controversy is often settled by one means or another. The company officers may maintain that they have made a mistake and will pay the full claim, or they may make a settlement favorable to the complainant. Sometimes the company officers contend

[6]After several attempts to see the case files of complaints in the PSB, I was finally allowed to examine the index cards to closed cases. On the cards were recorded the name and address of the claimant, the company against which the claim was filed, a simple code for the type of problem and solution, and the dates of the opening and closing of the case. I was not given direct access to the files to which these index cards corresponded, in accordance with California confidentiality laws. Despite these restrictions, the index cards did provide me with interesting data: precise geographic distribution of the claimants which could be correlated with census materials to yield an approximate racial distribution; correlation between companies and types of complaints, and between companies and results; and so on. By means of the data on these cards, I contacted 41 complainants for telephone discussions and personal interviews about their cases and their experiences with the PSB.

that the claim is too high, and they remit some lesser amount based on the new materials given them by the Department. If the claimant is unwilling to accept less than the full amount he originally claimed, the Department terminates its case and refers the claimant to an attorney to pursue the dispute further.

However, the company may simply refuse to accept the recommendations of the Insurance Officer. If no more information is forthcoming, the Insurance Officer may request an investigation of the company's claims records if he still feels that the claim is valid and that the company has not acted in good faith. He then requests an investigation by the Department's Investigation Bureau. This investigation must be authorized by the Chief or Assistant Chief of the Legal and Compliance Division and the head of the Investigation Bureau before it is carried out. Generally there is a brief investigation of the company files, searching out "acts of bad faith." The investigation may conclude in one of three ways:

1. Dropping the complaint because of insufficient evidence.
2. Submitting an inconclusive report, closing the case in favor of the company.
3. Presenting sufficient evidence to request again that the company cooperate.

If the company cooperates and pays the claim, the case is finally closed. If the company refuses to cooperate, the PSB may request that the Legal and Compliance Division prepare with the Attorney General an order to show cause—a request that the company prove its position on the case at a public hearing. Failure to "show cause" at the hearing may result in a fine and suspension of the company's certificate of authority to transact business in California.

In sum, the formal processes of complaint management in the Policy Services Bureau are relatively straightforward. However, the Insurance Officer's assessment of the validity of a claim is a complex task. For fairness' sake it requires an impartial evaluation of the evidence, an informed consideration of the legal rights of both parties, and equal treatment of all cases that are presented for judgment. Moreover, in cases of controversy, a fair disposition of a claim necessitates cooperation and a coincidence of interests between the acting Insurance Officer and his superiors in the Department. The Insurance Officer has available only the limited number of formal methods just discussed to settle disputes fairly. In the following pages we will see how these formal procedures are both manipulated and ignored in the informal day-to-day business of the Insurance Officers. We will also explore the limitations imposed on PSB employees by the Legal and Compliance Division and the overall Department bureaucracy. The result is that the actual workings of the Policy Services Bureau subvert fairness while maximizing efficiency.

Social Characteristics of the PSB Staff

There appear to be several internal considerations that discourage the Bureau's aggressive prosecution of consumer complaints. Here we will briefly explore the backgrounds and social status of PSB employees.[7] This discussion will permit a better understanding of the nature of the relations among workers in the Department of Insurance and between PSB employees and the public, for these factors have an effect on the complaint-management process.

Of the seven Insurance Officers in the San Francisco office of the Policy Services Bureau, six have been in the Department from 7 to 17 years. The staff of Officers has remained essentially the same for nearly 10 years, and the duties, responsibilities, and roles they perform have been relatively static during that period. The effect is a certain tediousness of daily activity that is aggravated by great pressure to keep up with a growing number of complaints in a chronically understaffed and underfinanced office. Insurance Officers are often curt when asked about the tedium and reply, "We don't have time to get bored." They tolerate the routine because the pay is relatively high and the benefits are good; furthermore, they are secure in their jobs, and there is little pressure to advance. In contrast, the secretaries have little personal interest in their jobs. The clerical staff turns over quickly because, as one Range B Typist declared:

> There is no way to continue to stare at the same office and the same blank faces of these men who seem to have lost interest in anything but the football games. . . . I've been filling out the same forms for the same people for eighteen months and recently I've been getting home and crying at night. I just can't take much more. I've asked for a transfer and I have been looking for a job elsewhere, but jobs are hard to find in the city.

The backgrounds of the Insurance Officers are remarkably homogeneous. All are white males between the ages of 40 and 45, except for one who is 30. All have West European heritages but were born in the United States: one on the West Coast, three in the Midwest, and three in the New York City area. All but two are from lower-middle-class back-

---

[7]The data for this and following sections come from two sources—participant observation and interviews. I spent 2 to 4 hours daily for a month observing the PSB staff as they carried out their duties. And I spent an additional 100 hours observing the interaction between Insurance Officers and consumers with their consent. The participant observation was supplemented by nearly 100 hours of loosely structured interviews after a formal interview schedule proved difficult to follow for time and rapport reasons. I interviewed nearly all the 13 San Francisco employees of the PSB, as well as several other Department workers. Two key informants supplemented the material. The Insurance Officers were cautious and tended to give idealized responses, which I corrected for by direct observation.

grounds: The father of one was a worker in a brewery; another was a worker in a public utilities office in New York; a third was a manager of a New York department store. All are from larger than average families, with three–seven children. All seven men worked at odd jobs while they were in high school, and none completed college: three attended part-time; three did not finish high school during adolescence but later attended night school for their diplomas. The jobs they held between high school and their employment in the Department of Insurance were varied, though all but two of the Officers worked for a time in some area of the insurance industry, usually claims adjusting. They also worked as truck or cab drivers, clerks in department stores or markets, functionaries in other government agencies, factory workers, or salesmen. All seven are veterans of the armed forces.

As striking as their homogeneous backgrounds is the similarity of their present life-styles. Six live outside the city limits of San Francisco, commuting from working-class and lower-middle-class suburbs because they insist that the suburban life is more relaxed and considerably cheaper. All are married and have one–five children, but none of the men is eager to speak of his family life, at least not to an outsider. The dispersed living pattern of the employees seems to reflect their attitudes toward each other. They are compatible co-workers; I never observed overt hostilities in the office, and my informants concurred that they seldom had intrabureau disputes. They spend considerable time together during office hours, often eating lunch together. Sporting events usually arouse the most conversation among them, but aside from an occasional meeting to watch sports events on television, the men rarely get together outside of work. They are not close friends, and most of their interaction is confined to formal, job-related activities. There is, then, little esprit de corps or overt enthusiasm for their jobs. But despite a lack of concerted effort, the similarities in background and life-styles guarantee a certain predictability in the ways the seven Officers handle their cases.

The men of the PSB have very low status in the Department. This may be a reflection of their long tenure and low level of mobility in the non-professional ranks of the bureaucracy. The men are aware of this low status and recognize that it is generally accorded to petty functionaries who are seen as having plodding minds and little ambition. Within the Department, their sense of inferiority is reinforced by the condescension and deliberate display of professionalism by the legal staff, who belittle the experience of the Insurance Officers. In a given situation, an Insurance Officer may actually have a much better acquaintance with a type of case than does an attorney, but the attorney will rarely consult the nonprofessional. In fact, the Insurance Officer is allowed no input into the general policymaking decisions of the Department even when they directly affect the Policy Services Bureau. One Insurance Officer expressed the resentment and sense of powerlessness that such a work situation engenders:

Sure, all the attorneys are friendly enough guys, but we don't socialize too often. They don't have much power around here either, but they are professionals and we are not. And they play that up all they can, by not eating or drinking with us, or by not even asking us for an opinion on something or letting us know what they're doing. Like a few months ago, I gave a case to an attorney because of a policy interpretation matter, well I never heard about it again, until the guy who made the complaint showed up in my office one day and told me that he was sent a note from the Department telling him the company interpretation was correct. Hell, he [the attorney] could have at least told me what he was doing.

The Insurance Officers' feelings of inferiority are compounded by the attitudes of the industry representatives with whom they attempt to resolve disputes. Insurance agents often threaten to consult an Insurance Officer's superiors when disagreements arise, thus implying that the bureaucrat's opinion is of little worth and that any innovative opinion can easily be overridden.

In the formal mechanism of dispute resolution, cooperation among Insurance Officers, company representatives, supervising counsels, and high administrative officials is necessary for the fair disposition of claims and the success of the Bureau. But at every turn the Insurance Officers find their opinions disclaimed and their work subverted. Even their secretaries accord them little respect as supervisors. The only relief from this continual belittlement is the respectful treatment given them by some members of the public who come in as complainants. Perhaps to compensate for their own frustrations, the Insurance Officers often demean complainants in the same ways the attorneys demean the Officers. Members of the lower social classes are the particular targets of their scorn and high-handedness. But except for these occasional stirrings of resentment and hostility, PSB personnel generally seem uninterested in their work, resigned to their inferior roles, and passive toward their potentially innovative and adversary role in consumer protection.

It is unclear whether these attitudes are selected for during the hiring process or whether they develop in the Insurance Officers out of their defeating experiences with uncooperative superiors, nagging consumers, complex and industry-biased laws, an enormous backlog of cases, severe budgetary constraints, and the pervasive influence and power of the insurance industry itself. In any event, my informants in the Department reported that the Department does not want "gung-ho" people at any level of the bureaucracy.[8] Far from being gung-ho, the Insurance Officers in the

---

[8]In my research on the career patterns of Department of Insurance attorneys, I found that the advancement of attorneys was greatly influenced by their attitude toward regulation. Attorneys who were resolute in their enforcement of the Insurance Code rather than rigidly following the company orientation of the Commissioner and the supervisors were not advanced, or not advanced as rapidly. See Serber, n.d.:34–47.

San Francisco office were under such great stress that most reported high blood pressure and stomach problems—probably ulcers or incipient ulcers. Absenteeism is high. Between 1969 and 1971 the only personnel changes followed on the deaths of two Insurance Officers—one at the age of 45, the other at 53.

In sum, the social and psychological characteristics of the PSB staff members and their uneasy status in the Department of Insurance make for a particular quality of human interaction, marked by outward resignation, conservatism, and businesslike sociability and by inward alienation, resentment, and hostility. Though secondary to certain institutional constraints, these social characteristics have some impact on the way disputes are handled in the PSB and contribute to that agency's self-restriction, ineffectualness, discriminatory procedures, and accommodation to the insurance industry.

The Deselection of Complaints

> ... interviews require unlimited tact, a thorough knowledge of human nature, sound judgment, extreme patience, wide experience in human relationships, a complete understanding of the many and varied kinds of insurance, as well as of the intricate and complicated policy provisions, together with a goodly portion of ordinary horse sense. The utmost discretion and diplomacy must be exercised in dealing with these very personal relationships thus established with a large group of individuals constituting a fairly representative cross section of every known type of human being. They very often involve persons who may be plunged into deep sorrow by the loss of loved ones, persons distracted by worry over doctors' and funeral bills, and the loss of their sole support and maintenance, and persons aggrieved by what is either rightfully or wrongfully considered by them as a grave injustice. On occasion claims have been presented by persons who are malingerers or are attempting to obtain the State's assistance in the collection of fraudulent claims. Here, where the human heart is displayed in all its vagaries, it is imperative to maintain harmonious relations to the end that a valuable public service may be rendered by the Department [State of California 1940:34].

Such was the declaration of the Insurance Commissioner in his Special Report to the Governor in 1940. But let us examine some of the interactional elements and informal procedures that *actually* occur in the PSB office.

Despite the poverty of access to the Department of Insurance, as many as 40,000 complaints were brought to the attention of the PSB in 1969 alone.[9] This certainly indicates a pressing need for the services of the

---

[9]The figure of 40,000 is a rough estimate based on several discussions with staff members of the PSB and upon my observations.

Bureau, but only a third of these complaints were processed.[10] As I have indicated, funding and staff were not increased to keep pace with the rise in population and policyholders in California. It would be physically impossible for the Bureau to resolve every incoming complaint; therefore, potential cases must be deselected by the staff. At the point of initial interaction between the complainant and the Insurance Officer or secretary, certain deselection and avoidance mechanisms operate to limit the Bureau's caseload.

These mechanisms are exhibited most clearly when a complainant appears in person at the Policy Services Bureau. Aside from the formal criteria previously cited, there are informal bases for refusing to assist complainants that are highly personalized and situational. The initial response of the Insurance Officer is directly related to his evaluation of the "status" of the complainant; the second response is based on a cursory evaluation of the complexity and difficulty of a case. There is a complex interaction between these two factors, but the first tends to be a more accurate predictor than the second.

There are four primary parameters by which an Insurance Officer and the secretarial staff judge the "status" of the complainant: sex, race, affluence, and articulateness. The interplay among these four factors is obviously very complicated, and it is difficult to determine which is most influential for the individual PSB staff member in any one case. Nevertheless, certain traits appear to have meaning for the Insurance Officer and staff in making the status determination, which is then rationalized into a basis for deciding whether to accept or refuse a case.

Although many of the people who come into the office are women, they are quite clearly treated as a less worthy group of complainants, and Insurance Officers frequently refer to them in derogatory and degrading terms. Race, too, is an immediate cue for discriminatory treatment. Ordinarily, if even the slightest trace of any race other than white is perceived in the complainant, he or she will be classified as a member of another group. Minority people very often are turned away without assistance, brusquely discouraged, or dismissed after a very cursory review of their claim. This attitude, though scarcely proclaimed in the Bureau, operates at all levels of the observed interaction between PSB staff and complainants. Blacks, particularly, are considered to be out to cheat the insurance companies, though recently the Department has been careful to be courteous and cooperative with articulate, middle-class blacks.

This is not to imply that white males automatically receive better

[10]State of California, *Annual Report of the Insurance Commissioner of the State of California*, for the year ending December 31, 1969, p. 27. The precise figure is 13,733, of which approximately 5,000 were processed by the San Francisco office. The amount of money recovered for the claimants by all three PSB offices was $3,159,909.08.

treatment; rather, other criteria are used and considered more important for them. In particular, neatness of appearance is perceived to be an index to relative affluence and an acceptable life-style.

In general it appears that the more closely an individual approaches a stereotype of middle-class respectability, the more likely it is that their complaint will be adjudged valid. In making this determination, probably the most important criterion is articulateness. This can be operationally defined as a better-than-average control of "standard" English, a college-level vocabulary, familiarity with insurance jargon, and at least enough information to discuss a case intelligently. The complainant must also be able to reply to most questions asked by the Insurance Officer. The further away the complainant is from this ideal, the more likely it is that the Insurance Officer and the rest of the Bureau staff will use avoidance mechanisms.

Although partially contingent on the aforementioned variables, the other primary source of deselection is the apparent complexity of a case; the operational measurement of complexity is the time it will take to resolve the complaint. Two indicators are especially considered: the personality of the complainant and the estimated straightforwardness of the case. The emotional state of the individual is important: If he or she is greatly upset, the Insurance Officer assumes that he or she will make constant inquiries and take up too much of the Bureau's time. Apart from determining the validity of a claim, the Insurance Officer must also determine its *resolvability* and must then evaluate the problems involved in recovering the claim. For example, if a poor black woman manages to get past the secretary to explain her case to an Insurance Officer, her complaint must be clear-cut in order to be accepted; clarity is more important for her case than justifiability is. On the other hand, if an articulate, well-dressed male appears with a highly complex case that is in PSB jurisdiction, it is highly unlikely that he will be dismissed or discouraged.

A number of techniques are used by the PSB staff to avoid processing complaints. They discourage walk-in complainants by requiring them to fill out long and unnecessary forms and by simply being rude. Complainants are frequently asked to leave and return some other time or to return with documents that are hard to obtain. The staff is often discouraging about the prospects of resolving a claim and speak in abstract, legalistic, or highly technical jargon that is incomprehensible to the complainant. Common techniques are to falsely advise complainants that their cases are not within the Bureau's jurisdiction or to simply inform them that their complaints appear to be invalid and that the Bureau cannot be of assistance. In situations where these types of techniques are successful, the staff not only avoids the complaint but misinforms complainants about their rights.

Written complaints are judged by their articulateness, neatness, informational content, and complexity. The Department will characteristically fail to answer or will "misplace" up to 50% of this initial complaint correspondence. Other letters are considered "inarticulate" or inadequate and are sent back for clarification and additional information. Again, if a case appears complex and an Insurance Officer is able to refuse it without formally recording a grossly inaccurate opinion, he is likely to do so. Otherwise, he may request that the writer appear in person and then discourage or refuse him. Also it is standard policy to be very uncooperative and to discourage all telephone inquiries. Long waiting periods on the phone are characteristic and informally encouraged by the supervisor. Up to 50% of phone complaints go unanswered.

The methods of excluding complaints exhibit a recurring pattern: They are directed at those people who can be fooled or who will not or cannot challenge the staff. The Insurance Officers deny this, but admit that some of their exclusions are based on their experience with different types of people. However, in the opinion of the researcher, this selective processing demonstrates nothing more than racist, sexist, and classist[11] prejudices that have become operative partly because of personal background and prejudicies but more importantly because of external bureaucratic constraints on the staff. Since a high percentage of the complainants who come to the office are women, minorities, or members of the lower classes who are then turned away, the Policy Services Bureau is able to limit its caseload simply, economically, and efficiently.

The Informal Process of Complaint Resolution

Although two-thirds of the complaints were discouraged and avoided, the Policy Services Bureau did process 13,733 cases in 1969. It is instructive to see how these complaints were actually handled, bearing in mind the official guidelines.

The most common type of complaint processed by the PSB concerns a dispute over the interpretation of a clause in a policy. Insurance Officers characteristically use three alternative methods for resolving this kind of dispute; two of these techniques are informal, and the third may be formal. Most commonly, a PSB staff member contacts the insurance company by telephone, requesting an explanation of the section under question. This explanation is then forwarded to the complainant as the Bureau's official interpretation, the claim being denied. But frequently, a mere telephoned inquiry by an Insurance Officer is sufficient to ferret out a bureaucratic mistake, which is immediately rectified to the claimant's advantage. Least frequently, disputes arise between Insurance Officers

---

[11]This term refers to the privileges and prestige attributed to people in the upper social and economic classes of society, and conversely denied to those of the lower classes.

and insurance companies that involve a lively exchange of formal correspondence and that may or may not result in settlement.

Underpayment of claims is a persistent practice throughout the insurance industry and is the second most common source of consumer complaints. In these cases, the Insurance Officer plays the role of mediator, deflating the expectations of the complainant and requesting that the company modify its position. The Insurance Officer then suggests to the insurance company a figure that he considers "reasonable compensation," and a compromise often results on an acceptable, if not fair, settlement figure. However, the Bureau rarely challenges a company's final offer. In this sense the PSB does not act as a consumer advocate; in the last analysis, the Bureau values settlement and a closed case over a "reasonable compensation" that would involve a court fight. If the claimant is not satisfied with the proposed settlement, he or she is referred to an outside attorney.

Regardless of the type of complaint, the Insurance Officer characteristically attempts to solve the problem over the phone. This has several consequences. Instead of consulting legal sources for policy interpretations, the Bureau simply refers the question to the company. This saves time, though at the expense of a potentially fairer independent determination. In fact, this procedure goes against legal guidelines which have held that when ambiguities arise in adhesion contracts in which the form is fixed and not mutually agreed upon (as are all insurance policies), the benefit of the doubt is to be given to the individual, not the company.[12] Telephone conversations also obviate formal written records. This is to the advantage of both the PSB and the companies, for illegal practices, breaches of good faith, and an Insurance Officer's mismanagement of a case thus can go undetected. As there is no record of damaging but unproven charges, the costly procedures for investigating a company are avoided. A call to clarify a "misunderstanding" or a "bureaucratic mistake" is considered a much more efficient method of resolving cases.

Other mechanisms are used to prevent the establishment of a damaging company file. The most common one is the widely reported destruction or "loss" of files by Insurance Officers. There is a pattern to this: Wealthy, old, local companies are much less likely to have complaint letters placed in Department files than are small new ones. The latter are considered potential public risks, and they are watched more closely. Even if they comply with a Bureau request, their files are often referred to the Legal Division for further examination and possible investigation.

Other more private considerations affect the disposition of cases. Commonly a member of the political elite—a state senator, a state assembly member, a city council member, or another government official with

---

[12]From interview with California Supreme Court Justice Matthew Tobriner.

influence—will intervene on a complainant's behalf. No matter what the question or the merit of the case, it is processed by the Department. The Insurance Commissioner and his representatives consider this a common political courtesy, and Insurance Officers are instructed to consider it official policy.

The following are two representative case histories reported by complainants. Both are from individuals who attempted to file complaints with insurance companies and then with the Department of Insurance. They illustrate the kinds of frustrations people experience and the sorts of informal procedures practiced by the Policy Services Bureau.

> My husband has worked for _____ Company [a large department store] for sixteen years. He tried never to miss work and wasn't sick very often. He never had any important illness, and was never in the hospital. He thought it would be a good idea to get insurance because of the children. Through the company we got life insurance and had paid on that for nearly twelve years.
>
> At fifty-two my husband got a heart attack and had to be hospitalized and the company health insurance covered the expenses for the month he was in the hospital. That amounted to over $6,000 about which the insurance company should have paid. They sent us a letter saying that the payment of the claim was being held up because of some sort of problem and that they were doing an investigation. The hospital and the doctors kept sending us the bills and more bills were being sent for the time my husband had to see the doctor after the hospital. Because we didn't have enough money to pay off our bill my husband had to go back to work after six months off the job. His doctor didn't think it was a good idea but he had to do it.
>
> And the insurance company still didn't pay the bill from the heart attack. We kept calling them to find out when they were going to pay it off. Every time we called we spent a long time on the phone waiting till they got the right person and then the file had to be found; we just were given the run-around. Always we got the same answer: it was under consideration and the payment would be made later.
>
> About two months after that the company sent us a letter that said they would not pay us the money because Bob had a heart murmur or something when he was twenty-five. They found this on an old army record. I don't know where they got it but they did. I guess they wrote the army for his health record but that was a long time ago. The doctor that examines him regularly didn't ever mention anything like that to him. They said that since he had this heart condition before he got the insurance and didn't report the insurance wouldn't cover a heart attack. What I don't understand is why they didn't do this investigation before he got sick.
>
> We went down to the company and spoke with a man and told him that he never had any problems that he was aware of, even our doctor said he didn't know about the heart murmur. My husband didn't remember that he had this problem in the army and during the war they didn't discharge him for this thing. The man at the company showed us the form we filled out for the

insurance and it asked if Bob ever had a heart murmur but he answered no because he didn't remember. He didn't remember because nobody had mentioned it to him since the service and then only once. We explained that to them at the insurance company that we didn't remember that he had a heart murmur then and that we had been paying our money all this time in case something happened. They said they wouldn't pay.

Not knowing what else to do we went to see a lawyer that a friend told us about. He said that he might be able to collect some money but that he would charge us $100 and 40% of the settlement. We couldn't afford to do that and we were so upset that we borrowed some money from friends and paid off the bill with our savings. We also got a letter that our life insurance policy was cancelled unless we paid an additional rate of quite a bit in thirty days because of the same reason our health insurance was bad.

Again we called them and told them that we didn't have the money and asked for an extension, but they said no and that they would cancel it out on the fifteenth of the next month. We let them cancel us out and bought some other cheaper insurance. I was telling a friend about the story and she said a brother of hers was an insurance agent and she would ask him what to do. She phoned me back the next day and told me that the brother said that unless it was written on the outside of the policy or in bold print that if he had a history of an illness the company didn't have the legal right to cancel us out for a problem in the past.

After filling out the forms, I spoke with the man [a PSB Insurance Officer] about the problems we have been having. He told me that he would contact the insurance company to get their files on the case. When I asked them if they were wrong he told me that they would have to look more closely at the case. He said that he would send me a letter as soon as he found out. After a month I got no letter so I called. I finally got to talk to him and he told me that he was examining the case and that I would get the letter. About two weeks after that I got a letter saying that there was nothing the Department could do.

But I went back and told him what my friend's brother said about the policy not having it written in bold print that if somebody had an illness before he couldn't collect. When I told him this he said he would investigate the problem and get in touch with me later. In about a week I got a letter from the Department of Insurance telling me that the company had offered to pay for the first week's hospitalization or about $1200 worth of the bill and that they would not do any more. If I was interested in the settlement I should contact the company immediately. We felt that there was nothing else to do and that that much money was better than nothing.

The second complainant is a man in his late fifties who owns a small grocery store in San Francisco. He was forced into sudden retirement by a mild heart attack, followed soon after by another. His physician instructed him to stay away from his business, and so his son and daughter-in-law have been managing his shop.

I had been paying my [health] insurance bill regularly for twenty years to the same company and had always had good service with them. In 1961 I cracked my hip and had to be in the hospital for a while. They paid my bills and took care of everything. And when I had my first heart attack they were just as good. But about three months after that they sent me a note that my payment was overdue. I didn't understand this. For one thing they didn't send me a bill. They have always sent me the bill and I had never made a late payment. Immediately I sent them the check and asked them why they didn't send me a bill.

About ten days later I got another letter telling me I had thirty days to pay or my insurance would be cancelled. The letter said that if I had already made my payment I should ignore the notice. So I ignored the notice. A couple of weeks after that I got my second heart attack. It wasn't bad but I was in the hospital for about twelve days, and the bill was about $2,300, and it was sent to my insurance company. Three days after I was out of the hospital, my wife got a letter from the insurance company cancelling my policy because I didn't make my payment.

She didn't tell me about it because she didn't want to upset me so she gave it to my boy. He got really mad then because he knew what had happened about the billing a month before. So he called them up and told them that I had made the payment about a month ago, and that I never got a bill in the first place. They refused to answer any questions on the phone and told him that they would investigate the problem and send me a letter. We got a letter from them about a week and a half later (remember I didn't know what was going on yet) with a copy of the bill I never got and a note saying that the check was never received. We also got a note from the hospital telling us that the company had refused to pay the bill. Then my wife finally told me what was going on.

I was sure that it was just a problem with the mail and that my company would understand. I checked the bank to see if the check went through and it hadn't. So I called the company and told them that it must have been lost in the mail and that I would send them another check. They made me talk to about three or four people and wait about an hour on the phone before they told me that they had sent me three notices and that it was simply too late. I waited for a few days and checked by bank again but no check had come in and I didn't know what to do. The medical bills were piling up so I paid some of them off and asked the hospital to wait. My wife and son went into the company with my checkbook, which was proof that I at least wrote the check to them. They were rude and gave them the run-around and told them that there was nothing that they could do.

A friend of my son's told him that there was a state insurance agency in San Francisco and that I should take my story to them. The next day my son went over there. They gave him the same run-around that the insurance company did. Waiting, forms, the whole bit. But he's a smart boy and talked to a man about the problem. My son was asked to come back with my policy, checks, and other stuff. I had to sign a complaint too. He went back the next day and had to wait two hours to speak with the same man. When he finally *got to talk to him all he did was take the papers and say he would notify us by mail.*

We didn't hear anything else from them for about two months. I called them back in November and talked to the same Mr. _____. He said that he would look at my file and return my call. The next day he called me back and told me that there was nothing he could do unless I had the canceled checks to prove I paid the premium. If you ask me, that bastard was worse than the company.

The above cases are typical in many ways; common patterns are displayed by both the insurance companies and the Policy Services Bureau. Unfortunately, my knowledge of these cases is limited to the complainants' recapitulations. The Department of Insurance held firm on its policy not to discuss individual cases, and so the data are no doubt biased. However, it appears in both cases that the insurance companies violated regulations of the California Insurance Code and that the Department of Insurance ignored its mandate to investigate cases in its jurisdiction.[13] In the first case, the Code stipulates that claim payments are to be made in full terms of the contract unless exceptions are listed in bold type or on the front of the policy. A claim may be denied because of previous medical history only if such a limitation is explicitly stated on the policy.[14] If these terms are not met, the company is acting in bad faith, and the Department should have taken coercive measures to eliminate the practice. Furthermore, the Department should have attempted to obtain a full remittance of the particular claim. In the second case, it appears that the company had no desire to continue insurance for a man who had become a bad risk, and thus it was acting in bad faith. Nevertheless, the Department did not pursue the dispute.

The Department of Insurance is not a court of law and cannot formally award a claim or reinstate an insured person, but it may "suggest" payment or reinstatement by its threat of other types of coercive action. It appears that in the first stages of both cases, the Insurance Officers made efforts to avoid handling these complainants but were forced to deal directly with the problems when the complainants persisted. In the second case, the efforts of the complainant and his family only resulted in an examination of the case that brought the grocer no remedy. It appears that the Insurance Officer took the simplest alternative—denying the possibility of violation—rather than formally investigating the problem. In the first case, it is likely that when contacted by the PSB, the insurance company denied a seemingly justified claim. The Insurance Officer then forwarded this information to the complainant. But because she had some

---

[13]See Articles 3a, 4a, 5a, Chap. 4, Part 2, Insurance Code, added by Stats. 1951, c. 570, p. 1719.

[14]Insurance Code 10270.94.

limited knowledge of her rights (gained through a friend—another common pattern) the complainant was able to state her case more strongly. The Insurance Officer then approached the company with the information of her awareness. He may even have threatened to take legal action. In any case, the Insurance Officer was able to convince the company claims agents that they would have to make some sort of a settlement offer to satisfy the Department and the complainant. They made a minimal offer, which at that point was gratefully accepted.

This is the type of action frequently taken by the Department when a case cannot be deselected, avoided, or ignored. The first complainant was fortunate that she was white, well-groomed, rather articulate, and somewhat knowledgeable about insurance regulations. Unfortunately, she was filing against a large insurance company that would not likely be the subject of any major coercive action on the part of the Department of Insurance. The second complainant, on the other hand, received pitifully little attention and no satisfaction whatsoever from the Policy Service Bureau.

Constraints and Restrictions

Whereas the interactions between PSB personnel and the public are often marked by discriminatory treatment, avoidance, and frustration, the relations between the Insurance Officers and the insurance representatives are cordial, cooperative, and mutually beneficial. A closer look at some of the institutional constraints on the Insurance Officer will clarify his position and illustrate how his hands are effectively tied by higher-ups.

Official procedures dictate that if a claim is deemed valid and the company is clearly acting in bad faith, then the Insurance Officer may request an investigation at the company's expense. This request must be approved by the Assistant Chief of the Legal Division and the head of the Investigation Bureau. Such requests are rarely approved, though investigations are sometimes used by higher Department officials themselves to intimidate executives of small companies. Investigations of large companies are discouraged; indeed, the standard policy is to afford the older, larger, more "reliable" companies the total benefit of the doubt. They are assumed to act in the best of faith vis-à-vis the consumer, and hence any complaints involving them are considered "bureaucratic mix-ups."

This attitude is but a reflection of the many ties between the Commissioner of Insurance and the larger companies. A background investigation of past Commissioners and Assistant Commissioners of Insurance found that since 1940 all but one previously had been insurance company executives or attorneys receiving large retainers from insurance companies. After their terms in the Department, all but one went on to fill more important roles in the insurance industry. Moreover, the larger companies in effect nominate the individual whom the Governor selects as Commissioner. Insurance companies are also extremely active in other aspects of California politics and administration, and in the past have made sizeable campaign contributions.[15]

Because investigations by the Department are discouraged, most PSB staff will not make a request for formal action for fear their actions might be interpreted as a challenge to the policies of Department superiors. Consequently, the Insurance Officer is forced to rely on informal methods for resolving most cases. Nevertheless he may *threaten* to pursue an investigation in an attempt to force a claim settlement from the company, but this tactic is not always successful. Frequently when such an investigation is requested, a company official will go over the Insurance Officer's head and contact the Chief or Assistant Chief of the Legal Division to try to suppress the request and to see that the Officer is rebuked. In these ways the Insurance Officer's potential effectiveness as a consumer advocate is undermined.

Occasionally a company remains intractable even after an investigation has proved that a complaint is justified and that the company has made a serious breach of good faith. It is within the Bureau's powers in these cases to request that the Legal Division issue an "order to show cause," requiring the company to appear at a formal hearing to defend its position. Such an order can be issued only if it appears that large numbers of consumers have been harmed. The PSB rarely requests an order, and when it does, it is even more rare for a company to have to appear at a public hearing. Before a public hearing occurs, informal discussions usually lead to a settlement and retraction of the order. There has not been a hearing of this nature in at least 10 years, and no major company in the history of the Policy Services Bureau has ever been publicly indicted by the Department of Insurance for a charge concerning consumer issues.[16]

In sum, how an Insurance Officer proceeds is determined in most instances by policy stipulated by the Chief of the Legal Division, over whom the PSB staff has no control. Informal procedures and "off the record" consultations with the industry are pervasive practices throughout the Department and are symptomatic of the close ties and accommodation between the Department and the industry it ostensibly regulates. This type of cooperation is considered necessary and efficient for "effective regulation."

---

[15]Personal correspondence with Robert Fellmeth from his research on the California Land Project.

[16]It is interesting to note that the Insurance Officer IV, who has been in the Bureau for ten years, informed me that the only court trial or public hearing case he ever helped prepare was against a young complainant who had been discovered attempting to cheat an insurance company.

Summary and Conclusions

The California Bureau of Policy Complaints, now known as the Policy Services Bureau, was established in 1927 to investigate and resolve disputes between individual consumers and insurance companies. Aside from the courts, to which access is difficult and expensive, the PSB is the only recourse for the California consumer involved in a dispute with an insurance company.

Despite the public's general ignorance of the existence of the PSB, as many as 40,000 complainants brought their disputes to the Department of Insurance in 1969. However, the Department was able to process less than a third of these. A severe lack of resources forces the PSB to limit the number of complaint cases it can consider. The most effective way to reduce the caseload is to limit the public's awareness of the Bureau. Even this technique has not been totally successful; so other means of discouraging, avoiding, and deselecting complaints are practiced by the PSB staff. Certain official guidelines for deselecting complaints are outlined in the state Insurance Code, but the actual likelihood that a complaint will be processed depends more on the social characteristics of the complainant than on the technical merits of the case. Complainants who are white males, who appear to be middle to upper-middle class, and who are articulate and persistent are more likely to get satisfaction than are women, members of minority groups, lower-class people, and individuals who are either inarticulate or angry. This deselection helps eliminate what is potentially a vast backlog of work and permits a smoother-running bureaucracy at the expense of a large segment of the population that is degraded and frustrated. The system is bureaucratically efficient if not just.

Once a case is accepted, the formal procedure dictates a technical evaluation of the complaint, the gathering of relevant documents, and, if the case merits it, a request that the company settle the complaint. If the company refuses to settle, the Insurance Officer may request an investigation or turn the case over to the legal staff for possible disciplinary action, including prosecution, if the case appears symptomatic of chronic violations or malpractice by a company. Ideally, detailed records are kept on the processing of each case accepted by the Bureau.

But formal procedures are only the rhetoric of complaint management in the Department of Insurance. In practice, informal procedures and policies are far more common, and they deviate markedly from the official line. If a PSB Officer suspects that a complaint is justified, he informally contacts the company to discuss it. In the majority of cases this method leads to one of two resolutions: Either the company disclaims the substance of the complaint but admits to some bureaucratic error and immediately settles with the complainant, or the company defends its position and convinces the PSB Officer of the rightness of it. He then forwards this opinion to the consumer as the Bureau's official decision. In this case, no settlement is accorded the aggrieved consumer, but the matter is closed for the PSB. Cases closed in such a fashion contain few written records that could be of use in further investigations.

Even when the complainants fall into social categories acceptable to the staff and even when detailed investigations support the complaint, the PSB does not aggressively pursue the disputes. Complex cases are often abandoned because of the costliness of resolving them and because informal PSB policy views pursuance of them as "harassment" of the company. Thus, both the process of dispute resolution and its outcome accommodate the industry. Patterns of company malpractice are not discovered, nor are they searched out; as a result, the Department of Insurance did not bring an insurance company to court or hold a public hearing involving an insurance company during the entire decade of the 1960s. In this sense, the entire complaint-management process as it currently operates in the Policy Services Bureau is self-restricting. Busying itself with informal solutions to a severely limited number of individual complaints, the PSB ignores the source of those complaints and so never effects structural changes that could remedy underlying problems.

Each step described in the complaint-management process appears, in the short run, to be bureaucratically efficient. Cases are simply and inexpensively selected and deselected. Those cases that are accepted are usually disposed of by informal methods demanding little time or paperwork from the staff. The costly procedures of investigating patterns of illegal practices, preparing and holding public hearings, building a legal case, and going to court are avoided. The result is that a large percentage of the cases processed are resolved in favor of the individual customer at an extremely low cost to the State. As far as the successful complainants are concerned, the PSB's intervention in dispute cases is effective. In 1969, cases processed generated slightly over $3,000,000 in settlements.[17] This figure no doubt represents a significant compromise, yielding the successful complainants considerably less than their claims. Considering the limitations on its resources, the PSB appears to be an efficient and successful operation on the official record. If the PSB procedures were to conform to its public rhetoric, the operation would be much more costly and possibly less successful in the short run.

As far as the industry and individual companies are concerned, the PSB operation is successful. A large company may continue practices that may be illegal or unjust (and immensely profitable) without fear of public exposure or prosectuion while those few customers who are the most

---

[17]Indicative of how minimal these results really are, the total claims of payments facilitated by the PSB represents one-twentieth of 1 percent (0.0005%) of the premiums paid by California consumers in the same year.

threatening are appeased by the PSB. The PSB's more resolute regulation of the smaller or "fly-by-night" companies restricts the most flagrant violations and avoids scandalous publicity that might draw unwanted public attention to the industry. What we find is that the bureaucratic interests of the Department of Insurance and the economic interests of the insurance industry mesh together and that the consumer is caught in between.

What are the factors that generate a complaint-management process that is so accommodating, self-restricting, and ineffective in the long run? One of the factors is the budgetary restrictions that have been mentioned. However, this may be merely a reflection of something else more important, for the way state monies are allocated is only a marker of legislative priorities that are influenced by a whole constellation of special interests and political machinations.

(An examination of the social characteristics of the PSB personnel suggests that predominant attitudes and biographical similarities may also have an effect on the complaint-management process. It may be that the investigators—uniformly white, male, and middle-class—are selecting in favor of complainants of their own social type because they consider their complaints more legitimate, their motives more honest, or, perhaps, their actions more threatening than those of other social types.)

Moreover, these workers exist in the world of the petty functionary. Judged by the standards set by American culture, they are unsuccessful and occupy a low status. They are certainly on the bottom rung of the prestige ladder within the Department of Insurance: Though their functions are potentially crucial for millions of insurance holders in California, they have the lowest status among the males in the Department. Alienated from their colleagues and largely powerless in their work, the Insurance Officers are unhappy and frustrated. It may be in defense of their insecure status that they treat those they consider their social inferiors—blacks, women, lower-class workmen, and the like—in such a high-handed manner. Or it may be because they are resigned to their status that they do not aggressively prosecute cases in a crusading spirit but rather routinely process them in a compromising way.

But the complaint-management process in its present form is not so much the result of these internal dynamics of the Policy Services Bureau as it is a reflection of the accommodating and industry-oriented administrative policies that dominate the entire regulatory process in the Department of Insurance. Industry orientation is a phenomenon discussed in much of the academic literature concerning independent regulatory agencies.[18]

---

[18]See Marver Bernstein, "Independent Regulatory Agencies: A Perspective on Their Reform," for an excellent summary of some of the academic literature concerning regulatory agencies, in *The Government as Regulator*, Bernstein, M., ed., *Annals of the American*

Government studies and journalistic research[19] have further documented this tendency of commissions to develop procedures that minister to the needs of the regulated group.[20] Louis Jaffee (1954) argues that "industry orientation" and "capture" are conditions that are endemic to both state and federal agencies that seek to regulate industry. Although my research did not focus on the external forces affecting the regulatory policies of the Department of Insurance, I nevertheless have presented considerable evidence to indicate that this agency, in fact, has been "captured" by the insurance industry and so corresponds to the general pattern.

The primary concern of continuing research, however, should not be the *extent* to which the California Department of Insurance or any other regulatory agency is influenced, controlled, or captured by the regulated industry, but rather the *process* by which private interests dominate government agencies that ostensibly regulate in the public interest.[21] If complaint management in complex societies is to be characterized first by the brokering of special interests and second by the intervention of third-party agencies, we should be very careful to discover just how these two features interact to influence the course of dispute settlement and so determine who benefits from their resolution.

Academy of American Political and Social Sciences, vol. 400 (March 1972); see Gabriel Kolko, *The Triumph of Conservatism* (New York: Free Press, 1963) for a discussion of the development of economic regulation by the state; Gabriel Kolko, *Railroads and Regulation* (Princeton: Princeton University Press, 1965); see also Mark Green, ed., *The Monopoly Makers* (New York: Grossman, 1973), which contains numerous references to the political science, law, and economic literature in the extensive footnotes, pp. 347–389.

[19]There have been five major governmental studies of problems and possible reform of agencies: by the President's Committee on Administrative Management (1937), the First Hoover Commission (1949), the Second Hoover Commission (1955), the Landis Report (1960), and the President's Advisory Council on Executive Organization, or the Ash Council (1971); see also M. Bernstein (1972), for a brief summary of the findings and suggested reforms of these studies and a summary of the arguments of their critics.

[20]See particularly Robert Fellmeth *et al., Nader's Raiders* (New York: Grove Press, 1969) on the Federal Trade Commission; Robert Fellmeth, *The Interstate Commerce Commission* (New York: Grossman, 1970); Mark Green (1973) on economic regulation in several sectors; Louis Kohlmeier, *The Regulators* (1969); and Morton Mintz, *By Prescription Only* (Boston: Beacon Press, 1967).

[21]Despite the great mass of literature, no study systematically describes and analyzes the roles of the regulated agencies in the process of regulation and the development of regulatory policies. A similar research perspective was discussed in an essay by Merle Fainsod in 1940 (cited in Bernstein 1972:15); however, "in the thirty years since the publication of Fainsod's essay, it would be difficult to claim any considerable advance in our analysis of the regulatory process beyond the framework of analysis suggested by his essay. ... Our thinking about the regulatory process and the independent commissions remains impressionistic, and the need for empirical research is largely unfulfilled (Bernstein 1972:16 and 21)."

References

Associated Press
  1973 *The official Associated Press almanac.* New York: Almanac Publishing
        Company.
Bernstein, Marvin H.
  1972 Independent regulatory agencies: A perspective on their reform. In The
        government as a regulator. In *Annals of the American Academy of Polit-
        ical and Social Sciences* **400** (March): 14–26.
Green, Mark (Ed.)
  1973 *The monopoly makers.* New York: Grossman.
Jaffe, Louis L.
  1954 The effective limits of the administrative process: A re-evaluation. *Har-
        vard Law Review* **67**(7): 1105–1135.
Serber, David
  n.d. *Lawyers in insurance regulation: A study of career patterns of depart-
        ment of insurance attorneys.*
State of California
  1940 *Special report to the Governor from the Insurance Commissioner of the
        State of California.*
  1969 *Annual report of the Insurance Commissisoner of the State of California.*

Angela Karikas

SOLVING PROBLEMS IN PHILADELPHIA:
An Ethnography of a Congressional District Office

Introduction

Every weekday night scores of Philadelphia citizens stream into a small row house on the corner of 24th and Wharton across the street from Reno's Cafe in South Philadelphia. Some have walked only a few blocks from their own front stoops, and others have driven in from the city limits. They try to park their cars close to the corner because the area is plagued by street gangs, and muggings are commonplace occurrences. Once they arrive, the visitors resign themselves to a 2- to 3-hour wait in the cramped office that serves as the district headquarters for Congressman William Aloysius Barrett.

The 76-year-old Democrat, who has represented Pennsylvania's First Congressional District for over 25 years, makes himself available almost every night to hear his constituents' problems. By 9:30 P.M., after completing a 280-mile round trip by air to Washington, D.C., the Congressman is ready to begin what he considers the most important part of his job. From his office in one of the city's most impoverished neighborhoods, he attempts to find jobs for unemployed workers, housing for evicted tenants, and shortcuts through the government bureaucracy for frustrated citizens.

In 1972 the Ralph Nader study of Congress described William A. Barrett as one of those congressmen who "worry little about affairs of state. They see themselves as tribunes of the people, and their highest calling is to serve their constituents' immediate problems [Green, Fallows, and Zwick 1972:216]." Barrett's reputation for listening and caring about constituent complaints raises the question of whether or not members of Congress should devote their time to solving problems for indi-

NO ACCESS TO LAW
Alternatives to the American Judicial System

vidual citizens. What are the costs and benefits of electing a representative who is so closely involved in his constituents' problems? Do the roles of complaint handler and national legislator conflict, or do they compliment each other?

The few studies analyzing constituent casework handled by congressmen reveal that congressional staffs spend a large part of their time handling individual problems. However, it appears that their success rate is disappointingly small. A group of Dartmouth College professors found that over half of the 80 House members they surveyed admitted that casework was one of the most burdensome problems confronting them (U.S. Congressional Joint Committee on the Organization of the Congress 1965:775). According to C. L. Clapp, some representatives reported that as much as 90% of a congressman's time is occupied by constituent casework (Clapp 1963:53–54).

In spite of the time and effort spent by representatives on constituent complaints, Walter Gellhorn asserts in *When Americans Complain* that congressional staffs claim only a 10% success rate when they intercede for constituents in government-related problems (Gellhorn 1966:79). The fact that most of the congressional aides Gellhorn interviewed admitted to the 10% figure would indicate that congressmen either lack the motivation to resolve the myriad problems brought to them by constituents or their effectiveness is indeed very limited. In either case, in terms of resolving problems and improving administrative policies, congressional staffs seem to expend much wasted effort.

The district organization of Congressman William A. Barrett appeared to be an exception to the general rule. During the months of June and July and 1 week of December 1973 I studied Congressman Barrett's system for handling complaints in South Philadelphia as a basis for my undergraduate honors thesis at Harvard University (Karikas, 1974). I attempted to study the complaint process from the viewpoint of the Congressman as well as the complainant. I also considered the nature of the district he represents and the political party structure in Philadelphia in order to evaluate his effectiveness as a problem solver.

A Note on Methodology

When I first contacted Congressman Barrett by telephone in May 1973, he agreed to let me come to his office to learn how he handled complaints. At our first meeting he rejected my offer to help his staff, and during my stay in Philadelphia, he gradually restricted my contact with constituents at his office. From the beginning Barrett made it clear that he would neither allow me to have access to his files or mail nor listen to his discussions with constituents. He did agree to let me interview people as they walked into his waiting room. However, I had observed the nightly sessions from the outer room for less than a month when the Congressman called me into his office one evening. He informed me that he could no longer allow me to interview his constituents there, because some people were refusing to come in as long as I was asking questions. I proposed an alternative plan which the Congressman approved. During the remainder of my stay in Philadelphia, I was permitted to question Mrs. Rose Kane, the Congressman's secretary, every morning about the problems that had been heard the previous day.

Because the sample of complaints I then received was filtered through Mrs. Kane, I attempted to supplement my data in two ways. First, I questioned the other members of the office staff, but this strategy met with little success. My questions were usually redirected to Mrs. Kane. On one occasion when I attempted to talk to a part-time worker in the mail-room, one of Barrett's aides called out her name, and she promptly stopped talking to me. Another of the Congressman's aides whom I questioned once told me, "I hope you're not going to write about any conflicts of interest." It was obvious that Barrett had warned his staff against giving me too much information. Second, I tried to interview residents of the First Congressional District who had asked Barrett for a favor. Directors of community groups and clergymen in the area referred me to residents who had been helped by the Congressman, most of whom were very willing to talk to me.

Since Congressman Barrett refused to let me observe the complaint-taking process from the inside, I did not focus on statistical analysis of the problems he received. Rather, the following account describes Barrett's organization largely in terms of my own observations and my interviews with others who had contact with the Congressman. In addition, I interviewed scores of elected officials and administrators of local agencies who service citizen complaints in Philadelphia. I also briefly observed the complaint-handling procedures of two other Philadelphia congressmen. I hope that by relating my first impressions of people and places in the complaint-handling process, I have helped to convey something of the complainants' experiences. My research was also supplemented by a study of the 40-year clipping files maintained on Congressman Barrett in the archives of the *Philadelphia Inquirer* and the *Philadelphia Bulletin,* by interviews with political reporters and editors of those newspapers, and by studies of the political machines that once controlled Philadelphia and New York.

The Political Context

The opposition party leader in Bill Barrett's home ward admitted, "You can't knock Barrett's political machine. It's the best in the city [interview with Bill Black, 9 July 1973]." The Congressman has ruled his

South Philadelphia domain for some 30 years. He remains one of the most powerful figures in Philadelphia politics because he delivers his district to the party without fail on election day. Barrett once told a reporter: "Organization is necessary to protect democracy [Lynch 1973:8]," and the organization Barrett has built in South Philadelphia is the very foundation of his version of democracy.

The Democratic Congressman's style of politics has a long history in Philadelphia. When Barrett first entered political life in 1935, a Republican machine controlled the city. The formal party structure that existed then remains today, and power is still measured by the number of people who are personally indebted to a politician. However, few today utilize the system as Barrett does.

A pyramidal structure characterizes political party organization in Philadelphia, providing politicians with channels for direct and binding contact with voters. The city is presently divided into 66 wards. Each ward contains several divisions (precincts), averaging six city blocks each.

At the base of the party pyramid (Figure 9.1) are two committeemen elected to represent each division by party members. They are the party workers who provide the link between the political organization and the voters. Committeemen perform two crucial functions. They get out the vote for their party's candidate on election day, and they service complaints brought to them by people in their divisions. As one committeeman explained, "If someone wants a ticket fixed or the streets cleaned, I take care of it, but if a family needs welfare or some type of assistance, I will go to someone higher up in the party who will contact the proper department [interview with James Jones, 20 June 1973]."

The person to whom a committeeman usually turns for help is the ward leader. He is elected by the committeemen and serves as a representative on the City Committee, which is near the apex of the party pyramid. The City Committee formulates party policy and draws the party slate for local offices. A ward leader's influence on the City Committee increases as his control over the voters through his division committeemen grows. The committeemen rely upon the party hierarchy to help them service

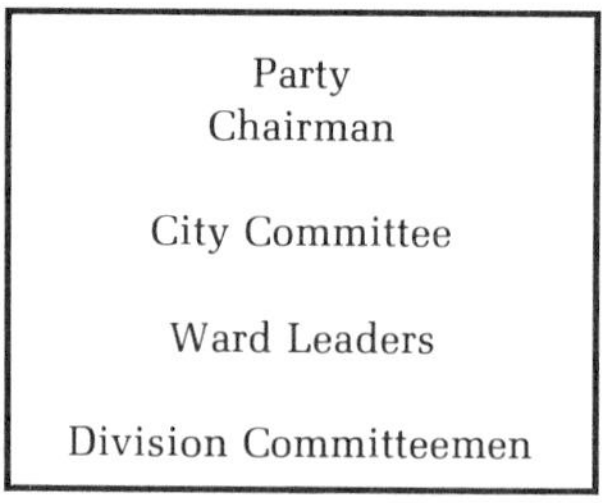

```
┌─────────────────────────────┐
│            Party            │
│          Chairman           │
│                             │
│        City Committee       │
│                             │
│         Ward Leaders        │
│                             │
│     Division Committeemen   │
└─────────────────────────────┘
```

FIGURE 9.1. *This pyramid represents political party organization in Philadelphia.*

neighborhood complaints, and the party depends upon the committeemen to deliver the votes for the party candidates. The ward structure in Philadelphia provides politicians with an excellent base of support, and it is no coincidence that most of the local, state, and federal officials in Philadelphia are also ward leaders.[1]

It was the Republicans who first used the ward structure to create a political machine in Philadelphia. They dominated city politics for over 80 years until 1951, when Richardson Dilworth and Joseph Clark successfully challenged the Republican bosses and were elected to the offices of District Attorney and Mayor, respectively. According to David Kurtzman, in his 1935 study of machine politics in Philadelphia, the Republican organization used two methods for controlling votes (Kurtzman 1935:28). The party obligated its committeemen by giving them positions on the city payroll. Because committeemen were under pressure to produce votes for the party on election day or lose their jobs, most sought to secure a Republican majority by making voters indebted to them. "[A] guiding principle in the days of the Republican machine was: Do a man a favor and you've got his friendship, do two favors and you've got his vote [Hartwell 1948:15]." The alternative was to use a variety of voting and registration frauds. However, if a committeeman or ward leader resorted to the latter method, a breakdown in the political process had usually already occurred.

Although the Republican organization no longer exists, some of the methods it once used to control votes are still practiced in Barrett's district. In some wards the committeemen attempt to maintain the same dependent relationship with the voters as that existing between ward leaders and themselves. A worker at a South Philadelphia settlement house told me:

> Before, if you wanted anything done you had to go to a politician. Today, there's agencies; but people still go to politicians first. When you want a job, the politician can help push it along. Politicians are always there. If you get drunk and are locked up, a committeeman will take you to someone higher up. There is no money or graft involved, only favors.

Not all ward leaders can keep as tight a rein on their committeemen as the Republican bosses once did. Members of the city's Reform Democratic camp have been elected in some South Philadelphia neighborhoods, and they have no allegiance to the ward boss or his machine. As a result, some politicians have continued to rely on various techniques of election fraud in order to ensure their victory. In the 1972 presidential

---

[1]In the summer of 1973, ward leaders in the city included the Philadelphia Sheriff, Chairman of the City Council, all four congressmen, and several state senators and representatives.

election, poll watchers were beaten up and prevented from observing the voting procedure in several South Philadelphia divisions (Wiley 1973:1). A state representative from the area admitted to me that in certain ger-rymandered divisions of his own district there were three pairs of legs in the polling booths on election day: "A Democrat, a Republican, and one of my committeemen showing them how to split the ticket." The buying of votes is not an uncommon practice in Philadelphia. A South Philadelphia committeewoman told me that her own ward leader, who is also a state senator, sanctioned the buying of a small number of votes at a preelection strategy session with his division committeemen (interview with Patricia Arney, 13 July 1973).

Although numerous election frauds have been reported in other South Philadelphia wards, Barrett's own ward, the 36th, has been un-touched by voting scandals. The effectiveness of his committeemen on election day rivals the past glory of the Republican machine. He is the last ward leader in the city to open his doors to constituents every evening (Lynch 1973:8), and, according to a state representative from South Philadelphia and a political reporter for the *Philadelphia Inquirer*, he is the only ward leader personally responsible for getting jobs for all 84 of his Democratic committeemen. In addition, these two sources claim that most of the Republican committeemen in the 36th Ward are also indebted to him for their jobs (interview with Dan Lynch, 15 July 1973, and with James Tayoun, 19 July 1973). The executive secretary of the Philadelphia chapter of Americans for Democratic Action told me:

> In the last state senatorial election we had a couple of Barrett's commit-teemen working for us against the man Barrett was backing. They were scared to death that he would find out—not of a physical threat but afraid that they or someone close to them would lose their job [interview with Shelly Yanoff, 20 July 1973].[2]

Whereas some wards resort to illegal political tactics to bring in the vote, Barrett confidently relies on the countless favors he has done for the people in his district over the last 30 years.

The Social Context

Pennsylvania's First Congressional District, which is the industrial heart of Philadelphia, extends across South Philadelphia from the Dela-

[2]In this special senatorial election, Barrett supported an Irish Catholic Democrat against a black Independent. The white Democrat carried the election as well as Barrett's own ward, despite the fact that the ward is nearly all black.

ware River in the east, westward beyond the Schuylkill River, to the western edge of the city. To the north, the district is bounded by Market, Lombard, and South Streets. It is evident even to the newcomer that South Street is the great divide between the white, upper-middle class, who reside in the downtown area known as Center City, and the ethnic neighborhoods of South Philadelphia. As one travels south of this divide into Barrett's district, the number of abandoned buildings with broken windows and paint-sprayed graffitti increases. Barrett's own 36th ward is composed of street after street of red brick row houses, interspersed with churches, taverns, funeral homes, and grocery stores. The alleys that bisect the blocks are unpaved and strewn with litter.

Until recently Philadelphia was a city of closely knit neighborhoods. This was especially true of South Philadelphia, where European immigrants who came to the city settled in small ethnic clusters. One committeeman told me that when he was a child, most people were born, raised, and buried within the same few blocks. The Republican machine traditionally had its strongest hold in the neighborhoods of South Philadelphia. It was natural for the immigrants who had just come to the city to turn to their local committeemen for help with citizenship papers, schooling, and a myriad of other problems. The committeeman was close by, and he was always available. Machine politics flourished in the tightly knit ethnic communities because news of favors spread quickly and was not forgotten (Kurtzman 1935:32).

According to Dr. John Shover, professor of history at the University of Pennsylvania, most of the ethnic neighborhoods have dissolved with the movement to the suburbs (interview with Dr. John Shover, 5 July 1973). The Irish and Jewish enclaves as well as the small Polish, Ukranian, Russian, and Lithuanian communities that once existed in the district have nearly disappeared. In 1960 the total foreign stock[3] still made up 32.8% of the district's population, but by 1970 that figure had dropped to 23.4% (Kupferstein 1972:5). The Italians remain the largest European group in the district. They dominate the 1st, 26th, 39th, and 58th Wards and represent 12.8% of the district's total population (Kupferstein 1972:5).

Whereas other ethnic groups have been leaving South Philadelphia, the black population has increased dramatically. In 1960 blacks made up 23% of the population in the First Congressional District, and by 1970 they were 39.2% of the total population (Kupferstein 1972:5). Today South Philadelphia forms a checkered pattern of white and black neighborhoods. Very few wards are racially integrated.

The turnover in district population is beginning to have an effect on the traditional party organization in South Philadelphia. The old

[3]According to the U.S. Census Bureau, "foreign stock" refers to immigrants and their children born in this country.

neighborhoods are now occupied by residents who are more mobile than their predecessors and not as receptive to political machines. A lawyer in a community legal service agency in South Philadelphia told me that the blacks who have moved into the district in the last 10 years and who do not live near Barrett's district office remain outside the political system. He said they more often take their problems to a local social service agency rather than to the local committeeman. At the same time, many Reform Democrats have been elected as committeemen from wards around the University of Pennsylvania and the area known as Queens Village, where some middle-class residents have recently moved from Center City. These committeemen do not work within the traditional party structure and contribute little or nothing to the power of the ward bosses.

Although the composition of Barrett's district is changing, the vital statistics remain the same. For example, according to the 1960 census, the First Congressional District was below the national average in median family income and median years in school.[4] In 1970 the median family income in South Philadelphia was $8690 whereas the U.S. average was $9433 (Kupferstein 1972:5). The district's median years in school in 1970 was 10.4 whereas the U.S. average was 12.2 (Kupferstein 1972:3).

The Complaint Process in Barrett's Office

One evening as Congressman Barrett saw me to the door of his inner office, he said with a slight smile, "I'm sorry you have to go, but I hear some penitents outside." Another time he ended an interview by saying, "I have to hear these people's confessions now." Although his references to religion sounded incongruous at first, the longer I stayed, the more appropriate they seemed. The nightly sessions in Congressman Barrett's office are not occasional events. They occur with as much regularity and meticulous attention to detail as any religious practice. The Congressman can be found at his district office on any weekday night after 9:00 P.M. and on Saturday mornings beginning at 8:30 A.M. During the months in which I conducted my research, he remained overnight in Washington only three times. Only occasional banquets or political functions interrupted the routine and prevented Barrett from showing up at his office when he was home. Even an electric power failure, which lasted for nearly an hour one evening, did not stop the ritual: Barrett refused to turn people away

---

[4]The 1960 census statistics show that the median family income in the First Congressional District was $5580 whereas the U.S. average was $5660 for that year. The median number of years in school for the people of the district in 1960 was 9.0, which was below the national average of 10.6 (U.S. Bureau of the Census 1963: 2–3, 428–429).

and close the office. He used candles until someone brought in a battery-operated light, and he instructed his secretaries to lead people in from the waiting room to see him.

On my first evening's visit to Barrett's district office, it was unusually hot and humid, and the office door had been left open. Inside, the small waiting room was filled with people, and the electric fan in the window gave little relief from the heat. The heavy wooden chairs that lined the walls were all occupied. During most of the evening people had to stand in the middle of the room and sit on the stairs leading to the unoccupied second floor. I learned later that a few people had come as early as 6:30 P.M. in order to be the first to see the Congressman.

The building is old, and the waiting room has never been remodeled. The dark wood paneling, the yellowed and blistered paint, and the cheap stained carpet on the floor made for a rather depressing scene. A couple of faded scenic photographs and pictures of Truman, Kennedy, Jefferson, and Barrett lined the walls. A single fluorescent bulb cast a harsh white light in the room, creating an atmosphere that hardly fostered conversation. Occasionally, a person recognized a neighbor and said hello, but most people waited in silence. I heard a woman remark to an elderly man, "The Congressman is too old to be doing this kind of work." The man replied that he was the only person around who was doing it. "The people know it and appreciate it," she agreed.

Barrett finally made an entrance at 9:45 P.M. He drove up in a black Lincoln Continental and was followed into the office by one of his secretaries. He walked in through the waiting room, making it a point to shake hands or nod to everyone. I was surprised to find that the man who suddenly brought life to the hushed room was a most unobtrusive figure. Bill Barrett was a short, stocky man fastidiously dressed in a conservative, three-piece suit in spite of the wilting heat.

I had learned in a prior conversation with one of the secretaries that the Congressman schedules no appointments. As a result, everyone must wait his or her turn to speak with him. However, he does have a policy of seeing city officials, community groups, and individuals escorted by committeemen first. Barrett emerged from his inner office a few seconds later and called, "First committeeman." The first man in line took two other people with him into the office. A man who had been waiting for over 3 hours became angry and left when he realized that Barrett was taking the committeemen first. About 5 minutes later Barrett escorted the first group to the waiting room door and called in the next committeeman. The same procedure was repeated several times. Each committeeman was accompanied by at least one other person, and some took two separate groups in succession into the office. Almost an hour later the last committeeman left.

As the next person was about to go in, Barrett announced that he wanted to see me next. I followed him into the small inner office, which contrasts sharply with the decor and atmosphere of the waiting room. The office has been made over into a sterile, businesslike compartment. It contains three small desks, file cabinets, a copy machine, and a water cooler. Barrett listened quietly as I explained the purpose of my project and the type of research I was interested in doing. He did not ask me any questions but smiled pleasantly and told me he would have more time if I came back in a few days.

I returned to the waiting room and remained there until the last person went into see Barrett at 12:30 A.M. About 90 people had entered the waiting room that night, and at least 70 people actually went in to talk to Barrett. In the evenings that followed, the procedure rarely varied. On one occasion Barrett invited a Senior Citizens group to be the first to come into his office, and another time he allowed a state representative to see him first. After the groups, officials, and committeemen had left the office, individual constituents went in to speak to the Congressmen according to the order in which they had arrived. They usually had a 2-hour wait. However, in the several sessions I observed, only one man was visibly angered by the long delay.

Barrett estimates that he meets about 700 constituents, personally accepts over 1000 telephone calls, and receives 300 letters every week. This personal contact in the complaint process ensures that Barrett's constituents feel that he, rather than a staff member, is taking care of their problems. He reserves for himself the duty of calling people into his office, but he rarely spends more than a minute and a half with each person. He told me, "After doing this for so long, I can usually analyze a problem immediately." He then directs the complainant to print his name on an index card and give the details of his problem to one of the secretaries. He does not allow his secretaries to intervene and take notes on a problem until he has first spoken to the constituent himself.

During my last interview with Barrett, he agreed to let me observe his sessions with the next two constituents waiting to see him. He called into his office a man with his young son who wanted to be nominated to the United States Military Academy at West Point. In a businesslike manner Barrett informed the boy that he would have to send him a letter in Washington with all the pertinent details. At one point the boy spoke in a very soft voice, and Barrett told him, "You'll have to speak up louder than that if you want anything done." Father and son spent no more than 2 minutes in the office, and on the way out a secretary handed the boy a stamped, addressed envelope. The next man who came in told Barrett that he had seen the Congressman previously about a permit to put a sprinkler system in his place of business. After a brief conversation with one of the secretaries, Barrett recalled the initial interview with the man and told him he had informed him earlier that it would be necessary to meet with the people who were going to do the installation. In both conversations Barrett was short and brusque. He did not seem particularly eager to put the men at ease.

One resident of the 36th Ward told me that the Congressman always lets a person know how he feels. "He may shout at you and tell you how wrong and stupid you've been, but he'll usually turn around and do you the favor." A woman who once took a group of neighbors in to see Barrett about trash that was piling up in an alley, told me that Barrett did not hesitate to take anyone to task. "We had a man with us who was being particularly obnoxious to Barrett, and the Congressman wouldn't stand for it. He told him, 'You big mouth, shut up!'" The Congressman firmly believes that the power of a single favor outweighs anything he might say or promise a constituent.

Barrett prefers to use the telephone when he works on district problems because it is faster and more direct than the mail. When a constituent wants help in finding a job or unraveling a mix-up with a government agency, the Congressman has a policy of phoning in the presence of the complainant. Because most calls cannot be made at night or on Saturday morning, when Barrett holds his office hours, the constituent is instructed to return to the office the following day, when one of the secretaries will put the call through. According to one of the aides in the office, "That way we tell the person the information as we receive it. If we get an unfavorable response, the person is told on the spot."

Barrett was not able to estimate the average time spent on a constituent's problem. "Sometimes it takes a couple of hours, and sometimes a couple of days." However, he did answer that the nature of most people's problems requires them to make a second trip to the office. An anecdote told to me by a reporter for the *Philadelphia Inquirer* indicates that the logistics of problem solving are not the only factors that determine how long a solution will take. The state senator from South Philadelphia, Henry J. Cianfrani, once had related to the reporter that he learned a valuable political lesson from Barrett. Cianfrani occasionally held "confessionals" for his own constituents, and Barrett observed him handle his casework one evening. On that particular occasion Cianfrani had been very successful. He had solved eight or nine problems immediately, and his constitutents had left his office feeling that there was nothing more to worry about. At the end of the evening Cianfrani turned to Barrett and asked how he had done. "Terrible," Barrett replied. "Don't you know that you should never solve a problem right off the bat? Make them come back again and get them used to returning to your office with their problems [interview with Dan Lynch, 15 June 1973]."

Although Barrett personally sees almost all of the complainants, he does not personally handle all their problems. He maintains two offices in Philadelphia, but he sees constituents only at the Wharton Street address.

The other office is manned by one secretary who answers phone calls and opens mail only. His total staff includes seven secretaries and an administrative assistant who works in Washington, D.C. Barrett often takes file cards with him to Washington to work on particular problems before he returns to Philadelphia at night. He leaves instructions with his Wharton Street secretaries on how to handle most of the other problems that came in the previous evening.

Barrett calls all his Wharton Street aides secretaries, but it is clear that he gives Mrs. Kane the most responsibility. She has worked for the Congressman the longest time, and she is very well known in the district. In addition to being Barrett's secretary, Mrs. Kane is also the Congressman's personal representative. Barrett attempts to make an appearance at the wakes of all the people he has known in South Philadelphia, but when he cannot attend, Mrs. Kane goes in his place. Some residents know that if they cannot come into the office to see Barrett at night, they can see Mrs. Kane about their problem during the day. Mrs. Kane receives a salary of $29,000 a year, considerably more than that of the other two secretaries, one of whom is Mrs. Kane's sister.

At different times, each of the three secretaries works with Barrett during his open office hours by taking notes on constituents' problems and answering the phone. They follow through on those problems until they are resolved. None of the secretaries specializes in solving particular types of complaints. The staff also greets constituents who walk into the office during the day. Daytime visitors consist of those who are concluding their business from the night before or those who are unaware of the Congressman's schedule. In most of the latter cases, the secretaries ask what the problem is and tell them to return at 9:00 P.M. During the several mornings I spent talking to Mrs. Kane, I noticed that both she and her sister, Mrs. Anna Corbet, gave out advice and resolved at least some of the problems that came up during the day. The secretaries tended to handle simple problems brought in by residents they knew that did not require much "pull." One morning an elderly woman came in to complain about an unpaved alley behind her house. Mrs. Corbet appeared to know the woman, and she had her wait while she called the City Department of Streets. Another time, Mrs. Kane gave advice to a woman whose ex-husband refused to pay alimony. However, at the end of the conversation she told the woman to come in and see Barrett anyway.

Bureaucratic procedures are kept to a minimum in Barrett's office. The Congressman does not keep detailed records on the problems he receives. He maintains a small card file on people who ask for jobs: "That way, if we hear of the right job opening for a person, we can contact him quickly and send him over." Unless a person's problem is time-consuming or involves correspondence, the most detailed records in the office are the secretaries' notepads. Very little time is spent on paper work. The complaint process is geared toward visible action.

Barrett also redirects some of the requests he receives at his Wharton Street office to his office in Washington, D.C. All decisions on nominations to the service academies and scholarship aid are made with the help of his Washington staff. Problems concerning potential legislation are also handled through the Capitol office.

Indirectly, the division committeemen play an important part in the complaint process. An individual constituent can save a great deal of time if he can get his committeeman to take him to Barrett's office. Barrett told me that about 40% of the people whose problems he handles are brought in by committeemen. He added that since the FHA scandal in Philadelphia,[5] about 15% of the people brought to him by committeemen were individuals who had been cheated in buying a house. I asked him if he used his committeemen to find people who were victims of this particular fraud. He answered, "No, honey, I never go out looking for trouble."

The Complainant

Unlike modern bureaucratic agents, Barrett has a reputation for listening to everyone and handling all types of problems. On 3 November 1950, the *Philadelphia Daily News* ran a half-page political advertisement, showing Bill Barrett meeting his constituents. The caption beneath the picture read, "In his modest office at 24th and Wharton, Congressman Barrett has an open door for all. From every walk of life he interviews people who come to him with Congressional, domestic and problems of all types. Every race, color, and nationality is given the same fair, square treatment by Congressman Barrett." It is obvious that Barrett enjoys his reputation for tackling all types of problems from rich and poor, black and white, alike. He once told me that in his 30 years' experience he had "heard every problem under the human umbrella."

[5]In 1971 low-income families in Philadelphia, represented by the local Legal Aid Society, brought suit in federal court, charging that the homes they had bought through the Federal Housing Administration (FHA) were substandard. Under the FHA program, commonly referred to as Section 235, the administration had insured and subsidized rundown houses that were repaired and resold by speculators. Investigations by the Department of Housing and Unemployment (HUD) revealed that some speculators had made only superficial improvements on the homes and had then influenced appraisers and tradespeople to give an inflated estimate of their value. The FHA approved mortgages based on these estimates and houses that were badly in need of repair were then sold to low-income families. In 1971 the Philadelphia Grand Jury handed down several indicments for fraud in connection with the appraisal and resale of houses under this program (*Business Week* 25 September 1971:39).

Each night a similar pattern may be discerned among the constituents who fill the Congressman's waiting room. Slightly over half the visitors are black. Most of the constituents are middle-aged or older, and, although nearly all the committeemen are male, there are an equal number of male and female complainants. The few young people whom I interviewed were asking Barrett for help in finding summer jobs, obtaining a scholarship or an appointment to one of the service academies, or fixing a traffic ticket. A young committeeman from South Philadelphia told me, "People my age just don't go to see Barrett."

Although some people who lived outside the district came to see Barrett with their problems, the Congressman insisted to me that he did not help them. He carefully explained to me in three different interviews that he observes a new congressional courtesy that requires all congressmen to refer complainants to their own elected representatives. However, several Philadelphia residents indicated that the Congressman does not always follow this policy. For example, a worker in a community housing organization told me:

> I know for a fact that Barrett will help people who are not in his district, because I ask him to. I brought him a family of six children who had been eating the lead paint in their apartment. Mr. Barrett saw to it that the family was put into a hotel while their home was repainted. He helped them even though Nix is their Congressman. Mr. Barrett is a whip with the people. They know him and like him.

Most of the people to whom I spoke in Barrett's waiting room had gone directly to a committeeman or the Congressman for help. Approximately half the constituents were brought in by committeemen. None of the constituents I questioned had taken their problem to an agency such as the Mayor's Office of Information and Complaints or the Legal Aid Society before going to the Wharton Street office.

When I asked people in the Congressman's waiting room how they knew about Barrett's office hours, I often heard the reply, "Why, everyone knows about the Congressman!" One man told me, "Anyone over the age of six knows about Barrett." A lawyer at a South Philadelphia Legal Aid Office estimated that anyone who had lived in the district for over 5 years knew all about the Congressman. Those who did not think that my question was too obvious to answer usually replied that they had been referred to the office by a friend, neighbor, or relative.

The people who spend an entire evening in Barrett's waiting room to see him for approximately a minute and a half have a variety of motivations. For some, the decision to see Bill Barrett is spontaneous and made in a moment of intense anger. For others, the trip to 24th and

Wharton is made only after a series of frustrating attempts to resolve their problems by themselves. One night a young, black man who had been cited by a white policeman earlier in the evening for gambling on the sidewalk and obstructing the street burst into Barrett's office, saying he was the victim of racial discrimination, and he demanded that the Congressman take some action on his behalf. That same evening a young couple who had tried for several months to obtain a school board authorization for their daughter to change schools quietly waited 2 hours to see the Congressman.

I received two types of responses when I asked Barrett's constituents why they had decided to take their problem to him. The first answer was a defensive "He's my Congressman. Why shouldn't I see him?" I received a different response from people who believed they needed the assistance of someone with influence. I often heard, "I wanted to go to the top first."

The Congressman was not exaggerating when he stated that constituents bring him every problem "under the human umbrella." For 5 mornings a week during a 5-week period, I questioned Mrs. Kane about the problems that had come in the night before. By using her daily summaries and my own interviews with constituents in the waiting room, I compiled a list of over 200 problems taken to Congressman Barrett by his constituents during that period. However, the list only partially represents the complaints received and processed by the Congressman. Mrs. Kane was often impatient and refused to give me a full accounting of the previous night's problems. She also failed to mention any cases in which the Congressman had used his influence to bend the law for a complainant. I found that the constituents were not as reluctant to discuss these types of requests. The following list ranks problems according to the volume of complaints and requests I compiled during June and July 1973:

1. Employment-related problems and requests   137
2. Delayed welfare and Social Security checks   30
3. Housing   10
4. Requests for appointments to service academies   9
5. Requests of military personnel and requests to prevent closing
   of military installations   8
6. Overdue light and water bills   6
   Complaints about condition of city streets   6
   Advice on immigration and naturalization   6
7. Evictions   3
   Traffic tickets   3
   Advice on family problems   3
8. Student scholarships   2
   Abandoned houses   2
   Lawyer referrals   2

Jail sentences	2
Admittance to mental hospitals	2
Placement in homes for the aged	2
Complaints concerning neighborhood contractors	2
9. Unemployment insurance	1
School transfer	1
Customs request	1
House remodeling permit	1
Payment on back taxes	1
Help in tracing a car license	1
Overpaid damages for a car accident	1
Help in real estate transaction	1
Request for a block party	1
Investigation of a gang killing	1
Request for a paved playground	1
Total	245

Even when Barrett cannot obtain what his constituents ask, they are often just as impressed with him for the personal attention he gives them.[6] One resident in Barrett's ward told me:

> He's one of a kind. He did a favor for my mother when my father passed away last year. My mother wanted a color guard at my father's funeral because he was a veteran. We called the army and everywhere, but they said they only did it for big shots. The night before the funeral at 11:30 P.M. I called Congressman Barrett, and he got the police honor guard for us. It wasn't the military, but it was almost the same thing. My mother bought him a bottle of whiskey for a present but he refused to take it.

And an elderly woman explained:

> My son was in prison and one evening I caught Congressman Barrett out on the pavement before he went into his office. I told him that my boy was going to be sentenced. He said he would do what he could for him. And when I went back for my answer, he told me that he had spoken to the Judge. And I'm sure that if it hadn't been for the Congressman, my boy would have gotten a much stiffer sentence. I think the important thing is that you see him. He doesn't brush you off, but he takes the time to talk to you. I really do believe in my heart that he tries to help everyone. I spoke to him myself and not through a committeeman. He told me, "Mrs. Reed, if there is ever anything I can ever do for you, please call on me, no matter what hour it is."

[6]Most of the constituents whom I interviewed either were waiting in the Wharton Street office to see the Congressman or were referred to me by someone who knew they had received a favor from Barrett. As a result, my sample was limited, and I talked to only a few people whom the Congressman was not able to help.

Many of the complainants' stories show that the Congressman rarely explains to his constituents how he has solved their problems. A man who lives on Barrett's street related his experience to me:

> I had a problem buying my house. After I put some money down, it didn't look like it was going through. I went to my committeeman first, and he took me to the Congressman. I finally got a telegram from Washington saying not to do anyting until I heard from him. I don't know what he did, but the Congressman solved it for me.

Another woman told me:

> I had a mix-up with my Social Security check and I didn't get it. So I went to see Mr. Barrett and then he notified me by mail that it was all cleared up. He doesn't do anything under the table. He's only getting something you're already entitled to.

Although the Congressman does not bother to explain to his constituents how he has resolved their problems, he is very careful to describe all his actions on their behalf when he is unable to help them. For instance, when Barrett fails to find a place in a housing project for constituents, he forwards to them the negative replies he has received from the housing authorities. Barrett prefers that the constituent receive the negative tidings directly from the official source.

Spokespeople from the community organizations and groups whom I interviewed were usually pleased with the Congressman's response to the problems they brought to his attention. Barrett estimates that approximately one-third of the requests and complaints he receives come from organizations rather than individual constitutents. During the 5-week period I tabulated complaints, the Congressman received visits from several formal organizations as well as from ad hoc groups of neighbors and workers. The most frequent group complaints concerned the closing or transfer of military facilities in the area.

Most of the established community organizations voiced their complaints to all the locally elected officials, but representatives of these groups believed that Barrett was among the most responsive. Members of a citywide organization for the elderly explained to me that they had tried to speak to other congressmen but were unable to see them. They felt that Barrett "was very cooperative." And the chairperson of a housing group called the Concerned City-Wide Homeowners said that Barrett was one of the most accessible and cooperative officials in the city. She said that a member of their group had written a housing bill that Barrett's Congressional Subcommittee on Housing had sponsored.

Informal groups of residents were even more enthusiastic about the Congressman's response to their problems. A resident of Barrett's ward told me, "Whenever I'm at a community meeting, I keep it at the back of my head that we can go to the powers that be—Congressman Barrett." Another resident of the 36th Ward reported:

> I'd say about 90 percent of the time when a community problem arises, a group gets together and sees their committeeman, and then goes to see the Congressman. We were having trouble with gangs, and we asked for additional police in the neighborhood. When our children were running rampant in the schools, and we couldn't impress the school officials to do anything, I don't know how he did it, but he got a new principal in. We've had trouble with our homes being burglarized, and through the Congressman we got more stake-out men. The burglary hasn't stopped but it has declined. He also helped get us housing in the area for residents with low incomes. Some of these people own $25,000 houses now because the government is subsidizing their rent. He's the only one around here who will do anything.

Resolving the Problem

A political reporter in Philadelphia once wrote that Bill Barrett is the "padrone" or godfather for the people of the First Congressional District (Lynch 1973:10). The title is an appropriate one for the Congressman, but it does not begin to describe the variety of roles he plays in the process of servicing complaints. In addition to representing his constituents in Congress, he gives out information and personal advice. He plays the role of advocate for constituents who are frustrated by the bureaucracy of government agencies. He has even come to the aid of some of the more notorious residents of South Philadelphia by testifying as a character witness at their trials. The Congressman probably provides more jobs than any employment agency in the city, placing his constituents in government as well as private industry. And, unlike many of the other politicians I interviewed, Bill Barrett does not hesitate to mediate in family or community disputes. Finally, he plays the role of judge in "bending the law" for or against a constituent.

Barrett derives the prestige and power to play so many different roles from two sources. First, the title of "Congressman" carries considerable influence. Mrs. Kane, as well as the assistants to the other Philadelphia congressmen, confirmed that administrative agencies are more willing to service a complaint when the call is made from their office than they are when the call is from a private individual or agency. Federal agencies are required to respond to a congressman's inquiry within 48 hours. But more important, the vast network of personal contacts Congressman Barrett has established in Philadelphia over 30 years enables him to intercede successfully for constituents when another congressman would be forced to draw the line at giving information, advice, and referrals.

Perhaps the easiest role for Barrett to assume in helping his constituents is that of a counselor dispensing advice and information. This service rarely requires the use of political influence, but it is important because it is appreciated by the constituent. The secretaries in Barrett's office spent at least part of every day advising immigrants on the naturalization process and helping constituents fill out Social Security forms or scholarship applications. Unlike other congressmen and agencies in the area, Barrett rarely refers his constituents to anyone else except when legal representation is needed. Mrs. Kane explained to me, "We don't send people to lawyers. We let them go in on their own, except for the charity cases. And if they tell us that they don't have a lawyer, and they never had dealings with one, Mr. Barrett will recommend a lawyer who specializes in their problem. When a constituent has a charity case, Mr. Barrett will recommend lawyers who will charge only $25." She quickly added, "You know, some people would think that if we had certain lawyers we always referred people to, we would be getting a kickback from them. So we just stay out of it."

In spite of the Congressman's alleged disinterest in legal problems and referrals, he does refer constituents to attorneys, and he benefits politically from providing the service. An attorney located in Barrett's ward told me, "The Congressman has always been very helpful to me. He often refers clients to me [interview with James Logan, 1 December 1973]." The advantages the Congressman gains by referring clients to attorneys and widening his network of debts and favors are more important politically than any kickbacks could be. The fact that Barrett handled legal referrals personally would seem to indicate that he considers it more than a routine service.

Barrett assumes the role of an advocate whenever he confronts a government agency or a private firm on behalf of a constituent. Many of his constituents believe that he can deal easily with uncooperative officials in unsnarling bureaucratic procedures when they have failed. One afternoon an elderly constituent told me, "Congressman Barrett got me my job 22 years ago. I want to transfer from heavy to light work. I appealed, but my supervisor just won't let me do it. I know all Mrs. Kane has to do is make a telephone call for me."

Mrs. Kane continually deemphasized the importance of the Congressman's influence and the political benefits he derived from servicing complaints: "We never pressure anyone when we make a call to get something done." And she added, "You know, we're not doing favors for people who come in here. It is their right to ask their elected public officials to get things done for them."

Barrett's success as an advocate does not depend entirely upon his network of influence. In several cases a government agency had failed to give the proper consideration or service to constituents, and Barrett merely helped them obtain what they deserved. However, it would be difficult to deny that the Congressman's intervention speeded up the process. A man who had lost his hearing while working for the government filed a claim to receive disability benefits and waited 3 years for a decision. Mrs. Kane made a phone call to the state insurance board and had the claim processed within 90 days. On another occasion Mrs. Kane contacted the water utility company to demand the rereading of a private meter because the constituent claimed her water bills were too high.

According to Mrs. Kane, the Congressman tackles consumer problems only occasionally. She said that the most common complaints were from residents who were pressured into buying defective products from door-to-door salespeople. "Even though a contract has been signed, Mr. Barrett steps in. We find that when someone from the government steps in for a person, the company becomes a bit shaky and listens."

When all other methods have failed, Barrett has introduced private bills in Congress to resolve a constituent's problem. For example, he authored a private bill in 1946 to prevent the deportation of a 17-year-old Italian youth who fought on the side of American servicemen in Europe during World War II (*Philadelphia Bulletin* 25 January 1946:3).

The employment agency that Barrett operates at 24th and Wharton is by far the most important service he provides to his constituents. It works better than an ordinary agency because every position Barrett secures widens his network of contacts in both the public and private sectors. The constituent is obligated to return the favor of employment by using his position to help others when Barrett calls on him or her. One local politician's description of Barrett as a "great big amoeba" is appropriate imagery.

Barrett's control of many patronage positions dispensed through the Democratic Party partially explains his extraordinary ability to find employment for needy constituents. According to a member of the South Philadelphia Community Council, 75% of the city employees are politically appointed, and "all city and state jobs are at Barrett's disposal." Although civil service exams are now prerequisites, a former Republican ward leader admitted, "There are still ways to get around them." As an influential member of the City Committee, Barrett undoubtedly enjoys a large share of the party spoils. It is accepted by many that Barrett is responsible for placing his long-time friend, Johnny Sills, in the position of patronage dispenser for the Democratic City Committee. Some ward leaders admit that Sills has control of 45,000 government positions in Philadelphia relinquished by Governor Milton J. Shapp in exchange for votes for his income tax legislation in 1972 (Lynch 1972).

The Congressman's ability to obtain employment for his constituents also extends into private industry. According to Mrs. Kane, if an individual applies for a position and never receives any notification, one of the secretaries calls the personnel director to find out his or her status. If necessary, the Congressman will then write a letter of recommendation on behalf of the constituent. Mrs. Kane once emphasized, "We don't hand out letters like circulars. We give recommendations if we know the person or someone in the area knows him." She told me that the Congressman has placed people in positions at Bell Telephone and the Philadelphia Gas Works. During my study Mrs. Kane reported that eight individuals had secured positions in private businesses through the Congressman.

Barrett's aides attempted to impress upon me that the Congressman does not actively seek work for his constituents. However, jobs are more important to Barrett than his aides were willing to admit, because they are the currency of Barrett's realm. The Congressman grants favors in exchange for employment opportunities for his constituents. An incident that occurred several years ago reveals that the Congressman will use his influence in Congress to maintain his local network of favors and debts. A Philadelphia public relations man once took a friend who was a supermarket executive to see Barrett about some legislation. Barrett agreed to help the man immediately, and when he was asked what it would cost, Barrett replied, "It'll cost you jobs. Give me thirty or forty jobs in your supermarkets. Let me hire people to fill them [Lynch 1973:8 and interview with Lynch, 15 June 1973]."

The Congressman is very proud of his role as a mediator of family and community disputes, and he was quick to recall several family problems that he had personally resolved. Thirty years ago a distraught mother visited Barrett because she wanted to place her son in a reform school. After a lengthy session Barrett finally convinced the woman to allow the boy to remain at home. Barrett also assumed the responsibility of reviewing her son's report cards in the future. The boy began making exceptionally good grades, and the Congressman later helped him get scholarships for college and law school. Barrett proudly concluded, "And today that boy is a judge." Although the Congressman refused to tell me the boy's name, it is commonly known in Philadelphia that Bill Barrett is the benefactor of Common Pleas Court Judge G. Fred DiBona. Barrett's willingness to intercede in a family matter had very practical results. Judge DiBona is another link in Barrett's network of influence.

Because many of Barrett's constituents are personally indebted to him, he is often successful in resolving community disputes when others would have failed. On 17 June 1970, white residents on the 2600 block of Gerritt Street in South Philadelphia set up barricades, blocking all traffic from the street in protest against a black family that had moved into the neighborhood. After standing their ground most of the day, they still refused to move until they had seen Barrett. Barrett did see them and held a series of meetings. The barricades were removed, and the black family stayed [*Philadelphia Bulletin* 17 June 1970:5]."

Servicing constituent complaints has sometimes involved Barrett as a character witness for convicted criminals. The case of George Barrow illustrates his effectiveness in this role. In 1963 George Barrow was convicted of carrying on interstate racketeering from his headquarters in South Philadelphia. He had a long history of felony arrests, but his sentence was reduced soon after he was convicted. Then, an "unprecedented second hearing" for reduction in sentence followed (Pennsylvania Crime Commission 1970:71). Congressman Barrett testified in his behalf, in spite of the fact that Barrow had been arrested three times for murder and was alleged to have had no legitimate occupation since 1926 (p. 71).

The Pennsylvania Crime Commission[7] stated that "all witnesses testified that they had known Barrow as a law abiding citizen with a reputation for honesty." At the time Barrett told reporters that he "came forward on a compassion basis" because Barrow was good to his wife and mother and "I think he has the gout [*Philadelphia Inquirer* 13 May 1967:]." According to the Commission, on 15 May 1967 Barrow's sentence was reduced to 1 year in prison, and he was declared eligible for parole after having served 4 months. The Crime Commission stated:

> Organized criminals endear themselves to officials and political leaders in a number of ways, creating many types of obligations. While evidence does not always exist of specific bribes, key officials go to bat for racketeers for unexplained reasons when the latter get into trouble with law enforcement authorities. . . . One of the commonest occasions for pressure applied on behalf of racketeers has been that of the criminal trials or sentence hearings. During trial, community leaders have appeared as defense witnesses, claiming that the defendant is of such impeccable character as to be incapable of the crime for which he is charged. At sentence hearings the burden of testimony is that the convict is an asset to his community and should be given a light sentence. The appearance of these witnesses is one way by which political leaders signal to judges and correctional officials that the convict is a person about whom they care [Pennsylvania Crime Commission 1970:68–69].

In March 1957, Barrett interceded on behalf of John Mollica, who had been sentenced to life imprisonment for murder in 1946. Barrett entered the case in June 1955 after Mollica's lawyer, G. Fred DiBona (later the Common Pleas Court judge), was told that another clemency hearing

---

[7]The Pennsylvania Crime Commission, a special investigative committee of the Commonwealth's Department of Justice, was established in 1968 to examine the extent of organized crime in Pennsylvania and to recommend legislation and administrative reforms to combat the problem.

could not be held until November of that year. After 11 years' imprisonment and two rejected clemency pleas, Mollica was released by Governor George M. Leader and the State Board of Pardons. Barrett later explained that he had interceded because of the "poor health of the prisoner's mother" and because "his case had not been presented in the proper light [Philadelphia Inquirer 14 March 1957:21]."

Barrett represents a district with many of the "toughest gangsters this side of Sing-Sing [Lynch 1973:8]," but he does not provide testimonials for all of his constituents. As the Crime Commission has suggested, the decision to defend certain convicted criminals is not easily linked to the offer of bribes. However, by aiding these men, Barrett may be placing others who are more influential than they in his debt. For example, the case of John Mollica might be viewed as a continuing exchange of favors between the Congressman and his protégé, G. Fred DiBona.

The Congressman's role changes from advocate to judge and jury when he uses his power to "bend the law" for or against a constituent. His highly placed contacts enable him to grant unusual if not illegal favors. A man who lived in Barrett's district once told me, "Barrett does everything. If it was anyone else but Barrett, they would say he was crooked and dishonest, but because it's Barrett it's all right." Incidents revealing how Barrett avoids or twists the law were reported to me by his constituents. A young resident of Barrett's district had driven off a small public bridge in New Jersey. The bill he received for damage to the bridge amounted to $12 for new wood and $700 for labor. He could not pay the bill and took his problem to the Congressman. Barrett told him to pay for the new material and forget the rest of the bill. And another example is that of a young nurse who lives in Barrett's ward and who once accumulated $400.00 in parking tickets. She worked the late-night shift at a hospital, and she could never find a legal parking place close to her home when she returned early in the morning. She parked illegally because she was afraid to walk alone in such a "rough neighborhood." Barrett told her not to worry about paying the tickets because he would take care of them.

According to a former employee at the Philadelphia Housing Authority, Barrett often pressures the agency to accept "tenants who are not exactly qualified [interview with Marilyn Weiler, 2 December 1973]." Administrators of the various housing agencies in the city are continually trying to please the Congressman because of his position as chairman of the House Subcommittee on Housing, which selects the housing projects that receive federal aid. In exchange for his cooperation in sponsoring favored bills, agencies such as the Philadelphia Housing Authority and the Redevelopment Agency grant favors to constituents of Bill Barrett. Those constituents recommended by the Congressman receive special consideration for housing placements as well as job opportunities. A former employee of the Philadelphia Housing Authority also admitted that most of the people hired by the Authority in 1973 were political contacts of Bill Barrett.

According to some South Philadelphia residents, Barrett uses his power to both help and harass others. One resident of the district claims that after opposing Barrett at a meeting, he was continually harassed in his place of business by health inspectors and the police. In April 1967, Francis Smith, Chairman of the Democratic City Committee, blamed Barrett for masterminding police raids on taverns in wards that opposed Democratic mayor James H. J. Tate's renomination (*Philadelphia Inquirer* 13 April 1976:5). One South Philadelphia resident claimed that the Congressman can easily have his contacts on the police force raid a home or a business to harrass an individual. He told me, "A few weeks ago a cop raided a place in Center City, and he was told to lay off. He knew the order came from Barrett. Barrett's been able to buy people by giving them jobs in city positions."

Until recently it was believed that no one could join the Philadelphia police department without a politician's recommendation. One of Barrett's constituents suggested to me that the Congressman is the "real power" behind the police force and that Barrett was the mentor of Mayor Frank L. Rizzo, who was formerly the chief of police.

The ease with which Barrett obtains light sentences and releases from jail for some of his constituents indicates that he has very close ties with the judicial branch. According to some of the Congressman's constituents, Barrett's friends on the bench include one federal judge, two Common Pleas Court judges, and one municipal judge.

Barrett began building his network of debts and favors long before he made his first bid for Congress in 1944. Early in his career, he became an appraiser of mercantile property and was thus in a position to grant favors to merchants by lowering the assessments on their businesses. Congressman Barrett once told me:

> I started out as an administrative assistant to a Congressman here, and I learned a lot from that. He lost a lot of friends because he did not see everyone personally. I made up my mind then that no matter how small or trivial a problem is, I would be available. A staff member doesn't have the same impact as an executive.

Barrett alone controls the vast network of debts and favors he has established. He has been in public office longer than any other politician in the city, and he has probably outlived most of those to whom he was indebted at the beginning of his career. More than one of Barrett's constituents told me, "He's been around too long to owe anyone anything." The Congressman tried to impress on me that he resolves constituents' problems on a reciprocal basis. Administrators, clerks, and employees of important agencies perform services for his constituents, and he grants them favors in return. However, Barrett never mentioned that most of the people he contacts are actually indebted to him for their jobs. Bill Cibotti, Philadelphia City Councilman, and Earl Vann, State Representative, are two important links in his network. They are also committeemen in the 36th Ward, and, according to several Philadelphia residents, they are Barrett's men. "Barrett elected them and he can unelect them [Lynch 1973:10]." The relationship that Barrett maintains with many officials as well as with lower-level employees in the city is not based on a mutual exchange of favors on a one-to-one basis. Barrett assumes the role of long-term creditor in providing jobs for his constituents, and they fulfill the Congressman's wishes in order to pay the debt.

A Comparison with Other Congressional Offices

Most politicians view Barrett's style of politics as the last vestige of an archaic system. He is the only ward leader in Philadelphia to "hold court" for his constituents every night (Lynch 1973:8). An administrative assistant of another Philadelphia congressman told me, "Barrett's method of handling complaints isn't necessary. The only thing he gets out of what he does is the notoriety of flying back and forth from Philly to Washington at age 76 [interview with Charles Duld, 10 July 1973]."

Although few elected officials regard Barrett's personal involvement in his constituents' problems as a model worth copying, the importance of constituent casework is undisputed. As Congressman Joshua Eilberg, a three-term Democrat from the Fourth District, succinctly put it, "Besides being very satisfying work, helping people is good politics. If a person remembers what I have done, he'll remember to vote." The importance the other three Philadelphia congressmen place on helping constituents is evidenced by the fact that they maintain large district staffs especially for that purpose. During the summer that I conducted my research I had the opportunity to compare the bureaucratic organization of two of these congressional offices with Barrett's virtual one-man operation.[8] The comparison yielded an interesting contrast in the attitudes of the congressmen toward their jobs.

[8]Most of my data are from interviews with administrative assistants to Congressmen Joshua Eilberg from Pennsylvania's Fourth Congressional District and William Green from Pennsylvania's Third Congressional District. I also personally interviewed Congressman Eilberg and Congressman Robert Nix from the Second Congressional District. However, Nix spoke with me only briefly over the telephone and would not allow me to interview any of his aides.

Congressmen Joshua Eilberg and William Green each have a staff of six people who work exclusively on constituent casework for the district. Unlike the secretaries in Barrett's office, some of these aides specialize in handling a particular type of complaint or request. The aides in both offices maintain complete records of every constituent's problem. In Green's office each problem is written on a standardized mimeographed form, assigned a number, and filed alphabetically. The number is then recorded in an index file for quick reference. Both offices produce far more paper work than is generated by either Barrett or his secretaries.

Unlike Barrett's employees, the other congressional staff members prefer writing letters to using the telephone when they are attempting to resolve a constituent's problem. An aide in Green's office explained, "That way we keep copies of everything that is done on a constituent's behalf, and our records are more complete." If Green's office does not receive a reply within 15 days after taking some action on a complaint, the file card is pulled for review in the near future. Every month the staff tallies the number of complaints and breaks them down into categories for review by the Congressman.

In addition to employing more bureaucratic procedures for handling complaints, the other two congressmen also give more authority to their district staff than Bill Barrett does. Whereas Barrett directs almost every movement in his office, the other congressmen are spared the details of the complaint-handling process. Their staffs, headed by experienced administrative assistants, are authorized to open and answer all mail, send letters in their names, and make proposals for legislation. It is revealing that Barrett chooses to call his district office workers "secretaries" whereas the other congressmen employ "administrative aides."

In spite of the seemingly business-like procedures for handling complaints in the other district offices, no other congressman claims to process as many complaints as does Barrett. Although aides to Congressmen Green and Eilberg estimate that their offices process 100 complaints a week, Barrett claims to handle at least 700 complaints and requests with the help of a staff one-half as large as that of the others.

The disparity in the results produced by Barrett's office as compared to those of Eilberg and Green might be explained best by a difference in attitude. Both of the other congressmen are concerned with maintaining a national image. As Green's administrative assistant told me, "The congressman believes that he is elected to represent the people in Washington." The aides in Eilberg's office told me it was their job to process problems related to the national government. Eilberg himself said, "Most people who come to see me fail to consider that I have only federal jurisdiction, and I usually must refer their problems to local officials." Although it later became apparent that Eilberg did process some local complaints, he does not encourage his constituents to bring all types of problems to him. Both Eilberg and Green draw the line at interceding in family or community disputes because the role of local mediator is not in keeping with their images or duties as national legislators.

The comparatively small amount of time that Eilberg and Green spend in their home districts is also an indication that they believe their most important work is in Washington. Eilberg usually flies home on Friday and meets with constituents on Saturday morning. However, all visitors are screened by his aides in advance, and meetings are by appointment only. A ward leader in Green's district admitted, "Truthfully, he comes down mostly at election time, but he does take care of us [Witkin 1972:20]." Congressmen Green and Eilberg further enhance their images as national legislators by striving to maintain good voting records in the House. In 1971 Green participated in 80% of the total house votes, and Eilberg's percentage was 84% (Congressional Quarterly Almanac 1971:95).[9] On the other hand, William Barrett's voting record for 1971 was only 63%, which was much lower than the 84% average of all Democratic congressmen that year (Congressional Quarterly Almanac 1971:95).

Conclusion

Albert Hirschman writes in Exit, Voice, and Loyalty (1970) that there are primarily two responses from dissatisfied consumers, citizens, and members of organizations: exit and voice. The dissatisfied consumer usually chooses to exit by buying a product from another company. However, in the political realm, where escape from the state is not a likely alternative, irate and unhappy citizens decide more often to voice their complaints.

The large volume of constituent casework handled by Philadelphia congressmen and the Mayor's Office of Information and Complaints indicates that residents are not reluctant to voice their problems.[10] This propensity can be explained by three factors. First, many of the citizens of Philadelphia are forced to complain, because the problems that affect them are crucial to their survival. The seriousness of their problems is reflected in the high percentage of unemployment, welfare, and housing complaints received by Barrett's office. Second, many of those who complain cannot afford to exit by moving to the suburbs, where housing is better and the crime rate is lower. Residents in three of the four congressional districts in the city have a median income below the national aver-

---

[9]The Congressional Quarterly Almanac arrives at a voting participation ratio by calculating the number of times that a Congressman votes either yea or nea. Although the Almanac warns that this method is only an approximation of an attendance record, it is the closest approach devised.

[10]With a staff of 26 members, the Mayor's Office of Information and Complaints receives 17,000 visitors a year who register complaints.

age (Boast 1972:5; Kupferstein 1972:5; Witkin 1972:5). And finally, the political ward structure provides Philadelphia residents with the means by which to complain. Residents in Barrett's First Congressional District do not have to leave their neighborhood in order to unburden themselves to a committeeman.

Barrett's system appears to be the most popular voice option in the city. The Congressman personally sees nearly 50,000 people a year at his Wharton Street office.[11] Barrett's constituents choose to wait 2 hours for a 2-minute conversation rather than exit from his complaint-taking system in order to select another voice mechanism in the city. Applying the theory of exit and voice to the service of complaint resolution, Barrett's constituents would have two options if the Congressman were unsuccessful in servicing their complaints. They could either vote him out of office or take their complaints elsewhere. It appears that the majority of Barrett's constituents have exercised neither of these options over the past 30 years.

Flexibility is the most important feature of Barrett's system, and it explains why he is more successful than any other complaint agency in the city. Unlike most elected officials or bureaucratic agencies, Barrett is willing to tackle city, state, and federal matters as well as personal and family problems. Every new complaint has the potential of changing the process and expanding Barrett's network of influence. Thus, constituents are doing more than voicing their complaints to the Congressman. They are also using voice to affect the complaint-resolving procedure. If the Congressman is confronted by a problem that his organization cannot encompass or resolve, it is an indication to Barrett that his network of influence is incomplete and that he must make new contacts. On the other hand, the system for handling complaints in the offices of Congressmen Eilberg and Green is clearly defined. If the complainant and his or her problem do not fit into the structure they have created for handling complaints, then he or she is sent elsewhere. The success of Barrett's system suggests that an effective voice mechanism must be defined by the problems with which it is confronted.

Barrett cannot afford to be too selective about the problems he decides to handle. The more services he provides for his constituents, the more contacts he acquires. The variety of people who are indebted to him ensures his success in resolving a variety of problems. Thus, the complainants and the problems they bring to Barrett shape the complaint-resolving process. If his constituents need employment, then Bill Barrett will demand that outstanding debts be paid back to him in jobs, or else he will help those who can hire his constituents.

Barrett may fail to use his influence to help a constituent when there

---

[11]This figure is a projection based on the number of complainants I observed in the Congressman's waiting room during June and July 1973.

are no political advantages in granting the favor, but he gives everyone the impression that he will try to solve each problem. He takes every opportunity to emphasize the fact that he listens to all types of complaints.

Barrett's responsive system for handling complaints contrasts sharply with those of our courts and administrative agencies. The most visible difference is the easy access Barrett's constituents have to him. Although there is often a 2-hour wait in his office, constituents can be assured of seeing the Congressman any night his office is open. They do not have to contend with busy telephone signals or crowded court calendars, nor are they required to pay for legal counsel. They know they will talk to the person in charge. In my informal survey of the people in Barrett's waiting room, half the constituents indicated that they went to Barrett because their problem required someone with influence. If they want the support and assurance of someone who is familiar with Barrett, they simply ask their neighborhood committeeman to accompany them.

Constituents of the First District may also prefer Barrett's system because they believe they have a special bargaining power with him that they could never have with civil service employees of administrative agencies. Barrett is a man who deals in votes, and they have votes to give him. This confidence—that they bring bargaining power to their meeting with Barrett—in addition to the belief that they have a right to utilize his influence gives the citizens of South Philadelphia strong reasons for choosing Barrett's service over any other.

Finally, one of the biggest advantages in going to Bill Barrett rather than to the courts is that the Congressman is often able to effect a more pragmatic solution to the constituent's problem. He is free to take into consideration the background of the parties and the circumstances involved. For example, he advised a constituent to ignore an inflated labor charge in a bill for repair of a bridge because the constituent could not afford to pay it. When Barrett bends the law for a constituent, he is essentially making a new law to fit the circumstances.

There are numerous benefits to voters in electing a congressman as attentive to their individual problems as is Barrett, but what are the costs? The most obvious criticism of congressmen who are personally involved in constituent services is that they are unable to perform adequately their "real" functions in Washington. In 1971 Barrett missed twice as many House votes as the average Democratic congressman (*Congressional Quarterly Almanac* 1971:95). His administrative assistant in Washington explained that his poor attendance record in that session was due to illness (Kupferstein 1972:8), but the Congressman's absenteeism in the past several years has been higher than average.[12] Perhaps that is the price

---

[12]The Democratic average for voting participation in the House in 1970 was 79%; Barrett's record for that year was 71% (*Congressional Quarterly Almanac* 1970:113). In 1969

to be paid for making a 280-mile round trip to the district every week night.

All of Barrett's congressional duties seem geared toward increasing his effectiveness as a problem solver at home. Important national issues must take a back seat to legislation directly affecting his constituents. One of the few times Barrett remained overnight in Washington during the period of my field research was when Congress was debating the new minimum wage bill; yet in 1971 he missed the votes on the two most celebrated national issues of the year—the war in Vietnam and the draft (Kupferstein 1972:8).

One can only speculate how much Barrett uses his vote in Congress to enable him to hand out favors at home. My data suggest that the Congressman is not above giving legislative favors to influential people who can give him the power to help his voters. Note, for example, Barrett's quick and favorable response to the supermarket executive who had jobs to give his constituents. And it is not altogether surprising that Barrett, who went on record as being strongly opposed to the construction of the Supersonic Transport (SST) (Kupferstein 1972:8)[13] was conveniently absent when a vote was taken to disapprove funds for the project. A $1,372,336 subcontract had been tentatively awarded to the city of Philadelphia for production of the SST, subject to final approval, and it is likely that Barrett would have had a hand in parceling out jobs (Kupferstein 1972:9).

The Congressman's use of the powers of his office cannot be examined justly without considering the context of Capitol Hill. The ways in which wealthy individuals and special interests have ingratiated themselves with legislators is well documented in the Nader Congress Project, *Who Runs Congress?* (Green, Fallows, and Zwick 1972). According to the study, soaring costs of campaigns have made it increasingly difficult for congressmen to remain outside the influence of those willing to line campaign coffers. Congressmen need money to pay for travel expenses and television time in order to be reelected. Special interests are willing to pay money to have "reliable" men in Congress. The exchange of money and

---

Barrett participated in 76% of the roll calls, which was well below the 85% Democratic average for that year (*Congressional Quarterly Almanac* 1969:1039). Although the Congressman's voting record was 2 points above the average in the second session of the 90th Congress in 1968 (*Congressional Quarterly Almanac* 1968:865), his record had dropped 15 points below the Democratic average in the first session in 1967 (*Congressional Quarterly Almanac* 1967:123).

[13]During the debate over the SST, Barrett stated, "This project . . . would distort national priorities for years to come. What we actually need is the construction of 26 million homes to eliminate slums and provide for our growing population . . . to help meet our national housing goals approved overwhelmingly by Congress. We are being asked now to hedge on that commitment . . . so that a few jet-setters can save an hour or two on their travels [Kupferstein 1972:8]."

favors seems almost inevitable, despite legislation curbing campaign contributions.

Barrett's organization may run on a similar theory of exchange, but with one crucial difference. Favors are exchanged for favors, and the constituent may personally benefit from the deal. Barrett consistently runs low-keyed campaigns because he realizes that his popularity with the people depends on his ability to grant them favors and to service their complaints. Thus, in exchange for backing certain legislation, Barrett gains the power to resolve his constituents' problems and stay elected. In Barrett's operation the constituent obviously gets something in return. Thus, weighing the costs and benefits of Barrett's entire organization is not a simple matter. What appears to be a cost in the context of everyday life in Washington can and very often is a benefit to Barrett's individual constituents.

Ultimately, however, Barrett's system fails simply because it does not provide for lasting change and improvement. The Congressman's organization is a responsive voice mechanism, but it resolves problems on a case-by-case basis only. For example, complaints about the Social Security Administration and the welfare department, when viewed collectively, underscore the failings of these institutions and point to areas needing improvement. However, as long as Barrett's primary goal is to service his own constituents' complaints and thereby remain in power, he has no incentive to make structural changes that would eliminate those politically valuable complaints.

And finally, Barrett's system is fragile because it depends upon the existence of one man. Barrett is at the center of a very intricate and delicate web of debts and favors. Only he can pull the strings to make people perform. His constituents are personally indebted to him rather than to his office or the Party. And, when Barrett leaves, the entire system he has spent over 30 years in building will disappear with him.[14]

References

Binzen, Peter
    1970 *White-Town, U.S.A.* New York: Random House.
Boast, Tom
    1972 *Robert N. C. Nix.* New York: Grossman Publishers.
Bulletin Almanac
    1973 Philadelphia: The Evening and Sunday Bulletin.

[14]Congressman William A. Barrett died on 12 April 1976. In final testimony to his influence and organization, he defeated his Democratic opponent by a three to one margin in a primary election that was held 2 weeks after his death (*Los Angeles Times* 28 April 1976:11).

Business Week
1971 "The fight on fraud in FHA programs." 25 September: p. 39.
Clapp, Charles
1963 *The Congressman*. Washington, D.C.: The Brookings Institutions.
Congressional Quarterly Almanac
    1971 Voting participation. Washington, D.C.: Congressional Quarterly Service 95.
    1970 Voting participation. Washington, D.C.: Congressional Quarterly Service 113.
    1969 Voting participation. Washington, D.C.: Congressional Quarterly Service 1039.
    1968 Voting participation. Washington, D.C.: Congressional Quarterly Service 865.
    1967 Voting particpation. Washington, D.C.: Congressional Quarterly Service 123.
Fagan, Irving K.
1948 "Corrupt and discontented." *Nation*, 3 July: p. 9.
Gellhorn, Walter
1966 *When Americans complain*. Cambridge: Harvard University Press.
Green, Mark; James Fallows, and David Zwick
1972 *Who Runs Congress?* New York: Grossman Publishers.
Hartwell, Dickson
1948 "Corrupt and Not Contented." *Colliers*, 7 August p. 15.
Hirschman, Albert O.
1970 *Exit, Voice, and Loyalty*. Cambridge: Harvard University Press.
Karikas, Angela
    1974 Complaint management in Philadelphia: In ethnography of a congressional district office. Unpublished undergraduate thesis, Harvard University.
Kupferstein, Linda M.
1972 *William A. Barrett*. New York: Grossman Publishers.
Kurtzman, Harold D.
1935 *Methods of Controlling Votes in Philadelphia*. Unpublished Ph.D. dissertation, University of Pennsylvania.
Los Angeles Times
1976 "Dead Man Nominated for Seat in U.S. House." 28 April: p. 11.
Lynch, Dan
    1973 "The Last Dinosaur." *The Philadelphia Inquirer Magazine*, 20 May: p. 8.
    1972 "Democrats Say John Sills is Nice Guy, Bad for Party."*Philadelphia Inquirer*, 25 June: p. B1.
Macky, Peter B.
1972 *Joshua Eilberg*. New York: Grossman Publishers.
Mann, Dean
1968 *The Citizen and the Bureaucracy: Complaint-Handling Procedures of Three California Legislators*. Berkeley: University of California Press.
Peirce, Neal R.
1972 *The Megastates of America*. New York: W. W. Norton & Co., Inc.

Pennsylvania Crime Commission
1970 Report on Organized Crime. Harrisburg: State Department of Justice.
Philadelphia Bulletin
1946 "Congress Asked to Let Italian Boy Remain." 25 January: p. 3.
1970 "Whites Barricade S. Phila. Street." 17 June: p. 5.
Philadelphia Daily News
1950   3 November: p. 21.
1957 "Congressman's Plea Freed Slayer After Board Balked." 14 March: p. 1.
1967 "Smith Blames Barrett for Bar Raids." 6 April: p. 5.
1967 "U.S. Attorney Labels Barrow a Top Crime Figure." 13 May: p. 21.
U.S. Bureau of the Census
1963 Congressional district data book (Districts of the 88th Congress): A statistical abstract supplement. Washington, D.C.: U.S. Government Printing Office.
U.S. Congressional Joint Committee on the Organization of the Congress
1965 Material prepared by Roger Davidson, David Kovenock, and Michael O'Leary for Hearings Pursuant to S. Congressional Resolution 2, 89th Congress, 1st Session. Washington, D.C.: 775, cited in Olson, Kenneth G. (1966), "The service function of the United States Congress." In The first branch, edited by Alfred DeGrazia. New York: Doubleday & Co., Inc.
Vare, William S.
1933 My forty years in politics. Philadelphia: Roland Swain Press.
Wiley, Doris B.
1973 "Judge and Councilman Accused of Election Fraud." Philadelphia Bulletin, 13 March: p. 1.
Witkin, James B.
1972 William J. Green. New York: Grossman Publishers.

10

David I. Greenberg

EASY TERMS, HARD TIMES:
Complaint Handling in the Ghetto

Introduction

This chapter seeks to explore the complaint-handling process in one inner-city, low-income neighborhood of Washington, D.C. Three separate organizations have been chosen as objects of study: Walker-Thomas Furniture, Co., an "easy credit," ghetto retail store supplying installment credit to welfare recipients and working poor people; the Neighborhood Development Center, an antipoverty, multiservice center helping individuals in a small geographic area of the city with problems ranging from welfare benefits to alcoholic rehabilitation; and the Mayor's Inter-Agency Committee to Improve City Services, a city government organization processing complaints about municipal services. The three organizations handle different sorts of problems but have in common one very important characteristic: Each is the most accessible avenue of redress for members of the community in its specific problem area.

The three groups are both in the community and of the community. Not only are they accessible; they are relevant. These remedy agents can serve their clients in simple, understandable ways; they minimize bureaucratic procedures, cultivate personal and social relationships, and avoid confusing legal jargon. The skill of these agencies in responding to low-income people within their realm of experience helps to create relationships of trust, loyalty, and dependency between complaint handler and client.

This highly informal set of relationships provides the remedy agent with a great deal of flexibility and a great deal of potential control over clients, who come to depend on the interpretations and information the agencies dispense. Thus, to most Walker-Thomas customers, the re-

NO ACCESS TO LAW
Alternatives to the American Judicial System

quirements applicable to monthly payments or repossession of goods are what the salespeople say they are, not necessarily what the District of Columbia laws state. Similarly, for many members of this community, the city's responsibilities for trash pick-up seem to proceed from the largesse of officials in the Department of Environmental Services rather than from the department's governing regulations. The informality is double-edged: Though the organizations in this study provide flexibility, they can also camouflage illegal coercive tactics and distort clients' notions of what they deserve or should expect. Which informal element comes into play—the "relevant" or the illegal—depends largely on the organizations' own institutional needs. Each group has its peculiar strains and pressures: inadequate resources, lack of power over marketplace or political forces, or the need to appear legitimate in the eyes of the community and law enforcement agencies.

Their complaint-handling techniques are rooted in these imperatives. If there is a surfeit of complaints, the remedy agency can respond symbolically, using its personal relationship with the client to assuage his or her anger about a complaint. Alternatively, the agent can manipulate "legal" requirements to make it appear that the client bears responsibility for remedying the complaint. The complaint-handling organization can also decide to select among complainants, for example, responding substantively only to those clients who might subject illegal procedures to outside scrutiny.

These characteristics and tactics exist in different proportions in the three organizations. In each, they demonstrate a sad fact of ghetto life: Not only must low-income people endure shoddy goods and inadequate services but also poor complaint handling. Both the people themselves and the institutions attempting to resolve their complaints run into the brick wall of severely limited resources and powerlessness.

A Note on Methodology

My data on the three organizations are drawn from over 3 months of field research in 1975, including interviews with staff and clients, participant observation, and analysis of relevant documents. The personnel of the first two complaint-handling agencies, and their clients are pseudonymns. For the Mayor's Inter-Agency Committee to Improve City Services and its staff and clients, actual names have been used.

The Ghetto Retail Store

Located on the Seventh Street "easy credit" corridor of downtown Washington, D.C., Walker-Thomas Furniture, Co., is a community institution of long, if somewhat notorious, standing. The retail store has survived a long series of litigations (cases bearing its name can be found in several law school texts); its owner has extricated himself from several physical attacks and robberies; and the store's former gun-packing collection manager managed to live through an often frightening 6 years of separating hundreds of Washington's inner-city poor from a fair percentage of their meager incomes.

Walker-Thomas's array of products includes living room, bedroom, and dining room furniture; major appliances, from washing machines, dryers, and refrigerator–freezers to television sets, radios, and stereo equipment; rugs, draperies, linen, blankets, wallpaper, lamps, patio furniture, cooking utensils, and even gold-plated pedestals.

The merchant markets these goods through a fleet of approximately 30 door-to-door sales representatives–collection agents who comb the neighborhoods in search of sales and payments. Combined with a substantial in-store staff, the sales force sees to it that Walker-Thomas maintains from 15,000 to 20,000 working accounts and an average yearly sales volume of $4 million. This business is derived almost completely from a very narrow clientele: welfare, Social Security, and Supplemental Security Income recipients; unemployed people; and segments of the working poor. All have one characteristic in common: an inability to obtain credit for major purchases in normal retail stores. It is to this group of people that Walker-Thomas devotes its substantial business know-how and intuition.

Monopoly

Walker-Thomas markets its goods through procedures that meet the needs of its customers. Responding to their lack of other retail credit, their vulnerability, and the day-to-day realities of life for low-income people, the merchant fashions a quasi monopoly hold over their purchasing power.

The primary need of Walker-Thomas customers is installment credit. Whereas downtown and suburban "name" stores turn away almost all unemployed and benefit-receiving credit applicants, Walker-Thomas abounds with easy credit. Its ex-credit manager, reflecting on his 6-year tenure, says that only a few dozen applicants were refused during that time (interview with Clinton Baker, 18 June 1975). In fact, credit is not merely available at Walker-Thomas; it is required. The company often tells customers that, for purchases above $100, credit is the only acceptable method of payment (Clinton Baker, 18 June 1975).

The way credit is dispensed also helps build consumer dependency: Through door-to-door salespeople, Walker-Thomas expands its geographic marketing area, widens its customer pool, and engages people in personal as well as commercial relationships.

The shopping radius of poor people is quite narrow. Community leaders stress time and again the need for residents to recognize the cheaper prices and better quality available in suburban stores and in other parts of the downtown area. In their own words, however, they fail to convince people that "stores exist outside a very small neighborhood." Walker-Thomas recognizes and utilizes this aspect of the community very effectively. The 30-odd "traveling" representatives—whose routes stretch into all four geographic quadrants of the District of Columbia and parts of the Maryland and Virginia suburbs—widen this shopping area so that Walker-Thomas often becomes the only accessible merchant of credit. Moreover, many customers who cannot or would rather not come to a store can be served in this manner, especially the elderly, the disabled, and the unacclimated rural immigrants.

The sales representative system also allows the extension of credit to many who could otherwise not qualify under normal circumstances. Most stores require customers to bring payments to the store or mail them; the burden is theirs. Walker-Thomas, in contrast, brings collection to its clientele. Collecting from people daily if necessary, Walker-Thomas reaches consumers on whom even other ghetto merchants would cast a wary eye. Federal Trade Commission interview reports reveal again and again that many customers, although unhappy with Walker-Thomas goods and services, feel that they have nowhere else to purchase needed products (Federal Trade Commission 1975).

Walker-Thomas's specialized collection procedures underlie its ability to sell to this high-risk clientele. Since its customers' prime source of income is the monthly benefits check, salespeople can schedule collections for days when checks are likely to arrive; in this way, they are guaranteed a steady source of payment—if they can get to the check before it is spent. The salespeople and postal employees therefore tend to arrive simultaneously; the salesperson then cashes the check, taking out the amount of the monthly payment. In order to conduct this service, Walker-Thomas salespeople keep on hand large amounts of cash; over $200,000 is disbursed at the beginning of each month (Clinton Baker, 18 June 1975).

This small aid is a good deal more significant than it might first appear. Not only do Walker-Thomas salespeople know the precise dates on which checks arrive, but so do other segments of the community. Unfortunately, many recipients cannot make it home with their money from the bank, credit union, or grocery store: The incidence of robberies is very high; the emotional strain and fear even greater. One community worker tells of gangs of young boys lurking outside homes for the elderly and housing projects in which mothers receiving Aid for Dependent Children are concentrated (interview with Teresa Fender [pseud.], 7 July 1975). Even when fear plays no role, convenience does; the lines begin to form at check-cashing establishments before sunrise, and the wait can take several hours (Teresa Fender, 17 July 1975).

Informality

Besides goods and services, the salespeople also provide intangible, psychological rewards for their customers. Many people are enjoying their first major purchase on credit, and the salesperson is the only link to the store and the goods. The customers naturally tend to personalize the source; thus, it is the salesperson who is providing the previously unattainable product. The salesperson, of course, takes full advantage of his or her role.

Mrs. Clark provides a good example of a new Walker-Thomas customer. She is a young mother of nine, living in a Northeast Washington housing project, supporting her family on a welfare budget of approximately $6300 per year. Because this income barely allows for rent, food, and clothing, the children sleep on floor mats instead of in beds. Mrs. Clark must also send them to school each day in dirty clothes, for she fears losing both clothes and wash money in the basement robberies her neighbors talk about.

Through her cousin, however, she meets a Walker-Thomas sales representative who says he can change all that. All she has to do is sign some papers, agree to give up a small amount of her check each month, and promise to let the sales representative know whenever she needs any other household furnishings; he will take care of the rest. Within a few days, one of Walker-Thomas's delivery trucks brings five new sets of bunk beds; after several prompt payments by Mrs. Clark, a washer–dryer combination follows. As he collects, the sales representative reminds Mrs. Clark of her newfound luck and its source:

> You know, Mrs. Clark, it sure wasn't very easy for me to talk our credit manager into taking you on. Yessir, he's a tough old bird. But I got you those beds and that fancy washer–dryer. Ever seen anything so nice? Now don't you let me down on those payments after I went out on a limb for you, hear? [interview with Mary Clark, 7 July 1975].

After such an auspicious start, the role of the salesperson continues in its exaggerated fashion throughout the collection process. He often follows up his well-placed reminders with small, inexpensive gifts for regularly paying customers (Clinton Baker, 1 July 1975), and special bargains or payment treatment for those who introduce him to friends, neighbors, and relatives.

Like the cashing of benefit checks, these things are very small on the surface but must be understood in the context of the treatment these consumers usually receive in retail stores. They are often abused and misunderstood because of language difficulties, watched suspiciously by security guards, intimidated from asking too many questions (Teresa Fender, 7 July 1975). In contrast, the Walker-Thomas sales representative is friendly, helpful, simplifying. He or she takes orders and produces goods without any effort on the customers' part, seems to understand payment difficulties, explains contractual arrangements in simple language, even keeps track of accounts in his or her notebook (Clinton Baker, 1 July 1975).

The tactics of the Walker-Thomas sales representatives add the final cement to the dependency relationship between customer and merchant. Their treatment of their low-income constituency encourages the transformation of a professional relationship into one of a highly personal, highly informal, mutually beneficial nature. Or so it would appear.

Control of Information

The personal nature of the customer–sales representative relationship touches the key to Walker-Thomas's success: the ability to emphasize the visible and informal while shifting the attention of the consumer from the structural, formal, and contractual. Utilizing the consumer's ignorance, dependency, and lack of information, Walker-Thomas obscures the governing legal rules and is able to manipulate the customer's expectations concerning total cost and financing charges, product quality, and collection requirements.

Total cost, including the very high finance charges, approaches and often goes beyond the legal limit of 30–31%, according to a Federal Trade Commission attorney (interview with Gary Laden, 30 June 1975). This total is largely irrelevant to the Walker-Thomas customer; merchant practice makes it even more so. A Federal Trade Commission investigation of Walker-Thomas reveals that many customers learn of the total cost and financing charge of their purchases long after the sales are consummated (FTC 1975:579). That transactions can be completed before such notification intimates what is important to the consumer: the monthly charge. Sales representatives mention total costs only when pressed. The upshot, of course, is that high costs and charges can go virtually unnoticed until it is too late. Thus, the sales representatives emphasize, as with one customer, the "great deal I've got for you for only $35 a month on this color TV [a set normally retailing for about $400; the customer paid, in total, over $700] [Gary Laden, 30 July 1975]."

Although product quality is naturally important to consumers, the Walker-Thomas customer has little opportunity to gain the necessary perspective from which to judge his or her purchases. Rather than using a formal system of newspaper or radio advertising, Walker-Thomas relies entirely upon word-of-mouth publicity, verbal descriptions, and salesperson promises. Door-to-door customers, by definition, cannot engage in comparison shopping (except with a catalogue that is rarely used). They tend to believe that the salesman has "just what you need." They sign a contract and receive their purchase later (as Mrs. Clark did). Mrs. Jackson told her Walker-Thomas salesman, Mr. Fritz, that she wanted a sturdy dining room set; he told her he would pick one out (FTC 1975:115). Miss Harding always allowed her salesman to choose the merchandise she purchased and to deliver it to her, sight unseen: a television set, two washers, rugs, and a deep freezer (FTC 1975:177). And Mrs. Jamieson bought two electric heaters, an electric fan, and a washing machine that were all selected and sent out to her by her salesman, Mr. Myers (FTC 1975:177).

Obviously, a pile of junk will not suffice in these situations. But this system does allow Walker-Thomas to engage in selling, quite profitably, used, repossessed, and repaired goods as new ones and in delivering products other than the ones requested by the buyers. A freezer whose promised "standard" ice-maker actually cost the customer $100 extra, and the "19-inch color TV," which was actually 14 inches, black and white, and $300 more expensive than desired, are suitable examples (FTC 1975:101).

The salesperson's unilateral control of payment collection strikes similar chords. The informal approach to missed payments often allowed by Walker-Thomas salespersons obscures the merchant's power to repossess upon customer default. Salespersons allow flexibility—up to a point—when customers can convince them of their good faith and have substantive excuses. The customer, therefore, comes to perceive a fluid, bargaining relationship rather than a strict, legal one. When Mrs. Sachs could not meet her $80-per-month payments—her welfare check was a little more than double that amount—her salesperson refused to refinance her installment contract but told her she could pay in smaller monthly amounts, which she did for a time. At a certain point, however—usually after the merchant's costs have been covered—the flexibility evaporates, much to the surprise of the customer. Thus, Mrs. Sachs watched sadly as a marshall took away a four-piece sectional couch, two table lamps, and curtains (FTC 1975:333).

That customers perceive the merchant—not the law—as arbiter emerges most clearly in situations in which they have "lost," that is, failed to convince the salesperson to extend payments. At that point, Walker-Thomas initiates all sorts of harassing activity: threatening letters, scaled on a continuum of increasing nastiness; early-morning and late-evening phone calls from the collection manager demanding immediate payment and vowing to send out the truck that very day; attempts to force payment through contacting customers' friends and relatives (whose names are conveniently provided on the "Buyer's Financial Statement," which all customers fill out before making any purchases); and repossession of goods from the customers' homes when they are absent (Clinton Baker, 18 June and 1 July 1975). After the customers revealed these tactics to me, I asked them whether the tactics were *illegal*.

They all replied, to the last one—no matter how angry or upset they may have been—"Oh, no. I missed my payments [interviews with Walker-Thomas customers, 7 July 1975]."

These informal procedures thus lay the customers' expectations at the feet of the Walker-Thomas salespersons and their individual discretion; the governing rules shift from formal consumer protection law to informal "merchant law." Mrs. Alexander, a long-time Walker-Thomas client, tells her community worker why she paid for a repair on a brand-new washing machine: "I know that the salesman told me that the washer has a six-month guarantee and I only bought it two weeks ago. But since he says I have to pay for the repair, I better do it or else he might decide to take it away [Teresa Fender, 7 July 1975]."

With its closed market, Walker-Thomas reverses the traditional relationship between merchant and customer: Here the merchant uses the resolution process to achieve his own ends rather than the satisfaction of the consumer. The complaint process serves to minimize his repair costs, insulate his tactics from outside scrutiny, and preserve an air of legitimacy.

Complaint handling plays a central role in the Walker-Thomas customer relationship for two very simple reasons: (a) the marketing process tends to create a large number of potential complaints, both through the sale of misrepresented and quickly deteriorating goods and also through the harassment of customers; and (b) the ever-present fleet of door-to-door salespersons seems to provide consumers with a costless and accessible avenue of complaint voicing. There is, of course, a tension in these two factors: If many complaints are caused and there is an easy way to voice them, then it stands to reason that Walker-Thomas will receive a veritable mountain of complaints. The company resolves this tension by using the very accessibility of the salespersons to control, both quantitatively and qualitatively, the complaint process. Specifically, complaint handling works on two levels of control: the level of consumer expectations and the level of merchant power and retribution.

Consumer Perceptions and Expectations

Consumers cannot assert warranty rights unless they are aware of them; the Walker-Thomas system tends to camouflage these protections. Hidden rights do not mean that repairs will not be made, however. On the contrary, the company repairmen are almost as accessible as the salespersons are; they often respond within several hours. But without a perception of rights, the consumer will pay for any needed repair work; the informal system transforms warranty complaints into repair requests.

When the transmission belt on Mrs. Anderson's 3-month-old washer broke three times within 2 weeks, she paid the Walker-Thomas repairman $15 each time to repair it even though the standard warranty provided for free service on all parts for 1 year (FTC 1975:32). An inadequate repair job on another washer was $36 for Miss Harding; the machine was less than 1 week old (FTC 1975:177). When the repairs are satisfactory, though, the consumer is not outraged to have to pay but rather quite pleased with the quick and efficient service rendered. Moreover, though repair charges are often illegally placed on a customer's bill, they add only marginally to monthly payments (Clinton Baker, 18 June 1975).

The informal, personal role of the salesperson also plays a large part in diffusing complaints at the level of consumer expectations. A fundamental maxim of the Walker-Thomas complaint process is that only the customer's salesperson receives complaints; anyone calling the store will be referred directly to the salesperson. This procedure brings into play an array of costless responses by the sales force.

1. *Complaint Resolution—Collection Linkage.* Whenever the salesperson receives a complaint, he always informs the customer that he will either examine the damage or malfunction on his normal collection day or else make a special exception and combine the two purposes into a dual trip. Customers thereby are reminded that the prospects for complaint resolution may very well depend on their making good their monthly payment. In this way, customers are socialized to "good" habits. Moreover, by shifting the focus from the complaint to the payment, the salesperson succeeds in making all but the up-to-date customers less secure about articulating their complaints. The informal system is likely to connect past consumer actions—payment record—with present merchant liability for complaint resolution. Therefore, the question becomes not whether the customer's complaint deserves response, but whether the customer himself deserves merchant beneficence (Clinton Baker, 1 July 1975).

2. *Consumer Internalization of Liability.* The salesman's proximity to most of his customers also allows him to know who can be convinced that product damage is customer-caused and thus that any ensuing repair is to be customer-financed. This tactic comes to the fore most frequently in complaints about furniture, some of which is purchased as damaged manufacturer seconds by Walker-Thomas and is repaired by the company's furniture finisher. When Mrs. Danton showed her broken couch to the salesman, she was greeted with the following argument:

> Hey, you know how the kids always jump around on the furniture, even though you tell them not to . . . I know, kids will be kids. Listen, I'll tell you what, he's very busy, but I think I can talk our repairman into making a special trip by here to fix this first thing tomorrow. You two can work out the terms [interview with Virginia Danton, 6 July 1975].

After hearing this logic, Mrs. Danton, although quite upset about the couch (which was barely 3 months old), wavered: "Maybe the kids did do that. . . ." And, first thing the next morning, she paid to have it fixed (Virginia Danton, 6 July 1975).

3. *The Repair or Complaint Ticket.* If the foregoing tactics do not convince consumers that the complaint is their fault, the symbolic value of the complaint ticket tends to soften any annoyance. When the salesperson responds to a complaint, no matter how seemingly small, he is required to write up a complaint ticket containing all relevant data surrounding the nature and source of the problem. The information, however, is less important than the process of collecting it.

The sympathetic and careful attention that the salesperson gives in filling out the ticket has a decidedly important purpose: It allays any hostile emotions toward the company from the very beginning of the complaint. No matter how angry, the customer cannot help but be disarmed by the serious hearing and the careful and official-looking transcription his or her complaint receives. Whatever the eventual disposition of the complaint, the ticket serves a useful function as a calming and symbolic show of company concern (Clinton Baker, 1 July 1975).

4. *Complaint Decisions.* Although salespersons receive the complaints, Walker-Thomas makes very explicit the fact that the reps do not make decisions about their resolution, that power rests with the store manager. This distribution of authority takes full advantage of the close personal relationship of the sales rep and his customer without jeopardizing it with arguments about the resolution of complaints. Salespersons, in short, can very easily appear to take the side of the customer in the dispute. After filling out the ticket, salespersons explain that, although they do not make the decision, they will attempt to exert pressure on the consumer's behalf to convince the manager to grant the repair. Even if the customer eventually receives a "TD" (turn-down), he or she often feels somewhat mollified by the salesperson's advocacy (Clinton Baker, 1 July 1975).

5. *Salesperson Financed Repairs.* If the consumer remains angry or the complaint escalates, the proximity of the salesperson allows for yet another costless response. Especially if the customer threatens to take a complaint to an outside remedy agent, the salesperson may offer to pay for the complaint himself. This offer has two possible explanations.

First, the salesperson may actually pay the repairer out of his own pocket. He might do this for a customer of long standing, many purchases, an excellent payment record, and a history of bringing new customers into the fold. The customer never fails to be touched by this action and does not neglect to tell friends, neighbors, and relatives about the special treatment from his or her salesperson. This action returns many times the small cost of the repair in good customer relations and new sales (Clinton Baker, 1 July 1975).

On the other hand, the salesperson's control of information can make it feasible only to appear to pay for the repair. For, as the FTC documents

show, Walker-Thomas salespersons commonly withhold receipts and payment books from customers; the customer, therefore, may not be able to
judge accurately the status of his or her account. In such an instance, the
salesperson merely states that he will pay for a repair that has been rejected
by the management—thereby placating the consumer—and then proceeds
to charge the customer for the repairer's services. This tactic is highly
successful in manipulating consumer perceptions and in keeping
complaint-resolution costs to a minimum—and it is illegal in addition
(Clinton Baker, 1 July 1975).

Merchant Power, Pure and Simple

When consumers know very well that they are unlikely to receive
satisfaction from the merchant, they often consider moving outside the
closed system. The company almost always attempts to prevent this action. Not only does customer contact with law-enforcement or complaint-
handling bodies threaten to expose the merchant's large illegal flank,
but it also tends to change the balance of the perceived power relationships surrounding a dispute. Consumers become less afraid and more
likely to pursue their complaints to full resolution. The head of the consumer division of a neighborhood legal services group explains:

> *Many of these consumers have little idea that they are being treated both
> unfairly and illegally. When we tell them that they are paying more than
> wealthier people pay in reputable stores, when we explain what their yearly
> finance charges actually are, and when we explain that they have often
> unknowingly been subject to illegal treatment, it usually has the effect of
> pushing them to pursue their [original] complaint—which may have noth-
> ing to do with these things—all the way down the line [interview with
> George Zweibel, 10 June 1975].*

In other words, the closed system starts to open.

In these situations the salesperson can express his power over the consumer in a subtle and personal way:

> *Hey, you don't want to do something stupid like complaining and ruin all
> I've done for you, do you? Why make your credit worse than it already is? If
> you start making trouble and we have to cut you off, then where are you
> going to go? Look's like that living room set is beginning to come apart—
> where you gonna get a replacement except from me? You don't want to spoil
> all this for yourself, now, do you? [Clinton Baker, 18 June 1975].*

This simple statement—one that the company's ex-credit manager characterizes as "company policy on complaint handling"—has the effect of
linking complaining to losing purchasing power, a cost that few consum-

ers are willing to bear for one specific complaint (Clinton Baker, 18 June 1975).

Another tactic used to cut off people's complaints from outside purview involves a threat of future inflexibility. Many consumers know that they are at the virtual mercy of the merchant in allowing them to miss payments or make partial ones. If this understanding evaporates—especially in light of the variability of these consumers' income streams—many are likely to lose their goods to the sheriff or the Walker-Thomas trucks. Most of them will not take any action likely to threaten their flexible relationships; the cost of pushing complaints too far, once again, is prohibitively high.

Yet the power of Walker-Thomas extends even beyond the products it sells. Not only does the store collect information through the sales and collection process, but it also employs six men whose express purpose is to assemble information about Walker-Thomas customers. If the company really needs to insulate a complainant, this network of employees—known in store jargon as "pimps"—can work in the following manner (Clinton Baker, 18 June and 6 July 1975).

Mrs. Arthur, a public assistance recipient, is involved in a bitter controversy over a malfunctioning color TV set: She demands to have it fixed; the store manager refuses, alleging that the set is no longer under warranty and was subject to consumer abuse in any case. Mrs. Arthur threatens to call an attorney and register a complaint with the Federal Trade Commission and does not budge before any of her salesperson's conciliatory arguments. Then one day she receives a call from her salesperson who promptly gives way to the Walker-Thomas manager. They talk for about a minute. Mrs. Arthur agrees to pay for the repair and abandon her idea of complaining to outside remedy agents.

What could have been said to sway such a recalcitrant customer in such a short time? Simple. On the basis of the pimp's information, Mrs. Arthur was informed that the management was aware of her husband's status "over the line" in Virginia (he was working at a construction site). Her continued obstinacy, the manager continued, would lead Walker-Thomas to make that information available to her social worker (whose name and telephone number were included on the Buyer's Financial Statement). Mrs. Arthur's welfare status therefore might have changed considerably, from "husband's whereabouts unknown" to that of ex-welfare recipient. With the family's sole financial support endangered—the estranged husband was not contributing anything—Mrs. Arthur chose the only rational alternative: changing her intent to contact outsiders and paying for the TV repair (interview with Jane Arthur, 22 June 1975).

Whether her welfare status actually could have been changed by Walker-Thomas's contact with the social worker is irrelevant. Drawing on Mrs. Arthur's uncertainty, Walker-Thomas succeeded in making the test of its credibility much too expensive. The store had threatened not only her goods and credit, but also the very income the family needed for food, rent, clothing. This is the full range of the merchant's power, pure and simple.

The description of this system, by necessity, has been a selective one. Walker-Thomas does resolve complaints. But, as has been demonstrated in the tactics described, one central theme stands out: Complaint handling serves the merchant's interest, which nearly always is opposed to that of the consumer.

Given past findings about ghetto merchants (Andreasen 1975; Caplovitz 1968; Magnuson 1968; Margolis 1968; Schrag 1972), the results of the Walker-Thomas complaint-handling system may not be too surprising. No one ever thought easy-credit stores had the best interests of the poor in mind. What is surprising, however, is that the same forces tend to operate, the same results ensue, from complaint-handling systems that are at least nominally designed to serve poor communities. It is to two examples of these that we turn.

The Neighborhood Service Center

The Neighborhood Development Center (NDC) stands three blocks from Walker-Thomas and serves a considerable number of the store's past, present, and future customers. According to a 1975 pamphlet describing its work, NDC is a multisocial service center supported through the United Planning Organization, the District of Columbia's federally funded antipoverty agency. The Group's staff of approximately 20 attempts to be the general complaint-handling organization for a ghetto area of 1 square mile and 24,000 population. Eight other similar centers—some publicly funded, others private corporations—exist throughout the poorest areas of Washington (interview with United Planning Organization Research Division staff, 28 January 1976).

Although the NDC assists its service area with a multiplicity of problems, my analysis will focus on only one: problems with the public benefit programs—welfare, food stamps, Social Security—which affect the ability of many low-income people to survive.

Monopoly

The NDC organizes its services and its approach to complaint handling in such a way that, like the ghetto merchant, it becomes an indispensable remedy agent with broad access to the community. The NDC's breadth, methodology, and personal treatment of clients all ensure its unique role.

Unlike most public programs, NDC treats the problems of poverty in broad perspective. Its expansive approach encompasses housing, public benefits, employment, food, education, and alcoholic rehabilitation. Theoretically, people who walk into the Center will not be turned away, whatever their problem; in fact, they are likely to receive assistance in more ways than they originally asked for. Not only is breadth important, but also approach. The Group staff helps clients in mobilizing private resources as well as in assembling the necessary documents to certify them for public aid. NDC workers even accompany particularly timid or inarticulate clients to the certification centers.

This holistic approach differs markedly from the assistance available from other forums. Many offices, like those of the Neighborhood Legal Services, require appointments and limit clients to legal questions. Others, like the District of Columbia Office of Consumer Affairs, tend to be one-problem agencies. Still others are so swamped with complaints that individual attention remains more theory than practice; all the programs of the City Department of Human Resources fit into this category.

Informality

The methodology, therefore, reflects NDC's concern for thoroughness, combined with sensitivity toward the individual's privacy. Because many female beneficiaries and applicants fear disclosing their addresses, phone numbers, and details of their personal life to public ears, the staff offices are structured to provide personal counseling rooms, contrasting sharply with the large, corral-like open spaces in the certification centers.

The NDC employs community people, and thus many of the community residents are acquainted with the staff. This familiarity is strengthened further by the NDC strategy of sending staff members door-to-door around the community actually soliciting problems, much as Walker-Thomas solicits sales. This practice provides contact with those segments of the community most in need of assistance and least likely to come to the Center: the elderly and disabled as well as people unaware of the NDC and its services. Many welfare checks and Social Security benefits are salvaged through the Group's presence in the neighborhood: The staff provides at-home assistance with rent slips (proof that the housing cost information given on aid applications is valid), instructions from social workers, and hard-to-understand letters from the Department of Human Resources (interview with NDC welfare staff, 23 July 1975).

The in-office approach to problems involves another form of discovery. Many low-income people have problems that they have no idea can be remedied; some merely misinterpret the avenues down which to proceed. Therefore, NDC personnel attempt to elicit all key information from their clients in informal converstion to make sure that no possibilities for aid remain concealed. Clients are shifted to a more expert NDC component if that becomes necessary. In this way, situations that at first seem to involve food stamp purchase prices but actually relate to a necessary upward adjustment of welfare benefits to reflect increased rent payments find their way to the most knowledgeable member of the staff (Neighborhood Development Center pamphlet, 1975).

Finally, the personal treatment and informal approach created by NDC structure and policy create a social relationship between staff and community. Many social functions—luncheons, field trips, youth gatherings—take place under the Group's sponsorship. Thus, as a professional and sociocultural force in its small community, the NDC outshines other types of assistance centers.

Control of Information

The NDC staff worker becomes the same type of complaint-handling focal point as the Walker-Thomas salesperson; all problems are directed to one problem desk. Similar, too, is the way in which the Group worker defines the problem and the possible array of responses. What seems to separate the two relationships is that Johnson Brothers explicitly pursues business goals; the NDC, on the other hand, seeks to alleviate clients' problems in their own best interests. Unfortunately, the NDC is not always free to pursue those interests.

Because it has no formal power over the benefit-granting process, the NDC, in intervening in the beneficiary–bureaucracy relationship, has developed informal problem-solving techniques; these, in turn, subject its staff to manipulation by the agencies. The NDC worker must depend on the agency worker for information about the availability of benefits, privileged access to case decisions, and personal trust and credibility in order to facilitate complaint resolution. Not only does this approach deemphasize the formal, legal relationship between the recipient or applicant and the agency, but it also affords the agency a very handy locus of control. If the community depends on the NDC to define problems, translate them to workable solutions, and smooth the process of documenting and qualifying for benefits, then agency manipulation of the NDC staff amounts to indirect control of the individuals who seek its aid, as we will see.

It is misleading to assume complicity on the part of the NDC; the problem is clearly one of inadequate structure, not intent. The Group is a reactive mechanism; it cannot grant benefits but must respond to people's problems in an ad hoc manner. In its approach to public benefit problems, then, the NDC responds to situations created by the agencies themselves.

The informal mechanisms that the NDC utilizes in solving benefit problems are symptomatic of the discretionary power of the agencies. Formal procedures are less clear in this context than in many others; strict regulations are more the exception, low-level agency discretion more the rule. In the words of a presidential commission:

> The determination of eligibility, need, and grant levels in public assistance on an individual case-by-case basis gives a great deal of discretion to officials at the lowest levels. They have the power to interpret regulations broadly or narrowly, to give or withhold assistance. Moral fitness requirements not characteristic of more impersonally run programs are often imposed, and administation of the program may be harsh and stigmatizing [President's Commission on Income Maintenance Programs 1970:244–245].

This low-level bureaucratic power allows agencies to confuse, frustrate, and "cool-out" beneficiaries and applicants to create the following sorts of problems. In each, the NDC response is necessarily an informal one.

1. *Special Access.* It often takes a client as much as 4 hours of phoning to reach his or her social worker to check on the status of a benefit application. The downtown food stamp office, for example, maintains only two public telephone lines. Knowledge and personal friendship with a social worker, however, allow NDC staffers to locate agency personnel much more quickly, often using telephone numbers unknown to the general public.

2. *Privileged Information.* Given discretionary power, public agency officials can often cut recipients from the rolls for a variety of reasons that the people themselves do not understand. To unravel these decisions, NDC staff need inside information that only the agency can provide. The recertification process provides an example.

When John Ownes returned to the Department of Human Resources office to be recertified for his family's food stamps, he answered all the questions truthfully. Yet 2 weeks later he received notification that the benefits were to be discontinued. He came to the NDC desperate, without a notion of the agency's rationale or what he should do. To uncover the appropriate information, the NDC worker had to use her personal friendship with a DHR caseworker to have the file reopened (NDC welfare staff, 19 August 1975). It turned out that a simple discrepancy in Ownes' statement about the number of people in his household—explained by his eldest son's long absences from home—convinced the certifier that he was lying, and therefore his application had been denied. Only the knowledge of whom to talk to and how to reopen the Ownes file saved the family's benefits. Moreover, had the caseworker not trusted the word of the NDC staffer, there would have been no recourse for the Owneses, for the explicit information John gave did appear to contain a contradiction of his former statement (observation, 19 August 1975).

3. *Personal Vouching.* Poor people's lives, especially in the economic sphere, tend to change very quickly; therefore, it is important to

adjust their benefits quickly, to avoid nearly catastrophic consequences. Once again, the NDC workers must rely on informal techniques.

Mrs. Green needed money to buy food for her children; that's all she was able to tell NDC staffer Jackson between sobs (observation, 19 August 1975). Mrs. Green's family had just been forced to move to a more expensive apartment and could not afford the purchase price of its monthly allocation of food stamps; her family was surviving on close to a starvation diet. Because of the increased rent, however, the Greens qualified for a reduced purchase price on their food stamps, a change that might take weeks to be approved. Miss Jackson of the NDC, through a friend among Department of Human Resources (DHR) personnel, arranged to speed the change and avoid substantial problems for the Greens. By providing an independent and trusted substantiation of the claim of increased rent, Jackson was able to avoid a multitude of forms and a long waiting period (interview with Constance Jackson, 20 August 1975).

New applicants for benefits often require the same sort of special access to avoid crises. Many potential recipients wait until the last moment to apply for aid, fearing the whole process of attempting to articulate and substantiate their claims. Once they do build up the resolve, however, they cannot afford to wait weeks for the bureaucracy to disgorge their benefits. The knowledge and connections of the NDC can be used to facilitate receipt of benefits in these situations, in effect shifting these emergency cases to the top of the agency pile. This NDC ability also becomes important when appropriate documentation cannot be found for an applicant; benefits here either can be denied or take months longer. The Group staff, however, can do one of two things: either find out what sort of alternative documentation might suffice or simply vouch for the applicant's honesty (based on prior knowledge and contact). Essentially, then, the NDC screens applicants for the agencies, taking care not to send any fraudulent cases to the certification centers for fear of losing its own credibility and access.

The combination of these forces—agency discretion and NDC personal influence—is the essence of an informal system. NDC staff workers—and therefore applicants and beneficiaries—become socialized to look to personal connections rather than to regulations. The process becomes one of the NDC staff's requesting assistance from the agency. The fact that clients may be legally entitled to benefits hardly seems to matter.

CONTROL OF AGGREGATE INFORMATION

At the base of the public agency's influence over the NDC complaint process is its ability to structure expectations and alternatives through controlling information; as intimated earlier, this control extends to the entire client population of the NDC. Three examples will illustrate.

NDC Consumer Aide James speaks of many emergency allocations supposedly available under the government welfare program: food allowances, money for furniture, clothing stipends, bus tokens, even emergency cash assistance (interview with Rev. Daniel James, 17 September 1975). Yet he admits that he cannot actually find out whether or not such allocations exist; he is forced, along with the remainder of the NDC workers, to assume that they do not. The Group's clients must obviously do the same.

Emergency food stamp allocations are also rumored to exist. These grants would cover the period between certification and actual receipt of benefits. In attempting to unravel this puzzle, James can make no headway; his social worker contacts all say that they are restricted from interviews on the subject (Rev. Daniel James, 17 September 1975).

Finally, NDC attempts to facilitate the benefit process are often stopped short by agency claims of low allocations. Mrs. Little, a NDC staff member, tells of calling a social worker again and again on an especially desperate food stamp allocation. Finally, she threatened to obstruct totally the social worker's schedule unless the benefits were speeded along. The social worker calmly replied:

> I'm sorry—we are short of stamps. Our budget was recently cut, and our allocation is very low. You can call all day long if you want, but my answer cannot help but be the same. I really am sorry [interview with Martha Little, 19 August 1975].

The effect of this statement, of course, can carry over to all the NDC's potential food stamp applicants in the allocation period. By determining what information is relayed to the NDC, the agency determines the realities of life for many needy families in the service area, for Group clients depend totally on the skills of the NDC staff. Like the Walker-Thomas customers, the applicants and beneficiaries who go to the NDC for help cannot assert rights they do not know exist.

EMPHASIS ON THE INDIVIDUAL CASE

This inability of the NDC to obtain aggregate information obviously gives broad discretion to the public aid agencies. It also determines that NDC complaint handling isolates problems from one another, developing no systematic approach or means of monitoring agency behavior. When staffers look to friends among the social workers for a key piece of inside information on how to work the system, clients begin to perceive their benefits as the result of special treatment rather than as their legal right, much as the Walker-Thomas customers may view complaint handling by their salespersons. The implications of this approach are documented by three NDC cases in September 1975.

Several welfare recipients came to the NDC with letters from the DHR (Department of Human Resources) stating that unless they could produce copies of their medical records (or physical exam reports), they would be dropped from beneficiary status. The communications gave them 6 days to do so. As it turned out, this demand was literally impossible to meet. D.C. General Hospital—where the data had to be gathered—was booked solid with appointments and record requests such that the backlog was at least 6 weeks. Thus, when Alvin Stone and George Caron were asked to produce exam reports by the end of September, the first available appointments were for October 26 (Rev. Daniel James, 17 September 1975).

From available evidence, these demands were not the result of a bureaucratic oversight. D.C. General Hospital is an arm of the DHR, the department that distributes welfare benefits. As the chief social worker at D.C. General told the NDC staff, the impossible demands did not reflect poor intradepartmental communications: "The welfare people have been warned and warned about how long things take here. Every caseworker over there knows better. But they do this all the time [Rev. Daniel James, 17 September 1975]."

The hospital official's comment intimates that the threatened cutoffs are a general policy. As the statement was made to a NDC staffer, the Group knew this to be the case, and yet its response to the two specific cases was flavored by the individual and the informal. In one case, a NDC consumer aide posed as a social worker at the hospital in order to obtain a rush copy of the medical records. In the other, he haggled with the beneficiary's caseworker to grant a special exception and extend the deadline for the documents in line with reasonable appointment dates. Only deception and begging, then, kept two legally qualified beneficiaries from arbitrary loss of their aid (Rev. Daniel James, 17 September 1975). The NDC, in rising to the emergency for two clients, failed to recognize that this tactic also might be affecting many other beneficiaries in Washington.

In a similar example, the NDC relied on private resources in the face of a tortuously slow agency response to qualified recipients. Two very old, largely incapacitated married couples who applied for welfare aid were not granted it for over 5 months whereas normal waiting periods are approximately 3–4 weeks (Rev. Daniel James, 17 September 1975). The NDC staffers suggest that this tactic is quite common; the process is so slow, they say, because elderly people cannot go to the certification centers to create personal advocacy for their applications (NDC welfare staff, 20 August 1975). But while acknowledging this pattern of agency unfairness, the NDC responded by mobilizing private aid rather than by demanding more efficient and equitable agency practices. Staff workers went to churches to obtain furniture, depleted the small NDC food and clothing banks, and even paid incidental expenses out of their own pockets (Rev. Daniel James, 18 September 1975). Although admirable in its concern to keep these couples afloat, the NDC helped to obscure the source of the problem: the public aid agency. For if agencies can rely on the NDC and similar groups to provide private support, the agencies will not need to improve their benefit-granting procedures. Delaying benefits in this manner is not a new idea; in the late 1960s a New York City Budget Memo suggested that, in order to save money on welfare expenditures, "the departments build up the maximum legal backlog between intake and final determination of eligibility [Pivens and Cloward 1971:147–148]."

The last instance of NDC response to problems with known widespread effects involves the arbitrary definitions of "employability" used to strip recipients from the rolls. The NDC staff describes the continual flow of 40- to 50-year-old men cut off under this redefinition. As one of the Group's employment experts expostulated:

> There is no way anyone is going to hire these men. I have tried everything I know, used every resource I can think of . . . I challenge the DHR to find them a job [Little, 20 September 1975].

Yet implicitly, the NDC accepts the definition imposed by the Department. For when the men come to the Group for assistance, staffers do not try to have their benefits reinstated. Instead, they search vainly for jobs they know are not available. The men are thrust on the community with predictable effect: Without any job or means of public support, the men will turn to small crime. Not stealthy enough or even physically strong enough for major crime, they make a paltry living stealing from local stores and newsstands (selling papers at half price) or as couriers in the numbers racket (NDC welfare staff, 19 August 1975).

NDC staff workers realize and admit that the reinstatement process would be both time-consuming and harmful to their own good relations with the agency (observation, 7 September 1975). Accepting the agency's arbitrary and demonstrably inaccurate definitions, then, is the most "rational" NDC response. The NDC implicitly participates in the shifting of public responsibilities onto the meager resources of the neighborhood. Only the myopia of this informal system could make that appear "rational."

THE INFORMAL SYSTEM IN REVERSE

As can be seen, many of the tactics of the NDC depend on the good graces of agency personnel; with no formal power, the success of Group complaint handling depends on the virtual whim of the benefit bureaucracy. The agencies can easily turn off the informal spigot. This possibility may explain the NDC reluctance to pursue certain complaints, for to fight too hard may be to upset one's perilously privileged position.

Staffers say that they perceive a schizophrenic response on the part of the agencies: Sometimes the friendliness and willingness to provide help turns quite cold. Old acquaintances suddenly become distant and non-committal. Easy access is transformed into a series of unreturned phone calls and unanswered questions. Connections into the guts of benefit agencies instantly, and without apparent cause, change to fuzzy messages about long lunches, vacations, and staff meetings (NDC welfare staff, 19 August 1975). Consumer Aide James, for example, in trying to uncover the reason for particularly long food stamp certification periods, was told by a social worker friend—one who regularly helps him out—"I'm sorry, I cannot give you an interview on that. I am instructed not to speak about the issue [Rev. Daniel James, 18 September 1975]." This type of closing off leaves the NDC with no real means of problem resolution except through private resources.

Agencies can create a similar effect by personally intimidating applicants and beneficiaries. By handling them in such a way that they will not come back to the public office, agencies utilize the NDC to avoid depleting their own budgets.

Mrs. Biggs provides a case in point. She needed bus fare to transport her two young grandchildren back to their home in North Carolina, something her $35-per-week income would not provide. She came to the NDC for help, explaining that the boys lived with her parents (their great-grandparents), very simple people who would not tolerate any type of "welfare" investigation. She therefore asked NDC's James to help her obtain funds for the trip without any such investigation. James wrote a very explicit note to that effect to the appropriate DHR official, offering to utilize the services of a local clergyman who knew the family well and could vouch for the home's "suitability." When Mrs. Biggs arrived with the note, she was told that an investigation would be conducted (contrary to the official's earlier promise to James on the phone). Frightened, Mrs. Biggs left and returned to the NDC office; she told James that under no circumstances would she accept DHR funds, for she feared her parents' reaction to the threatened investigation. Rather than questioning the official's purposeful scare tactics, James merely arranged the aid through a local, private charitable organization (Rev. Daniel James, 18 September 1975).

Other agency tactics create the same effect: Applicants who are refused information and assistance at certification centers refuse to go back, considering it a waste of time and effort (observation, 16 September 1975); are made to wait hours for certification, only to be told that they have no appointment or lack the appropriate documentary evidence (observation, 12 September 1975); and are refused access to the social worker handling their case. When they come to the Center for help, they often refuse to go back to the agency alone, demanding that a NDC staffer accompany them (observation, 19 September 1975). That, of course, would be a large drain on NDC resources; it seems much more rational to look for available private means.

The unwitting effect, however, is to absolve public agencies of their responsibilities while implicitly condoning their delaying and abusive tactics. Here, then, the agency can raise the costs of problem solving to the point that NDC has neither the time nor the incentive to bear them.

The NDC system of complaint handling begins to resemble a political machine. In order to retain specific services for its constituency, the Group must give up any designs on policymaking or aggregate issues. Individual complaints are solved—at the agencies' discretion—as far as agency resources allow. But the choice is the agencies', not the NDC's, nor is it the clients'.

All the NDC power is derivative in nature: The agency giveth and taketh away; NDC must accept the agency rules of the game, which ultimately serve agency interests. In the end, the overall power position of low-income consumers of government benefits—as well as the material benefits they derive—looks unfortunately similar to that of Johnson Brothers' customers.

The City Government Complaint Handler

On Wednesday afternoons, the NDC office clears out early, as many of the staff members travel several blocks to the Anthony Bowen YMCA for the weekly meeting of the Mayor's Inter-Agency Committee to Improve City Services.

Created in 1970 by Mayor Walter Washington, the MICICS divides the District of Columbia into nine separate service areas, each with its own service area committee (SAC). Each committee meets weekly in its own area, bringing together primarily city agency representatives and leaders of community organizations. Chaired by members of the Office of Community Services, the Mayor's appointed public liaison group, these meetings have broadly stated goals: "Improving service delivery at the neighborhood level, increasing effectiveness and efficiency of government, and insuring and increasing the responsiveness of government to citizens [District of Columbia Office of Planning and Management 1974]."

Service Area 6 includes both the NDC and Walker-Thomas. One of the poorest areas in Washington, it contains a disproportionately large percentage of the city's poverty-level citizens and benefit recipients. Nearly 55% of the area 6 residents live in households whose yearly income is less than $7000 (D.C. Government 1975).

The poverty of this community is matched by its city service deficiencies. Week after week the same problems come to the attention of the SAC: abandoned cars, alleys and vacant lots full of trash, streets in serious need of sweeping, clogged sewers, large bulk trash littering front yards and sidewalks. In three SAC 6 meetings of late July and early August 1975, 47 such complaints were registered, largely from one part of the area; by mid September, only three had been resolved (observations, 30 July–17 September 1975).

Such results contradict the SAC image as the major forum for government–citizen interaction, and yet its legitimacy remains intact. In Service Area 6 at least, the SAC constituency, structure, and approach explain this contradiction.

Monopoly

The Service Area Committee holds a monopoly on its specific brand of complaint handling of city service problems. Aside from being the only "official" body designed to treat such disputes, the SAC creates an approach that compliments the needs and experience of its complainant group, the leaders of community organizations.

Access to local decision makers has long been a major priority of low-income groups; many studies document the detailed strategies leaders of poor neighborhoods use to gain the attention of city officials (see Alinsky 1946 and 1971; Lipsky 1970). The SAC resolves this problem: Access is systematized. Wednesday afternoons brings government officials to the community. City publications suggest using this easy alternative to individual agency channels (D.C. Government 1975).

SAC structure allows for a necessary "whole community" approach to problems. The wide range of departments on the roster resembles the one-stop shopping provided by Walker-Thomas. Furthermore, the SAC creates a personal, face-to-face relationship between citizens and bureaucrats, one designed to provide greater acountability from the agencies. When presented with a problem, the departments in theory cannot shift the complainant from office to office. The same representative from each city department is supposed to attend the SAC meetings each week.

This personal contact tends to create greater understanding and flexibility in the representatives of both the agencies and the community; social relationships also become important. Many of the city representatives are community people, old friends or schoolmates of the organization leaders and workers. First names are the rule; the chairperson corrects any new participants on this point. The social atmosphere of the SAC is underscored by its use as a forum for intraneighborhood communication about community events and private gatherings. Finally, group cohesion flows from the chairperson's continual search for unifying issues and opportunities to stress solidarity. Long, wandering group discussions, seemingly irrelevant to the purposes of the SAC, serve this purpose (observation, 27 August 1975).

The key element in the structure of the SAC shows through this quest for unity: The SAC is geared to serving not only the complaint-handling needs of the community but, more particularly, the personal needs of the community's leadership. The two, unfortunately, are not always the same.

Informality

This concern for the temperament of community leadership hints at the informal nature of the SAC. The uneven participation of both agencies and neighborhood representatives combines with the SAC approach to servicing complaints to create an informal, bargaining environment.

Community participation in the SAC remains largely a narrow one. The area contains over 80,000 people, and yet many of the meetings are dominated by the representatives of three or four neighborhood organizations who often comprise 80% of the attendance. Their concerns, quite naturally, relate to the problems in their immediate area. Groups and organizations that choose not to participate on a regular basis provide their constituents with inadequate representation before the city government. Thus, although the SAC purports to deal with problems of the entire service area, its actual work relates to the needs of a much smaller part of that area.

City agency representation is also less certain than might be expected in a face-to-face organizational scheme. On the average, 11 of the 25 SAC agencies are absent from a given meeting (observations, 30 July–17 September 1975). Among the most frequently absent are departments that tend to receive a large number of complaints: Environmental Services (responsible for trash hauling and street cleaning), three absences out of eight meetings in the sample; Department of Human Resources, three absences; National Capital Housing Authority, four absences; Police Department, five absences; and Social Security Administration, six absences. Obviously, this attendance record weakens the personal accountability model on which the SAC stands; it also makes personal connections and access to departments outside the auspices of the SAC more important.

SAC procedure adds to the informal process. All complaints are treated in a nonhistorical, value-free manner; the edict of "first complain, first served" seems to operate. No matter what a given situation's history or circumstances, it is designated, at first mention, a "new request for services" (SAC 6 Minutes, 30 July–24 September 1975). This definitional scheme seems to give implicit approval to any past inadequate and unequal service patterns by the agencies, and it combines with the unequal representation of neighborhoods and organizations before the SAC to allocate greater attention and resources to those most often present.

The day-to-day experience of community representatives reinforces the informal atmosphere. Leaders of organizations like the NDC have learned that making friends in agencies and discovering bureaucratic pressure points produce results. Their sophistication, therefore, suggests the need to drive hard bargains rather than to rely on "paper" rights.

Although this perception could lead to an adversary approach to government representatives, it normally gives rise to mutual trust within the SAC. Community leaders listen to good excuses and accept partial, good-faith responses from the officials they work with from week to week. When presented with over 20 complaints about trash service, Mr. Johnson, the Department of Environmental Services (DES) representative, described eloquently the pressures on him, his long hours, and the difficulties of navigating the turgid departmental waters. His statement received sympathy and a cautious word for maintaining the good relationship the community leaders had developed with him. As one of them said, "The man's trying, we must see that. We better understand what a hard job he has, how hard he's trying or else we'll end up with someone who won't even explain himself [observation, 6 August 1975]."

The informal environment stresses requests rather than demands, explanations rather than strict accountability: "Please, Mr. Johnson, if you can't do something about these things, don't promise that you can. We've heard too many promises. Just give it to us straight [observation, 6 August 1975]." Here again, the legal responsibilities of the department do not seem to matter; perceived fairness instead dominates. Although Mr. Smith of the NDC stated that his purpose at the 6 August meeting was "to force the DES to pick up the trash," he accepted the agency counteroffer to clean the alleys but not the vacant lots. And in response to Elder Parker's request for four trash cans for a certain block, the DES's willingness to provide only two was accepted by a consensus of the meeting (observation, 6 August 1975).

Perhaps the prime example of the informality of the SAC system is the practice of agency representatives to disclaim responsibility for problems outside their own personal jurisdiction. Mr. Johnson of the DES forswore liability for his department's lax street-sweeping, claiming "I'm just the solid waste man, you can't blame me for that. You better talk with someone else if you want some answers [observation, 6 August 1975]." And, according to SAC minutes, Officer Ewing of the Metropolitan Police Department turned away Elder Parker's request for increased surveillance of street gambling, stating that "Elder Parker should contact First District Headquarters as that area is not part of the Third District." [observation and SAC 6 minutes, 13 August 1975.]

These statements contradict the purpose of the SAC, which is to bring citizens into contact with *representatives* of the city agencies directing services; no one expects the individual representative to have complete knowledge or answerability for his or her department, but he or she is supposed to channel complaints to the appropriate official and then to inform the SAC of the agency response. Here, though, the officials refused this referral role, preferring instead to delve into the informal realm of "blame." Thus, not only does the SAC system tend to obscure the formal relationships between agency and citizen—witness the foregoing excuses and partial remedies—but it even violates its own internal rules. Yet, to the participants, this informal system must appear rational and fair; community leadership did not object one bit to the blanket refusal of accountability by agency representatives.

Control of Information

In late July, Mrs. Anderson *asked* whether the DES trucks were authorized to pick up the trash in the alleys. At the same meeting, Mr. Hines *suggested* that weekly street and alley cleaning were needed in his part of the service area (observation, 30 July 1975). The next week, Elder Parker *demanded* weekly services for his Ridge Street blocks (observation, 6 August 1975). All of these requests or demands were completely removed from the issue of what the agencies *owe* the community. The approach of the community leaders leaves complete discretion to the agencies. The relationship is reduced to one of power: The DES can either respond or refuse; the community must either accept the result or try to force a different one. In any case, the relationship is removed from the most appropriate context—that of government responsibility—to the most beneficial one for the agencies—that of governmental discretion.

The informal quality of the aforementioned requests flows directly from consumer ignorance of the services to be provided—when, where, and how they are supposed to occur. One of the major problems in the community is how to dispose of large bulky items like old furniture and used major appliances. Very specific DES procedures for removing such trash exists: "Bulk" removal takes place on Wednesdays for large wood and nonmetal items; "white" removal, on the other hand, is available by request only for metallic items such as refrigerators and washers. This distinction was revealed at the 6 August meeting; not one of the community leaders present had fully understood that before (observation, 6 August 1975). It seems safe to assume that the residents' tendency to throw these large items onto vacant lots and curbs and into alleys was a direct result of this ignorance.

This consumer ignorance, more insidiously, is coupled with a repeated failure of agencies to respond to requests for information. The clearest example involves the trash removal schedules and regulations which would have eliminated a major area of ignorance. Five years of SAC meetings are virtually littered (an appropriate term) with requests for the distribution of these printed schedules (SAC 6 Minutes, 1971–1975). In 1975, the first such request came on April 2 (SAC 6 Minutes, 2 April 1975). On 23 April, as part of a demonstration project, SAC assigned the agencies the task of advertising their schedules through leaflets, postcards, and the media

(SAC 6 Minutes, 23 April 1975). Yet on 6 August, the leaders of the area community still did not know how to dispose of bulk trash. Elder Parker asked for schedules on 6 and 20 August, and Mrs. Jackson asked for them on 27 August (observations, 6, 20, and 27 August 1975). But through the end of September, none had been distributed (SAC 6 Minutes, 10, 17, and 24 September and 1 October 1975).

Neither do people understand the division of responsibility between agency and community. They cannot fulfill obligations of which they are not aware. References to the care of tree boxes—the unpaved areas at the base of trees that line the streets—dot the minutes of the SAC meetings of late summer 1975. In each instance, both the community leaders and the agency representatives seemed to accept the premise that tree-box maintenance was the responsibility of the city. Mr. Smith announced that the tree boxes in his area had been cleaned the week of 30 July; he thanked the city for prompt attention (observation, 30 July 1975). Elder Parker noted the need for tree-box cleaning in his area on 13 August; the complaint was promptly referred to the Department of Transportation, whose representative, Mr. Hairston, acknowledged it (observation, 13 August 1975).

At the 10 September meeting, however, a group of citizens in a very large area requested that all tree boxes in their neighborhood be cleaned. At that point, the agencies and the chairperson revealed that the tree boxes were actually the legal responsibility of the individual owner or tenant; therefore, the city would not respond to the request (observation, 10 September 1975). Yet for 5 weeks (and presumably much longer), specific requests had been met by the DOT without a whisper of this responsibility. It seems, then, that at times the ignorance of the community can become too expensive.

Just as the leaders attempt to obtain information, they also seek perspective from which to judge agency service. One of these attempts came in late September, as Mrs. Cress questioned the city DOT representative about his department's activities in the city as a whole. In the end she asked, "Do you provide the same services in Georgetown and on Capitol Hill that you provide here? Do they have to scream and beg every week like we do?" The SAC chairperson refused to allow a response, shifting the meeting to a minor procedural issue. When Mrs. Cress continued to press her demand for a response, the chair instructed the DOT representative to bring to the next meeting copies of his agency's regulations. Mrs. Cress interrupted, stating that her query remained unanswered. The chairperson then suddenly retook the floor, accused Mrs. Cress of wasting valuable time, and banned the topic—all highly out-of-character procedures for these normally informal meetings (observation, 10 September 1975). Mrs. Cress had raised the issue of selective delivery of services, and the chairperson did not care to discuss it. The closed system does not allow for such comparisons.

A fairly strong argument can be made on the basis of the nearly 50 unresolved complaints mentioned earlier (only 3 of 47 were responded to) that municipal services demanded outnumber services within the agencies' resources as allocated. The inadequate trash services, for example, appear to be caused systematically by the patterns of pick-up within the Department of Environmental Services. The DES representatives to the SAC have little or no effect on those patterns; any complaint handling they can provide must come only at the margins of service, only where no expensive shifts or changes in services are required. Ultimately, the SAC must work within priorities and service patterns established by higher officials. It cannot create more resources, nor can it magically create efficiencies that will solve what is a fiscal and political problem.

What it can do is change people's perceptions of what the government should provide and to whom; manipulate the informal SAC relationships to produce rifts within the community and competition for a finite amount of services; and take care to preserve its own legitimacy through a show of forceful complaint resolution in a limited, well-chosen, and relatively costless manner.

VICTIM BLAMING

Dependent on the agencies' discretion to resolve complaints and lacking information about the levels of service they should expect, the community leaders in SAC 6 are reduced to convincing agencies that their requests are fair. In this context, a definition of fairness excludes those instances in which the community has not upheld its part of the bargain, not fulfilled its proper responsibilities. Therefore, the agencies can avoid complaint handling by blaming inadequate services on community deficiencies.

Lack of citizen participation is a frequent example of this very concept. In reference to the trash-filled vacant lots in parts of the service area, DES representative Johnson commented: "There is just no way, no how to eliminate this problem without community participation, and we're not getting any [observation, 10 September 1975]." The real source of the problem, however, already has been revealed: The community, unable to find out either the procedures or the times for removal of bulk trash items, inevitably deposits them in vacant lots and alleys.

The DES accused another part of the community, the Ridge Street residents, of being unable to learn the difficult art of putting trash into cans. Again, Mr. Johnson: "Folks just won't containerize," he replied to questions concerning the department's failure to maintain a decent level of trash removal in the area. "The alleys, vacant lots, tree spaces: They're all full and we just can't handle it when it gets that far," he continued (observation, 10 September 1975).

In reality, the Ridge Street area was not being given the opportunity to "containerize." Elder Parker literally begged for four trash containers for the street during the 6 August meeting, but his request was slighted by

Mr. Johnson. Mr. Johnson's explanation for the denial points to a reason far different than the community's inability to negotiate throwing away garbage: "Not only are we already overextended in our capability to pick up the trash, but those containers are expensive, easily stolen, and frequently torn up [observation, 6 August 1975]."

The problem seems to be one of agency priority, not community deficiency. Johnson's accusation, however, pinpoints the character traits of the low-income residents of Ridge Street. Not only are they being blamed, but the inadequate trash removal is being justified on that basis. On reflection, this ability to blame the community—thereby saving agency resources—resembles Walker-Thomas's ability to save money on repairs by convincing consumers that product malfunction is their own fault. In both instances, the informal system subjects people's expectations to outside control.

DIVIDING THE COMMUNITY

The residents of Ridge Street became embroiled not only with the DES but also with representatives of other areas of the city. The understanding attitude that community leadership commonly exhibits toward the agencies correlates strongly with the complaint-handling response they themselves receive. Thus, although the Ridge Street residents berated the DES representative, the members of another area took up the agency cause (manifesting the victim-blaming approach): "You all know why the man can't do the job over there. It's your own fault. You gotta clean up the community yourself first. That's what we did. Don't be crying to him." Yet, as demonstrated earlier, the Ridge Street problem was largely one of too few containers for too much trash and lack of information on how to dispose of large items. The agency position, though receiving only partial community support, won out in the SAC informal decision-making process (observation, 6 August 1975).

An interchange between two leaders of different sections of the area illustrates the method to this intracommunity madness. The leaders of the better-served neighborhoods have little patience with the demands and threats of the poorly served; the service pressures and tight resources of the agencies are made quite explicit, and the leaders perceive that only resource shifts, not expansion of services, are possible. Because gains in service to one part of Area 6 are perceived to come only at the loss of service to other areas, the leaders of different areas often become adversaries.

In the context of the tree-box debate, one lady commented, "That's not the way we operate . . . you can't always expect others to do things for yourself. . . . Can't always expect the city to do it." Amidst general smiles from the chairperson and the agency representatives, a young man pointed out his neighborhood's dilemma: "I'd just like you to explain, ma'am, how you expect my people to clean tree boxes when they don't even know they're supposed to, when no one advises them of their responsibility. You know, we all don't have it as easy as you, ma'am." Though the issue was dropped for the moment, the meaning of the young man's statement was illustrated in the complaint section of the meeting. As the chair opened the floor to complaints and requests, the heavy-set woman just quoted was the first to raise her hand and be recognized. She was greeted by the chairperson in the following fashion: "I see, Mrs. Brown, that, as usual, you have your list all ready." She then proceeded to read several specific complaints and service requests from a yellow pad. The requests were received, acknowledged, and acted upon within a week (observation, 10 September 1975).

It is within the agencies' power, therefore, to define some complaints as acceptable and others as unacceptable. While one segment of the community is denied resolution for questioning overall departmental policy and information control, another is rewarded—by expeditious resolution of specific complaints—for siding with the agencies. Within this system, then, it becomes quite clear which is the more productive action. Without any power, the community must play within the rules of the agencies or else go unheeded and unserved.

LEGITIMACY: THE BURST-OPEN COMPLAINT

Perhaps the most telling example of how the SAC applies its selective brand of definitions is the Community Educational Demonstration Project. One of the subcommittees of the SAC, the Cleanup Subcommittee—headed by DES representative Morgan—found evidence of systematic service deficiencies and agency laxity in many parts of SAC 6. Its ultimate response—the proposed resolution of the problem—focused on only one part, Ridge Street.

Ridge Street, it will be remembered, was the street a group of residents attempted to improve by requesting more containers, alley cleaning, and removal of bulk trash. The Ridge Street representatives were rebuffed and accused of creating the problems themselves through lack of cooperation and "containerization" skills (observation, 6 August 1975). What separated Ridge Street from other denied complaints, however, was Elder Parker. Parker harped on Ridge Street week after week, collecting information, soliciting promises of citizen support for a cleanup campaign, and even calling agency people during the week. Slowly, the SAC–agency approach began to change (observations, 30 July–17 September 1975).

The specific complaints about Ridge Street were originally contained in a list of over 20 problem areas drawn up by the Cleanup Subcommittee, with no special priority attached to any of them. None of the other problems was ever mentioned again during the 6 weeks of my study, but Parker never quit screaming about Ridge Street.

The watershed came with the unveiling of the Community Educational Demonstration Project, a multiagency effort directed at just one area: the Ridge Street blocks (SAC 6 Cleanup Subcommittee, 27 August 1975). Although the chairperson had received the original complaints about Ridge Street quite calmly (saying nothing), as soon as it became defined in this special role, he stated: "The filth of Ridge Street is a deplorable condition demanding quick and effective action; that's what this project will give us."

The agencies also promised to redouble their efforts a scant 3 weeks after the area had been refused additional trash containers. The following tree-box discussion between Elder Parker, the chairperson, and the DOT representative is illustrative:

> DOT: *How many tree boxes need to be cleaned?*
> PARKER: *About five on the south side of the street.*
> DOT: *Only five? I thought there were about ten. . . . You only want me to do one side of the street?*
> PARKER: *Look, I counted the ones needing work and there's—*
> CHAIRMAN: *(breaking in) Pete, can you do them all?*
> DOT: *Sure, we might as well get them cleaned up and put this whole thing in order."*

Those at the meeting ignored the fact that an educational project should not undertake misleading activities like cleaning areas that are the responsibility of the residents and the fact that there were other, more pressing problems within two blocks of the demonstration project: clogged sewers, piles of trash rotting in alleys, vacant lots full of broken-down cars, and abandoned refrigerators. Unfortunately, they received no special mention or attention (observation, 10 September 1975).

Once the demonstration area was designated, it became a symbol of the SAC and its legitimacy. With the entire institutional ego of the organization invested in the Ridge Street area, any threats to the importance or viability of the project received quick rebuffs. The Department of Licenses and Inspections, as its part in the multiagency effort, was assigned "vigorous enforcement" of the housing code on the block (SAC 6 Cleanup Subcommittee, 27 August 1975). Someone, however, brought up the serious question: What if the multiple code violations of an absentee landlord caused the eviction of extremely poor Ridge Street residents? The chairperson quickly and strenuously pointed out that the city's ample relocation funds could be used to remedy that possibility should it arise. The only problem, though, as Mr. Sims of the Center City Community Corporation pointed out, was that there was literally no place to relocate to: Other private housing was too expensive for the people in the area, and the city Housing Authority had a 3- to 5-year waiting list for public housing.

The chairperson had absolutely no answer; his desire to further the project left him completely vulnerable. Finally the Licenses and Inspection representative admitted lamely that displacement was extremely unlikely to occur: His resources limited him to a very superficial inspection; only those people actually requesting an inspection would receive one. The vigorous enforcement had disappeared (observation, 10 September 1975).

The redefinition of the Ridge Street problem brought with it an increasingly complicated analysis of the source of the problem. From lack of citizen participation and an inability to throw away trash properly, the SAC focus shifted to the gambling taking place in a vacant house on the street (which Elder Parker had also been emphasizing for several weeks). Letters were drafted from the SAC to the Mayor, police chief, and precinct captain calling for more police activity in the area. DES representative Morgan, speaking for the Cleanup Subcommittee, labeled the gambling the "major problem, in need of drastic action." When asked to explain the new emphasis on gambling and why the ring had not been broken up earlier, the chairperson explained that such action was extremely difficult: The owner of the house had to be found, a delicate strategy planned, various agencies notified.

At that point, a wizened old man stood up and put the situation, the demonstration project, and the entire SAC mechanism into perspective:

> I just don't understand all this. You say you got a gambling problem and the gambling goes on in a vacant house. Well, I'll tell you something—I'm no saint. I guess I've done about all the things that a man can do, gambling included. No sir, I've lived in this city all my life, wasn't just born yesterday.
>
> Yeah, I play some poker; win a little money, too. We play in a nice residential house, nice neighborhood . . . not making too much noice, not bothering anybody. But the police can break down the door, mess up the game, throw us in jail—like they've done coupla times. Kick in the door is what they do.
>
> Now you say you got a tough problem with them guys gambling on Ridge Street—playing cards, shooting dice in a vacant house. You also say it's bothering the neighbors, teaching bad habits to the kids, somehow keeping the trash from being picked up and the alleys from getting cleaned, although I don't quite understand how. You even tell that there's been some shooting going on . . . that somebody might get hisself killed one day.
>
> Now if the police can come in and kick the damn door down on our game—the one that's not bothering anyone—how come they can't do the same thing with this one? Hell, this place don't even have no doors or windows . . . police can just walk right in. Seems to me that they could do it today and that they coulda done it a long time ago if they or anyone else had wanted [observation, 10 September 1975].

The old man made a lot of sense; no one listened. They dismissed him as unsophisticated and went back to their complex plans.

As demonstrated by the selective treatment of certain groups and the exaggerated attention given to the Demonstration Project, complaints are more important in source than in substance. The needs of a particular neighborhood for trash service are weighed according to its leaders' ability to make those needs too costly for the agencies to ignore. In the end, only the most capable and persistent individuals—like Elder Parker—succeed. The result, as in his case, is often cooptation: His considerable organizing skills were utilized to mobilize support and provide coordination for a largely symbolic project—a project, ultimately, that drew attention away from the wider needs of the community.

Ultimately, the SAC, as a complaint handler, cannot face those needs and survive as an institution. The agencies simply do not have the resources required to alleviate service deficiencies for Washington as a whole. The SAC cannot create those resources. Its only other choice is to create an atmosphere in which minimal treatment of complaints is achieved.

Conclusion

The chief finding of this analysis should be clear by now: Complaint handling serves the needs of ghetto stores, the social agencies, and the city departments rather than those of low-income people. Beyond this central conclusion, though, three broad themes emerge that help bring this case study into overall perspective: (a) Many personal characteristics imputed to low-income people actually, when viewed from inside these relationships, represent rational responses on their part to the power and opposing interests of the institutions they deal with; (b) these institutions use complaint handling to serve interests and meet constraints imposed on them from outside by larger social forces; and (c) any actual change in levels of satisfaction for the complainants will probably come not from improvements in complaint handling but rather from different social choices.

Consumer Characteristics

Low-income consumers appear to be characterized by apathy, lack of public orientation, and irrational fear. All three organizations in this complaint-handling saga of low-income consumers seek to reduce costs to themselves through an array of techniques: defining away complaints through selective control of information, making successful voicing of complaints too costly to pursue, and threatening to eliminate goods and services to their consumers. In turn, consumer reactions to these organizational tactics seem to demonstrate personal deficiencies on their part.

All the systems provide accessible and simple mechanisms for complaint voicing. Through experience, however, consumers learn that the costs, ultimately, are too great in relation to the benefits derived. Although the ghetto merchant responds quickly to complaints, he also imposes large costs (often unperceived) for such service. One long-time customer, aware of the charges for repair service, continues to buy from Johnson Brothers but refuses to complain: "It always ends up costing me too much," he explains (FTC 1975:187). City welfare agencies raise the costs of voicing by confusing or by ignoring both present beneficiaries and new applicants. Many individuals respond by demanding to be personally accompanied by Neighborhood Development Center aides on their next visit to the agency—a demand that is virtually impossible to meet (NDC welfare staff, 18 September 1975). And the inadequate or halfhearted participation of many community groups in the Service Area Committee is rooted in their inability to receive information and responses to their complaints about municipal service. Since resolution often depends on area and past connections with the agencies, this response of consumers—like the others mentioned—exhibits internal rationality, not apathy. The key for the agency here is the ability to manipulate services and expectations to reduce the number of complaints.

The lack of public orientation in the response of poor people also serves the organizational needs of the merchant, social agencies, and city departments; it, too, is an induced characteristic. The informal systems work to eliminate general, issue-oriented complaints: Consumers do not know and cannot find out their rights; legal and administrative responsibilities are turned, therefore, into special treatment, rights into favors. Walker-Thomas hides warranty rights (FTC 1975:4); welfare agencies obscure requirements for aid and the existence of special grants (Rev. Daniel James, 17 September 1975); and city departments fail to release service information and thus succeed in creating an atmosphere in which people blame one another rather than seek needed policy changes (observation, 6 August and 10 September 1975). All these obfuscations cut consumers off from one another, giving them no opportunity to perceive complaints in generalized, publicly oriented ways but instead helping ensure that they continue to look inside the system, rather than outside, for all resolution.

Finally, the seeming "irrational fear" poor people exhibit, at least in the context of these institutions, roots itself in a high degree of rational cost-consciousness. Ultimately, Walker-Thomas exerts control over customers' purchases by creating the possibility that the goods can be taken away at the salesmen's whim; over their purchasing power by making explicit the threat that credit can be withdrawn; and even over their financial resources, by the information collected through the "pimp" system (Teresa Fender, 7 July 1975). Given these incentives, that people may fear to push a complaint too far makes eminent sense. The discretion given to the welfare agency induces a similar sort of power-conscious fear: The arbitrary cutoffs, manipulation of "employability" status, and impossible documentary demands explain why, in the words of NDC's Little, "People just don't know what's gonna get that check taken away from them, and they're near scared of their shadow because of it [Martha Little, 25 September 1975]." And in the community's dealing with the city service departments, the need to compete with and downgrade the complaints of others flows from the fear that agency attention will shift away from one area's needs to those of another. In such light all these responses are highly rational and at the same time highly effective in serving ends that oppose the needs of most of the consumers involved.

Systematic Causes

In all these complaint-handling relationships, problems are not accidental, but rather they are logical and predictable outcomes of the nature of the merchant, the welfare agencies, and the city departments. In responding to its "captive" consumers, Walker-Thomas creates an abundance of potential complaints through its unique marketing process: It sells shoddy goods (many manufacturer seconds) that deteriorate rapidly, and it engages in illegal and unfair collection methods and harrassment. Its complaint-management techniques—in part the outgrowth of its other methods—are necessary to redistribute and reduce the costs of its marketing and collection.

Welfare agencies create complaints because of their inability to serve all qualified applicants. A New York City survey in 1971 found that for every person on welfare, at least one more is eligible (Pivens and Cloward 1971:147–148). Another survey conducted in an urban renewal district of Manhattan found that 10% of those not on the welfare rolls qualified for emergency assistance (Pivens and Cloward 1971:147–148). A Massachusetts study made in 1970 states: "We can see that many families are potentially eligible for AFDC [Aid for Dependent Children] and provide [sic] a reservoir of needy families that will continue to try to join the AFDC rolls [Beer, S. ed. 1970:90]."

Estimates from within the area of my fieldwork confirm these national trends. NDC consumer aide James suggests that, on every block, there are two or three qualified families either unenrolled in welfare or underbudgeted (Rev. Daniel James, 18 September 1975). Consumer aide Lyla Peterson states that the number of people on welfare in the NDC service area could easily be doubled (interview with Lyla Peterson, 15 September 1975). Thus, the discretionary power of the agencies, which creates so many complaints, is necessary to maintain the resource levels that agencies themselves admit are low.

The inadequate delivery of services that underlies the complaints in SAC 6 also flows from resource inadequacies. Washington, D.C., is currently fighting major deficit problems, including proposed layoffs of city workers and an ill-fated commuter tax. City departments not only will be unable to expand services to meet the large need but may even fail to maintain current levels. The SAC process makes clear this allocation problem, informally by enforcing the competitive atmosphere among community groups, and formally through its governing pronouncement, "The government will respond within resource limits [District of Columbia Office of Planning and Management 1974]."

Complaints and Social Choice

The resource constraints that cause many of the complaints we have looked at reflect choices made outside the context of the retail store, the social agencies, and the city departments. The tensions of resource limitations result from social, economic, and political choices. Consider that labor and insurance costs, shoplifting, inability to secure lines of credit, and bad debts combine to push business out of the ghetto and make profit a virtually impossible goal except for the unscrupulous firm like Walker-Thomas (see Andreason 1975); that the inadequate resources of welfare agencies represent a political decision not to fund them so that full statutory entitlements can be translated into full material benefits; and that only the political will of Washington area residents and the federal government can expand resources enough so that service levels meet adequate standards.

This perspective points directly to one conclusion, a conclusion that overpowers any discussion of complaint-handling reform measures: The complaints of poor people, as represented in these case studies, represent a "trickle down" from the choices made by the politically and economically powerful. The complaints of the poor therefore derive from the same sources as their poverty. To castigate Walker-Thomas and the welfare and service agencies, then, is ultimately to criticize the political and economic choices we make as a society.

References

Alinsky, Saul A.
   1946 *Reveille for radicals*. New York: Vintage Books.
   1971 *Rules for radicals*. New York: Vintage Books.
Andreasen, Alan R.
   1975 *The disadvantaged consumer*. New York: Free Press.
Beer, Samuel (ed.)
   1970 *The state and the poor*. Cambridge, Mass.: Winthrop.

Caplovitz, David
1968 *The poor pay more.* Toronto: Macmillan.
District of Columbia Government
1975 *The people of the District of Columbia* (pamphlet).
District of Columbia Office of Planning and Management
1974 *The Service Area system* (pamphlet).
FTC (Federal Trade Commission)
1975 *Investigation of Walker-Thomas Furniture, Inc.*, Complaint Released to the Public, 31 October 1975, Commission File No. 732 3064.
Lipsky, Michael
1970 *Protest and city politics: Rent strikes, housing, and the power of the poor.* Chicago: Rand McNally.
Magnuson, Warren, and Jean Carper
1968 *The darker side of the marketplace.* Englewood Cliffs, N.J.: Prentice-Hall.
Margolis, Sidney
1968 *The innocent consumer vs. the exploiters.* New York: Trident.
Pivens, Frances Fox, and Richard Cloward
1971 *Regulating the poor.* New York: Random House.
President's Commission on Income Maintenance Programs
1970 *Poverty amid plenty: The American Paradox.* Washington, D.C.: U.S. Government Printing Office.
SAC (Mayor's Inter-Agency Committee to Improve City Services, Service Area Committees)
1975 SAC 6 Cleanup Subcommittee Report. 27 August.
1971–
1975 SAC 6 Minutes.
Schrag, Phillip
1972 *Counsel for the deceived.* New York: Pantheon.

11

Gregory Wilson
Elizabeth Brydolf

GRASS ROOTS SOLUTIONS:
San Francisco Consumer Action

Introduction

This chapter describes the efforts of one local voluntary consumer organization to improve the position of the consumer in the marketplace.[1] Until 1971 in San Francisco, a city of over 700,000 people, there were but three nonjudicial agencies to which consumers victimized by unfair business practices could turn for help. These three, the President's Office of Consumer Affairs, the California Department of Consumer Affairs, and the Better Business Bureau, together were unable to handle the problems facing San Francisco consumers. Other government agencies either did not handle individual complaints or functioned simply as referral centers. Founded in May 1971 by local volunteers, San Francisco Consumer Action (SFCA) was designed as a community service to fill that void by offering individual complaint assistance.

Our description of SFCA illustrates the evolution of the organization from a complaint switchboard to a much larger consumer organization

[1]San Francisco Consumer Action was chosen for study because of its local reputation and the convenience of its location to the University of California, Berkeley. Wilson observed the organization from September to December 1973 and made random visits in February, March, and August 1974 in order to complete a review of SFCA's records. Brydolf participated for 6 months in 1976 in one of SFCA's complaint-resolution committees, and later in the same year she was a participant–observer in the Cleveland Consumer Action complaint chapters. Both authors conducted interviews with the staffs during their periods of research. This report covers the period to March 1977.

The researchers' access to information from both organizations was excellent. The personnel of SFCA were generally receptive to the proposal that a report be written on the organization's development and operation.

involved in a broad range of activities. The organization did not spring from a preconceived blueprint. Rather, through a process of learning, the group repeatedly sought to address problems of increasingly broader scope.

The purpose of this chapter is to communicate an understanding of how such organizations develop and to illustrate the interplay of ideas and experience as a way to redirect organization. The group was not static but dynamic and changing—a product of the relationship between the group's ideals and the realities confronted in order to survive and be effective.

An essay on public involvement in consumer issues might well mention de Tocqueville's notion that the power of the American state is best limited by America's proclivity to form associations. A powerful state and an apathetic mass society, he thought, must be balanced by local self-government and voluntary associations to ensure the stability of a democratic political system. By such means central power is limited as well as challenged.

Most voluntary associations are formed for the purpose of bringing about change in society. They serve to temper feelings of powerlessness: "Being reduced to a stage of virtual impotence as an individual, the urbanite is bound to exert himself by joining with others of similar interests into organized groups to obtain his ends [Wirth 1938:22]." By virtue of their loosely structured form, such organizations are able to innovate in a way that established business and government organizations cannot.

SFCA was founded in May 1971 by Kay Pachtner and several other volunteers as an outgrowth of the now defunct Association of California Consumers (ACC), a statewide group. None of the SFCA volunteers professed any expertise in resolving complaints. As Pachtner noted, "We just dived in without knowing anything about the law or complaint handling. But we learned fast." Pachtner and the other volunteers, primarily middle-class housewives, worked from their living rooms. An early decision was to give free assistance with complaints while urging complainants to become SFCA members with a donation of $4 or more.

A month after its founding, in June 1971, the group found space in a Methodist church and moved into its first office—a tiny room with a desk and one telephone. It has made three moves since then and now occupies spacious quarters on the second floor of the Odd Fellows Building, which dates from the turn of the century and is located in a rundown but colorful area of central San Francisco. The advantages of the present location are low rent, easy access to public transportation, and proximity to City Hall.

Through the end of 1971, SFCA operated on a very small scale, with Pachtner and other volunteers handling consumer complaints on a caseworker basis, each complainant being counseled individually by a single staff member. In 8 months of operation in 1971, 130 consumers requested assistance with a complaint. Through year's end, 14 of these complaints were resolved by SFCA, 10 completely or partially successful.

After 3 years of growth, SFCA greatly changed its methods of complaint handling in August 1974. Doing away with the old procedure of counseling complainants on an individual basis, SFCA switched from staff grievance committees to consumer-run "complaint resolution committees," based on a model developed by the Consumer Education and Protective Association (CEPA) in Philadelphia.

The four general goals of SFCA help determine its dynamic structure:

1. To maintain an effective procedure for resolving consumer complaints and grievances with the active participation of the individual concerned through any legal means available.

2. To maintain a program of public education on unfair business practices and governmental actions affecting consumer interests.

3. To be a constant watchdog over the policies and activities of the public agencies that have consumer protection functions and enforcement powers and to act as a consumer spokesman in relevant issues.

4. To stimulate the development of and to act in concert with neighborhood consumer groups.

SFCA has never had any formal or informal ties with government regulatory bodies, and none have been sought. Federal regulatory agencies, state attorneys general, and local district attorney offices do not, as a matter of policy, act on individual complaints but rather channel their limited resources into investigation of businesses that evidence numerous violations of laws and regulations. In these offices, complaint assistance is a by-product of a larger function and as such is not usually available to individuals.

SFCA has been able to provide a unique service that both government and business have failed to provide, and though it alone cannot possibly meet the enormous need for better consumer complaint handling, it hopes that its efforts will spur other organizations into creating new and diverse mechanisms to do the job.

A Note on Methodology

Although we as investigators and writers had complete cooperation from the people at SFCA, there were some methodological difficulties in carrying out this study that were related to the changing nature of the organization. It is difficult to write about something that is fluid and developing. It is perhaps endemic to an entirely volunteer organization that during its first 2 years of operation record keeping at SFCA had a very low priority. Those who volunteer to fight corporate dominance and unfair business practices like least of all to imitate the habits of business. When time is short and so much needs to be done, there is little enthusiasm for transcribing permanent records. Records for the first 2 years of SFCA operation are especially uneven. However, completeness of the organization's files showed considerable improvement over time, a development that corresponds to the group's realization that records are valuable tools for instruction and improvement, and essential in documenting the group's effectiveness as a consumer protection organization.

Voluntary Organizations and the Role of the Individual

SFCA's political and social orientation is derived primarily from the two key figures in the organization's development, Kathryn Pachtner and Neil Gendel. Pachtner was the prime mover in the establishment of San Francisco Consumer Action. Holding the title of executive director until her resignation in December 1976, she was indisputably responsible for the organization's survival and growth. Sylvia Weiss, a co-founder who left SFCA in 1971, described Pachtner as "an incredibly hard worker." In addition, Weiss noted that "Kay has a greatly attractive personality which makes it easy for people to work with her." Gendel, a San Francisco attorney who began working with SFCA early in its development, acknowledged Pachtner's central role: "Kay has always been deeply concerned with making SFCA work. It's her organization." In conversation, Pachtner easily demonstrates the qualities that helped mold SFCA. Generating an infectious sense of urgency, she is at once committed, pragmatic, and optimistic.

Saul D. Alinsky, the late consummate community organizer, discussed in his writings "the items one looks for in identifying potential organizers . . . [Alinsky 1971:72]." Alinsky said that, among other things, an organizer should possess a "free and open mind," be capable of "political relativity," and have strong doses of curiosity, irreverence, imagination, humor, ego, and optimism (Alinsky 1971:72–80). Pachtner rates well in each category, and the same attributes define most of those working at SFCA today. She professes no familiarity with the literature on organizing groups, and her background is devoid of any experience in organization or administration. "If there's one thing you should emphasize in your report," she said, "it's that anybody could set up an organization like this anywhere."

Her belief in the importance of a consumer constituency surfaced in a discussion of other consumer protection endeavors. Pointing to the efforts of Ralph Nader, she indicated that his work would continue to be a necessary stimulus for grass roots action but that substantial nationwide changes could be obtained only with widespread participation by consumers. She sensed danger that Nader and other consumer advocates would become institutionalized and isolated, and she emphasized that the public must respond actively to such vanguard efforts and not become complacent about them.

But this hoped-for active support of the citizenry has been slow to develop. Early in history of SFCA, Pachtner realized that consumers were not greatly motivated to aid SFCA financially. That realization suggested that consumer complaint assistance could attract widespread financial contributions *if* it provided a service that many members of the public needed. That service ultimately was supplied by SFCA's complaint resolution committees.

The complaint committee, as we shall see, was to be an organizing tool, a mechanism to educate people and tempt them into becoming involved. As SFCA continued to develop, Pachtner wanted individual complaints handled by complaint committees in order to have the core staff at SFCA, with the backing of an active membership, working on developing influence in the political arena. As one staff member stated, "We'd like to become a movement. We want to influence the world rather than pick up complaints all the time." Referring to the SFCA's executive director, the informant continued, "Kay wants to handle our growth like a campaign."

Pachtner had widespread contacts among consumer groups that served to complement and inform activity at SFCA. Her overriding concern was to strengthen her own organization through such connections. She sat on the executive committee of the Consumer Federation of California and was a board member of the Consumer Federation of America. She also held a board position with San Francisco's Public Media Center, Electricity and Gas for People, and several other consumer and public interest groups.

Pachtner expressed concern over the future development of SFCA. "My main worry is . . . whether we're going to become a service organization—complaint assistance, shoppers' guides, educational lectures—or a service-plus group with an active, growing membership." Pachtner said that she did not want to see SFCA reduced to "holding people's hands and become a passive information receptacle."

A prime obstacle to a broadening of the consumer movement, in Pachtner's view, has been its lack of rapport with organized labor. AFL-CIO officials view consumerists and environmentalists as potential threats to jobs that unions are dedicated to protect. Pachtner noted that SFCA has yet to convince organized labor that there exists an essential identity of consumer and union concerns. "Our experience with unions here in San Francisco has been pretty negative. They don't seem to want to cooperate."

The second important force at SFCA was attorney Neil Gendel, a man deeply involved with SFCA's development from its inception. At the time of SFCA's founding, Gendel was a California deputy attorney general whose concern with better shaping of governmental regulatory efforts led him to attend SFCA's inaugural meeting in May 1971. He was interested in the group's potential for building an alternative mechanism for regulating business behavior. For over a year, Gendel offered advice, moral support, and regular donations to SFCA while continuing his government position. In June 1972 he resigned from his state post and 4 months later began working as a full-time volunteer consultant to SFCA.

Gendel earned his LLB in 1964 at the University of California, Berkeley, School of Law and in October 1965 joined the staff at the Attorney General's office. After several years of casework, Gendel appreciated the problem of operating within a framework of overlapping regulatory agencies at three levels of government. In April 1970 he joined and eventually headed a voluntary association of federal, state, and local law enforcement agencies with responsibilities including consumer and investment problems. This group, the Bay Area Consumer Protection Coordinating Committee (BACPCC), was one of several committees in various parts of the country sponsored by the Federal Trade Commission (FTC). At the same time, Gendel helped form and later chaired the Bay Area Prosecutor's Association Fraud Committee (BAPAFC), a group comprised of representatives from the District Attorneys' offices of nine Bay Area counties and Sacramento County. Both committees, BACPCC and BAPAFC, worked together to share information and expertise on common problems of regulation and prosecution.

In his 6½ years as deputy attorney general, Gendel stated that he exacted civil penalty awards of over $250,000 and orders to refund over $2,500,000 to defrauded investors (Gendel 1973). But he left the Attorney General's office in June 1972 because he found "a lack of real commitment to protecting the investor and consumer on the part of the administration [Los Angeles Times 1972:]." Specifically, Gendel objected to interference from the administrative office with his aggressive prosecution of the Boise Cascade Recreational Communities Corporation for real estate fraud.[2]

The previous month Gendel had felt forced to resign as chairman of BACPCC and BAPAFC when the Attorney General ordered the committees' coordinating work deemphasized in order to highlight the establishment of the Attorney General's own Consumer Fraud Advisory Task Forces. These groups, Gendel observed, were not composed of law enforcement personnel and met only sporadically. At the time of his resigna-

[2]The Contra Costa County District Attorney continued the prosecution after Gendel left his post. Suits brought by private parties against the corporation yielded a settlement for an unprecedented $580,000,000 and forced the corporation out of the recreational communities development business. A vice-president of Boise Cascade, George McCown, stated simply, "It was no longer financially viable to continue [Los Angeles Times 1972]."

tion, Gendel concluded, "It's as cynical an attitude as I've ever seen. Just do the PR stuff and ignore the other agencies, which is guaranteed to insure the consumer doesn't get protection [*Los Angeles Times* 1972].[3]

After his resignation, Gendel departed on an extended vacation to relax and ponder his choices. At 32 he was an attorney, unemployed, but intensely concerned with confronting consumer problems. Acting on that interest, in October 1972 Gendel returned to San Francisco and began working as a full-time volunteer consultant to SFCA. To explain his viewpoint, Gendel referred often to Ramsey Clark's (1970) perception of white collar crime as the most corrosive of all crimes, because it questions the moral fiber of advantaged people.

Gendel noted that after a century of legislation and government enforcement, consumers face an unchecked deterioration in business practices. He was convinced that "the changes necessary to insure consumers a 'fair deal' in the marketplace cannot be made by government." Gendel without reservation agreed with Pennsylvania Insurance Commissioner Herbert S. Denenberg's pronouncement that "government has been the biggest consumer fraud around [Denenberg 1973]."

Gendel subscribed to an essentially conservative classical economic interpretation of consumer problems. He expects consumers to act only in their individual self-interest and make rational decisions on what to buy. Acknowledging that few semblances of free enterprise exist today, he added that through "the mobilization of shopping power in the market place, we can move toward such a system." Gendel views government regulations as efforts "to facilitate the proper functioning of a free enterprise system" and concludes "Consumers need two very basic things today—corporations and entire industries which produce the best possible prices and government agencies which are truly responsive to the needs of consumers and not the industries which they have been mandated to regulate in the public interest. We have neither of these [Gendel 1973]."

In his work with SFCA, Gendel chose not to involve himself in routine operations but instead worked on specific projects to which he felt he could best apply his skills. Before Gendel came to the organization, he noted, it was essentially a consumer grievance committee. Through his initiative, SFCA diversifed its efforts and thereby gained a more substantial reputation as a force in consumer matters. It was Gendel who first led SFCA into the investigations of banking and finance, his own area of expertise. And next to complaint handling, financial organizations have remained SFCA's most persistent concern because of their pervasive role in consumer affairs. Gendel's specific contributions were his fund-raising

---

[3]A spokesperson for the Attorney General's office at the time termed Gendel a "disgruntled deputy" and offered no comment on his specific allegations of interference in the Boise Cascade suit [*Los Angeles Times* 1972].

efforts, the preparation of the book *Break the Banks: A Shopper's Guide to Banking Services,* and a review of the effectiveness of the California Department of Consumer Affairs. Since beginning a practice as a private attorney, he has continued to work with SFCA as an occasional consultant.

Background Events

The Association of California Consumers was formed in the early 1960s by members of local consumer groups who wished to expand the scale of their involvement in consumer issues. Initially, they wanted to establish a statewide organization to act as an umbrella for local groups and to press for a consumer council within the state government's executive branch. Its founders also hoped that ACC would serve eventually as an advocate of consumer interests backed by a considerable statewide membership. ACC never emerged, however, as a substantial force in consumer affairs, primarily because of financial and structural weaknesses. Its founders had envisioned a hierarchy in which local consumer groups throughout California would respond to a central office's initiatives. But the approach employed for developing a membership base tended to stifle such aspirations. The bulk of ACC's claimed membership consisted of consumers already belonging to local organizations which in turn affiliated with ACC.

ACC also tried on its own to establish a number of local chapters. Through occasional consumer education meetings, attempts were made at outlining a basis for consumer activism and at discussing specific issues, such as a proposed telephone rate increase in 1969. Generally, those in attendance voiced approval of an activist posture but offered only a tentative assurance of responsiveness to a remote state coordinator. In effect, ACC represented an attempt to generate by fiat a statewide consumer interest group. Sylvia Siegel, ACC's executive director from 1969 to 1972, readily admitted that the organization "was a paper tiger, a sort of board of directors. It was organized upside down, from the top down."[4]

Pachtner, in a search for "something interesting and meaningful to do," contacted ACC in the fall of 1970. Siegel suggested that she work with Sylvia Weiss, who was in charge of the San Francisco chapter of ACC. Pachtner was plainly disappointed with the extent of ACC's organizational efforts, but Pachtner and Weiss found they worked well together. After several months of exploring the limits of ACC's consumer education

---

[4]In March 1972 ACC merged with the Consumer Farm Information Committee (CFIC) to form the Consumer Federation of California (CFC). Commenting on her former organization's history, Siegel observed that "without grass root support, ACC couldn't grow. But for its time, it served a useful purpose." Siegel herself declined to continue with CFC and went on to form her own utility watchdog group, Toward Utility Rate Normalization (TURN).

meetings, Pachtner and Weiss began thinking of forming an autonomous local organization. Ideally, they wanted to imitate the apparent success of the feisty Consumer Education and Protection Association (CEPA), spawned in impoverished areas of Philadelphia.

An opportunity to move toward that goal arose in November 1970, when the organizers of a Call for Action complaint center at local radio station KABL expressed interest in having a San Francisco consumer organization to refer complaints to (see Chapter 13). Pachtner eagerly volunteered to have KABL direct grievances to them at home in the name of ACC. With no idea of how they would handle grievances, Pachtner and Weiss nevertheless started taking calls. Initially, as a precondition for assistance, both asked complainants to join ACC and pay the accompanying $6 membership fee. They quickly found that such a request effectively quashed whatever interest callers had in the procedure. "ACC simply had no credibility," Pachtner explained. "Why shell out six bucks to an organization you had never heard of?" After dropping the membership prerequisite, Pachtner and Weiss started to accumulate a small number of requests for assistance.

To help finance mounting telephone bills, transportation costs, and consumer education meetings, Pachtner and Weiss found themselves drawing increasingly on their own and their husbands' bank accounts. ACC could offer no financial assistance; instead, Siegel continued to ask that membership fees be collected and forwarded to the state office. ACC seemed ready to absorb whatever funds were available from the local chapter without providing concomitant advantages. Moreover, with San Franciscans telephoning to register their complaints directly, Pachtner and Weiss had entered a new arena with new priorities for their time and the consumers' money. The inclination to form an autonomous consumer protection organization grew correspondingly.

After concentrating on consumer complaints through the winter, Pachtner and Weiss became convinced that such grass-roots activity was essential to the development of an effective consumer organization. They also felt strongly that continued affiliation with ACC would hinder the growth of such a group. These views were shared by the other active members of the chapter, and in May 1971 these consumers planned to announce the formation of an autonomous consumer protection organization that would primarily serve San Francisco and be named San Francisco Consumer Action.

Plans were made for an elaborate announcement meeting complete with a panel of speakers. Pachtner rented a room large enough to hold 300 at the University of San Francisco and thought of asking for donations to help finance the venture. Announcements were mailed to ACC members, a press release was distributed, and on 21 May 1971, San Francisco Consumer Action (SFCA) was inaugurated. As Pachtner put it, "Maybe fifty people showed up, including the panel, their friends, and relatives. We lost money renting the room." Media coverage was mixed. Neither of San Francisco's daily newspapers mentioned the meeting, though articles did appear in the twice-weekly *San Francisco Progress* and the biweekly *Bay Guardian*. The next day local radio stations KABL and KBCA carried brief announcements about the new organization.

Among the people who came to the founding meeting of the group were several attorneys from a San Francisco law firm that had established a group legal services program. They were enthusiastic about extending the group legal services program to SFCA. The firm offered an arrangement whereby any member of SFCA could receive legal services on a reduced fee schedule. SFCA's arrangement for these group legal services continues today, and a wide range of other organizations, including union chapters and neighborhood associations, also subscribe to the services.

In the months after SFCA's founding, the lawyers spent a great deal of time instructing Pachtner in basic consumer law. She recounted, "I had no training in the field, just interest. I didn't even know there was such a thing as a small claims court." The attorneys suggested that Pachtner incorporate SFCA as a public, tax-exempt, nonprofit organization,[5] and, donating their time, they drew up the incorporation papers.

The Organization and Activities of SFCA

At the head of SFCA's formal structure is a 13-member board of directors composed of community figures who are elected annually by the membership. In practice, because few members outside the staff appear at the annual meeting, the staff's selection is virtually certain to win. The staff, including volunteers, also chooses an executive director, who supervises regular operations and can approve expenditures up to $100. Operating decisions are made at weekly staff meetings by consensus or by majority vote.

Staff Members

From its inception through early 1973, SFCA was operated solely by volunteers contributing their services on a full- or part-time basis. But from the beginning, SFCA volunteers believed that a paid staff was crucial

---

[5]Under the Internal Revenue Code a "public" 501(c)(3) corporation is one that receives more than one-third of its contributions from the general public. Those corporations not meeting such a standard are accorded "private" status. The distinction is important because of differing restrictions placed on lobbying activities. A public 591(c)(3) organization can devote only an "insubstantial" part of its activities to lobbying; a private 501(c)(3) organization cannot lobby at all (Nader and Ross 1971:81).

to the organization. As one staff member put it, "What in the end will differentiate a group of part-time do-gooders from an effective reform organization is the measure that comes only from a paid staff."

By 1976 SFCA had a paid staff of 16, although it still drew upon volunteer help. In March 1977, at the close of the period covered by this report, there were 12 full-time staff members (10 of whom were paid), 12 nonstudent part-time volunteers, and 10–15 student part-time volunteers. Most staff members, both men and women, are white, and they tend to be young—those who can afford to live on an uncertain salary of $500 per month. This financial insecurity causes a high staff turnover and limits the staff to individuals who do not have dependents or large financial commitments. In the words of one staff member, "The most frustrating thing about this place is that we keep losing good people who have to leave because of lack of funds." Some staff members "burn out" because they expend too much energy too fast, and non-self-starters drop out because staff shortages do not permit close supervision.

SFCA's structure has been kept purposefully unbureaucratic and is characterized by a horizontal distribution of power. In theory, at least, each staff member and each full-time volunteer has an equal voice in SFCA's decisions. The work, too, is distributed horizontally. Each person handles his or her own secretarial tasks. Each pitches in on the larger newsletter, bulk mailings, emergency, and fund-raising activities that require periodic concentrations of energy. Staff members sometimes voice frustration that so much effort is required merely to keep the organization functioning.

As SFCA has grown, the staff has tried to develop ways of coordinating its work in various areas without developing hierarchical work relationships. SFCA's activity task forces—food, utilities, media—various research projects, and Consumer Advocates—who handle its political lobbying—have all been attempts at alternative organizational structure. In addition to each staff member's substantive involvement in one or more of the mentioned areas, each is responsible for seeing that certain tasks are done in media publicity, production, publication distribution and marketing, accounting and general business, newsletter organization and production, and coordinating the work of volunteers on the grievance switchboard.

The Staff members relate comfortably to each other and to the volunteers. Often large groups of staff members and volunteers eat lunch together, and occasionally staff members hold parties at their homes for the group. The staff members uniformly exhibit a genuine concern for consumer protection and an enthusiastic pursuit of a fair economic setting in the marketplace. Their dedication to consumer protection is undoubted; only those who value the organization's goals would persist in a situation devoid of conventional remuneration and security.

Volunteers

Since the fall of 1973, 30–40 volunteers have worked at SFCA in an average month, most of them students. The summer months attract far fewer volunteers, as the Bay Area universities empty. Student numbers change with every quarter or semester, and the amount of time individual students spend at SFCA varies widely. Most volunteers attend the University of California at Berkeley or the University of San Francisco. Both institutions allow students to earn academic credit in a variety of subject areas while working at SFCA for 10–12 hours per week. Law students come from three Bay Area schools; several prelaw undergraduates have worked full-time at SFCA for a quarter or a semester, earning academic credit.

The attitudes of student volunteers toward their work at SFCA closely approximate that of the staff. For some students, academic credit for independent work is a sufficient incentive, but most of those who choose to work with SFCA do so because they are interested in consumer protection and are attracted to its working environment.

Nonstudent volunteers come from a wide variety of backgrounds. Most of them contribute time from other consumer-oriented activities and jobs; others have responded to SFCA advertisements for volunteers. SFCA's membership does not represent a personnel resource to be drawn upon. During Wilson's research period, only two volunteers indicated that they had been SFCA members before beginning work at SFCA. Full-time volunteers, although they would be ideal for the organization, are not common. Wilson noted only two full-time volunteers, and both left SFCA during his period of observation. Most volunteers receive no monetary compensation, but some are occasionally paid small amounts.

The orientation sheets given to new volunteers conclude with the invitation: "Enjoy yourself. Your time spent with us should be not only educational and interesting for you but fun too. If you have problems or questions, let us know. We're easy." This casual working environment is both an incentive for continuing at SFCA and an unstated compensation for the lack of pay. This environment produces what some observers would call inefficiency in daily operation—though a cost-effective analysis might prove them wrong—but it allows the concomitant advantage of a relaxed work place in which no one is exclusively consigned to tasks of drudgery and routine.

Educational and Political Activity

In the early years of SFCA, executive director Pachtner, continually aware of the organization's fragile nature, concentrated on broad efforts to increase its impact on the consumer protection arena. Her priorities included fund raising, cooperating with similarly oriented consumer groups, and developing positions on broad political questions that affected consumer protection. Her enthusiasm for organizing was demonstrated repeatedly.

The incident that all connected with SFCA agree first promoted the group's reputation as a determined, action-oriented group was their skirmish with British Motor Car Distributors, Ltd., San Francisco:

In July 1971, SFCA accepted a complaint from a young woman who had bought a used automobile from BMC for $1900. BMC had given her a 30-day warranty; in 45 days the car had stopped running. After fruitless complaints to the California Department of Motor Vehicles, Pachtner wrote BMC, concluding: "In view of the obvious unsafe condition and serious mechanical defects, we feel that Miss —— deserves to have her contract rescinded, the car returned, her past payments refunded and her obligation discharged [Pachtner 1971]."

After further correspondence, Pachtner and an SFCA volunteer went to BMC in December to ask what the corporation intended to do about the matter. They were shunted to the office of BMC's lawyer, who told them matter-of-factly that BMC had no further legal obligation to the car's owner. When Pachtner protested that SFCA's client was being unfairly treated, she was told that fairness had nothing to do with the matter. As Pachtner recalled, "I was furious. We had to do something." Several volunteers urged picketing BMC's showroom, and Pachtner agreed. The picketing was planned for 22 January 1972, a Saturday. Press releases were sent to the media 5 days in advance, and elaborate handouts and placards were made up. Pachtner recalled, "We were pretty excited." That day 10 SFCA members picketed—until Pachtner was handed a notification that a $6-million libel suit had been filed charging her and 50 John Does with "slander, libel, extortion and conspiracy." SFCA had not yet incorporated, and Pachtner was therefore sued personally. The Sunday San Francisco Examiner and Chronicle reported that she gasped, "Six million dollars! I haven't got six cents! [1972:A6]."

In addition, Pachtner was served a summons to appear at a hearing at which BMC planned to seek a temporary restraining order. At the hearing a Superior Court judge granted an injunction against further picketing on the dubious grounds that SFCA pickets might be mistaken for union pickets. Although the situation was serious for SFCA, it at times touched on the absurd, as when the BMC general sales manager stated the corporation's position: "We've tried to help and to be fair, but when it comes to driving a car into the ground and then a strong-arm attempt—just like the Black Panthers . . . you've got to draw the line [1972:A6]."

Pachtner rushed to the Northern California office of the American Civil Liberties Union to ask for help in appealing what was, in Pachtner's view, "a constitutionally ridiculous" ruling. "It took the ACLU representative about 5 seconds to agree to take the case," Pachtner recalled. A meeting was held at SFCA to determine a course of action. It was felt that the group should quickly attempt to overturn the injunction, because a number of consumer groups were springing up in surrounding counties and SFCA members didn't want the BMC order to intimidate these new organizations. It was decided that the most expeditious action was to violate the injunction. This was for SFCA a crucial decision, as the pickets might wind up in jail.

SFCA members wrote to every organization they could think of to gather support for their cause and prepared press releases announcing their intention to violate the injunction. On 1 and 2 March 1972, SFCA again picketed BMC, bearing fresh placards denouncing BMC's attempted suppression of consumers' freedom of expression. More people turned out to violate the injunction than had appeared at the initial picket line. But the San Francisco police declined to arrest anyone. The action did yield its intended result, however. Pachtner was issued a contempt citation and fined $100, and this allowed the ACLU to go to court over the citation immediately. The case went to the California Court of Appeals, and in October 1972 that Court struck down as "patently overbroad" the antipicketing injunction.

In March 1973, BMC finally agreed to settle with the car owner and to pay SFCA $100 to drop the whole matter. "We wanted more to pay all expenses, but the hundred helped. BMC's attempt at intimidation failed," Pachtner concluded.

Publicity from the BMC affair was substantial and served to establish SFCA as a determined group dedicated to helping consumers. As Pachtner described it, "After the BMC incident, things started to happen at SFCA." Memberships began to increase, and volunteers became more numerous. In 1972, 625 consumers requested assistance with specific complaints, an increase of nearly 500 over its 8-month existence in the previous year.

In 1972, a member of the city's board of supervisors asked SFCA to help draft an ordinance creating a department and commission of consumer affairs for San Francisco. On submitting the proposal to the city council for approval, SFCA saw the commission's proposed powers to make regulations and impose fines deleted. Believing that no department would be preferable to a powerless one, SFCA came out in opposition to the amended proposal and garnered sufficient opposition to cause the board to reject the watered-down proposal. In the same year, SFCA had a more successful encounter with the city government. Participating in a temporary coalition of community and labor groups, SFCA was able to help stop Mayor Joseph Alioto from cutting the city District Attorney's Consumer Fraud division budget.

In the summer of 1972, SFCA attempted to convince the Bay Area broadcasting media to air a counteradvertisement on the dangers of recalled Chevrolet automobiles. SFCA's action prompted numerous television news stories, and reports of its activity were also carried in *Advertising Age* and *Automotive News*. At the same time, the group investigated the state of recalled autos in dozens of Chevrolet used car lots and reported the results to district attorneys' offices. Executive director Pachtner contacted the California Highway Patrol with a list of the affected Chevrolet models. The CHP acknowledged the correspondence and incorporated a warning into its inspection team procedure.

In 1973 executive director Pachtner and others were instrumental in organizing boycotts against high meat prices and in starting the California Food Action Campaign. Pachtner, commenting on the effect of SFCA's coordination of the meat boycott in San Francisco said, "We were not naive enough to think that the boycott would lower prices. The boycott was a catalyst for a consumer movement that is going to be unbelievable. . . . Talk about consciousness raising!"

In 1973 Pachtner twice testified before U.S. Senate committees investigating corporate concentration in food industries, and consultant Gendel made several appearances before California state legislative committees. In 1974 the SFCA staff joined Electricity and Gas for People (E&GP) to fight utility rate increases, and with San Francisco's All People's Coalition it monitored gasoline prices at service stations.

A SEPARATE CORPORATION FOR LOBBYING

In January 1974 SFCA personnel decided that their consumer protection efforts should expand to include substantial political lobbying. But to accommodate this interest within SFCA's operations would jeopardize its status as a public, nonprofit, tax-exempt corporation qualifying under Section 501(c)(3) of the Internal Revenue Code to receive charitable contributions tax-deductible by the donors. To circumvent this problem, SFCA decided to sponsor a separate corporation for lobbying, known as San Francisco Consumer Advocates, and to seek certification for it as a 501(c)(4) nonprofit, tax-exempt corporation.

Certification was granted for Consumer Advocates in June 1974. The new corporation has a separate board of directors, budget, and record keeping, and is staffed primarily by volunteers; any paid SFCA staff member who "crosses over" is held strictly within the bounds required to maintain SFCA's 501(c)(3) status—that "no substantial part" of his or her activities consists of active lobbying.

Since its founding, Consumer Advocates has helped draft and support a wide variety of state bills of interest to consumers, including ones concerning rent control, data banks and the right to privacy, the destruction of surplus food, collection agency practices, default and repossession of motor vehicles, used-car warranties, drug labeling, malpractice insurance, item pricing, product safety, and milk price controls. In SFCA's monthly newsletter, Consumer Advocates also tallies the consumer voting record of California's U.S. senators and representatives, calling it a "tale of heroes and zeroes."

THE TASK FORCES

In 1975 and 1976, SFCA created three separate units, or "task forces," to work in specific problem areas—food, utilities, and the media. Each was to operate and to apply for grants from foundations independent of the main organization. The strategy was adopted for two main reasons. First, it was hoped that funds would be attracted more easily to separately identifiable units, each of which had narrowly focused interests and goals. Second, the task force concept was expected to gain publicity and recruit volunteers interested in particular issues. The idea began promisingly when the Food Task Force landed a grant of $10,000. But hope was short-lived: The task forces withered away in 1976, unable to sustain themselves financially. SFCA continues to carry out research in a number of different areas, but the projects are no longer formally organized.

While they existed, the task forces devoted themselves to several issues of great importance to the consumer. The Utilities Task Force concentrated on utility price structures in the state and on local rates for consumers and business users. The Media Task Force was formed in opposition to San Francisco's public television station's dependence on corporate monies and its lack of accountability to the public audience. The Food Task Force was perhaps the most active, outlining as its goals "the distribution of accurate information about the food industry, government policies, and developments in nutrition and agriculture; the participation of consumers on all food-related government bodies; and the exploration of new priorities and new assumptions about the economics and politics of food." Its philosophy was reflected in the creation and coinage of the lifeline food concept, which urged "the distribution of nutritious food at low, fixed rates" to the elderly and the needy.

Among its activities was a citywide Food Day in which some 35 organizations participated and which was attended by over 2000 people. The task force also published a number of informational pamphlets on agribusiness, food advertising, labeling, unit and item pricing, and the "gross and highly questionable practices" of Del Monte Corporation in its production and distribution of canned goods.

The Food Task Force also provided testimony at a number of Federal Trade Commission and state legislative hearings, and placed a representative on a state Department of Agriculture ad hoc committee for about a year. One of its most successful local investigations was a study of Bay Area food salvage outlets. Task force members found the stores' claims of "pure and fresh, 100% guaranteed" goods to be false. Although much of the canned food was in good condition, staffers found numerous examples of severely dented, rusted, and swollen cans, and opened and unrefrigerated food sold in unsanitary conditions. These items, potentially containing poisonous bacteria, were sold to nursing homes, schools, and other public and private institutions in addition to private consumers. In response to the task force's study, the owners of the largest salvage chain contacted SFCA. Negotiations resulted in the stores' agreement to strictly monitor food quality, display health shopping guidelines in their stores, and end their misleading advertising.

FEDERAL TRADE COMMISSION HEARINGS

In November 1975 SFCA opened an important chapter in its history by participating as a representative of consumers in the trade regulation hearings of the Federal Trade Commission (FTC). SFCA had the distinction of being the first private organization ever to be reimbursed by a federal agency for participating in agency hearings as a representative of the public interest. The organization received funds from the FTC for this purpose under provisions of the FTC Improvement Act of 1975.

In general, FTC hearings are an important forum for the consumer because it is there that the Commission hears testimony from industry and other interested parties concerning its proposed trade regulation rules. The purpose of the rules is to set out in specific terms those industry practices that will be considered "unfair or deceptive." The FTC has the power to enforce its rules by the use of civil penalties.

The first FTC hearing in which SFCA participated concerned the vocational school industry and its widespread use of high-pressure sales techniques to sign up customers for courses costing thousands of dollars while misleading them as to the total amount and terms of payment as well as to what they would probably accomplish by taking the courses. Along with FTC and industry representatives, SFCA was permitted to present and cross-examine witnesses on this consumer abuse.

In 1976 SFCA participated in other FTC hearings on a variety of issues, including food protein supplements and eye care. So far, it is impossible to say whether consumer groups' participation in FTC hearings will make any real difference in the final regulations adopted. As it is, all the proposed rules that SFCA dealt with—along with thousands of pages of testimony—are still on the Commissioners' desks. Moreover, SFCA's role in the hearings is limited; it must work with a proposal already formulated by the FTC and has little opportunity to advocate its own vision of consumer law.

Without a doubt, the hearings offered many benefits to SFCA. Apart from giving it a prime opportunity to promote its own views on issues of consumer law, the FTC grants had become by early 1977 a major source of income. As a result, a substantial portion of the staff's energy continued to be devoted to some of these projects. Five staff members, for instance, were occupied in preparing for the vocational school hearings. In addition, the hearings served to increase SFCA's public exposure and prestige.

The FTC projects have their disadvantages, too. They offer substantial rewards only when they tie into areas of continuing concern to SFCA and contribute to its expertise. Finally, SFCA has not found that its association with the FTC has helped it raise money for its own purposes. It seems that many foundations prefer to aid new groups struggling for survival but turn elsewhere once these same organizations become established.

CONSUMER BOOKS

SFCA has published four major works on consumer problems. In December 1973 SFCA released the results of a 12-month study of 16 California banks in *Break the Banks: A Shopper's Guide to Banking Services*. This 63-page booklet furnished comparative tables on checking and savings account costs and services, and analyzed loan services in helpful detail. Cost comparisons were made of bank cards, check overdraw loans, personal unsecured loans, installment loans, and deeds of trust. Most valuable were the straightforward explanations of unfair and questionable banking practices. It was this guide that first demonstrated the advantages that many small banks have for the consumer. Publication of the guide was noted in San Francisco's daily press as well as in major, out-of-state newspapers, including the *New York Times*. By March 1977 almost 20,000 copies had been sold at $3.50 a copy.

In 1974 staff and volunteers conducted an in-depth investigation of California's Department of Consumer Affairs (DCA). Following 2 months of interviews and reviews of the department's statutory authority, budget, and data, SFCA published a 154-page exposé entitled *Deceptive Packaging: A Close Look at the Department of Consumer Affairs*. It called for major changes in the DCA's structure to prevent its control by business interests. The report received considerable media and legislative attention, and about 3000 copies had been sold by March 1977 at $3.10 each.

Consumer Action's *Auto Insurance Guide* was released in January 1976 and had sold about 11,000 copies (at $3.50) by March 1977. The guide clarified insurance practices and provided price comparison charts for 16 auto insurance companies, thus giving ordinary California consumers their first chance to become educated shoppers in this area.

As part of its continuing interest in the banking industry, SFCA followed up *Break the Banks* with another publication in November 1976 entitled *It's in Your Interest: The Consumer Guide to Savings Accounts*, the first comprehensive guide of its kind. Its purpose was to help clear up the mysteries surrounding the savings programs at 47 California banks and savings and loan companies, to aid consumers in making meaningful comparisons among the programs. Technical terms and practices were defined and explained; the 47 programs were ranked using a formula designed by the author, J. B. Moore; and checklists were provided to help consumers do their own effective comparison shopping. SFCA hoped that the guide not only would help consumers find the best savings programs but also would have an influence in changing banking practices through the pressure created in the market by a growing corps of informed consumers. *It's in Your Interest* received praise from the experts, and between 4000 and 5000 copies (at $4 each) had been sold by March 1977, 4 months after publication.

Other Consumer Action books include a study of the eye care industry and a comparative drug pricing survey. SFCA's first publication, a pamphlet entitled *A Guide to Public Records, or Getting It Straight from the Horse's Mouth,* achieved great popularity among journalism students by teaching them how to find information in city records.

Public Relations

As an organization with all local consumers as a potential constituency, SFCA relies on visibility for its continued operation. A substantial part of its income and its entire consumer complaint-resolution service rely on public awareness of SFCA. Efforts directed primarily at maintaining and improving SFCA's public relations image can be categorized as newsletters and leaflets plus irregularly scheduled speaking engagements, media interviews, free media announcements, and press conferences.

Newsletters

From its inception, SFCA has produced one- and two-page mimeographed newsletters at irregular intervals. In April 1973 it began printing a regular monthly newsletter, which was intended primarily for the paid membership but was also distributed at public meetings to increase public awareness of the group. In April 1975 newsprint was used for the first time, to give a more professional appearance to the paper. About 6000–8000 copies of the newsletter were being printed monthly by the end of 1976.

Current issues of *CA News* consist of 10–20 11" × 18" pages. A review of the issues printed between April 1973 and March 1974 showed that roughly 40% of the space was devoted to detailing SFCA's activities, including case studies from the grievance committee's work. An additional 20% of the newsletter regularly provided both useful and obscure bits of information on consumer protection and business fraud. Each newsletter also includes a membership form, to encourage new members to enroll. The newletter, under the direction of editor Michael Heffer, provides SFCA's contributing members with a valuable tool for their annual dues of $15.

Leaflets

SFCA produces an enormous volume of mimeographed leaflets proclaiming its existence that are distributed free at press conferences and public meetings. Specific leaflets promoting the SFCA consumer guides are also mimeographed in large quantities.

Speaking Engagements

As SFCA's visibility increased, its staff began to be invited to address local gatherings. The number of acceptances of invitations to speak is irregular, depending on staff availability. The group has reorganized its speaking engagement procedures with a series of consumer education lectures, so that a specific topic can be requested by interested organizations. Initially, the income potential of these speaking engagements went unrecognized, and no fee was charged. Eventually, as the number of invitations increased, SFCA adopted a policy of asking a minimum $25 donation for each appearance, though groups unable to afford that amount were usually accommodated free of charge.

Radio and Television Interviews

Consumer protection has become an increasingly popular topic on radio and television, and SFCA has benefited accordingly. Staff members say that there are more media requests for information than SFCA can satisfy, and invitations to participate in radio and television interview programs are frequent. SFCA personnel make such appearances as the group's other activities permit. In one 6-month period, they made 18 scheduled media appearances, and in addition SFCA activities were reported on radio and television news programs in 6 separate instances. No one at the organization has systematically evaluated the comparative advantages and rate of return of increasing media appearances in terms of broadened public support.

For more than 2 years, SFCA had its own weekly 1-hour talk show on KQED, a local public radio station. The programs ended in November 1976 after KQED attempted, in the words of the SFCA staff, "to censor and stifle" the program (CA News 1976:1). The dispute arose after the show's moderator read to the listeners the names of businesses and professionals that had been disciplined by state licensing boards, the names coming from a public list published by the California Department of Consumer Affairs.

Free Media Announcements

At one time, volunteers from another San Francisco group, Public Interest Communications (PIC), prepared public service messages and announcements for SFCA and contacted radio and television stations that were likely to be receptive to the group. Now SFCA prepares its own messages, which, if accepted, are broadcast free. In one 18-month period, SFCA averaged six radio spot announcements per month accepted by local radio stations. For the more elaborate television spots, the group averaged one acceptance a month. The messages and announcements ranged in duration from 30 to 60 seconds and were broadcast in English, Spanish, and Chinese.

News Conferences

Newspaper and television news coverage of SFCA's activities is frequent, and on several occasions front-page articles about the SFCA have appeared in San Francisco daily newspapers. The organization has a prepared format for calling a news conference of press and television personnel, complete with a list of vital names and telephone numbers. News conferences are used to publicize major issues that SFCA is working on and to herald the publication of new books.

In sum, SFCA has steadily exploited low-cost media promotion.

SFCA's Financial Base

Many volunteer associations have problems with funding, a theme which in part accounts for changes in the scope and activities of such organizations. Pachtner and Gendel worked to generate income from a number of sources: membership fees and donations, speaking engagements, foundation grants, publication sales, and individual fund-raising events. In 1971 and 1972, the first 2 years of its existence, SFCA raised $800 and $3600, respectively. The most significant factor in SFCA's early development was the securing of substantial foundation grants in 1973. These for a time eased the constant financial crises that had plagued the organization. For 1973 as a whole, SFCA received $33,400 in support from a dozen foundations, specified for three purposes: $22,700 for consumer complaint assistance, $8200 for activity in the California Food Action Campaign, and $2500 for general support.

In the first quarter of 1974, SFCA embarked on a concerted effort to market its banking guide and to duplicate the success of the previous year in attracting foundation grants. At the same time, consultant Gendel began organizing a group of university students to undertake a study of the California State Department of Consumer Affairs, and the SFCA staff made plans for another consumer guide—its comparative study of prescription drug prices.

The search for additional operating funds, however, did not yield sufficient monies to meet SFCA's rising operating budget, and in May 1974 the group was forced to shut its doors for the month in order to devote all its efforts to a fund-raising drive. By June SFCA had collected $8200 in consumer guide sales, membership dues, and donations. At the same time, Consumers' Union responded to a grant proposal and added

$9800 to SFCA's account. This $18,000 kept the organization at its previous level of operation for an additional 4 months. Since then the SFCA annual budget has continued to expand. By 1976, with an approximate budget of $8000 a month, SFCA needed to raise nearly $100,000 a year to meet its expenses.

In the fiscal year ending in March 1977, SFCA received $11,800 in dues and extra contributions from its 1200 members, $30,000 from the sale of its books, $6000 in donations, and $80,000 in grants—a total of $127,800. The figure for grants requires explanation. Most of this money came from the Federal Trade Commission to be used specifically for SFCA's participation in trade regulation hearings (described earlier). The FTC grants thus inflated SFCA's income and redirected some of its energy away from projects it had initiated itself.

The income from memberships and donations fluctuates widely from month to month, though membership dues are the steadiest source of income. The rise in memberships directly reflects increasing public awareness of SFCA. Apart from FTC funds, foundation grants have been its single largest source of money, but SFCA has found them uncertain. SFCA avoids money from business corporations, fearing a loss of autonomy or cooptation.

Evaluation of Consumer Complaint Assistance

Throughout its publications, SFCA states as a prime goal "to maintain an effective procedure for resolving consumer complaints and grievances with the active participation of the individual concerned and through any legal means available."

Operating Procedures

For purposes of exposition, the efforts of the grievance committee readily divide into two components: consumer advice and individual casework.

CONSUMER ADVICE

Telephone activity varied randomly throughout the week, though a consistent daily pattern was observed in which incoming calls are most frequent from opening to noon, diminishing steadily through the afternoon. On the average, grievance workers received 50–60 initial consumer contact telephone calls daily. Most of the initial contacts were requests for information or advice, and the completion of the call terminated the grievance committee's assistance to the consumer.

Grievance committee members drew on information accumulated since 1974 to aid consumers: floor-to-ceiling bookcases crammed with handbooks and "how to" paperbacks on auto repair, personal bankruptcy, tenants' rights, and small claims courts, as well as dozens of government publications on specific consumer problems; publications by the Bay Area Consumer Protection Coordinating Committee (PACPCC) and various San Francisco associations listing available local, state, and federal government consumer services; and useful summaries by the San Francisco People's Law School and San Francisco Tenants' Union on legal resources and landlord–tenant problems. All of these were referred to sporadically in response to a specific consumer inquiry.

A smaller group of favored reference works, however, served to handle most inquiries. One, a publication of the San Francisco District Attorney's office, *Summary of California Consumer Law and Authorities Handbook*, proved an invaluable cross-referenced sourcebook which allowed grievance workers to pinpoint violations of the law. As one staff member recalls, "I was in the D.A.'s office one day and spotted it. I said, 'I want one,' and they let me take it." Two publications by a group of California attorneys, *The California Guide to Small Claims Courts* and *The California Tenant's Handbook,* give concise information in those areas. Another favorite has a catalogue compiled by the grievance workers themselves and is termed, appropriately enough, the "Bitch Book." Divided into two parts, the looseleaf notebook started with a series of summary chapters on common consumer problems. Written in a format that presents "the problem, the law, what to do, references," the chapters provide the essential elements for resolving many complaints in the areas covered: advertising, chartered plane flights, door-to-door sales, eviction, health spas, how to break a lease, security deposits, telephone solicitations, tenant housing, repairs, and warranties. Chapters are added continuously. The second section lists the names of contact people in business ·and government who have proved helpful to the grievance committee in resolving past complaints. It is here that SFCA demonstrates one of its important strengths. As a local organization, the group has become quite familiar with Bay Area businesses and the law and government agencies supposedly regulating such business. The accumulated information about these elements has formed the basis of the group's ability to aid in consumer protection.

Staff members and volunteers indicate that about half the consumer advice calls concerned either automobile purchase and repair complaints or landlord–tenant problems. In those areas the grievance committee staff exhibited an excellent understanding of the consumer issues involved and was uniformly capable of concisely stating the relevant laws or indicating the most favorable method of approaching the difficulty. In less heavily traveled areas, in particular real estate matters and insurance, grievance workers could offer little advice or assistance. Consumers were told frankly in such cases that SFCA could not help. After the grievance worker suggested other possible agencies to turn to, the conversation was ended.

The grievance committee records contained a percentage breakdown of initial consumer contact calls by complaint area logged during 1 week in August 1973. The number of calls was estimated at 200. In a sample week in December 1973, the preponderance of initial contact calls were recorded both by complaint area and action taken (see Table 11.1).[6]

Since SFCA's inception, the advice procedure has been a straightforward one, providing the consumer with all available information so that the individual's position is strengthened.

Individual Casework

SELECTION

In a small percentage of initial consumer contacts, usually less than 25%, the caller requested assistance with a specific complaint. The grievance worker then inquired about the specifics of the case in order to decide if SFCA's assistance was warranted. The basis for that decision was primarily the determination of whether the consumer had been treated unfairly. If the caller's complaint seemed valid, a second determination—whether further action by the complainant was warranted, before the grievance committee accepted the case. At the beginning of the research period, this second determination was not made: If a consumer stated a fair grievance, the person was told that SFCA would accept his or her case. As the grievance committee's staff changed and resources tightened, some questions were raised as to whether the complainant could take another step in attempting a resolution. Complainants would typically be told that they could pursue the case in small claims court individually or that they could begin correspondence with the defendant firm. These considerations, though, only marginally affected the selection of individual cases. If a consumer evinced despair or seemed uncertain how to proceed, the complaint would be taken without hesitation.

[6]Before January 1974 no regular records were kept of the number of consumer calls received. After that time grievance committee workers attempted to record on an interview file card each consumer's name, address, and complaint category. This compilation had a two-fold purpose: First, recording inquiries by complaint category could indicate the areas in which grievance workers should become more proficient; second, the interview cards could be used to mail consumers a request for membership. Compliance with this procedure was erratic, though membership pitches on the telephone were increasingly common.

TABLE 11.1
Consumer Complaint Assistance in Initial Telephone Contacts

Complaint area	Week August 1973 (percentage)	Week December 1973 (number)	Grievance worker estimates
Landlord–tenant	(20)	76	50%
Auto purchase–repair	(37)	24	
Finance–credit	(8)	21	
Other		95	
		216	
Grievance Committee Action			
Information or advice		151	70–80%
Referral		30	
Individual casework offered		35	20–30%
		216	

Observation of grievance workers handling calls indicated some individual variation in the amount of effort expected of the complainant before SFCA accepted the grievance case. This variation had narrow limits, however, and, in general, any consumer who requested assistance with a specific complaint was accommodated.

PROCEDURE

After the grievance worker decided that the consumer's case warranted assitance, the date, the complainant's name, address, and telephone number were recorded on a 5″ × 8″ card along with a brief account of the complaint. Complainants were then mailed a "grievance kit" to be completed and returned to SFCA, after which work on the case commenced. Before concluding the call, the grievance worker offered a brief description of SFCA and urged the complainant to join the organization and contribute funds.

Grievance kits were usually mailed to complainants the same day as the initial contact and consisted of three mimeographed sheets: a cover letter, membership form, and summary information sheet. The cover letter instructed the consumer to fill out the summary information page, to write an additional, detailed history of the complaint, and to enclose copies of all written materials and receipts pertinent to the case, including any letters of complaint already written to the complainant. Consumers were also requested to sign and date an authorization statement printed on the summary information sheet, which carried over from the practices of the Association of California Consumers. It was designed to protect

SFCA from legal difficulties with clients and to permit SFCA to publish case histories in newsletters and elsewhere.

The cover letter closed with a request for consumers to become SFCA members and contribute membership dues. The second page of the kit consisted of a brief statement of organization goals and a membership form, asking whether the consumer would be willing to volunteer time at SFCA. The complainant was also asked if he had some specialized knowledge that he would be willing to share with grievance workers on the resolution of complaints, such as familiarity with television repair or automobile engine overhaul.

The summary information page, useful as a reference sheet for caseworkers, recorded the complainant's name, address, business and home telephone numbers, the defendant company's name, address, telephone, and any contacted representative's name, the product or service involved, the signature date of any contract, and the dollar amount paid. It asked for information on how the client heard of SFCA; what, if any, government agencies the client had already contacted; and what specific resolution the client desired.

After the kit was mailed, the interview card was placed in the alphabetized "Kits Sent Out" section of the interview card file. The next step was left entirely to the client. The returned, completed forms were placed in a folder along with the interview card, and the case was noted in the case logbook and assigned a case number. The numbered case material was then dropped into a box marked "Cases to Be Opened."

All cases were opened at the twice weekly grievance committee meetings. Before a meeting, several caseworkers read through the folders in the "Cases to Be Opened" box so that a brief presentation could be made on each case at the meeting. Then any caseworker with experience with the same type of situation or with the same defendant could either take the case or offer specific suggestions on how to proceed.

After carefully reading the case folder contents, the caseworker's first action was to telephone the client, to inform the client of his working hours at SFCA, and also to review his understanding of the case with the client, probing for information until satisfied that he had a clear conception of the transaction. In most cases, if the client had not already done so, the caseworker strongly urged him or her to complain to the California Department of Consumer Affairs. This course was prescribed not in the hope of effective action but to build pressure to improve the Department.

The caseworker next attempted to contact the case defendant in order to uncover both versions of the case. For local businesses, communication by telephone was preferred. Outside the Bay Area a form letter sufficed. Through either means, caseworkers attempted to appear polite but firm, interested in the defendant's story but insistent on a fair settlement. The initial defendant communication form letter illustrates the method.

TO WHOM IT MAY CONCERN:

The below named consumer has asked us for representation in a matter involving your firm.

We are sending this form letter first to open an opportunity for you to air your side of the matter since the consumer has presented one side already. Briefly the consumer has alleged:...

The consumer has indicated that to effect satisfactory resolution of the problem the following is needed:...

Your prompt attention to this matter may obviate the necessity for legal and-or civil action.

Sincerely yours,

SFCA Grievance Division

cc: [consumer]

In a small number of cases, these communications uncovered a basis for settlement. Otherwise, the caseworker began attempts to reach a fair resolution of the grievance. Often the defendant responded to caseworker contacts with a compromise offer, and a series of counteroffers could eventually produce an agreement. The consumer client was consulted at each stage.

If a reasonable settlement could not be negotiated, caseworkers might recommend legal action. San Francisco's Small Claims Court imposed a $500 award ceiling, so that if the settlement sought was less than that amount, the caseworker suggested small claims court. Grievance staff workers regularly served small claims court papers and accompanied clients to court to provide moral support. Grievances with more than $500 at stake pressed the upper limits of the committee's capabilities. Consumers were then referred to the group legal services firm with which the organization had an arrangement. SFCA could also pursue the complaint through public pressure tactics such as picketing, but this option was not regularly considered because of the resources required to conduct the effort effectively.

Consumer complaint cases were closed at grievance committee meetings. If a resolution was unsuccessful or only partially successful, further possible strategies were discussed collectively and a decision reached on whether to close the case. If the committee decision was to conclude SFCA's involvement in such cases, a call or letter to the client ended the case.

The caseworker noted the committee's action in the case logbook, summarized the case's disposition on the interview card, transferred the card from the "active" to the "closed" section of the interview card file, and put the complaint case folder in the file of closed cases.

Evaluating the Data

Early in our study of SFCA, a variety of sources provided us with the means for evaluating SFCA's consumer complaint assistance service. Wilson's observations and interviews in 1973 and 1974 were supplemented by a complete tabulation of the closed cases in SFCA's complaint files.

He reviewed the grievance committee's case logbook and prepared a summary for each of the 926 folders of closed cases in the committee files in an attempt to discover whether grievance case characteristics had changed in the course of SFCA's development. He found that a year-by-year comparison was unhelpful because the casework had increased rapidly in the more recent years and because a substantial number of case histories overlapped calendar years. A simpler procedure was chosen, in which the number of closed cases was divided in half and characteristics were compared between halves. Cases numbered between 163 and 1598 comprised the first 463 case folders; these completed cases were opened between March 1971 and March 1973. The second 463 case folders were numbered between 1603 and 2470 and included all completed cases opened from March 1973 to March 1974.

Questionnaires were mailed to all complainants with whom the committee had opened a case from January 1972 through December 1973 and whose addresses were available. A total of 910 questionnaires were mailed, 766 to consumers whose cases were closed as of 1 January 1974 and 144 to complainants who were still being assisted. The purpose of the questionnaire was to profile the grievance committee's clients and discover their assessment of the committee's effectiveness.[7] Of the 910 questionnaires mailed, 220 were returned—a 24% response rate. Although the number of responses was disappointing, the questionnaires did serve to verify the accuracy of case folder information. Questionnaires had been encoded with the original case number so that the consumer's evaluation of the case result could be compared with the grievance worker's notes recorded in the case folder tabulation. In no case were there indications

[7]Wilson patterned the questionnaire closely after that used in an analysis of the Pennsylvania Department of Insurance's effectiveness. Originally, it was hoped that a comparison of the Department of Insurance's complaint responses and SFCA's client answers would prove useful, but our low response rate discouraged such a venture.

TABLE 11.2
Sources of Consumers' Information about SFCA

	Number of responses	Percentage
Television	68	(32.8)
Friends	52	(25.1)
Radio	48	(23.1)
Newspaper	18	(8.6)
Better Business Bureau	11	(5.3)
Telephone book	10	(4.8)
Other	21	(10.1)

that the caseworker had exaggerated the effectiveness of the grievance committee's action. In fact, the at times pointed prose of the case folders, in a number of instances, was more pessimistic than the consumer's recollections of the case.

The questionnaire also asked clients how they had learned of the existence of SFCA. Table 11.2 categorizes the answers of the 207 responses.

Case Duration

Of the 926 closed cases, 757 had a closing date noted, which provided a measure of how long the grievance committee had worked on a complaint case. From a 333-case folder sample with opening and closing information, a mean duration of 2.3 months was computed. Similarly, a later sample of 424 cases averaged 2.2 months between opening and closing dates.

Consumer Complaint Case Closing Record

Closing date	Total cases closed
1971	28
January 1972	3
February	4
March	10
April	4
May	2
June	7
July	8
August	12
September	7
October	12
November	21
December	7
TOTAL 1972	97

(continued)

Consumer Complaint Case Closing Record—*Continued*

Closing date	Total cases closed
January 1973	14
February	29
March	33
April	54
May	36
June	48
July	67
August	41
September	28
October	58
November	22
December	22
TOTAL 1973	452
January 1974	76
February	40
March	64
First Quarter 1974	180
(169 Missing Observations)	
1971	47
January 1972	5
February	8
March	9
April	7
May	11
June	13
July	17
August	16
September	14
October	35
November	51
December	29
TOTAL 1972	215
January 1973	66
February	75
March	70
April	91
May	56
June	81
July	63
August	55
September	42
October	53
November	23
December	40
TOTAL 1973	715

(continued)

Consumer Complaint Case Closing Record—*Continued*

Closing date	Total cases closed
January 1974	104
February	78
March	27
First Quarter 1974	209

Complaint Category

Closed case folders were examined to identify major areas of consumer complaints. The tabulation (see Table 11.3) served primarily to underline the vast range of consumer problems, as only complaints about automobile purchase and repair accounted for more than 10% of the total. No substantial shifts in complaint category were observed during two different periods in 1973–1974.

Case Disposition

Of the 926 closed case folders, 832 contained sufficient records to categorize by case disposition. Three hundred fifteen of these 832 were closed though unresolved through grievance committee procedures (see Table 11.4).

There were, for the period under study, records of 517 consumer cases resolved by SFCA. These were divided into categories of successful,

TABLE 11.3
Consumer Complaint Categories

Complaint categories	Number of cases (%)	Number of cases (%)	Total cases (%)
Automobile purchase–repair	126 (27.8)	113 (24.9)	239 (26.4)
Appliance–electronic equipment purchase–repair	35 (7.6)	37 (8.1)	72 (7.9)
Finance–credit	41 (9.0)	28 (6.1)	69 (7.6)
Mail order	44 (9.7)	25 (5.5)	69 (7.6)
Home furnishings	32 (7.0)	29 (6.4)	61 (6.7)
Clothing	21 (4.6)	26 (5.7)	47 (5.2)
Landlord–tenant	7 (1.5)	35 (7.7)	42 (4.6)
Insurance	21 (4.6)	16 (3.5)	37 (4.1)
Home repairs	15 (3.3)	21 (4.6)	36 (4.0)
Movers	14 (3.0)	4 (0.8)	18 (2.0)
Other	97 (21.4)	119 (26.2)	216 (23.8)
	453	453	906

447

TABLE 11.4
Disposition of Closed but Unresolved Cases

Lost contact with client	95
Advice given; client continued without further assistance	63
Client withdrew	49
Client resolved without SFCA assistance	22
Client referred to group legal services	20
Client retained private attorney	19
Client referred to government agency	19
Client wrong	19
Client referred to another citizen consumer action group	9
	315

partially successful, and unsuccessful (see Table 11.5). "Successful" indicates that the client received most or all of the action originally requested on the summary information sheet; "partially successful," some; and "unsuccessful," little or none. No trend was evident between the two samples of cases taken during 2 different periods in 1973–1974.

Four hundred six cases (354 successful and 52 partially successful) generated specific results for the clients. The main result categories were cash payment, merchandise replacement–repair, and revision of contract (see Table 11.6).

There are several objective measures by which to judge SFCA's handling of complaints. These include percentage of cases successfully resolved and broad estimates of monies, merchandise, and services recovered for complainants. Another, more subjective, measure would be the general satisfaction of consumers who relied on the grievance committee.

The questionnaire, directed to a sample of consumers who utilized the grievance service, attempted to explore their satisfaction, though the term "satisfaction" was deliberately left undefined. In all, five questions related to this issue (see Table 11.7).

TABLE 11.5
Categorizations of Resolved Closed Cases

	Number of closed first half cases (%)	Number of closed second half cases (%)	Total (%)
Successful	190 (69.5)	164 (67.2)	354 (68.5)
Partially successful	22 (8.0)	30 (12.3)	52 (10.0)
Unsuccessful	61 (22.5)	50 (20.5)	111 (21.5)
	273	244	517

TABLE 11.6
Specific Results in Resolved Closed Cases

	First half (%)	Second half (%)	Total (%)
Cash payment	84 (39.6)	68 (35.0)	152 (37.4)
Merchandise replacement– repair	32 (15.1)	48 (24.7)	80 (19.7)
Contract revision	22 (10.4)	9 (4.7)	31 (7.6)
Other	74 (34.9)	69 (35.6)	144 (35.2)
	212	194	406

Evolution of Consumer Complaint-Resolution Groups

By 1976 SFCA was the sponsor of five consumer complaint-resolution committees meeting regularly at various places in the San Francisco Bay Area. These self-help committees, composed almost entirely of volunteers, were the subject of the study made by Brydolf, the

TABLE 11.7
Consumer Reaction to SFCA Assistance

1. Satisfaction with complaint outcome independent of SFCA's efforts (N = 189)

	Number	%
Very satisfied	92	(48.7) } (58.2)
Somewhat satisfied	18	(9.5)
Mixed feelings	20	(10.6)
Somewhat dissatisfied	13	(6.9) } (31.2)
Very dissatisfied	46	(24.3)

2. Satisfaction with SFCA's complaint handling (N = 207)

	Number	%
Very satisfied	111	(53.6) } (70.5)
Somewhat satisfied	35	(16.9)
Mixed feelings	26	(12.6)
Somewhat dissatisfied	13	(6.3) } (16.3)
Very dissatisfied	22	(10.0)

3. Would ask for advice and help from SFCA again (N = 206)

	Number	%
Definitely yes	127	(61.7) } (76.7)
Probably yes	31	(15.0)
Maybe	28	(13.6)
Probably not	11	(5.3) } (9.7)
Definitely not	9	(4.4)

(continued)

TABLE 11.7—*Continued*

4. Would recommend SFCA to a friend ($N = 196$)

	Number	%	
Definitely yes	132	(67.3)	} (87.2)
Probably yes	39	(19.9)	
Maybe	11	(5.6)	
Probably not	8	(4.1)	} (7.2)
Definitely not	6	(3.1)	

5. Trust SFCA ($N = 204$)

	Number	%	
Definitely yes	148	(72.5)	} (88.7)
Somewhat	33	(16.2)	
Mixed feelings	15	(7.4)	
Not much	4	(2.0)	} (4.0)
Not at all	4	(2.0)	

junior author of this chapter. Only two paid staff members, who help with organizing, work with the complaint committees. Membership on the committees is open to anyone, subject to two conditions: principally, a willingness to work with the committee for at least the duration of one's complaint, which means attending weekly meetings and participating in complaint-handling activities, and second, paying a yearly SFCA membership fee of $15, of which $5 is retained by the committee.

Most members find out about the committees through the SFCA switchboard, which receives consumers' complaints on a well-publicized telephone line. The switchboard caseworkers also give consumers information over the phone and help them find other complaint mechanisms when their problems cannot be handled well by an SFCA committee—for instance, when the merchant is located out of town. Consumers are referred elsewhere, too, if the type of complaint is not one that SFCA deals with; the committees do not work on complaints against government agencies (such as Social Security or welfare agencies) and do not handle landlord–tenant problems.

The number of members in an individual committee ranges from 10 to 40, with 15–20 members as an average. Although their characteristics vary from committee to committee, most members are middle- and working-class adults in their mid forties to late fifties. Women tend to make up more than half of any committee, and most members are married. Attendance generally reflects the racial composition of the particular district. In San Francisco, for example, the downtown committee's members are a racially heterogeneous group reflecting its large Asian, Spanish-

American, and black population, while another committee in the suburban peninsula area is largely white, middle class. Notably absent from all are upper-class residents and young, single adults in their early twenties; also absent are the very poor.

All committee members whose complaints have been resolved are encouraged to remain with the committee to help provide a stable core membership of experienced volunteers to assist newcomers and establish the committee as a permanent power base within the community. However, most committee members come and go with introduction and resolution of their complaints, and thus each committee owes its continuity to a small core of perhaps three or four loyal members. Core members are separated from less permanent volunteers by their general interest in the broader consumer movement. The core sets the tone, expectations, and ethical standards of each group and in large measure determines its success in complaint resolution. These members have also developed an expertise in complaint handling and are able to offer opinions and strategy suggestions based on their experience on the committee as well as the needed leadership, enthusiasm, and support. They hope that the social nature of each committee, combined with its success in complaint handling, will draw new permanent members. Lacking this dedicated core, committees can exist for only short periods, and SFCA has seen some complaint committees fade away without it.

Committees meet weekly in libraries or other community buildings; meetings are publicized through thousands of fliers and through government agency referrals, the local media, word of mouth, and SFCA's consumer hot line. Each committee is run by a group leader, a secretary, and a treasurer who are elected by the members about every 6 months. Each week new members are included and given complaint forms to complete. A typical form begins:

> Welcome to the committee. If you have a complaint you would like the committee to help you investigate, please complete both sides of this form and give it to the chairperson. Later on during the meeting you will have a chance to explain your complaint. Thank you, we are glad you decided to come....

The form requests the name of the merchant involved, a description of the complaint, and a summary of the action already taken by the consumer.

After the meeting is called to order, the committee leader gives a brief introduction to the group and its activities. After preliminaries, old cases are discussed. The complainant (member with the complaint) gives a brief history of his or her complaint. (All committees maintain a policy that a case is not discussed unless the complainant is present.) The committee member who has volunteered to try to resolve the complaint then outlines any action that has taken place since the last meeting, and members discuss and decide on any further action to be taken. Both old and new members are encouraged to voice their opinions and give advice based on their own experience. For example, members sometimes relate accounts of previous encounters with a particular merchant.

Following discussion of the old cases, newcomers present their complaints and what each believes would be a fair resolution of the problem. Committee members dicuss the new cases and decide whether or not to accept them. If a complaint is accepted, a member volunteers (or is chosen if no one volunteers) to handle it and is then in charge of all further communications with the merchant, though any final settlement must have the approval of the complainant.

Older members tend to take special care to treat new members politely and with respect. They offer condolences and try to give support to any discouraged victim who comes to the chapter for help. Implicit in all the committees' actions is a belief in the honesty and judgment of the complainant—provided he or she does not prove to be untrustworthy at a later date.

After all new cases have been presented and any other miscellaneous items announced, the meetings are adjourned. Core members like to keep the meetings to 1½ hours, as they otherwise tend to drag on and bore those attending.

The complaint committee follows essentially the three-step resolution procedure developed by the Consumers Education and Protective Association (CEPA) in Philadelphia: letter writing, group negotiation, and educational picketing. First, the complainant is asked to make an initial contact with the merchant to explain the complaint (if he or she has not already done so). If a negative reply (or no reply) is received or if the complainant has already contacted the merchant before coming to the committee, the committee member who volunteers to handle the case completes a form letter that briefly states the facts and the committee's idea of a satisfactory resolution.

About 20% of the complaints are settled at this stage. In these cases, the committee's intervention is generally successful in clearing up any misunderstanding existing between the consumer and the merchant or in placing further pressure—that of a consumer group—on the merchant to reach a resolution.

If a resolution is still not reached after a follow-up phone call from the committee representative, committee members may form a delegation, generally five or six people, to visit the merchant and negotiate a settlement. Of the consumers who have stayed with the committee up to this point, roughly 80% see their grievances resolved at the delegation level. The following is one such case:

In one example, a young couple came to the San Francisco committee with a complaint against a jewelry chain from which they had purchased an engagement–wedding ring set for a substantial sum. When the diamond came loose from the setting, they took the ring to another jeweler, who told them the set was worth only half what they had paid.

After the committee wrote the company and received no response, members had the set appraised at a number of jewelry stores, where they, too, were given lower estimates of the set's worth. They then arranged for a delegation to the merchant's office. Twenty members, an unusually large group, attended the negotiation session, at which the chain manager agreed to refund the couple's money.

If the delegation and a subsequent second phone conversation prove unsuccessful, the third and final step may be an informal picket line outside the merchant's place of business. This step requires nearly unanimous committee approval, some previous experience with other committee picketing, and the preparation of informational leaflets describing the complaint and approved by the central office. Once a decision to picket is made, the committee is responsible for its continuance until the complaint is resolved. Careful planning is required at this stage. The success of the pickets is crucial to the committee's ultimate success in all its complaint resoltuions, for it is the threat of pickets that provides the real leverage in the entire process. And that threat remains potent even though SFCA has resorted to picketing no more than a dozen times in its entire history.

Operating Principles

In this study of the operation of the complaint committees, five major principles were observed. First, in their evaluation of whether the individual consumer has been treated unfairly, the committees grant a strong presumption of accuracy to the consumer in weighing a complaint; this attitude has rarely proved unwarranted. The ideal is for all committee members to review and discuss each case so that from many perspectives the complaint is considered valid.

Second, committee assistance is intended to supplement the consumer's own attempts to resolve the complaint. The group's resources are made available along an information–advice–assistance continuum, depending on the complainant's own capability, the specifics of the complaint, and the responsiveness of the defendant. Consumer participation is intended to ensure that the complaint committee works with and not for the individual complainant. In fact, it is standard policy for a committee not to take a case until the complainant has exhausted all avenues available to him or her as an individual.

The third operating principle is that the committees are willing to use dramatic, imaginative, and unorthodox means—as long as they stay within the law—to maintain constant pressure until a fair resolution is reached. This persistence is illustrated in the case of an elderly couple who bought a new but malfunctioning $28,000 Dodge–Pace Arrow motor home in October 1974 for their retirement. The committee tried letters, negotiations, educational picket lines, and even a mock funeral procession for the car before it persuaded the agency's president to negotiate. Members from other complaint committees as far as 50 miles away drove to picket in support of this claim.

The fourth operating principle is that consumer complaint assistance involves a series of judgments to be made collectively, not individually, though the individual consumer is the one who must finally decide whether to accept a particular settlement offered by the merchant.

Last, the committees are seen by core members as having the potential for organizing consumers and involving them in a larger movement.

Cleveland Consumer Action: A Comparison

We thought it might be useful to compare SFCA with a similar organization, Cleveland Consumer Action, which also has complaint-handling groups, called "chapters." Although Brydolf's contact with the Cleveland group (CCA) covered only a few days, she found notable similarities. Both groups, founded in 1971, boast impressive track records. Through 1976, Cleveland's three chapters had saved their members $200,000, and San Francisco's five committees had saved $250,000. The Cleveland chapters charge somewhat smaller dues—a yearly membership fee of $2 plus 50¢ a month dues, or $8 per year—compared to San Francisco's total of $15 yearly.

As complaint-handling services, both groups appear to be highly successful in attracting and resolving consumer complaints. Both organizations estimate that each of their committees receives up to 15 new complaints weekly, and few complainants are turned away. On the whole, the committees vote to accept any complaint that seems to be an honest one brought by any consumer who is willing to work with the committee in its resolution process. The committees in both cities accept many complaints that other agencies for various reasons refuse to consider, such as complaints involving binding contracts regarded as unfair or unethical. However, if members think that a complainant has a strong legal case that could be won in small claims court or would be quickly handled by a government agency, they will recommend that course of action.

For both groups, the only consumers who come to the complaint resolution committees are, for the most part, those with complaints involving sizable sums of money, and more than half of all the cases handled concern automobiles or other large vehicles. Most of the other cases involve major purchases, such as refrigerators or stoves. Most consumers with minor grievances decide that it is not worth their while to spend 1 or 2 hours a week in committee meetings in order to receive satisfaction on a minor purchase. As most consumer gripes involve small amounts, the limitations of the committee approach are apparent. Simpler, more efficient mechanisms must be devised to handle minor consumer grievances.

Very few of the complaint cases accepted by either group result in no compensation of any kind for the complainant. Many end in a resolution close, if not equal, to the complainant's idea of a fair settlement, disregarding the time and effort spent working on the case; other cases result in a compromise with the merchant—one that usually could not have been achieved by the individual alone. One primary reason for the committees' success in both places is their dependence on members' own judgments of whether or not a complaint can be resolved. In practical terms, the likelihood of winning depends on whether complaint resolution is amenable to the groups' negotiation and picketing methods.

Both groups seek to educate their own members as to problem solving and prevention. The committees provide opportunities for participants to learn from each other's experiences. Members have an opportunity to develop skills in handling their own complaints and to learn how to avoid further consumer problems.

The impact of the complaint groups at the community level is harder to gauge because of the extensive developments of consumer protection along many fronts in the last few years. In Cleveland, according to one participant, the parent organization, Cleveland Consumer Action, has had an impact in two areas. First, its presence has had preventive effects, serving to eliminate the most obvious abuses and fraudulent business practices in the area. "We just don't get cases of clear consumer fraud the way we used to," observed one CCA member. Second, the chapters' success in resolving individual complaints and CCA's positions on city issues have pressured other local consumer groups and agencies to become more forceful in order to maintain their own standing. Similarly, in the San Francisco Bay Area the presence of the SFCA committees appears to be having a preventive effect.

In both cities the groups' primary strategy of approaching businesses from a position of collective power—through contact, negotiation, and finally picketing—is integral to their success in complaint handling. Second, each group's refusal to be tied to the traditional legal framework and its insistence on the use of its own ethical criteria for judgment enable it to define the ethics of business relations. Instead of being subject to a merchant's definitions and decisions, these committees take control, using consumer buying power as leverage. The third and most crucial step, picketing, is an effective combination of voice and exit (Hirschman 1970) in a marketplace that is little influenced by complaints from individuals (voice alone) or their silent changes to other brands and other merchants (exit alone).

Although essential to the complaint committees' success, these strategies are not without their limitations. The three-step resolution process is generally unable to handle complaints about nonstorefront operations, where consumer picketing is not possible or effective. In addition, because the complaint committees are nonprofessional, they have little validity in some people's minds, and some merchants are reluctant to give serious attention to complaints brought by them.

Perhaps the major long-term limitation of the complaint committees is their failure to obtain block solutions to consumer problems—solutions that benefit numerous consumers. Their policy of solving individual complaints often necessitates their acceptance of an explicitly stated exception to a store's general policy in order to settle a complaint.

SFCA's experience with the chain of jewelry stores mentioned earlier is an apt illustration of how difficult it is to bring about general changes in company policy. SFCA had received a number of complaints about the same chain over the years. In each case the store had agreed to refund the purchasers' money, but no changes were made in the manipulative sales techniques that led to the grievances. Evidently there was more profit to be gained by continuing the hard sell; the few dissatisfied customers who used SFCA to pressure the company into resolving their complaints were only a minor irritant. Then a local television station stepped in and exposed the problem on its consumer show; the company still did not relent. Even intervention by the San Francisco District Attorney seemed to have little effect, as the company's policy fell into that shady area where there was no clear violation of a law.

On the positive side, a number of structural checks strengthen the committees and ensure both their validity and their responsiveness to people's problems. First, group acceptance, discussion, and advocacy of complaints require majority agreement and support of each decision. Second, the educational pickets are required to have both convincing and truthful leaflets approved by the committee. Third, the committees' sole dependence on member participation for negotiations and pickets—in fact, for their existence as a whole—forces them to be accountable and effective.

Concluding Remarks

San Francisco Consumer Action has made important contributions in its attempt to improve the position of the consumer in the marketplace. It has demonstrated the virtues of flexible organization; it has evolved a philosophy of dispute settlement that recognizes disputing as an activity related to broad economic and political structures in this society. As an organization that educates people in government, it has reminded us of the importance of a social consciousness, a factor missing from so many of our nonvoluntary institutions, which are sometimes more concerned with the continuity of their organizations than with any social mission. It has trained people in leadership. As of March 1980, SFCA was no longer handling consumer complaints. Affected by a shortage of resources, it is presently an organization dedicated primarily to consumer education and regulatory effort.

We have mentioned throughout that the organization has had constant worries about sources of support. The very instability caused by the fragile financial base at SFCA has been a source of esprit among workers who have received little or no remuneration. The fact that some have stayed in spite of the absence of tangible reward and of a strong financial base is interesting in itself.

Innovation has been rewarded at SFCA. Members first experimented with complaint mobiles in poor neighborhoods; now such mobile units are used as part of the work of the Consumer Fraud Division of the San Francisco District Attorney's office. After SFCA began to provide aid and advice in languages other than English, the Consumer Fraud Division likewise adopted the practice. SFCA was not embarrassed to borrow good ideas from elsewhere if they contributed to its overall goals. The idea of complaint committees, which was being tried by consumer groups in Cleveland and Philadelphia, was used in answer to the perceived need for greater awareness and self-esteem among consumers in trouble. The many and successful consumer booklets SFCA has published were undoubtedly influenced by similar activities that were an integral part of Herbert Denenberg's term while he was Commissioner of Insurance in Pennsylvania. That such innovation and borrowing was common practice at SFCA may be related to the absence of hierarchical organization, so that its leaders were not separated from direct interaction with clients of and colleagues in the organization.

SFCA has lived up to many of its goals under difficult circumstances, as the previous discussion has documented. One of its important functions is educational. This function is recognized by local colleges and universities and is the reason academic credit may be earned by SFCA's student volunteers. SFCA has given many hundreds of prelaw and law students the opportunity to participate in a developing organization with goals that are social in nature rather than antisocial or solely profit making. Lawyers do not get such training in law schools, where the concern is usually corporate in nature or at least more abstract in relation to problems of the poor. SFCA is an experiment in problem solving at the local, private, and voluntary level. Here both undergraduate students and law students learn the difficulties inherent in solving problems one by one in a mass society. Some of those who learn, like Kay Pachtner and Neil Gendel, become leaders. Furthermore, the business community learns of the need for changes in business practices, of the need to arbitrate or to improve its practices. Small claims courts, too, are encouraged to live up to their purpose by teaching citizens how to use them.

To evaluate SFCA, then, requires us to view it and similar organizations as places for leadership training, as classes in learning about democratic procedures, as experiments in solutions and organizations—all in addition to their broad goal of furthering social welfare. Such organizations are an important part of the crucial relations between private and public activity in this country.

In its evolution from a small consumer complaint switchboard to an organization involved in a wide range of activities from public relations work to education, advocacy, and complaint handling by geographically scattered committees, SFCA illustrates how an organization can develop in response to the needs of its clientele and in terms of its goals as stated at the outset. Such an evolution is quite in contrast to the development of organizations that respond principally to the needs of the organization itself, as illustrated in Chapter 10 on complaint mechanisms in the ghetto. SFCA started out servicing complaints one by one and gradually came to realize that such a procedure was inefficient if its goals were indeed to improve the position of the consumer in the marketplace. Its members' concern appropriately shifted toward block solutions and prevention, and toward the exercise of consumer power through the use of shoppers' guides and self-help complaint committees.

References

Alinsky, Saul
  1971   *Rules for radicals.* New York: Random House.
CA News
  1976   "CA Blasts KQED for Censorship, Ends Program." Nov.–Dec.: p. 1.
Clark, Ramsey
  1970   *Crime in America. Observations on its nature, causes, prevention and control.* New York: Simon and Schuster.
Denenberg, Herbert
  1973   Address to the Consumer Federation of America Assembly, Washington, D.C. 26 January.
Gendel, Neil
  1973   Background and goals statement. Testimony before the U.S. Senate Judiciary Subcommittee on Consumer Laws, Los Angeles, 25 October.

Hirschman, Albert
  1970 *Exit, voice and loyalty: Responses to decline in firms, organizations, and states.* Cambridge: Harvard University Press.
Los Angeles Times
  1972 28 June.
Nader, R., and D. Ross
  1971 Action for a change. New York: Grossman.
Pachtner, Kay
  1971 Letter to British Motor Car Distributors, 12 October.
San Francisco Examiner and Chronicle
  1972 23 January: p. A6.

12

Elaine Combs-Schilling

GRIEVING AND FEUDING:
The Organizational Dilemma of
a Labor Union

Introduction

At the outset, it should be said that the types of complaints we will be examining in this chapter, as well as the organizational structure intended to handle these complaints, are fundamentally different from those examined elsewhere in the book. Most of the studies in this book are concerned with grievances of persons or organizations against *other* persons or organizations; complaints by customers directed to stores where they make their purchases; complaints against insurance agencies lodged by those who bought their insurance; problems and complaints concerning governmental agencies filed with a congressman by his constituents; and complaints against numerous business firms and government agencies received by media "action liners" from private citizens. These complaints can be labeled *external complaints.* Either the mediator who receives the complaint is not a part of the organization against whom the complaint is directed, or the person filing the complaint is not a member of that organization.

In this chapter we shall be examining "in-house" complaints and an "in-house" procedure for their solution. The organization I use to illustrate this type of complaint and complaint-handling procedure is the UAW—the International Union, United Automobile, Aerospace and Agricultural Implement Workers of America. My concern is with the complaints UAW workers have about their own union, and with the union's own mechanism for handling these complaints. Complaints against management are not considered here unless they manifest themselves in the

NO ACCESS TO LAW
Alternatives to the American Judicial System

workers' grievances against the union, such as the failure of the union to adequately handle its workers' complaints against management.

The union provides a particularly fascinating example of what I have labeled *internal complaints* and complaint-handling procedure, for its members see themselves very much as an in-group that is in more or less constant conflict with an out-group, the management. This structural position has some important ramifications for both the complaints voiced and the arena available for settling them.

UAW—Management Relations: The Institutionalized Feud

The relations between the UAW and management perhaps can be appropriately characterized as that of an institutionalized feud. The two groups see their interests as directly conflicting and have basic misgivings about the repercussions of the other group's actions upon themselves.

In the traditional feud, according to Evans-Pritchard (1940 and 1949) and Emry Peters (1967), conflicts within the in-group are submerged as the energies of the group are directed toward the opposition—the out-group. In these traditional feuds, actual conflict between the in-group and the out-group is only intermittent. In times of peace, the in-group's united front ceases to be so united; conflicts within the group reemerge and necessitate some kind of mechanism for solution.[1] Positions of authority within the in-group are temporary, flexible, and of limited scope, being greatest during times of conflict and least during times of peace.

The UAW–management feuding situation differs from the foregoing description in some fundamental ways: (a) Within the in-group, authority positions have been institutionalized and are permanent in nature. Union, as well as management, has a formalized bureaucracy to deal with the feuding situation; (b) The in-group and the out-group see themselves in constant, rather than intermittent, opposition (although the intensity of the conflict is certainly variable). The two groups are in daily contact, and their differences are graphically portrayed; the management's attire includes white shirts and ties whereas the UAW workers wear overalls or colored shirts and pants, and no ties.

Despite these differences, there remain certain similarities between the institutionalized and the traditional feuding situations. From our standpoint, probably the most important similarity is the in-group's per-

---

[1]In egalitarian society, the "solution" might be the channeling of aims and desires, the creation of consensus, rather than the open expression and subsequent solution of conflicts. For an incisive discussion of this question, see Colson 1974:31–59.

ceived need to submerge in-group conflicts, maintaining a united front against management, particularly in times of crisis. It is this structural position that presents a most interesting problem for complaint management.

Before beginning to examine the substance of the UAW complaints and its complaint-handling procedure, two important points need emphasis. First, the UAW was chosen, not for the weakness but rather for the strength of its attempt to tackle the complaints of its workers. Of the large, established unions in the United States, the UAW appears to have the best procedure, and maybe the only procedure, for handling the internal grievances of its members. In this chapter I will note what I perceive to be some of the deficiencies in this system, but no other organization, including management, need gloat over these shortcomings, for it can be seriously doubted that there exist many, if any, organizations that equitably handle the complaints of their own members against themselves, not only solving personal grievances but remedying the structural weaknesses that precipitated the grievances. I remain unconvinced that Americans have as yet developed organizations that: (a) have effective lines of communication between the multiple levels of the organization (i.e., the top and the bottom, the bottom and the middle, and so on); and (b) have the organizational capacity and flexibility to respond to the problems exemplified in internal complaints by reorienting their own structure so that these same problems do not reemerge. In fact, this problem is what this whole book is about—trying to find ways to develop flexible, open organizations that can quickly respond to the problems and complaints posed by its members, organizations that operate with self-confidence rather than fear.

The second point that needs emphasis is the paucity of data on the use and nonuse of the UAW complaint-handling mechanisms by its constituents. Although this study was meant to be a preliminary one, it turned out to be rather more preliminary than we had hoped. Although I am fairly certain of the findings concerning the formal structure of UAW complaint-handling procedure, my discussion of the use and nonuse of it by UAW members rests on shakier ground. Data on the latter question were extremely difficult to obtain.

A Note on Methodology

There were two main periods of research: (a) November–December 1973, during which time I amassed data on the formal structure of the UAW and conducted interviews with local UAW officials and line workers. The total number of initial interviews was small: 15 line workers (who had been in the union for 7½ to 29 years), five local officials and shop committeemen, and two International Representatives. Although I have reason to believe that these workers' answers represent major trends, it was thought that additional data were required to verify preliminary findings. (b) Therefore, an attempt was made to collect these data during a second period of research in July and August 1975. Interviews were the first line of attack, but this attempt proved to be unproductive. The extent of my personal network of contacts had been exploited, and other workers were extremely reluctant to talk. Although I myself am fundamentally distrustful of questionnaires, it was decided, given the short time period available, that this was the best alternative means of attack. Seven hundred questionnaires were distributed, but only 38 were returned, and only 36 were completed. I am aware of the extremely limited nature of the data.

There is probably good reason for this lack of access to data. Union members form an in-group who typically are distrustful of "outsiders" who come to "study" them, offering little or nothing in compensation for their intrusion. For all the workers knew, I might have been in collaboration with management or antiunion legislators who would have liked to foment conflict within the union. Furthermore, in 1975, the union was in the midst of a particularly critical time. The automobile industry was anything but thriving. In one of the union locals I was examining, 1500 workers had been laid off. The union had a weaker bargaining position with management than it had had in years.

This crisis probably had two results that made it much more difficult to gather data on complaints by the union about the union. The first consequence was that the union, like any in-group in the midst of a feuding crisis, had drawn more closely in upon itself. Second, the workers and committeemen simply had less time and tolerance for talking to an anthropologist (who they may well have doubted knew the meaning of an honest day's work) about what they then saw as a peripheral problem (complaints against the union) when the central problem (directed toward management) of how many more workers were going to lose their jobs loomed so ominously in the foreground.

Despite the limitations of the data, we decided to proceed with both the presentation of the formal structure and the discussion of apparent patterns of use and nonuse of it by constituents. Any misrepresentations are unintentional, and apologies are sincerely offered for them. Further data, research, and comments, in either negation or support of the findings in this chapter, are more than welcome. It is hoped that this study will be only a beginning to the dialogue concerning the generalized problem of in-house complaints and grievance-solving procedures.

Structure of the UAW: Allocation of Responsibility

We begin our discussion with a brief look at the structure of the UAW, focusing on the tasks of the local committeeman, as many complaints appear to revolve around him. We then examine the three main formal systems of complaint management within the UAW structure: trial proceedings, local recall proceedings, and appeal procedures. Our focus finally turns to the actual complaints of line workers and to a discussion of the use and nonuse of formal UAW complaint-handling procedure.

Briefly stated, the UAW is organized in the following way: A convention of the UAW, with delegates from each local, meets every 2 years. The convention is the highest authority of the union. In between conventions, the International Executive Board, which meets quarterly, has final say on all union matters. The International Constitution states, "The International Executive Board shall execute the instructions of the International Convention and shall be the highest authority of the International Union between Conventions, subject to the provisions of this Constitution, and shall have the power to authorize strikes, issue charters and punish all subordinate bodies for violation of this Constitution [UAW 1972a:22]." The Executive Board is currently composed of the UAW President, Leonard Woodcock; the Secretary–Treasurer, Emil Mazey; 7 vice-presidents; and 18 regional directors. The officers are elected at each International Convention. Between the quarterly meetings of the UAW Executive Board, the president is the highest authority in the union.

The regional directors serve as the apex of the regional structure. Each region has several international representatives who serve as the liaison between the local unions and the regional directors. The regional director in turn serves as the link to the International Executive Board.

On the local level, there are two groups of important officials, the local officers and the shop officials. In some locals the same men fill both roles, but in the local this writer observed, the roles were separate. The local officers are the president, vice-president, recording secretary, financial secretary, treasurer, three trustees, a sergeant-at-arms, and a guide. These officers, all ex-officio members of the Local Executive Board, are elected every 2–3 years.[2] The local officers, with the exception of the financial secretary, work for the union only part-time, retaining their regular jobs in the plants. The financial secretary is a full-time employee of the union; he gives up his plant job for as long as he remains elected. These officers carry on the functioning of the local union, paying the bills, conducting the meetings, forming committees, and such. They have their offices in the local UAW hall.

The official "shop" positions of chairman, unit committeemen, and district committeemen are all full-time jobs of the union. Their offices are located in the actual plant where production occurs. These officials, also elected every 2–3 years (depending on the length of the contract), are the ones who ensure that the contract between the company and the union is

[2]Elections coincide with union–management contract renewals. Thus, the length of time between elections is dependent upon the duration of a contract, usually a period of 2–3 years.

honored. The shop chairman, also called the building chairman, is the official head of the "shop", that is, all the UAW members in an entire manufacturing plant.[3] Under him are three unit committeemen, each in charge of one unit in the plant. The unit committeemen and the shop chairman make up the official bargaining committee that negotiates contracts and contract disputes. Each unit is divided into districts of 225 men, and each district has its own district committeeman, usually called simply the committeeman. The most important and time-consuming job of the committeeman is the settling of grievances. An understanding of the grievance procedure is important for our purposes, because it is the committeeman's handling of these proceedings that is the source of many complaints.

The Grievance Procedure

The grievance procedure provides the mechanism for members of the UAW to complain against management, particularly in terms of contract violations. This procedure helps insure that contracts are honored. For instance, under the UAW contract, foremen, who are a part of management and consequently salaried workers, are not allowed to work on the production line. If a line worker observes a violation of this clause, he can file a grievance against the foreman. If he sees a foreman working for an hour on the line, the line worker can go through the grievance procedure, and if he wins his claim (by having sufficient proof of the offense, usually the word of other witnesses), he will be financially compensated for the time the foreman worked.

A substantial number of grievances every month are against foremen who have been working on the line. In the Union's monthly plant report, if the grievance is won, the results are listed like the following: "Ch-6290–J. R. Thompson, 5849-Paid ½ hour—Foreman Bayer working ... Ch-6080–M. Jimenez, 9752-Paid 4.0 hours—Foreman Carrillo working" (UAW Local——, Plant Slants, November 1973:3). The other most common grievance is misassignment of overtime. Again, workers are compensated financially if they win their grievance. Some grievances concern the lack of safety equipment, and others often involve reducing discipline penalties. There is an intricate hierarchy of discipline procedures, and if a man feels he has been too harshly disciplined, he can file a grievance.

A grievance must be filed for a worker by his committeeman, that is, his district committeeman. The committeeman then tries to settle the grievance with the foreman. If they cannot settle it, the grievance goes to

---

[3]The UAW is organized not by craft but by plant. Although different craft workers often have subcommittees within the local organization, they do not comprise different locals.

the unit committeeman. If again the grievance cannot be settled, it goes to the shop chairman. If he cannot obtain a settlement of the grievance with management, the grievance goes to the shop umpire, who is ostensibly an impartial judge, a member of neither the union nor the management. He is an outsider selected by joint agreement of union and management officials.

The grievance procedure is vital to the line worker. Not only can he be financially compensated for certain grievances, but his very job may depend on the grievance procedure. According to some workers interviewed, if a foreman is "out to get a man," he can repeatedly discipline the man for offenses he did not commit or for which he had reasonable explanations (e.g., for being late for work). Reprimands and warnings in writing go on a man's record and remain there for 5 years. After a man has a certain number of these reprimands, he can be fired from his job. The way a man prevents this from happening is by the filing of grievances. The worker is dependent on his committeeman for this filing.

In general, the grievance-filing procedure appears to be a good one, as it relieves the worker from the paperwork involved with the filing as well as allows a few people, the committeemen, to specialize in the intricacies of the contract. However, the system does leave the worker in a rather vulnerable position. A grievance is supposed to be filed by a committeeman upon request by the worker. After the actual filing of the grievance, the committeeman can then investigate and decide whether it is a meritorious or un unmeritorious grievance. In reality, this appears not to be the normal procedure. The committeeman (who often may be pressed for time even in the handling of what he considers very serious grievances concerning marked violations of the contract) can overtly or covertly discourage the filing of a grievance that he for some reason does not wish to handle.

Formal Complaint-Handling Procedures of the UAW

If a union member has a complaint against another union member that involves a violation of the UAW Constitution, he can press charges against the accused and bring him to trial. Trials against members follow one of two procedures, depending on whether they concern international executive board members or regular union members.

TRIALS OF INTERNATIONAL OFFICERS AND INTERNATIONAL EXECUTIVE BOARD MEMBERS

The following is the procedure outlined in the UAW Constitution for charges and trials of international officers and executive board members:

Charges against International Officers of International Executive Board Members may be filed in either of these manners: (a) Upon written affidavits signed by five (5) or more Board Members filed with the International

Secretary–Treasurer. (b) Upon written affidavit signed by a Local Union and by at least ten (10) additional local unions in the International Union, or in the case of charges against an International Executive Board Member, upon written affidavit signed by the Local Union member and endorsed by his own Local Union and by a majority of the Local Unions within the region from which the International Executive Board Member is elected [UAW 1972a:49].

When the charges are against the International Secretary-Treasurer, they are filed with the International President. Otherwise, when the charges are received by the International Secretary-Treasurer, he sends a copy of them to all members of the Executive Board, including the accused. The accused is notified that he has 15 days to prepare a defense. A special meeting of the International Executive Board is held 10 days after the charges are filed. The accused stays in office until the outcome of the trial is known, unless the International Executive Board, at the special meeting, votes by two-thirds to suspend the member.

The first order of business at the special meeting is to choose a trial committee. By lottery, the names of 50 delegates to the last convention are drawn. These delegates cannot be officers or employees of the International Union or members of the International Executive Board and must be currently in good standing with the union. "After these names are drawn they shall be read by the International Secretary–Treasurer in the presence of the International Executive Board and each name in succession shall be set opposite a number from one (1) to fifty (50) [UAW 1972a:50]." The accused and the accuser each have the right to strike 10 names from the list. After these names have been stricken, the first 12 persons remaining are taken to serve on the trial committee, the remaining names serving as alternates if any of the original 12 cannot attend the trial.

According to the Constitution, the trial is to be conducted in the following manner:

Section 12. The International Trial Committee shall go into session immediately upon arrival of the full panel and shall hear the charges brought by the accuser and all the witnesses named for substantiation, and shall hear the defense of the accused and all his witnesses for substantiation. The Trial Committee shall decide its own rules of procedure relating to the conduct of the trial and may elect its own Chairman and Secretary, providing that verbatim minutes of all evidence shall be reported by a court stenographer. The accused and accuser shall have a right to be represented by counsel.

Section 13. The Trial Committee, upon completion of the hearing of the evidence and arguments, shall go into closed session to determine the verdict and penalty. A two-thirds (⅔) vote shall be required to find the accused guilty. In case the accused is found guilty, the Trial Committee may, by a majority vote, reprimand the accused or it may, by a two-thirds (⅔) vote, assess a fine not to exceed five hundred dollars ($500.00) with automatic suspension, removal from office or expulsion in the event of the failure of the accused to pay the fine within a specified time; or it may, by two-thirds (⅔) vote, suspend or remove the accused from office, or suspend or expel him from membership in the International Union.

Section 14. In case a Trial Committee finds the accused innocent they may determine the honest or malicious intent of the accuser. If they find the accuser guilty of obvious malice in filing the charges they may assess a penalty against him in accordance with Section 13 of this Article (UAW 1972a:50–51).

TRIALS OF MEMBERS

Trials of members are held locally and follow the same basic procedure as excerpted with the following exceptions: Any one member of the local can press charges against another. The charges are submitted to the Local Recording Secretary. They are reviewed by the Local Executive Board, which judges whether or not they are legitimate according to the Constitution. The time periods between notification and trial proceedings are shorter than those on the International level. The trial committee is chosen (also by lottery) from the local membership present at the first meeting after the charges have been filed. The number of names drawn as well as the number of names the accused and accuser are allowed to strike depends on the size of the local union. After the trial committee arrives at its verdict and decides upon a sanction (a fine at this level cannot exceed $100), it must present its findings at a meeting of the local union membership. The members in turn must pass by majority vote (on secret ballots) both the verdict and the penalty before they can go into effect.

If the accused is found innocent, as in the International trials, the trial committee may determine the honest or malicious intent of the accuser and may, if the case warrants, impose a penalty upon him.

Either an acquittal or a conviction can be appealed to the International Executive Board, which:

> shall review the record of the trial and subsequent proceedings in the Local Union and such other matters relevant to the charges and the appeal as it feels necessary in order to assure justice. The Board shall be empowered, if it finds that the verdict was against the great weight of the evidence, to set it aside and order a new trial by an International Union Trial Committee [UAW 1972a:59].

This decision in turn can be appealed to either the Convention Appeals Committee or the Public Review Board, as is explained in the coming section on "Appeals Procedure."

RECALL OF LOCAL COMMITTEEMEN

A local committeeman can be recalled according to procedures in the local bylaws. In the local I studied, recall procedure could be started by a petition containing the signatures of 25% of the workers in the committeeman's district. A district meeting would then be held at which both sides would present their viewpoints. At this meeting, two-thirds of the men in the district had to be present before a recall vote could be taken, and then a majority of those present had to vote to recall him.

APPEALS PROCEDURE FOR MEMBERS

A member of any local union can appeal any action, decision, or penalty of his unit within 60 days of that action. He must first appeal to the Local Executive Board or to the local membership (unless the International President from some reason waives this restriction or unless the local group does not meet to vote on the appeal within 45 days after it is submitted). The appellant has a right to counsel (UAW 1972a:62). Most appeals are complaints of improper action of a committeeman on a grievance or complaints about the way in which an election was conducted.

The local membership can overturn the action the worker is appealing. If, however, they do not and the appellant continues to believe he has a legitimate complaint, he may appeal to the International Executive Board. He does so in writing to the International President and the International Secretary–Treasurer. At this level either of two procedures may be followed: (a) The International President may investigate and decide on the appeal; and (b) a two-member committee of the International Executive Board may investigate and make a decision that must be ratified by the larger nine-man Appeals Committee of the Executive Board in order to become effective.[4] Copies of the decision made by either the International President or the Appeals Committee are sent to all Executive Board members and become the decision of the International Executive Board unless one or more members of the Board protest the decision, in which case it is decided at the next International Executive Board meeting (UAW 1972a:63–64).

If again the appellant is not satisfied with the decision given him, there are two options still open, either of which is final. He may appeal either to the Constitution Convention Appeals Committee of the International Union, or alternatively, he may appeal to the Public Review Board (UAW 1972a:64–66).

The Constitution Convention Appeals Committee is made up of delegates selected from different regions by lot at the Constitutional Convention. They meet semiannually and decide any appeal cases before them. Only six cases were decided by them in the period from 1970 to 1972 (UAW 1972b).

The Public Review Board, established in 1957, was proclaimed a

---

[4]The Appeals Committee consists of nine members of the International Executive Board, selected by the Board to handle appeals.

significant innovation, for workers now could appeal to a board comprised of nonunion people who would ostensibly be nonpartisan in terms of union decisions. The 1972–1974 Public Review Board was comprised of the following people: the Right Reverend Monsignor George C. Higgins, Chairperson of the committee and Director of the Division for Urban Life of the Department of Social Development of the U.S. Catholic Conference; Harry W. Arthurs, Associate Dean of York University Law School, Toronto, Ontario; Robben W. Fleming, President of the University of Michigan; James E. Jones, Professor at the University of Wisconsin Law School; the Honorable Frank W. McCulloch, now Professor at the University of Virginia Law School and former Chairman of the National Labor Relations Board; Jean T. McKelvey, Professor at the New York State School of Industrial and Labor Relations, Cornell University; and Rabbi Jacob J. Weinstein, Rabbi Emeritus of Temple K.A.M. in Chicago (UAW 1972b:129). The Public Review Board meets whenever it deems it necessary to consider the cases before it. The Board may dismiss a case before a hearing if it does not think there is sufficient evidence to warrant a hearing.

Use and Nonuse of Complaint Procedures

The most striking feature of these three systems—the trial, the recall procedure, and the appeals procedure—is the nonuse of them by most of the workers. All UAW members I interviewed agreed with this finding. Of the 20 local workers I interviewed, none had ever used the trial or appeals procedure, and only one of them was aware of anyone who had. Of the 36 workers who completed the questionnaires, 32 said they had never even considered bringing another member to trial, and 28 had no idea what the trial procedure involved. The recall procedure was that with which workers were most familiar, but this procedure, too, remained largely unused. Of those who returned questionnaires, 14 said they were familiar with the union's recall procedure, and 19 said they were not familiar with it. Only 2 had actually participated in a recall proceeding (although 10 said they had considered attempting to recall a committeeman or local officer). Of union members interviewed, only 1 had participated in recall proceedings, and it was unsuccessful. In the local I studied, no committeeman had been recalled, at least not within the last 24 years. Nor did any of those interviewed, including the officers, know of any Local or International Officer or Executive Board members who had come to trial. One of the local officials related that several years ago there had been a trial in the local union, and it was such a rarity that no one knew quite how to proceed.

What is apparent in proceedings on the local level is even more striking in complaint-handling mechanisms on the national level. None of the line workers interviewed had ever heard of the Public Review Board, and only two had heard of the Convention Appeals Committee. Of the five local officers and committeemen interviewed, I was most surprised that three of them had never heard of the Public Review Board. One of these men had been a loyal member of the union for over 30 years and a committeeman for over 10 years, and he had made it his policy to know all about the union. He stated that not only had he not heard of the Public Review Board, but he was sure it did not exist. He told me I must be thinking of the Convention Appeals Committee.

Only 1 of the 36 workers who completed the questionnaires said that he had ever considered taking a complaint to the UAW Convention Appeals Committee, and none had ever considered taking a complaint to the Public Review Board. Over two-thirds of those completing questionnaires said they had never heard of either of these groups.

Thus we can conclude from these preliminary data that workers apparently do not, as a rule, use the available UAW complaint-handling procedures as a mechanism for voicing their grievances about the union. Local officials agreed with this finding, stating that unless a complaint were very serious, the formal procedures available were not viable ones. Statistics from the national level support this view, as only six cases were heard by the Convention Appeals Committee in the 1970–1972 period and only 23 by the Public Review Board, a tiny number of cases considering the total UAW membership of over 1,300,000.

Hypotheses Concerning Nonuse

In asking why the union mechanisms for complaint management are not used, we must first caution the reader that, given the amount of information available, we cannot decisively answer this question. Rather let us look at various possible explanations, examine the data that support or refute them, and try to reckon with their consequences.

The most obvious explanation for nonuse of the UAW complaint-handling system is that UAW workers have no complaints, as one committeeman, in a 2-hour interview, claimed. Half the workers who returned questionnaires said they had had no complaints against the union in the last 2 years. However, given that the others who returned questionnaires as well as those interviewed all had some sort of complaint (though most of the workers considered their complaints to be minor ones), we can dismiss this rather far-fetched possibility out of hand. In addition, because our concern in this book is with "minor" as well as "major" complaints, our interest in why UAW workers do not use the available union mechanism for voicing their complaints is in no way diminished.

Some local officials posed an alternative possibility. They claimed that one reason for nonuse of the union complaint-handling mechanisms was their complexity. The system involved simply too much work. One former committeeman summed it up by saying, "It'd have to be something really big to go through all the trouble it is to file an appeal." Another committeeman stated, "I've found the more paperwork involved, the less likely the men are to use that procedure." Several stated that a man would not bother going through the union mechanisms when he could complain much more easily to the National Labor Relations Board (NLRB) or to the Equal Opportunity Commission (EOC).[5] According to the local officials interviewed, more complaints against the union have been filed by local workers with these two commissions than with the UAW mechanisms. The estimates of the number of complaints filed were very small, ranging from guesses of three to five complaints filed by the local UAW workers with these two agencies within the last 5 years. Only 1 out of the 36 people who returned questionnaires said he had ever considered filing a complaint with NLRB or EOC (but did not, in fact, file). None of those interviewed had ever considered going to either of these agencies. It appears that neither of these "external" agencies serves as a substitute forum for handling UAW complaints, both because of their circumscribed areas of concern and the fact that, according to UAW local officials interviewed, a complaint would have to be really serious for a worker to win a case in these agencies.

It is interesting and perhaps informative to note that all the officials questioned had a certain amount of negativism about workers who complained; whether or not this negativism was warranted is not our concern here. One official stated that the only time a man would complain was if he had been having trouble at home and was taking it out on his committeeman. Another official said that workers who complain are usually "those who 'kiss-ass' with the company and try to undermine the union any way they can." Another said that "those who complain are just anti-union. There are some of that kind in every crowd." He portrayed them as "grasping at straws" in terms of their complaints. Although this study offers no conclusive evidence, it seems very possible that because the committeemen and officers have negative attitudes toward complaining, they may discourage workers from taking their complaints any farther than themselves. As it is the local officials who have the greatest access to

[5]The NLRB and the EOC are federal agencies that have administrative offices in local areas to deal with the problems that come under their purview. The NLRB was established in 1935 by the Wagner Act and is the federal board that regulates labor–management relations. The EOC, established in 1964 with the passage of the Civil Rights Act, deals with questions of discrimination in employment and housing on the basis of race, color, religion, sex, and national origin.

information on how to use the complaint-handling procedures, the line workers are very dependent on the officials' advice if they are to pursue their complaints within the UAW system.

So, another obvious possibility for the nonuse of the formal UAW complaint-handling system is simply the lack of encouragement and the lack of knowledge of how to use it. However, as long as those who have the most information on these procedures—the local officers and committeemen—retain a negative attitude toward complaining, it is unlikely that this information will be disseminated to the local line workers.

The line workers interviewed offered an additional explanation for their pattern of nonuse of the UAW complaint-handling procedure. Even though they lacked knowledge of the available forums, they each expressed doubts about whether there was anything to be gained by going to these union forums because, they thought, the local line worker would not be likely to get a fair shake. None of them mentioned the complexity of the system or antiunionism as reasons for not pressing their complaints. However, each of the line workers interviewed mentioned that, in one way or another, the higher up one went in the union, the less people cared about the local line worker. Thus, they reasoned, if a local worker were to come in conflict with the union in some way, no matter what the validity of his claim, these "higher-ups" would be unlikely to rule in his favor.

Not all the workers interviewed agreed about how good or bad the union was. Some, especially the older ones, were quite enthusiastic about it. Others, especially the younger ones, had many complaints. But none wanted to live without it! However, whether they judged the union as excellent or poor, all agreed that there were at least some things wrong with it and that unless a line worker's complaint was really big, there was little, if anything, he could do about it.

Most of the line workers' complaints concerned the committeeman's not doing his job. Those interviewed agreed that it was not worthwhile to call in a committeeman about a grievance unless the problem was something really major. All those interviewed gave instances of when they had called in a committeeman and he had not come or had come too late to do any good. The feelings of these line workers are best summarized in the statements of the following worker:

> When you're having a problem, you can call in a committeeman, but it sometimes takes one or two weeks before he gets to you, and a lot of times it's all finished by then. Sometimes a committeeman will come, but he'll just talk to the foreman and not do anything until months later, and by that time you're on a new job and it doesn't matter anymore. . . . Most men I know don't even bother to call committeemen in. It just won't do any

> *good.... Committeemen make all kinds of promises in the campaign, but after you get them in, they completely change.*

Another man gave the following statement:

> *Say something is wrong with the health and safety requirements in your department and you call in the committeeman, but he doesn't come. Or he comes and says he'll straighten it out, but he doesn't do anything. He's a guy who's weak on the union and strong on the company. Well, if it is something really bad and you want something done, you could go to the building chairman, but he would probably side with the committeeman, since they work together all the time. You could call in International if you wanted to, and some men do and if the case got real big, they might have the Regional Director come down. But I'm not saying he'd do anything for you. The higher you get, they're real weak for the guy on the bottom. Those International Reps are making 18–20 thousand year, and he's not going to put his job in jeopardy by siding with you. You don't get a fair shake. He doesn't care about the little guy on the bottom, so the chances are he'd rule in favor of the committeeman.*

Statements of the other line workers supported the view that a line worker could go to another committeeman[6] or to the building chairman or to an International Representative, but the chances are they would rule in favor of the first committeeman. Whether or not this is the case cannot be determined from this study. How many workers take their complaints to these people and are given a "fair shake" is not known. Nonetheless, the feeling is present among line workers that these officials would not rule in favor of the man on the bottom—the line worker. One would presume that this attitude alone would keep many men from trying to take their complaints through the union system.

When I talked with the building chairman of one local union about this view, he said that although he did not totally agree with it, he could see how the men might get this impression. He gave the example of his local union's Fair Practices Committee, stating that five out of the seven members of the committee were local committeemen. He said that from his viewpoint, this was helpful as they were used to working with each other, but if he were a line worker with a complaint against a committeeman for discrimination, he would not want to go to that committee.

---

[6]Technically, a worker is not supposed to go to another district committeeman if he is dissatisfied with his own. Instead, he should take his complaint to the next higher level of committeemen—his unit committeeman—and then if not satisfied, he should go to the building chairman. However, workers do in fact occasionally take complaints to other district committeemen. These committeemen can either refuse to deal with the complaint (because it does not come within their jurisdiction) or they can try to arrive at an informal solution with the worker's own district committeeman.

Other complaints concerning the union mentioned by the line workers interviewed included the following:

> The union [local] just doesn't know very much. They didn't even know
> when we were supposed to go out on strike. You can learn more from read-
> ing the paper than you can from going to union meetings.

Another worker said the union was ineffectual because of lack of attendance at union meetings. He gave the following example:

> For instance, one dollar out of the worker's union dues goes to paying off the
> UAW building, even though the building is already paid for. They need 150
> people at a meeting to vote it out but they've never had enough there. The
> closest they ever got was 120. People don't even go to the meetings to ratify
> the contracts. Out of 5000 workers at GM, only 1000 voted on the new
> contract, 800 for it, 200 against it. Most men don't have anything to do with
> the union except have their dues taken out.

A few workers complained that the committeemen and International
Representatives were "company men." One said, "When you see the contract they give us, you can tell they are company men." Next to complaints about committeemen not doing their job, the most common complaint was in terms of the "distance" of International Representatives, the
links between the union locals and the Regional Director. As one man
humbly expressed it, "it appears that many of the International's decisions are not always in the best interest of the average worker." Another
complaint was that committeemen knew about better jobs and could get
them without the necessary seniority if they ever got voted out of being
committeemen.[7] Three men with whom I spoke were especially angry
about what they said had happened at General Motors during the 1972
cutback. They stated that everyone with 5 years' seniority or less had to
"go out the door" but that committeemen with just 3 years' seniority had
been able to stay. They could not understand how this had happened and
thought it was most unfair to the average worker.

As we have seen, line workers indeed do have complaints about the
union, but apparently they do not believe that there is a viable union
mechanism for expressing or solving these complaints. What of the possibility of bringing them up in local union membership meetings? The
workers interviewed agreed that this was probably a dead-end track. None
of those interviewed and only two of those who returned questionnaires
regularly attend meetings. This finding does not seem to be a sampling

---

[7]There is no limit on the number of times local union officials, including committeemen, can be reelected.

error but rather is reflective of the current state of the union. The majority of workers nationwide do not attend meetings. In the local union I examined, the secretary stated that over half of the monthly membership meetings cannot be held because they do not have the required 82 members present (this local has over 4000 members).

The line workers I interviewed stated that one of the main reasons they do not attend meetings is that there is always so much arguing at them. One very loyal union worker who has been in the union for 29 years stated he no longer goes to meetings because "all they do is argue." Another line worker vividly expressed his feelings about union meetings in the following way:

> I was thinking about becoming a committeeman. I was a shop steward at the time. So I decided to get more involved in the union. I went to union meetings for eight months straight and kept trying to bring up some of the things bothering me, but I never got a chance to talk. I'd try to say something during old business, and they'd say, "Sit down. You can't bring that up now. That's new business." So I'd sit around and wait for new business to come up, and I'd then try to bring up the same point, and they'd say it was old business and I should've brought it up then. I'd say that I had tried but they'd told me to bring it up in new business, and then they'd say, well, it had some old and some new business in it and so it was supposed to be brought up in old business and that they couldn't help me now so I'd have to wait till the next meeting. I went for 8 months straight and never really got a chance to talk. I got so disgusted I quit.

From the line worker's perspective, union meetings do not provide a suitable forum for them to express their complaints about the union, nor do they consider any of the other forums (formal or informal) practicable. Those interviewed agreed that by far the most likely thing a worker would do (unless his complaint were really big) is "lump it." They simply would do nothing, except perhaps complain to their friends. As one worker put it, "Workers would rather do just what they can themselves or otherwise just forget it."

As for the important question of *why* these workers "lump it," no conclusive hypotheses can be made on the basis of this research. Several important suggestions, however, are brought to mind by this material. It is on these that we now focus.

There is the question of whether or not these men "lump it" because "lumping it" is endemic to American life, as some have suggested. However, this answer remains unsatisfactory because it does not address the question of how and why these particular people lump it. How is the system of the UAW similar to or different from other structures in American life? What is there in the UAW organization, in labor–management relations, in the workers' personalities, or in the environmental ambiance that causes these workers to "lump it"—to fail to voice their complaints? (What are the characteristics of people who do not?)

Judge George Brunn, in a lecture at the University of California at Berkeley in November 1973 spoke of the pervasive sense of fatalism among Americans—a fatalism that makes them think they cannot change the system and consequently fail even to try. This fatalism seems to be present among UAW workers, in terms of both company management and their own union organization. Why is there this fatalism? Why do line workers apparently feel so powerless despite the ostensible strength and power exhibited when they go out on strike? Do they really experience a sense of power when striking, or do they, even then, feel like pawns in the game, not being able to decide among themselves when they will strike but rather receiving instructions from the International Executive Board?

As yet, we simply do not know the answers to these questions. However, returning to our discussion at the beginning of this chapter, we may see the structural position of the union as a crucial factor in explaining the line workers' pattern of not voicing their complaints. Perhaps workers fail to complain because their complaints seem to them too minor to warrant the cost of voicing that complaint. This supposition seems even more likely if we remind ourselves of the nature of the relationship between the worker, his union, and the "outside" world. As previously mentioned, the union forms an in-group of which the worker is a member, an in-group that is in constant conflict with the out-group—management—though that conflict varies in intensity. There is a perceived need on the part of union members to maintain a united front in the face of the opposition.

Furthermore, not only from the perspective of the health of the union as a whole but also from the worker's personal perspective, he may decide not to voice his complaints about the union. This decision could be a resultant of either positive or negative restraints. On the positive side, upon weighing benefits against complaints, the worker might decide that the benefits from the union are so great that it would be ungrateful to complain about the minor problems that do exist. It is true that the improvements brought about in the working conditions of automobile factory workers since the 1940s have been astounding. Many workers, especially the older ones, are acutely aware of this fact and consequently see complaints against the union as unjustified. Workers in general see the union as their only protection against management—a management that, as far as many workers are concerned, does not give a damn about them. Not only may the worker not want to seem ungrateful for what he has received at the hands of the union, but also he may fear the cutting off of these benefits if he should get on the "wrong side" of union officials. He may fear that complaining would leave him defenseless against possible abuse by management. Whether or not in reality this is the case, the possibility is quite easy to envision.

If a worker has a grievance he wants filed—for example, if he believes he has been too harshly disciplined—whether or not he wins that grievance depends in large part on how hard the committeemen are willing to fight for him. The union must sometimes compromise with management, and it seems quite reasonable to assume that they would be most willing to compromise on grievances of those workers who are not in good standing with themselves as committeemen or with the union in general. From either of these perspectives, that of gratitude or that of fear, a worker's complaint may seem to him too minor to warrant filing.

Problems Inherent in the Complaint Procedure

Undoubtedly it is a combination of all the aforementioned factors that accounts for the pattern of nonuse by line workers of the UAW formal complaint-handling structure. However, from our perspective there is an additional factor, mentioned neither by workers nor by local officials, that significantly contributes to the pattern of nonuse of the system. This factor concerns the nature of the complaint procedure itself. The UAW complaint-handling system seems, at least in part, to be modeled on the American legal system and, consequently, has some of the same advantages as well as the same problems. It is on the problems that we will focus, for it is the nonuse that we are trying to understand. The question we will be focusing on is: What is it in the structure of the system itself that makes it an unsuitable mechanism for handling the typical complaints of local line workers?

The first problem we see as inherent in the structure itself is that of physical and social distance from the worker. The appeal procedure does not take into account the importance of face-to-face relations for the local workers. All the line workers interviewed as well as about two-thirds (23 out of 36) of those who completed questionnaires said that if they had a complaint about the union, they would prefer to have it heard and settled by a group of local union members. This finding is interesting in light of the fact that most of the reforms of the complaint-handling procedure in recent years have taken place on the national level. It is our contention that the Public Review Board, the innovation of which the UAW is most proud, is too distant from the workers for them to see it as a practicable forum for handling their complaints. The Public Review Board can only be reached by first appealing to the local membership, then to the International Executive Board (which decides whether the case merits a hearing), and finally to the Review Board itself. As we have seen, line workers apparently have a skepticism about people "higher up" in the system.

If the union wants to change its appeal procedure to more adequately handle the complaints of workers, it may well be that a local review board might be more effective than one that is so removed from the workers' everyday situation. Although it may be prestigious to have deans of law schools, professors, and religious leaders on the Review Board, it seems likely that this roster may cause more disuse than use of the system. The local line worker is aware that he is low on the totem pole, and it seems probable that he or she would be more reticent about taking a "small problem" to a Review Board comprised of such distinguished members, than if there were the possibility of taking a complaint to a local Public Review Board composed of people the worker deems social equals.

The need for devising a forum in which the local worker feels physically comfortable and mentally at ease is most important in the development of effective and equitable complaint-handling procedures. An important point—one all too often forgotten in grievance-handling mechanisms—is that in the complainant's eyes the *process* may well be as important as the end result, or, at least, the end does not justify the means. In other words, even if the complainant is likely to receive a just decision, he is unlikely to use the mechanism if in the process he is made to feel ignorant, afraid, uncomfortable, and ill at ease, as undoubtedly often happens in our complaint-handling forums. As we have seen in rape cases handled by the American legal system, if we want people to take their grievances to court, we have to scrutinize our process (as well as our outcomes) to see if we are abusing the complainant in the course of the hearing. The same undoubtedly holds for other grievances handled by our legal and extralegal grievance-handling systems. In terms of the complainant, our focus has been perhaps too singly upon the outcome, the "just" decision, rather than the process (whereas perhaps the opposite holds for the defendant). The process itself, and what is communicated to the complainant during this process, deserves careful scrutiny.

The second aspect of the complaint-handling procedure that is affected by whether or not the complainant feels physically comfortable and mentally at ease concerns the end result—the actual judgment arrived at in the case. The question of the complainer's feeling at ease and its connection to "justice" is a complex one that can be touched upon only briefly in this chapter. In this country, our ideas concerning objectivity and impartiality typically have resulted in our seeing a professionally trained outsider using carefully controlled procedures as the person most capable of providing a "just" decision. This is probably one reason why the UAW is so proud of its Public Review Board. There are many points in favor of this argument (too familiar to warrant enumeration), but on the other hand, there may be some weaknesses in it also. One of the major pitfalls in this argument is that it all too glibly assumes that communication between complainant and judge can take place.

How great is the problem of communication in the forums we have devised for the settling of grievances? If the complainant feels ill at ease, can he adequately communicate his complaint? And without an understanding of his complaint as well as of the social environment out of which it emerges, can the judges offer a fair and just decision? We admit that this is not a question of right versus wrong; rather it is a question of relative costs. In what types of forums are the relative costs the greatest? Perhaps for the kinds of complaints we are considering in this book, some of our fundamental conceptions about how best to achieve justice need thoughtful reconsideration.

The UAW formal complaint-handling procedure has the additional problem of being oriented toward specific actions rather than toward the handling of underlying social unrest (again like the U.S. judicial system).[8] Under the present system it would be easier to remove a committeeman who has stolen some union money than to remove one who has failed to do his job well, despite the fact that the latter may cause more discontent among the workers. This brings to mind the related problem of how we define what a major and what a minor problem is—by the dollars and cents involved or by the number of lives affected. Undoubtedly we need forums for handling both types of grievances (which sometimes but not always overlap). We suspect that the current UAW forum is best at handling specific wrongful actions of a fraudulent nature rather than at handling generalized neglect, although it is the latter kind of problem that seems to form most of the workers' grievances.

In the UAW system, as in the American legal system itself, attempts at reform tend to be made within the parameters of the current structure rather than extending beyond the limitations of this structure. In other words, what we find is modification, not change. However, we postulate that because of some of the problems discussed, reforms made within the boundaries of the current structure will not be sufficient to make the grievance-handling system one that is suitable for most of the workers' problems. We are not proposing the razing of the current system. On the contrary, it is probably a good one for handling specific actions that are flagrant violations of the UAW Constitution. What we are proposing is an additional system—an alternative system geared toward the everyday grievances of workers and obviating some of the problems that we have postulated make the current system an unlikely forum for the average workman.

An Alternative Forum

What would be some of the characteristics of an alternative forum for handling complaints? Only the briefest sketch can be offered here.

---

[8] I am indebted to Professor Laura Nader for this observation on the American legal system. See Nader 1975.

Ideally, the forum would be geared toward handling "minor" complaints. It would encourage the expression of vague discontents as well as the reporting of specific violations. Of course, it would have to be fully endorsed by the union hierarchy and the local workers themselves. From our preliminary research it appears that ideally the personnel would be local union members (who perhaps would work half-time on complaints and half-time in their regular jobs) who are committed to the idea that an effective complaint-handling forum would make for a stronger union by encouraging those who have complaints to file them. The personnel would not be committeemen (given the fact that committeemen already have a vital and time-consuming task handling workers' grievances against management and that many of the workers' complaints involve questions about the handling of these grievances), but they would specialize in the same kinds of knowledge as the committeemen.

It is interesting and not surprising that it is against committeemen that complaints are directed. Committeemen are nodal figures connecting the network of line workers with the network of management. As occupants of these positions, they have access to personal contacts and to information that directly affect the line workers' lives but that are not easily accessible to the line workers. This phenomenon is simply that of specialization of tasks—a phenomenon inherent in the bureaucratic structure and one that has many beneficial side effects. However, bureaucracy's forte is also its weakness. Monopoly of contacts and information in and of itself is a special form of power and can be easily abused (withholding of knowledge or misrepresenting information to those seeking it provides a powerful lever for these holders of knowledge). Even if this power is not abused, the man who is dependent upon it may have lingering doubts about the accuracy of the information he is given and, consequently, about whether or not he is receiving a "fair shake."

By developing an alternative forum for workers that is not connected with either the management or the union hierarchy, it should be possible to solve some of the problems we have addressed. The cost of complaining also would be considerably reduced. It would be possible for the worker to obtain information about whether or not he is receiving fair treatment without feeling disloyal and without fearing repercussions.

It may well be that simply having an alternative forum for obtaining information may solve some of the workers' complaints about the union, as many complaints may rest on a worker's unfounded doubts about whether or not he is being treated fairly. With the proposed forum, he could receive that information (without fear of costs) and then on the basis of that information could better judge the accuracy of his complaints and the cost involved in pursuing them. Access to information in and of itself makes the workman's position less vulnerable, complaining less costly, and abuse more subject to scrutiny.

We speculate that if the UAW were actually to develop such a grievance-handling forum and its use were fully supported by workers and the hierarchy, it would provide a means of communication and evaluation between different levels of a hierarchy in a way that is currently unknown in most of our organizational structures. Not only could problems of individuals be solved (thereby perhaps combating the organizational problem of apathy) and abuse of power gained by monopoly of information be held in check, but also the UAW itself could learn in what places it was most in need of change.

We speculate that, at least in part, the development of an effective grievance-handling procedure might provide a mechanism for focusing the gaze of the union upon itself. It would be one way not only of encouraging the exchange of information but also of feeding that information into the organizational form itself, allowing it to respond gradually to changing conditions rather than do what we suggest is done in most organizations: perceiving needed changes only when forced "up against the wall."

Furthermore, we suggest that the organizational form discussed in this chapter (an in-group involved in a more or less constant institutionalized feud with an out-group) is one of the most problematic and important for the development of effective and equitable grievance-handling procedures. We have frequently mentioned why in this organizational form complaints are unlikely to be voiced and why, in turn, the organization is unlikely to respond to them (the outward-focused gaze, the need for a "united front"). This form is comparable not only to many other institutions in our society but also to the nation–state itself, which so often has turned its gaze outward and has failed to provide an effective mechanism for listening to the complaints and grievances of its own citizens.

References

Brunn, Judge George
    1973   Public Lecture. Anthropology 157, University of California, Berkeley, November.
Colson, Elizabeth
    1974   *Tradition and contract: The problem of order.* Chicago: Aldine.
Evans-Pritchard, E. E.
    1940   *The Nuer.* Oxford: Oxford University Press.
    1949   *The Sanusi of Cyrenaica.* Oxford: Oxford University Press.
Nader, Laura
    1975   Forums for justice: A cross-cultural perspective. *Journal of Social Issues* **31**(3):151–170.

Peters, Emry L.
    1967   Some structural aspects of the feud among the camel-herding Bedouin of
            Cyrenaica. *Africa* **37**(3):260–282.
UAW
    1971   Fourteenth Annual Report of the Public Review Board. International
            Union, United Automobile, Aerospace and Agricultural Implement
            Workers of America.
    1972a   Constitution of the International Union, United Automobile, Aerospace
            and Agricultural Implement Workers of America, UAW. Adopted at At-
            lantic City, N.J. April.
    1972b   Proceedings of the 23rd UAW Constitutional Convention. Convention
            Hall, Atlantic City, N.J. 23–28 April.

13

Michael C. Mattice

MEDIA IN THE MIDDLE:
A Study of the Mass Media
Complaint Managers

Introduction

> When a married student could obtain no explanation from the Veterans
> Administration of why his GI Education Bill payments were four months in
> arrears, he complained to the cost-free dispute-assistance service known as
> KABL Radio Call for Action. There a volunteer caseworker contacted an
> officer in the Veterans Administration who had earlier agreed to accept
> similar complaints from Call for Action. As the student had recently
> changed his address, the "VA contact" explained, his next check would not
> be issued for a month. The volunteer pleaded for greater haste in deference
> to the couple's increasingly critical financial need and to the proximity of
> the Christmas holiday. The sympathetic contact obtained a $1,000 check for
> the student within two weeks.
>
> The student called Call for Action again when, three weeks after the due
> date he had not received his next regularly-scheduled check. Again the
> volunteer conferred with the contact, who learned that Administration
> computers are programmed to reject any new disbursements for veterans
> having recently received large amounts. The contact again arranged special
> processing of the grateful student's account.

In the United States there are approximately 400 complaint managers, often called "action lines," that are either suborganizations of or
contractually associated with mass media organizations. Using methods
described in this chapter,[1] media complaint managers provide cheap and

[1]The author is deeply grateful to Mary B. Mattice for the hundreds of hours she invested
in this project, and to Nancy Zerbey Gray, whose hard work and clear thinking influenced
this entire chapter. Additional thanks go to those kind people, too numerous to list, who also
contributed uncountable time and effort.

frequently effective dispute-assistance service to literally millions of Americans. The operations and methods of four such complaint managers are described here, and many others are referred to. The intent is to explore the relationship between media association and complaint management.

In the early 1900s the *Chicago Tribune* published a reader service column entitled "Friend of the People," which featured local problems such as potholes in the streets, according to that newspaper's present action-line editor (telephone interview with F. Kennan Heise, 10 March 1973). When the economic base of the newspaper industry shifted in the twentieth century from subscriptions to advertising—that is, from readers to business—editorial policy followed suit (telephone interview with journalism professor Frank Pollock, 15 February 1973). As wars and depressions followed each other, newspapers became even more interested in reporting news that concerned business and government rather than little events in the lives of their readers.

In the late 1950s newspapers began to feel the effects of business' shift of advertising to television (Emery 1972:618–626). Growth rates for advertising accounts and circulation figures fell, giving new incentives to newspapers to reintroduce reader service columns. Old "Mr. Fixit" and other household hint features were revived. In 1961 the *Houston Chronicle* introduced "Watchem," a column that printed answers to complaints and questions called in by readers (*Editor & Publisher* 1966:9). The action-line column became a new form of reader feedback. By the late 1960s consumerism was a hot issue, and more and more newspapers and radio and television stations discovered that the action line provided a unique combination of human interest material and public service. Action lines became popular features that simultaneously boosted ratings, discharged public responsibilities, and enhanced the media's public image. However, like similar institutions created to respond to issues as defined by changing times, action lines have a short life span.

The four action lines described in this chapter are: "Action 7" of KGO Television, San Francisco;[2] "Call For Action" of KABL-AM Radio, San Francisco;[3] the "Ombudsman Service" of KABC-AM Radio, Los Angeles; and a newspaper column, "Action Line," published in the *Oakland Tribune*, Oakland, California. Although two of these action lines have ceased to exist, we use the present tense in describing them.

KGO-TV's "Action 7" is at once a 3-minute segment of the weekday evening "Channel 7 News Scene" program as well as a small team of KGO-TV newsroom employees. The team generates program material by

---

[2]Action 7 ceased operations in mid 1974. See later discussion.

[3]The KABL chapter of Call for Action, Inc., ceased operations in March 1975. See later discussion.

soliciting and processing complaints about consumer goods and services and about governmental services. Each week Action 7 receives about 120 complaint letters, which are culled by the Action 7 staff for items that might interest the KGO-TV audience. From one to four complaints are selected daily as potential broadcast material, whereupon they receive the full attention of the Action 7 reporter. He or she spends all day putting the Action 7 story together for the audience. Another Action 7 staff member deals with the remaining complaint letters primarily by sending them, accompanied by Action 7 form letters, to complainees or to government complaint managers. The Action 7 team's purpose is to produce an interesting broadcast, and managing individual complaints is a means to that end.

Like all 37 chapters of Call for Action, Inc., KABL Radio's Call for Action is an autonomous volunteer organization that assists local residents who have complaints or who require information about community services. Under a standard form contract between KABL Radio, San Francisco, and Call for Action, Inc., the radio station furnishes offices, telephones, and office supplies for the 30 or so volunteers and advertises the Call for Action service at least five times per day. The carefully organized volunteers research local complaint managers and other services, and man the telephones during scheduled hours. When a citizen calls to complain or request information, a volunteer refers him or her appropriately, using an extensive catalogue built up and maintained by volunteer research. With each such referral the volunteer says, "Tell [the complainee] that KABL Call for Action told you to call him." After giving citizens several weeks to use the proferred information, volunteers call back those with more difficult problems to check on progress and to offer more help. In about 10% of complaint cases, volunteers must directly intervene by calling less tractable complainees ("I am calling from KABL Radio Call for Action"). Volunteers compile statistics on calls for purposes of self-measurement and to spot common citizen problems. When either individual complainants or the statistics indicate critical community problems, the volunteers present data to the managers of KABL Radio, who then use the information to editorialize on the need for change.

Each Call for Action chapter is a subdivision of Call for Action, Incorporated, a highly structured, nonprofit company headquartered in Washington, D.C. Intending to create an inexpensive complaint-assistance mechanism and to study problems endemic to New York City, Ellen Strauss founded the first unit in 1968 at the family-owned WMCA Radio Station. She subsequently built Call for Action into a 40-chapter national network with financial help from the Urban Coalition and the DeWitt Wallace Fund. Vertical and horizontal communication abounds throughout Call for Action via policy communications, national conventions, and interchapter visits and letters. Chapters exchange out-of-town complaints and send statistical information to Washington in suitable form for congressional study.

KABC-AM, Los Angeles' most popular radio station, initiated the Ombudsman Service under Dr. Michael Sommers, then the station's public affairs director, in response to the California legislature's failure in 1967 to pass the Unruh Ombudsman Act. The Service was intended to act as a powerful intermediary between citizens and their government. Soon the Service was helping as well with consumer complaints against businesses, and the total number of all types of complaints surpassed 50,000 annually. Under the direction of a KABC executive, this case load is managed by 18 volunteer students. Most complaints are simply forwarded to complainees, who are told in unmistakable terms in a cover letter that they are dealing with an interested radio station as well as with complainants. The few complainees who do not respond are subjected to a series of escalation techniques until the complainant indicates reasonable satisfaction. If all else fails, KABC Radio may broadcast an editorial statement about the need for particular government policy or rule changes, or for particular forms of government regulation of business. As with Call for Action, Ombudsman Service volunteers do not engage in broadcast-oriented tasks. Rather, they concentrate almost exclusively upon complaint management.

Each weekday an "Action Line" column appears on page 2 of the *Oakland Tribune*. It is researched and written by three staff members who attempt to balance the two goals of individual complaint resolution and column presentation. Whereas KGO-TV's Action 7 first segregates all letters into the two classes of "potentially broadcastable" and "nonbroadcastable," the newspaper Action Line staff first determines whether the complainant can be helped best by referral to a certain contact in the complainee organization or by the more active participation of Action Line. The Action Line editor selects from concluded cases the ones most likely to interest column readers.

In the following discussion several concepts will emerge. Chief among these is that a media complaint manager has access to a great deal of power. State and federal courts and enforcement agencies use power that is specifically granted to them by constitutions and statutes. In contrast, action lines wield power that is granted by complainants and, sometimes begrudgingly, by complainees.

A Note on Methodology

This study was initiated in September 1972 when I sent questionnaires in three waves to all the 322 newspaper action lines known to exist; 113 of these eventually responded. I sent similar questionnaires to the 14 non–Call for Action broadcast action lines then known to exist; 11 answered, including Action 7 and the KABC Ombudsman Service. Library research revealed the Call for Action network of 51 broadcasters (since reduced to fewer than 40).

To research the KABL chapter of Call for Action, I made 9 day-long visits to the chapter's office, accompanied on the first visit by fellow student Polly Tyson, and made 6 calls to chapter members. I supplemented these conversations by studying numerous internal documents of the organization and by library research. Polly Tyson and I conversed with 20 of the chapter's 30 members and observed some 50 telephone calls in progress. Sally Livingston, then one of the chapter's two coordinating chairpersons, read and commented on a brief description of this action line written by Tyson and myself.

I obtained the Action 7 materials during 4 day-long visits to that office, and Marian Eaton and I spent 4 additional days studying the 123 letters received by Action 7 in 1 week. John Brian and Nancy Iida of Action 7 also provided many internal documents. Over a 10-month period I observed 70 Action 7 broadcasts.

The Action Line data were obtained during 1 interview of the staff by Eaton and 2 day-long visits by me. I made numerous telephone calls and examined 50 Action Line columns. Finally, Clifford Pletschet of Action Line completed two versions of my newspaper action-line questionnaire.

I obtained most of the data about the KABC Ombudsman Service in an 8-hour tape-recorded interview with Nelkane Benton, the Service's director. I prepared for this interview in part by reading a study of the Service completed in 1971 by students of Stanley V. Anderson of the University of California at Santa Barbara. Benton examined and corrected the full transcript of this interview and also provided an extensive collection of public relations material and internal Service documents.

In telephone conversations the leaders of each of the four action lines criticized draft ethnologies of their respective units.

Why Do Media Have Action Lines?

Action lines can be expensive operations. In 1968 they cost larger newspapers from $100 to $1600 per week or an average of about $500 per week in salaries, equipment, and promotion (APME 1968:i). KABL Radio spends $6000 annually on behalf of its Call for Action partner, a medium-sized chapter (telephone interview with Knowles Hall, 31 December 1975). These investments support active participation in disputes, a role quite different from the well-known media function of dispensing information. Why do media have action lines?

Modern commercial newspapers and broadcasters generate income by selling advertising, a service, to other businesses who seek thereby to attract customers. Because large audiences contain large numbers of potential customers, advertisers are willing to pay higher fees to the more popular media (Emery 1972:333–335; Summers and Summers 1966:107–108). Thus, media executives constantly search for new features to lure readers and listeners away from competing media.

Action 7 was initiated in 1972 to enlarge KGO-TV's share of the evening news audience, according to Nancy Iida, as that station had suffered poor ratings in 1971. The effort succeeded, as it has with many newspapers: In a 1968 poll of newspaper action-line editors, 59% responded favorably when asked whether their features had boosted circulation. Only 7% gave a definite "no" (APME 1968:ii–v; Gray 1975:6); Bellay (1970) describes one newspaper's unsuccessful use of an action line to enhance circulation.

Under the terms of the license granted by the Federal Communications Commission, a broadcaster has a duty "to take all reasonable measures to eliminate any false, misleading or deceptive matter [from its programming] [FCC 1960:7295]." A responsible newspaper presumably has a similar duty, although the First Amendment to the Constitution proscribes regulatory control of newspapers (Barrow 1975). The action line can assist by giving notice of impropriety and by deterring some offenders.

Ellen and Peter Straus of WMCA Radio New York formed Call for Action as an inexpensive alternative to judicial dispute resolution (*Washington Post* 28 February 1971:E7) whereas the KABC Ombudsman Service was developed because a California State Ombudsman office was not. An action line is but one way to serve "public convenience, interest [and] necessity" as the FCC requires of all broadcasters (Federal Communications Act of 1934:Sec. 307).

Who Runs Action Lines?

Some action lines see program or column production for the general audience as their foremost duty, with complaints constituting the source material. Not surprisingly, such action lines are often administered by people with predominantly journalistic, media-based backgrounds. John Brian, the Action 7 producer and reporter, has a degree in radio–television communications and 10 years' experience in television news. Brian conducted most of the research and planning for the Action 7 television program and has piloted the unit since its inception in August 1972. Brian's primary responsibility is to prepare the 3-minute Action 7 broadcast each weekday evening, using one or two interesting complaints. He makes phone calls, visits the parties, directs filming, edits, confers with other newsroom employees, writes a script, and performs all other such production work. At 5:15 P.M. he reports the story to the News Scene audience. The other full-time Action 7 staff member is Nancy Iida, a young woman with about 5 years' experience in television, primarily as an assistant to the program director at KGO-TV. Iida handles the 120 or more complaints per week that are not chosen for broadcast. She classifies these letters according to Action 7's battery of strategies, writes answers, looks up Bay Area complaint managers for referral, forwards complaints as necessary, files complaints and complainee responses, and manages the Action 7 office. Action 7 also shares a secretary with another KGO-TV department and calls upon several KGO-TV technicians when Brian chooses to film a story.

Journalism training and experience is probably the most common background for senior action liners, who are called "action-line editors" in the newspaper business and are sometimes called "action-line reporters" or "talents" in broadcasting. Twelve of the 113 newapaper survey respondents described their action-line editors as "veterans," and of the 42 responses that stated the number of years the editor had engaged in journalism, the mean was 16.4 years. All nine of the responding broadcast action lines have experienced journalists as reporters, and five of these reporters are known to guide their units.

Journalists appear to be well-suited for the action-line forms of complaint management, as they are trained to uncover and communicate facts in a cogent manner, to use resources, and to discover who is responsible for certain events. It must be recognized, however, that if the raison d'être of the action line is to produce a daily feature, the talents of the senior journalist are expended on the feature story, which may not be a typical complaint. An average of 5.8 items appear in each column, according to 102 newspaper survey respondents, and even fewer items appear in the typical action-line broadcast.

Call for Action has not found a need to employ journalists. The KABL chapter is staffed by about 30 volunteers and a half dozen substitutes, most of whom are young or middle-aged women with diverse educational backgrounds and often with community service experience. Chapter members typically contribute 6–10 hours per week each. To qualify for Call for Action, one must have a great deal of interest and above-average communicative ability. Fifteen volunteers are engaged exclusively in answering the telephones and working with callers. From 10 A.M. to 2 P.M. each weekday, two or three volunteers and one of the five day-captains handle individual complaints and other calls, and study the action line's reference sources. Day-captains also tally daily statistics, assist the other volunteers with unusual problems, and attend monthly meetings with the chapter's various chairpersons. Another volunteer handles all written correspondence. Two volunteers research local complaint-management agencies and compile statistics from the action line's files. The publicity chairperson keeps abreast of community events of interest to the action line and promotes Call for Action publicity. One woman, in cooperation with KABL management, works on editorials about community problems. Still another recruits and trains new volunteers and substitutes. Finally, a coordinating chairperson (or two co-chairpersons) oversees the work and also communicates with the national organization. Volunteers exchange jobs about once per year to avoid organizational inertia.

All volunteers have been specially trained to handle difficult telephone calls. As prescribed by the national organization's program, the coordinating co-chairpersons pose as drunks and drug addicts, worried mothers, concerned neighbors, and angry consumers; they call the other volunteers, using numerous devices and deceptions to confuse and distract them. The object of this training is to teach the volunteers to help callers even under the most adverse conditions.

The KABC Ombudsman Service of Los Angeles has a staff of 16 volunteers guided by Nelkane Benton, a full-time executive of KABC Radio, who also is an associate director of public affairs for the station. Benton directs Ombudsman activities, maintains personnel requirements, and institutes KABC policy. She reads all incoming Ombudsman mail to discover community trends and to make tactical decisions about unusual complaints. As one of five members of the KABC Editorial Board, Benton sometimes suggests broadcasts on subjects that the Service has perceived are critical to the community. Benton's background includes a degree in English and 12 years' experience in public relations.

Most of the Ombudsman Service's volunteers are college seniors or graduate students in the social sciences, journalism, public affairs, or liberal arts, who receive credit from a half dozen local colleges and universities for their Ombudsman work. Much like the Call for Action volunteers, the student workers handle telephone calls (9–10 A.M. and 1–3 P.M. weekdays) and written complaints and requests. The Service also receives help from two middle-aged women volunteers, one of whom acts as senior tactician in Benton's absence.

The editor of the Action Line column, Clifford Pletschet, was an *Oakland Tribune* reporter for 16 years. For 5 years he was assigned to the government offices of a Bay Area city. Pletschet, who holds a degree in journalism, makes most of the tactical complaint-management decisions, writes all the Action Line columns, and communicates as necessary with the *Tribune*'s executive editors.

Pletschet has two assistants, Jon Fox and Rose Alston, who spend most of their efforts in managing individual complaints. Fox studied journalism and political science for 3 years and has worked for several newspapers as well as for a radio station. Alston, whose journalism training has been on the job, has been a *Tribune* librarian and a secretary. In addition to its journalistic staff, the Action Line shares a secretary with other *Tribune* departments.

Fourteen of the 113 newspapers responding to our survey have no staff structure known as an action-line staff. Problems addressed to these newspapers are distributed, generally by city editors, to reporters whose beat gives them particular knowledge of the complaint or the complainee. These reporters then investigate and seek resolution. Each of three other responding newspapers has one action-line reporter who does some of his own action lining and who receives investigative help from the other newspaper reporters when he needs it. One newspaper has an action liner who writes a column and assigns complaints to members of the town's Junior Chamber of Commerce, who investigate and try to obtain solutions to complaints.

Ninety-nine newspaper respondents had clearly delineated action-line staffs, of which the largest had the equivalent of 7 full-time members (*Minneapolis Star*) and the next largest, 6.5 (*Akron Beacon-Journal*). These figures include clerical helpers who are shared with other newspaper departments, as they are on nearly one-third of the 99 staffs. The average staff size among this group of respondents is equivalent to 1.8 full-time members.

The nine broadcast action lines responding to our survey reported staff positions as summarized in Table 13.1 (staff and division of labor within nine broadcast action lines). Six reported that "researchers" (sometimes called "investigators") categorize and interpret the complaint input, and research and apply some of the strategies. Three respondents

TABLE 13.1
Staff and Division of Labor within Nine Broadcast Action Lines

Station	Number of staff members	Reporter	Researcher Full time	Researcher Part time	Secretary	Producer	Camera operator
KNBC-TV	8	1	3	2	2		
KCRA-TV	2	1	1				
KCBS[a]	?	1					
KPIX-TV	3	1	1			1	
WQXI-TV	5	1	1	2			1
WLS-TV	4	1			1	2	
WOSU	7	1	3	2		1	
WXYZ-TV	3	1				2	
WCCO-TV[a]	2	?	1(?)			1(?)	

[a] Staff organization was not clearly stated by respondent.

said they delegate these duties to the reporter, secretaries, or producers. Five of the nine responding broadcast action lines have "producers," who are responsible for the technical aspects of actual broadcasting. The term is used as a catch-all phrase in the industry. KPIX-TV's action-line producer, for example, has research and scriptwriting duties in addition to his technical tasks. Table 13.2 outlines the reported backgrounds of these action line researchers (training and experience of researchers for nine broadcast action lines).

Recently some law school students have assisted broadcast action lines for credit. Under Professor Donald Rothschild of the George Washington University law faculty, for example, some law and undergraduate students help run action lines for WRC-TV and WTTG Radio in

TABLE 13.2

Training and Experience of Researchers for Nine Broadcast Action Lines

Action Line station	Number of researchers		Does researcher have one or more degrees?	Degree major	Previous experience
	Full time	Part time			
KNBC-TV	3		Yes	[a]	
			Yes		
			Yes		
		2	Yes		
			Yes		
KCRA-TV	1		Yes	Political Science	
KCBS	?	?			
KPIX-TV	1				[b]
WQXI-TV	1		Yes	Sociology	VISTA
		2	—	—	Retail Sales and Public Relations
			—	—	Medical Research
WLS-TV ("Producers")	2		Yes	Broadcast	4 years TV
			No	—	8 years all media
WOSU	3	2	[c]	[c]	[c]
WXYZ-TV ("Coordinators")	2		Yes	American Studies	2 years TV
			60 units	—	1 year Radio and TV
WCCO-TV	1(?)		—	Speech & Journalism	

[a] "Majors run from sociology to psychology and journalism."

[b] Original researcher had prior experience as nonlegal investigator for Washington State Attorney General. Her replacement's training and experience was not reported.

[c] "All Ombudsman Service personnel are professional broadcast journalists."

Washington, D.C. In New York City similar relations exist between WABC and Fordham University Law School, and between WNET-TV and New York University Law School (Weisman 1975:7).

Complaining to an Action Line

Action lines reported that their daily volumes of complaints and requests for information ranged from 1 (for 10 newspapers) to 500 or more (for the *New York Daily News*). The second highest daily volume was 360 (for the *Santa Ana* [California] *Register*). Uncontrollable factors such as the size of the parent media's audience, local population density, and the presence of other complaint managers may account in part for the number of complaints an action line receives, whereas other factors are under the control of the action line. An action line wishing to expand its volume may employ several forms of publicity. KABL Radio's Call for Action has advertised on television and on posters, and KGO-TV provided full-page magazine advertisements for Action 7, inadvertently causing the latter's complaint volume to exceed its administrative abilities. Action 7's complaint volume fell soon after the magazine campaign was discontinued. Several staff members of the KABC Ombudsman Service park a distinctively-labeled truck in large shopping centers for 2 or 3 days per month. Having some knowledge of the social composition and residence patterns exhibited by the KABC audience, the Service staff members take the truck to shopping centers where they are least likely to find KABC Radio listeners, and discuss consumer and government problems with curious onlookers. The Service also dispenses a variety of consumer- and citizen-oriented pamphlets from the mobile unit and, when appropriate, hands out complaint forms to be completed and mailed to the Serivce's office. This mobile unit accounts for about 25% of the Service's total volume.

As the number of complaints addressed to an action line rises to thousands or tens of thousands, the effort of merely receiving this volume assumes large proportions. The action lines studied illustrated four input methods. The *Tribune*'s Action Line and television's Action 7 accept only written complaints, as do 51 (45%) of the newspaper action lines sampled. A second group of action lines, including the nearly 40 Call for Action chapters, prefer telephoned complaints, although Call for Action readily accepts letters as well. For 50 (44%) of the newspapers surveyed, the telephone is a regular input method. A third way to receive complaints, initiated by the *Houston Chronicle*'s "Watchem" in 1961 (*Editor & Publisher* 1966:9), is to tape-record callers' messages for later study by an action liner. This method is used on at least some occasions by 37 (33%) of our newspaper respondents and by three broadcast action lines. The fourth and by far least popular input method is a personal interview with the complainant. The KABC Ombudsman Service regularly interviews, although only in the mobile unit. The Service prefers written complaints but also receives phone calls during scheduled hours. Twenty-seven (24%) of the responding newspapers also interview on occasion.

Several factors enter into an action line's selection of input method. With a "letters only" policy, the action line can easily photocopy a record of each case and, if not equipped to render effective assistance, can forward the letter to some other complaint manager or to the complainee, all without risk of compromising its own image of objectivity with an incorrect interpretation of facts. But to handle written complaints, the action line must frequently solicit further information from complainants, one-third of whom, according to Pletschet of Action Line, do not provide all necessary facts. Furthermore, many complainants send original documents in support of their claims, even if the action line's advertisements request copies only. Chicago's WLS-TV found this to be such a problem that their Action 7 staff developed a form letter to accompany documents being returned to complainants. Documents may be lost, and if the action line falls behind in opening its mail, complainants are hindered in seeking effective help elsewhere.

With telephoned input the action liner can solicit all pertinent information on the spot while gauging the caller's emotional investment in the problem. KABL's Call for Action volunteers find that without immediate emotional support, some callers just stop talking and decide to "lump it." But telephoned complaints take time; KABL volunteers spend at least 60–70 hours per week handling about 70 problems by phone. In contrast, Iida and Brian of Action 7 expend 40 hours per week on the 120 written complaints not deemed broadcastable, and the Ombudsman Service, receiving three-quarters or more of its input by mail, expends a mean time of less than 6 minutes per item. Telephoning frequently inconveniences both callers and action lines, although the latter can minimize this problem with adequate staffing or with tape recorders, both requiring additional expense. Taped callers, like letter writers, tend to supply insufficient information. An added problem in some states is that up to 23% of the households have no telephone (*American Almanac* 1973:494).

With personal interviews the action line can generally obtain the maximum amount of information. However, because the action line performs best when its information collection is close at hand, the complainant must travel, at the action line's convenience, to an office that may seem awesome and forbidding.

Once a complaint is received by an action line, it is then classified. In each case the first question is whether the action line should work on the complaint at all, or reject it. Conventional grounds for rejecting complaints and questions include the fact that the problem is not interesting to readers because it is repetitive (mentioned by 17 newspaper survey respondents); too difficult for the action line to solve (16); a legal (6), medical (5), or "personal" problem (5); or because the complainant is a "crank" (8). When asked about the nature of "legal problems," all respondents rendered denotative rather than connotative definitions. An action line might refuse to act if an attorney has entered the picture, or it might consult the parent medium's attorneys in debatable cases. Although no examples of "crank" cases were submitted, one action liner suggested that facetious or "clearly unreasonable" complaints fit this category. Action 7's Iida states that about 5% of its cases are rejected in all whereas Call for Action chapters do not recognize rejection as a means of dealing with their customers.

KABL's Call for Action volunteers classify queries by problem type, for example, "automobile repair" or "insurance." Having researched local complaint managers and having set up its classification system before accepting any complaints, the volunteers were from the first day of operation able to help about half their callers (more recently 63%) by merely directing them to extremely helpful people. In contrast, Action 7 had neither a complaint taxonomy nor a catalogue of references for dealing with the first influx of complaints it received, and a backlog quickly accumulated until Brian devised a classificatory scheme.

Complaint-Management Techniques of Action Lines

Gathering appropriate information is the life blood of the mass media. In contrast, citizens are far less able to develop useful knowledge about corporate and governmental structures. In fact, some action liners report that all too many citizens are unable to effectively use telephone books, some of which identify numerous government regulatory agencies under a heading such as "Consumer Complaint and Protection Coordinators." An action line cognizant of such listings has a double advantage, for many media offices collect directories from dozens of cities. The federal and state governments publish rosters and organization guides[4]

[4]Examples are (a) U.S. Office of the Federal Register, National Archives and Records Service, *U.S. government organization manual* (now called *United States government manual*) (Washington, D.C.: Government Printing Office, Stock No. 022-003-00910-8), available annually from Superintendent of Documents, Government Printing Office, Washington, D.C. 20402; (b) *U.S. Government telephone directory* ([for Region 9] San Francisco: Government Services Administration), available at any U.S. Government bookstore; (c) *California roster for 1972–1973: Directory of state services*, edited by E. G. Brown, Jr. (Sacramento: Documents Section, Office of Procurement); and (d) *State of California telephone directory* (Sacramento: Documents Section, Office of Procurement).

that action lines quickly accumulate, along with private complaint guides[5] and pamphlets from public service groups.

A well-managed file system can constitute a vital source of information. The *Tribune's* Action Line keeps records of all cases in a problem-oriented file, which staff members consult for tactical ideas in particularly baffling situations.

A complaint-assistance technique of critical importance to the KABC Ombudsman Service, to Call for Action chapters, and to the *Tribune's* Action Line consists of *recruiting a specialized network*. As used here the term "network" refers to "the chains of persons with whom a given person is in actual contact, or with whom he can enter into contact [Boissevain 1968:546]." A person on familiar terms with the mayor of a town can probably use this relationship to get fast action in a complaint about potholes in the street. But few ordinary citizens know the mayor or corporate executives or regional directors of federal agencies. Even fewer people know a large enough number of such powerful individuals to be able to select from among them the one or ones most likely to help with a particular complaint. Many action liners, during their previous years in newsgathering, in business, or in governmental consumer protection, have incorporated powerful business and government officials into their own networks.

Network recruitment is a constant process for the KABC Ombudsman Service. KABC-AM Radio, with one and a half million listeners, has developed a reputation for public service through such programming as the "Mini-Specials," in which knowledgeable people discuss important issues and social trends. In one Mini-Special eight State Superior Court judges discussed "justice" (KABC News Release 1972:1); in another, Ralph Nader discussed "consumerism" (KABC News Release 1973:1). Backed by the power of its reputation and its huge audience, KABC hosts monthly "Leadership Luncheons" to which prominent businesspeople, educators, minority leaders, politicians, and other powerful individuals are invited.[6] There the Ombudsman Service and the problems it encoun-

---

[5]The private guides most commonly seen were (a) M. Gast, *Getting the best of Los Angeles* (Los Angeles: Torcher/Southern California Guide, 1972); (b) Joseph Rosenbloom, *Consumer complaint guide 1974* (New York: Macmillan Information, 1974); (c) J. D. Weaver, *Los Angeles handbook* (Los Angeles: Proce, Stern, Sloan, 1972); and (d) Jack White, Gary Yanker, and Harry Steinberg, *The angry buyer's complaint directory* (New York: Peter H. Wyden, 1974). The Rosenbloom and White Books, when used as a pair, comprise a comprehensive list of corporate executives for thousands of U.S. corporations and of municipal, county, state, and federal complaint assistants.

[6]A partial list of guests who attended KABC Leadership Luncheons during 1971–1972 includes the White House Director of Communications, 4 U.S. senators, 17 U.S. congressmen, the governor and the lieutenant governor of California, several superintendents and directors of departments of California state government, 18 California legislators, 7 county supervisors, 17 other county officials including 4 Superior Court judges, 20 Los

ters are explained to the guests, whose frequent offers of assistance are filed for the Service's future use.

The volunteers of KABL Call for Action, like those in other chapters, built a network over a period of nearly 3 months before accepting a single complaint. They poured over public service leaflets, advertisements, and telephone listings, and contacted newspapers, libraries, friends, the public schools, and the health department, to name a few. Armed with the names of nearly 60 private and government organizations, 20 volunteers set out in teams of 2 to interview well-placed officials. Besides informing these officials about Call for Action, they collected data on each agency, including the name and position of the person interviewed, hours of operation, the services provided, any fees required or restrictions upon who could receive help, and whether the agency would accept referrals from KABL. They also noted any new leads, which were then pursued in the same way. After a year of operation, the volunteers surveyed the files to identify the most common subjects and origins of complaint, and investigated further. They categorized the complaint-assistance data and reproduced them in loose-leaf binders that are regularly updated and kept at the desks where volunteers take telephoned complaints.

To help maintain relationships with contacts and to make them feel like friends, the *Tribune*'s Action Line sends Christmas cards to the 25 most helpful ones. Benton for the Ombudsman Service occasionally calls contacts just to say "hello" and to offer them her help as they find necessary. KABL holds annual banquets at which they extend "Most Helpful" awards and their thanks to contacts.

Having accumulated many references and developed an extensive network, an action line can then dispose of half or more of its input by the straight referral method, *directing the complainant to a helpful person or agency*. The premise of this simple technique is that many complainants can fend for themselves if they know where to go to press their claims, especially simple ones. If a complainant is not reaching the segment of the complainee organization best prepared to deal with his or her problem, there is, from the complainee's standpoint, no complaint. Complainants showing great facility in formulating and communicating their arguments are most likely to be treated as straight referrals.

When taking a call of the straight referral type, a Call for Action volunteer listens carefully to the complaint and asks questions to ensure her own understanding of the problem. From the loose-leaf directory the volunteer then selects one or several names for the complainant's use. Other action liners use analogous techniques. Straight referral can be used

---

Angeles city officials including the mayor, 14 "business leaders" of whom at least 6 were board chairpersons or presidents of major U.S. corporations, 15 education leaders, 14 "minority leaders," and other powerful individuals.

again and again for one complaint until the action line and the complainant achieve a reasonable result.

The Ombudsman Service reports that 5% of its cases must eventually be referred to enforcement agencies because complainees' conduct comes within these agencies' statutorily defined jurisdictions. Benton adds, however, that the Service can generally get action faster than can government agencies in consumer problems, despite the fact that many such agencies ask the Service to turn over more of the latter's work load. A test of the need for government intervention often used by other action lines is the frequency with which a common pattern of complaints arises against one firm.

A simple variation of straight referral, normally used by Action 7 and by the Ombudsman Service, is to mail a complainant's letter to the complainee along with an action-line form letter. Action 7's letter has a wildly colorful letterhead proclaiming "Action 7!" and an eye-catching bottom line stating: "KGO-TV San Francisco[,] an ABC owned television station." The KABC Ombudsman stationery features a pair of star-spangled scissors cutting through red tape, surrounded by the words "KABC Radio 79" and "Ombudsman." Although the media affiliation is unmistakable, implication is preferred to intimidation. The cover letter neither attributes blame nor explicitly threatens publicity; it merely requests the complainee to look into the problem and notify both the complainant and the action line of the results. The primary intent of such stationery is to *grab the complainee's attention,* a universal action-line tool. Its use may accomplish no more than to put the action line user at the head of the complaint line, but this objective appears to be legitimate when time is of the essence, as in the following case:

> *A woman complained to Action 7 that the public works department was cutting down all the trees on her city's main street. She said that most of the residents wished to preserve the trees, but that complaints to the city manager's office were falling upon deaf ears. Protests to a city council member and to a local newspaper had not helped. The problem required immediate attention as the tree removal was proceeding rapidly. Using the Action 7 name as much as possible, Brian was able to reach the city manager by telephone. The tree-cutting was discontinued. On the same day the city council chastised the city manager for his earlier unresponsiveness and adopted a moratorium on tree removal until the problem could be studied by a local committee. The woman who had complained to Action 7 was appointed chairperson of the ad hoc committee. KGO-TV aired the story on its evening news program.*

The attention-grabbing device may be used successfully without any action-line effort, for Call for Action volunteers described cases in which ex-complainants had called to report that mere threats of enlisting the action line had caused previously unresponsive complainees to make satisfactory settlements. The users of Call for Action and of Action Line are always advised to mention the action line when introducing themselves to complainees.

When complainant and action line agree that no reasonable response is forthcoming from the complainee, dispute escalation begins, a common form being to *penetrate the complainee organization by circumventing normal channels* (Cyert and March 1963:117–127). The essential element in this technique is a well-developed complaint-assistance network. Benton related the following case:

> The KABC Ombudsman Service received a complaint that the California Department of Social Service had failed to send the food stamps due one woman, who had not the money to purchase food. The problem was further complicated by the fact that the complainee was a diabetic, and that her disease was controlled by insulin injections. Since a diabetic must precisely balance doses of sugar from food, the woman stated that it was unsafe for her to take insulin without having food at hand. The situation was potentially life-threatening, but the complainant was unable to contact her social worker, the one link she had with the Department. An Ombudsman Service worker telephoned the complainant's social worker, who refused to discuss the matter. The Service worker then telephoned the social worker's supervisor, but he was attending a meeting and was therefore unavailable.
>
> At this point Benton telephoned the Service's contact in the Department, a secretary in the office of the Director of the entire organization. Within ten minutes the complainant's social worker telephoned the Ombudsman Service and listened to Benton's description of the complaint. The social worker promised to personally deliver the food stamps to the complainant at the end of the Department's work day. Benton relayed this message to the complainant. (Curiously, the complainant rejected this as an inadequate solution, saying that since food purchases with stamps required some cash and that since she had no cash, her life was still threatened. The Service collected several dollars from other KABC employees, and delivered the donation to the woman.)

This case illustrates five noteworthy concepts. First, use of the action line's specialized network is reserved until the lower-echelon complainee representative has evidenced unwillingness or inability to resolve the problem; that is to say, the Ombudsman Service always first tries to use the complainee's routine input channels, which sometimes take the form of a "company ombudsman" (as it does at Chrysler Corporation and Westinghouse). This policy gives rise to the second concept: The action line's network contacts do not receive ordinary complaints that may well be adequately resolved at lower levels, for these problems are screened out by the action line. Consequently, the action line does not overburden the contacts. Third, the action line usually does not reveal its network to complainants. Action lines differ in this policy, but Benton of the Ombudsman Service explains that future Ombudsman users are the ultimate beneficiaries of network anonymity. Benton and her volunteers, unlike many complainants, maintain a cool and impartial attitude; thus appreciative contacts are willing to continue helping the Service. When one student volunteer broke the anonymity rule, a harried contact complained to Benton, who reproved the student. It is possible, but unverified, that other action liners consider Benton's argument for anonymity when deciding whether or not to use the straight referral method for particularly angry callers. Fourth, many network contacts are not executives although, like the secretary, all are said to be structurally close to the centers of power in their organizations. Indeed, in their network-building Call for Action volunteers consciously attempt to avoid recruiting executives, for, in the words of Sally Livingston, "executive officials do not do the work of routine complaint management." Fifth, the Ombudsman Service did not exert direct "pressure" on the social worker or even on the Department. Instead, the social worker was galvanized by her own superiors or by someone appearing to represent her superiors. The contact was, in turn, stimulated by Benton's amicable use of her personal network.

Clifford Pletschet remarks that government agencies are more difficult to penetrate than are commercial firms. Call for Action folklore holds that government complaints take twice the time required for consumer problems. "Bureaucrats try to remain anonymous," said Pletschet, "by using regulations and protocol to construct fences around themselves." For this reason the small *Tribune* staff, rather than investigating for itself, relies upon network contacts whenever possible to discover the source of a complainant's problem.

In a broad sense, the function of all action lines is to help complainants and complainees communicate. In about 10% of the cases reported by KABC and KABL, this assistance assumes the more specialized form of *interpretive communication*. While trying to resolve their dispute, complainant and complainee often end up talking past each other because of different expectations about their relationship or because they consider different facts to be most important in the disagreement. Sometimes the problem is exacerbated by the complainant's inability to comprehend his adversary's language; he or she may misinterpret prolix warranty provisions or directions, or simply be unaccustomed to "corporatese."[7] In these cases an interpreter who can understand both positions must enter to reduce the dispute to basic facts and to translate for the parties, as in the following hypothetical case, which was approved by Benton of Ombudsman and Fox of Action Line.

---

[7]Several states have recently enacted legislation requiring that insurance and credit provisions for consumer purchases be stated in simple language (*Time* 1975:74).

A man buys a set of stereo audio components under warranty and finds, after assembly, that the system produces undesirable background noise. Upon complaining to the seller he is told that if it is excessive he has probably failed to follow assembly instructions. He checks the system carefully, determines that he has followed instructions, and decides that the fault lies in two of the components. He does not wish to dismantle the system to return it to the seller, as he will thereby dismantle his evidence of systemic malfunction. He again complains to the seller, but receives the same reply. The seller also states that it is not the policy of the firm to send repairmen on house calls. Now angry, the man calls an action line.

The action liner first must analyze the complaint to discover factual issues, in this case whether the system operates correctly and, if not, whether the fault lies in the seller's components or in the buyer's assembly. Next the action liner must try to strip the dispute of emotional content and reveal underlying principles. Our hypothetical complainant is convinced that because he has purchased an expensive and highly specialized instrument and has taken due care in its assembly, the company has a positive obligation to ensure his satisfaction with the product. The seller operates under different considerations. Businesses complain that purchasers in fact fail to follow instructions and then complain about an appliance that they allege does not work or that indeed they have ruined. Considerable company expense goes into sending repair personnel out on these false alarms (FTC 1971:271). In this case, the parties have become mutually suspicious, and their positions polarized.

To salvage this or similar situations the action liner must appear dispassionate, objective. An irate worker is an unsuccessful one and must be dismissed, as has happened to a KABC volunteer, especially if he or she badgers the more cooperative and useful contacts. Call for Action uses intensive telephone training to help new volunteers become sensitive to this problem.

In these situations the action liner neither injects his or her own opinions and suggestions nor relies upon special subject-matter expertise. I have observed middle-aged suburban volunteers at Call for Action earnestly discussing automobile warranties, appliance repairs, and financial instruments with both dispute parties, but they were not arguing principles of automotive mechanics, electricity, or credit. Rather, they were ensuring that each party had a detached, rational description of the other's position.

The *Tribune's* Action Line also uses interpretive communication but generally does so by letter, because the staff believes it is easier to be successful on the justified complainant's behalf when letters are used. According to Pletschet and Fox, a skilled conversationalist can obfuscate the issues more easily by phone than by a letter, which is subject to careful scrutiny for faulty argumentation. Moreover, if a complainee rejects the action liner's telephoned proposals, the complainee, by alleging that he has already explained himself once, can severely restrict further action-line attempts to communicate.

The KABC Call for Action volunteers dispose of roughly 60% of their cases by the straight referral method. In the other 40% the volunteers maintain relationships with complainants through an elaborate call-back system. The record of a new case not clearly amenable to straight referral is placed in a postdated chronological file so as to appear as part of the original volunteer's work load 30 days hence. The Tribune's Action Line uses a similar system (by mail), but all other groups studied leave to the complainant the burden of keeping the relationship alive. The purposes of calling back are to determine whether the agency first suggested came through with its service; to offer additional suggestions and encouragement if the dispute is not yet settled; and to help clients maintain their belief that their complaints are important. Call for Action continues to call back until a satisfactory settlement is reported, or the volunteer discovers that no settlement will satisfy the complainant, or the complainant manifests loss of interest, or a complainee's apparently unreasonable position requires either court or government agency action. On one occasion a volunteer excitedly told me, "We just heard from one woman whom we have been calling back for a year. She just won her case in small claims court." The complainant was quoted as saying that she "never would have done it if KABL had not kept after [her]."

A complainant may allege that an advertisement publicized by the action line's own parent medium is unfair or untrue, in which case the action line may notify its parent's advertising department:

> In a television advertisement a large garment manufacturer offered a special discount on the second of two garments to be bought by each customer. A number of complainants told Action 7 that the firm was not sending the garments as promised. After finding that KGO-TV broadcast the ad, Nancy Iida described the complaints to KGO-TV's advertising sales department. A few days later Iida received apologetic letters from the firm explaining that the demand created by the ad far exceeded the firm's expectations. The firm promised to fill the orders as soon as possible.

This procedure both helps the individual complainant and alerts the station or newspaper of possibly improper advertising to the benefit of all in the parent's audience. Iida states that the advertising department resists this method because of the time demands, primarily in research requirements, upon a department "not in the business of complaint resolution." Pletschet reported no such resistance in the Oakland Tribune's advertising department. An action line may surmount the objection by first completing all necessary research and then turning its findings over to the responsible department:

> Several Los Angeles radio stations, including KABC, carried advertisements for "invention marketing companies." One or more of these companies was in the business of soliciting listeners' inventions and "assessing the inventions for marketability." If the invention was "found to be marketable," the inventor would pay the company between $500 and $1000 for "development of a market," i.e., for sale of rights to the invention to manufacturers. The KABC Ombudsman Service was receiving numerous complaints from inventors who had spent $750 only to be told months later that "no one bought the invention."
>
> After some research (which she did not describe), Benton discovered that such companies probably were making efforts to sell the inventions. However, she also discovered that in many cases the marketing companies probably should have been far more selective in their assessments of the marketability of the inventions. Benton carefully described her findings to the advertising executive. KABC no longer carries advertisements for such companies.

Trade associations often have the express mission of creating good public relations for their members, and at least one action line has learned to take advantage of this orientation, as shown in the following case:

> A woman complained to the Tribune's Action Line about a carpet installation which had been performed by a local discount warehouse. Jon Fox forwarded the letter to the firm. After weeks had passed with no answer, Fox discovered that the local carpeting firms had recently cooperated to form a public relations office similar to a specialized better business bureau. Fox sent a copy of the woman's letter to this office which in turn promptly enlisted several local carpet-workers. This group spent a number of hours repairing the poor installation work. (According to Marion Eaton, potential customers of this firm who check with the Better Business Bureau about the complainee's reputation are told the firm "has indicated its unwillingness to reply to complaints submitted through [the BBB]."

The better-funded and more heavily staffed action lines rarely, if ever, enlist the aid of other privately operated complaint-management services as Fox did, for they usually have worked out extensive procedures that include the ultimate sanction of notifying government agencies of complainee wrongdoing.

Action liners and their observers (Waters 1975:70) assume that they can exert much pressure on local businesses. Said Action 7's Brian, "A word or two one way or the other on television may cost that business hundreds of dollars."

Its wish to maintain an image of objectivity and to avoid unfairly injuring complainees usually proscribes an action line's use of explicit threats of bad publicity. But an action line may still use *implicit reminders of its power.* Thus, Benton carefully reminds Leadership Luncheon guests that KABC can and may broadcast a complaint when necessary. Complainees who have not responded to a gentle Action 7 inquiry are told in a dispute-escalating letter: "Thus far, we have not received any response from you. As this is one of the few inquiries we have selected for use on our broadcast, . . . we would appreciate any resolution or response you can provide as soon as possible . . . [Action 7 form letter no. 8]." Pletschet often prods complainees with "Action Line hopes your silence means that you are hard at work on our reader's problem."

When do action lines use *publicity* in complaint management? There is no simple rule, as one action line's governing considerations differ from another's. An action line heeding the listener and viewer ratings looks for material that will attract the audience, perhaps by showing how much power it has or by emphasizing the human interest aspect of an elder's complaint. However, many of the most common complaints (e.g., late Social Security checks, mail-order problems) generally are not deemed sufficiently interesting to broadcast very often. An action line seeking to establish itself as a "watchdog" for consumers to deter questionable businesses uses publicity to create for itself a powerful "no holds barred" image. But if the primary interest of an action line is to resolve individual cases, there is great concern for an image of objectivity, and publicity is used only as a last resort either to campaign for structural changes that will prevent the complaint from recurring or, rarely, to pressure an obstinate complainee.

There may be a greater tendency among action lines to use publicity pressure against government than against private-sector complainees. A nonrandom sample of 201 newspaper columns sent to us by some 70 action lines reported 514 disputes (in addition to 748 requests for information from noncomplainants). Of these, 308 (60%) concerned the private sector and 206 the public sector. The action lines reportedly were more successful with the private sector complaints (see Table 13.3). More im-

TABLE 13.3
State of Conflict in 514 Published Action-Line Cases from 201 Sample Columns

	Private sector	Public sector
Complainant won	187 (61%)	87 (41%)
Complainant lost	32 (10%)	18 (9%)
Conflict not yet resolved	89 (29%)	101 (50%)
Totals	308 (100%)	206 (100%)

portant, in 29% of the private-sector complaints but 50% of the public-sector complaints, the action lines reported the cases as still open and requiring further efforts at resolution.

The following two cases illustrate the technique of publicizing a complaint to cause government to react. The first is taken from the *Oakland Tribune:*

"Sound Off"

What recourse do we have against those who drive like maniacs in our residential neighborhoods? Hilltop Drive in El Sobrante is a favorite spot for these screwballs. On the 40 miles-per-hour stretch it is common to see cars going 55 to 65. On the 25 miles-per-hour section they slow down to 40 or 50. There have been many accidents. A girl was killed last month when a speeder hit her car from the rear. The police seem powerless. Where is the radar?— E. F. El Sobrante [*Oakland Tribune* 1972b:2].

The second is from a radio action line:

A woman complained to KABL Call for Action that she had been bitten by a neighbor's large dog. Fearing retaliation by the neighbor, the woman had not complained to the police. The volunteer, who happened to live in the woman's neighborhood, called the police although preserving the complainant's anonymity. The police claimed there was nothing they could do, since they did not have jurisdiction to enforce the city's leash law. The volunteer discovered with considerable research that *no* city agency had been given power to enforce the statute, as the board of supervisors had failed to grant any funds for this purpose.

After deciding that an editorial was in order, the volunteers approached the KABL program manager, who wrote the following message, which was broadcast on three successive days:

"It is against the law in San Francisco for animal owners to allow their pets to roam the streets out of control. Yet, according to KABL's Call for Action volunteers, violations of the leash laws are high on the list of complaints from the community. Filth on the sidewalks is a significant factor, but not to be overlooked is the increasing menace of dogs actually attacking people. Last year over 3400 such cases were reported in San Francisco. Many of the attacks were serious, and certainly not necessary if the leash laws had been properly enforced. Fortunately, something can be done about it. Find out for yourself. Call for Action at 398-5225. That's 398-5225" [KABL 1972:i].

At least one member of the board of supervisors publicly complained that by editorializing, Call for Action "pressured the board into a corner." The board held public hearings, the volunteer testifying as one of several witnesses. In December 1974 funds were allocated to the police department so that one police officer could assume the full-time assignment of giving citations to the owners of unleashed dogs.

Neither the KABC Ombudsman Service nor KABL Call for Action has ever used broadcast pressure against an *individual* private complainee, although both action lines preserve the tacit suggestion of such broadcasts. Because both are jealous of their images as objective complaint assistants, both wish to avoid all risk of appearing to blackmail either government or business complainees into action. If a business appears guilty of blatantly bad conduct, the action line alerts appropriate state and federal officials. And if bad conduct is symptomatic of an entire industry, the action lines campaign for government regulation of the industry.

The *Tribune's* Action Line has a similar policy of not naming complainee businesses in the column. The sole exception to this rule occurs when Action Line is aware of government proceedings against a business and the subject of such proceedings resembles complaints previously directed to Action Line. Then the column describes the proceedings and recommends that related complaints be sent to the appropriate government agencies.

In short, an action line concerned first and foremost with complaint management generally reserves the very strong publicity technique for those complaints that either cause stress throughout large segments of the community or point to situations involving high risk for individual citizens.

All action lines studied reported that some complainants attempt to use the power of the action line to achieve favorable results even when not justified by the facts. One Call for Action volunteer ventured the opinion that this group makes up the approximately 11% of the complainants who upon being called back state that they have lost interest in the dispute and want no further contact with Call for Action. "They do not wish to face the possibility of being exposed," stated the volunteer. Keith Smith, executive producer of the WOSU Ombudsman Service in Columbus, Ohio, is alert to "unjustified" attempts by consumers to use the Ombudsman as a weapon for clubbing complainees into submission:

> We deplore being used in such a manner and say so on the air, frequently pointing out in complete detail the actions taken by the person threatened as he went about satisfying the complainant. We strive for fair, accurate and balanced reporting and sometimes bend over backwards to neutralize blackmail attempts by publicly chiding such listeners for doing so [Smith 1973:1].

Action 7 has a similar outlook, as shown by the following case:

> A man wrote that "No Parking" areas around a local museum were inadequately marked and that the parking ticket he had received was therefore unjust. The complaint was broadcast, with film showing "No Parking" signs that Brian described as "so close and so numerous that we could not take a picture of the building or the area without including the signs."

Complaints such as this may indicate that citizens who feel powerless (Nader 1977) are experimenting with action lines as a way to regain power. According to Nelkane Benton, this effort is realistic, for a publicity-conscious businessperson may well capitulate to a complainant using an action line, even though knowing the claim is absolutely false.

Action liners exhibit profound concern for their own images of objectivity because they believe that the true source of their power rests not in their ability to cause severe economic damage to complainees, but in complainee's willingness to hear them out. The personal network-building so crucial to many action liners requires that the action line not hinder its own access to members of its audience. In short, the action line must legitimize itself.

The WOSU Radio Ombudsman Service of Columbus, Ohio, uses publicity for the purpose of *deterring* anticonsumer behavior. The goal of this Service is "to improve . . . the standard of consumer services and domestic protection and education [Gillard 1973:69]." WOSU, a noncommercial station, is funded by the Ohio State University Tele-communications Center and the Corporation for Public Broadcasting (WOSU 1973:1). Eighteen different Ombudsman programs are aired each day (WOSU 1973:3). Of the approximately 1600 complaints the station receives annually (Smith 1973:1), nearly three-quarters are generated by WOSU Ombudsman programs (*News in Engineering* 1972).

The complaints not rejected by WOSU for the standard reasons (see earlier discussion) are investigated by an Ombudsman worker who, visibly armed with a tape recorder, visits the complainees' offices and records everything:

> even the anguished cries of "Oh my God, you can't put this on the air," . . . When a [cemetery] operator, answering complaints of overcharging, presented for signature a lawyer's agreement giving him the right to approve or reject any broadcast, the WOSU people declined to sign—and read the proposed agreement on the air. Names are named in all their programmes, . . . [Gillard 1973:70].

There is something to be learned in every action-line broadcast or newspaper column, although sometimes only that "the natives are restless." In some instances action lines have manifestly assumed the task of *educating citizens* about complaining and related social concepts. The following case illustrates how an action liner can, without squarely addressing the merits of the complaint, help a citizen to mitigate his tension by changing his expectations:

> *A man called KABL Call for Action to complain of his union's "unjust demand." The union had struck for an extended period and had then ordered all members to contribute to the depleted strike fund. The KABL volunteer, a member of another union, explained that the arrangement was*

a matter of contract with which Call for Action could not interfere. The volunteer went on to explain that such contracts are "probably necessary," and that they constitute "just one of those things that goes with working in a union." The conversation apparently relieved the caller's distress, and he made no further complaint to the action line.

In the case next described the volunteer argued with the complainant about the merits of his case:

A typewriter was ruined in a residential fire. The owner argued with his homeowner's insurance adjuster that the latter's company should cover the original price of the machine, which was ten years old. Upon calling KABL Call for Action, the owner was told by a volunteer that she "understood the problem." The volunteer then talked with the complainant for about twenty minutes, finally convincing him that the machine could not possibly be worth its original price.

The same volunteer later stated that this form of action lining is rare and that she undertakes it only when a complainant or complainee indicates uncertainty with an untenable position. Benton of the Ombudsman Service agrees, adding that argument is very rarely necessary, especially in light of the risk of alienating a party.

Members of all four action lines that were closely studied pointed out that many disputants reach impasses because anger, frustration, or other emotions prevent them from communicating further. Although many such people no doubt "exit" the dispute (Hirschman 1970:4, 21–29), others call upon action lines to damage opponents with adverse publicity. Action lines, jealous of their reputations for impartiality, do not grant such requests. Rather, they try to teach such complainants to control their own emotions:

A schoolteacher complained to the KABC Ombudsman Service that her supervisor had dismissed her with insufficient cause and had engaged in immoral activities. The service returned the complainant's original letter with Benton's explanation that as written it was probably slanderous. After receiving a second, more temperate letter Benton called the supervisor, who was unfamiliar with the Service and who remained unconvinced of the origin of the call after several minutes of discussion. Upon Benton's suggestion the supervisor hung up the phone, called KABC, and asked for the Ombudsman Service, but still refused to discuss the dispute with Benton. However, she asked that Benton forward the letter and promised that she would carefully consider and respond to the allegations.

Pending further notification Benton considers the Service's participation in this dispute to be both successful and complete. The Service was successful because the complainant was taught to describe her complaint in the sober, temperate terms required to make it meaningful to the com-

plainee. As the disputing parties have agreed to communicate with one another, no further Service action is required.

All Call for Action chapters regularly analyze their files using statistical methods. Among other data, such studies reveal what community conditions most bother callers. Action lines unable to commit labor resources to such studies can learn to recognize chronic problems by arranging to have one staff member read all incoming mail or by holding regular information-sharing meetings of the staff. Several community problems then may be publicized for *preventive education* purposes:

> A complainant requested Action Line to ask a correspondence school to acknowledge several requests for information and applications. Action Line's response in the column was: "This is a switch. Usually readers are asking us to get them out of mail-order school, not into one. We contacted the school and a representative called on you and signed you up. We hope you don't have to write us in the future about troubles with the school [*Oakland Tribune* 1972a:2].

Under the direction of Arthur E. Rowse, a newspaperman and former Executive Director of President Johnson's White House Consumer Office, a syndicated action line called "Help-Mate" began publishing in several newspapers in the United States in January 1973. "Focusing on widely distributed products and services [personal letter from Rowse, 8 January 1973]," Help-Mate selects representative complaints and inquiries from its client newspapers' readers, investigates thoroughly, and publishes twice weekly a column that names all persons involved. Help-Mate's stated goals are to "spot buyers' problems" and then "suggest what [buyers] can do about them ... before they explode into federal cases [Rowse, 8 January 1973]."

Who Uses Action Lines and for What Problems?

My action-line research included some examination of complaints and case records. Action 7 permitted me to read the entire input for 1 week, which consisted of 123 letters, before Iida or Brian processed any of them. This material may have been skewed by the broadcasts of the previous week, for a televised complaint often draws comments and complaints about similar problems. Six of the sample letters requested help in finding local services and information; other letters were complaints. Where not otherwise stated, the Action 7 figures in the following tables concern complaints.

A different type of sample was obtained from KABL Call for Action. In the year between 16 March 1972 and 15 March 1973, this action line received approximately 3500 telephone calls and letters, of which about 2210 were disposed of by the straight referral method. Of the remaining 1290 (37%), I examined every tenth case record, a total of 129, finding 65 complaints by the aforementioned working definition. As both samples are small and not strictly comparable, the data cannot be interpreted as exhaustive or representative but rather as suggestive of general trends among complainants in the San Francisco–Oakland region.[8]

There are few data from which to infer sociological generalizations about the people whom the samples represent. Men and women use these two action lines in equal numbers, and almost all complainants are individuals representing themselves or nuclear family members. Twenty of Action 7's users and 16 Call for Action users complained or asked questions for friends or small groups. Presumably, larger groups such as unions, neighborhood associations, and businesses have access to information, influence, and economic sanctions sufficient to effectively press their grievances elsewhere. No data in the samples indicate whether ethnic, racial, or religious factors affect the choice of whether or not to use an action line.

The samples give some indication of what people complain to these action lines about (Table 13.4), although complaint subject matter is not easily susceptible to categorization. "Consumer" complaints involving commercial complainees are heavily represented in this sample whereas neighbors, family members, and close associates are less likely to be contested with by these means. Students of other action lines report comparable figures (cf. n. 8).

Although each action line received several complaints concerning landlords, both usually treat these complaints as being "too legal" for extensive action-line participation. Call for Action volunteers often warn complaining tenants that recruitment of third parties invites retaliation from many landlords; callers are then given the names of several local tenant advisory groups.

My newspaper survey indicates that magazine subscriptions, appliance repairs, landlord–tenant disputes, and fights with utility companies are serious and chronic problems. Computers are occasional but highly potent opponents, as one frustrated action liner discovered:

> Once a mistake is programmed into a computer's account, getting that mistake out of the electronic monster is a real chore. . . . This editor recently attempted to straighten out a subscription problem for a reader, sent his

[8]For similar analyses of complaint samples from two newspaper action lines, see Horton 1972:10–23, which also shows among Action Line's users a vast majority of *local* residents; and Palen 1972:10–24.

TABLE 13.4

Summary of Complaint Samples to Action 7 and KABL Call for Action

Complaint subjects	KGO-TV Action 7	KABL radio Call for Action
General consumer services	18	18
Automobile sales–service	11	9
General merchandise	19	10
Mail-ordered merchandise	11	7
Private contract of sale	2	—
Deceptive advertising	4	2
Landlord	4	5
Tenant	—	1
Municipal–county government	8	—
State government	8	1
Federal government	5	2
Police	5	1
Courts	1	1
Neighbors	3	4
Employers	3	—
Prior business partner	1	—
Estranged husband	1	—
Son	1	—
The action line	5	—
Miscellaneous	7	4
Totals	117	65

complaint to the magazine, along with a covering form letter of the column. Next thing we knew, we began receiving the magazine as a new subscriber and haven't been able to stop it yet! [Bicknell 1972:2].

The monetary values involved in 57 of the 117 Action 7 complaints and 22 of the 65 KABL Call for Action complaints are summarized in Table 13.5. The other letters and case records gave no figures. Like small claims courts, action lines hear complaints involving sums that are too small to warrant normal legal action but are sizable enough to concern average households. In some ways small complaints are more difficult to settle than are larger ones in that the value involved is often outweighed by the concomitant inconvenience. The persons empowered by the complainee to resolve disputes are hidden within a bureaucracy, and when found they do not take threats of legal action seriously. Action lines can help because they are uncommonly visible, easy to mobilize, and inexpensive for users. Finally, action lines do not concern themselves with questions of jurisdiction, which are threshhold issues for every court.

As accessible as action lines may be, numerous complainants seem to treat them as last resorts in problem solving. Thirty-two complainants

TABLE 13.5
Monetary Value of Complaint Samples

	KGO-TV Action 7 (57 values reported)	KABL Radio Call for Action (22 values reported)
Mean	$ 367.01	$ 257.37
Median	81.00	185.00
High	5294.55	1000.00
Low	1.10	6.75

mentioned having consulted at least one other agency before calling on Action 7, and five complainants said that the action line was the fourth stop. The last-resort analysis finds some support in the length of time some complainants waited after their problems arose before consulting Action 7. Table 13.6 summarizes these data as reported by 71 complainants.

Although she did not indicate whether or not Action 7 was a last resort for her problem, one woman perceived the action line as a catalyst for structural change when she wrote:

> My neighbor is wanted by the police for murder... his [unoccupied] house stinks with garbage, chicken manure and rotten boxes.... The county health department or the police won't help, ... So what can you do for us?

How Successful Are Action Lines?

Access to the letters and case records described earlier was conditioned on the researchers' promises of confidentiality. Although justified on the basis of complainants' privacy, these restrictions prevented investigation of the best source of data on whether and to what extent action lines are successful in their complaint-management efforts. Consequently, we must rely upon action liners themselves for this information.

All four of the action lines closely studied agree that a dispute is "successfully resolved" if both parties express satisfaction. This happens, for example, when one party offers a resolution that the other party ac-

TABLE 13.6
Time Interval between Onset of Problem and Complaint to Action 7

Mean interval	141 days
Median interval	60 days
Shortest interval	1 day
Longest interval	4 years

cepts. Proffered resolutions come in several forms, the most obvious being refunds, repairs, and the like. Action liners add that some complainants are satisfied merely with reasonable explanations of complainees' conduct, which have not been forthcoming because of breaches of communication.

Each action line recognizes that some complainants will be satisfied with any reasonable solution the action line may help to bring about. In these cases the action liner decides that further action would be useless and indeed counterproductive in that continued pressure on a personal network contact would damage the rapport so vital to the interests of future complainants.

Benton estimates that 80% of the Ombudsman Service's 50,000 annual complainants ultimately gain satisfactory results, and that the Service annually recovers $250,000 for its users. These figures are derived from semiannual file sweeps and follow-up letters to complainants. The KABL Call for Action data reveal that 22 complainants (58%) obtained favorable results in the 38 disputes completed on or before the last date sampled whereas 6 (or 16%) expressed dissatisfaction with case conclusions. In 10 cases (20%), volunteers noted that complainants had lost interest in further action. No success rates were available from KGO-TV's Action 7 or the Tribune's Action Line, but both claim "a wide majority" of successful efforts.

Conclusion

Throughout the 1960s and early 1970s the action-line concept of adapting early twentieth-century question-and-answer columns into consumer and citizen service features proliferated among the mass media. But action liners do not have an easy task and must navigate numerous choices and pitfalls. Certain policy judgments critically affect an action line's influence in the community and, hence, the effectiveness of its complaint resolution. The action line must first choose an identity: Is it to be a primarily entertaining, circulation-conscious feature, a news report of special classes of consumer-citizen problems, or a complaint-management and -prevention center? If the last path is chosen, how much independence is the action line to have from the journalism enterprise that sponsors it? This decision particularly affects the action line's incentives to generate meaningful data for the use of legislatures and government enforcement agencies as well as to warn consumers away from malevolent businesses. Also critical is the relative emphasis to be placed on the two diverse goals of individual complaint assistance and promotion of broad structural changes, each requiring substantial resource allocations.

More technical matters then arise. Administrative planning encompasses at least the following tasks: recruitment and organization of volunteer or paid personnel; acquisition and arrangement of general reference works and information; cultivation of a comprehensive complaint assistance network; reception, whether by mail, telephone, recording equipment, or personal interview; classification of complaint input; and intermediating disputes.

Strategic choices will include whether it will generally refer complaints or will assume a more active and persistent communicative role, or even outright advocacy. The nature and form of messages to appropriate officials concerning structural problems must be carefully considered. A decision must be made whether to build staff expertise in certain subjects at the possible expense of greater skill in generalized complaint assistance.

As varied as they are, action lines exhibit a certain consistency of style in complaint management. Thus, there are few formalities in action lining beyond the customs of polite, businesslike conduct. Most of the action lines studied remain neutral and act as message bearers rather than advocates. Publicizing disputes is not an exception to this policy, as even then action lines attempt to appear objective. Unlike courts, action lines expend little effort establishing facts as foundations for legal conclusions. More important, action lines do not generally adjudicate, as they might do were they to use publicity as a primary tool of complaint management (see Lazarsfeld and Merton 1965:462). Rather than handing down enforceable decisions, action lines encourage negotiation, in which parties contend, with or without outside help, through argument, moral force, physical threats, and a variety of other means, each party hoping thereby to gain the best possible outcome in the form of a mutually tolerable settlement (Gulliver 1969:17). If negotiation breaks down entirely, an action line may help the complainant seek adjudication (through courts or government agencies, for example), or it may encourage society to make structural changes within itself (by editorializing or by preventive education).

My study did not include examination of individual complainants. The great majority of sampled complaints, however, concern ephemeral, highly specific, often "one-shot" or single-stranded transactions between parties who are unlikely to interact again (see Table 13.2). Intrafamilial disputants, neighbors, co-employees, and others with strong, often multistranded relationships rarely recruit the media assistants, perhaps because such parties draw upon relatively equal sources of power: other family members, clergy, banks, employers, or courts. In contrast, corporate or government giants and individual citizens do not interact with equal strength in disputes arising from single-stranded relationships. My samples also indicate that many complainants have sparse information about complainees, their organizations, and how to penetrate and stimulate them into action. In short, these complainants are powerless to vindicate their rights.

An action line can amass power of considerable, although peculiar dimensions. Its power derives from the status of its parent medium; as an action line becomes known for objective, fair work, its power multiplies. Another derivative power stems from the economic sanctions that a media audience can apply against complainees receiving the worst publicity. Action lines can frequently use their personal relationships with various government officials and their knowledge of corporate procedure to get explanations or offers of settlement from complainees. Through these networks, backed again by the threat of publicity, action lines can elicit responses from individual bureaucrats who abhor being branded as troublemakers by their superiors. Conversely, the action line may render quick, positive feedback to complainees in the form of good publicity when warranted.

Common obstacles inhibit action lines from becoming skillful dispute-assistance alternatives. They are expensive for the parent media to operate, and their unsuitability to cost–benefit analysis makes them difficult to justify in the eyes of media executives. KABL Radio, for instance, began supporting a Call for Action unit in 1970, when the latter was still a new and unique concept in the electronic media. Annual expenses approached $6000. In the next 5 years, independent switchboard referral systems flourished in the San Francisco Bay Area and to this date perform many of the services offered by Call for Action. During this period, the owners of KABL opened an Oakland community center and committed themselves to maintaining it for the duration of their ownership of the station. Call for Action, Inc., had concurrently separated from the Urban Coalition and the latter's funds, and was charging annual fees to stations sponsoring Call for Action chapters. Lost uniqueness and mounting financial burdens, then, account in part for the March 1975 severance of the relationship between KABL Radio and Call for Action (telephone inverview with KABL station owner Knowles Hall, 31 December 1975).

Fiscal dependence upon its parent medium may cause an action line to neglect certain of its more powerful complaint prevention tools. For example, fewer than half the respondents to a 1973 action-line survey by the Associated Press Managing Editors Group (APME) said that they routinely named malevolent complainee businesses in their columns (Levine 1975:45). Although some action liners claim not to need this tool, some observers reasonably argue that such a policy reduces an action line's deterrence power and its ability to warn endangered customers (Levine 1975:42–51). In addition, a muzzled action-line staff may lose morale. To be sure, the no-name rule reduces the risk of driving away current and potential advertisers who support the action lines as well as their parents.[9]

To further justify themselves to expense-conscious commercial media, many action lines exhibit greater concern for audience enlargement than for effective complaint management and prevention. Thus 53 (47%) of our 113 newspaper survey respondents neither answer nor act upon complaints that have little audience appeal. Because repetitive complaints (e.g., Social Security) are frequently in this class, the most common problems paradoxically receive the least attention. Moreover, cost consciousness inhibits many action lines from attempting to instigate structural changes with the masses of rich data they possess concerning their readers' problems. Another 33 (29%) of the survey respondents stated that they seek quick, individualistic solutions whereas only 16 (14%) of the respondents claim to analyze their files regularly to expose community trouble spots. A complainee dealing with one of the former group has little incentive to adjust his policies; if he does have an interest in reforming, he can obtain little help from such an action line.

As audience acquisition is an economic goal, an action line formed for this purpose is unlikely to be granted the substantial staff and equipment required for the greatest effectiveness in complaint management. The staff, being concerned with program or column production, tends to use the easiest means of complaint handling—straight referral, occasional telephone calls, and personal interviews—and tends to work hardest on those complaints with the greatest chance of success, such as repair or replacement of defective appliances purchased from large department stores. Over the long run such an action line may fail to meet the expectations of its parent's management. This process contributed in part to the mid 1974 demise of KGO-TV's Action 7, as described by the news director who made the decision (telephone interview with Steve Skinner, 8 January 1976). Such a decision reemphasizes the need for total commitment by the parent to the action-line concept.

Some media may be inherently well suited to action lining and others not, the distinction resting upon how variegated a medium's audience is. For example, at least 50 radio stations compete with KABL-AM for Bay Area listeners. In such a crowded market (compared with three or four competing daily newspapers and four major television stations), each

---

[9]Horton (1972:19) documents a case in which the *Gainesville* (Florida) *Sun* publicized numerous unresolved complaints against mobile home dealers. The local trade association was so enraged that each member dealer withdrew its advertising account from the *Sun*, and the association created a public relations-oriented complaint-resolution mechanism much like that of the carpet industry in Oakland. The newspaper lost income but gained prestige as a responsible advertiser.

radio station is bound to attract a small, loyal audience, as KABL has done with its "smooth" music program of orchestrated popular tunes. According to Call for Action's executive director, such a program is not likely to attract listeners with problems most amenable to the action-line process (Brown 1976). Hence, despite generous multimedia promotion by KABL Radio, that chapter's complaint input fell below Call for Action's expectations, and the national corporation agreed to dissociate with KABL in 1975. The organization now seeks contractual agreements with major television stations, which tend to have the largest and most diverse audiences.

Their difficulties notwithstanding, action lines hold great promise. Their powers virtually equal those of government. Few other organizations can marshall such evidence of the weak points in our bureaucratic society as they see every day, and only they are prepared to broadcast their findings.

References

Allison, Graham T.
1971   *Essence of decision: Explaining the Cuban missile crisis.* Boston: Little, Brown.
Anderson, Stanley V.
1972   *A preliminary report: KABC Ombudsman Service.* Santa Barbara, Calif. Unpublished manuscript.
APME (Associated Press Managing Editors Association)
1968   *Preliminary action line study for the Content Committee.* New York: Internal report.
Barrow, Roscoe
1975   The fairness doctrine: A double standard for electronic and print media. *Hastings Law Journal* **26**:659–708.
Bellay, John T.
1970   *A content analysis of three action line columns.* Unpublished M.A. thesis, Kent State University.
Bicknell, Dwight
1972   Statement made before the Division of Consumer Protection, Ohio Department of Commerce, 22 August.
Boissevain, Jeremy
1968   The place of non-groups in the social sciences. *Man, the Journal of the Royal Anthropological Institute* **3**(2):542–56.
Brown, E. G., Jr.
1972   *California roster for 1972–3: Directory of state services, State of California.* Sacramento: Documents Section, Office of Procurement.
Brown, Sandra
1976   Personal telephone call, 6 January 1976.

Bureau of Census and U.S. Department of Commerce
  1973 *The American almanac: The U.S. book of facts, statistics and informa-tion.* New York: Grosset & Dunlap.
Cyert, R., and J. March
  1963 *A behavioral theory of the firm.* Englewood Cliffs, N.J.: Prentice-Hall, Inc.
de Tocqueville, Alexis
  1965 *Democracy in America.* Edited by Henry Reve and Rev. Francis Bowen. Abridged by Andrew Hacker. New York: Washington Square Press.
Eaton, Marian
  1971 *An ethnography of BBB Oakland: One consumer's view.* Unpublished undergraduate thesis, Department of Anthropology, University of California, Berkeley.
Editor & Publisher
  1966 "Newspapers get ACTION for readers." 31 December: pp. 9–10.
Eisenberger, Ken
  1975 Personal letter, 25 September 1975.
Emery, Edwin
  1972 *The press and America: An interpretive history of the mass media,* 3rd ed. Englewood Cliffs, N.J.: Prentice-Hall, Inc.
Federal Communications Act
  1934 Section 307.
Federal Communications Commission
  1960 Report and statement of policy, network programming inquiry. *Federal Register,* FCC 60–970, 29 July: p. 7295.
Federal Trade Commission
  1971 Report of the Task Force on Appliance Warranties and Services. In *Con-sumerism: Search for the consumer interest,* edited by David A. Aaker and George S. Day. New York: Free Press.
Gillard, Frank
  1973 "Call Don Moffat." *Listener* **89** (18 January): 69–70. Reprinted as "A Con-sumer Ombudsman Keeps Them Listening in Ohio." *Media & Consumer* (June): 69–70.
Gray, Nancy
  1975 *The media in the middle: A study of mass media complaint managers* (adaptation of working paper of the same name by M. Mattice, 1974). Unpublished working paper, Department of Anthropology, University of California, Berkeley.
Gulliver, P. H.
  1969 Case studies of law in non-Western societies. In *Law in culture and society,* edited by Laura Nader. Chicago: Aldine Publishing Company.
Hall, Knowles
  1975 Personal telephone call, 31 December 1975.
Heise, F. Kennen
  1973 Personal telephone call, 10 March 1973.
Hirschman, Albert O.
  1970 *Exit, voice, and loyalty: Responses to decline in firms, organizations, and states.* Cambridge: Harvard University Press.

Horton, A. H.
  1972 *Consumer advocacy at the* Gainesville Sun: *The first six months of Action Line, September 15, 1971 to March 15, 1972.* Unpublished graduate studies report, University of Florida, Gainesville.
KABC
  1972 KABC News Release 72–63. 26 April.
  1973 KABC News Release 73–45. 19 April.
KABL
  1972 KABL Editorial. 25, 26, 27 July.
Lazarsfeld, Paul F., and Robert K. Merton
  1965 Mass communication, popular taste, and organized social action. In *Mass culture: The popular arts in america,* edited by Bernard Rosenberg and David Manning White. New York: Free Press.
Levine, Arthur
  1975 "Better than deep throat." *Washington Monthly,* April: pp. 42–51.
Nader, Laura
  1977 Powerlessness in Zapotec and U.S. societies. In *Anthropological studies of power,* edited by R. Fogelson and R. Adams. New York: Academic Press.
News in Engineering
  1972 "Ombudsman by radio" (reprint). May.
Oakland Tribune
  1972a Action Line. 5 September: p. 2.
  1972b Action Line. 10 June: p. 2.
Pacific Telephone and Telegraph Company
  1975 *Oakland telephone directory.* June.
Palen, Frank S.
  1972 *Newspower—A newspaper as a problem solver.* Unpublished report, State University of New York at Buffalo, Faculty of Law.
Pollock, Frank
  1973 Personal telephone call, 15 February 1973.
Rowse, Arthur E.
  1973 Personal letter, 8 January 1973.
Skinner, Steve
  1976 Personal telephone call, 8 January 1976.
Smith, Keith D.
  1973 Personal letter, 27 August 1973.
Summers, Robert E., and Harrison B. Summers
  1966 *Broadcasting and the public.* Belmont, Calif.: Wadsworth Publishing.
Time
  1975 "A new lega-ease." 22 September: p. 74.
Warner, Ralph, and Peter Jan Honigsberg
  1975 *How to legally beat the bill collector,* California ed. Berkeley, Calif.: Nolo Press.
Washington Post
  1971 "Ellen Straus: She's a volunteer's volunteer." 28 February: pp. E1, E7, E8.
Waters, Harry F.
  1975 "Consumer Galahads." *Newsweek,* 15 September: pp. 69–70.

Weisman, John
1975 "How Tony got his free hamburger." *TV Guide*, 20 September: pp. 7–8.
WOSU
1973 News '73 (release by WOSU News/Public Affairs Production Unit). Columbus: Ohio State University Telecommunications Center.
WQXI-TV
1973 *Action Line* (script of 5 July broadcast).

AUTHOR INDEX

Numbers in italics refer to the pages on which the complete references are listed. Numbers in parentheses are footnote reference numbers and indicate that an author's work is referred to although the name is not cited in the text.

SUBJECT INDEX

A

Access, 18, 46, 57, see also Complaint handling process
  to congressional intermediaries, 373
  to legal system, 3, 4, 60, 62
Action line, 27, 28, 485–519, see also Media complaint handling; Intermediaries
  Action 7, 488, 505
  administration, 490
  advertizing, 33
  Call for Action, Inc., 487–491
    complaint procedure, 504
    staff, 499, 501–503
  community influence, 515
  complainants, 511, 514–515
  complaint-handling, 496, 499, 502, 504
  complaint-management techniques, 497, 502, 508, 518
  complaint resolution, 504, 514
  complaints, 495, 509, 512, 513, 516
  conflicts of interest, 33, 36, 517, 518
  as consumer advocate, 516
  costs, 489, 517
  education, 509, 511
  evaluations, 511, 515
  formation, 486–487
  functions, 502, 506
  goals, 28, 515, 518
  government regulations, 508
  limitations, 28, 36, 517
  media affiliations, 500
  Ombudsman Service, 488–489, 499, 505, 508

  formation, 488
  staff, 492
  newspaper, 488, 509
  power, 506, 508, 516, 517, 519
  rationale for, 489–491
  staff, 493
  use of public opinion, 36, 506–08, 516–517
Adjudication, 76, 78–86
  government, 80
Advertising, 5, 33, 46, 97
  action lines, 33
  Better Business Bureau, 241–243
  and consumers, 97
  deceptive, 69, 145–146
  regulation, 258–260, 265, 278
  retail ghetto store, 384
  self-regulation, 239–240
Aggregate action, 45, see also Class action law
Aggregate complaint handling, 86–98
  advantages, 86–88
  class actions, 91–94
  consumer interest, 88
  preventing sanctions, 97
Alioto, Joseph, 430
Alternatives to judicial system, 44–49
  adjudication, 76–86, 99
  aggregate action, 86–99
  Department of Economic Justice, 84
American Civil Liberties Union, 429, 430
American Medical Association, 126
  criticism of, 124, 125, 131
Anti-trust, 87, 89, 92, 95

529